DATE DUE

DEC 3 1 2002		

THE
NEW METROPOLIS

New York City, 1840-1857

EDWARD K. SPANN

COLUMBIA UNIVERSITY PRESS
NEW YORK

Edward K. Spann is professor of history at Indiana State
University, Terre Haute

Columbia University Press
New York   Guildford, Surrey

Copyright © 1981 by Columbia University Press

This book is the recipient of the 1977 New York
State Historical Association Manuscript Award

Library of Congress Cataloging in Publication Data

Spann, Edward K., 1931–
   The new metropolis.

   Bibliography
   Includes index.
   1. New York (N.Y.)—History—1775—1865. I. Title.
F128.44.S734   974.7'103   81-91
ISBN 0-231-05084-4 (cloth)   AACR2
ISBN 0-231-05085-2 (paper)

End papers: Greater New York, 1859

p 10 9 8 7 6 5 4 3 2

To
BRYANT,
Who will always be nine

CONTENTS

[vii]

CONTENTS

PREFACE

THIS IS A STUDY of New York City and its suburbs during
the formative period of modern American urban society. The
nineteenth century brought rapid economic development and
urbanization both to the United States and to Western Europe.
As the chief commercial and cultural link between these two
modernizing societies, New York became a primary focus of,
and agent for, those generally beneficial but often disruptive
changes which the hopeful called "Progress." Although denied
the political importance of such European capitals as London
and Paris, this largest of American seaports was able to transform itself into a major world metropolis with a preponderant
economic and cultural influence over the nation. It was during
the two decades before the Civil War that New York completed
the essential phase of its metropolitan development. By 1860,
it had established itself as the chief market and source of supply

for most of the United States. It had also become the dynamic center of a loosely knit metropolitan area which in population and productive power ranked among the great urban regions of the world. During this same twenty-year period, New Yorkers, acting in both private and public capacities, created the supply systems and institutions needed to sustain a concentrated population which not only tripled in size but grew socially and ethnically more complex. In many ways, the new metropolis was a magnificent expression of human intelligence and enterprise at work in an age of progress.

In other ways, it was a disturbing example of human failure. Having attracted a large and diverse population from both Europe and America, it failed to resolve the problems associated with this massive migration. In large part, the city was a victim of forces beyond its control. As the nation's metropolis, New York was burdened by a disproportionate share of the nation's troubles, while it received little assistance from either federal or state government. It is also true, however, that the self-interested individualism, civic carelessness, and other defects in the city's character compounded its problems—as did its rapid growth, which both strained its resources and forced a transformation of its internal structure that disrupted social and political life. Whatever the causes, the new metropolis was confronted by a comprehensive range of such troubles as social disorder, ethno-religious discord, mass poverty, and physical squalor which were to challenge most of the nation during the next century. Government, the principal instrument of public purpose in the city, not only failed to resolve these problems but itself became an object of widespread civic concern, thus opening the way for the direct intervention, in 1857, of New York State in the affairs of the metropolis. Even in its indisputably messy politics, however, New York must be accounted far more a success than a failure as a human society.

There is no easy way to find and disclose the essential truths of a city so frustratingly yet rewardingly complex and unfinished as was the ante-bellum metropolis—no prominent heroes or villains to explain its successes and failures, no convenient formulas for assessing it, no ready means for determining its

PREFACE

character. Respect for this complexity has led me to avoid either a specialized, monographic approach to one facet of New York life or a specific methodology such as that of the "New Urban History." Such approaches, however, have greatly enriched the common stock of understanding from which we all derive great benefit. Certainly, my own understanding owes much to the work of Sam Warner, Peter B. Knights, Stephan Thernstrom, Edward Pessen, Seymour Mandelbaum, David Ward, Zane Miller, and other innovators in the field of urban history as well as to the many specialists who like Robert G. Albion, Thomas Bender, Robert Bremner, John Duffy, Robert Ernst, Carl Kaestle, Jermome Mushkat, and James Richardson have in recent decades contributed volumes to our knowledge of life in New York.

My special thanks to Professor Bayrd Still of New York University for his inspiration in the field, to Mr. Wendell Tripp for his valuable assistance as Director of the New York State Historical Society, to the staffs of the Indiana State University Library and the New York Public Library for their generally courteous and efficient service, to the Indiana State University Research Committee for its financial aid, to Mss. Rita Phillips, Virginia Banfield, Joanne Hyde, Kelly Anne Rambis, Debra Raichel, Karen Hickman, and Patricia Strader for their contributions to the final typescript, and to Joanne Spann for her faith in my work.

Terre Haute, Indiana
April 1981

The engraved overview of New York in 1852 conveniently sections off, with light and shade, the city. The shaded area at the tip of Manhattan from Battery Park (to the right are the slips of the Long Island Sound steamers and the Staten Island ferries; to the left is circular Castle Garden) northeast to the East River covers most of the old commercial district oriented toward foreign trade and the South Street waterfront. Part of Brooklyn can be seen on the other side of the river; note the three Fulton Street ferries.

The rest of downtown commercial New York is included in the light area from Fulton Market (the large building with the cupola on the right) near the East River to West Street on the Hudson. The large domed Merchant's Exchange marks Wall Street; the prominent church is Trinity. The wharves at the extreme left are in Jersey City.

Above the Wall Street area in the center of this overview can be seen a large triangle formed by the convergence of Broadway and the Bowery, the most prominent streets in view. The shaded portion at the bottom of the triangle covers most of the Sixth Ward including City Hall and its Park and, to the right, the Five Points slum area. Most of the lighter portion of the triangle is the Fourteenth Ward with its Centre Market (the building with the cupola).

The large dark buildings in the upper part of the triangle mark Astor Place and its ill-fated Opera House. Broadway, on the left, runs north past City Hall to an apparent end at the apex (the white building is Grace Church) of the triangle in the upper center of the view. Immediately to the left is Union Square (14th Street) with its circular fountain. Below and farther to the left can be seen the trees of Washington Square Park; Fifth Avenue runs northward from the center of the Park. The light area even farther to the left is Greenwich Village.

On the right side of the triangle, the Bowery runs south from Union Square past Astor Place to Chatham Square where it meets Chatham Street (lower side of the triangle) and Catherine Street (running south to the South Street waterfront). To the left of Catherine Street is the Fourth Ward; to the right is William M. Tweed's Seventh Ward extending eastward to Corlaer's Hook. To the north can be seen the East River shipyards, Williamsburg (Greenpoint), the open lands of Queens County, and Blackwell's Island.

Most of Manhattan above 14th Street is yet to be developed. The northern limit of the built-up area is below 59th Street on the West Side (Sixteenth Ward) and 23rd Street on the East Side (Eighteenth Ward). Fourth Avenue can be seen extending north from Union Square to Yorkville in the distance.

FIGURE 1. An Overview of New York City in 1852
Courtesy of the Prints Division of the New York Public Library (Eno Collection)

THE
NEW METROPOLIS

Chapter 1

COMMERCIAL
NEW YORK

EVEN WITH ITS LOW-LYING SKYLINE, New York in the 1840s visually inspired a sense of power and of destiny. The vitality and magnitude of this, the greatest of the Atlantic ports, made an impressive picture for the thousands who on entering its harbor observed, like one European traveller, "the many sails which were tending toward it, the expanding river and opening harbor, and at last the broad way, with its tall ships setting in from the sea . . . and the Great Metropolis itself stretching into the distance, with its domes and spires, its towers, cupolas and 'steepled chimnies' rising through a canopy of smoke, in the gray dawn of a cloudless September morning." Visual New York was a great and growing work of many men on the Atlantic shore of a still largely virgin America. Despite its grandeur, however, the soul of the city could best be told not in poetic images but in numbers, since the source of its being was far less a striving for the awesome than a humbler though more complex instinct for money. Although in 1840 New York's skyline was still dominated by the spires of its churches and the cupola of its City Hall, no one could mistake the chief business of the some 300,000 people who clustered at the southern end of Manhattan Island. Except for its graceful bayfront promenade at the Battery on the tip of the island, the city's waterfront was solidly devoted to trade.[1]

Viewed from its harbor, this "Tyre," this "London," this "Empire City" of the western Atlantic impressed even travel-wise Europeans with its commercial greatness. South Street on the East River was the primary center of American foreign trade—a street of merchants' stores and warehouses screened by a winter forest of masts and spars of sailing ships from many nations; in 1835, more than a thousand ships (the number would triple by 1849) had entered New York harbor from some 150 foreign ports. The forest of masts was less dense on the Hudson River side of Manhattan, but the scene there, with its scattering of smokestacks belonging to steamships, bay steamers, and river boats provided a glimpse into the future; in 1838, the English had inaugurated transatlantic steam service with the great western port. During the previous 25 years, New York had become the wonder of the commercial world and the chief American focus of North Atlantic trade. Both its foreign commerce and its population had increased nearly three times since 1815. By the 1840s, it handled over half the imports and nearly a third of the exports of the United States, and these shares would grow larger over the next decades. It supplied the greatest variety of goods, the greatest number of ships, the greatest quantity of money, and the greatest range of commercial skills in a nation whose expanding society was increasingly infused with commerce. It was fast becoming the American metropolis and a major world city, even though unlike most other great cities it was not the capital of its nation nor even of its own state.

In response to the needs and pressures of its growing commerce, New York was remaking its internal structure.

COMMERCIAL NEW YORK

Affluent citizens had begun to abandon their homes in the once quiet streets of the lower city west of City Hall for new neighborhoods to the north around Washington Square and elsewhere above Houston Street. When in 1836 ex-Mayor Philip Hone sold his home on Broadway across from City Hall Park, he predicted that in the entire area "all the dwelling houses are to be converted into stores . . . , and the old downtown burgomasters who have fixed to one spot all their lives, will be seen during the next summer in flocks, marching reluctantly north to pitch their tents in places which, in their time, were orchards, cornfields, or morasses." Indeed, the City Hall area soon became the focus for businesses, hotels, and entertainments (including by 1841 P. T. Barnum's "museum") especially intended for the thousands who came from outside to do business in the city. Hone had been persuaded to move by the construction nearby of the massive, plain-fronted but lavishly appointed 300-room Astor House.[2] Broadway itself was becoming the busiest and most luxuriant retail street in America, remembered by thousands of visitors both for the fashionable dress of its women shoppers and for the noise and crush of its traffic. As the chief link between the expanding residential areas to the north of City Hall and the bursting business district to the south, it was increasingly glutted with carriages, coaches, wagons, and omnibuses during the work-day. One observer later counted 1200 horse-drawn vehicles pass City Hall in an hour.[3]

The tear-down and build-up spirit of the emerging commercial metropolis was as much at work in the area half a mile south of City Hall. On the west side of Broadway, historic old Trinity Church had been razed in 1839 to make way for a grand new Trinity to be completed in 1846. Even the prospective new church, however, could not overshadow the great financial street which ended on the other side of Broadway. Wall Street had been briefly humbled in 1835 by the Great Fire, which had ravaged much of lower New York, but it had soon been reborn in even grander form. An English traveller in 1838 called it the most "concentrated focus of commercial transactions in the world. . . . The whole money-dealing of

[3]

New York is here brought into a very narrow compass of ground, and is consequently transacted with peculiar quickness and facility."[4] Here, in Greek temples and behind granite façades, were located some of the nation's biggest banks, insurance companies, and a rich variety of offices devoted chiefly to the business of finance.

Especially grand was the new Merchant's Exchange, completed in 1841 at a cost of nearly $2 million to provide a meeting place for the fast expanding business community. With its great columns and its dome which rivaled the spires of churches, it seemed to one observer as if it had been carved out of a granite mountain. To another, it was an architectural folly where efficiency was sacrificed to false grandeur: "A New York merchant loses every year at least thirty-two hours in ascending and descending the steps of the exchange." Whatever its deficiencies, however, it served to symbolize the power of the commercial city, its rotunda "the very sanctuary of Trade and Commerce" where, said one New Yorker, "the wealth or poverty of hundreds of thousands—the price of stocks, the quotations of flour and cotton, the plenty or scarcity of money—all will be decided."[5]

Wall Street was only the most conspicuous part of a maze of streets which made the one square mile of land at the "golden toe" of Manhattan Island the greatest concentration of wealth and energy in America and, considering its limited size, in the world. The simplest explanation for this concentration was that Nature had made New York the most convenient and efficient point for the exchange of goods between the Old World and the New. When Washington Irving introduced his playful *History of New York* with a disquisition on the creation of the world, his humor expressed a fundamental truth, for Creation had indeed given the city an impressive array of advantages over its fading rivals in the Atlantic trade, Boston, Philadelphia, and Baltimore. Its harbor was broad, protected, and readily accessible from the Atlantic—a safe refuge which, boasted one New Yorker, could hold all the shipping in the world. From its docks, New York had the easiest natural access among the

Atlantic ports to American producers and consumers. Through protected Long Island Sound (once the perilous "Hell Gate" between the Sound and the East River was passed), it could more readily reach industrializing southern New England than could Boston. To the North, the Hudson River provided a convenient avenue to rapidly growing upstate New York as well as to western New England. By way of the Hudson, the city could also reach the Erie Canal (completed in 1825) and easy access to the developing West; of the four major port cities, only it had the advantage of a natural break in the Appalachian Mountain chain, a still formidable barrier to trade between the East and West. In an age where water travel was king, New York had the cheapest and most efficient system of transportation.[6]

It was thanks largely to its natural advantages that the city achieved several special relationships with key areas of the American and North Atlantic economies. Eventually, New York's trade with the West would be the source of immense profit, but two other American relationships were more important in the four decades before the Civil War. One was with the Northeastern coastal states from Massachusetts to Maryland, which formed the most densely populated, developed, and prosperous section of the United States. This section, already a leading urban and industrial area in the world, provided an especially lucrative market for New York's imports and for its varied commercial and financial services. In spite of the efforts of Boston, Philadelphia, and Baltimore to reverse the trend, New York by 1840 was becoming the metropolitan center of the Northeast, to the point that it was able to benefit from the economic growth of its rivals and their hinterlands.[7] New York's second relationship was distinctly different though no less profitable: As part of its growing command over Atlantic commerce, it had acquired a major role in the trade of the staple-exporting South, a role revealed by the fact that one of its chief exports was cotton shipped to it from southern ports; 325,000 bales of cotton was exported in 1844, a banner year. Whether or not it engaged in the actual export of the nation's most profitable crop, however, was less important than the larger and even more profitable role which it played in furnishing goods and services to the Cotton Kingdom.[8]

These special relationships in turn depended on an even more important one which New York had developed with the very center of the North Atlantic economy, Great Britain. At the end of the Napoleonic Wars in 1815, the British had chosen the city as the focus for their trade with the United States, a blessing which New Yorkers took care to cultivate. As a result, the South Street merchants, who in 1810 had been closely rivaled by Philadelphia and especially Boston in the import trade, imported in 1825 nearly three times as much as those two cities combined. New York enjoyed a particularly favored position as the American market center for Britain's chief export, drygoods, especially silk, woolen, and cotton fabrics. So dominant was the city as a place where Americans bought their cloth and their clothing that even New England textile mills chose it over Boston as the chief place to market their domestic production.[9] As most imports were bought and sold on credit, the drygoods trade in particular gave South Street and Wall Street special access to British capital, and so was an important factor in making New York the financial center of the United States. The leaders of New York's generally conservative mercantile community took particular care to maintain their special relationship with Liverpool and London, the export and financial centers of Great Britain, for that was the crucial element in their success. With the backing of British capital, they were able to provide the credit and the loans on which American domestic trade and economic development came increasingly to depend.[10]

By 1840, New York's advantages had attracted the business talents and energies required to make it an international center of exchange—a wealth of outside skill and ambition infused into what had once been the sleepiest of the major Atlantic ports. Some merchants came from Europe, especially from Britain. It was through the initiative of a transplanted English merchant, Jeremiah Thompson, that the city first developed its line of transatlantic packets, the fast sailing ships whose

[6]

speed and adherence to schedule helped seal the special relationship with his native land. Many more merchants were drawn from the northern part of the United States, most notably from New England, much of whose accumulated mercantile skill served New York at the expense of its Yankee rival, Boston. The prominance in the business world of such names as Macy, Grinnell, Fish, Dodge, Phelps, King, Howland, Goodhue, and Whitney prompted one New Englander to boast that, though they formed only a small part of the total population, "the Yankees took New York long ago . . . , and this city may henceforth be regarded as the capital of the 'universal Yankee nation.'" Boastfulness aside, it was true that the New Englanders and their descendents contributed heavily to the growth and welfare of the city, giving them a stronghold not only on business but also on social and political matters. As important as they were, however, the Yankees were only the most conspicuous element in a cosmos of talents and skills which had concentrated at New York. Collectively, this cosmopolitan merchant community formed the great system of knowledge required to manage the exchange of goods in both the national and international economies.[11]

The special combination of natural advantage and command over human power enjoyed by commercial New York seemed to give it a special and profitable destiny as an agent of world progress. Freeman Hunt, editor of the *Merchant's Magazine*, wrote: "Commerce is now the lever of Archimedes; and the fulcrum which he wanted to move the world is found in the intelligence, enterprise, and wealth of the merchants and bankers, who now determine the questions of peace and war, and decide the destinies of nations." Commerce, declared another New Yorker in 1840, promoted world prosperity, civilized and refined nations, encouraged freedom, and stimulated public improvements and the development of human knowledge. Man, brought into contact with opportunity, would awaken in ambition and productivity; brought into contact with a higher moral culture, he would awaken to new expectations for self. Thus, out of the increasingly complex web of commercial relationships being woven by cities like New York there

Commercial New York: I

FIGURE 2. (left, above) The engraved view (1828) of the South Street docks looking south from Maiden Lane gives some idea of the "forest of masts" during the simpler days when New York was first asserting its dominance of the import trade. The ship in the center background is tied up at Coffee Slip at the east end of Wall Street.

FIGURE 3. (left, below) The lithographed view (1850) of the north side of Wall Street looking west toward Trinity Church was drawn from a point at the corner of the Merchant's Exchange. This Sunday-like scene centers on the Custom House (under the flag), built in 1842 on the site where George Washington was first inaugurated as President; the building is located at the corner of Nassau Street.

Both views courtesy of the Prints Division of the New York Public Library; the first in the Stokes Collection, the second in the Eno Collection.

was developing a progressive, modern civilization.[12] Indeed, South Street and Wall Street were instrumental in spinning a network of exchange and interdependence which drew Americans out of local isolation and into a modernizing society to the general economic benefit of all and the special benefit of New York.

This optimism, however, was confronted by a deepening mood of anxiety and impotence which afflicted the business community in the early 1840s, for commercial New York faced hard times when the great engine of exchange which it managed sputtered amid exploding ambitions and faltering businesses. In the previous decade, the city had prospered from a spectacular expansion of foreign trade which peaked in 1836 when American imports reached a value nearly double that of only five years earlier. Unfortunately, this extraordinary period ended with the Panic of 1837, which brought ten years of commercial uncertainty and unnerving deflation. In 1840, young George Templeton Strong compared the recent fortunes of businessmen to a string of firecrackers, "pop-pop—one after another they go off—and their substance vanishes in fumes." So uncertain were the times, wrote Strong, that he would "hardly trust John Jacob Astor with twenty dollars unless secured with real estate worth a hundred." The confidence of New Yorkers was further shakened when a few months later one of New York's most respected businessmen, the recently retired Nathaniel Prime, committed suicide by cutting his throat from ear to ear.[13]

Shrinking fortunes and a rising number of bankruptcies brought hard feelings as well as hard times. Early in 1840, outraged stockholders in the Manhattan Bank demanded an explanation for the bank's heavy losses, prompting an investigation which determined that bank officers had made large loans on stock that subsequently had sharply depreciated in value. After the report of the investigators was made public, the Cashier of the bank, Robert White, attempted a rebuttal by attacking one of them with a club on Wall Street. This was only one of a series of bankruptcies, defalcations, and other scandalous business events which undermined the confidence of

COMMERCIAL NEW YORK

the business community in the world and in itself. Even the mountainous Merchant's Exchange, built by a corporation of businessmen to crown the glories of Wall Street, proved to be a crumbling rock, for the Exchange corporation was forced to default on its interest payments in 1842. Only the timely aid of English bankers saved the merchant community from the mortifying financial ruin of its own exchange.[14]

These troubles were symptoms of fundamental afflictions which since the Panic of 1837 had made business increasingly uncertain, fitful recoveries alternating with fitful collapses. In August 1840, the *Journal of Commerce* saw signs of improvement: "Whirled in the air and crashed to earth as New York has been, she is on her feet again." In 1841, however, the city was once more crashed to earth by new financial troubles resulting from the collapse in Philadelphia of the giant United States Bank of Pennsylvania. The ruin of the nation's biggest bank eliminated Philadelphia as a serious rival to Wall Street, but it also precipitated a depression that bottomed out in the winter of 1842–43. The trouble brought a sharp decline in American imports which made the new collapse especially hard on the nation's chief importing city.[15] It was a grim time of rising unemployment and spreading poverty—a time that cast a long shadow over the city's future. If the poor and powerless were hurt, so too were many businessmen and property-owners who were caught in the grip of faltering trade, falling rents, and collapsing property values. The ensuing decline in the assessed value of property was to trouble the politics and government of the city throughout the decade.[16]

Dismal reality was highlighted by the stark contrast between New York's troubles and the good fortunes of Boston. While property values fell in New York, they rose sharply in New York's commercial rival, making the Hub, on a per capita basis, the wealthiest city in the United States and perhaps the world. While New York's population increased by a substantial but not spectacular 18 percent between 1840 and 1845, Boston's grew by 34 percent. Even with this growth, Boston in population and total wealth was still a puny rival, but in a world of commercial rivalry one city's spectacular gains were seen as another city's equally spectacular losses.[17] Especially disturbing was the possibility that Boston's success was less the result of temporary good luck than of Yankee ingenuity and energy, which had given it a head start in harnessing the power of the dawning age of steam.

While New York had plowed much of its money into expanding its existing water system, Boston capitalists concentrated on the development of railroads, most significantly on a rail line to Albany where they could reach the eastern terminus of the Erie Canal and thus divert the traffic of New York's great artery to their own city. Even before Boston completed its Western Railroad to the Hudson, some New Yorkers warned that New York's future was threatened by the project. In 1840, the editor of the *Journal of Commerce*, himself a transplanted New Englander, predicted that the far-sighted Yankees were planning to extend their system to the Mississippi and beyond. He urged New York to strike back with its own railroad to Albany to counter the fact that navigation on the Hudson was restricted if not closed during the winter months. Boston's threat did not confine itself to railroads, he warned, for England had decided to make that city the western terminus for its new Cunard line of steamships. Was it not possible that soon most of the import and export trade between England and America would be carried by steam-power through Boston?[18]

The call to action, however, evoked only a weak response. Although a railroad system had begun to develop around New York, it was a thing of bits and pieces. To the west, the New York and Erie Railroad ran neither to New York nor to Lake Erie, one terminus being on the west side of the Hudson at Piermont, some 20 miles north of the city, the other at the end of the track in the wilds of southern New York. To the east, the Long Island Railroad straggled out from Brooklyn into Long Island. The only railroad which actually terminated in New York, the New York and Harlem, was aptly named, for it ran to a point only slightly beyond the Harlem River, Manhattan's northern boundary.[19] Little was done to improve this system in the early 1840s, largely because the city's willingness to finance new ventures was paralyzed by the anxieties of the merchant's troubled world.

As a great center of exchange, New York was hurt by a worldwide crisis of confidence which pinched and narrowed the channels of credit on which international trade depended. The confidence of foreign lenders in the United States was severely shaken by a long series of American defaults and business failures after 1837. In 1843, Philip Hone anguished: "The English papers do abuse us shamefully for swindling, repudiation, cheating, and other trifling departures from rectitude, which abuse is all the harder to be borne from the difficulty we have in many of the cases of contradicting the truth of the charges." In response, New York moneymen retreated into a program of financial conservatism. Mindful that the city's predominance as a center of exchange obligated it to restore the confidence of the creditor classes, merchants and bankers practiced a policy of restraint that left little room for investments in enterprises as untried as railroads.[20]

The revival of commerce in the mid-1840s, however, restored the initiative to New York, with the help of a lesson in the growing importance both of the West and of railroads. Aside from the loosening of British credit restrictions, the chief stimulus for recovery came from an exceptionally strong European demand for American agricultural commodities as the result of crop failures in Ireland and on the Continent. A flourishing western export trade promised to stimulate domestic demand for New York's imports, a point made by Hunt's *Merchant's Magazine* when in 1845 it was able to report a general increase in agricultural prices which "will react upon the Atlantic cities in enhanced purchases of goods." The importance of railroads to this promising trade was quickly demonstrated when in November of that year the coming winter prematurely closed the Erie Canal, leaving much western produce on the frozen canal at a time of high demand in New York. The message was repeated in 1847 when unusually cold weather cut the shipping season on the Hudson by more than two weeks.[21]

Although railroad promoters continued to complain of an often apathetic and occasionally hostile business community, the lesson of frozen water and stalled trade soon had its effects. The Erie Railroad, revived by its success in raising a much needed $3 million in New York, was able to push its tracks steadily westward to Lake Erie by 1851. That same year also brought a second all-weather route when the Hudson River Railroad was completed to a point near Albany, enabling New York to tap into a line of upstate railroads which ran west to Buffalo; this was the beginning of the future New York Central system. In such ways did the awakened city succeed not only in countering the western designs of Boston and other rival ports, but also in making itself the chief Atlantic terminus of the expanding national railroad network.[22]

New York's recovery was clinched by comparable achievements in its transatlantic navigation. In the 1840s, shipping rates on the Atlantic were sharply reduced by the introduction of faster and larger vessels, many of them built in the city's expanding shipyards. Sailing ships continued to predominate, but the most dramatic change came with the increasing use of the ocean-going steamer whose size and speed promised both further reductions in shipping costs and the more efficient use of mercantile capital; the *Journal of Commerce* in 1840 estimated that the faster steamships, by reducing the time that goods were at sea, enabled the merchant to use his money four times as frequently as was possible under sail. Although New York had long taken pride in its Hudson River boats and Long Island Sound steamers, it waited until the mid-1840s to initiate an international system of steamships partly subsidized by Federal mail contracts under the Ocean Mail Act of 1845. By 1850, steam lines had been established to Cuba and to the Isthmus of Panama, to Le Havre and Bremen on the Continent, and to Liverpool.

The Liverpool route, covered by the Collins Line, attracted particular attention, since it brought New York shipping interests into direct competition with Britain's formidable Cunard Line. The Collins Line eventually foundered, but not before it had helped to drive down transatlantic shipping rates and to concentrate ocean steam traffic at the mouth of the Hudson. Between 1840 and 1860, when American ocean steam tonnage increased more than six times, New York's share of that tonnage rose from 38 to 75 percent. Even the Cunard Line, which initially had selected Boston as its western terminus, shifted most of its business to the Hudson, with its concentration of markets and cargoes.[23]

New York was thus able to preempt Boston's dream of a steamline from Liverpool to the Mississippi. Having consolidated its position as the great exchange point between Europe and the United States, it achieved an unprecedented dominance over the rapidly expanding American economy. By 1850, it had become the unchallenged metropolis of America, while its former rivals were left to play reluctant roles as subordinate regional centers. With its suburbs, the metropolis was home to some 650,000 people (the number would rise to well over one million by 1860) whose domestic needs, when added to its export demands, made it the largest market in America for producers ranging from the textile men of New England and coalmine operators of Pennsylvania to the wheat and cattle raisers of the West; New York had, boasted one New Yorker, "become so enriched that she may call Ohio her kitchen-garden, Michigan her pastures, and Indiana, Illinois and Iowa her harvest fields." Similarly, its imports combined with its growing manufacturing output made it by far the chief source of supply for Americans, from the wholesalers of interior cities to the southern women who wore clothing made by New York seamstresses.[24]

Even more, it was the great money-market for the United States, the magnet for investment money from both Europe and America, and the major source of the capital and credit required for economic expansion. "Capital is attracted to this central point," said the Chamber of Commerce, "because it finds scope and objects for investment and distribution. . . . The interests of agriculture and manufacturing, no less than those of commerce, share in the benefits of centralization. The productive industry of the Union, thus becomes, in various ways, a partaker in the prosperity of our city, as joint contributors to a common cause, and common sharers in the public weal." Certainly, the prospects of a profitable investment in the nation's largest and most diversified money market drew money to New York from most of the rest of the United States, including New England—and from overseas as well. When European and American investors began to pour their funds into the railroad boom of the 1850s, Wall Street handled most of the transactions.[25]

The commercial metropolis thus became a great agency for human progress with a special opportunity to direct the new powers of the progressive age. In 1850, the departure of the steamer *Atlantic* from New York inspired a minister to apotheosize both steamships and railroads: "These pillars of cloud by day and of fire by night are heralding our modern civilization to conquests and results not possible before. The fast-flying gigantic shuttles are weaving the nations inextricably together in the bonds of mutual acquaintance, friendship, and commercial intercourse. They will soon make war impossible. . . . They will lift the masses. . . . They will make—are making—a highway for our God." In a similar way, the new age inspired the novelist James Fenimore Cooper to more concrete thoughts regarding the city's place in the world future. From his home upstate at Cooperstown, Cooper was able by 1850 to devine the metropolitan destiny of New York and its contiguous areas, a destiny which he believed should be appreciated and promoted by every citizen in the state: "The money of the towns at the mouth of the Hudson is finding its way into every village, and to the summit of every mountain-top. . . .Demanding in exchange supplies of the most familiar and minute character, giving additional value and a certain sale to every pound of butter that is churned and to every egg that is laid." To complete the natural economic unity of greater New York, the novelist proposed the construction of a great chain of docks built of stone to run from the Hudson River waterfront to Governor's Island to Redhook to Flushing Bay and then to the Harlem River, which collectively would form "the noblest dock in the work," equal to the destined role of the metropolis as the great port for an ever-expanding national and world economy.[26]

Before he could publish his plan, Cooper died and so was spared what would have been the disappointing 1850s when New York's port facilities seemed more to deteriorate than to improve and when a resentful state, far from assisting the metropolis, actively interfered with its affairs. Indeed, many shadows had begun to form over the happy prospects of the progressive age. New York's increasing dominance of the economy, for instance, evoked resentment as well as admiration elsewhere in America. That was made clear when in 1851 several representatives in the nation's Congress launched an attack on, as Isaac Holmes of South Carolina put it, the "wealthy and overgrown city." Southerners led the attack, resentful of New York's success in gaining control of the South's commerce, but the most noteworthy expression of hostility came from Willis A. Gorman of Indiana:

> Sir, the city of New York occupies a position this day in regard to America, that Paris does toward France. The great city of New York wields more of the destinies of this great nation than five times the population of any other portion of the country. The efforts that are made . . . warn the people of the West, the South, the Southeast, and the Northwest, what they must expect from the absorbing, mighty, and increasing strength of the city.
>
> The city of New York controls at the present time, with its immense monetary power, the commercial destinies of the Union.[27]

Such attacks, although prophetic of the crusades against Wall Street after the Civil War, had as yet little sting. It was more difficult, however, for the commercial city to ignore some deep troubles which had developed within itself. In part, they resulted from the rapid expansion of business which disrupted the old merchant community, replacing it with a disturbing new world that became increasingly complex, impersonal, and competitive. Freeman Hunt, whose *Merchant's Magazine* had often lauded the civilizing tendencies of commerce, was driven to warn of a counter-tendency toward "mercantile degeneracy and mercantile ruthlessness." Hunt traced the trouble to what he believed was an excess of competition among ambitious men attracted to New York by the hope of quick wealth; this was "the calamity of a great city." The result was speculation, fraud, and a deification of the almighty dollar—old sins in disturbing intensified forms threatening to his ideal of the merchant as a "liberal and intelligent commercial man." Although Hunt's warnings were often lost in the roar of business, they could not be ignored. In the chaotically growing world, with its increasingly complicated transactions, how was it possible to have full faith in other businessmen or, given the temptations of wealth, even in one's own clerks?[28]

Business-minded New Yorkers, however, were less concerned about the disorders of their own world than they were about the social and political degeneracy they saw around them. Despite its defects, the commercial city so evident in South Street, Wall Street, and Broadway could be clearly identified with progress; the real threat came from its sordid twin, a seemingly alien social and political city associated with crime, disorder, dirtiness, political deceit, governmental corruption, and burdensome taxes. New York had never been a model of civic order and virtue, but the situation seemed significantly to worsen during the generally depressed and depressing decade after 1837. Even with the return of prosperity, it persisted—a disturbing contrast and challenge to the glittering successes of the progressive commercial world.

Much of the trouble originated in New York's chronic, often a-social and occasionally anti-social individualism, which flooded public places with, as the *Tribune* complained in 1842, "confusion, disorder, incoherent action, conflict of effort," and general civic carelessness. In bad times and even more in good times, the city seemed to be in a state of flux, its people floating atoms in turbulent space. The rootless character of individual life was dramatically illustrated annually on May 1, the great moving day, when the streets were filled with people who, having given up or lost their annual leases all at once the previous February, now all at once were caught up in the frenzy of moving their possessions to some new place in town, temporary nomads in the upheaving city.[29] Most New Yorkers, like humans elsewhere, sought and found commitments which gave them a stake in some kind of collective life, but their society involved special discouragements against the development of a strong sense of community: Moving day, the inadequacy and high cost of housing, the common practice of residing in boarding houses as well as rented rooms and houses, the diversity and anonymity of life in a large metropolis, and the necessary disruptions of life and home associated with a fast-growing, transforming commercial city. Perhaps in no other city were even citizens so much strangers to each other.

The problem of molding a civic order in such a place was formidable enough, but there were still deeper shadows associated with a social fact for which the progressive ethos had little room—the ever growing masses of poor and often degraded people who had migrated to New York. From this mass came the laborers, carters, porters, seamstresses, and others whose callused or nimble hands were vital to the successes of the commercial world. Yet these hordes of strangers—who were crowding into the side streets off Broadway, the region east to City Hall, and other areas close to the business city— were a deeply disturbing presence associated with poverty, disorder, crime, and with nearly every other problem that increasingly afflicted the city. Like other ports, New York had long known the rootless and the poor, but not in such disturbing numbers. By the 1840s the accumulating mass seemed to be congealing into an alien world at least vaguely menacing to the hopes, values, and interests of the progressive city.[30]

If the magic of steam promised to unite the nations of the world, this strange mass threatened to deeply divide society. Under the pressure of migration as well as of its own uneven economic fortunes, New York appeared to be breaking down into two social extremes—of wealth and poverty, of virtue and viciousness, of sunlight and shadow, of citizens and strangers. These appearances obscured a more complex reality, particularly the presence of a broad middle range of human existence;

BROAD-WAY.

Commercial New York: II

FIGURE 4. (left above) The lithographed view (1850) drawn by Aug. Kollner of the area south of City Hall is from the tip of the Park at a point formed by the convergence of Broadway and Park Row. At the right on Broadway is the Astor House, one of America's first luxury hotels. The columned façade to the south belongs to St. Paul's Chapel; Trinity Church can be seen slightly left of center in this view. The building with the exotic pictures on its front is Barnum's Museum.

FIGURE 5. (left, below) Barnum's also appears on the left in the engraved view (1849) drawn by J. H. Hill of the lower city from the steeple of St. Paul's. The row of buildings in the immediate right foreground (note the Gallery of the pioneer photographer, Matthew Brady) are located on Fulton Street. Broadway runs at an angle from the front of St. Paul's southward past Trinity Church in the background. To the left of Trinity can be seen the dome of the Merchant's Exchange. The hills and buildings in the distance beyond the masts of South Street on the left are in Brooklyn at the western end of Long Island.

the expanding commercial city provided many opportunities for the development of the modern middle class, in which eventually most of the seeming strangers would find an acceptable place. The increasingly conspicuous extremes were real enough, however, to constitute the central problem of the nineteenth-century urban world, a problem aptly named by a later candidate for Mayor of New York, Henry George, in the title of his influential book published in the late 1870s, *Progress and Poverty*. Certainly, the increasing concentration of the poor, especially the foreign poor, in New York intensified a devil's dozen of interrelated problems which were long to trouble the progress of the new metropolis.

Chapter 2

STRANGERS AND CITIZENS

THOUSANDS OF STRANGERS followed the trade routes to their focus in the commercial metropolis. In 1850 the census-taker for the Fourteenth Ward listed the following among those living in dwelling number 39 on his rounds: Solomon Hearris, a clothier from Poland; Abram Christina, a Russian cap-maker; Patrick Lilly, a shoemaker from Ireland; Philip Henry, a German cabinet-maker, and Thomas Pike, a lamp-maker from England. These men, with their wives and children (some American-born) and an assortment of other people who also lived in dwelling number 39, formed part of the vast cosmopolitan world of New York.[1] Nearly 60 percent of the 515,000 New Yorkers in 1850 had been born elsewhere, either in America or in Europe—a mass of Yankees, New Jerseymen,

Long Islanders, Pennsylvanians, Irishmen, Germans, Englishmen, Frenchmen, and others, from cities, towns, farms and
peasant hovels.[2]

A society of many peoples: this was part of the strength of
the metropolis, but it was also very much part of its burden. In
1855, the *Tribune* predicted that soon Manhattan Island would
"hold three millions of human beings, gathered from the
uttermost ends of the globe. . . . Such an impending agglomeration of blended yet jarring myriads drawn hither by the
haste of commercial gain, or the thrust of incisive poverty, will,
and in a large degree already does, present a social phenom-
enon with few, if any, parallels."[3] The dark side to this diversity
could be summed up in a compound question: In a society
with such an unstable and uncertain character, what warranty
for the public welfare, what protection for the weak, what
assurance of community? How could strangers, to each other
and often to their city, become citizens with meaningful roles
in a common society?

This question challenged every rapidly growing and changing city, but it was magnified for New York by a rising flood
of foreign immigrants who followed the transatlantic trade
routes to the American import center. Between 1840 and 1855,
over 68 percent of the 3,298,000 foreign immigrants to the
United States landed at the port of New York. Most continued
on into the interior along the expanding domestic trade routes,
but many remained—especially the ablest and most ambitious
on the one hand and the poorest and most unwanted on the
other. In the decade between 1845 and 1855, the proportion
of foreign-born New Yorkers increased from one-third to one-
half. In 1860, the city was home to 6 percent of the English
immigrants in the United States, 7 percent of the French, 9
percent of Germans, and over 12 percent of the Irish.[4]

Immigration was of recognized benefit to both the city and
the country. In 1850, *Banker's Magazine* asserted that money
brought by the newcomers had added substantially to the
capital available at New York and so contributed to the city's
supremacy as an investment center. Immigrant expenditures
for transportation, said *Hunt's*, helped finance improvements

in the means of travel and trade. Robert B. Minturn, a New York shipowner, declared that income from the immigrant traffic served to reduce transatlantic freight rates and so to subsidize the expansion of Atlantic trade.[5] The immigrants also brought valuable skills and physical strength. Nearly 70 percent of those who came to the United States were between the ages of 15 and 40. Ready to work, they had been reared at the expense of their abandoned countries. Among the workers were many skilled artisans: blacksmiths, carpenters, shoemakers, and tailors. When immigration declined sharply in 1855, the nation lost $100 million, according to T. S. Lambert of New York.[6]

Other New Yorkers, however, were more inclined to view most of the newcomers as an oppressive burden. Such nationality groups as the English, the French, and the Scotch found ready acceptance. Generally, they had the money, the experience and the skills required for success in urban life. In their backgrounds, capabilities, ambitions, and often in their religions, they closely resembled the native Americans who were also migrating to the city. Considerably different were the great mass of immigrants, the Germans and the Irish, most of whom had been uprooted and thrust unprepared into the alien world of the American city by the economic, social, and political troubles of their native lands. Often poor, they seemed like a burdensome surplus of people in a city already overflowing with people.[7] Even these two nationalities, however, differed significantly in their abilities to find acceptance and an acceptable place.

The Germans, in some ways, should have been the most indigestible element in the ethnic stew. They spoke a strange language, they were often Catholics or free-thinkers, and they tended to cluster together, forming a "Little Germany" (*Kleindeutschland*) on the east side of the city. Moreover, their alleged addiction to lager beer and their conspicuous enjoyment of Sunday pleasures offended New York's small but active class of New England Calvinists who favored prohibition and a quiet Sabbath.[8] In a city as proud as it was fearful of its cosmopolitan diversity, however, Germans were soon type-cast as useful, contributing members of society. Although sometimes poor, they brought with them the skills, habits and the leadership which enabled them to make a rapid adjustment to an urban-commercial way of life. They soon appeared in disproportionate numbers in many of the skilled trades and in petty businesses: In 1855, when they were less than 20 percent of the total population, Germans constituted more than one-half the city's bakers and confectioners, cabinet-makers, tobacconists, shoemakers, tailors, and woodworkers. Conversely, they appeared in disproportionately small numbers among the unskilled workers. They were also able to establish an ethnic community which gave them protection and identity and supplied conditions for a flourishing culture.[9]

Their successes, however, compounded the troubles of the Irish, who in contrast looked like a major problem to the problem-ridden city. In the 1850s, when the Irish-born constituted about 30 percent of the total population, they made up nearly 60 percent of the almshouse population and nearly 70 percent of the recipients of charity. In 1859, it was estimated that over one-half those arrested by the police were Irish.[10] Such figures seemed to confirm the established stereotype of the Irish as drunken, improvident, and disorderly, and to consign them to the very bottom of society, where they found themselves in competition with another much-stereotyped group, New York's small black population.[11]

Few New Yorkers cared that the troublesome newcomers had been left peculiarly unprepared to cope with city life by their devastating social experiences. Under British rule, most of the Irish had been tenants and fieldworkers mired in a primitive state of agriculture which, in comparison to the American farmer, gave little experience with a commercial society. Poor even under normal circumstances, in the 1840s they were dislodged even from this miserable state. Many were forced to abandon their hovels when English landlords decided to consolidate their lands into larger farms.[12] On top of this came the great famine which in the mid-1840s brought death, debilitation, and desperation. From the horror of home, the Irish poor fled to the horror of the Atlantic passage: Stinking ships, bad food, and disease—then to be herded ashore, often to be robbed and swindled by immigrant runners and boarding house keepers. This experience, which telescoped the troubles of a lifetime into a few months, left many of the immigrants further enfeebled and bewildered, aliens in an alien land.[13]

Even if they were lucky enough to bring some money and to have friends or relatives in America, the Irish often failed to find a secure place in their new world. The great majority were Roman Catholics in an overwhelmingly Protestant society often hostile to Catholicism. As a deprived rural people, they had few of the skills respected and wanted by the established population. Many were unemployed or underemployed—a useless surplus in a city concerned about an excess of people.[14] More found low-paying, unskilled jobs: In 1855 60 percent of Irish men and women with recorded employment were domestic servants, laborers, porters, laundresses, carters, and coachmen. Such employment frequently brought them into competition with blacks, which thrust them unwillingly into New York's sensitive and complex racial situation. Many of the Irish did find employment in skilled trades, but, just as they helped block off employment opportunities for blacks, so were many opportunities closed to them by the Germans who were able to move into society at a higher point.[15]

Poverty, however, was not the last broken rung on the ladder of misfortune, for with it came the frequent disintegration of the Irish family, resulting from the death, disappearance, or disability of husbands and fathers. One statistic generally overlooked by contemporary social observers was the high ratio of women to men, a striking contrast to the general preponderance of immigrant males both in the city and in the nation. In the 1860 census, one-third more Irish females than males were reported, a disproportion which also characterized the black population.[16] The death rate for the Irish males in the United States seems to have been higher than it was for natives and considerably higher than it was for Germans.[17] Other Irishmen disappeared, either temporarily or forever, as they went inland constructing canals and railroads. Among those who remained, poverty intensified family tensions and encouraged male desertions. Absent fathers, working mothers, crowded living quarters—these led many juveniles to a life in the streets, frequently to delinquency and occasionally to crime and prostitution.[18]

Even in the land of opportunity, poverty threatened to perpetuate itself unless there were positive assistance; and for the Irish in New York there was little of that. The city, to be sure, was able to provide some aid from a variety of public and private sources, but in the great and growing city with its apparent infinity of problems that aid was sporadic, distant, and begrudging. The import center had to bear a disproportionate share of the immigrant burden with little help from its state and none from the nation.[19] Like other immigrant groups, the Irish had to depend largely on themselves to succeed in America—a difficult task, for their institutional life was weak. The community of desperation which had helped them survive in their native villages disintegrated as they spread out through the vast, impersonal metropolis.[20]

The Church, which had served at home as a refuge, was in America unprepared to meet the massive needs of an uprooted population scattered throughout the city. The tavern continued to serve as a necessary social center for the male population, but it also was an encouragement to the alcoholism which was to long burden the lives and reputations of the Irish. To make matters even worse, the habit of village clannishness which they brought from Ireland often encouraged divisive competition and open conflict among them, which not only weakened their unity but also reinforced their reputation as a factious, riotous, and brutal people. No wonder that Thomas D'Arcy McGee in the 1850s urged them to leave the city and referred to the Irish of the Fourth Ward as a "perverted peasantry."[21]

In reality, of course, the great majority were not jobless, not drunken, and not riotous. Eventually, the Irish did muster their resources sufficiently to create a strong institutional life; perhaps they even overcompensated for their earlier weaknesses, but their achievements brought new problems both for themselves and for the city. Like other peoples burdened by their poverty and by an oppressive stereotype, their effort to establish a place in New York aroused strong opposition, because they threatened to upset existing social, political, and cultural arrangements. This became especially evident in the early 1840s when they found a dynamic spokesman in the person of Bishop John Hughes.

Hughes, a strong-willed Catholic leader, believed that his religion was vital to the social as well as the spiritual welfare of his people. In 1857, he stated his objectives and role:

> The people of this country, and especially those among whom I have lived, have great respect for a manly, straightforward, and outspoken vindication of any rights. . . . I had to stand up among these people as their bishop and chief; to warn them against the dangers that surrounded them; to contend for their rights as a religious community; to repel the spirit of faction among them; to convince their judgment by frequent explanations in regard to public and mixed questions; to encourage the timid; and sometimes restrain the impetuous—in short, to knead them up into one dough, to be leavened by the spirit of Catholic faith and Catholic union.[22]

As the "bishop and chief" of a divided and dispirited people, Hughes devoted himself to a double lifetime of labor. His church was pitifully weak for the task he assigned it. In 1841, for more than 60,000 Catholics, there were ten churches burdened with debts totaling $300,000. Observing that there was only one priest for every 8000 people, Hughes asked: "What . . . can be his influence among such a mass of people? Where can be his influence in the first great elementary division of society—the family? Where his superintendence of the children?" His efforts to provide strong leadership encountered resentment and resistance from some of his own flock.[23] Within fifteen years, however, he succeeded in establishing doctrinal unity, in paying off the debts, in tripling the number of churches, and in creating a variety of charitable, social, and educational organizations which became a strong basis for Irish Catholic community life in New York.[24]

The Bishop gave special attention to the problem of creating a system of Catholic schools. As an America, he believed in the necessity of education for the formation of a sound, moral citizenry. As a Catholic, he believed there could not be sound morality without strong religious training. Earlier Catholic leaders had attempted to establish a system of religious education, but by 1840 the results of their efforts were frustratingly inadequate: a few private schools for Catholics able to afford private education and some eight church schools struggling, with little money, to educate a growing mass of poor children. Under such conditions, the great majority of poor Catholic children would receive no education in the Catholic religion, a prospect dangerous not only for the church but, as Hughes believed, for society. If religious training was necessary for morality, the failure to train the growing masses of Catholic poor would weaken the moral foundations of the social order, a matter of great concern in the increasingly disordered city.[25]

Hughes, therefore, could believe that he was acting in the public interest when in 1840 he asked the New York Common Council to provide financial support for the struggling Catholic schools. His request for public tax monies did not seem to threaten public education, for in New York there was no public system in the modern sense. Rather, there appeared to be a system very much like the one Catholics were building for themselves. On top, there was a variety of secular and religious private schools; below, a flourishing organization of free schools under the direction of the well-established Public School Society, an educational corporation chartered more than thirty years before to educate those who could not afford private education. Although governed by a private board, the Society by 1840 had broadened its operations and established a claim to nearly all public education money.[26]

Catholic children were entitled to attend the Society's schools, but Hughes believed that the Society was a Protestant organization whose educational philosophy and practice threatened Catholic morality in one of two ways: Either it taught Protestantism and ridiculed Catholicism or it taught no religion at all. In either case, it threatened to turn Catholic children against both the religion of their parents and the parents themselves. The existing educational system, then, was incomplete in that it failed to provide a sound moral education for New York's large Catholic population. Public aid for Catholic schools would not destroy that system but complete it as an effective agency to maintain the moral order of the city. A pluralistic school system for a pluralistic society—the idea had already been expressed by the Governor of New York, William H. Seward, who in 1840 had advocated the creation of schools where the children of immigrants "may be instructed by teachers speaking the same language as themselves and professing the same faith."[27]

Whatever its logic, the Bishop's request for public money to support his schools precipitated a controversy which was to embitter Protestant–Catholic relations for a century and to change the character of public education in New York. By linking Catholic dogma to morality, Hughes challenged a powerful Protestant establishment which had developed its own way to create a moral basis for society. This establishment, headed by a small group of wealthy merchants like the influential Tappan brothers, had made New York the capital of an evangelically inspired "benevolent empire" intended to convert Americans everywhere to an essentially Protestant version of Christian morality. The commercial metropolis was the natural communication center of the United States and so also the logical place to establish the offices of such national benevolent organizations as the American Bible and Tract societies. These two societies, with their headquarters near City Hall, had printed millions of religious pamphlets and Bibles for national distribution since their formation in the 1820s. In order to reach the doctrinally diverse Protestant community, such organizations had developed a nondenominational approach to their mission which avoided religious doctrine as much as possible. Thus, they seemed to have found a nonsectarian, nondogmatic moral base for a Christian America.[28]

This benevolent approach colored the philosophy and practice of the Public School Society. Although it was rightly criticized for allowing anti-Catholic bias in its classrooms, the Society believed that it had contrived a nonsectarian yet strongly moral system capable of uniting and educating "the children of the rich and poor, of the American and the Foreigners, all mingled as a band of brothers."[29] That system, however, had been increasingly hampered by insufficient funds. When Catholics petitioned for a share of the already inadequate school money, therefore, they posed a double threat to Protestant hopes of maintaining the good order of the expanding city.

In the 1840s, New York's diverse, ever-changing, ever-growing society seemingly required a strong, unified agency to foster unity and preserve morality. The division of the school money would both seriously weaken that agency and promote the division of society along religious lines, a fear seemingly justified when the Catholic petition was soon followed by similar requests from one Presbyterian and two Jewish congregations. Such schemes involved an invasion of the "educational police" of the city, warned one writer, which threatened to "map out the metropolis into an infinite number of little plots and subdivisions; each with a characteristic religion and discipline under the governance of its own priests and teachers; here a little scarlet patch of Romanism, there a blue one of Presbyterianism"; did anyone believe "that a community so diverse and heterogeneous could . . . hold together a twelve month?"[30]

Both sides made some effort to settle the issue. The Catholics offered to place their schools under the general supervision of the Society, while it promised not only to eliminate anti-Catholic bias from its schools but to permit the use of its school buildings for Catholic religious instruction.[31] They could not, however, resolve the most basic question, one which was to progressively poison relations between the two sides: What was the basis for morality? If the Society was committed to a nonsectarian, nondoctrinaire Christian basis, Catholics were equally committed to the idea that morality was rooted in Catholic religious doctrines, as they made plain in a reply to the nonsectarian professions of their opponents: "If they do not [exclude sectarian doctrine] . . . they are avowedly no more entitled to the school funds than your petitioners. . . . If they do . . . exclude sectarianism, then your petitioners contend that they exclude Christianity."[32]

STRANGERS AND CITIZENS

Unable to resolve this basic question, the two powerful institutions fell into an increasingly bitter conflict which neither could win. The Catholics lost the first round, when the Common Council rejected their petition by an overwhelming majority. Victory for the Society, however, proved to be a prelude to its destruction; the beginning of its end came in 1842 with the passage of a state law (the Maclay Act) setting up a new city school system headed by a popularly elected Board of Education. The Society was permitted to continue its schools, but they declined in importance until 1853, when they were quietly absorbed by the Board of Education.[33]

Although the Maclay Act altered the situation, it failed to resolve the basic question; in fact, it produced a fresh controversy over Bible reading in the new schools. The act prohibited the expenditure of public money for sectarian purposes, a defeat for those who favored public aid for Catholic schools, but it did not specifically exclude nonsectarian religious training. Protestants insisted that a reading of the Bible "without notes and comment," was a nonsectarian way of communicating the message of Christianity. Spokesmen for the Catholic position objected to the practice, in part because the Bible generally used was the Protestant King James version but, more profoundly, because the very notion of Bible reading without interpretation was Protestant and anti-Catholic.[34] If, then, Bible reading was nothing less than Protestant sectarianism, it should be eliminated from the schools—a position that won the support of others who objected to any kind of Christian religious training.

The controversy confirmed and deepened prejudices on both sides. For Protestants, the Catholic Church had shown that it was opposed to public religious instruction and so proved that it was in favor of perpetuating an ignorance that led to immorality: The disorderliness and poverty of the Irish Catholic poor, therefore, stemmed less from their troubled life in Ireland than from their Catholicism.[35] For Catholic leaders, public education was either a Protestant conspiracy to subvert the Catholic faith, or, when religious instruction was eliminated from the schools, a "godless" conspiracy to subvert Christianity.

They also developed similar suspicions of other public institutions. "How many of our orphan children," wrote Hughes,
"are now sent either to Long Island farms or to the Protestant
asylums, to be brought up in hatred of that religion which was
the only and last consolation of their dying parents?" His
response was to intensify efforts to build a Catholic system
apart from the public institutions, thus darkening the line
between the Catholic Church and the rest of society.[36]

The school controversy, by focusing religious hostilities on
a public issue, added a new complication to the already
disordered politics of the city. In 1841, a committee of the
Common Council warned that special legislation in favor of
any particular religious group would "open a door to the
unholy connection of politics and religion which has so often
cursed and desolated Europe." The next years, indeed, did see
the emergence of an unholy connection between politics and
religion, but it came in an American and not in a European
form. Although anti-Catholic, anti-foreign nativism had previously surfaced in New York, not until the 1840s did it become
an important factor in the society and politics of the city.[37]

Nativism was a vent for popular anxieties and frustrations,
which grew especially strong in 1842 when the school controversy merged with the economic gloom caused by a stagnation
of trade. The decline in business and employment opportunities raised resentments among native tradesmen and workers
against the competition of immigrants. Licensed retailers were
particularly incensed by the rivalry of unlicensed shopkeepers
and peddlers. In 1842, dealers in dry goods, crockery and
glass, groceries, hardware and tinware, stationers, clothiers,
and confectioners met with watchmakers, cabinet-makers, and
other artisa. s to protest against peddlers who with maddening
audacity sometimes stood in front of licensed shops to sell the
same goods available inside. Similarly, the competition of
foreigners for jobs hurt the "laboring and mechanic classes in
this city," said the Association for Improving the Condition of
the Poor, "both by crowding them out of employment, and
diminishing the rewards of industry."[38] Immigrants, then,
seemed to be aggressive invaders of what, by prevailing views,

[34]

was a largely Protestant and native space and, as such, responsible for a variety of noxious problems which had assumed disturbing proportions.

For many New Yorkers, society seemed to be disintegrating with the uneven growth of the city. New faces and new places—the old was changing and, so it seemed during depressed times, rarely for the better. Anxiety and resentment were focused especially on the public streets. Here was the accumulated dirt, manure, and garbage of a crowded city. Here was a cacophonous clutter of carts, wagons, carriages, and omnibuses. Here was the raw world of struggling petty entrepreneurs whose business spilled out on the sidewalk: Saloonkeepers, retailers, butchers, newsboys, and peddlers. Here was the site of riots, fights, raucous behavior, and crime.[39] Thomas Ritter of 104 Cherry Street complained that he and "other peaceful citizens in my neighborhood have long been disturbed by gatherings of youth and adults around the grog shops of the corners of Oliver St. and Cherry and the apple and cake stand at Catherine corner of Cherry. . . . At the apple & cake stand . . . is almost constantly a crowd of boys either fighting or hooting, pitching coppers & blocking up the sidewalk." After protesting that nothing had been done to close "a most abominable brothel" located only two buildings away from him, Ritter concluded: "It is almost impossible for me to find opportunity to worship God quietly in the closet of my house on the Sabbath because of the noises from the causes above mentioned."[40]

Citizens looked to government to restore order in the streets, chiefly by enforcing existing laws. Brothels and disorderly houses should be closed; unlicensed grog shops, carters, retailers, and peddlers put out of business. The government, however, seemed unable or unwilling to act. The dirt, disorder, clutter, noise, conspicuous immorality, and competition continued to grow—and, to compound frustrations, so did taxes and government expenditures. Also disturbing to active citizens and partisans was the apparent corruption of the political process, glaringly illustrated by election violence and fraud.[41] What had gone wrong?

The answer seemed obvious: Both society and government

were being corrupted by the growing host of foreigners. It was the Irish—the Irish, Catholic poor—who provoked the most resentment. Aside from their poverty and their identification with a sectarian Catholicism, their numbers made them conspicuous competitors for jobs and in petty business as well as a major presence in the troubling politics of the city. As it was widely suspected that many of the newcomers had been illegally naturalized in order to manufacture partisan voters, they were associated with what seemed to be a cheapening of citizenship and an accompanying degeneration of the election process. Since they generally supported the Democratic party, the Irish especially antagonized many Whigs, but native-born Democrats also frequently resented them as competitors for places, privileges, and patronage—for the many petty rewards of political activity.[42]

Normally, party loyalties could be expected to restrain these nativist tendencies, but in 1842 the school controversy and economic troubles combined to focus public attention on the presence of immigrants. With the Maclay Act and its provision for the popular election of the Board of Education, nativism found a political arena in which it could act without regard to established party loyalties and issues. In the summer school elections in both 1842 and 1843, Democrats and Whigs joined to elect men who favored the continuation of Bible-reading in the schools.[43] Having won sweeping victories in favor of an "American" school program, nativist Whigs and Democrats in 1843 jointly organized the American Republican Party as an agency of civic reform.[44]

The new party pledged to extend the naturalization period for immigrants to 21 years (the period then required for the native-born to grow to voting age) with the promise that, once foreigners were thus eliminated from politics, then: (1) Because party leaders would no longer compete for foreign votes, elections would be more honest and orderly, (2) the benefits of government in the form of offices and licenses would be reserved to citizens honestly committed to the interests of their city and country, (3) Bible reading and nonsectarian religion would be preserved in the public schools, (4) foreigners would be thoroughly Americanized before they assumed the power and responsibilities of citizens.[45] George B. Cheever, minister of the Allen Street Presbyterian Church and anti-Catholic nativist, promised that, once the 21-year requirement was enacted, "the temptation to buy votes and to sell them, to bribe and to be bribed, and to drag foreign paupers to the polls as soon as they landed would be in great measure taken away. The great source of evil in our elections would be cut off, and the whole play of our affairs would be easier and fairer."[46]

Both the program and the promise were politically naïve, but in a time of social stress this very simplicity appealed to the many voters who had grown tired of the inability or unwillingness of government to solve the problems of the city. If nothing else, the nativist party was a new broom which would sweep an inept and unheeding leadership out of office—and sweep it did. Before the city elections in April 1844, many experienced officeholders sensed the public mood and discretely refused to stand for reelection, thereby assuring the nativists one of the most complete victories ever achieved by a political party in the city. Running in a three-man race, their candidate for Mayor, James Harper, carried 51 of the city's 73 election districts, while American Republican candidates won an overwhelming majority in the municipal legislature; only four of the 34 newly elected Alderman and Assistant Aldermen had served in the previous Common Council.[47]

James Harper, the new Mayor, seemed to be the ideal champion of the movement. A devout Methodist and ardent temperance man, he believed that Sunday was made for religious worship and not for drunken revelry. Like many New Yorkers, he had come from the countryside in pursuit of his ambitions. Unlike many, he had found success in the city as a founder of the great Harper Brothers publishing house known both for the Bibles it published and for the efficiency of its operations. Moreover, he was new to politics. Here was a businessman, free from political commitments and preoccupations, who seemed capable of ending administrative waste and mismanagement in the name of a godly government.[48]

Harper's fate, though, was to be the first in a long line of reform-minded mayors who vanished from government almost as quickly as they came. In this case, his exit through the revolving door of city politics was quicker than most, because his term was for only one year. He was modest enough to recognize his inexperience. Soon after his election, he compared himself to a small boy who had climbed a tree to free his trapped kite, climbing out on smaller and smaller branches until he found himself stuck—and stuck he was, with a commitment to fill the unattainable promises of nativist reformers.[49]

The new Mayor received an especially frustrating lesson in the difference between promises and practices when he attempted to impose order on the streets. Harper committed his administration to enforce ordinances against the sale of liquor on Sunday, the commercial use of sidewalks by peddlers and shopkeepers, and fast and dangerous driving; in July 1844, he stationed a "posse" on Broadway to arrest those guilty of fast driving.[50] A clean, orderly, safe city—the effort to fulfill that promise was, as later reformers would also discover, both politically dangerous and futile. Since these ordinances most affected the poor, the administration soon provoked charges that it was discriminating against widowed apple sellers and other poor street vendors as well as against workingmen who had only Sundays to spend at leisure in the saloons. On the other hand, having stimulated high expectations for law enforcement, the nativists soon proved unable and, in some cases, unwilling to follow through. Harper might urge that all drinking places be closed on Sunday, but some of the Aldermen, who had great influence over law-enforcement, closed their eyes to Sunday drinking; that the glass continued to be lifted in downtown hotels at the very time that the poor man's saloon was closed seemed further proof of class discrimination, especially since at least two members of the Council were hotel owners. [51]

In less than two months, the crusade had broken down in a cloud of protest, recrimination, and frustration. In July, "A Real Native" complained: "I went through many Wards for the last Sabbath, and found the porter-houses, taverns, cigar and candy shops the same as heretofore. . . . Let any person go through the Markets and see if the laws are there enforced? . . . Have the newspaper boys been stopped from bawling through the streets on Sunday? Are the billiard tables connected with houses 'licensed to sell spirits' suppressed?" Were the streets any cleaner and less cluttered? The answer was, of course, No.[52]

The failure of law-enforcement in the spring and summer of 1844 intensified demands for a disciplined, professional police force to replace the haphazard, ineffectual system of watchmen and constables which the city had inherited from the previous century. After months of delay, the Common Council finally brought forth an ordinance which, as with other nativist efforts, tended more to antagonize than to please. Disregarding an opportunity to establish a completely new professional enforcement organization, the Aldermen created a small, uniformed, salaried police force to supplement the existing system. The new police did make some improvement in law-enforcement, but they were too few to be an effective guarantee of order; moreover, they were set apart from much of the population not only by their uniform (a "blue frock-coat, with covered buttons, and dark vest, and blue pantaloons") but by the Council's requirement that they be American citizens. The fledgling force won few friends and was quietly buried soon after the American Republicans lost power.[53]

In less than a year, it was evident that the new party had stumbled and would fall. It had failed to persuade either Congress or the state legislature to extend the naturalization period to 21 years. Moreover, it had failed to deliver on the reform promise of honest, efficient, and low-cost government. The self-proclaimed good citizens had not worked the miracle of honesty and order in the chaotic city of strangers.[54] As they began to lose steam, the American Republicans became increasingly vulnerable to counterattack by the leaders of the two established parties. In preparation for the city elections in April 1845, Whigs and Democrats alike condemned the nativist approach. The nativists, warned one Whig, "wish to tear assunder the bulwark of our liberties, civil and religious, and thereby throw us as a people into civil strife." A decade later,

[39]

Thomas R. Whitney, a member of the movement, was to complain that his party had been destroyed by the smear tactics of politicians who had unjustly fastened upon nativism "charges of 'bigotry' and proscription."[55] Although Mayor Harper remained popular with many voters, he ran a poor second in a three-man race, finishing some 7000 votes behind the Democrat, William F. Havemeyer. The defeat of his party was as complete as its victory had been only a year earlier. In 1844, American Republican strength was spread throughout the city. They had no particular stronghold, so that when their support fell off they were left with nothing, losing every seat in the Common Council. Within two years, the party was dead.[56]

Political nativism was to revive in the mid-1850s, again as a temporary channel for the frustrations and resentments of many of the native-born and also of some naturalized voters who set themselves apart from less assimilated foreigners. Nativism was many things to many different voters, a catch-all for a wide variety of feelings, but above all it won support because it promised to cut the roots of the social and political problems which afflicted the metropolis. Poverty, disorder, immorality, political corruption, inefficient government—all were a part not of the "real" America but of a diverse and disordered cosmopolitan society which had crept upon the city. The conservative Whig, Philip Hone, gave this view an unusually disgruntled and undemocratic form in 1840:

> Scenes of violence, disorder, and riot have taught us in this city that universal suffrage will not do for large communities. It works better in the country, where a large proportion of the voters are Americans, born and brought up on the spot, and where if a black sheep comes into the flock he is marked immediately. But in our heterogeneous mass of vile humanity in our population of 310,000 souls, the men who decide the elections are unknown; they have no local habitation or name, they left their country for ours to better their condition by opposing everything good, honest, lawful and of good report, and to effect this they have banded themselves into associations

to put down at all hazard the party in favor of order and good government.[57]

The nativists attempted to preserve both urban democracy and social order by establishing a homogeneous electorate which would be committed to the interests of the community. In their eyes, they were not bigots, for they did not seek the political exclusion of either immigrants or Catholics as such. They condemned "Popery," not Catholicism; they rejected "foreigners," not immigrants. They demanded that the newcomers assimilate themselves into an essentially Protestant society not as Protestants (this involved divisive religious dogma) but as upholders of nonsectarian Protestant values. Citizens, then, would not be strangers.[58]

The nativist solution, however, ran counter not only to fundamental American values but also to the realities of the modern city. The commercial ties which New York's merchants had created with Europe made the immigrant traffic both profitable and inevitable; even the nativists did not publicly oppose immigration. As the great center of exchange, then, New York was destined to be the great cosmopolitan mixing bowl of the nation. In such a context, nativism was not so much a solution to problems as a naïve and ineffectual effort to avoid the inevitable. Worse, the movement threatened, as many Americans recognized, the very evils it set out to cure. It was, preeminently, the party of unity and order, but its attacks on foreigners and "Romanists" tended both to deepen the ethnic fissure in society and to generate new forms of disorder in which the fine distinction between "Popery" and Catholicism would be lost. Even many of those who believed that the Irish were political and social nuisances could agree with Bishop Hughes when he warned that nativism "was calculated to destroy social confidence—producing feelings of rage on one side and revenge on the other; and among the least enlightened portion of the community of all sides, to produce that welling up of bad passions which an additional drop might have caused to overflow, breaking down every barrier, and leaving our fair city a scene of desolation."[59]

If nativism was no answer, then what could give unity, order, and purpose to a diverse and disorganized city population? What would be the conception of society needed to define the public interest? What should be the nature of community restraints on the freedom of the individual? Perhaps the most common answer was to accept diversity and disorganization not as problems but as essential virtues. New York was *the* American metropolis precisely because, unlike Boston or Philadelphia, it both encouraged individuality and accommodated cultural diversity.[60] It was here in Gotham that men learned to benefit from and to live with a variety of distinctive peoples and ideas.

In 1852, for instance, Daniel Curry argued that the essential character of the city derived from its having been settled by individuals seeking commercial opportunity rather than by an organized group with common goals. In such a society, no single group had the power to assimilate all others, "nor were the various elements of character found among the several classes such as could be harmonized into a consistent unity." New York, therefore, became a confederation of individuals each seeking to live his own life in his own way. This individualism was balanced by each man's recognition that he depended on others to achieve his goals, by a "community of wants and interests" which encouraged the development of tolerance and rationality while permitting the free play of individual energy. To become a member of society it was necessary only to accept the right of every other person to freely pursue his private goals. New York was thus able to accommodate a great diversity of distinctive groups and to transform all of them "into genuine Americans" by teaching the members of such groups to act as individuals in disregard of group interests: "New York energy acts as a solvent to fuse the motley masses that Europe is pouring upon our shores into a consistent body of valuable and happy freemen."[61]

Others saw this live-and-let-live character as a powerful stimulus to the development of individual talents and personality. Thomas R. Gunn said of the city: "It is the most free and easy place conceivable. The right to do as you d——n please

[42]

... is nowhere so universally recognized or less curbed by authority. Individual character, therefore, whether of men or social institutions, is apt to be forcibly developed."[62] At its best, then, New York was a model of cosmopolitan diversity well adapted both to commercial civilization and to individual ambitions. New York was literally the world in which all differences could exist, whose character was the absence of any restrictive character. Assimilation? Homogeneous community? These were not important, because in time all differences would be Americanized. Group distinctions and loyalties would disappear as all men learned to become individuals, tolerant of individual freedom. The city would become a cosmos of human diversity where in public all could meet as brothers in disregard of the diversity of the private worlds from which they came.

The ideal of cosmopolitan individualism was better adapted to the realities of the metropolis than was nativism, but it, too, was flawed. It involved little understanding of the very real ethnic, religious, and racial tensions which permeated the common life of the city, especially of the emotions and needs which lay at the roots of these tensions. Moreover, it tended to sanctify some very troubling elements of New York society. Its easy toleration of differences could degenerate into an indifference to all values. Its acceptance of an amorphous cosmopolitan character could encourage an indifference to the public welfare, for who could be sure what "public" really meant? Its emphasis on the right to do as one "d——n pleased" could justify the selfish pursuit of individual interests. Materialism, corruption, ruthless individualism, an indifference to the plight of the weak, the sense of individual helplessness—these formed the negative side of any large city, but perhaps nowhere more than in New York were they so closely aligned with the prevailing ethos.

In 1843, while New Yorkers were lashing themselves with invidious comparisons with Boston, an observer of both cities described them as representatives of two very different kinds of society. Boston was a model of order and respectability, where a well-established uniform code of behavior guided and regulated human behavior. In New York, on the other hand, "every man you meet . . . walks, with his countenance free of any sense of observation, any dread of his neighbors. He is an integer in the throng, untroubled with any influence beyond the risk of personal accident." This same "stand-alone character" was evident in much of the petty business life of the city: "The drays, instead of belonging to a company are each the property of the man who drives it; the hacks and cabs are under no corporate discipline, every ragged whip doing as he likes with his own vehicle; and all the smaller trades seem followed by the same individual impulse, responsible to nothing but police law." Two years later, N. P. Willis observed more darkly that, in comparison to Boston (which he termed "a Utopian beau ideal of efficiency and order"), New York was more "vicious" and turbulent.[63]

Although they failed to note that Boston had its share of civil disorders, these men made a point which few New Yorkers cared to refute: That New York was both disorganized and disorderly, a city troubled and divided. Having rejected the nativist solution, New Yorkers were still left with the basic problems. How to solve them? Whatever the opinion, the city government had to be an important answer. Government, however, as nearly all could agree, was very much also a part of the problem.

Chapter 3

THE TROUBLE
WITH GOVERNMENT

BY THE 1840s, the government of the city of New York had contracted a variety of perplexing and seemingly incurable ailments. The trouble, in part, was external. As a municipal corporation created by the state legislature, the city was increasingly subjected to interference from Albany. A particularly painful reminder of this dependence on the whim and will of upstaters came in 1842 when the legislature compelled the city to collect a new annual state tax as part of the municipal tax levy, thereby adding some 10 percent to that levy at a time of rising discontent with city taxes. State interference, however, was only one strand in an ever more frustrating situation, for the Municipal Corporation failed to keep up with the needs of the expanding, changing city. Essentially, its duties were simple:

to protect the individual and to promote the public welfare. But what was simple in the rural village or even in the eighteenth-century town had become a bewildering, complicated task in the expanding metropolis. In 1842, an ex-Alderman noted that "Our city is as populous as many of the States, and requires more laws and regulations, and collectors and pays out more monies than any State in the Union"— including the parent state on which it was dependent.[1]

The responsibilities were many. The government was to maintain order in a disorganized society. It was to enforce a multitude of laws and ordinances. It was to apprehend and punish criminals. It was to make, pave, clean, and light the streets. It was to regulate the markets where food was sold, to regulate hacks, cabs, and omnibuses, and to regulate the disposal of ashes, garbage, manure, and the contents of privies. It was to protect the public health. It was to protect the city from fires. It was to take care of the insane, the orphaned, and the dependent poor. Moreover, it was to manage an extensive property in public buildings and streets and also in all the unappropriated lands within the city, all the land between high and low water mark along the city's extensive waterfront, and all ferry rights, "together with the rights of dockage, wharfage, and all the rent, issues, and profits arising or growing out of same; also all rivers, creeks, caves, ponds, etc.; fishing, fowling, hunting, etc., and all the mines, minerals, etc., within the limits of the city."[2]

By its decisions over streets and lands, it could influence the future development of sections of the city. Through its laws and its grants of privileges, it could bring pleasure or pain to the city's thousands of petty businessmen. It could befriend individuals; it provided public works employment for some 750 men through a jobless winter in 1839–40.[3] It could annoy and enrage taxpaying citizens, as well as protect their property. It could punish the vicious and protect the weak—or, it could punish the weak and protect the vicious.

In human terms, the government was a small army of decision makers, agents, and workers; in 1844, there were 3691 men and one woman (a prison matron) directly identified with the governing process. They included the Mayor, 17 Aldermen and 17 Assistant Aldermen, 100 City Marshals, 12 Watch Captains, 24 Assistant Watch Captains, 976 Watchmen, 13 Dock Masters, 1 Commissioner of Health, 16 Health Wardens, 1 City Inspector, 1 Keeper of Potters Field, 15 Night Scavengers, 1 Superintendent of Public Privies, 1 Superintendent of Roads, 1 Superintendent of Streets, 17 Street Inspectors, 7 Inspectors of Manure, 217 Sweepers, 1 Superintendent of Lamps and Gas, 90 Lamplighters, and 34 Assessors. In addition, there were various keepers, guards, and other employees in the prisons and asylums managed by the Almshouse Department, as well as 1661 volunteer firemen.[4]

The City Corporation had the responsibility for doing many things. The trouble was that it seemed to do all of them badly. In striking contrast to the progressive tendencies of the city's commerce, its domain reeked of decay: Decrepit, dirty, cluttered public docks and markets; dusty, muddy, garbage-laden, stinking, disorderly public streets. One citizen complained that a walk through Broadway "has been perilous to the lungs and the eyes, and certain ruin to one's clothes." Another New Yorker said that in many areas of the city, "heaps of offal and garbage are thrown into the streets . . . and ten thousand swine are steadily engaged in rendering this reeking mass of filthy and putrescent matter still more offensive."[5] The obnoxious character of the streets stretched beyond simple dirt to include the noise, clutter, and all-around disorder increasingly typical of New York public life. As the brief reign of nativism showed, many New Yorkers believed that their government had failed to enforce necessary civic discipline, especially among undisciplined newcomers to the city.

Even worse, the piles of filth were matched by mounting costs of government. Those who took the long view estimated that in the forty years before 1841, city expenses had increased some 24 times, but of more immediate concern was the fact that expenditures doubled during the 1840s and then increased threefold in the next decade.[6] With growing expenditures came rising taxes. Between 1839 and 1846, the tax rate doubled, the biggest increase coming in 1842 when the rate jumped by

38 percent—not enough, however, to keep the government from spending more than it received during the next two years.[7] The warning of a special committee of the Common Council in 1839 was to be repeated in the future: "Notwithstanding the great increase of the city taxes, the debt has been constantly accumulating."[8]

Most of the financial burden was a natural result of New York's growth as a modern commercial metropolis. Streets had to be extended and paved to facilitate the growing flood of carts, wagons, carriages, cabs, and omnibuses which helped sustain the expanding metropolis. An expensive water system (the Croton system) had to be built to replace the increasingly polluted wells of a thickening population. Public schools had to be erected to meet the educational expectations and needs of an urban population. Almshouses, asylums, prisons and police organizations had to be expanded in reponse to the problems posed by an increasingly diverse people, many of whom were poor.[9] To meet such a wide range of needs meant not only heavy investments and debts, but a consequent increase in expenditures to maintain the enlarged system. More paved streets meant more street cleaning. More police meant more prisons and station-houses which in turn required more money for maintenance. Throughout the public system, an increase in one component influenced the operations of other components. Usually, the influence boiled down to the need for more money.[10]

Such expansion became particularly onerous when the depressed state of the economy in the early 1840s both increased social needs and shrank the city's tax base.[11] The spectacular jump of the tax rate in 1842 came not only from an increase in spending but from a decline in assessed property values of nearly $14 million in that year alone; between 1840 and the bottom of the decline in 1843, values diminished by over 9 percent ($29 million). Not until 1848 did assessed values return to the 1840 level.[12] In contrast, Boston during this period managed to maintain a far stronger tax base to support its government, as *Hunt's Magazine* pointed out in 1852: "Although the rate of taxation per head is much larger in Boston than in

[48]

New York, the burden upon property is less, the wealth of the former city being much greater in proportion to its inhabitants than that of New York."[13]

What could be done? One answer was to find new sources of revenue, especially new property to tax. There were persistent suspicions that much personal property, particularly in the form of financial securities and business facilities, had escaped taxation because their well-to-do owners either were on vacation during the summer assessment period or lived elsewhere, in the suburbs or in Europe.[14] "Poor men in business who have but little capital or personal property are taxed in full," complained one New Yorker, "while the rich, richer, and richest pay little in proportion."[15]

Despite such complaints, however, little was done to reach deeper into the rich man's pocket, in part because the issue involved a dilemma which increasingly was to trouble the makers of financial policy. More intensive efforts to tax the rich, especially the business classes, threatened to drive them out of New York to its independent suburbs, particularly to fast-growing Brooklyn, then a separate city, which publicized itself as a refuge from onerous New York taxes. However, the failure to tap this wealth for revenue purposes meant a higher tax rate on that property which was assessed or a deterioration of government services, either of which also threatened to encourage the flight of wealth to the suburbs. In 1847, reformers warned "that property is continually tending from our city to escape the oppressiveness of our taxation. . . . Thus, while every suburb of New York is rapidly growing, and villages twenty and thirty miles distant are sustained by incomes earned here and expended there, our City has no equivalent rapidity of growth, and unimproved property here is often unsalable at a nominal price."[16] In the 1840s, this dilemma was only dimly realized, but it was to give birth in the next decade to the long-frustrated but eventually successful effort to annex Brooklyn and other adjacent areas into a greater New York City.

The reasons why New York failed to find adequate sources of revenue are complex (one cannot completely discount the possibility, for instance, that the alleged untaxed wealth simply was not there), but whatever the reasons the result was that city government had to face a class of strongly dissatisfied property holders. Rarely did the complainers think of their taxes as basically a necessary payment for the social and economic benefits of metropolitan life. Enamored with a social ideal modeled from the simple world of the rural village, inclined to treat the city as a resource to be exploited for their own particular private benefit, they saw the city budget far more as an index of municipal bungling than as the bill due for maintaining the public space so essential to their well-being.

If government was such an obvious and obnoxious failure, critics reasoned, then the best way to reform it was to reduce its responsibilities and powers as much as possible. If street cleaning seemed to be a costly mess, let the streets be cleaned by businessmen acting under contract with the city rather than by the government itself. If public markets and docks cost more than the revenues they produced for the city, then dissolve the markets and sell off the docks. Such steps would both simplify administration and reduce the costs of government.[17] The Corporation, too, should disentangle itself from its role as the city's largest property owner. Faced with mounting debts, the Common Council in 1844 decided to sell off all unnecessary and unproductive property, especially in land, in order to provide for the redemption of the city debt, a step which would also place more property in private hands and so increase the tax rolls.[18] Retrench, reduce costs, simplify government, let businessmen do what politicians so obviously could not do—these were rallying cries for reform which suited not only the interests of taxpayers but the rising faith in the virtues of private enterprise as well.

They were difficult to achieve, however, in part because they encountered strong opposition from interests entrenched in the public domain. The food vendors and others who had purchased places in the public markets, for instance, opposed the abolition of the markets unless they were amply compensated for their loss, while the threatened loss of jobs and patronage in the Street Cleaning Department made many voters and politicians hostile to the contract system. Even when enacted, such measures fell short of reformers' promises. The contract system, tried on an off-again, on-again basis, failed significantly to reduce either cleaning costs or the level of dirt in city streets.[19] The sale of city property also was far from satisfactory. To achieve a modest reduction in its indebtedness, the city auctioned off lands in the 1840s at bargain prices. Most of the properties, located in the area between 39th and 42nd Streets and Fifth Avenue and Broadway, skyrocketed in value during the prosperous 1850s, leading one critic to complain that the Corporation had virtually given away lands whose later value was more than sufficient "to wipe out at once the entire debt of the city."[20]

Reform programs were only partly realized, reform goals rarely achieved. Taxes continued to rise and services seemingly to deteriorate. Why? Although it was obvious that the economic troubles of the 1840s complicated the task of governing the growing city, critics preferred to believe that the failure to combine low taxes with good services was the fault of a corrupt and bungling government. Critics readily found evidence to support their views in the bicameral Common Council of Aldermen and of Assistant Aldermen which enacted the laws, passed the taxes, selected the programs, and in general managed or mismanaged the affairs of the city. By the early 1840s, the Council had become the object of public concern and contempt as well as the most formidable problem of government.

Even its friends admitted its defects but blamed the situation on the fact that the people's representatives—who received no salary—were overworked. Certainly, the work of the Aldermen had become a complex and time consuming task involving a boggling variety of responsibilities, great and small. One Council, for example, during the last six months of its term (1841–42) acted on some 260 resolutions covering taxes, streets, the markets, the watch, water supply, ferries, lands, appointments, the fire department, docks and wharves and other matters—all this being done at once-weekly meetings generally held at night. "The infinite variety of peculiar circumstances incidental to an artificial state of society as is created in a large commercial city," said Alderman Josiah Rich in 1841, "calls for intellectual labors which are arduous, complicated, and difficult in the extreme."[21]

What would encourage men to take on such arduous tasks? Certainly not the nonexistent pay, nor a devotion to the public interest which—as Alderman Rich pointed out—was weak in New York: "Among the changing population or our city there are comparatively few whose interests become permanently identified with its prosperity. . . . Of those who become permanent residents, few have leisure to attend to anything except their private affair, and that few are generally men of wealth, who are not remarkable for public spirit." Who, then, would be willing to serve as Aldermen? "The people are confined in their choice of their municipal legislators to the very small class of men who have a strong thirst for distinction, and can afford to sacrifice the necessary time, or who have some unseen and unsuspected private object to obtain."[22]

Rich, perhaps, was unjust as well as unkind to his colleagues, but most of these amateur Aldermen gave much more time to their own business affairs than to the complex job of protecting the public interest.[23] Often they were not even experienced amateurs, for elections brought, substantial changes in membership each year.[24] Distracted, unprepared, tired—they lent at least some substance to the hostile description in 1843 of the Council as appearing more like "a hen roost than that of an assemblage of dignified representatives of our city—the members inclining in all positions, some asleep upon their desks, the President *pro tem* gracefully sitting with his feet placed a considerable distance above his head, and his eyes, if open, presenting a very *leaden* appearance."[25] These men governed a troubled city of over 300,000 people.

A logical response to the situation was to provide the Aldermen with salaries, a step which, as Alderman Rich pointed out, was in harmony with the emerging social ethos of the metropolis: "The organization of society, which provides for a division of labor among its members, does not demand voluntary sacrifices of time and talent from any member of the community."[26] This, however, ran against a deep rooted commitment to amateurism in government. The earlier—and smaller—city had been governed by enlightened amateurs—and governed well, so it was remembered. Moreover, the idea of professional paid legislators was at odds with the current democratic belief that only those representatives who shared directly in the ordinary working life of the people could be trusted to understand the people's needs. Thus, the Whig party, more closely aligned with the city's merchant elite than the Democrats, boasted in 1843 that its slate of candidates for the Council included 18 "mechanics" and only 6 merchants, whereas the opposing ticket included (among others) 11 merchants and only 5 mechanics.[27]

If critics would not agree that the Council was underpaid, they often could agree that it was overworked; but they blamed that defect on the Aldermen themselves. In 1842, an "ex-Alderman" asserted that the members of the Council, out of "a love of jurisdiction and power," had taken on too many offices and given themselves too much unrestrained power: "Is it not an anomaly that the same individuals, as a Committee on Public Offices and Repairs, build our prisons; as Watch and Police Committee, arrest and examine us; as a Market Committee, contract for our food and raiment; as Supervisors tax us, and as Common Council men audit all their own, or rather our, accounts, make all City Laws."[28] Virtually unrestrained, the Council controlled patronage, contracts, revenues, and an array of other matters—enticements to venality as well as burdens to conscientious effort.

The result, as seen by the critics, was extravagance in expenditure and inefficiency in operation. If the Aldermen depended on the votes of street-sweepers and other employees whose appointments they controlled, if employees were appointed on the basis of their political support, who then could enforce efficiency, who could assure that the streets would be cleaned? The way to reform the Council, then, was to reshape it to conform to the current ideal of government as a simple machine with simple, definite responsibilities. How to disentangle the Council from its own web? How to simplify administration, check legislative wickedness, and clarify responsibilities? These were emerging as the central questions of nineteenth-century political reform—ones which posed work for giants and for decades.

Unlike many future reformers, the first man to grapple with this problem was a professional officeholder who had considerable experience in the labyrinths of the governing process. Robert H. Morris (1802–1855), the son of a New York merchant, was one of the city's most successful lawyers and a major presence in the local Democratic party. When he was first elected Mayor in 1841, he brought with him the experience gained as an assistant District Attorney, state legislator, and City Recorder. After completing three consecutive one-year terms as Mayor, he was to serve as Postmaster of New York (an important Federal patronage post) and, in his last years, as a Justice of the State Supreme Court.[29]

During his first year, the new Mayor made no effort to change the basic form of government. His principles, as he expressed them in his first annual message, were the pious ones of virtually every newly elected executive. After urging the Democrat-controlled Council to maintain the "strictest economy in the city government" (already a timeworn cliché), he declared that "the government should be so systematized as to be carried on by the least number of agents compatible with its importance. This will not only ensure efficiency in its operations, but will lessen the chances for peculation." His most significant proposal to achieve governmental simplicity and efficiency was for the sale of unneeded city-owned property when real estate values recovered from the depression.[30]

Soon after his reelection in April 1842, however, he was made aware of the need for more basic change. Although Morris's personal popularity had carried him to victory, popular dissatisfaction with government gave the Whigs control of the Council. The Whig Aldermen did attempt some reforms; they reduced salaries and established the contract system for street cleaning.[31] Good intentions, however, were partly cancelled out by the irresistible political impulse to enjoy the spoils of victory. Nowhere was this more evident than in the Whig manipulation of the watch system. Traditionally, the city had depended on part-time watchmen to protect the persons and property of its citizens, but by 1842 it was evident that this system of amateur policemen was no longer capable of maintaining order. The problem of creating an effective police had become, and was long to remain, one of the troublesome elements in the larger problem of city government. The response of the Whigs, however, was not to change the system but to turn it to their advantage.

After winning public applause by reducing the pay of the watchmen, they then took control of the system away from Mayor Morris and vested it in the Council by overriding the Mayor's veto. Having done that, they next ousted Democrats from the Watch force and replaced them with Whigs, for the thousand watchmen represented a thousand useful, partisan votes. The next step, however, was not politically helpful. The Council had created a Whig watch force, but it proved to be an angry Whig force which threatened to turn against the party unless their pay was restored to its earlier level. In November 1842, the Aldermen capitulated, thereby adding back to the city budget almost as much as they had eliminated earlier.[32] As the tax rate jumped by more than one-third that year, this act was, for outraged taxpayers, the easiest to remember and the most difficult to forgive.

The Whig Council was no worse than the average in the 1840s (and measured against the Councils of the next decade it resembled an assemblage of Solons), but in its short year it failed to affect the miracles of reform demanded by an impatient city. It had not conquered the rising tax rate, made the streets notably cleaner, or created a more effective police system to maintain order.[33] Moreover, the Council had maneuvered itself into open combat with a personally popular mayor, especially over politically important patronage matters. Certainly, it did little to ease public unrest. The year 1842 was one of the most troubled of many troubled years for New York. The school controversy had begun to excite those tremors which produced the nativist landslide of 1844. Commerce declined; unemployment rose; property values fell. Both the new school system established under the Maclay Act and the recently completed Croton water system added heavily to the costs of government. Frustrated and outraged, New Yorkers gave vent to their feelings in the next annual election in April 1843 by returning Morris and his party to complete control of the city government.[34]

Victory, however, brought with it the responsibility of re-form, as Morris recognized. His struggles with the Whigs had convinced him that the problem was the failure of the Aldermen to respect the separation of legislative and executive power. Not content simply with making the laws, the Council also attempted to implement them through executive committees which, Morris charged, had become irresponsible miniature governments: The committees "determined, legislatively, that work was necessary to be done; executively, they made the contract or employed the workmen; in many instances took the contract themselves or were interested in it; executively they determined whether their own work was properly done, and directed payment to themselves out of the City Treasury." Thus, much money been wasted, and large sums had been paid out to members of the Council. Although the money was spent for services and supplies (shortly, Morris was to refer to "pretended, unnecessary and half-performed services"), it could easily lead to corruption: "Such practice will lead persons to obtain seats in the Common Council with the express object of making money out of the City Treasury."[35]

Morris sought to restrict the influence of the Aldermen, but significantly he also refused to increase his own power as Mayor. Although his veto had proven ineffectual against the Whig Council (it could be overridden by a simple majority) he did not demand a stronger veto, nor did he try to transfer the Council's control over appointments to himself. Instead, he proposed a plan to divide the patronage power among various independent executive departments, the heads of which were to be elected directly by the people.[36] His distaste for central-ization of power, even in his own office, was fully demonstrated when some ten weeks later he supplemented his original proposal by urging an even more radical decentralization of government.

Morris urged the Council to give up its power to appoint

city functionaries as an act of self-purification which would both ease its workload and protect it from the corrupting influence of the spoils system. In place of the patronage system, the Mayor proposed a scheme for the appointment of all city employees either by the popularly elected department heads or by the people themselves; each ward would elect not only an Alderman and Assistant Alderman, but also a Justice of the Peace, two Assessors, an Overseer of the Poor, a Clerk, a Street Inspector, two Captains of Police, and the requisite number of policemen. Most radical of all, the Mayor envisioned the creation of ward councils, consisting of the Alderman, Assistant, Justice of the Peace and Assessors, which would "prescribe the internal government of the Ward," although all decisions were to be consistent with the ordinances of the Common Council. Conflicts over such matters as the paving or cleaning of streets separating two wards would be resolved by joint meetings of the local Councils. Such a plan, said Morris, would give the people a direct role in the governing process and bring greater honesty, lower taxes, and more efficient administration. Reform would be achieved by adhering to the simple Jeffersonian formula: "The best, most efficient and least expensive government is that which is brought the nearest to the people."[37] Thus did Mayor Morris attempt to restore the virtues of town government to a disorganized urban political society.

The plan was a pleasant dream, one which was to have a powerful appeal and some influence in the future, but it stood little chance of being realized. It required that political leaders give up their own dreams of power and prestige in favor of an untested popular system of government, a system doubly suspect in a city sharply divided by ethnic and religious controversy. Perhaps Morris was encouraged in his hopes for decentralization by the enactment of the Maclay Act, which provided for decentralized decision-making, but the conflict over Bible-reading within the new school system did little to make the essential idea popular with political and social leaders.[38] The response of the Common Council was predictable. After politely shelving the proposal, the Aldermen thumbed their collective nose at the very idea of self-sacrifice in patronage matters by increasing both the size and pay of the watch force in preparation for the state elections of November 1843. Six months later, both the Council and Morris's plan were swept away by the nativist landslide.[39] Neither Mayor Harper nor the new Council gave much thought to changing the structure of city government, if only because there were committed to the hope that fundamental reform could be achieved by changing the nature of the electorate.

The belief that the Common Council was the central problem in government, however, did not die with Morris's decentralization plan. When a Democratic victory in the city elections of 1845 ended the hopes for nativism, the stage was set for another attack on the legislative octopus. The new Mayor, William F. Havemeyer, declared that misgovernment in New York was a well-established fact, but denied that the blame rested with those who governed. Rather, the fault was in the system itself: "The Government of the City remains substantially the same as when it was instituted to regulate the affairs of a petty municipal Corporation, while the community upon which it acts, has grown until it embraces a larger population than several of the States of the Union." As Morris had done, he attacked the Council's entanglement with patronage as the major evil which corrupted both the legislators and the voters.[40] Under the existing system, government tended to be "a mere machine for the distribution of public favors." It is notable that like Morris and virtually every other reformer, Havemeyer attempted to solve the problem not by establishing a civil service system of permanent tenure for municipal functionaries but by reallocating the patronage power at the expense of the Council.

Havemeyer's call for structural reform demanded action. Public dissatisfaction was too strong to be ignored, especially after the Council in early 1846 applied to the legislature for authority to levy $2.5 million in taxes, nearly twice as large as the tax some six years before.[41] Change, yes—but what kind of change? Although the Aldermen prudently showed some willingness to give up their executive power and to reduce their influence over patronage, reformers were divided over the question as to whether that power and influence was to be centralized in the Mayor or be apportioned among various popularly elected department heads, as Morris had suggested in 1843. When the Council proposed a plan to concentrate the appointive power in the Mayor, it provoked loud debate within the Democratic party; a meeting at Tammany Hall broke into such violent wrangling that it reminded one observer of "a council of monkeys."[42]

The dispute over structural reform focused on two related issues. One involved the question as to who would constitute the most responsible and responsive executive power, elected department heads or department heads appointed by a mayor? Some reformers supported elected heads on the grounds that they would naturally be more sensitive to the people's wishes; in contrast, a strong mayor with strong appointive power posed the threat of "executive tyranny." Others, however, believed that the division of power among a number of elected departments would simply reproduce the same irresponsibility that had plagued government in the past.[43] The second issue involved the patronage power, a vital question for the many party faithful who held or wanted to hold office. Would they benefit if the power to make appointments were concentrated in the Mayor's office or if it were divided among elected department heads closer to the rank-and-file? Especially among challengers of the party's leadership, the tendency was to favor a system which divided and diffused the appointive power.[44]

The dispute over these matters came to a head in the summer and fall of 1846, when the question of reorganization was taken up by a special City Convention established by the state legislature for that purpose. As 33 of the 36 popularly elected delegates were Democrats, the controversies within the party threatened to reappear at the Convention. Perhaps this is why the delegates, when they first met in City Hall, decided against reporting their deliberations to the public.[45] With a minimum of publicity and with what seemed to be a minimum of effort (the convention adjourned for the month of August), they finally put together a new city charter, most of which was later to be adopted in 1849 as the city's frame of government. The delegates satisfied one reform hope by stripping the Council of its executive functions. They were, however, either unable or unwilling to construct a coherent executive power. While they gave the Mayor a strong presidential-style veto, they divided executive responsibility by establishing distinct executive departments, each headed by an elected head, and then further complicated the executive arrangement by giving the Mayor power over most, though not all, appointments in the departments.[46] The proposed government was, despite its complications, an improvement over the existing sytem, but it was not the kind to inspire much interest, especially since the convention had avoided publicizing its work. This absence of public discussion was unfortunate, for in November the proposal was submitted to the electorate for approval in company with a proposed new state constitution. Faced with the responsibility of voting intelligently on two frames of government at the same time, many New Yorkers responded by not voting at all on the charter, and it was defeated by more than 1000 votes.[47]

As a result, the old government was left to muddle through its increasingly more complex responsibilities. "At present," said the *Evening Post*, "the care of our finances, of our hospitals, of our prisons, of our alms houses, of our police, of our streets, of our wharves and other public property, is thrown upon a miscellaneous body, who are half bewildered by the superintendence of these vast institutions of a vast population."[48] What had stalled reform? Why had not the Council been relieved of its bewildering tasks? Why, too, had the city's political leadership been so unenthusiastic about the proposed charter? One obvious answer was that reform, like every other governmental matter in New York, was entangled with the politics not only of the city but also of the state and nation. Politicians, though they might favor reform in the abstract, were not inclined to change the existing system for fear that they might jeopardize their power in the larger party as well as at home. There were, for instance, important state and federal offices in New York which could be won only if the politicians had influence in

Albany and Washington—and they were likely to have that influence only if they controlled appointments to city offices.[49]

The logical response to this situation seemed to be some new nonpartisan political organization which would take the affairs of the city out of state and national politics and out of the hands of the politicians. The hope of disentangling municipal affairs from party politics had been the basis for most of the ephemeral strength of the American Republican Party. In January 1847, after political nativism had withered away, the nonpartisan approach was revived by a group of reformers headed by two men destined to become mayor: a Democrat, Daniel F. Tiemann, and a Whig, Caleb S. Woodhull. Their new City Reform party soon faded away, but not before it had helped convince the leaders of the two major parties of the need for change. By threatening a citizen's revolt against the parties, it had raised a signal which politicians could read and appreciate. What had been bipartisan indifference to reform in 1846 became bipartisan interest in the cause, as both Whigs and Democrats took up the issue of reorganization. As a result, when a new reform charter was submitted to the voters in April 1849, it was overwhelmingly approved.[50]

It was the first significant change in municipal government in nearly twenty years. Like so many future changes, however, it raised hopes only to turn them into ashes and bitterness. Although the new charter brought some improvement, it disappointed the expectations for a fundamental reorganization of government. Reformers had dreamed of a simple, efficient, responsible governmental organization, but compromise had turned their lean, swift horse into an ungainly camel. On the positive side, the Charter attacked the central problem of the past by eliminating the authority of the Common Council to make appointments or to perform executive business. As a further restraint on its tendencies to connive and to spend, its members were prohibited from having an interest in any work or transaction involving the expenditure of public money. In general, the work of the Alderman was both simplified and more sharply defined.

The Trouble with Government

The Council, however, was left with a variety of legislative functions which in themselves were to assume formidable proportions with the growth of the city. It retained not only its crucial powers to tax and to spend but an increasingly important responsibility for the use, sale, and leasing of city property. Much unproductive land could be sold off, but the city could not disassociate itself from other forms of property which were becoming of ever increasing value, especially ferry leases (enhanced by the rapid growth of the city's suburbs in New Jersey and Long Island) and franchises for the use of public streets (of great importance to the street railways, which would appear in the early 1850s). If reform had succeeded in diminishing the Council's involvement with patronage, the course of events was increasing its power over wealth.[51] Left to face these awesome—and tempting—responsibilities were essentially the same amateurs who had managed and mismanaged council business before; unlike the rejected charter of 1846, which would have provided for salaries of $400 a year for Aldermen, the revisions left them to scramble for whatever legitimate income they could find.[52]

In other ways, too, the new charter disappointed hopes for a solution to the governmental problem. The solution toward which the period was awkwardly moving was to shift the locus of government from the Council to the executive power in order to simplify government and to establish a system of well-defined responsibilities for the management of municipal affairs. The defeated charter of 1846 would have strengthened the Mayor by giving him a presidential-style veto and some effective, although muddled, power over executive appointments. The charter of 1849 gave him neither, leaving him only slightly stronger than he had been before, although it did extend his term from one year to two. His greatest single strength lay in his position as head of the Police Department, a fact of great consequence in the 1850s. Otherwise, he was denied a wide range of executive powers, which were scattered among nine other departments headed by independent elected officials who, with a few exceptions, controlled appointments within their departments.

THE TROUBLE WITH GOVERNMENT

This complicated arrangement had its appealing side. Each department, in theory, would be responsible directly to the people for carrying out clearly defined executive tasks. The new Finance Department would collect and pay out all city revenues. The Street Department would be responsible for constructing the streets and maintaining the public wharves and piers. The Department of Repairs and Supplies would maintain all public roads, buildings, and machinery. The Department of Streets and Lamps would be responsible for both lighting and cleaning the streets. The Croton Aqueduct Department would manage the city's water supply. The City Inspector's Department would supervise all matter relating to public health. The Almshouse Department would manage the prisons and almshouses. The Law Department would conduct all the legal business of the city. And the Fire Department (whose chief was to be elected by the city's all-volunteer force) would put out the city's fires.[53]

Together with the Police Department, ten executive powers would respond to ten different municipal needs. One trouble, of course, was that in the complex and interdependent city no one had found a way of creating ten sharply defined executive domains over which the ten executives would have exclusive responsibility. This was particularly the case in regard to that festering sore of municipal administration, the streets. The Streets and Lamps Department had the responsibility for cleaning them, but not for extending them, paving them, repairing them, or tearing them up—all of which affected their condition, all of which were influenced by decisions made in other departments. Such blurred and overlapping jurisdictions both interfered with efficient management and reduced the level of responsibility in each department.

This scattered power might have been unified for effective executive action, if the people had been able to elect ten conscientious and responsible men as department heads; but this was impossible. As shrewd politicians must have recognized, people were not likely to make responsible and meaningful decisions when they had to choose among twenty or more candidates for executive positions. As if to boggle the election

THE TROUBLE WITH GOVERNMENT

process further, the new charter also moved the city elections, which had been held in April—apart from state and national elections—to November; consequently, voters had to choose among a bewildering variety of candidates for Congress, state senate, state legislature, governor, lieutenant governor and judgeships as well as for mayor, alderman, assistant alderman, comptroller, street commissioner, city inspector, corporation council and other positions in city government. This electoral chaos made partisan labels even more important than before. When the Whig General Committee submitted its slate for the elections in November 1851, it urged voters to consider first "our CAUSE, and MEN afterward"—no wonder, since citywide there were 165 Whig nominees for 165 state and municipal posts ranging from state assemblymen and judges to ward school commissioner. In each ward, the Whigs presented a minimum of 26 candidates. The Whig ticket was simple in comparison to those of the factionalized Democrats, who in many wards ran competing candidates.[54] Inept structural reform, born out of democratic good intentions as well as political expediency, thus served to make it more difficult for the public to select honest and capable men to manage the affairs of the city.

It was not surprising, then, that 1849 should prove to be simply the first of several false dawns of reform in the city's history. Reformers had hoped to eliminate the influence of politics from the administration of government; instead, that influence grew both more complex and more pervasive. They had hoped to stem the rise of taxes, expenditures, and the city debt; all continued to rise. They had hoped to mold government into an instrument to achieve civic order; civic disorder seemed to grow even more threatening than before. They had hoped to restrain those tendencies toward dishonesty in government which had led the *Tribune* some months before the new charter was approved to compare the Aldermen with the fabled "Forty Thieves"; less than three years later, New Yorkers elected a Common Council which soon won the title of "Forty Thieves" by out-spending and out-conniving any previous Council.[55]

[64]

The Trouble with Government

What had gone wrong? The question would continue to impel political reformers to tinker with the structure of government. Perhaps a more valid question, however, is whether anything had gone wrong, for behind all of the anguished cries regarding rising taxes, corruption, and dirty streets there was a fundamental satisfaction with the political system. Even at its worst, government did meet the basic needs of most New Yorkers. It was the lynchpin of a political system centered on party loyalty and patronage which provided prestige, jobs, comfort, and places for thousands of people. It assured a basic order, as dirty and crime-ridden as it was, which guaranteed the exercise of that right which was most precious of all, the right to do as one would "d——n please"; its management, or mismanagement, of public space aided far more than it inhibited the New Yorker's favorite pursuits, especially the pursuit of wealth. Despite the periodic anguish of taxpayers, the tax burden was actually light by the standards of later days and of some other contemporary American cities. In general, the demands of civic responsibility rarely interfered with individual self-interest. "If things go wrong in the city government," wrote one observer of the New York scene, "if the streets are neglected, if the public purse is plundered, if taxes are high, our citizens console themselves with the reflection that their own private affairs are all right."[56]

Undoubtedly, the growing public contempt and concern for government was justified. Neither the personnel nor the structure of the Municipal Corporation constituted a satisfactory agency of public purpose for the big and growing city. Half-enlightened amateurs faced a bewildering variety of half-understood problems which they were expected to solve with powers and budgets better suited to the eighteenth-century town than to the modern metropolis. Yet this is one way of saying that the trouble with government was also very much the trouble with society. Disorder, crime, dirty streets, and the incompetence and corruption which so conveniently explained why these ills had not been remedied—all had their causes in the crowded, disorganized city of citizens and strangers. The Corporation was expected to remedy problems without seriously disturbing their roots, without trespassing on the private rights and interests of citizens. When it failed, it was rewarded with public contempt and concern which further undermined its integrity as a reliable instrument of public purpose.

Much of the trouble with government can be traced to two characteristics of the great and growing metropolis. One was the general devotion of society to the proposition that each man had the right to strive for wealth with a minimum of distraction from government or anything else, a right which many citizens fully exercised at the expense of their civic responsibilities and ultimately of the public interest. The other was the city's large and growing mass of poor people. Both characteristics formed the stuff not only of many clichés about New York but of its essential troubles. Poverty especially was a pervasive problem as a major source of disorder, disease, and disreputable politics, as a drain on the municipal treasury, and as an insult to the city's self-image as the metropolis of a happy, prosperous, and progressive America. Although the poor had long caused concern in New York, the troubles of the early 1840s significantly deepened that concern and brought new efforts to cope with the problem. In these efforts, government played an inevitable role, but its work against poverty, as with other matters, was diminished by the then popular attempt to shift responsibility over important public matters from the political sphere to the realm of private enterprise.

Chapter 4

POVERTY

IN DECEMBER 1846 a young and poor German immigrant was quietly separated from the great mass of New Yorkers. When he had arrived in the city some two years before, he had not been able to find a job, became a rag picker, got sick, had to depend on the meager earnings of his wife and the sale of their household effects, was finally cornered by poverty in a dank, cold cellar room in 13th Street, and died of starvation on a bed "consisting of a few shavings and his old rag bag being rolled up for a pillow." Three months later, an Irish woman— a wife and mother—died in another damp, cold cellar on James Street. Her body was discovered "uncared for, in its rags on some wet straw scattered upon the floor in one corner, while the father and children were sick and moaning with hunger—all near the center of this great metropolis! Two of the children were near dying; in their abode, no fire, no food, no table, no shroud or coffin for their dead, no friends to console them!"[1]

Social New York: I

FIGURE 6. (at right, above) The lithographed drawing by John Perry Newell features the city residence in the 1850s of Daniel Parish at the corner of 16th Street and Fifth Avenue (in the Eighteenth Ward). Parish was one of New York's richest men, but his wealth did not entirely exempt him from the crowding so typical of the city.

FIGURE 7. (at right, below) A much different kind of crowding is portrayed in the lithograph (1852) by Charles Parsons of the infamous "Old Brewery" in the Five Points slum area. This abandoned brewery building allegedly housed as many as a thousand people at a time before it was taken over by the Ladies Home Missionary Society and torn down in 1852.

Courtesy of the Prints Division, New York Public Library, Eno Collection.

POVERTY

Poverty was rarely so grimly final. Few people died of starvation in nineteenth-century New York. Yet poverty had become an ever increasing presence in the life and death of the city. It was seen in the thousands who resorted to charity or to the municipal almshouse—and in the beggars who posed a ragged insult to the land of opportunity. It could be seen in the swarm of peddlers and apple sellers who clustered before the Merchant's Exchange and on the Ferry Landings—and heard in the sing-songs of the hot-corn girls who peddled their wares to street crowds until late in the night:

> Hot corn! Hot corn!
> Here's your lily-white corn.
> All you that's got money
> Poor me that's got none—
> Buy me lily-white corn
> and let me go home.

It could be seen in the *chiffoniers*, or rag-pickers—men, women, and children—who searched through the city's trash and garbage for anything of value, including scraps of food.[2] In good times as well as bad, poverty shadowed the increasingly conspicuous wealth of New York's successful citizens. For one November night in 1848, for instance, the *Tribune* could report both that a "brilliant and fashionable" audience had attended the Astor Place Opera House and that the coming of winter had "already trebbled the ranks of beggars in the streets. . . . In dark and dreary alleys, barefooted and ragged children delve among the filth for bones and cinders."[3]

Many, perhaps most, successful New Yorkers dismissed poverty in these forms as an irrelevant exception from, or even an affront to, the true nature of American society. Beggars, vagrants, *chiffoniers* . . . these were foreigners—the paupers, idlers, and degraded overflow of European society to be (as the nativists especially urged), ignored, discouraged, and excluded. Yet, it was difficult to ignore the thought that behind these outcasts lay a deeper well of poverty embracing unknown thousands of unseen poor, those "who are not beggars, and

yet are liable at any moment to be reduced to beggary."[4] Estimates of the number of poor, especially of the great many tucked away in side streets and back alleys, were mere guess-work, at best pliable facts shaped to fit varied contentions. Horace Greeley, the reform-minded editor of the *Tribune*, for instance, supported his plea for a rearrangment of American society with the assertion in 1845 "that there are Fifty Thousand People in this City who have not the means of a weeks comfortable subsistence and know not where to obtain it." Greeley was soon upstaged by the Reverend Samuel I. Prime, who supported his own plea that ambitious Americans not migrate to misery-laden New York with the contention that not one-seventh but fully one-fifth, some 75,000, of New Yorkers had been forced to resort to charity.[5]

As uncertain as the statistics were, they demonstrated the unavoidable truth that many New Yorkers were poor. Most of the trouble stemmed from the city's failure to find full use for the skills and muscle of its expanding population. In the bleak early 1840s, the slowdown of commercial activity brought both a rise in unemployment and a fall in wage rates. In 1845, Greeley estimated that at least two-thirds of New Yorkers subsisted on hardly more than one dollar per week per person. "On this pittance, and very much less in many thousands of instances, three hundred thousand persons within sight of Trinity steeple must pay City rents and City prices." He supported his contentions with the following "facts": (1) the average wage for shoemakers had fallen until it was less than $5.00 per week; (2) the regular daily pay of laborers was $1.00, the average laborer being fortunate to earn $200 a year; (3) of some 50,000 employed women, at least half earned less than $2.00 per week when employed. A year earlier, striking New York tailors had demanded an increase in their average pay to 75 *cents* per day for 10 to 15 hours of work.[6]

Even with steady work, it was impossible for many New Yorkers to accumulate savings or property on which to fall back in time of need. In 1850, of some 3700 families comprising most of the population of the Fourteenth Ward, only 125 were listed by the census-taker as owning real estate, in amounts ranging from $190 owned by an Irish-born laborer to $90,000 owned by an English-born glass cutter. The Fourteenth was not the poorest ward in the city.[7] One grim reality of New York in the 1840s was the yearly downturn of the economy during the winter months when the canals froze and ocean commerce dwindled. While merchants warmed themselves in Holiday cheer, many of the poor were left jobless, forced to scramble to avoid starvation.[8] It was then that the almshouses and the various charitable organizations were hard pressed to meet the needs of the poor.

Low wages, periodic unemployment and a bare margin for existence was especially the lot of many of the estimated 30,000 to 50,000 women—unmarried, married, widowed, and deserted—who attempted to make their living in the city. Women, especially those who worked as domestics or in the needle trades, were the most poorly paid and exploited class in the city. Seamstresses were lucky to earn between $1.50 and $2.00 per week when employed; Greeley estimated that the some 10,000 sewing women who worked on a piecework basis made between 75¢ and $1.50 per week.[9] The plight of the working women brought periodic complaints that they were denied employment opportunities by men who filled some jobs, especially in retail stores, which were better suited to females. Despite occasional demands that the men give up such effeminate work as clerking in millinery shops, however, males continued to dominate the employment scene.[10] Moreover, mothers, especially widows with young children, were virtually forced to take needlework, which could be done at home. It was not until the 1850s that a few feeble efforts were made to establish nurseries for the care of children of poor working mothers, and even these did little to free women from the restraints of child care.[11] Entrapped in such circumstances, it is little wonder that women crowded the almshouse and the breadlines or drifted into prostitution.

Whether male or female, the poor had to face the same basic problems in a world they could not control. They had little influence over their wages or their working conditions; not even the very skilled and fortunate workers were able to organize effective unions until the 1850s. Nor could they control their living costs. Although rents declined during the early 1840s, they were still higher in New York than in other places—and became even higher with the increase after 1842 in property taxes, which landlords tried to pass on to their tenants.[12] Wholesale food prices also fell during this period, but Greeley may have been right when he charged that the poor were victimized by one feature of New York's haphazard economy—an overabundance of petty retailers who tried to assure their survival by inflating prices. In 1846, he said that an investigation showed "that the profits made by the small family Groceries to be found four on a corner in many parts of the City, average more than one hundred per cent" squeezed out of the customer by high markups on small quantities, watered milk, and doctored weights and measures; patronage at such stores was small but sure, since customers generally found themselves in debt to the grocer.[13] Even without such interference, prices generally rose in the wintertime, making it doubly cruel for the poor. In the winter of 1845, when New York exporters began to profit from a rise in European demand for American breadstuffs, the increased price of bread left many in want. No wonder that Greeley could write on Christmas Day: "The gorgeous rainbow that spans the whirling torrent of metropolitan life rests its base on such dark depths of misery and crime as it makes one shudder to think of."[14]

Although there was no accurate gauge of the depths of misery and crime, New Yorkers were sure that poverty had become an oppressive burden on their society. They were proud of the city's benevolent work. While they believed that in democratic, prospering America there was no cause for the degraded poverty of Europe, they accepted the traditional notion that the unfortunate poor would be an inevitable part of society. Abandoned children, widows, lunatics, the blind, the sick—all those who fell victims of life unfortunate accidents were society's responsibilities. To meet this responsibility, the city created an ever-growing network of public, semi-private (privately managed but receiving some public aid), and private charitable organizations. In 1853, one New Yorker proudly estimated that New York supported 22 asylums, 8 hospitals, 7 medical dispensaries, 90 benevolent societies, and 75 benefit societies, the last established by particular groups for their own members.

The charities list included the following: The Sailor's Home (for destitute white seamen), The Colored Sailor's Home, the Marine Society (for the widows and orphaned children of deceased seamen), the American Female Guardian Society (intended to protect female virtue by assisting indigent women and girls), The Society for the Relief of Poor Widows with Small Children, The New York Orphan Asylum, The Colored Orphan Asylum, The Protestant Half Orphan Society, The Roman Catholic Orphan Asylum, the New York Hospital, the Demilt Dispensary, The Bloomingdale Lunatic Asylum, The New York Institution for the Blind, The Prison Association, and The Home for Female Convicts. Important enough to be mentioned separately was the powerful and pervasive New York Association for Improving the Condition of the Poor. Such were some of the "great institutions of mercy and world-wide charity" in which "wealth and talent and enterprise have at length been employed in making men less selfish, and to bring them nearer to one another in kindness."[15]

There were, however, limits to benevolence, especially when it involved the most public and the most enforced form of charity, the municipal almshouse establishment. By the early 1840s, the Almshouse Department had acquired several distinct roles: It provided care for homeless children at its nursery on Long Island. Especially during winter months, it supplied outdoor relief in the form of food, fuel, and money to thousands of the poor who were able to maintain homes for themselves; among these were sick and aged "pensioners" who received regular aid. As if to confound its charitable role, it also managed City Prison and the Penitentiary on Blackwell's Island in the East River. This was not so anomalous as it might seem, since in the 1840s the majority of those sentenced to prison were vagrants. On that same island, it also took care of some 300 to 400 patients in the municipal Lunatic Asylum.[16]

The centerpiece of this charitable empire was the almshouse

itself, located at Bellevue on some 30 acres between 25th and 29th Streets near the East River. The three-story main building was described in 1846 as containing "60 apartments, a chapel, and two large dining rooms," these being the chief accommodations for some 1400 inmates. Also on the property was Bellevue Hospital, with nearly 500 poverty-stricken patients. The inmates, said the *Tribune* in 1843, "are well-fed, comfortably clad, have excellent medical attendance, and are treated with kindness." But they also were uncomfortably overcrowded, and that condition was destined to get worse.[17] In 1847, the Prison Association of New York charged that both the almshouse and the prisons, deluged by a flood of poor immigrants, had become so crowded "as to render them rather places of torture, than secure and comfortable asylums"—and places of death where some ten to twelve persons died each day. In 1854, the City Inspector estimated that in all the public institutions of the city more than 25,000 persons had died in the previous eight years, about 15 percent of deaths in the city during this period.[18]

Taxpaying citizens, however, were concerned less with almshouse accommodations than with the rising costs of relief. In the early 1840s, public concern over increasing taxes frequently focused on the Almshouse Department and its growing number of inmates. Available statistics were inconsistently reported, distorted by the inclusion of criminals with the relief population and certainly primitive, but they seemed to point to three conclusions: (1) that the pauper population supported by the city was growing rapidly; (2) that almshouse expenditures had increased even faster than the number of relief cases and much faster than the growth of the city (between 1840 and 1846, overall expenditures nearly doubled, while the population of New York grew by only 20 percent), (3) that a great and growing percentage of those who received public assistance were foreigners.[19]

Most New Yorkers were inclined to treat the problem as one thrust upon the city from outside. The Prison Association, for instance, complained that "the rapid growth of this city and its geographic position, the *point d'appui* of the emigrating masses which are traveling westward, and also the reservoir for the scum of the cast-off population of Europe, crowds our prisons with vagrants and our almshouses with paupers, many of whom prefer the comforts and leisure of even our criminal establishments to that ceaseless unrequited toil of liberty."[20] Given its presumed origins, the problem of poverty might have been viewed as a national problem to be solved with the assistance of the Federal government, but, except for the unsuccessful nativist effort to persuade Congress to exclude pauper immigrants, nothing was done in this direction.

In 1847, the state government did ease some of the burden when it created the Emigration Commission, which provided assistance for needy persons who had been in America for less than the five-year naturalization period; money for this work came out of a tax on immigrant ships. During its first eight years, the Commission provided some medical care, food, lodging, and transportation for more than 600,000 immigrants.[21] It was established in time to lessen the pressures on the city from the rapid increase of immigration in the late 1840s and early 1850s—pressures such as those in the winter of 1846–47, before the creation of the Commission, when a flood of destitute foreigners crowded the public institutions beyond capacity. "Every hole and corner under a roof," complained the *Tribune*, "down to the very vaults and cellars within the jurisdiction of the city, have become resting places for the swarms of foreign paupers and idiots emptied daily upon our shores by the governments of a portion of Europe."[22]

The Commission, however, could not protect the city from the growing number of native-born and naturalized poor who even before 1846 had filled the almshouse. What could be done about them? One answer was to reorganize the Almshouse Department so that it would not only provide assistance to those in need but would also help solve a problem which reformers saw as the primary cause of poverty—pauperism. On the assumption that, except for extraordinary periods of economic paralysis, every able-bodied American could find employment, it was easy to conclude that the hundreds of apparently healthy men and women who asked for public assistance were unwilling to work. These were the paupers, so degraded in spirit and character as to prefer dependence on charity to the rewards of good, honest labor. "Pauperism is a great social disease, and it lies near the very heart of our city," warned a writer in *Arcturus*. "As a question of economy, of police, and morals, it is urgent in its demands upon our attention."[23]

To deal with the problem, Mayor Morris in 1841 called for a total reorganization of almshouse operations, beginning with the transfer of the almshouse from Bellevue to new buildings on Blackwell's and Randall's islands in the East River. This new construction would supply jobs for the unemployed; more important, it would provide the physical basis for coping with the pauper problem. The key to Morris's program was his proposal for a workhouse which would isolate the pauper element from "the virtuous and unfortunate poor" who would be housed in separate buildings rather than in degrading proximity with paupers, as was the case at Bellevue.[24]

The workhouse idea was at the heart of developing reform hopes that the city's social problems could be clarified, classified, and then solved in a systematic way. The treatment of the deserving poor would be upgraded, once their corrupted cohabitants were shunted off to a separate place. At the new workhouse, it was hoped, the able-bodied poor could be assigned to productive labor that would lessen the costs of maintaining them and also impose on them the skills and habits required to make them self-supporting once they were released. Vagrants, rather than being imprisoned among criminals, could be placed in an institution more likely to cure them of their idle ways than—as in the case of prison life—to complete their corruption. Removing them from the Penitentiary would make that foreboding place, said Morris, what it was intended to be—a place to confine those guilty of "acts of moral turpitude and misdemeanors which require exemplary punishments as a warning to the community." Benevolence, rehabilitation, and punishment would, then, be so separated as to enable the Department to perform all three functions more efficiently and at less expense.[25]

POVERTY

The workhouse idea evoked the enthusiasm of Horace Greeley, although he treated it as a means less to cure pauperism than to provide needed employment. Unlike most New Yorkers, Greeley believed that especially in times of depression many men who wanted to work simply could not find jobs. On the assumption that society should supply work for the unemployed, he suggested that the city establish a massive "House of Industry" (he rejected the term workhouse for its degrading connotations) which would educate poor and orphaned children to habits of industry, provide temporary adult work during periods of extensive joblessness, and save the depraved, degraded, and indolent from their own bad habits. This would enable the inmates to support themselves without expense to the city and would also, by providing a refuge from degrading circumstances, encourage the poor to develop the character and talents which would soon make them free, independent, contributing members of society. "As things now are, a man possessing the talent of a Fulton, the strength of Sampson, the uprightness of Job, may perish of want in the streets of our most civilized and enterprising city, because no one knows his abilities or chooses to employ him."[26]

Most advocates of the workhouse idea, however, were less interested in actualizing the talent of a Fulton than in reducing the costs of poor relief. In 1843, for instance, the Common Council expressed interest in establishing a workhouse as an effective way to discourage "our dissolute and idle population" from seeking public aid; able-bodied relief-seekers would be given the choice of work or denial of any public assistance.[27] Given the growing displeasure of the city's taxpayers, it was not surprising that the hope of improving the treatment of inmates in public institutions should be subordinated to the fruitless effort to reduce municipal spending. Nor was it surprising that the workhouse idea itself should be swallowed up in a larger and different scheme for the solution of the relief problem.

By 1843, New Yorkers were beginning to give serious attention to Mayor Morris's earlier proposal for the removal of the almshouse from Bellevue to the islands in the East River.

Among other virtues, this scheme would more effectively isolate paupers from the surrounding society. The Commissioners of the Almshouse complained that the growth of the city around Bellevue, by opening more contacts between the inmates and the population outside, was beginning to interfere seriously with "discipline." As a bonus, the isolation of the inmates would also lessen the chance that they would be voted *en bloc* in city elections, a source of complaint especially from the Whigs. Moreover, the scheme would enable the city to sell most of the extensive almshouse site for development as city lots, a step which would both ease the city's debt burden and encourage the growth of the East Side north of Fourteenth Street.[28]

In 1844, Mayor Harper and the nativist majority in the Common Council decided to move the almshouse to Randall's Island, together with the "nursery" for poor children, which was then located on Long Island. At this new site, both the adult poor and "infant paupers" would systematically be taught the habit of labor. Randall's Island, which previously had been rented to market gardeners, would be made a garden spot capable of feeding the inmates and of making profits for the city.[29] By the spring of 1845, the nativists had nearly completed the buildings for a children's Farm School (set in "a spacious garden of beauty," said one visitor to Randall's Island), and had laid the cornerstone of a great new almshouse, planned as "a vast structure six hundred feet in length, the width and height in proportion." An ambitious expression of urban pride—but one which in that same year abruptly collapsed. The American Republicans not only lost control of the city government to the Democrats but saw their hopes for a permanent change vanish in the smoke from a fire which destroyed the new buildings of the Farm School.[30]

The ruin of the nativist experiment left the Democrats free to carry out their own scheme. Although they rebuilt the children's Farm School on Randall's Island, they rejected that place as the site for the new almshouse in favor of a location on Blackwell's Island. To complete their system of public charity, they created a new administrative organization in the form of a single popularly elected Almshouse Commissioner who replaced the unwieldly body of commissioners previously appointed by the Common Council.[31]

The new Commissioner, the prominent Democrat and ex-Congressman Moses G. Leonard, attempted to improve the care of the needy poor and, especially, to put paupers to work. Leonard was especially unhappy with the failure of the city to concentrate all the poor at one point (Randall's Island), for he shared with other reformers the faith in the virtues of classification and systematization. Give him the power "to bind the integral portions of this Department in a more solid phalanx," he promised the Common Council, and he would create a system that would improve conditions for the aged and infirm poor, educate poor orphans, put paupers to work efficiently, and save the city money.[32] Instead of consolidating Leonard's control, however, the Whig-dominated Council actually reduced his power, to the outrage of reformers and Democrats who accused the Aldermen of making a partisan grab for the growing patronage of the almshouse. The power to appoint guardians for the poor and the authority to grant the destitute immediate access to public charity was too important a source of votes for the Council to vest them in a single administrator, particularly a Democrat.[33]

Just as Mayor Morris's conflict with the Whig Council in 1842 had awakened interest in administrative reform, so now Leonard's troubles focused public attention on the fact that the good ship charity had long been buffeted by the storms of partisan politics. In 1842, Charles Dickens had observed that, while the newly constructed Lunatic Asylum was a handsome building, the treatment and care of the inmates inside was depressing both for them and for himself. Dickens attributed these conditions to the influence of "the miserable strife of Party feeling. . . . Will it be believed that the eyes which are to watch over and control the wanderings of minds on which the most dreadful visitation to which our nature is exposed has fallen, must wear the glasses of some wretched side in Politics?"[34] The creation of the office of Almshouse Commissioner in 1845 was intended to insulate charity administration from the annual shifts in New York politics, but the conflict between

Leonard and the Council pointed to the need for more fundamental administrative reorganization. This came in the spring of 1849, when the state legislature created a Board of Almshouse Governors designed to provide stable administration and also, if not to exclude politics, at least to replace partisan with bipartisan political influence. The ten commissioners were to be elected for five-year terms, one to be elected every year from the nominees of each of the two major parties.[35]

For the first time, New York had a stable almshouse administration free from the control of the Common Council. For the first time, too, the city had a formal workhouse; the new board were able to open one on Blackwell's Island in 1850. By absorbing many of those sentenced to terms for vagrancy, this work place relieved some of the pressures on its sister institution on the island, the penitentiary. The commissioners also could boast of impressive improvements in the care of the sick poor at Bellevue Hospital. In the 1850s, they erected new buildings for the hospital, expanded its activities, improved management, made it a center for medical internships, and cut its notorious death rate in half, reducing it from 20 to 10 percent.[36]

They failed, however, either to lower the cost of the almshouse establishment or to devise an institutional solution to the relief problem. Between 1853 and 1856, expenditures for the Almshouse Department increased by 240 percent, the fastest growing item in the municipal budget.[37] Certainly, the workhouse did little to reduce relief costs or to solve the problem of pauperism, for it was able to employ only a small minority of the almshouse population. Contrary to popular belief, the majority were not indolent paupers but children, the insane, the sick poor, the aged—and convicted criminals.[38] Even for those who were capable of work, the beneficial effects of forced labor were limited. Workhouse operations were restricted by strong public opposition to the employment of paupers in direct competition with free workers at a time when unemployment was a persistent problem. Thus, the new institution soon became an agency less to cure pauperism than to punish vagrancy. Vagrants, complained the warden of the Workhouse, were sentenced to terms that were too short to teach them steady habits but long enough to convince them that the law despised their apparent shiftlessness.[39]

Greeley's dream of a great House of Industry which would provide meaningful work and education for the destitute remained only a dream, counterpointed by a system in which the most conspicuous forms of work were breaking rocks in a prison quarry and washing clothes in prison laundries. The Almshouse Department, far from evolving into an agency of public beneficence and education, developed into an institution designed chiefly to provide custodial care for society's rejects: the unreclaimable and irredeemable.[40] Probably, this was an inevitable consequence of the growing tendency among tax-paying citizens to view government generally less as an agency for public good than as a public nuisance and burden, at best a necessary evil. If government could not be trusted, it was logical to assume that constructive charity work should be placed in the supposedly safer hands of private beneficence.

Beneficence was not a notable attribute of money-making New York. Undoubtedly, many citizens shared the view of one "J.F.K." who, with ruthless logic, proposed in the *Tribune* in 1843 that the best solution to the pauper problem was simply to eliminate any public aid which might keep paupers alive: "They who will marry and beget children in dirty cellars are a curse to the world."[41] Let them die. The idea was in harmony with the competitive individualism of the city, but it did not fit a strong contrary tendency toward practical benevolence promoted by a small number of merchants and professional men, chiefly from Calvinist or Quaker backgrounds, who believed that intelligent self-interest as well as Christian charity demanded attention to the poor. One of them, Charles Loring Brace, warned that no New Yorker could afford to remain indifferent to the growing masses of poor people in the city's spreading slums: "There they live, breeding each day pestilence and disease ... raising a brood of vagrants and harlots— retorting on Society its neglect by cursing the bodies and souls of thousands whom they never knew and who never was them."[42] Brace, Robert B. Minturn, John H. Griscom, and Robert M. Hartley—such men helped to give form to the diffuse, often contradictory, thinking of New Yorkers regarding poverty. The chief instrument for their practical benevolence was the powerful New York Association for Improving the Condition of the Poor (AICP) which, even before the workhouse was opened in 1850, had supplanted it as the great cure for pauperism.

Although the AICP, in both its means and ends, resembled an earlier organization, the aptly named Society for the Prevention of Pauperism founded in 1817, it originated in the 1840s from still another organized effort, this one designed to meet not the material but the spiritual needs of the poor. Religious-minded New Yorkers had long expressed concern over the spiritual and moral debasement of the poor. Out of this concern came the founding in 1827 of the New York City Tract Society, chiefly by Presbyterians and others from a generally Calvinistic background. The Society was intended to be a city-wide organization which would convert the spiritually deprived to a nondenominational form of Protestantism. As they penetrated into the dark alleys of poverty, however, the missionaries of the Society became increasingly sensitive to the material, as well as spiritual, destitution of poor New Yorkers. Charity work began to interfere with missionary work to the point that in 1843 the directors of the Society decided to set up the AICP as a separate organization to grapple with the problem of poverty.[43]

The Tract Society had long depended on the support of some of the city's most influential merchants, especially on Anson G. Phelps and his son-in-law, William Dodge, James Brown of Brown Brothers, Robert B. Minturn of Grinnell and Minturn, James Boorman, and Apollas R. Wetmore, a wealthy hardware merchant. Along with a few other prominent men of wealth such as George Griswold and James Lenox, they became the mainstays of the AICP, constituting a charity establishment which was long to have a strong influence on benevolence in New York. They formed a compact group

[83]

united by a common class and religious background—and by location as well, for most of them lived in the Fifteenth Ward on or near Washington Square.[44]

To handle the day-by-day work of the new association, the Board of Managers appointed Robert M. Hartley as their Executive Secretary. It was Hartley who gave shape to their thinking and direction to their good intentions, in the process creating the foundations for nineteenth-century professional social work. Born in England in 1796 and brought to America by his merchant father three years later, he began his career as a businessman in New York. His real interests, however, were in religious work. A God-driven Presbyterian, he became a leading force in both the Tract Society and in temperance work. His experience as Secretary of the City Temperance Society between 1833 and 1842 especially deepened both his interest in the problems of the poor and his conviction that they could not improve themselves without systematic support from the more fortunate. Thus, he eagerly gave up his business career entirely for full-time work as Executive Secretary of the AICP, a position he held for some three decades.[45]

Under Hartley's management, the AICP quickly became the dominant influence in determining the nature of, and solution to, the problem of poverty. Why, in a progressive and benevolent age, did poverty grow rather than diminish? Why had the work of 33 charity societies and the expenditure of over $150,000 in 1842 neither relieved the wants of the poor nor limited "pauperism," which had increased faster than population? Hartley's answer was not that society did not give enough, did not try hard enough (hardly a popular response to groaning taxpayers or preoccupied businessmen) but that society had not yet learned how to give intelligently. "If we except the pauperism occasioned by immigration," wrote Hartley in breezy dismissal of that fateful problem, "the chief cause of its increase among us is the injudicious dispensation of relief."[46] Ignoring the substantial unemployment occasioned by the hard times of the early 1840s, Hartley and other charity reformers blamed indiscriminate alms-giving for encouraging many of the poor to depend on handouts rather than to support themselves. In

1840, for instance, the *Evening Post* attributed the increase in "pauperism" to the managers of public charity who "were so grossly lavish and so careless of the consequences, that to them we must attribute a great deal of the demoralization, improvidence and misery that exists."[47]

It seemed obvious to Hartley that the situation required a reorganized relief effort which, while relieving the physical wants of the destitute, would also discourage such pauper habits as idleness and improvidence. This meant reeducating the charitable as well as the poor to the philosophy of the AICP. Generous New Yorkers had to be convinced that the only sure cure for poverty was the improvement of the character as well as the condition of the unfortunate. As they had neither the time nor the knowledge to work that improvement themselves, they were to channel their charity through the Association, which had the skill, experience, and organization needed to cope with the problem in the massive and anonymous city. Should a beggar approach them on the street or at home, they were not to give him aid other than directions to the nearest agent of the Association.[48]

Hartley hoped to make the AICP a charity monopoly under the twin banners of Christian benevolence and "scientific philanthropy." The two were synonomous in his eyes, for he believed that God was the creator of all science. By directing benevolence through one city-wide, expertly managed system, he believed it possible to provide a cheap, efficient cure for poverty. Moreover, the Association would serve as "a chain of union" between the rich and poor. By giving the rich an opportunity to express feelings of brotherhood and by giving the poor an appreciation of the intrinsic virtues of society, it "connects the extremes of society—not by fear or dependence, but by affection and gratitude, and binds all harmoniously together"; thus would human community be maintained in the impersonal city.[49]

The elaborate system devised by Hartley was headed by a central Board of Managers, which handled finances and also guided the operations of District Committees, each of which managed the charity affairs of a Ward in the built-up portions of the city. Each ward, in turn, was divided into from 6 to 32 sections, each section being the province of a "visitor" who was to exercise "a voluntary individual guardianship over the poor." Thus, the talent and benevolence of some four to five hundred volunteers would be organized in a permanent effort, headed by influential men able to raise the funds, public support, and volunteer effort needed to sustain it. The organizers prided themselves on having created an organization which could cover the entire city without losing the ability to meet the varied needs of a highly diversified mass of poor.[50] In 1845, Hartley boasted:

> Its machinery, though extensive, is easily managed, and works with admirable precision, economy, and effect. It has proven its adaptation to the wants of the city, by doing for the benevolent what they cannot accomplish for themselves, inasmuch as, by its personal intercourse with the poor, it offers a permanent channel through which charities will reach their object with beneficial results; and, with the general cooperation of the public, they see not how it can fail to expel idleness and beggary from the city.[51]

The vital link in this system was the visitor, who was expected to act as a charity policeman as well as a benevolent guardian of the poor. It was his task to determine which cases of poverty should become the Association's responsibility. Those persons who were physically or mentally incapable were directed to the appropriate institutions, especially to those managed by the Almshouse Department. Recent immigrants after 1847 were referred to the Commissioners of Emigration. Those persons who obviously would not help themselves, the incorrigibly debased and pauperized, were consigned to the almshouse, workhouse or penitentiary. In these ways, the visitor acted as part of "a vast sieve" which separated "the precious and the vile." In an effort to prevent "incorrigible mendicants" from continuing to sponge up the resources of private charity, the AICP established a central office "where is kept a register of persons who received aid from this and other benevolent associations, and from city authorities," to aid in the detection of professional paupers who made a livelihood by tapping several benevolent sources.[52]

Having played his part in disposing of the unworthy poor, the visitor could then concentrate both on relieving the physical wants and on ministering to the moral necessities of those who could be reclaimed as useful members of society. To these, the visitor was to bring sufficient aid to help the unfortunates over hard times, but not so much as to encourage a sense of dependency. Physical assistance was to be sparing: Enough food to assure health; enough clothing, fuel, and medical attention; enough, but no more than necessary. More important, the visitor was expected to bring to the poor two particularly precious gifts: First, a "friendly intercourse" initiated by a respectable citizen who obviously cared for their plight, a sign that society was not ready to leave them to suffer in isolation. Second, advice on how to overcome those character defects such as improvidence which presumably had led to the initial fall into poverty; an eight-page pamphlet entitled "The Economist," for instances, provided money-saving hints, including how to make four gallons of soup for 22 cents. Thus, the visitor would both overcome the alienation of the poor and convert them to the habits of self-reliant, responsible citizens.[53]

By its own standards, the AICP was a success. In 1848 Hartley claimed, with a characteristic addiction to statistics, that in five years its 298 "philanthropic laborers" had made more than 135,000 visits of sympathy and aid. "What an immense expenditure of means and of effort is here exhibited." This massive effort reached into every corner of poverty in New York, bringing with it assistance shaped to the particular needs and circumstances of the individual poor. From its files of visitors' reports, the AICP could supply proof of its success in meeting those particular needs. To one immigrant family left moneyless and friendless in a strange city, a visitor provided food, clothing, and "religious instruction and consolation." He brought medical care for the ailing wife, and he found jobs for the father, two sons, and three daughters. Another visitor encountered a poor Irish family, the husband dangerously ill, the wife weak and sick, with two helpless children and little food. Besides providing food, he found a doctor who was able to bring the husband back to health, and to the point where he was soon able to find a job.[54]

The AICP also seemed able to reach into every corner of wealth and influence. By 1850, it had some 4000 contributing members, among whom was a veritable social register of prominent names running from William B. Astor to George Zabriskie.[55] Such men not only supplied it with money but also provided direct social and political backing for its increasingly ambitious efforts to improve the environment as well as the character of the poor. Once they were confronted with the realities of poverty, the leaders of the AICP recognized that improvement in character frequently depended on an improvement in living conditions. Therefore, it promoted a variety of projects which required support from society and government: the establishment of dispensaries to provide medical aid; a bath and washing house to enable the poor to practice its precepts of cleanliness; savings banks to encourage habits of thrift; efforts to improve housing conditions, and the Juvenile Asylum to which the children of depraved parents could be sent to get them out of their corrupting environment.[56]

By the 1850s, the AICP under Hartley's leadership had made itself the dynamic center of a broad benevolent effort to solve the problem of urban poverty. It had created a citywide organization capable of finding and assisting the poor in every street and in every alley. It had established a bureaucratic organization based on the theory, if not the practice, that the poor and their problems had to be understood as individual cases if poverty were to be eliminated. It supplied aid, consolation, and advice to thousands of desperate people; by 1870, it claimed that it had aided some 180,000 families during the previous 27 years.[57] It was a major force behind efforts to improve the urban environment, especially in the form of improved housing, sanitation, and education. Above all, by offering the hope for a widespread regeneration of human character, it seemed to be an inexpensive solution to poverty and its attendant social disorders. In the 1840s and early 1850s, it spent annually an average of between four and five dollars on each of the thousands of families it visited.[58]

An inexpensive and successful war on pauperism and on disorder—Hartley believed that he had devised the organization and acquired the knowledge needed to eventually solve the social problems of the metropolis: "The various objects of the Institution are now resolved into an intelligible system, and the means for the attainment of these objects are believed to be guided by principles which are accordant to reason and Revelation. By observing these principles, success, with Divine favor, appears as certain as are the laws of antecedent and result." The remedy had been found to "that great and difficult problem which now so extensively agitates the world—the best remedy for social evils, in populous communities."[59] This, for Hartley, was America's answer to the Communist Manifesto, which had exploded out of pauper-ridden Europe in 1848. In 1850, he noted that the number of persons aided by the AICP in that year (25,762) was less than the number in 1844 (28,062), despite the growth of population.[60]

Characteristically, he gave little credit to the gradual improvement in the New York economy after 1844, as if that had had no effect in diminishing the proportion of persons who required aid. If there were such good years as 1850, however, there were also bad years like 1852, when the AICP had to appeal for additional funds to meet suffering and want which it claimed was unprecedented in its eight years of experience, and like the devastating winter of 1854–55, when a combination of high food prices and great unemployment drove more than 60,000 people to seek its aid.[61] Faced by such pressures, even Hartley had to concede that a disturbing change was taking place: "Marked changes are transpiring in the social condition of the poor, which become apparent every year. The laboring population, constituting a large part of the community appear not to obtain a proportionate share of the growing prosperity around them."[62]

The significant social changes of the 1850s, however, did not markedly shake Hartley's faith either in American society or in the AICP approach to poverty. In his mind, there was little doubt that the trouble came from the flooding of the city with Europe's poor. Not only did the immigrant wave carry with it thousands of degraded, vicious, and irredeemable paupers, but it also glutted the labor market to the detriment of the city's laboring classes. Hartley believed that the poor could find ample employment in the interior but that they preferred to remain in New York, where they could take advantage of its many charities.[63] He veered toward a Scrooge-like stance, therefore, when during periods of distress kind-hearted New Yorkers adopted relief measures, such as soup kitchens, out of harmony with the AICP philosophy. "There is unfortunately amongst us, though not peculiar to our city, a false philanthropy—a sickly sentimentality." Thanks to such unwise benevolence, he complained in 1855, the city was "overrun by an unmanageable crowd of men, women, and children" who demanded relief as if it were a right, an evident sign for him of growing pauperism.[64]

Hartley thus backed himself into the position of advocating a hard-hearted relief program in order to drive the poor out of and away from the city. He did make some effort to find jobs for the unemployed with farmers and manufacturers outside the city, especially during the period of mass unemployment which followed the Panic of 1857. Like similar efforts, however, his plan failed; by 1861, Hartley could report that only ten employers had responded to his plea for jobs. His explanation for this failure was predetermined by his philosophy: It was not that employment was unavailable; rather, it was the fault of the poor themselves, because they made little effort to take advantage of existing opportunities. If so, then let them suffer at least a little; when possible, compel them to labor in the workhouse or, as Hartley proposed in 1858, on city-owned farms.[65]

This view of the poor undoubtedly was shared by many New Yorkers. Poverty was seen as the result of "pauperism" or, if not of an absolute refusal to work, as the result of a reluctance to seek employment outside the city in areas where labor was needed. By ignoring the possibility that rural America had little room for the urban masses, it was easy to conclude that the poor were the self-made victims of a fatal preference for easy living. It was this perverse preference for urban life rather than any serious defect in society which best seemed to explain the widespread unemployment, low wages, and mass misery of New York. In such a view, the poor—especially the foreign-born poor—were far less suffering victims than annoying spoilers of the American dream of a happy, prosperous society. Especially with the return of prosperity in the late 1840s, they were often dismissed from the conscience and consciousness of those many citizens who were eager to exploit the opportunities of their rich and growing city.

Social New York: II

FIGURE 8. (left, above) The idealized picture (1849) drawn by C. Bachman of New York south from Union Square gives another view of the crowded city below Fourteenth Street. At the extreme right center, between Washington Square and the northern end of the Hudson River Waterfront, is Greenwich Village. At the extreme left center a cluster of trees marks Tompkins Square. Shipbuilding activity can be seen on the East River, especially at Corlaer's Hook (marked by the large building with the smoking chimney). Rich and fashionable New York dominates the foreground of this view. The tree lined street to the right is Fifth Avenue. The short, wide avenue (right center) from Union Square to Washington Square Park is University Place; New York University is the white building immediately to the left of the Park. The prominent church on the left side of Broadway (left center) is Grace Church; the steepled Greek Temple to the south is the Astor Place Opera House. Intruding on this scene to the left of Broadway is the Bowery with its horse-drawn cars of the Harlem Railroad.

FIGURE 9. (left, below) The more impressionistic but also more truthful view of the Bowery looking south from Cooper Square was painted by an unnamed artist in 1864. Although it lacks the prominent buildings and the visual clarity of the preceding view, it is unusually successful in conveying a sense of the unkempt vitality of the Bowery and of work-a-day New York generally.

Both views courtesy of the Prints Division, New York Public Library, Eno and Stokes collections.

Chapter 5

A RICH AND GROWING CITY

POVERTY WAS A MAJOR PRESENCE in New York, but it was a presence which successful New Yorkers ignored whenever possible. The poor, tucked away in side streets, alleys and cellars, and behind almshouse walls, were easily forgotten, despite such reminders as street beggars, chiffoniers, hot-corn girls, and the concentrated riffraff of the notorious Five Points. Perhaps even in the minds of the poor themselves, they were not the real New York. For natives and visitors alike, the real city was the wealth and power so clearly expressed in Wall Street and, even more, in Broadway which had become the great thoroughfare for the march of business northward up Manhattan Island.

It was lower Broadway, especially the mile between Bowling

Green and Canal Street, which best summarized the destiny of the city. Once a place for the solid residences as well as for the businesses of a part of the merchant class, the street was becoming the great stage for the display of metropolitan wealth and success, a great "agglomeration of trade and fashion, business and amusement, public and private abodes, churches and theatres, barrooms, and exhibitions, all concentrated into one promiscuous channel of activity and dissipation."[1] The commercial depression following the Panic of 1837 slowed its development, but the return of prosperity after 1845 soon made it the centerpiece in the reconstruction of the lower city. Scattered along Broadway were some of New York's most conspicuous monuments: Lavish new Trinity Church, its spire pointed toward the Heavens and its front facing Wall Street; Barnum's American Museum, decorated with brash advertisements of the Ethiopian Serenaders, the Feejee Mermaid, and other human curiosities inside; graceful St. Paul's Chapel, and the marble-faced City Hall with its park, both already too small for the growing city.

In the 1840s, the Park, with its fountain, was a verdant focal point of busy city life. At its north side terminated the Harlem Railroad; at its southern point merged two great streams of traffic from upper Broadway and the Bowery. Nearby were the famed Astor House, the Mercantile Library, the buildings of the American Bible Society, and a hodgpodge of two, three, four, and five story buildings: boarding houses, restaurants, stores, and hotels.[2] Over all and around all there was the daytime noise of a street crowded with people, working people and people at leisure, with lumbering wagons, scurrying carts, hurrying carriages, thundering omnibuses. The noise of a people in a hurry, of iron wheels on granite pavements, a noise which one listener compared to "the sound of Niagara heard from the Cataract Hotel, not so deep and thunderous however, but sharper and harsher—a great corroding roar, that seems to gnaw the earth like corroding fire."[3] Broadway was not a street for conversation but for looking.

Much of its haphazard character was a reflection of the constant building and rebuilding which was becoming the predominant feature of lower New York. By the late 1840s the homes which had once graced the street had either been converted into stores or torn down to make way for newer and bigger buildings. Broadway seemed perpetually unfinished, its sidewalks encumbered by piles of timber and iron and mounds of brick and stone, its guiding genius an urge for change which gave little heed either to the future or the past. When excavating work in 1845 for a new building uncovered the cornerstone of old Washington Hall, Philip Hone, who as a young man had contributed to its construction, complained: "Overturn, overturn, overturn! is the maxim of New York. The very bones of our ancestors are not permitted to lie quiet a quarter of a century, and one generation of men seem studious to remove all relics of those who precede them." Such ambitious presentism might produce individually fine and occasionally magnificent buildings, might make lower New York a richly varied concentration of architectural styles, but it did not inspire the making of a street of permanent visual beauty.[4]

Broadway, in truth, was a showcase far less for architecture than for people, a role well-suited to the intense individualism of New Yorkers. It was, without challenge, the fashionable street of the nation, *the* place in democratic America for the successful to display their superior social status. Hundreds of men and women, said the *Tribune* in 1846, "spend their lives in sauntering through Broadway during fashionable hours seeing and being seen." Whatever the merits of their strivings, the status-seekers contributed heavily to the most striking visual characteristic of Broadway, its fashionable dress: successful businessmen in suits of an appropriately conservative cut, the dandy with his beard and thin trouser legs, and, above all, the women in their fluttering ribbons, rainbow silks, and latest Parisian fashions.[5]

As the nation's great showcase of fashion, Broadway played a significant role in stimulating among Americans a revolution of expectations regarding luxuries and comforts. There was a continuous interplay between its roles as a stage for the fashion-conscious and as the city's leading retail street. Wealthy women, often conveyed down Broadway in their private carriages, came not only to see and be seen but also to buy the best and the latest; the shopwindows grew bigger in order to attract the notice of the carriage trade. In 1846, the prosperous shopper could purchase a rich variety of elegant articles from all parts of the world, including jewelry at Tiffany, Young & Ellis, housing furnishings at J. & C. Berrien, wines at John Duncan and Son, books at Appletons, and toys, jewelry, perfumes, and many other items at the Lafayette Bazaar which, as its contribution to the history of mass-merchandising, announced that it had stationed "a couple of darkies in regimentals at the door" to hand out catalogues listing the merchandise for sale within.[6] Above all, Broadway was the street where the fashionable and the would-be fashionable could buy the latest clothes.

Clothing shops there were beginning to benefit from what the *Tribune* in 1845 called a "revolution in the price of fashionable clothing" comparable to the revolution in newspaper publishing which had produced the penny-press, since New York clothiers had learned how to make quality reproductions of London and Paris fashions at half the cost of imported clothing.[7] By the mid-1840s, many of New York's great clothing shops had established themselves on or near Broadway, where they advertised the latest European styles for sale: James Beck & Co., H & L Peck, Hearn Brothers, A. Arnold & Co. (Aaron Arnold was an uncle of the Hearn Brothers), and, outshining them all, the great store of Alexander T. Stewart.[8]

Recognizing that much of the time of fashionable women was spent in shopping, Stewart erected a marble palace to meet virtually all of their shopping needs. When it was opened in September 1846, it impressed even the worldly-wise with its grandeur: "The main entrance opens into a rotunda of oblong shape, extending the whole width of the building, and lighted by a dome seventy feet in circumference. The ceilings and sidewalls are painted in fresco, each panel representing some emblem of commerce. Immediately opposite the main entrance . . . , commences a flight of stairs which lead to a gallery running around the rotunda. This gallery is for the ladies to promenade upon."[9] The essence of the store was not in its marbled magnificence, however, but in its advanced merchandising techniques. Stewart offered a wide variety of quality goods conveniently provided under one roof and at comparatively low prices achieved by his shrewd use of the mass buying power of the store. Particularly after its enlargment in 1850, the store seemed a model of modern progress with its two acres of floor space and three hundred salesmen and clerks. For thousands of women in New York and elsewhere in America, Stewart offered, through his retail and wholesale departments, a portal to the fashionable life of the metropolis.[10]

If the A. T. Stewart store and its lesser rivals served Broadway's function in facilitating and encouraging a widespread enchantment with fashion, another prominent Broadway institution enlarged American expectations regarding comfort. New York's hotels were located throughout the lower part of the city, but it was the Broadway hotel which, since the completion of the Astor House in 1836, best served to introduce Americans to a new and more comfortable life. Many people experienced the benefits of gas-lighting, interior plumbing, and steam heat for the first time in one of the public mansions which lined lower Broadway. With the return of prosperity in the late 1840s, hotel owners, anxious to attract the patronage of European as well as American travelers, intensified their efforts to produce the latest refinements in comfort.[11]

In 1853, for instance, the Astor House attempted to brighten its faded image by experimenting with climate control in the form of a glass and iron "exchange" built in the courtyard of the hotel: "The immense space is heated in winter by warm air from below; and in the summer, jets of cold air will be blown into the room, moistened by the perpetual play of Croton fountains; and at all seasons the ventilation from the roof will keep the atmosphere fresh and pure. There is every accommodation provided for merchants and gentlemen of leisure, to meet, talk, smoke, drink and read the newspapers."[12] In such ways, the hotels represented a constantly advancing frontier of almost sinful luxury, which taught thousands of travelers and local inhabitants new expectations regarding physical comfort. "This word *comfort*," remarked *Hunt's*, "which referred formerly to a few wants which the best host could not have imagined to reach beyond a half-dozen, now comprises a vast list of real necessities (some of them the luxuries of former times), conveniences, and elegancies."[13]

New York's 45 hotels (in 1854) were the most conspicuous part of a downtown complex designed to excite and fulfill the desires of well-heeled travelers and inhabitants. In 1853 Broadway could boast of the "largest and most elegant restaurant in the world" in Taylor's Saloon, where "the walls are covered with mirrors in rich gilt frames; the chairs and sofas are covered with rich cloth of crimson and gold; and the ceilings are ornamented with gildings and scroll work of great beauty." This was the most lavish of hundreds of downtown eating places—restaurants such as Delmonicos, oyster cellars, coffee houses, and "ice-cream saloons." A few, such as Taylor's and Thompson's, were especially designed for the lady shoppers of Broadway, but most respectable—and unrespectable—restaurants catered to downtown businessmen and male commercial travelers.[14]

Eating places satisfied only a part of the increasingly cosmopolitan palate. Although New York's theaters usually provided only a mediocre dramatic fare, their heavy dependence on the plays, themes, and actors of the English stage did give their audiences a chance to commune with the sophisticated life of Europe. Less respectable but very much a part of emerging New York nightlife were the gambling houses and brothels, the most lavish of which were generally located a few tempting blocks from the hotels. With the northward movement of business and fashion in the years after 1847, a concentration of brothels appeared on Mercer Street, just a block west of Broadway. So "open, free, and undisguised" were these houses that the *Tribune* could declare sarcastically they could not be houses of prostitution; surely, their respectability was attested to by the fact "that they are frequently visited by gentlemen of the best standing . . . such as aldermen, judges, lawyers, assemblymen, state officers, country merchants, and others."[15] Hotels, restaurants, theaters, gambling houses and brothels—all were essential elements in the day-and-night life which for many Americans characterized Broadway and, by extension, all of the metropolis.

The development of this center of sophistication, however, was simply the most flamboyant part of a larger change which was altering the character of the downtown areas—in fact, was making a downtown. Adult New Yorkers could remember when "downtown" had been the whole city, where merchants, mechanics, and others lived as well as worked. By the 1830s, though, the expansion of commerce had begun to displace residents from their old homes to new areas farther up Manhattan Island, initiating a process which in the next century would increasingly separate city dwellers from their places of work. Temporarily slowed by the commercial troubles after 1837, the process accelerated again in the late 1840s. By the 1850s, some sections of the lower city had become so specialized as places of business that they were virtually deserted after working hours.[16]

The major force among the many forces behind the reconstruction of the lower city was the spectacular expansion of the clothing and drygoods business. New York had become the great American emporium for fabrics from all over the globe. As such, it benefited from the revolution in clothing which was making Americans the best dressed people in the world. During the decade after 1845, the drygoods business, once confined largely to Pearl Street near the East River waterfront, moved north and especially west as wholesalers looked for larger quarters and cheaper rents. Anxious to locate near places where out-of-town buyers were likely to stay, drygoods dealers tended to follow the uptown march of the hotel business along Broadway. Initially, they converted stores and private residences into showrooms and warehouses, but by 1850 their expanding business was ready to burst out of the old buildings and out of the restricted space and tangled streets of old New York.[17] The result was a building boom in the Third Ward, located west of Broadway. After the widening of Liberty Street in 1852 furnished an excuse for a wholesale leveling of the dilapidated buildings there, a rush began for commercial properties in the Ward. Anticipating a mass flight of business from the high rents and restricted quarters of the lower city, builders constructed "palatial" warehouses, often in fashionable marble, which seemed to signal a new era in New York business: "We do not hesitate to predict," asserted one New Yorker, "that in ten years the finest buildings now in New York will be far surpassed by the growing taste and wealth of builders. We have seen the last of the plodding business life, which even within our recollection, bought and sold contentedly in the primitive regions of Pearl Street and Coenties Slip."[18]

The westside building boom was a conspicuous piece in a larger pattern of change which was altering the spatial character of the city. Significantly, the "palatial" warehouses and other new business buildings constructed in the Third Ward did not have residential quarters. Although the old combination of dwelling and store continued to be erected for shopkeepers in many parts of the city, the emphasis downtown was on meeting the needs of large businessmen. Redevelopment, then, meant the elimination of dwellings and the displacement of population to other sections of the city. While property values more than doubled in the Third Ward between 1840 and 1855, population declined by over 30 percent.[19]

With little thought as to the consequences, New York was turning its downtown areas over to business. If people stood in the way of the expansion and movement of commerce, then they were to move or be removed. After the great fire of 1845, for instance, the *Evening Post* urged the elimination of narrow streets and alleys in the burned-over portions not only to facilitate traffic but to reduce population density. Nearly a decade later it returned to this theme when it supported a proposal to build a new city hall farther uptown on the grounds that it would draw population northward, "making more room for merchants and others" in the lower part of the city.[20] If lower New York was to be consigned to business, then why not the rest of Manhattan as well? As early as 1843, Caleb Woodhull, an influential Whig leader and a businessman who gave much thought to the physical development of the city, noted that "a few years ago no building in this city was uninhabited—now whole quarters are devoted to stores alone in which no one dwells. This will continue to be the case until, in the course of time, it is probable that the whole island will be covered with store houses, and the residences of those doing business there will be on the opposite shores and in contiguous counties."[21]

Certainly, by the end of the 1840s, it was evident to most observers that Manhattan was in the process of an extensive rebuilding which would affect not only the downtown areas but all of the island. As lower New York became the province of commerce and of fashion, New Yorkers with the money to do so moved into the territory surrounding the old city. Some westsiders tried to cling to the houses of their earlier years, but the thrust of their society was uptown. The rich and fortunate classes were abandoning old New York to commerce; the environment deteriorated for living, and so in the end even the stubborn moved, selling out or leasing out their property either for business or for housing the poor. One of the most stubborn was the father of young George Templeton Strong who for nearly a decade clung to his home on decaying Greenwich Street, resisting his son's entreaties that they move uptown. Finally, in the late 1840s, he was persuaded "that a street of emigrant boarding houses and dirty drinking shops is not a pleasant place to live," and the Strong's migrated uptown to East 21st Street on Gramercy Park, one of the last of their class to abandon lower Manhattan.[22]

In such ways were many New Yorkers convinced that in their progressive society nothing was permanent and nothing more valuable than the money needed to take advantage of changing times. In his *Washington Square*, Henry James has one of his characters comment regarding a small house he had taken for himself and his wife-to-be: "It doesn't matter, . . . it's only for three or four years. At the end of three or four years, we'll move. That's the way to live in New York—to move every three or four years. Then you always get the last thing. It's because the city's growing so quick—you've got to keep up with it. It's going straight up town—that's where New York's going."[23]

The uptown movement was the most conspicicuous part of a broad redistribution of population and of property which, though long in the making, only became a significant factor in the two decades after 1840. Nowhere was this change more evident than in the old Twelfth Ward, which in the early 1830s covered all of the island north of 14th Street. Below that street was the city; above, a largely rural space of market gardens, estates, waste land (much of it owned by the municipal government), and villages such as Manhattanville and Harlem at the north end of the island. In 1836, population growth brought the creation of the Sixteenth Ward for the area between 14th and 40th Streets. Even by 1840, however, only 33,811 lived north of 14th Street, with perhaps a third of that number engaged in agriculture.[24] In the 1840s, the population of the two north wards more than tripled. This was only the beginning, for by 1860 the population in the area would triple again; by that date, 40 percent of New Yorkers, some 344,000 of them, would live where only 30 years before there had been barely 12,000. Row houses and tenements would grow up where gardeners once tended their fruits and vegetables, and where rich men had once taken their leisure.[25]

This rapid expansion of population was made possible only by the hasty development of the middle third of the island. By the 1840s, development was a well-established and simple science. In 1811, New York had been given a combined boon and curse in the form of a state-ordained plan which imposed a geometrically simple gridiron pattern of streets on the varied and occasionally rugged terrain of the island. Critics would later condemn the plan for committing the city to a ruthless, expensive, and destructive confrontation with nature which obliterated the natural beauty of most of Manhattan.[26] Most New Yorkers, however, wanted straight streets and easy grades to speed the flow of horse-drawn traffic; and they wanted rectangular surveys and rectangular lots to provide easily developed and saleable parcels of land. Who would prefer otherwise if Manhattan was especially to be the home of expanding commerce? Thus, they transformed the landscape to conform to their rigid geometry, leveling hills and filling in ponds, swamps, marshes, and portions of the waterfront. As early as 1840, a New Yorker complained of "the millions already so freely expended in blasting rocks, in removing immense hills, in reducing to a regular grade so vast an extent of rugged surface as would already conveniently locate thrice the present inhabitants of the city."[27]

Not all development was destructive. In the 1830s, Samuel B. Ruggles, perhaps New York's most far-sighted developer, spent years and some $180,000 in leveling hills and filling in swamps on the East Side between 19th and 22nd Streets. Out of his work came lovely Gramercy Park, one of New York's few squares to preserve a good residential character. "Come what will," Ruggles told a friend, "our open spaces will remain forever imperishable. Buildings, towers, palaces, may molder and crumble beneath the touch of Time; but space—free, glorious, open space—will remain to bless the city forever." Blessed the city was—in a few select locations. In 1878, Ruggles would assert that the squares established in the decade between 1833 and 1843 (Union, Tompkins, Stuyvesant, and Madison) had served to raise property values in their surrounding areas, but he noted bitterly that despite their value for the city, no squares were opened between 1845 and 1853, when developers set the character of "the whole broad belt of the city" between 26th and 57th Streets, leaving an area of four square miles "without one single breathing space other than adjacent roads and avenues."[28]

Perhaps Edgar Allan Poe best summed up the future of the island when in 1844 he observed that the East Side furnished some of the world's most picturesque sites for villas, yet the whole area, including its mansions, looked neglected and unimproved. Why? "In fact, these mangnificent places are doomed. The spirit of Improvement has withered them with its acrid breath. Streets are already 'mapped' through them, and they are no longer suburban residences but 'town lots.' In some thirty years every noble cliff will be a pier, and the whole island will be desecrated by buildings of brick, with portentous *facades* of brown-stone. . . ." A few days later, viewing the waterfront from a skiff in the East River, he made a more depressing forecast that as "a necessary result of the subdivision of the whole island into streets and town lots," New Yorkers in twenty or thirty years would "see here nothing more romantic than shipping, warehouses, and wharves."[29]

Through most of the 1840s, the spirit of Improvement was dampened by the city's slowness in opening and grading new streets and avenues uptown; bad times after 1837 had cooled enthusiasm for street projects. The return of prosperity at the end of the decade, however, provided a new spur to uptown development. By 1850, it was evident that the exodus from downtown was carrying many different New Yorkers and their wealth to outside suburbs, especially to fast-growing Brooklyn. Erastus Benedict, who wanted the rapid settlement of uptown areas, charged that New York had lost 70,000 people and $50 million in taxable property, chiefly because it had so neglected street development that "not one lot in fifty in the out wards, was at all accessible, even for the purposes of cultivation, much less building."[30] Faced with the erosion of its tax base, the city was eager to facilitate the opening of new residential areas on the island in order to stem the tide. Having sold off most of its uptown lands for private development in the 1840s, it now launched an ambitious program of street improvement which helped make that development possible. Manhattan by 1858 was built-up almost solidly as far north as 36th Street on the East Side and 50th Street on the West. In the fifteen years after 1845, the population of the area north of 14th Street increased by 290,000, almost as many people as the entire city contained in 1840.[31]

Although government made such expansion possible, it did little to control the results. Instead, the nature and distribution of population in the area was governed primarily by the desire of property owners and builders to maximize the value of their property, chiefly by attracting the rich and excluding the poor whenever possible. At its best, this meant Ruggles' Gramercy Park. More often it involved the kind of speculative development described by Charles Astor Bristed, a grandson of the great landlord, John Jacob Astor. In his *Upper Ten Thousand*, Bristed noted that owners of land frequently joined with some of their friends in building houses on their property in the hope of establishing its reputation as a fashionable place to live: "The upper part of the city is dotted over with little spots, which have tried to be fashionable places and couldn't be."[32] Some developers attempted to guarantee a good character for the neighborhood; one advertised that his property on Eighth Avenue and on neighboring blocks between 24th and 26th Streets was "secured against shanties or nuisances in the neighborhood by a clause in the deed of all lots . . . that Brick or Stone Dwellings only shall be built upon them." The deeds of property owners in the Gramercy Park area specified the kind of dwellings that could be built and prohibited any "noxious or dangerous trade or business." In one form or another, builders constructed homes designed to attract the right people and to exclude the wrong, an obvious and persistent tactic that raised both expectations regarding living comforts and the costs of housing.[33]

Development was also governed by some common assumptions as to the allocation of territory on the island. The downtown areas were assigned to commerce and to those too poor to afford a better residential environment. The same thinking prevailed uptown. Both river fronts were treated as the future home of commerce.[34] Nearby lands were intended for the poor, as were those areas which had a reputation for unhealthiness. In 1866, the Sanitary Inspector for the Fifth Ward noted that a low-lying region within the ward was deemed "undesirable for a good class of population" and so "an inferior class of building" was constructed there, a practice which in the neighboring sixth ward had long before produced a monstrous result: the Five Points slum.[35] Elsewhere, the poor were permitted to squat on undeveloped rocky ground or the sunken lots left by the elevation of street grades in low-lying areas. In 1854, the *Evening Post* described the situation of the uptown poor:

It is found that during the last few years, an immense population of Irish and Germans have settled on the vacant lots, between 37th and 50th streets. They have build their own cabins and live there, the dogs, goats and pigs often all in the same room with the family. Their business is the poorest street or house labor. Picking rags, selling goats' milk, gathering cinders from the ashes to sell to other poor, cleaning the new houses, working on the docks; and, among the Germans, making the wooden splinters for match manufacturers.[36]

This independence on the frontier of the expanding city however, was soon to end. The continued development of the uptown area displaced most of the poor to the growing slums, where they were packed either into converted old homes or, with increasing frequency in the 1850s, new-style tenement houses built especially to contain them. The results of this kind of social planning were fully evident by the mid-1850s. In 1855, the inhabitants of the seven river wards of the lower part of the city owned less than 10 percent of personal property in the city even though they constituted nearly one-third of the population; on a per capita basis, the more advantaged classes in the interior wards uptown owned nearly five times as much personal property.[37]

If property-holders and builders could, consciously or unconsciously, agree that the place for the poor was in the leftover space of the commercial city, they could also agree more openly that there was a definite place for the rich, on the better sites whose value only the rich could afford. In the old city, the merchant class had often preferred to reside near the water where their businesses were located. The most fashionable addresses were generally west of Broadway, particularly on Park Place, Murray, Warren, Chambers, and other streets near Columbia College. The wealthy were near their businesses and the institutions central to their lives: City Hall was close by, as were the Broadway shops and churches like Trinity and Old Grace (located at Rector and Broadway), while the fashionable promenade at the Battery was within easy walking distance.[38]

With the expansion of commerce in the lower city, the rich looked for new residential sites uptown, especially on the high ground in the middle of the island, between Second and Eighth Avenues. Here were the healthiest sites in New York and also the ones farthest removed from the to-be-commercialized waterfront. By the mid-1850s, the great majority of affluent westsiders had migrated to areas north of Houston Street, taking their institutions with them. Grace Church, for instance, was removed to a more fashionable location on Broadway between 8th Street and Union Square, while the First Presbyterian Church relocated from Wall Street to Fifth Avenue. The elite Union Club migrated first to 4th Street and then in 1855 to 21st Street and Fifth Avenue. In 1857, Columbia College relocated at 49th Street and Madison Avenue, leaving its original campus to be divided up into downtown lots.[39]

Located somewhere between the two geographic and social extremes was New York's ill-defined but rapidly expanding middle class of professional men, small enterprisers, clerks, and skilled workers. Development for them generally took place uptown on the more desirable lands situated between the commercial areas near the riverfronts and the wealthy residential zone in the middle of the island. After 1845, encouraged by the expansion of shipbuilding in the East River yards, middle and working class neighborhoods sprang up in the Drydock area around the east end of 14th Street. In 1850, the *Evening Post* reported extensive construction in the area between 30th and 45th Streets on the East Side, which included "handsome dwellings" for those able to afford $300 or $400 in rent, as well as new tenements for the less affluent. Two years later, it expressed the hope that the subdivision of a number of estates located north of 14th Street and east of Second Avenue would encourage the "hardy sons of toil in the 18th Ward" to settle their families near their work places in the city rather than across the river in either Brooklyn or Williamsburg.[40]

Farther north on the East Side, Yorkville, the region north of 76th and south of 100th Streets, became a favorite residential area for a middle class of skilled workers and of clerks and other white-collar workers, many of whom commuted to their places of work "downtown." In 1852, a real estate broker advertised over a hundred lots for sale in the northern part of the area as being "very desirable for persons of small means to purchase a fine building lot or for capitalists to make safe and profitable investments."[41] Yorkville developed into a decent place to live, especially for those on salaries or earning steady wages. Despite some sanitary problems, it was generally a healthy place to live. Housing was good and comparatively inexpensive, consisting of small one, two, and three family dwellings, frequently built of wood (Yorkville was north of the fire limits of the city) but providing both the space and the convenience the middle class desired. Within the area, a variety of small factories provided jobs in light manufacturing. From the beginning, Yorkville attracted an ethnically mixed population of native-born Americans, Irishmen, and Germans.[42]

Thus was New York crudely organized on the basis of economic class. Isaac Kendall, looking back from the 1860s on two decades of growth, noted how the city tended to move northward: "The river fronts are taken up for business purposes, for brick, stone, and lumber yards, factories and machine shops. In the streets and avenues next to them congregate the workmen and laboring classes, next the leading avenues on each side become the great marts for retail business. . . . In the centre of the island, and following the line of Broadway and the Fifth avenue are found the residences of the wealthier classes. And as the city grows, each of these columns pushes out from its own base." Kendall also noted, however, that the process of growth was not quite so simple; the city was not simply moving northward, but was also gradually being filled in by the growth of such uptown centers as Yorkville, Manhattanville, and Harlem, which were expanding independently of the downtown areas just as Greenwich Village in the West Side Ninth Ward had done earlier.[43] Moreover, as other observers recognized, segregation by zones was both imprecise and unstable; the expansion of commerce and the growth in the number of poor people was too rapid for either to be contained within an established zone.

In the 1860s the sanitary inspector for the Ninth Ward noted that the Greenwich Village area had long enjoyed a reputation for unusual healthiness and that it had attracted a heavily native-born, middle-class population. He also reported, however, the existence in the ward of nearly 400 tenant houses, converted from private dwellings, "which have gradually degenerated into tenements of the worst description, because they were never designed for more than one family."[44] The needs of the poor and the desire of property-holders to maximize their incomes posed a threat to the residential stability of middle class areas; such decaying, overcrowded tenant houses were the seeds from which future slums often would grow. As one New Yorker observed, there was a general tendency of those with sufficient money to avoid "the immediate neighborhood of tenement houses."[45] Some areas, thus, were destined to decline, a fortunate tendency for the poor, as it assured them at least some housing in a city whose makers were reluctant to consign them any but the most meager share of precious residential space. Not even the rich in their central residential zone were entirely safe. In the 1860s, a sanitary inspector for the Eighteenth Ward noted that the population in the lower part of the ward shaded away from the wealthy people and superior living conditions of Fifth Avenue and Union Square eastward to the mixed population and conditions of the blocks between Third and First Avenues and then to the bad conditions, smelly gasworks, and largely Irish population of the area near the East River: "Let the wealthy resident upon Fifth Avenue walk along Seventeenth Street from First Avenue to the East River, and examine the houses and look at their population as he pursues his way; and if he can read certain results in these causes, he will see enough to diminish his sense of security in his own house."[46]

Fortunately for their peace of mind, few well-to-do New Yorkers looked eastward or westward. Instead, their eyes followed the avenues, southward to the expanding commercial areas, northward to the lengthening strings of increasingly lavish homes for the rich in the region above Washington Square. This was the new and progressive New York which both citizens and visitors preferred to see. In the 1840s, a fashionable residential area developed around Union Square. Opened in the previous decade, the area attracted many eminent citizens, including Samuel B. Ruggles, whose Gramercy Park five blocks to the north had succeeded in attracting such equally respectable citizens as Cyrus Field, Peter Cooper, and Samuel J. Tilden.[47] Despite its splashing fountain, however, Union Square was not destined to be a permanent focus of fashionable life. By 1850, instead, it was becoming the target for two converging streams of commercial activity working their way from the south up the Bowery and Broadway. Several blocks of Broadway to the South remained fashionable into the mid-1850s, but by that time Charles Astor Bristed could see definite signs of the withering breath of commerce: "Even here the dwellings are interspersed with shops; elegant mansions are beginning to be elbowed by dentists and boarding-houses, and to assume an appearance of *having been* in the aristocratic precincts."[48]

By the late 1840s, fashionable attention had already shifted from Broadway fo Fifth Avenue, which was protected at its southern end from the march of commerce by Washington Square. Adorned on the east by the Gothic building of New York University and graced on the north by the brick row houses of some of New York's most solid merchants, Washington Square was the heart of the city's wealthiest ward, the Fifteenth. To the east, the rich lived on Waverly Place, on the still fashionable blocks of Broadway between 4th Street and Union Square and, beyond them, on Bond and Great Jones Street and in the grandly colonnaded La Grange Terrace on Lafayette Place. Some lived to the south and west of the square, but the principal direction for future development was north, not so much along the few short blocks of University Place (which terminated near Union Square) nor on Sixth Avenue (which thrust north out of the tangled streets of Greenwich Village) as on Fifth Avenue. Opened in 1837, the Avenue began its march to gilded immortality in the late 1830s when William G. Rhinelander and Henry Brevoort, as part of the general migration away from lower Broadway, built houses north of Washington Square. In 1847, George Templeton Strong reported "Several new palazzos rising in the Fifth Avenue; it is built up without any very great gaps nearly to Twentieth Street." By 1851, the blocks below 23rd Street housed such notables as George W. Morris, James Lenox, Robert B. Minturn, August Belmont, reformer Myndert Van

Schaick, George Griswold, Moses Taylor and Mayor-to-be Ambrose C. Kingsland.[49]

This column of wealth, as it rose northward from its base in Washington Square, produced immense profits for the owners of land on both sides of the Avenue. Thomas E. Davies, second only to the great Astors as a landowner, bought 400 lots north of 20th Street in 1840 for between $200 and $400 each; some of them were worth fifty times as much after a decade of development, much of the increase coming from Davies' own work in building blocks of fashionable residences on his lands. Some lots on West 37th and 38th Streets, purchased by ex-Mayor William V. Brady in 1847 for $300 each, were valued at $6000 each ten years later. When in the mid-1850s Amos R, Eno reportedly paid $170,000 for 14 lots in the area of 23rd and Fifth, the *Tribune* commented on the increase of land values: "The secret of their high prices we presume lies in the fact that an idea prevails to a certain extent that no lots on this island are fit to place magnificent structures upon except those situated upon the narrow strip lying between Fourth and Sixth-avs and Tenth and Fortieth-sts."[50]

Profits and better living conditions—the triumphant march of residential New York up the island was, in its own way, as grand and as hopeful as the march of the American people westward. In 1848 George G. Foster, in proposing that Canal Street be converted into a great market street, predicted that within ten years "the whole upper part of the Island will be encrusted with beautiful palaces and exquisite cottage residences, starting out or hiding modestly like the fairy pictures one sees in dreams."[51] It was a pleasant dream, but it was not suited to the real hopes and ambitions of the progressive city. Although much of Manhattan was soon covered with new homes, it was "encrusted" with something other than fairy-like cottages. Palaces, yes—the princely mansions of the rich crept north on Fifth Avenue, which seemed to grow more princely with each new block. The future of uptown, however, was set not by a fairy godmother but by a host of speculative builders anxious to maximize their investments in Manhattan's increasingly expensive land.

A Rich and Growing City

Much of that future was evidenced in the lengthening strings of houses constructed on the side streets of the central residential zone during the prosperous early 1850s. The increasing demand for uptown homes and a plentiful supply of money brought a building boom which peaked in 1853–54. During these hopeful years, ambitious builders, with little capital of their own, were able to buy lots on credit and to build on credit, paying off their borrowings from the sale of completed houses. Some built a few "showy dwellings replete with 'modern conveniences,'" said *Hunt's*, in order to increase the value of their surrounding lands which were then sold at a handsome profit. The interiors of the new homes were designed to meet the rising expectations of affluent New Yorkers: Plastered walls, coal furnaces, gas lights and plumbing systems complete with inside water closets and laundry rooms—the material good life and respectability on sale at prices ranging from $8000 to $16,000.[52]

The good life, however, also tended to be a crowded life. As builders were reluctant to waste valuable land on yard space, they constructed dwellings which covered the entire frontage of the city's ubiquitous 25 by 100 foot lots, though ingenuity in many cases reduced the frontage to 20 feet or less. Gaslighting and coal furnaces along with water and sewerage systems made possible a comfortable, even elegant, crowding of homes. In the 1850s, Charles A. Bristed described a typical gentlemen's house as being wide enough to permit only one front room alongside a not very wide hall. To compensate for its narrowness, it was built four stories tall and 70 feet long, leaving only the back 30 feet available for a meager yard. As the houses were build close together, middle rooms were generally dark, unless the house was on a corner lot (the reason why some New Yorkers preferred to live on corners despite the fact that they got the "dust and noise of two streets instead of one"). One irritating defect of such an arrangement, noted Bristed, was that it demanded small entryways—mere closets when compared with the grand entryways of the rich; or, he added, "you must dispense with a private staircase altogether."[53]

Under such conditions, why not dispense with a private

stairway? This logic led straight to the idea of a European-style apartment house. In 1857 Calvert Vaux, one of the architects of Central Park, proposed that modified Parisian (Paris was the model for fashion-conscious New Yorkers) apartment buildings be constructed for the well-to-do. The price of city land, said Vaux, had grown so great as frequently to make it impossible for respectable people to buy or rent single-family dwellings. Substitute for the European inner court a "well-hole" to supply light and air to the interior rooms, move the parlor to the front so that wives could look out on the street, restrict the height of buildings to four stories (in the absence of elevators, apartments on higher floors might rent at lower rates and so attract the poor), make the public staircase as bright, airy, and elegant as possible ("or a prejudice will be likely to be excited on entering the premises")—and the result would be a comfortable living arrangement suited to the new conditions of the metropolis.[54]

It was a good idea, one also promoted by Horace Greeley as the most efficient way of developing New York's crowded space for a comfortable and healthy human existence, but it was premature. Although many New Yorkers would eventually abandon their prejudice against apartment houses, most attention in the central residential zone before the Civil War was lavished either on the increasingly grand palaces of the increasingly magnificent rich that dominated portions of Fifth, Madison, and other avenues, or on the spreading ranks of brownstone row-houses that soon were to oppress observers with their seemingly endless monotony, an ominous prophecy of future slums.[55] That prophecy had already been realized downtown, where the old homes of the well-to-do had either been abandoned to commerce or turned into crowded and increasingly squalid pens for the poor.

Despite its defects, the development of uptown was generally accepted as progress for the rich and growing city. New York, went the current cliché, was constantly building and rebuilding itself, moving northward, leveling the trees and hills, filling the island with people, and growing better. "New York is continually rising like a phoenix from the ashes," said one citizen, "and at each revival with increased elegance and splendor."[56] At least a few observers, however, noted the not-so splendid ashes which the rising phoenix had left behind. One of them was Henry P. Tappan, a New Yorker who had gone west to become Chancellor of the University of Michigan. In a speech before the New York Geographical Society in 1855, Tappan complained that in its expansion up the island the city had carelessly ravaged a place once "remarkable for its natural beauty":

> Where the Tombs [City Prison] now stand, there was once a little lake which connected with the Hudson, by a little outlet through Canal Street. Near the lake was a hill with a natural and abundant fountain. Had the shores of that lake and fountain been preserved and embellished, had the outlet been left open and spanned with tasteful bridges, how charming that portion of the city would have been! Now there are the Tombs and mean shops and dwellings; the hill with its fountains is sunk to fill up the lake, and the running stream is changed into a covered sewer. . . . The upper portion of the city may yet be redeemed, but the beauty of the lower is gone for. . . . The heights of Brooklyn, the shores of Hoboken, might have been preserved for enchanting public grounds. They, too, are lost forever.[57]

For Tappan, this had occurred because New Yorkers lacked love for, and pride in, their city, the kind of love and pride which would make them work to enrich and embellish it as their permanent home, "continually becoming dearer to us as it becomes more beautiful and contains more objects to render it worthy of our love." Like Americans generally, New Yorkers were too much in motion to form strong local attachments, too rootless to perfect their civilization, and too concerned with economic growth to prefer enduring works of beauty to "mere works of utility." Had the rich and growing city produced anything immortal, anything worthy preserving, anything that would be preserved? "Were New York now to experience the fate of Athens, or Rome, or Venice . . . what would she be but a mere mass of bricks and clay and sunken sewers. And if she goes on increasing and flourishing, must not all the works of the present and prosperous generation sink into insignificance, and leave not a trace behind in the more magnificent prosperity of generations that follow?"[58] Build and rebuild, more and bigger—that was the principle of progress for most New Yorkers. Build better, build something immortal? Why, when a new and, one hoped, better world would soon appear in some new and better uptown? And so New York grew and decayed.

In their work and ways, New Yorkers rather resembled the pioneers who had tamed frontier Michigan only shortly before Tappan became chancellor of that state's new university. Some would heed his appeal to "love your city, love your homes, and become wise benefactors of your city and your homes."[59] Generally, however, they were busy urban pioneers, preoccupied with developing and exploiting the unfolding possibilities of the rich and growing city. The result of their efforts was considerably less than an enduring civilization; yet, like their western brethren, there was also a grandeur to their work. They were, in their awkward way, successfully reorganizing a small eighteenth-century municipality into a great modern metropolis, creating a downtown for its expanding business and an uptown of exceptional comfort for its rapidly growing upper and middle classes. In establishing their "mere works of utility," they had accomplished an imperfect miracle, an urban miracle: They had created by 1860 the physical basis for the survival and often for the prosperity of 800,000 individuals on the southern half of Manhattan, on some ten square miles of land.

Chapter 6

MANHATTAN
SURVIVAL MACHINE

ON OCTOBER 14, 1842, New York celebrated its greatest civic triumph with speeches, music, parades, and massive public good cheer. After seven years of discussion, politics, and labor, after the expenditure of some $12 million, a river of fresh water had been brought through some forty miles of aqueduct and pipes from the Croton Reservoir in Westchester County to Manhattan. Marked by the opening of the city hall fountain, with its plume of water 50 feet high, the Croton Water System promised a new era of civic order, beauty, cleanliness, health, and security.[1] Horace Greeley predicted that the new river would find its way into public baths, which would induce cleanliness of both body and mind, and into public fountains, which "will display their grace amid utilitarian rows of brick."

MANHATTAN SURVIVAL MACHINE

Even the generally disgruntled Philip Hone, though he fussed about the costs of the system, could dream that pure water would replace alcohol as the city's favorite beverage and so be a powerful force for morality and order. Believing that the new supply would serve to quench the city's fires as well as its thirst, Hone, with other conservative-minded members of his class, also ventured into the fire insurance business. Hone soon ruefully recognized that the moral and physical power of Croton water was limited, particularly when in July 1845 a $5 million fire in the lower city drove his insurance company into bankruptcy.[2]

Whatever its limitations, the Croton System was an essential part of the life-support system required by the growing metropolis. Development, with its leveling of hills and filling of swamps, had seriously disrupted the lower island's natural water supply, while the natural wastes of New York's crowded population had polluted wells and springs. Even a generation ignorant of the germ theory of disease recognized that contaminated water caused disease and death. Without the Croton System there could not have been a doubling of the narrow island's population between 1845 and 1855. Nor could the city's economy have developed as rapidly, for the hotels came to depend on the water, as did the growing number of steam engines and steamships.[3]

The new system also brought a revolution in urban living standards. Since the distributing pipes entered the city from the north, Croton water was readily available to service the kitchen sinks, bathtubs, and water-closets, which were being built into the new uptown residences. For the middle class in particular, the new magic of tap water promised to reduce the costly dependence on domestic servants without the risk of a humiliating decline in cleanliness.[4] Downtown, the marbled magnificence of Stewart's department store was evidence of a revolution in fashion. Now, uptown these new arrangements in urban living were symbolized by the massive, Egyptian-style walls of the great Distributing Reservoir at 42nd Street. Flowing south from that reservoir through some 180 miles of pipe in 1848 approximately 15 to 16 million gallons per day filled the needs of 14,507 dwellings, 91 steamboats, 253 steam engines, 166 manufactories, 41 fountains, 24 bathing establishments, 43 hotels, and a variety of other users.[5]

The Croton System was a triumph of enlightened public enterprise, but most of the progress in living arrangements was left to private hands and the profit motive. By the 1850s, coal had supplanted wood as the primary source of the city's energy. In 1858 the Chamber of Commerce estimated that more than 2 million tons, one-third of the total production of the eastern coal fields (Maryland, Virginia, and most especially Pennsylvania) was shipped to the New York area, mostly over the Delaware and Raritan, the Morris, and the Delaware and Hudson canals.[6] It had become a necessity not only to steam ships and railroads but to the expanding industrial production of New York and Brooklyn as well.

The broadest influence of coal was on urban living standards. When improved transportation drove down its price, it supplanted wood as a heating and cooking fuel in middle class households, making possible the rapid spread of centralized heating systems in the new uptown residential areas. More, it brought the brightness of coal-gas lighting to replace the dim flickering oil lamps and candles of the past. With the decline of coal prices and with the organization of gas production and distribution, gas lamps became standard in the principal streets and squares as well as in the new homes of uptown residents.[7] The city was taking one long step toward extending day into night, lengthening the time available both for work and for leisure, and intensifying the contrast between the rhythms of urban life and the age-old natural rhythms of sun-up and sun-down.

Progress—it was a wonderful thing. In 1853 a New Yorker at least half seriously predicted that electric communication and power would be brought to every house in less than fifty years: "Men and women will have no harassing cares, or laborious duties to fulfill. Machinery will perform all work. Automata will direct them. The only task of the human race, will be to make love, study, and be happy." By the 1850s the urban revolution in living habits was well under way. Modern conveniences were making life more comfortable and creating the basis for intensified family life. The comforts of home, the automatic delivery of gas and water, the lessened need for daily purchases of food and fuel, the declining dependence on obstreperous and intrusive "help," the growth of leisure time and of the habit of reading enabled the urban family, especially the middle class family, to find refuge from an increasingly obnoxious public world in the more private interior life of the home.[8]

Progress, however, had its shadows, especially in the form of a growing gap in living standards and styles which separated the middle and upper classes from the great mass of the city poor. While the more fortunate readily took advantage of urban services, the poor were left to wait for the new amenities slowly to trickle down to them—much as they did for Croton Water. The Croton System was managed according to the principle that users would pay the costs of its construction and operation. For those who wanted water in their homes, the Croton Aqueduct Board required payment of installation costs plus a minimum of $10 a year in water rent. For the poor, the Board provided public hydrants where water could be obtained without charge. Six years after the opening of the system, two-thirds of New Yorkers still had no water in their homes, in part because pipes had not yet been laid in their districts and in part because landlords were reluctant to pay the costs of installation. While the fortunate enjoyed their advantages, the crowded inmates of tenant houses made do with backyard privies and basement water closets.[9]

Eventually, water and such other advantages of the urban supply system as central heating and gas lighting would come to the poor, but only after those advantages had first accrued to the more fortunate classes. Waiting at the end of the line, the poor were less likely to reap the benefits than the obnoxious byproducts of the system with its railroad tracks, coal yards, slaughterhouses, and gas plants. In the 1840s, a number of gas tanks were erected near the East River. Because of leaks in the tanks, a foul stench invaded the East Side between 14th and 23rd Streets. Who, but the poor and the disreputable, would live there? And so the city's notorious Gashouse District was born.10

Whatever the apportionment or malapportionment of its benefits, the urban supply system did sustain, in 1860, over 800,000 people on the 22 square miles of Manhattan Island, a population larger than that of 20 of the 33 states. Food for this massive urban appetite was transported to the city by a variety of means.[11] Much of it arrived by water, in Erie Canal barges, in market boats from the gardens of Long Island, the Hudson River counties, New Jersey and Connecticut, and in a miscellany of oyster boats, fishing boats, sloops, schooners, and steamers with cargoes as humble as beans, as exotic as pineapple and bananas. For decades, the Erie Canal was the great channel for basic breadstuffs. Before 1845, supply by land was limited to farm wagons, droves of cattle herded on the hoof, and New York's still feeble rail system. Railroad development after 1845 rapidly opened up new inland areas. By 1850, besides its connections with New England, New York was served by some 762 miles of railroad; by 1860 the figure was 1110. The railroad may not have increased the area of the city's food supply by the 4600 percent estimated by rail enthusiast Henry Varnum Poor, but the new system did effectively supplement, and increasingly supplant, the older water and land routes by providing faster and more flexible service.[12]

Before the railroad, for instance, cattle had been herded on foot from New England, upstate New York, Pennsylvania, Virginia, Kentucky, and most especially from Ohio, which was the Texas of the 1840s. At least one New York cattleyard established a hotel to accommodate the drovers, some of whom had spent as long as ten weeks on the road.[13] The coming of the railroad, however, put an end to the long drive in the East just as it was later to do on the Great Plains. By 1854, the *Tribune* reported that few cattle came by foot, while many were shipped by special weekly expresses run by the Erie Railroad from its western terminus at Dunkirk. The city's appetite for meat was beginning to affect areas west of the Mississippi. In 1855, Solon Robinson, agricultural expert for the *Tribune*, reported the arrival of Iowa, Missouri, and Texas cattle, which had first been driven to the Midwest for fattening. Robinson predicted that the westward movement of cattle raising would be followed by the meat-packers, but in the 1850s the cattle yards and slaughterhouses generally remained in New York, making it the most extensive cattle market in America.[14]

The city also drew heavily on its surrounding waters and farming areas to complete its urban diet. By the 1850s, the demand for seafood had made oyster raising a major business which, so estimated the *Citizen* in 1854, directly and indirectly employed some 50,000 people. The $5 million and more spent by New Yorkers in oyster saloons, restaurants, and markets encouraged the systematic planting and raising of oysters on the sea bottom off Long Island. So successful was the practice that the *Tribune* urged that it be adapted to the raising of fish to replenish the rapidly declining natural supply in the New York area, noting that to make fish "as plentiful as formerly, would prove one of the cheapest modes of lessening the price of human food."[15]

Improvements in farming the waters, however, were overshadowed by changes in farming the land. Although competition of western staples hurt eastern corn, wheat, and cattle producers, in compensation, transportation improvements also brought the more fortunately situated easterners into profitable contact with the growing urban market for perishable fruits and vegetables. Between 1840 and 1860, the value produced by the market gardens in the surrounding areas of New York and New Jersey increased eight times.[16] The horticulturist Andrew Jackson Downing, who helped guide the adjustment to this new market situation, noted in 1851 that the previous decade had seen a great increase in the cultivation of tomatoes and other vegetables; fifteen years before the tomato was hard to find, but now "there are hundreds of acres devoted to its culture for the supply of the New York market alone." With tomatoes came asparagus, cabbages, cauliflower, peas, beans, carrots, and potatoes—brought to the city by railroad, market boat, and market wagon from the gardens and farms of Long Island, Westchester County, and New Jersey. The New York market also demanded increasing quantities of fruit. In the early 1850s, for instance, as many as six steamboats a day brought in peaches from Middlesex County, New Jersey, while, at the same time, the railroads were beginning to stimulate cultivation of orchards in western New Jersey counties.[17]

The city had an even greater interest in the growth of the dairy industry. In 1841, New Yorkers consumed over 16 million quarts a year; in 1853, they drank more than six times as much, nearly 100 million quarts. At its best, milk was health, but unfortunately its increasing use was accompanied by a shocking increase in New York's already criminally high rate of infant mortality. In 1814, children under ten accounted for 37 percent of all deaths in the city; by 1852, the percentage had risen to 62. The primary cause seemed to be the heavy consumption of local swill milk, produced in what might politely be termed milk factories in the city, Brooklyn, and in surrounding areas.[18]

In 1852, some 58.5 million quarts a year came from cows fed almost entirely on swill, the waste product of the thriving distilleries. In one swill milk factory, connected with the city's largest distillery, an observer found 2000 cows crowded together in a stench-filled atmosphere that could be smelled as far as a mile away. Many of the poor creatures showed their condition "in the rotting of their teeth, the tenderness and extension of the hoofs, which are turned up like the point of a skate, . . falling of the hair, ulcers upon various parts of the body, etc." Some 12 percent of the herd died each year, a modest death rate when compared with one such factory in neighboring Williamsburg, where 50 to 65 percent died annually. As swill milk was thin and had a bluish tint, it was doctored to the right color and consistency by the addition of magnesia, chalk, stale eggs, flour, molasses, burnt sugar, and other exotic substances; then, after these adulterants had conveniently increased the volume by perhaps as much as a fourth, it was sold at five cents a quart. Milk and whiskey and death. Medical authorities in the 1850s blamed swill milk for cholera infantum, diarrhea, and other killers of children, especially of infants under two.[19]

In the face of this devastation of its children, New York looked to the railroads and to the Hudson River counties for salvation. By 1850, the Erie and Harlem railroads had brought the city in touch with the dairy regions of Orange, Westchester, Putnam, and Dutchess counties. By opening up the city market to areas with good pasturage, they created a profitable trade in country milk. In 1852, New York's milk shed sent over 30 million quarts to the metropolis, roughly twice as much as the whole supply a decade earlier.[20] Yet, some two-thirds of the supply still consisted of swill milk. The opening of the dairy regions had stimulated a vast increase in the consumption of pure milk, especially among the more fortunate, but production and distribution were not sufficiently organized to make "good" cheaper and more available than "bad," even when country milk was watered down by city distributers. The children of the poor continued to drink swill milk—often delivered to the door by carriers who dipped it out of a can—and they continued to die.[21]

In other ways, too, the opening of new sources of supply was not followed by immediate improvements in general health and well-being, chiefly because, as with its water and energy, the city was slow to develop an efficient system of distribution for its inhabitants. Steamboats and railroads were replacing sails and horses, but progress was faltering before the problem of moving the mounting mass of food from the wharves and depots to the family table. Nowhere was this paradox of disrupted plenty more evident than in the city's markets, at once a source of pride and of shame. The names of the markets were an alphabet of abundance; Catherine, Centre, Clinton, Essex, Franklin, Fulton, Gansevoort, Gouverneur, Jefferson, Monroe, Tompkins, Union, and Washington. In 1850, the *Evening Mirror* described Fulton Market:

> We saw a display a fruits, vegetables, and flowers from all parts of the world. . . . Messina oranges; a heap of pineapples from the Bahamas, and bunches of ripe bananas from Cuba . . . Alpine strawberries in little Long Island baskets . . . a heap of Virginia water-melons. . . . There were Valparaiso pumpkins,

[124]

manna apples from Cuba, peaches from Delaware, lobsters from the coasts of Maine, milk from Goshen, chickens from Bucks County, Pennsylvania, hens from Cochin China, potatoes from Bermuda, peas, beans and squashes from Long Island, white-fish from Lake Michigan; there was beef that had been fattened on the banks of the Ohio; hams smoked in Westphalia; sausages stuffed in Bologna; mutton from Vermont; and cheese from the region of the St. Lawrence.[22]

With their equally rich variety of people—of foreigners and natives, of farmers, dealers, butchers, wholesalers, retailers, and housewives—the markets were the romance not only of abundance but of human community as well, where the citizen could experience some of the joys of urban living. An observer described one early Sunday morning at Catherine Market: "Young bloods who have been larking all night go there to get their coffee and cakes, and antiquated codgers to get some eels and other belly timber for their families, and a few drinks and some sport for themselves. Here and there a darkey may be seen dancing for pennies, and every thing and every body seems as gay as a cricket."[23]

Ideally, the markets were centers of meaningful public life. The market system had long been an instrument for the public regulation of the price and quality of food, with monetary profit for the municipality. Under it, retailers and wholesalers bought from the city privileged positions in the sale of meat and other fresh provisions; these market-men were expected to accept regulations prohibiting the sale of unwholesome food, unsanitary premises, and price fixing.[24] In theory, the system bound the muncipal government and the established tradesmen of the city together in a common devotion to the public good. The public side of some of the markets was enhanced by the presence of other municipal activities. Centre Market, opened in 1839 with a grand "Butcher Ball and Supper," provided drill and exercise space on the second floor for several militia units. Later, the Fourteenth Ward police used the upper part of the building as a stationhouse. When the new Essex Market was built in 1852–53, space was provided for courts, the Tenth

Ward police, the Eastern Dispensary and, in a dome capping the building, for the fire watch.[25]

Plenty, community, public order—the markets might have summed up the glory of the city. In fact, they were dirty, disorderly, and dissatisfying. If they were emblems of urban abundance, they also had become bottlenecks in the distribution of the rising flood of food. Washington Market, the greatest in the city, was strained beyond capacity. On one morning during the produce season in 1848, some 230 market boats, sloops, schooners, and barges thronged the Hudson waiting to unload their cargoes. The result was chaos. Wholesalers, retailers, and country people elbowed each other for market space, while the streets outside were clogged with wagons, carts, and wheelbarrows.[26]

While some markets like Washington and Fulton were overburdened by expanding business, others declined as the competition of private shops and the uptown movement robbed them of most of their prosperous customers. Weehawken Market on the West Side and Monroe Market on the East Side were abandoned in the 1840s, while others in the lower city, such as Franklin and Union, were left with vacant stalls. Although the few uptown markets saw an increase in patronage, the market system generally was severely disrupted by the rapid social and physical changes in the expanding city.[27] Its decay was plainly written in the dirty, weather-beaten appearance of many of the market buildings. Solon Robinson, who dreamed of neat market buildings complete with reading rooms for visiting farmers, called the motley collection of wooden sheds at Washington Market a disgrace and an abomination. What might have been agencies of municipal control and centers of neighborhood life, part of the progress of the city, were in fact a shameful reminder of municipal incompetence and, with their smells, disorder, clutter, and rats, a source of neighborhood decay.[28]

A well-established, significant urban institution was degenerating. Was it worth saving? A number of political leaders thought it was, if only because the city had a million dollar investment in the system and a strong moral and legal obligation to the marketmen. In 1841, the Market Committee of the Board of Aldermen urged the city to convert the less profitable parts of existing buildings to other purposes and then to erect a number of small markets in convenient locations.[29] In 1849, Mayor Woodhull proposed the complete rebuilding of Washington Market and the construction of a new market in the upper part of the city. The 1850s indeed did bring some effort to reverse the trend. Between 1852 and 1859, Essex, Gouverneur, Catherine, Union, and Tompkins markets were rebuilt.[30]

The system, however, continued to decline, for there was little public commitment to it. Many New Yorkers saw it as a costly anachronism in an age of triumphant individual enterprise. During the early 1840s, it became a political issue, as both Whigs and Democrats attacked the "Market Monopoly" for compelling housewives to walk long distances to pay monopolistic prices.[31] The law against the sale of meat in private shops was largely ignored, as judges and juries tended to treat it as an unconstitutional restraint on free enterprise and, in 1843, it was revised to permit meat sales. By 1850, an observer noted that "it has become so fashionable to have a meat-shop on almost every corner and fruits and vegetables in almost every grocery, and fish and oysters well nigh swimming through the streets that our large markets are to some extent foresaken." As their retail trade declined, the larger markets became wholesale sources of supply for private shops. Public markets were becoming simply the central part of an expanding system of private enterprise.[32]

In 1854, City Comptroller A. C. Flagg, a respected authority on public finance, urged the city to complete the process by leasing the markets for wholesaling purposes to businessmen or business associations, "leaving all the market arrangements to be made only on enlightened, liberal and simple business principles." Under the new arrangement, said Flagg, the wholesalers would be able to pay higher rents than existing marketmen. Moreover, once freed from the bungling interference of government, enlightened business enterprise would supply consumers with food more conveniently and cheaply than before, while also upgrading market facilities to a level equal to the city's "splendid hotels."[33] Neither Flagg's plan nor another simply to sell off the market properties was enacted into law. Instead, the system was allowed to drift—and to die as a truly public institution, without either the predicted gains in revenues or the upgrading of the market facilities. Junius Browne later described the markets as "Old rickety, unclearly, patched, and added to until they seem like old garments."[34]

The market situation, with its ill-kempt vitality and its ill-distributed abundance, was a microcosm of the vital and dynamic but haphazard and careless city. In less than two decades, the public and private enterprise of New York created a delivery system of canals, ships, and railroads sufficient to meet the expanding needs of a great population and to sustain its ambitious individualism. In this sense, the city had become a more efficient means of meeting human needs than nature herself. Water, coal, meat, flour, vegetables, and fruit—in thousands of tons, gallons, and bushels—formed the abundance so essential to an age of human progress. It was a marvelous system of human survival and development, but it was a carelessly managed one, in which abundance was accompanied by such waste and wastefulness that the city seemed likely to choke on its successes.

This wastefulness was especially evident in the use of water. The Croton system was capable of delivering 30 million gallons a day, enough apparently to meet the city's needs for many years. Yet, in little more than a decade, consumption threatened to exceed supply. In 1852, the chief of the Fire Department, Alfred Carson, warned that the city had to begin an immediate expansion of the system or run the risk that a water shortage would lead to a disastrous fire. Undoubtedly planners had underestimated legitimate demand, but equally certain, as the Croton Commissioners complained in 1846, there was an "extraordinary use and abuse of the water."[35] Water was left to flow, unused, from faucets, hydrants, and leaks in pipes in homes and in markets, on wharves and on the streets. Every year, Croton officials pleaded and threatened, but the waste continued, abetted by their failure to install meters to measure consumption in private households. In 1855, they estimated that more than half the water supply was wasted; other critics put per capita consumption in New York at twice that of Philadelphia and three times that of London.[36]

New Yorkers were also careless in their use of other resources. Solon Robinson, who combined his interest in agriculture with an effort to improve conditions for the urban poor, charged that because of inefficient heating systems the city wasted three-quarters of its coal; much of it was unburnt coal, thousands of tons of which yearly "are carried off in ash carts to fill up and build out some wharf on which to land more coal." Robinson also complained that more food was wasted than was eaten, as a result both carelessness in the keeping, cooking, and eating of food in the home and bad management "in our markets and store houses, where whole cargoes of grain, meal, flour, meat, fish, fruits, and vegetables are continually being wasted."[37]

This waste added to the normal byproducts of crowded living. Having created the system required to sustain a coal-burning city, a tearing-down and building-up city, an industrial city, and a growing city, New Yorkers faced the increasingly complex task of removing the collective tons of scattered ashes, broken building materials, junk, dust, and most especially the wastes of an intensely animal world. By the 1850s, besides its more than half a million human inhabitants, the city had a large four-legged population. In 1854, some 22,500 horses pulled omnibuses, streetcars, hacks, and other public conveyances in the city; the number used for private purposes was uncounted.[38] Thousands of pigs were kept in pens or left free to roam the streets. Thousands of cows and beef cattle were found in city milk factories and cattle yards.

What to do, then, with the tons of animal manure? What also to do with the byproducts of dying as well as living? In 1850, Mayor Woodhull estimated that there were 206 slaughterhouses, 11 public markets, and 531 private markets or butcher shops, in other words 748 "places in each of which there is generally a greater or lesser amount of animal matter, undergoing decay."[39] Bones, blood, and offal left by the slaughtering process; dead cows, pigs, dogs, and cats; steaming

[129]

piles of manure; the stench from privies, overflowing cesspools, and defective sewers—such was the nauseating evidence that as many as a million living and dying, consuming and excreting creatures crowded New York. Manhattan had become one great, haphazardly constructed, and inefficient survival machine, which converted a growing volume of the resources of the nation into life and the wastes of life.

This inefficiency alarmed those few New Yorkers who had developed an interest in conservation. In 1851, Andrew Jackson Downing warned that rising urban consumption was depleting the nation's agricultural resources: "We are in some respects like a large and increasing family running over and devouring a great estate to which they have fallen heir, with little or no care to preserve or maintain it." Observing that the last decade had seen both a significant decline in soil fertility and a shift of Americans away from agriculture to the cities, Downing predicted that, unless agricultural practices were significantly improved, the United States would begin to face the spectre of famine soon after it reached a hundred million in population. He noted a fundamental weakness of the existing system:

> "What matter it," say the wise men of our State legislature, "if the lands of the Atlantic States are worn out by bad farming? Is not the GREAT WEST the granary of the world?" And so they build canals and railroads, and bring back from the west millions of bushels of grain, and send not one fertilizing atom back to restore the land. And in this way we shall by-and-by make the fertile prairies as barren as some of the worn out farms of Virginia.[40]

A few other men also recognized the necessity of returning to the soil the billions of fertilizing atoms scattered around the city. In 1853, at a meeting of the City's Farmer's Club, Robert Ellis of Ulster County charged that New York, by discharging its human excrement into the surrounding rivers, was wasting each year enough nitrogen to raise 180 million pounds of wheat. Two years later, George E. Waring, Jr., who was to be a major influence in sanitation after the Civil War, estimated that the city and its suburbs threw away over $5 million in fertilizer a year, and warned that this enormous waste was debilitating not only the soil but the people themselves: "What with our earth butchery and prodigality we are each year losing the intrinsic essence of our vitality." Horace Greeley echoed this warning when, after condemning the "inexplicable stupidity" which led New York to waste a treasure more valuable than the gold of California, he declared that earlier societies had been weakened by "the exhaustion of the soil through the loss of such manures in their capitals."[41]

New York had not totally ignored its fertilizing treasure. For years, the city had been selling its street manure to surrounding farmers at considerable profit for itself. As early as 1840, a special committee of the Board of Aldermen, in urging public support for a railroad, argued that it would expand the market for manure. Similarly, some of New York's "nightsoil" (excrement from privies) had been sold as fertilizer, chiefly in the form of Poudrette, made by the Lodi Manufacturing Company and advertised as increasing agricultural yield by one-third.[42] Despite the warnings of the conservationists, however, the city devoted its attentions far less to using than simply to getting rid of its ominously growing tons of waste as quickly and as conveniently as possible.[43]

This preoccupation was particularly evident in the management of the sewerage system New York developed in the two decades after 1840. Although some sewers had existed earlier, it was not until the completion of the Croton Aqueduct that they were accepted as necessary improvements. Early in the 1840s, it was feared that the inpouring of this new river of water would compound Manhattan's drainage problems, especially since the opening and grading of streets as part of uptown development had disrupted the natural drainage of the island. Wet, swampy ground meant disease. To this problem posed by the new embarrassing abundance of water was added an opportunity to remove what had become an annoying abundance of human feces. The city's 300,000 people depended almost entirely on backyard privies and cesspools to meet their daily necessities.[44]

[131]

Aside from contributing to the stenchfull atmosphere, these waste traps posed a major problem of removal, since periodically they had to be emptied of their accumulated nightsoil. This work was done by night scavengers, whose disposal techniques left much room for nose-wrinkling complaint. In 1842, Dr. John H. Griscom, then serving as City Inspector, charged that the scavengers, on their way to the docks, managed to spill part of the nightsoil on the city streets. The noxious stuff was dumped into the river, to at least the occasional outrage of boatowners: "Small boats, which may happen to be within the reach of the avalanche and they are generally unseen in the darkness, are either wholly or partially filled, and instances are said to occur of their being carried to the bottom with their unnatural loads." As a result of the constant dumping of an estimated 750,000 cubic yards a year, some slips had become so filled as to be useless for shipping, while the general accumulation had compounded the filth and stink of the shabby waterfront. As a solution, Griscom urged the city to adopt the practice of Boston and Philadelphia in converting the nightsoil into fertilizer, but others saw an easier answer in the development of a sewerage system.[45]

Sewers could use Croton water to carry excrement underground, out-of-sight and out-of-smell. The presence of an abundance of water made it possible to replace outhouses with waterclosets on a large scale, an improvement which it was hoped would not only purify the atmosphere, advance human comfort, and protect the public health but also, by removing the need for obnoxious outhouses, increase land values and rents, open more space for urban occupancy, and make possible denser habitation. The Aqueduct, waterclosets ("these admirable modern combinations of utility, cleanliness, and decency," said one proponent in 1840), and sewers were essential parts of modern progress.[46]

Having invested exhausting millions in a water system, however, the city was reluctant to spend millions more on sewers. It moved slowly until 1849, when a combination of circumstances pushed it into its first massive sewerage program. In that year, the Croton Aqueduct Department was reorganized and was given responsibility for constructing a comprehensive sewerage system. That same year saw an outbreak of a massive cholera epidemic, which killed over 5000 New Yorkers. The disease frightened even complacent citizens into a greater interest in public health, especially since it was observed that it struck hardest in the developing upper wards close to where the more fortunate were establishing their homes. Aside from their value in preventing future epidemics, sewers promised not only to service the modern conveniences demanded by uptowners but also to prevent the flooding of cellars by ground water. "In many of the streets up town," said the *Evening Post* in 1851, "it is next to impossible to erect houses without first having a sewer built in the same street," in part because the introduction of Croton water had raised the water level "many feet." Under the spur of such concerns, the Croton Department between 1850 and 1855 laid some 70 miles of sewers in the upper and lower parts of the city.[47]

The system, however, was hardly complete. In 1859, the AICP complained that nearly three-quarters of the 500 miles of paved streets, especially those in poor neighborhoods, were still without sewers. Moreover, even on the sewered streets many property-holders were slow to connect to the system, as they were under no legal compulsion to do so. The landlords of the poor generally left their tenants to suffer in the stink of privies and cesspools. In 1856, there were 1361 baths and 10,384 water closets in a city of more than 600,000 people. No wonder that the AICP could complain that millions of gallons of sewage were left to accumulate "in courts, sinks, and cesspools, and in the streets and gutters to putrefy in the sun, and send out their poisonous miasmas to engender disease and destroy life."[48]

If construction was too slow, in another sense it was too hasty. After having observed hundreds of workmen "digging deep channels in the street," one New Yorker said that little thought had been given to the operation of the system and warned that the situation should be carefully considered before "we find pestilence among us from the exhalation of our sewers." In 1866, nearly twenty years after this warning, a medical inspector complained that the original sewerage plan was better suited to a village than to a city and that, far from being improved, it had been further weakened by haphazard additions often made with the thought of simply getting "the filth out of sight *somewhere*."[49] But not out of smell. Sewers built on this principle often were overloaded, especially since many had been laid with little thought to assuring the maximum flow. As a result, much of the solid waste matter was left to decompose in the pipes. The sewers became, as the AICP complained earlier, "one elongated cesspool," which, owing to the city's failure to install traps at sewer openings, emitted noxious gases during the warm months. Even when the system worked well, it simply removed the problem from the island to the surrounding rivers into which the raw sewage poured. Since the East River in particular carried off the discharge slowly if at all, much of the sewage remained to contaminate the water and to pollute the surrounding air.[50]

Sluggish sewers, filthy streets, and smelly air—these were the stuff of a popular lament: that New York had become one of the dirtiest cities in the world and also one of its deadliest. In 1854, George Templeton Strong wrote in his diary: "The stinks of Centre Street lift up their voices. Malarious aromata rampage invisible through every street, and in the second-rate regions of the city, such as Cherry Street, poor old Greenwich Street [where Strong had once lived], and so on, atmospheric poison and pungent factor and gaseous filth cry aloud and spare not, and the wayfaring man inhales at every breath a pair of lungs full of vaporized decomposing gutter mud and rottenness." Although neither Strong nor any other New Yorker recognized that the great city sustained not only a million living creatures but, in its filth, billions of microorganisms, their noses told them that in the "gaseous filth" there lurked a threat to the life and health of the city. Their noses were right, for the summer of 1854 brought an outburst of cholera only a little less deadly than the great epidemic of 1849, when one out of every one hundred New Yorkers died.[51]

Although the cholera years were especially devastating, every year was a threat to the life and health of the inhabitants, especially of children; less than one-half of those born in the city in the 1850s would survive to the age of six.[52] Between 1840 and 1855, the mortality rate mounted with ominous regularity. In 1840, of every 40 New Yorkers, one died; in 1845, it was one death for every 37 inhabitants; in 1850, it was one for every 30; in 1855, one for every 27—until the deadly increase began to falter.[53] So frightful was the general mortality that, in some years during the 1850s, deaths exceeded births. In 1856, there were a reported 16,191 births and 21,658 deaths (14,809 children). Three years earlier, before the establishment of a birth-reporting system, the City Inspector attempted to calculate the natural increase or decrease of the city and reached the tentative conclusion that "our only increase arises from emigration, without which the city would in a few years be depopulated."[54]

Debilitating sickness was even more common than death. Although there was no accurate way of determining its extent, Dr. Stephen Smith estimated in the early 1860s that there were 28 cases of sickness for every death and that in some areas 50 to 70 percent of the population was sick at any moment in time. Death and disease especially devastated the poor, leaving the fatherless families, orphans, and sickly parents so common to slum life. In 1845, Dr. John H. Griscom, a leading authority on public health, asserted that sickness among the poor meant an immense loss of human labor. More, it was intimately connected with the rising pauperism and crime which was proving so costly to the finances and good order of the city. So long as bad health undermined self-sufficiency, self-respect, and morality, he warned, so long will there be "a class in the community more difficult to govern, more disposed to robbery, mobs, and other lawless acts, and less accessible to the influence of religious and moral instruction."[55]

Thus, by the 1850s, the Manhattan survival machine had also become a death machine, destroying human lives and depleting human potentials—a menace to its citizens and to the rest of the country. In the early 1860s, a health inspector noted the extensive travel from the downtown areas of the city, where smallpox and typhoid fever were strong, and asked: "Is it any cause for surprise that cases of these diseases are here contracted, to be carried to the distant section of the country, there to develop themselves to the surprise and alarm of whole neighborhoods?" This menace was posed by a city which, aside from its naturally healthy location between two rivers, could boast of its medical talent (1,252 physicians and at least 12 surgeons in 1855) and of its four general hospitals, five dispensaries, two eye-and-ear infirmaries, and other medical facilities (these had provided free treatment of 151,000 cases of disease in 1853).[56]

There were almost as many explanations for this paradox as there were diseases. Smallpox, yellow fever, cholera, cholera infantum, typhus, typhoid fever, measles, scarlet fever, dysentery, tuberculosis—who could readily explain these and various other killers, especially in an age which had not yet discovered germs? Some New Yorkers blamed the city's growing trade with disease-ridden areas elsewhere in the world. A great many others blamed the sufferers themselves, the poor and especially the immigrant poor: Intemperance, bad diet, and slovenly habits explained why so high a proportion of the deaths were among immigrants and their children. Others, more sympathetically, attributed the problem not to the newcomers but to their debilitating experience in Europe and on shipboard.[57] Victims of outside forces beyond their control— New Yorkers preferred to think in such terms, but they could not ignore the smells and general dirt of the city, reminders of its murderously bad sanitation. Some, at least, recognized that many of the deaths among children, especially from diseases like dysentery and cholera infantum, resulted from the failure of the city to clean up its wastes. Though the germ theory was unknown, it was common to blame disease on the filth and poisonous air generated by ill-managed, densely crowded cities.[58] Dr. Griscom estimated that in 1860 alone bad sanitation was reponsible for 5248 deaths and 149,944 cases of sickness, while over the previous 20 years 75,000 people had died needlessly from the same cause.[59]

Here, for him and other critics, was proof that the city had failed miserably to protect the health of its citizens, especially its poor. It seemed obvious to Griscom that New Yorkers bore a collective responsibility for the urban mess they had created. What men had done, they must and could undo, for the development of urban civilization had brought with it the power to conquer disease and to improve the environment. Since the early 1840s, a few men like Griscom had attempted to shame and to frighten New York into adopting a program for the improvement of sanitation and public hygiene which would reverse its rising death rate, but with little effect. In 1860, Griscom complained that "one of the most surprising phenomena in the political economy of this state and city, is the indifference of the people to their own death records. . . . There is no denial that the mortality of this city is much greater than that of many others of far inferior advantage for salubrity and longevity, and yet the trump of the archangel sounds in their ears in vain."[60]

Eventually, there would be some significant gains for public health. Even before 1860, the sewerage and water systems were extended and Central Park begun. In 1866, Griscom and other health crusaders like Robert M. Hartley scored a significant victory over the Manhattan death machine when the state established the Metropolitan Board of Health; under the Board, sanitation was improved and the death rate brought down to the pre-1840 level.[61] Their triumphs, however, fell far short of their hopes, for a comprehensive program of public hygiene which would establish "wise precautions . . . relative to the soil we dwell upon—the houses we live in—the drainage of waters—the food and drink we consume—the places of public gatherings—the filth that poisons the air."[62]

In theory, the city might be perfected as an agency of human survival and improvement. In reality, New York was too carelessly individualistic to solve the problems of its chaotic growth. Between 1840 and 1855, its population more than doubled, while the volume of its animate and inanimate wastes undoubtedly grew even faster. There developed a city of extraordinary wealth and power but also a city of equally remarkable filth, a sparkling gem set in a pile of garbage. Given the character both of the problem and of New York, it

[137]

was not surprising that the health reformers should discover that their task far exceeded that of Hercules. Certainly, their efforts to clean up Manhattan Island brought them face-to-face with a variety of problems far more complex than the building of sewers and the cleaning of streets. To achieve their goal required that they discipline an ill-disciplined people, reform an inefficient government, and, above all, carry through the very complicated task of managing an increasingly crowded and increasingly valuable urban space.

Chapter 7

THE USE
OF URBAN SPACE

VISITORS AND CITIZENS were attracted to the glitter and power of Broadway, Wall Street, and Fifth Avenue. The City Inspector, however, was obliged to know another New York. As the chief municipal officer for public health, his attention focused on the less glamorous and more repellent uses of urban space: The garbage in the street, the manure piles, the ill-managed slaughterhouses, the defective sewers, the over-flowing privies—all those things which both offended the eyes and nose and threatened physical well-being. Although he was chiefly responsible for streets and other public places, the conscientious City Inspector also came to know the more private space occupied by the poor and the obscure, the alleys, backyards, courtyards, cellars, and grimy apartments which spawned the fetid atmosphere of the expanding slums.[1]

[139]

The Growing City I

FIGURE 10. (left above) This highly stylized view (1850) features the department store of A. T. Stewart at Broadway and Chambers Street shortly after its costly expansion from about three-quarters of an acre to nearly two acres of floor space. The fence and trees on the right are part of City Hall Park. North on Broadway in the distance can be seen the steeple of Grace Church at the point where Broadway bends toward Union Square. Fashionable New York is on display here, complete with two prancing horses, but even this antiseptic lithograph does not completely shut out the work-a-day reality of omnibuses and carts which made fashionable stores like Stewart's possible.

Courtesy of the Museum of the City of New York.

FIGURE 11. (left, below) J. W. Orr's wood engraving (1852) for *Putnam's Magazine* catches some of the haphazard vitality of the growing city in its depiction of the rebuiling of Liberty Street on the West Side; the Hudson River waterfront is in the background. Liberty Street, with other streets in the area, was completely rebuilt for the stores and warehouses required by New York's expanding dry-goods trade, including the wholesale and retail business of A. T. Stewart. *Putnam's* said that after the completion of this project one "would hardly recognize in the handsome, fresh, and almost palatial Liberty-St. of 1853, the dusky, tumble-down and seedy lane ... of the spring of 1852." This early form of urban renewal transformed most of the once residential Third Ward into the warehouse sector of the city.

Courtesy of the New York Public Library, Prints Division.

THE USE OF URBAN SPACE

Dr. John H. Griscom was both conscientious and well-qual-
ified. A graduate of the University of Pennsylvania Medical
School, he had served the poor in the 1830s as a physician for
the New York Dispensary.[2] Appointed City Inspector in 1842,
Griscom gave much of his time to making a comprehensive
survey of city health conditions, with particular emphasis on
the submerged mass of people. He discovered some 33,000
souls—a tenth of the population—who had been packed away
amid filth and vermin in dark, damp, ill-ventilated cellars and
crumbling backyard tenements. In a 200-page report to the
Common Council in 1843, he pointed out the many dangers
to the public health and urged an extensive municipal effort
to improve physical conditions, especially for the poor.[3] As a
reward, he was ousted from his post in 1843 when the
Democrats regained the Council and rejected for reappoint-
ment the next year after the American Republicans won
control; the nativist Aldermen added to injury the sneer that
its appointee would prove competent even though "he may
not, perhaps, succeed in framing a report quite so scientific
and speculative on the 'Philosophy of Diseases'" as that presented by Griscom. The ex-City Inspector, however, had some
influential friends, such as Mayor Harper and Peter Cooper,
who helped subsidize the publication in 1845 of his *The Sanitary
Condition of the Laboring Classes*, a milestone in the long effort
to improve public health.[4]

Although Griscom attacked a wide variety of physical an-
noyances, he emphasized the dangers inherent in the city's
cramped and crowded housing. He believed that a plentiful
supply of pure air (about 10 cubic feet per minute for each
adult) was essential for good health. The noisome atmosphere
of the crowded city was threatening enough; worse was the
condition of the cramped, dirty, ill-ventilated space occupied
by the poor. In 1844, he asserted that during the previous
year the city dispensaries had treated some 50,000 cases of
"disease originating chiefly from the occupation of crowded,
filthy, ill-ventilated inhabitations." Although he criticized the
poor for their indifference to the laws of health, Griscom
indicted the landlords for failing to provide their tenants with

the space and the "household conveniences," such as Croton water, required for a healthy atmosphere. Because the poor had no space to store fuel or food in large quantities, they were forced to purchase by "the small" from neighboring grocers at prices from 10 to 50 percent higher than those paid by the more advantaged. The result was sickness, poverty, and also immorality, for the physically depressing effects of illness, especially when associated with a dirty and shabby environment, often led to moral degeneration.[5]

Griscom and his friends recognized that the environment forced on the poor would produce a physical and moral degeneration in almost anyone, that the sufferings of the unfortunate were not simply the consequence of defects in their characters but were also the results of a mismanagement of space for which society, by its neglect, was ultimately responsible. So long as the city ignored the problem of bad housing, so long would it pay heavily for its neglect in the form of disorder, crime, vice, and pauperism.[6] To effect what he was later to call "a sanitary regeneration of society," Griscom proposed a comprehensive program of public action. Society would, by law, regulate both existing and new housing to assure clean, well-ventilated apartments and to prevent overcrowding. Aware of the importance of enforcement, he also proposed the creation of an effective Health Police, a professional organization of medical experts, which would have the power to investigate all dwellings, to compel landlords to clean up their buildings, and to close any places unfit for human habitation. Infringements on private property rights? Griscom pointed out that municipal government already prohibited the construction of wooden buildings in specified areas and imposed other limitations on private rights in order to protect the welfare of a crowded city. If those laws were proper, then "equally proper should be one respecting the protection of the inmates from the pernicious influences of badly arranged houses and apartments."[7]

Griscom recognized that regulation itself would not provide the housing needed by an expanding city. In fact, effective regulation would reduce available residential space for New

Yorkers unless combined with a program to encourage the construction of new dwellings. One of Griscom's allies—a City Tract Society Missionary—said that government should build or at least actively encourage the building of housing, "so constructed that each family may have at least two rooms."[8] Griscom, however, rejected the idea of public housing, in favor of the hope that benevolent capitalists would fuse philanthropy and profits by building homes for the poor:

> Blocks or rows of substantial buildings, in open spaces, where the air would have free access, with the internal arrangements such as would conduce to the well-being of the tenants, and with the facilities for warming, washing, drainage, and storage of fuel and food, which science has so greatly improved, might doubtless be made to yield a good interest for investment, while a return would be received in the increased happiness, health, morals, and comfort of the inmates, and good order of society, which cannot be estimated in money.[9]

Griscom's call for model housing was taken up in 1847 by the Association for Improving the Condition of the Poor (AICP), of which he was a member, with the warning that, because of defective housing, "social habits and morals are debased, and a vast amount of wretchedness, pauperism, and crime are produced." Having studied the example of English philanthropists, the AICP initially planned to set up a "chartered company" which would construct model dwellings, apparently on a plan it published early in 1847. For its time, the plan was an ambitious effort for the efficient use of urban space, involving the construction of eight buildings on a block of ground 200 feet square. Each building, four stories high, would be divided into three houses with separate entrances; each of the houses would have eight three-room apartments, each of which would be supplied with running water, a water closet, adequate ventilation, and privacy. Philanthropy would yield profits, for the AICP estimated that the apartments could be rented at one dollar per week "and yield a handsome income to the owners of the building."[10]

The Association was unable to get state legislation for a

chartered housing company, but it continued its appeal to philanthropic capitalists by offering to supply them with free plans for model housing. Results were negligible. In 1850, Silas Wood did build what he considered a model tenement on Cherry Street, consisting of two long, narrow buildings capable of housing 126 families. Three years later, R. E. Haight erected some "model dwellings for the industrial classes" on 37th Street near Eighth Avenue. They provided modern conveniences, including gas lighting, in each apartment and Croton Water on each floor. Haight, who set his rents so as not to exceed a 10 percent return on the costs of the property, took the opportunity to blast some of his fellow capitalists for attempting to get "from the helpless the greatest amount of income for the smallest minimum of expenditure of capital."[11] Even the philanthropic Mr. Haight, however, expected to make a decent profit, an expectation which soon subverted the dream of model housing: "After a time," complained the AICP in 1853, "an unlooked for deterioration in the character of the buildings was manifested. Many were erected on so contracted and penurious a scale as to be inferior as it respects the essentials of a dwelling to the old buildings whose places they were intended to supply."[12]

In 1854 the AICP finally acted on its own by organizing the Working Men's Home Association which a year later built a six-story model tenement in the Fourteenth Ward between Mott and Elizabeth streets. The experiment was not successful. The rents, designed to assure a 6 percent profit, ranged from $5.50 to $8.50 a month, which seemed rather high to one missionary who estimated that the "lowest poor" lived in rooms costing less than $4.00 per month. Despite its superior conveniences (gas, water, and a meeting space "designed for lectures, concerts, or moral and educational uses for the inmates") and some initial effort to supervise the behavior of the "inmates," the Association's "Big Flat" itself soon degenerated, to the point that some 30 years later a committee of the AICP condemned the building as unfit for human habitation. By that time, Silas Wood's Gotham Court had become one of the most noisome slum pockets in the city.[13]

[145]

The Use of Urban Space

Model housing was a noble dream. In 1850, the *Independent*, the influential Congregationalist weekly, concluded a four-part series on health reform with the hope that "Christian landlords" might even join together in a great corporation to buy up the Five Points area, New York's most depressing slum, and rebuild it with model houses: "Such a renovation would do more to improve the morals of that section than a dozen churches built in the area."[14] Good intentions, however, did not make for beneficent housing inventions. Rich New Yorkers, reluctant to invest either their money or their time in housing for the poor, left that field to small landlords who treated their tenements as a business rather than as benevolent enterprise. New York's rampant self-interest received little check either from benevolent impulse or from law; Griscom's hopes for an effective sanitary police remained a dream. Thus, during the two decades before the Civil War when the dwelling pattern of the metropolis was firmly set, housing was governed by impersonal market forces which favored the development of commercial and upper-class residential areas.[15] In a booming city where both space and capital were in short supply, the poor had to accept the meager leftovers of both.

Downtown, the poor inherited the abandoned homes of the uptown-moving rich, where they were packed into cellars, one-room apartments, and jerry-built backyard tenements. In a home that had once enclosed the good cheer of Knickerbocker New York, an observer found horror: A room, 12 feet by 20, with five resident families of 20 persons and only two beds—a much smaller room inhabited by a man, woman, and three children who helped pay for their miserable abode by renting it as a rendezvous for women of the street—an attic room, 7 by 5, whose only bed was occupied by a man burning with fever, his exhausted wife "struggling with the dirt on the floor and a little child asleep on a bundle of rags in the corner"—another room, scarcely larger, haunted by "the terrific screams of a drunken man beating his wife, containing no article of furniture whatever." The observer closed his descriptions with a quotation:

THE USE OF URBAN SPACE

—All life dies, death lives and nature breeds Perverse, all
monstrous, all prodigious things, Abominable, unutterable.[16]

Few places were as monstrous as this, but the lot of many
persons, especially newly arrived immigrants, was to be crammed
into tiny rooms, often roughly divided out of larger rooms, the
crowding made worse by the familiar expedient of taking in
boarders to help pay extravagant rents. Landlords, often men
who had leased the houses from their original owners, were
prone to charge all that the traffic would bear. The AICP
might believe that benevolent men would be content with a 6
percent return, but it soon complained that some landlords
were exacting 20 to 50 percent profits by charging high rents
for meager space. It cited a case in the Fourth Ward of one
"miserable rear building" where 10 small apartments, occupied
by 14 families, rented for an average of $1.50 per week each—
at a time when many of the poor were lucky to earn $8 to $10
per month.[17]

Although often condemned as monsters of avarice, the
landlords were governed less by sin than by the essential logic
of their city. Many of the poor stayed close to the downtown
areas, where they had the greatest chances of finding jobs and
housing. These areas, however, were equally the most expensive
and least stable of all residential space, since they were assigned,
by general agreement, to the domain of commerce. Land
values were high. Houses might soon be destroyed by the
march of business, as did happen in the Third Ward during
the early 1850s, or by the widening and lengthening of streets
demanded by expanding commerce. Pack the tenants in; let
the property deteriorate; charge rents high enough to cover
the anticipated decay or destruction of the house—this was a
natural formula, given prevailing attitudes and values, to
govern the use of space in the lower wards.[18]

The results of this system were particularly evident in the
Fourth and Sixth wards on the Lower East Side, where by the
1840s the worst kind of inner city slum appeared—to the
dismay of many New Yorkers, for the Sixth Ward happened

THE USE OF URBAN SPACE

to include City Hall (as well as Five Points). Situated close to the East River waterfront, the two wards became the home of immigrants, especially the Irish. In 1845, half the population of the area was foreign born. Ten years later, the proportion had risen to 70 percent, an increase which suggests that the wards served both as an entryway for newcomers and as a place for the rootless; a stable area would have produced an increase in the number and percentage of native-born children. In 1850, some 45,000 people crowded one-quarter of a square mile and 2626 houses, one person for every 140 square feet and nearly 18 people, on the average, per house.[19]

Worse was to come as street improvement and the expansion of business in the next decade both reduced the number of buildings for residential purposes. Much of the space was preempted by businesses which met some of the less respectable needs of downtown commercial areas, especially liquor stores and brothels as well as the stables of omnibus, railroad, and express lines. In 1866, a sanitary inspector reported that in the Fourth Ward such developments had reduced residential space by one-third since the early 1850s, without reducing the total number of inhabitants. By that time, the area had developed into a full-fledged slum. The population was crowded, at the rate of 28 persons per tenement, into drab and decaying houses, many of which, more than twenty years after the opening of the Croton System, still were not connected to sewers. Much of the food sold at corner groceries and butcher's shops was unfit for human consumption. There too was human decay, a pervasive physical and moral degeneration which the sanitary inspector labeled "TENANT-HOUSE ROT."[20]

The slums of the Fourth and Sixth Wards were only the most conspicuous of the social cancers spreading through much of New York. In the mid-1850s, the *Journal of Commerce* warned that "in nearly every portion of this city are the most unnatural aggregations of humanity—monstrous excrescences on the social fabric—where amid filth, squalor, degradation, and vice, are endangered a diseased off-spring, and of whom lives of infancy or a premature death may be confidently predicted." Again and again, concerned New Yorkers pointed out the

[148]

need for action, but without significant results. In 1853, Griscom complained that "with all the new light furnished by Philanthropy and Science, dwellings are crowded into alleys and cut up into smaller and smaller sections for separate occupancy—cellars and blind courts are more thronged than ever." In the long run, science and philanthropy brought some gains, but their most pervasive products were to be the new-style tenements especially designed for the poor—not, however, the AICP's "Big Flat," with its patina of philanthropy, but four, five, and six story buildings which used available space with a ferocious efficiency not envisioned by early reformers. The model houses proposed as a solution to the slum problem in the 1850s were, like some shabby parody of good intentions, destined to develop into the slum problem of the future.[21]

Certainly, the combination of science and philanthropy was only a weak counterpoise to the essential values which governed the use of urban space. The slums played a key role in the social economy of the expanding metropolis. New York had, in its commercial progress, become the reluctant guardian of hundreds of thousands of people whose misfortunes had begun elsewhere. In the face of this unwanted deluge of poor, the city received little guidance and even less aid from either the state or the nation. Domestic space had to be allocated for the poor, the luckless, and the vicious as well as for everyone else, but to these unwanted people the city would give only its unwanted space. Frequently, slums were called the "cesspools" of great cities, a word which had more meaning than intended, since the slums were, in fact, receiving basins for those persons for whom society had no use. Thus grew the slums—entrances to society for those who could prove their value, exits for those who could not. While Griscom dreamed of a society which would govern urban space for the good of humanity, development proceeded under the rule that space was a valuable commodity, to be allocated for the use of those who could best pay for it.

Decades before the uptown movement had actually reached the northern limits of Manhattan, far-sighted New Yorkers had become sensitive to the limited confines of their island. In

1847, one of them estimated that, of the 168,000 potential building lots on the island, 148,000 would be occupied by 1883 at an average density of 10 persons per lot, without subtracting that land which would be used for streets, trade, and industry; by that date "the whole island will be covered with buildings containing a million and a half souls!" In the commercial city, the logic of this prospect seemed clear: It would be foolish for New York's 14,784 landowners (in 1855) to sacrifice their property to house the poor when either the rich or commerce would likely pay more for it.[22]

The result of this logic was a great disparity in the amount of living space accorded to the rich and to the poor, best evidenced by the sharp contrast between the Fifteenth and Sixth wards. Although the poor had not been entirely excluded from the Fifteenth, it was the wealthiest ward in the city. Here, a population almost exactly as large as that of the Sixth in 1850 lived on three times as much area; 3685 families occupied 2269 houses in the vicinity of Washington Square in 1854, and only one person in sixty died each year, the lowest death rate in the city. In the Sixth Ward, less than two miles to the south, each person had less than one-third the space enjoyed by the fortunate; 5099 families crowded 1270 houses, and there one in every 28 people died. Samuel Halliday, a health and housing reformer, perhaps best summed up the disparities in the division of space when he noted that the two miles of Fifth Avenue between Washington Square and 42nd Street provided space for about 400 families, while a typical tenement block contained 700. Like most reformers, Halliday blamed the landlords for the failure to correct the situation: "The amount invested in tenant-houses in New York, together with the enormous percentage they pay, has created an interest so great that the work of reforming abuses connected with them will be no child's play."[23]

Slum-housing, however, was not so much the special product of wicked landlords as it was the result of the city's general housing shortage: that dwellings were both expensive and cramped was an evident and painful fact for most New Yorkers. In 1853, the *Tribune* said that only one in eight families owned a house of any kind, while no more than one-third were able to rent a dwelling exclusively for themselves. Six years later, Halliday estimated that of the city's 116,000 families, only 14 percent lived in single-family houses, owned or rented, and another 12 percent in two-family dwellings.[24] High rents and crowded housing was a subject of much concern. It was a standing plaint among those interested in municipal finance that the situation drove thousands of taxpaying citizens to Brooklyn and the suburbs. Others saw the boardinghouse life and frequent changes of residence forced on many New Yorkers by high rents as encouragements for a dangerous rootlessness which undermined family feelings and a meaningful sense of community.[25]

Parke Godwin, a radical social critic, proposed that the propertyless themselves solve the housing problem by organizing building associations through which they could accumulate money to buy their own homes. As he figured it, if 300 men each put $2 per week into a common fund, at the end of every year during a ten year period, 30 men would be able to borrow $1000 to buy a house.[26] Godwin's idea betrayed the innocence of the scholar, but it was taken up by others in a more practical form. In early 1848, the American Benefit Building Association was put into operation under the banner of "Every Man His Own Landlord." It was sufficiently successful to inspire the organization of a second association to "enable the members to purchase their own houses with the money they now pay for rent."[27]

There was a rush to organize building associations in the early 1850s after the state provided for their legal incorporation. By 1852, there were nearly seventy in operation under such names as the People's Association, the Industrial Home Association, and the Irving Building and Mutual Loan Association (which headed its advertisement for members with the promise of "Home, Sweet Home!")[28] It soon became evident, however, that for many of the organizers the real sweetness lay not in homes but in money. *Hunt's* warned of the growing number of associations which "profess the most generous designs, but pocket the money of the gullible," a warning it repeated several months later. Many innocent investors, however, had to learn the hard way when, as the result of a shortage of money in the mid-1850s, many of their associations went bankrupt, leaving them not with homes but with debts.[29]

With or without associations, New Yorkers discovered that the high cost of money prevented them from owning their own homes. It seemed logical, then, to concentrate on improving rental accommodations. At the same time that the AICP was attempting to promote model tenements for the poor, a few other housing reformers proposed that superior dwellings be furnished to the working and middle classes in the form of what Godwin described in 1848 as "unitary dwelling-houses, or a whole square of buildings, united so as to be capable of being lighted, warmed, ventilated, etc. by a common apparatus." Four years later, the *Democratic Review* urged that an area west of Broadway be set aside for tall buildings with "a dwelling house in each floor," to be served by elevators ("a car or omnibus, handsomely fitted up for the conveyance of passengers up and down"). The *Tribune* declared in 1853 that high rents for good housing, estimated at $1000 to $1500 a year, required "Houses for the Million on a totally different scale from any now existing."

> Now it is just as demonstrable as any problem in arithmetic that by taking an ordinary block of ground and building thereon a six-story edifice, with stores on the ground floor, refectories and laundries in the basement, dividing the upper stories and suites of rooms of diverse capacities for working men's families and the highest of all into bedrooms for single men (or women) alone, the cost of rent might be sensibly reduced . . . and with Croton water, hot air, gas, etc., in every part and refectories, provision stores, etc. in the basement, the cost of living may be essentially reduced.[30]

The manner of New York home construction, however, was far more complex than the *Tribune's* arithmetic. Although it seemed logical to view the block as the natural unit for an efficient use of space, both builders and landowners thought more in terms of the standard 25 by 100 foot lot. Those few

THE USE OF URBAN SPACE

families who owned large parcels of land were encouraged to
fragment them by the prevailing tendency to treat real estate
as a commodity to be retailed to consumers at the highest
possible price; thus large tracts generally were broken down
into lots either to be sold at auction or to be leased on a long-
term basis. As few wealthy men deigned to invest their time
and money in housing except for themselves, home construction generally was left to small builders who had neither the
means nor the inclination to build large unitary dwellings.
Even when a sizable tract was developed as a whole, as was
done on the north side of Washington Square, the emphasis
was on building row houses, self-contained units separated by
common walls; the lookalike brownstones that emerged in
monotonous rows in the 1850s were constructed on the same
principle.[31]

Probably, the greatest obstacle to the development of an
urban form of housing suited to New York was that home
construction was oriented by the preferences of the affluent
rather than by the plight of the average New Yorker—and the
affluent had not accepted the idea of apartment-house living.
When in 1857, Calvert Vaux urged the American Institute of
Architects to promote that idea, most of his colleagues in the
Institute protested that this European style had no place in a
nation where land was available for single-family houses.[32] As
housing construction was left largely to small contractors who
required substantial and immediate profits, it was not surprising that builders should build, just as architects should design,
to suit the tastes of the well-to-do and their uptown world.[33]
Late in 1850, the *Journal of Commerce* noted that of the 300
buildings then being erected at an estimated cost of $3.5
million, few were worth less than $10,000, while some cost as
much as five to seven times that figure. Such a situation evoked
a comment from *Hunt's*: "If the money invested in 1,000
dwellings last year had been expended upon 2,000, they would
all have been comfortable, and some of them elegant, while
none would have been extravagant, and the rents of all to the
inhabitants would have been less."[34]

Builders did not wholly ignore the housing needs of the

average man. Even in areas intended chiefly for the well-to-do, they sometimes provided accommodations for others in order to maximize their profits. In 1853, the *Tribune* reported that 15 "first-class" brownstones had been built on 14th Street to sell for between $18,000 and $20,000 each, while 13 others were built "in not so costly a style" in the rear. Moreover, a substantial number of new tenements were constructed for the working class. Between 1846 and 1850, more than 1200 buildings were erected in the two chief middle- and working-class wards below 14th Street, the Eleventh and Seventeenth. These wards, which embraced the Drydock area south of the Gashouse District, doubled in population between 1845 and 1855, in part because of the inpouring of German immigrants, and became the most populous in the city.[35] Here, in particular, the emphasis was on the new-style tenement house. Much of the construction was shoddy. In 1850, after the collapse of two unfinished buildings, Philip Hone noted that he had seen, "especially in the eastern section of the city, blocks of new buildings so slightly built that they could not stand alone, and, like drunken men, require the support of each other to keep them from falling." As hasty as it was, however, construction did not keep up with population growth, with the result that housing in the two wards was among the most crowded in New York.[36]

The emphasis on uptown construction indirectly benefited many New Yorkers by opening up a stock of cheap housing in downtown areas deserted by the more fortunate; but this fell far short of meeting housing needs, if only because these areas were particularly subject to two forces which partly cancelled out the increase in dwelling units in the city. One, a source of much shame and outrage, was fire, the most spectacular case being the great $5 million conflagration in 1845 which destroyed nearly 300 buildings in the business area south of Wall Street. Less noticed but more destructive of housing were the many smaller fires such as the two which in the spring of 1842 left more than 400 families homeless. Between 1837 and 1848, there were more than 2500 fires in the city.[37] Even with the introduction of Croton water, the fiery destruction continued at a faster pace than in comparable cities. In 1856, Enoch Hale, Jr., after observing that New York seemed to be "forever burning," estimated that the rate of fires was more than twice that of London; he charged that many of the fires were set in order to collect insurance. Not only were fires more frequent than in London but they were also more destructive, despite the proportionately greater size of the New York fire department.[38]

If citizens were outraged by the fiery destroyer, they took pride in the destruction of residential space caused by the expansion of business. Even in the depressed early 1840s the conversion of downtown into prime commercial property had not stopped. With the return of prosperity after 1845, the redevelopment of the area for business purposes came with a rush. The construction of new stores and hotels in the Broadway area and of new warehouses and other business buildings nearby eliminated much housing, especially during the early 1850s, when the building boom reached its peak. The extension and realignment of downtown streets had the same effect, to the satisfaction of more fortunate New Yorkers who saw in redevelopment a way to eliminate the shabby buildings which disgraced the lower city. Progress meant the elimination of housing for those too poor to add to the golden glow of commercial New York; even the *Tribune*, despite its interest in dwellings for the poor, could declare in 1855 that land in the First Ward on the West Side was "too valuable to be given up to such hovels as now cover whole blocks along Washington and Greenwich-sts."[39]

As a result of these influences, New York, while it grew in splendor, fell far short of meeting the housing needs of the majority of its growing population. In the 1840s, more than 13,500 buildings (many of them commercial) were constructed in the city; even without considering the unknown number of dwellings destroyed during the period, this was a poor showing for a city whose population had increased by 200,000 people during the decade.[40] Thus it was that New York fixed its character as a city of crowded houses and high rents. The shortage of housing, in turn, intensified other traits, some of which had a positive side, especially the New Yorker's prolific use of public space. Crowded, vibrant street life was a source of romance for those accustomed to the staidness of more private styles of life, and a source of nostalgia for those who had left the crowded Old World behind. For all, it was an expression of urban community.

For those most concerned with the social life of the metropolis, however, crowding was not romance but a sickness, a source of disease, dirt, vice, crime, family breakdown, and high taxes. Mike Walsh, a self-proclaimed spokesmen for the common people, asserted that crowding "is the cause of more vice and misery, more suffering in every way, sickness, debauchery, seduction, assaults, and even murder, than all other causes put together." New York had not created its problems—they could be traced to sources beyond its control (to the troubles of Ireland and Germany and to tendencies inherent in American society); but the city's management—or mismanagement—of space had intensified its difficulties. In 1856, Fernando Wood, the most broadminded if hardly the most honest of New York mayors, warned that "we have shown a want of prudent management of the great estate we have inherited," and went on to declare that the failure to provide cheap and healthy housing had driven "a large part of our best population" to the suburbs.[41]

For some, perhaps most, observers it was easy to assume that the results were the inevitable and essential outgrowths of urban development, something to be ignored, avoided or escaped whenever convenient. The failure to develop the kind of housing suited to an urban environment and in other ways to humanize a crowded situation served to strengthen the Jeffersonian suspicion of cities and to encourage the well-to-do to flee from the results of their mismanagement. In 1849 the *Journal of Commerce* commented on the significance of the annual summertime exodus of New Yorkers to rural areas: "Man made the cities. It had been a serious question whether the congestion of masses in the crowded houses of their Babels is, or is not, a violation of the laws of our nature. Certainly, its effects are often terrible. The pestilence finds its victims ready

... and the fire sweeps off millions of property, the very air of heaven is tainted and the waters of the ocean are foul and muddy, as they pass our piers. Every year witnesses the growth of vice, and the increasing corruptness of the mass, and the results would appear to be inevitable."[42] God made the countryside; corrupted man made the corrupted city—the cliché was a convenient way to dismiss New York as the wicked, hopeless city—a great place to make money but otherwise beyond redemption.

Yet the growth of the city also encouraged New Yorkers to Griscom's belief that what thoughtless man had done enlightened man might undo. Such an outlook was nurtured by the recognition that the physical and commercial growth which had enabled New York to surpass its urban rivals had made the city no mere place but the American metropolis which was to be compared less with a Boston or Philadelphia than with the great European metropolises. More and more New Yorkers were brought into contact with urbanizing Europe by the expansion of trade, travel, and trans-Atlantic culture. What they found was not simply the festering ulcers about which Americans had warned themselves since the days of Thomas Jefferson, but enlightened urban societies committed to improving the human condition. Although reformers like Griscom may not have traveled abroad, they were aware from their reading that the American metropolis lagged behind Paris, London, and even such lesser cities as Edinburgh and Manchester in its provision for the well-being of its citizens. Moreover, the increasing travel of well-to-do New Yorkers convinced some of them that the European metropolis was far ahead of their city in urban design, in the arrangement of its public space and buildings.

The rebuilding of the city after 1840 stimulated both an interest in urban design and the uneasy sense that New York was falling short of European standards and American hopes. After applaunding the spread of the "spirit of beauty" in uptown areas, the *Tribune* in 1848 went on to express concern over "the absence of anything like concert of action and design among owners of property." It was "every way desirable that the millionaire and the architect should go hand in hand—or instead of a magnificent city of palaces, domes and temples, we shall, at least, have nothing but unmeaning heaps of costly rubbish on the one hand, and comfortless and desolate dwellings on the other."[43]

Unfortunately, there were no great merchant princes and no Medicis with breadth of mind to match their powers; rather, there was the Astor family, content to reap profits from fragmented properties. Despite the work of Samuel Ruggles in Union and Gramercy Squares, the city failed to develop a commitment to urban design sufficient to guide its dynamic growth, to soften the rule of change and exchange, the new and the profitable. The result was a "modern city of ruins," said the New York *Mirror*, where "no sooner is a fine building put up than it is torn down to put up a better . . . the pear-tree is pulled up to make room for the lamp-post. . . . Lovely hills are dug down, and green villas are undermined, merely that the mounds of unseemly buildings may be put up in their places." In the process, the builders of the city created many individually fine structures, which were to help make New York a place of varied architectural delights, but, overall, they produced a city with little meaningful form, an exciting city which, as Henry Tappan complained, evoked far more awe than love.[44]

"Progress is a terrible thing." William James was not the first New Yorker to recognize the dark side of rapid and haphazard growth. In 1856, the editor of *Harper's Monthly* warned that the knock-em-down, build-em-up genius of New York had little left of the past around which citizens might associate their lives: "New York is notoriously the largest and least loved of any of our great cities. Why should it be loved as a city? It is never the same city for a dozen years together. A man born in New York forty years ago finds nothing, absolutely nothing, of the New York he knew." Yet progress was also yielding more positive results, strengthening the hope that New Yorkers could be rallied away from their money-making, privatistic inclinations to, in the words of Tappan, "love your city, love your homes, and become wise benefactors of your city and your homes." In the 1850s, the city's persistent and often worsening troubles were balanced by a growing interest in social, political, and physical improvement. Especially noteworthy was one great triumph of urban design with which nearly all New Yorkers could identify, the establishment of Central Park. In this achievement could be found some of the major strengths—and also some of the weaknesses—of the new metropolis.[45]

The park was intended to compensate for half a century of failure to provide adequate public space for the city's population. Part of the trouble developed out of the Plan of 1811, which had outlined New York's future spatial growth. That plan, unalterable except by state action, provided an inordinate amount of space for streets, thus ordaining Manhattan to be, more than other American cities, fragmented and paved over. Although the planners were ready to concede space for commerce, they yielded little of it for people. Having satisfied themselves that the population of the city would be 400,000, part of which would be concentrated at Harlem, they slighted their legislative mandate (the plan was drafted by a temporary commission appointed by the state) "to secure a free and abundant circulation of air." Defensively, they explained "that so few vacant spaces have been left, and these so small," because the Island was embraced by two arms of the sea, the Hudson and East Rivers, which would assure an adequate supply of air.

The planners did set aside some 450 acres mostly for park squares and a large parade ground, but they were practical men reluctant to waste space on public purposes in a city where "the price of land is so uncommonly great." Thus, despite some provision for public well-being, the plan mirrored the guiding spirit of the city, one which emphasized convenience for commerce and for property owners. Later, critics would condemn it as a major cause of New York's problems. Isaac Kendall complained that, under it, development preceded on a simplistic "parallel rule system" which destroyed the island's topographical advantages. Others were to see its simple geometry, its provision for a nearly unbroken gridiron of streets, as the cause for the crowding and monotony that afflicted extended areas of the new city.[46]

The plan was defective, but less so than its detractors would claim. It was no act of original sin, but an effort to meet human needs in the context of an intensely commercial and practical city. Its simple geometry was made to bear the blame for the effects produced by the more fundamental influences which formed the guiding genius of the city. Much of the trouble stemmed from the fact that while New York had a plan it had no effective planning authority. In theory, this role might have been played by the city government, which had a wide range of powers to govern the use of urban space. As the city's largest landowner, possessor of one-seventh of the island in the early 1840s, government could have excercised much influence over land use. As the protector of public well-being, it might, as some sanitary reformers demanded, claim the power to regulate the industrial and domestic use of space. "Might" and "could," however, had little reality for a government which had become increasingly harassed by the day-by-day management of an expanding city. In 1807, when it asked the state to create a commission to draft a plan, the city council had accurately stated the nature of the problem: "The diversity of sentiments, and opinions which has hitherto existed, and will probably always exist, among the members of the Common Council, the incessant remonstrances of proprietors against plans, however, well devised or beneficial, wherein their interests do not concur, with the impossibility of completing those plans thus approved, but by a tedious and expensive course of law, are obstacles of a serious and perplexing nature."[47] The full extent of these perplexing obstacles was yet to be discovered, for the growth of the city multiplied and strengthened contending interests as rapidly as it created or deepened its problems.

The expansion of commerce, for instance, was matched by the deterioration of city-owned piers and wharves to the point where they became as much a civic shame as the public markets. Under pressure to improve the waterfront, the Common Council also had to heed the demands of taxpayers and shippers, one wanting economy in expenditures for wharves as for other matters, the other wanting low wharfage rates in order to preserve their competitive advantage over Boston shippers, who paid more for their superior facilities. The result was that the city resorted to patchwork expedients which neither stilled the complaints nor stemmed the deterioration.[48] Similarly, residents protested against such nuisances as slaughter-houses and stables in their neighborhoods, but the Council had to weigh these protests against the interests and political power of property. In the face of powerful, hard-edged, self-interested pressures from taxpayers, property-owners, merchants, retailers, butchers, omnibus companies, landlords, and other interests, government tended to ignore the softer, more amorphous public interest unless it coincided with the needs of private property.[49]

By the 1840s, it had become apparent that this process involved the sacrifice of space for people. The New York *Mirror*, in 1840, complained that the city fathers "have destroyed nearly all the green shady nooks which the commissioners who laid out the city designed as public squares." In fact, the city had discontinued many of the open spaces provided in the 1811 Plan; by 1838, the original 450 acres had been reduced to 120.[50] In the mid-1840s, the city threw away a golden opportunity to provide space when it began to sell off its public lands. Harassed by financial concerns, government emphasized the need to get the lands into private hands and on the tax rolls rather than to use them for public purposes. Among other property, it disposed of some 80 blocks of ground, most of it north of 48th Street, part of which it was to buy back for Central Park a decade later.[51]

The city was not wholly inactive. It continued the development of some of the squares provided by the original plan, especially Union Square, and also, in 1846, laid out a public park on the grounds surrounding the Distributing Reservoir between 40th and 42nd streets. By 1849, New York could boast of having 19 public parks of 170 acres. Boasts, however, were not realities, for of the total acreage more than half was in four large proposed parks, none of which had been developed for public use.⁵² Not much more satisfying was the one significant enlargement of public space in the lower city, the completion of the long-discussed, long-delayed proposal to double the size of Battery Park at the toe of the Island by filling in the waterfront around Castle Garden. Revived in the late 1840s as a way of using the dirt left from the laying of sewers in the lower city, the project encouraged the *Tribune* to dream of a New York with the most magnificent sea promenade in the world, "a scene of gaity and splendor which would rival the far-famed Cassine of Florence, the Parks of London, or the Prater of Vienna."⁵³

The city, however, was slow to act, partly because it encountered opposition from shippers and merchants, who feared that enlargement would interfere with their business. In 1849, the *Journal of Commerce* made a counter-proposal that the Battery, in whole or part, be converted into a site for wharves and railroad tracks: "We can't afford to make a deer-park where land is worth $150,000 an acre, and where there is so little to be had at any price. If waste land is wanted for solitary meditation, or for the concealment of villainy, it would be better to select a site where land is cheaper." Eventually, in the mid-1850s, the project was completed, only to have part of it converted into the site of New York's first Emigrant Depot at Castle Garden. A decade later, the *Tribune's* magnificent sea-promenade had become little better than an open slum: "The grass has disappeared, the iron fence is broken, the wall promenade near the sea goes to decay, freshly arrived foreigners, ragged, tattered, and drunken men and women sit under the old trees, and the Battery is now as unsafe a place at night as can be found in the city."⁵⁴

The decay of the Battery was paralled by the deterioration of the few other open spaces in the lower city, including City Hall Park, once the pride of New Yorkers. The subject of complaint in the 1840s because of its unkempt appearance, the Park was diminished in size in the early 1850s by street widening and by such improvements as a comfort station. A committee of the Board of Aldermen even proposed that the Park be used as the site for a new Post Office, because it was no longer needed as "a pleasure ground" by the uptown-moving rich. Such reasoning was common. As the lower city was assigned to commerce, little attention was given to the space needs of the downtown masses.[55] Rather, concern focused on the failure of the city even to provide adequate space for the people of the rapidly expanding residential areas north of Houston Street. Washington, Union and, in the 1850s Madison Squares were showpieces of the city, suited to the needs of the rich, but for the great majority, especially in the increasingly crowded East Side, there were few open spaces other than the streets. New York, in an age that emphasized the physical and psychological importance of nature, was discovering that it was walling the great mass of its people off from natural influences by grimy curtains of brick and brownstone.[56]

Some New Yorkers recognized the need for a remedy to this situation. As early as 1842, the New York *Mirror* urged the need for parks as "the lungs of the city" to purify and regenerate the atmosphere; it proposed the creation of a park on each river front. Others, observing that builders had neglected to plant trees in developing areas, warned of the need for foliage to purify the air and provide shade. In 1848, the *Democratic Review* proposed that the city systematically plant shrubbery in connection with street development so as to turn New York into "a city of gardens." Two years later, Mayor Woodhull asked the Common Council to provide for more public squares both to beautify the city and to act as *"great breathing* places of the toiling masses."[57]

A few New Yorkers also emphasized the need for recreation space for the laboring classes and their children. In 1855, Charles Loring Brace, a reformer much concerned over the city's social problems, warned that New York was contributing to the growth of its "dangerous classes" by failing to provide the recreation required for the full human development of an urban population: "This question of amusements has become one of vast importance to our cities." Decision-makers, complained Brace, continued to think in terms of rural society and rural pleasures, without regard for the fact that for the city dweller the dinginess of home and the drudgery of life brought

[163]

a special need for pleasurable surroundings: "They breathe bad air; they have no amusement; they have no books; they are mere machines of society, wound up to work fifteen hours a day." No wonder that they picked up the chance for pleasure where they could, in saloons and beer gardens, at boxing matches and riotous play. To wean the masses away from their coarse amusements, Brace proposed the creation of parks for the working classes with fountains, flowers, statuary, and also chapels: "Here it would be natural and healthful for the laborer to worship; out of the sunny, dusty, nauseating streets, amid sweet smells and pleasant sounds."[58]

Ideally, these fragments of thought might have been formed into a plan to weave natural and recreational space into the fabric of the expanding city, an idea advanced in 1857 by the City Inspector who proposed that, when built-over areas were reconstructed, attention be paid to the need for "making squares and free spaces as useful as possible, for exercise and recreation." Ideally, parks, fountains, and play space might have been fused with streets and buildings into a humane cityscape which would permeate the everyday experience of all. The ideal city, said the *Express* in 1849, was for its citizens "a perpetual study of delight, like the unfolding of a new book, each day adding page upon page, chapter upon chapter, in the shape of new houses, hotels, resorts of art, fountains, parks, and avenues."[59] In some ways, the metropolis measured up to these standards, but the book of New York as it unfolded was less a saga of human satisfaction than a collection of tales from the pen of Edgar Allan Poe. Reformers might preach the need for recreational and natural space designed for the masses just as they might urge the importance of model tenements, but there was little chance that the city would set aside either space or money for the mass alone. Instead, when the demand for natural space was brought to a focus, it was in a form which suited not so much the needy majority as the affluent minority. The result was Central Park, a magnificent exception to a badly flawed city.

The park was a natural outgrowth of the increasing sophistication of wealthy New Yorkers. Many had been conditioned to a strong interest in natural landscape by the art and literature of the times, especially by the painting of Thomas Cole and the poetry of William Cullen Bryant. It was natural that those who took an interest in the city should give special attention to landscape architecture, especially since it harmonized with the prevailing emphasis on the healthful importance of fresh air. Moreover, an increasing number of sophisticates traveled in Europe, where they soon recognized the superiority of the great public parks there over those at home. One boastful New Yorker purportedly received a shock when he first saw one of London's parks: "Good heavens, what a scene! And I took some Londoners to the steps of City Hall last summer to show them the park of New York." The Americans were impressed by the expansive beauty of these urban landscapes and by the good order and decorum of those who used them—a remarkable contrast to the shabby chaos of the American metropolis. For them, New York would never become one of the world's metropolises until it could boast of a great park.[60]

It was Bryant, popular poet and influential editor of the *Evening Post*, who began the campaign for a new park when in the summer of 1844 he urged the city to acquire Jones' Wood, a wooded area between Third Avenue and the East River and 68th and 77th streets.[61] The *Evening Post* soon received support from its great political rival, the *Tribune*, which predicted what would happen if New York threw away the opportunity to acquire Jones' Wood: "Does not the experience of the past show that in a few short years, the lovely waste may be covered with close, dusty, dingy streets and endless piles of bricks and mortar?" The proposed 160 acres would have doubled the park space of the city, a startling reversal of the prevailing trend. As the *Post* observed, however, New York, though too busy for humble public squares and clean streets, was attracted to projects of magnificence like the Croton Aqueduct. In 1851, Mayor Ambrose C. Kingsland submitted the idea to the Common Council. After predicting that the entire area south of the proposed park would be given over to commerce, Kingsland made a special appeal to the paternalism of the rich with the argument that the money expended for the park "would be

[165]

returned to us fourfold, in the health, happiness and comfort of those whose interests are especially entrusted to our keeping—the poorer classes." Although paternalism was hardly strong in New York, the city did move to acquire Jones' Woods—only soon to reverse itself and to consign the Woods over to commerce and bricks and mortar in favor of an even more magnificent project at the center of the island.[62]

Central Park was especially the inspiration of Andrew Jackson Downing, a suburban landscape architect and editor of the influential *Horticulturist*, who emphasized the social as well as the aesthetic and sanitary importance of parks. In 1848, he warned Americans that they lagged far behind aristocratic Europe, especially Germany, in providing one essential feature of a democracy, a common meeting place where all classes could meet on an equal plane: "With large professions of equality, I find my countrymen more and more inclined to raise up barriers of class, wealth, and fashion, which are almost as strong in our social usages, as the law of caste is in England," an observation which was particularly applicable to New York. To counter these tendencies, he proposed public parks, gardens, art galleries, and libraries where the poor and the rich, the ignorant and the educated, could meet together for enlightenment and enjoyment.[63]

When Kingsland made his proposal for Jones' Wood, Downing supported him by denouncing the "timid tax-payers" who opposed the project, but then went on to suggest that the Mayor himself was too timid, for the Woods was "only a child's playground" by European standards. Instead, Downing suggested a great "People's Park" of no less than 500 acres in the middle of the island. Here would be space enough to combine landscape with public pleasure grounds, a place for solitary communion with nature or for communal relations with others free from the harsh noise and hard brick of the city. This new Central Park would be used for culture as well as nature, a place for works of art, for monuments, for music, for zoological gardens, and for the meetings of horticultural and industrial societies. It might also contain "winter gardens of glass, like the great Crystal Palace, where the whole people could luxuriate in groves of the palm and spice trees of the tropics, at the same moment that sleighing parties glided swiftly and noiselessly over the snow-covered surface."

To those doubters who remained reluctant to spend money for a people's park, Downing repeated his warning that, while the political tendencies in New York as elsewhere in America were "ultrademocratic," the most intelligible social tendencies were toward class exclusiveness. The Park would be a way of raising the masses to the level of responsible citizens while reversing the class tendencies: "It is republican in its very idea and tendency. It takes up popular education where the common school and ballot-box leave it, and raises up the man of the working men to the same level-of enjoyment with the man of leisure and accomplishment. The higher social and artistic element of every man's nature lie dormant within him, and every laborer is a possible gentlemen . . . , through the refining influence of intellectual and moral culture."[64]

Thus, through the civilized use of open space, New York might bridge the disturbing and deepening social gap between Fifth Avenue and the slums of the Sixth Ward. The development of Downing's genius abruptly ceased in 1852 when he died in the burning wreckage of the steamboat *Henry Clay*. Others, however, took up the Central Park idea, though in the interests less of the masses than of the upper classes. By the mid-1850s, the growth of the lower city had diminished its value for fashionable activity. Both the Battery and City Hall Park were degenerating as fashionable promenades, as was lower Broadway, with its sidewalks increasingly crowded by the foreign poor and its pavement congested with carts and omnibuses. The sporting set, too, had cause to rue the progress of the city, for the appearance of horse-cars had disrupted the trotting course on Third Avenue, where horsemen were accustomed to show off their steeds and themselves. The Central Park would be large enough for a fashionable promenade, a drive for carriages and a new trotting course—and large enough, also, to satisfy the desire of New Yorkers to have something similar to the great European parks.[65]

Moreover, the practical-minded readily recognized that the

new park would protect and extend the wealthy residential zone which was being pushed northward along Fifth Avenue. One noticeable feature of the proposed site was its rocky, swampy, uneven topography, which made it unsuited for building. A committee of aldermen estimated that street-grading alone would cost twice the value of the land, without even including the additional expense of laying the sewers required for uptown development. Since the area had not been considered suitable for building, it had been given over to the poor, who squatted there by the thousands. For those who anticipated the northward movement of fashion, the squatters were an eyesore and a sanitary menace who contaminated the air and depressed the land values of surrounding areas with their bone-boiling and rag-picking, and their pigs, cows, and assorted other animals which they raised on the garbage of the city. The park would be a convenient way of eliminating this nuisance. For those city fathers who were concerned with the expense of such a great project, there was comfort in the thought that the consequent rise in land values in the surrounding areas would increase tax revenues and so help pay for it.[66]

Thus, in 1853, New Yorkers discovered that in their enthusiasm they had decided on two large parks, this in a city where a man, said Charles Astor Bristed, might "buy two hundred dollar handkerchiefs for his wife, or pay a fancy price for a fast trotter, but to lose the interest on a town lot by making a garden of it, is an extravagance not to be thought of." In such a city, two parks were too much. A committee of aldermen recommended that the Jones' Wood project be dropped, in part on the grounds that its location on a river invited crimes of violence by making it easy for criminals to hide the bodies of their victims in a watery grave. The decision to eliminate Jones' Wood, however, appears to have been made in the interests not of potential victims but of landowners and merchants who wanted the area for commercial and residential development, the New York Chamber of Commerce having opposed the project on the ground that all of the city's waterfront should be reserved for commercial purposes.[67]

Even one large park appeared to be too much for some New Yorkers. One warned that it would seriously diminish space for residential purposes and so would "increase the intolerable grievances of high rents and crowded tenements," while another estimated that the Park would deprive the city of 13,521 building lots which might accommodate 190,000 people.[68] When the expense of acquiring the site mounted rapidly with the inflation of land values in the area, the Common Council in 1854 considered scaling down the Park by shifting its southern boundary from 60th Street to 72nd Street and taking 400 feet from both its eastern and western borders. Proponents of the change argued that the existing plan would slow the growth of the city by enhancing lots in the surrounding areas "to a price beyond what they would otherwise bear, and beyond the means of the humble classes; and thus impoverish or depress, or drive them from the island for habitations." Why should the interests of the mass be sacrificed, simply that the rich might have "an elegant and inviting drive" and pleasure ground? Why, especially since the majority of New Yorkers neither needed it or desired it? "Squares, such as we now have, are in every respect more useful, more convenient and ornamental, and much preferred by all classes."[69]

The Council in 1855 passed a resolution along the lines suggested the previous year, but the Aldermen encountered a storm of protest from the defenders of the Park who condemned them as corrupt and benighted Yahoos. There was much applause when Mayor Fernando Wood, an early advocate of a Central Park, vetoed the measure as short-sighted and "entirely unworthy of even the present position of this metropolis, to say nothing of a destiny now opening brilliantly before us."[70] New York had committed itself to a project worthy of its metropolitan dignity. Central Park was on its way to acquiring the sacrosanct character, so exceptional in a city of practical men, which was to protect it from much future tampering with either its scale or its design.

Under the Central Park Commission, set up by the state in 1857 and largely insulated from the meddling of the Council, it became a magnificent example of the power of a city to

perfect its space. No crude chunk of nature preserved from
the encroachments of the city, Central Park was a triumph of
urban design, a work of art and engineering created by one of
the truly great geniuses of the nineteenth century, Frederick
Law Olmsted. From that early triumph, too, came a major step
toward modern city planning, for Olmsted and his partner,
Calvert Vaux (previously Downing's partner), designed not
only parks but street systems as well—as close as upper
Manhattan and Brooklyn, as far away as Chicago and Berkeley.[71] In the 1860s, the Central Park Commission was to design
the streets and parks for the northern tip of Manhattan, which
had not been covered in the 1811 Plan, leading Isaac Kendall
to remark wistfully in 1865 that if most of the island had not
been laid out until the advent of the Commission, "the whole
residence portion of the island might have been a park—a
perfect pleasure-garden of delight."[72]

Central Park was much more than a pleasure garden of
delight, for it was designed to counter the inhumane influences
of a great city. It turned a pestilential area into a healthful spot
which acted as the lungs of the city. It was a landscape designed,
as Olmsted put it, to "secure an antithesis of objects of vision
to those of the streets and houses which should act remedially
by impressions on the mind and suggestions to the imagination," a tranquilizer, stimulus to noble intentions, discourager
of bad passions, a place where urban man could meet not in
competition or suspicion but in peace and in harmonious
community. It was recreational space for walking, rowing,
skating, and ball-playing, a place for exercise which would
reverse the physical degeneration which seemed to come with
crowded urban living. It was a point of civic pride, perhaps the
only point in the city where New Yorkers could agree to be
proud. It was the triumph especially of a talented designer
and humanist who later described his creation as "a single work
of art . . . framed upon a single, noble motive," that motive
being to assure the future millions of New York not simply
refuge from urban life but "conditions remedial of the influences of urban conditions."[73]

The Park, moreover, was a triumph of design capable also

of pleasing the most practical of men. Some of its supporters had early recognized that it would encourage the right development of the upper half of the island. It would attract and hold the wealthy to the city, raise uptown land values, and increase taxable wealth, which in the end would more than repay the city for its expenditures. By 1860, in fact, assessed values around and above the park had increased by two-thirds over the value four years earlier, to the satisfaction of both the city and those who owned the land. As time would prove, the Park served to stabilize the surrounding areas and to slow decisively the seemingly endless changes which accompanied city growth, preserving, as was hoped, much of the central spine of the island as a residential zone for the well-educated, well-heeled upper classes so necessary to the sophisticated character of the metropolis.[74]

If it was a triumph for metropolitan design, however, the Park fell at least one important step short of Downing's dream of a great "People's Park," for its major strengths involved some sacrifice of the interests of the mass to the interests of the upper classes. High land values in the surrounding areas assured that the well-to-do would most consistently and directly reap the benefits. More, the very character of the Park seemed to require the exclusion of certain institutions suited to the people. When in 1857 *Harper's Weekly* reported the rumor that beer-sellers and barkeepers were buying up lots outside the park, it warned that "if the streets adjacent to the Park are peopled with traders of this class, the Park itself will be nothing more than a great beer garden where the drunken will resort to sleep off their liquor." *Harper's* solution was to urge the rich to buy up the surrounding land, at least on Fifth Avenue, and to develop it as a fashionable residential zone.[75]

Olmsted, too, was concerned that the rowdy, ill-disciplined mass might spoil his design: "A large part of the people of New York are ignorant of a park, properly so-called. They need to be trained to the proper use of it." Recognizing that in a democracy discipline could not be enforced by authoritarian means, he hoped to make the design itself a force for good order by excluding anything which might attract or encourage disorderliness, anything which, as he put it, might convert the Park into "a great, perpetual metropolitan Fair Ground . . . a desultory collection of miscellaneous entertainments."[76] Thus, despite the urbanized character of its landscape, the Park was deliberately denied some of those elements of urban character which the mass of city dwellers found most familiar. Neither this nor the difficulties of reaching the Park completely excluded the masses, but both served to make it less useful to the majority than it was to the fortunate few.

In itself, this class bias would not have been important, if the city had heeded Olmsted's plea in 1853 that it provide, "at points so frequent and convenient that they would exert an elevating influence upon all the people, public parks and gardens, galleries of art, music, athletic sports and other means of cultivating taste and lessening the excessive materialism of purpose in which we are, as a people so cursedly absorbed."[77] Having made its metropolitan gesture, however, mid-century New York did little more to provide public places other than streets for the crowded poor of the lower city. Instead, money and attention was turned to the development of parks uptown, with a result best described by Junius Browne in 1869 when he noted that the Battery had been converted into an emigrant depot and St. John's Square (a private square once owned by Trinity Church) into the site for a railroad depot, while Tompkins Square had been allowed to run to waste. Browne concluded that "City Hall, Washington, Union, and Madison are really the only public grounds, and they have been so much neglected that they have lost most of their attractions. The downtown enclosures have of late years, especially since the opening of the Central, been given up to disreputable loungers, children, and nurses."[78]

Rather than weaving humane and humanizing space into its changing fabric, New York chose to set one great park against its city self, a magnificent exception to its rampant commercialism, disorderliness and congestion, but an exception nonetheless. Olmsted's noble design would ameliorate some of the problems of a troubled city. It could not, however, eliminate the effects of the prevailing mismanagement of space. As a refuge for the wealthy and the influential from those effects, it complemented the principle that Manhattan Island be developed chiefly in the interests of commerce rather than as an urban society of civilized men. Great triumph of metropolitan design though it was, Central Park was the product of a flawed metropolis and metropolitan way of life, of a society which served to encourage many of its citizens to dream of escape to better places beyond the limits of the city.[79]

The Growing City II

FIGURE 12. (right, above) This wood engraving (1852) by J. W. Orr features Genin's Bridge, the ingenious use of Broadway's increasing traffic problem to advertise the business of a hat seller. Note the death-defying feats of the few pedestrians foolhardy enough to risk crossing the street. The street's notorious traffic jams demanded extensive improvements in mass transit, leading in the early 1850s to the establishment of street railways and to a new era of corruption in city government. The glut of vehicles and of commercial activity depicted here also seemed to require a counter-influence in the form of Central Park.

FIGURE 13. (right, below) John Bachman's rather fanciful drawing of Central Park in 1875 does catch some of the essential spirit of Frederick Law Olmsted's great design. This view looks toward the southeastern corner of the park at 59th Street and Fifth Avenue. The flowing lines of the roads, paths and lakes in the park contrast with the cluttered geometry of the city which was growing up around it, a manifestation of Olmsted's hope that his creation would serve as a counter and remedial influence to the psychological effects of frenetic New York life. Although for those in the park the urban background is hidden by trees and a rolling topography, the fact that this is an urbanized "Nature" is evidenced by the presence both of a reservoir of the Croton water system (left corner) and of park buildings intended for mass use by city dwellers.

Both views courtesy of the Prints Division, New York Public Library, Eno and Stokes collections.

Chapter 8

ESCAPE TO SUBURBIA

CENTRAL PARK WAS HUMANIZED NATURE set against the unnatural influences of the congested city. It was the product of an age which, though ready to celebrate urban power and prosperity, also generally viewed the crowded, frenetic life of big cities as a malignancy which threatened the moral, mental, and physical health of man. New York's failure to humanize its increasingly congested space, visible most notably in its spreading slums, intensified the feeling that the city was unnatural and poisonous. It was a hell, said the radical reformer Lewis Masquerier, where "huge buildings covering whole blocks pack the thousands of humans in them, stifled with gasses and putrid air, breeding plague and raising puny half-formed children to fill up the cemeteries. . . . The water and gas are costly and bad. Street cleaning and sewerage are destroying the fertility of the soil. Thus not only physical but moral value is destroyed."[1] Others believed that the crowded anonymity,

[176]

the dependence, the hectic pace and frantic materialism of big commercial cities threatened to pervert the character even of their more fortunate inhabitants. "We live in a state of unnatural excitement," wrote a New York physician; "unnatural because it is partial, irregular and excessive. Our muscles waste for *want* of action; our nervous system is worn out by excess of action. . . . Excessive anxiety by disordering the animal economy, weakens the mental powers." In such ways were many Americans inclined to view big cities as "sores upon the body politic" at least vaguely menacing to the promise of American life, and New York ("this corrupted Gotham," said one critic) was the most dangerous menace of all.[2]

It was common belief that the metropolis was at least vaguely un-American, that the real America was somewhere else in the midst of a glorified Nature and a sentimentalized rural life. Even Walt Whitman, perhaps the most urban of American poets, concluded his *Specimen Days* with the warning that "Democracy most of all affiliates with the open air, is sunny and hardy and sane only with Nature. . . . American democracy . . . must either be fibered, vitalized, by regular contact with out-door light and air and growth, farm-scenes, animals, fields, trees, birds, sun-warmth and free skies, or it will certainly dwindle and pale."[3] Sublime landscapes, smiling skies, prosperous farms, healthy farmers, virtuous country villages—this happy picture, set in contrast to the physical and moral diseases of the congested city, embellished the frequent warnings of both city and rural leaders that Americans stay away from New York. "Why leave the land of your fathers, and home of your mothers," asked Dr. Joel H. Ross of his fellow upstaters, "to seek your fortune in the city? Is it that you may be more *happy*? Ponder this question well. A city life is *artificial*. True, there are some things which are real; such as trials, losses, frowns, failures, pestilence, poverty, and hypocrisy." Stay away, remain on the farm or in the village, go West in search of opportunity— the message repeated almost endlessly by Horace Greeley's influential *Tribune* was a well-worn accompaniment to the platitude that New York was a dangerous, wicked, un-American place.[4]

Whatever their sentimental devotion to Nature and to agriculture, however, Americans continued to flock to, and stay in, the city. Certainly, the census figures indicate that after 1840 the population of New York grew much faster than the population of its state, region, and nation. In 1840, New Yorkers constituted 4.6 percent of the population of the Northeast and 1.8 percent of that of the United States; in 1860 the percentages were 7.7 and 2.45. Most of the city's increase came from foreign immigration, but the migration of native-born Americans contributed a substantial share; in 1850, approximately one-quarter of the native-born population, some 70,000 people, was born outside the city.[5] Why did Americans continue to come, despite the mounting evidence of the dangers of city life? The answer for some observers was simply defect of character in the migrants: an enfatuation with city fashions and excitements, a lazy desire to escape hard work for easy living, and a simpleminded exaggeration of one's talent for success in the big city. The wicked city snared the weak and the thoughtless: "Cities are, to dwellers in the country, very like what white lights at night are to flies—brilliant and attractive, but certain ruin."[6]

Even critics of urban life, however, had to concede that the city did have some advantages over the countryside. Dr. Ross, though he emphasized city dangers in his book, *What I Saw in New York*, was too evidently impressed by the power, successes, and achievements of the metropolis to convincingly support his cause. Others more openly admitted that there were serious defects in the pretty pictures of country life. When in 1855 an economic crisis led some New York newspapers to urge the unemployed to find new lives for themselves in rural areas, *Harper's Monthly* noted that prospects were not good, since it was evident that farming was hard and dull work: "A little investigation reveals that these pastoral pleas are written by men who have chosen the city, and have not the slightest intention of taking their own advice." Even urban newspaper editor Horace Greeley, who so often gave that advice, agreed that there were social and economic limitations to rural life: "Until some marked change shall have been wrought in the character and condition of rural industry, so as to render it less repulsive than it now is, our cities must continue overcrowded and full of misery."[7] Greeley himself had shaken off the dust of his native rural New England to seek and eventually to find his fortune in the metropolis.

Defective, destructive city; defective, limited countryside— this tandem of weakness seemed to suggest that the troubles of the city were attributable less to urban life itself than to deficiencies in rural society which would have to be remedied if the spread of urban ruin was to be reversed. While cities suffered from the congestion of people, Greeley believed, rural areas were deadened by the opposite condition, an excessively sparse and scattered population which denied them the concentrated power and concerted effort which had made the cities centers of wealth and culture; the result was ignorance, dullness, and inefficiency—qualities which were becoming increasingly "repulsive" with the spread of urban standards. The solution was to raise the density of the rural population (to about one person per acre) so that it might adapt modern technology and organization to its needs.[8] Greeley dabbled in too many reforms to develop a coherent program of rural regeneration, but he did draw on a deepening well of social feeling which was long to have an influence on many attempted reformers of American life, one of the most significant being his contemporary, George Henry Evans.

Evans, a printer by trade, had long dedicated himself to the interests of urban working men. His *Workingman's Advocate* had been a center of labor-minded radicalism in New York until in the late 1830s poor health had forced his retirement to a farm in New Jersey. From there, he had pondered and analyzed the problems of the city and had concluded that they stemmed from one central cause, a surplus of labor not only in unskilled jobs but in the skilled trades. This surplus drove down wages to the advantages of the employing classes, producing a growing inequality of wealth, power, and opportunity which was making the conditions of workers progressively worse in the city. Low wages meant that working men could not accumulate property, leaving them dependent on exploitive employers and on equally exploitive landlords, who took one-third of the worker's already meager wages for crowded inadequate housing. Under such circumstances, the American dream of a society of prosperous, happy independent individuals was being lost in the cities: "This country cannot be a republic till every man can live in his own dwelling."[9]

To achieve that dream, Evans demanded a public land policy which would guarantee all Americans the opportunity to become independent landowners in rural areas. Independence, however, did not mean the isolated life of the subsistence farmer. As an advocate particularly of the interests of the skilled workers, Evans recognized the benefits of some inter-dependence among men. Therefore, he proposed a system of public land management designed to assure, along with the possession of land, the development of a diffuse society of rural villages which would maintain the essential advantages of urban living, free from the curse of urban dependence and crowding. He hoped to organize communities within the frame-work established by the major national land survey unit, the 36-square-mile-township. Most of that area he set aside for farms, each restricted to 160 acres to prevent the excessive scattering of population as well as to assure land for everyone. He also reserved one central square mile for a public park, a school, a town hall, and for lots to be owned by manufacturers, mechanics, tradesmen, and others required to meet the needs of surrounding farm families, all of whom would be within one hour's walk of the center. Such an organization would enable a population of between 1000 and 2000 in each town-ship, to support itself in independence and prosperity. By expanding rural opportunities, land reform would both stem the flow of ambitious rural youths to the city and gradually lessen the existing density of city populations by attracting surplus workers to the countryside, a development which Evans hoped the city government would subsidize with part of the $300,000 a year "now paid for the support of pauperism." The resulting national system of communities "would support the population on the smallest space consistent with health, comfort and happiness, reversing exactly the crowded city and isolated country system now in vogue."[10]

Thus did Evans attempt to translate the Jeffersonian ideal of the independent landed yeoman into terms meaningful for an urbanizing age.[11] He died in 1856, but his essential vision was to reappear in more sophisticated forms in the future. All were based on a common assumption that American society was breaking down under the pressure of "Progress" into two defective fragments, the congested and poisonous city—the sparse and stultifying countryside. To reverse that trend, it was necessary to create a new kind of society, neither rural nor city but suburban—a blend of rural and urban advantages. "Of course," said *Harpers Monthly* regarding the two fragments, "we know that the pleasantest life is the union of the two—the country enlivened by the intelligence and amenity of the city."[12] Ruralize the city, urbanize the countryside—this was the hope of a line of social prophets who placed the American dream of prosperity, comfort, independence, and virtue in a diffuse society of decongested cities, towns, and villages. With the right management of technology and of the land, America could escape to suburbia, which would conserve all that seemed threatened by the bloated metropolis: Human beings, natural resources, and American values.

Social visions, however, were not social realities. Virtually nothing was done in the nineteenth century even to begin the complex task of truly urbanizing the countryside, and so much of rural America was left to appear increasingly backward and benighted in the light of spreading urban influences and expectations. As Greeley and others had warned, the failure to adapt urban organization and technology to the needs of the countryside led to a widening gap between urban and rural living conditions. Although many of the rural poor (especially in the South) were to remain in the countryside until the twentieth century, and although the frontier west was to continue for a half century to be a promised land for restless farmers, the metropolitan future nevertheless had begun to reveal itself by the 1850s, as ambitious Americans flocked to rapidly expanding towns and cities. Cities had become the safety valves for the pent-up material, social, and cultural ambitions of rural areas. The crowded, congested, wicked city? Against that, successful city-dwellers were preparing a more practical escape than that proposed by the visionaries; in fact, they had already found a more realistic suburbia especially suited to their needs.

By the 1850s, the migration of both Europeans and Americans to the mouth of the Hudson caused a boom in the population not only of Manhattan but also of a metropolitan complex of interdependent cities, towns, and suburbs centered on New York. In 1852, Daniel Curry predicted that by 1895 this complex would form a city of four million people covering "the whole western end of Long Island, the whole of Staten Island, a vast extent of the coast of New Jersey, and a considerable portion of Westchester County beyond Harlem River":

> Already these places are becoming the seats of villages, built by capital from the city, and occupied by a teeming population from the city, who continue to spend their hours of business in the great metropolis. Here, too, in every direction, are springing up the suburban villages of more opulent citizens, who seek beyond the din and dust of the city proper, the quiet that is denied them. Here too, are rising a multitude of public institutions—charitable, religious and literary—and by all of which the recent scenes of rural industry are becoming transformed into scenes of the animated toil of city life. . . . Fifty years hence a city of cottages with gardens, and villas with parks and pleasure ground, and clusters of dwellings among cultivated fields and miniature groves will cover a circular area of fifty miles diameter, centering at the present site of the City Hall.[13]

Even in his failure to reconcile his dream of quiet suburban cottages with the expected expansion of the city's "animated toil," Curry proved to be an accurate prophet of the metropolitan future.

Three years later, the author of a glowing article on "Great Cities" for *Putnam's Magazine*, noted the existence of "The

Metropolitan City of New York" with more than a million people within a five-mile radius of City Hall, "whose residence there is caused by that proximity, and is dependent upon the city's business, directly or indirectly." Within the metropolitan city, a system of communication encouraged a "continued intermingling" of people; the inhabitants of Williamsburg, for instance, were kept in contact with those of Jersey City by "a line of vehicles across the island of New York, specially provided for that purpose." This growing interdependence and mingling of people in Long Island, New York, Westchester, Staten Island, and New Jersey had created a community of feeling and interest which transcended political boundaries: "A mere legislative act framing a common municipal government for its present divisions could hardly increase the general sense of this spontaneous unity."[14]

The long struggle to unite New York and Brooklyn, not achieved until the consolidation of Greater New York in 1898, would indicate that unity was neither spontaneous nor complete, but census data indicated that a great metropolitan city was at least being born. While New York grew faster than either the state or nation between 1840 and 1860, its growth was outpaced by the areas surrounding it; the city's population increased more than 2.5 times (from 312,710 to 813,669) by 1860, while that of the ten counties of New York and New Jersey surrounding it more than tripled (from 211,464 to 690,255). These figures measured a development more complicated than the emergence of dormitory suburbs, a fact which those who contemplated suburban growth then, as later, tended to ignore. More than half of that growth took place in just three counties (Kings in New York and Essex and Hudson in New Jersey) whose population quadrupled during the period.[15] These counties soon acquired an urban dimension of their own, much of their development occurring in and around a group of semi-autonomous cities.

In Essex County, Newark grew from 17,000 to nearly 72,000 people under the stimulus of New York's expanding trade. Hudson County, across the Hudson from lower and midtown Manhattan, was more directly dependent on the city, but much of its spectacular growth after 1840 (600 percent between that date and 1860) took place in urban areas. Jersey City, founded early in the century by New York developers, grew nearly tenfold during the period to almost 30,000. Hoboken, a favorite playground for New Yorkers (and the site of the first recorded baseball game), grew rapidly after 1838, with the formation of the Hoboken Land and Improvement Company; by 1852, Curry described it as "now becoming a thickly settled embryo city."[16] Such places were centers of industrial activity as well as residence. In 1860, more than 1000 manufacturing establishments in Essex and Hudson counties provided nearly 25,000 jobs. These and other employment opportunities attracted a substantial immigrant population. Over one-third of the inhabitants of Newark in 1860 were foreign born, as were nearly 40 percent of the residents of Jersey City, where the Irish were particularly numerous. Hoboken attracted so many Germans that as early as 1851 the *Evening Post* could declare that it was "half-Germanized already."[17]

The same development occurred on the other side of New York across the East River in Kings County. Most spectacular was the growth of Williamsburg from a place of some 3000 people in 1835 to a city of nearly 40,000 in 1852, as it became a favorite home for the skilled workers employed in the booming shipyards on both banks of the river. Williamsburg's history as a city, however, was short, for in 1855 it was absorbed by Brooklyn, making that city, with its 205,000 people, the fourth largest in the country. Although Greater Brooklyn provided manufacturing employment for over 13,000 people in 1860, there was some basis for the complaint that Brooklyn was a mere "dormitory" or "parasite" which skimmed the cream off New York's population by pursuing a course designed to attract those with some money, particularly businessmen and skilled workers.[18] Certainly, Brooklyn real estate developers, aided by that city's government, played up the advantages of a suburban escape from the high taxes, exorbitant rents, bad housing, and social misery of New York. When in 1854, James Cole and Sons advertised the auction sale of 450 lots near Carroll Park, they were careful to note:

ESCAPE TO SUBURBIA

> The distance of these lots from the Merchants Exchange, New York, is the same as to Tenth Street in that city, but requiring only half the time to pass, on account of the rapid transit over the long ferries between the two cities . . . ; the consolidation of Brooklyn and Williamsburg will have a tendency to reduce and permanently fix the tax on property which is at present far less than the taxes of New York, while the actual cost of real estate in Brooklyn does not exceed one-fifth of what it is in corresponding parts of that city.

Erastus Benedict, who blasted New York leaders for their failure to counter this policy, declared that it was so successful that Brooklyn could "hardly supply low priced dwellings fast enough for the throngs of people who sought to occupy them."[19]

While developers were busy manufacturing cheap dwellings to meet the dreams of the middle and working classes, they also were crafting a residential environment for New York's businessmen at Brooklyn Heights, which combined the elegance of a Washington Square with clean sea breezes and a glorious view of New York and its harbor. Here, in an environment described by one observer as "a sweet specimen of the *rus in urbe*," lived Lewis Tappan (merchant and reformer), Samuel Sloan (President of the Hudson River Railroad), James A. Leggett (Secretary of the Eagle Insurance Company), and other successful city men who lived quiet lives less than 30 minutes, by ferry, from the rush and clamor of Wall Street.[20] Perhaps their situation was best summed up by their favorite minister, Henry Ward Beecher, whose popularity as a sermonizer in his fashionable Plymouth Congregational Church was a powerful influence in attracting the rich to Brooklyn. For Beecher, Brooklyn Heights and its citizens formed a benevolent urban influence, which contributed its talents to the city, yet was insulated from urban malignancies. On the Heights, people escaped the depressing, degrading atmosphere of the city, in favor of a magnificent panorama (as Beecher himself could see from his back windows) of New York Bay, and of a vibrant nature which stimulated the spiritual and moral side of man. The inhabitants were better than most urbanites because their environment was better, but they were not isolated from the city, for it too was part of the panorama— a challenge and excitement in its distant magnificence: "Yonder, too, lies that great city with a thousand shining eyes, crouched down, but always watching, always measuring, night and day, like some huge, muttering behemoth, waiting for its prey in the reeds by the seashore."[21]

Beecher's idealization of the Heights of Brooklyn was suggestive of the fact that city and suburb were integral parts of the same society. George Henry Evans and others might place their faith in the autonomous, suburbanized village; the real suburbia was locked in the embrace of the great city. By the mid-1850s, some 60,000 native-born New Yorkers had removed themselves to Brooklyn, Jersey City, Hoboken, and scores of other places which grew up around New York.[22] Though they escaped from some of the problems of the city, they remained very much a part of its economic and cultural life. Many earned their living in New York; others depended on businesses which, though outside the city, were sustained by its economy. Frequently, they read its newspapers. Often, they depended on its organized food supply; in the 1850s, Solon Robinson observed that the villages along the route of the Harlem Railroad were "mainly supplied with marketing from the city, instead of their own vicinity." Especially for those who prized the wealth, talents, and skills of suburbanites, the suburbs played an equally vital role in sustaining the economy and culture of the city. In 1851, Erastus Benedict wrote that "The city is but one: like the human body it has many parts, of different beauty and honor and value, but they are all necessary to all. . . . Broadway and Wall Street are as necessary to the suburbs as the suburbs are to them."[23]

As Benedict emphasized, the vital arteries of this metropolitan body were its streets, ferries, ships, and railroads which by the 1840s were beginning to form a loosely integrated transportation system. As the city was well served by natural waterways, ships played an important role in the movement of goods and people. By the early 1840s, steamers were making at least one scheduled round trip a day during the warmer months between such comparatively distant places as New Rochelle, Glen Cove, Croton-on-Hudson, and New Brunswick, New Jersey, for the particular benefit of those fortunate few who could afford to arrive in New York late in the morning and depart by mid-afternoon. The more frequent ferries linked New York with Newark and Staten Island, the second of which, said Philip Hone, was "a sort of terra incognita to the people of New York" until the establishment of a regular ferry service in the mid-1830s.[24]

These were overshadowed, however, by the far more massive service provided for the suburban cities immediately across from New York. The ferry lines to Jersey City, Hoboken, Williamsburg, and Brooklyn were the earliest form of mass transportation, involving especially designed steam boats for commuter traffic and requiring extensive capital; when the Union Ferry Company was established in 1853 to consolidate the Brooklyn ferries; it was capitalized at $776,200. Often closely aligned with suburban real estate promoters, the ferry companies attempted to provide fast, efficient, and comparatively cheap service.[25] By the early 1850s, ferries left New York for Jersey City every 10 to 15 minutes during the work day, the fare being three cents per person for the one-mile ride across the Hudson. In 1855, an estimated 7 million people a year used the Jersey City ferries. The East River lines were organized for an even more massive commuter service. Williamsburg, for instance, was served by six steam ferries scheduled to leave at intervals of ten minutes from Peck Slip and every five minutes from Grand Street during the work day; the annual commutation rate was $10. For a time after the formation of the Union Ferry Company, service was provided between New York and Brooklyn for one cent a ride. In 1860, the East River ferries carried 32,845,950 passengers, a massed humanity pleasing to the eye not only of ferrymen and suburban developers but of Walt Whitman who four years earlier had celebrated the Brooklyn Ferry:

On the ferry-boats, the hundreds and hundreds that cross, returning home, are more curious to me than you suppose.[26]

[187]

This spectacle would not have been possible without at least some kind of land transportation to funnel passengers to suburban ferry landings. In the 1840s, probably the majority of passengers walked from their homes to the landings; yet, even then, some depended on stages and omnibuses. By the 1850s, the desire to facilitate the movement of these and other vehicles brought an upsurge of interest in plank roads. The sellers of suburban lots at Bergen Heights and other places noted that the Newark–Jersey City plank road would give the potential lot buyer access to New York in an hour or less, on any one of the 40 stages which traveled on the road at ten-minute intervals.[27] Similar roads on Long Island connected Flushing, Newtown, Jamaica, Coney Island and other places with the East River ferries.

Planks, however, were quickly overshadowed by rails. By the late 1850s, horsecar lines were operating in the more crowded suburban areas around Brooklyn and Jersey City. Even more significantly, steam railroads were beginning to promote the diffusion of population by developing a commuter service. Across the Hudson, Jersey City had by 1857 become a major focus for commuter traffic coming over varied lines from places in Bergen, Passaic, Morris, Union, Hudson, Essex, and Middlesex counties. The rail route between Jersey City and Newark had become one of the most heavily traveled in the world. According to Dinsmore's *Thirty Miles Around New York*, a guide to the city and its suburbs, the commuter might at least hope to travel in an hour or less by ferry and railroad to such places as Newark, Elizabeth, Rahway, North and South Orange, Boiling Spring (Bergen County's first suburban development, later renamed Rutherford), and Paterson. A two hour ride was the lot ot these few commuters who dared to settle at the outer limits of suburban New Jersey in places like Morristown and Somerville.[28]

The railroads also brought the beginnings of suburbanization to Queens and Westchester counties on the New York side of the Hudson. Queens was poorly served by the Long Island Railroad, especially after that line was prohibited in the mid-1850s from running steam locomotives through Brooklyn.

ESCAPE TO SUBURBIA

While the ferry and rail route through Jersey City promised to deliver the passenger to a place like South Orange (16 miles from New York) in 60 minutes, the Long Island required 85 minutes to get to Jamaica, only 12 miles away. The 1850s, however, did bring some improvement to the area when the New York and Flushing Railroad was opened between Hunter's Point and Flushing. The work chiefly of real estate speculators, the railroad brought a boom in suburban properties at Maspeth, Newtown, and Flushing by bringing them within 50 minutes of New York.[29]

Even with this, Queens grew slowly before the Civil War, especially in comparison with neighboring Kings County. A more promising suburban frontier in the 1850s was southern Westchester County. Before 1850, the areas to the north of New York both in upper Manhattan and in Westchester lacked the efficient system of mass transportation which, to the disgust and concern of leading New Yorkers, was encouraging the flow of people to the other sides of the Hudson and East rivers. The 1850s, however, brought the beginnings of mass commuter traffic on the three railroads which had been completed through the county. As two of them—the New York & New Haven and the Hudson River—had been built as long distance routes, neither initially gave much attention to developing a mass local traffic, but they did acquire a year-round commuter business, especially after suburban development reached such places as Yonkers (which more than doubled in population during the 1850s) and Mount Vernon (a new suburban town founded early in the decade).[30]

Suburbanization moved northward especially strongly along the tracks of the New York and Harlem, the oldest yet shortest of the three lines. Before 1840, the Harlem, having been slow to cross the river of the same name, specialized in the movement of passengers on Manhattan Island—with considerable success, for in that year it carried some one million people. In the 1840s, as it extended its lines into Westchester County north of the river, it brought much of its passenger business with it. By 1853, it was running seven trains a day to Croton Falls, six more to White Plains, and 15 to Williamsbridge in southern

Westchester, leading the *Tribune* to predict that "the line of this road will be nearly one continuous village as far as White Plains before 1860." The *Tribune's* editor, Horace Greeley, was later to be a commuter on the Harlem, having purchased a farm to escape the anonymity of his city residence: "Who, if he has any choice, prefers to grow old and die at No. 239, unknown to, and uncared for by, the denizens of Nos. 237 and 241?"[31]

Few New Yorkers, however, were permitted such a luxury. Despite the *Tribune's* optimism, the Harlem did not provide convenient access to White Plains or even to many places south of that town. In 1849, a critic charged that its White Plains train averaged less than 13 miles an hour, a condition which, if anything, seems to have worsened by 1857, when it took nearly 90 minutes to reach Bronxville, 19 miles away.[32] Moreover, like other railroads, its commutation rates ($37 a year to Morrisania in 1853) were a financial burden for all but the most favored. When in 1854 the company decided to raise its rates (by almost 25 percent for Morrisania), it set off a commuter revolt. At a series of meetings, angry passengers denounced the company for poor service and high fares, one of them making a charge, to be repeated many times a century later, that the Harlem's directors were deliberately sacrificing passenger traffic to their more profitable freight business: "They might say 'We do not want this local travel, but places for our freight trains.'" Despite the protests and accompanying threats to tear up the Harlem tracks or to start another railroad, commuters continued to use the line.[33]

Like its two counterparts, the Harlem contributed to the development of upper Westchester as the special suburban preserve of the well-do-do. Unlike the other two railroads, however, it also acted as a significant mass transit influence in determining a different development for the southern part of the county. In the 1850s its depots at the lower end of the line became the nuclei for such suburban places as Mott Haven, Morrisania, and Fordham, which were promoted by developers as retreats for workers as well as for businessmen and members of the middle class. The extent of the commuter protest in 1854 testified to the success of these developers. Certainly, the combination of real estate promotion and the railroad tripled the population of southern Westchester between 1850 and 1855. Thus, while the northern two-thirds of the county remained apart from the city, the lower third had begun that drift which was to lead to its eventual annexation to New York as Bronx County.[34]

Although the futures of specific suburbs were unclear, it was evident by the 1850s that the Age of Steam had, by encouraging both the concentration and diffusion of urban population, created the beginnings of the metropolitan city. By 1860, New York and its surrounding ten counties on each side of the Hudson had become a thickly settled region of some 1.5 million people. It was true that more than half of that population was crowded onto the 22 square miles of Manhattan Island, but suburban Kings and Hudson, most directly the product of steam ferries, had developed a respectable urban density of 2700 people per square mile, while there was a notable thickening of population in other counties along the railroad lines. The old world of semi-independent farms and villages vanished, to be replaced by a loosely organized and sprawling, if immature metropolis.[35]

Although most New Yorkers looked on the growth of the Metropolitan City with pride, that pride was often mixed with resentment and anxiety. A persistent complaint was that the suburbs skimmed off the "best people" from New York itself and left it with the worst. "Many of the rich and prosperous are removing from the city," said the AICP in 1850, "while the poor are pressing in." Some of this concern colored the protests against misgovernment in the city, especially as it contributed to the deteriorating environment and rising taxes which seemed to drive citizens to the suburbs. In 1859, Samuel Halliday charged that, because of the city's "horrid" housing conditions and misgovernment, "there are half a million of people, not living here, who are more or less connected with the business of New York" who otherwise might have made for a city population of one and a quarter million. Along with people went taxable property—$50 million estimated Erastus Benedict in 1851, lost to Brooklyn alone.[36]

How to reverse this loss of people and property? The question had special significance in the frequent disputes over transportation policy. As early as 1840, Alderman Daniel F. Tieman, who was later to become Mayor, opposed a measure to improve the East River ferry service with the warning that it would encourage the growth of Brooklyn at the expense of the city. This same point was made subsequently by other Aldermen, including one who proposed the ferry fares be raised from 3 to 25 cents in order to keep people in the city. More frequently, the hope of reversing the flight of wealth bolstered the agitation, especially strong in the early 1850s, for streets, street railways, and parks to hasten the development of upper Manhattan as residential territory within the city limits. Raise land values and broaden the tax base by holding and attracting people—the objectives pleased both land owners and politicians, but it involved the paradox of an already crowded city committing itself to a policy of further crowding.[37]

While policy makers pursued a policy designed to keep people on Manhattan, however, a few reformers saw in the outward movement something not to be resisted but to be actively encouraged. For them, the metropolitan city was not a political thing with an appetite for tax revenues, but a new social world in which the dream of ruralizing the city and urbanizing the countryside could be realized. When in 1849 some New Yorkers protested a proposal to extend the Harlem Railroad south to Chambers Street, the city reporter of the *Tribune* denounced the opposition as "striking evidence of the tenacity of human stupidity. . . . We hope yet to see every part of our City penetrated by railroads, so that nearly every citizen may take a car within two blocks of his store or shop, and be swiftly carried out to his residence amid green fields and waving forests for a trifle, and the unhealthy packing of ten thousand human beings into three or four blocks of buildings be gradually overcome." Charles Loring Brace, who sought to move the poor out of the great city, expressed the hope that

ESCAPE TO SUBURBIA

New York would diffuse its congested population through "An underground railway with cheap workman's trains, or elevated railways with similar conveniences, connecting Westchester County and the lower part of the city, or suburbs laid out in New Jersey or on Long Island expressly for working people." Whether they gave particular attention to the poor or not, such people shared a common hope that railroads would enable a growing proportion of New Yorkers to escape from the baneful atmosphere of the congested city to the benevolent influence of nature and property-ownership in decongested suburban villages.[38]

Like so much else in the period, this suburban thinking was inchoate and superficial, but it had powerful appeal to a society caught in the widening gap between its faith in progress and the grosser realities of an urbanizing age. It offered the hope that the suburbs would become the final frontier where the restless American people would at last settle, permanently at home in an environment which combined the best of both urban and rural life. Eventually, the overcrowded, unnatural city might even disappear. "There would never have been a city," said Nathaniel Parker Willis, "if there had been railways in Eden. Commerce would have been done at places like wharves, where nobody stayed after dark, and from which clerks and merchants went home to their country residence by railroad." The new Eden was within reach, declared John A. Dix in 1852, for the railroads progressively were bringing city people into touch with "the work of nature and nature's God" and into an open world where home ownership would encourage the formation of the local attachments and associations, the love of home and place, needed to stabilize and enrich life. If New Yorkers would spend even half the money they wasted on "frivolous embellishment in improving the area around New York," said Dix, that area would become "the most beautiful suburban district on the face of the globe."[39]

This hope that the new metropolitan city might be truly suburbanized was given special force by Andrew Jackson Downing, who spent much of his all-too-short career attempting to direct the development of the suburban frontier. Although

[193]

he had proposed Central Park as a way of humanizing the city, Downing was not a city man, nor did he have strong ties with New York. The son of a successful nurseryman at Newburgh, he inherited both the nursery business and lifelong roots on the banks of the Hudson River. As a horticulturist and land-scape architect, he paid particular attention to the needs of those who had the time and money needed to settle well away from the city on estates and in villas in the Hudson Valley. A sensitive and private soul who shied away from the rough, masculine world of the commercial city, Downing showed a particular affection for this elite which, with his help, modeled its lifestyle on that of the English country gentleman. Yet he was no mere landscaper for the rich but a man with a powerful vision of an America of beauty and harmony which permeated his popular books on horticulture and rural architecture, especially in *Rural Essays*, a collection of his writings as editor of the influential *Horticulturist*.[40]

He recognized that the progressive character of his age was opening the preserve of the gentry to more and more city people. Because of increasing wealth and the extension of the railroad, "hundreds and thousands, formerly obliged to live in the crowded streets of cities, now find themselves able to enjoy a country cottage, several miles distant—the old notion of time and space being half annihilated." This invasion of his private world disturbed him, but he also saw it as an opportunity to guide the development of a new and better society in an urbanizing nation. If the new society could be modeled on his principles, he hoped that Americans would be weaned from their restless habits to become a domestic people, happily rooted in their homes, amid beautiful surroundings.[41]

Downing noted that many city people had rushed to rural retreats in the belief that Nature would solve all their problems, only to be bored by an isolated existence and shocked by the expense of country living resulting chiefly from the cost of American farm labor. For such people, Downing's advice was to scale down the size of their properties to suit their means and characters. Although he gave his special affections for the country seats (places of 30 to 500 or more acres) of gentleman farmers, he urged others of more modest means to choose "a suburban country life" where more compact suburban places of five to thirty acres would provide a neighborly social life and reduce the costs of labor.[42] He was especially anxious that, whatever the specific nature of suburban life, it not be corrupted by what he termed "cockneyisms," i.e., the unconscious tendency of city people to thrust their city-bred social and aesthetic tastes into the countryside. Tall, rectangular city houses suited crowded environments, but planted in rural areas they disrupted the harmony of nature and violated the essential canon of Downing's aesthetic creed, that there be "union between house and grounds." City ways, unless adapted to the countryside, would eventually destroy the beauty and serenity which made life there so desirable for city people.[43]

As a landscape architect, Downing attended primarily to the improvement of individual houses and grounds, because, in the words of a friend, they were "dependencies and ornaments of home and home was the sanctuary of the highest human affections."[44] He emphasized his privatistic inclinations by declaring that he was "no communist." He also recognized, however, that it was the destiny of Americans to live their home lives not in isolated country places but in towns and villages, which he generally found, dull, graceless and "distressing to a man of taste." Americans were a town- and village-building people; yet they gave little thought to their work, there not being "a single plan formed" to guide their efforts. Downing saw some hope in some of the new suburban towns which were being laid out by land companies around New York, but not much. The governing ideal of these places was "not down to the zero of dirty lanes and shadeless roadsides," but it rose no higher than that of the better city residential neighborhoods with their fifty-foot frontages, rows of houses, and right-angled streets with (as a gesture to Nature) their planted trees: "And this is the sum total of the rural beauty, convenience, and comfort of the latest plan for a rural village in the Union."[45]

To counter this invading cockneyism, Downing offered his plan for a suburb which would establish and preserve a union between human culture and nature. The essential element in his plan was a large, commonly owned park in the center of the village. Around this nucleus, the people would live in single-family cottages on lots with frontages of no less than 100 feet, the best and largest homes located, in conformity with Downing's elitism, around the park. Wide tree-lined streets diverging from the park would provide every family sufficient space, circulation of air, and visual contact with nature to assure their physical and psychological well-being. Inhabitants would achieve a measure of independence as miniature farmers and horticulturalists by dedicating their private lots to the raising of fruits and vegetables. Much of their lives, however, would center on the park as a public pleasure ground and gathering place which would offer "beauties and enjoyments" beyond the capacities of private gardens. Here, "little arbors would be placed near where in midsummer evenings ices would be served. . . . And, little by little the musical taste of the village (with the help of those good musical folk—the German emigrants) would organize itself into a band." Music, visual beauty, serenity, comfort and good cheer: "Do we over-rate the mental and moral influence of such a common ground of entertainment as this, when we say that the inhabitants of such a village . . . would have something more healthful than the common gossip of country villages."[46]

Downing's interest in suburban planning was cut short by his death at the age of 37 in 1852. In death, he was not forgotten. His friends erected a monument to him in Washington, D.C., which bore the inscription:

I WAKE, I CLIMB THE HILL: FROM END TO END
OF ALL THE LANDSCAPE UNDERNEATH,
I FIND NO PLACE THAT DOES NOT BREATHE
SOME GRACIOUS MEMORY OF MY FRIEND.[47]

His influence survived in the form of his books (*The Theory and Practice of Landscape Gardening* went through six editions before the Civil War) and the work of his associate, Calvert Vaux. It was Vaux who emphasized the importance of street planning in determining the permanent character of towns. Rather than the gridiron pattern of right-angled streets with which Americans insisted on mangling the landscape, let town-builders make graceful, curved roads which would respect the topography, preserve nature, and maintain the quiet, leisurely character of a rural environment, a proposal which became a fundamental rule of planning for Vaux's later partner, Frederick Law Olmsted.[48] Even before Olmsted began his notable career as a landscape architect, Downing's spirt was embodied in the planned suburb, Llewellyn Park, developed in the mid-1850s by a wealthy chemical manufacturer, Llewellyn Haskell. Situated on the eastern slopes of New Jersey's Orange Mountains, overlooking New York and its harbor, this community, in its commonly owned park, curving roads, extensive plots, and exclusion of commercial activity, was the prototype for the romantic suburbs which in the next half century were to be planted around most major cities.[49]

Men like Downing were attempting to bridge the widening gap between the expectations and the realities associated with the growth of the metropolis. The big city meant progress in wealth and culture beyond the dreams of country villages, but it also meant a frantic, rootless, artificial existence which threatened to corrupt the American dream of a happy, moral, and independent life. How could progress, with its changes, be reconciled to the need for roots? How could human art and invention be harmonized with the beneficial influence of the landscape? For Downing, the answer was to teach Americans the moral and social advantages "of orderly, neat tasteful villages; in producing better citizens, in causing the laws to be respected, in making homes dearer and more sacred, in making domestic life and the enjoyment of property to be more truly and rightfully estimated." He saw signs of hope, especially in the new technology of steamboats and railroads which made the landscape more accessible to the city and in the growth among the wealthy of a cultivated taste for rural life. In his own special world on the east bank of the Hudson River between Tarrytown and his home at Newburgh—a world of beautiful estates and cultivated gentlemen (including the two grandfathers of Franklin Delano Roosevelt), he could dream that rootless, hurryup America would eventually become a society of happy, virtuous, home-loving people governed by benevolent, high-minded country squires.[50]

It was an appealing vision, but wealth and technology could, in the wrong hands, be brutal, as Downing's death in the burning wreckage of the *Henry Clay* illustrated. The steamboat and the railroad had opened the way for the development of a humanized landscape, but they could also bring the disadvantages as well as advantages of city life. Washington Irving soon complained of the railroad whistles which disturbed his sleep at Sunnyside, "these unearthly yells and howls and screams indulged in for a mile on a stretch and destructive of the quiet of whole neighborhoods." Irving and his friends also were repelled by the railroad itself, which ran like an ugly scar up the Hudson Valley. Others complained that the railroads were introducing city rowdyism and city crime to the countryside. Worse, the new forms of mass transportation threatened the wholesale invasion of those city ways, those cockneyisms, which Downing feared would permanently destroy the landscape. Even his early death did not spare him from at least one disturbing glimpse into the suburban future furnished by a development near Tarrytown which, having been carved up into rectangular blocks of lots, was described in 1853 as having "streets gullied by every rain, and basement-houses tottering upon the meagre patches of grass."[51]

The inefficiencies and high costs of the existing transportation system long protected the outer suburbs from most mass developments, but the dreary side of the suburban future was already appearing in those areas served by the ferries. As early as 1844, Edgar Allan Poe, complained that New Yorkers had already badly disfigured the natural beauty of the areas around the harbor with tasteless suburban "palaces" of painted white pine, rough boxes dressed up by builders with gimcracks and gee-gaws such as a fountain "giving out a pint of real water per hour, through the mouth of a leaden fish." In the rush to build cheap housing which followed in the late 1840s, builders ignored even the gimcracks; when George Templeton Strong walked from the new suburb of Greenpoint through Brooklyn to Fulton Ferry he traversed "what seemed an infinite region of monotonous shabby streets and small cheap houses." Places near the ferry landings like Williamsburg, Hoboken, and Jersey City became the terminals for railroads and horsecar lines, which brought crowds, commerce, industry, and the dirt, noise, and pace of city life. In less than half a century, the builders of the metropolitan city had spoiled the suburban fringes of both the East and Hudson Rivers in and around New York; regions which once had furnished an escape from the ugly city were being swallowed up by it.[52]

The decay of these first suburbs was accompanied by the rise of new ones; many were built during the suburban real estate boom of the 1850s in nearby places in Long Island, southern Westchester, and New Jersey. Anticipating that the expanding system of railroads, omnibuses, and horsecar lines would create a mass demand for suburban properties, developers boomed Fort Hamilton, Bushwick, Newtown, East New York, Flushing, Morrisania, Fordham, East Newark, Clinton, Bergen Hill, and other places as suburban retreats from city taxes and city problems. Often, they made some attempt to maintain a decent environment. They planted trees; a few boasted of a park or, as in the case of West Flushing, a park and a lake. Some, like the developers of Newtown, offered deeds containing "the usual nuisance clause against the erection of buildings of an objectionable character." Others attempted to guarantee a suburban environment by establishing minimum plot sizes. One of the developers of Fordham, having purchased a farm there, divided it up into "villa lots" of two acres or more and advertised that he intended to bind all owners of land there "not to sell, lease, or contract any of the above premises excepting for the use heretofore mentioned [i.e., for "villas"]. Purchasers will be bound to erect buildings which shall not cost less than $2,000 on each plot sold, within two years from the date of purchase. The object of the above restrictions . . . is to endeavor to secure a good neighborhood, and prevent nuisances and little village lots from being laid out."[53]

Not even the best of these schemes, however, had the integrity of Downing's romantic suburb. For good or ill,

ESCAPE TO SUBURBIA

Downing had planned an environment which would maintain the union between man and nature by excluding the disruptive commercialism of the city; the gleam of greed and the rampant power of material progress would be as distant as Newburgh was from New York. On the other hand, the developers were creatures of a commercial culture, the mass merchandisers of a dream suited to the realities of the marketplace. The dream was not Downing's romantic suburb which, for the great mass, was no more than a rainbow, but the more practical one of escape from city taxes, dirt, and dependence to some kind of possession, some kind of home, some kind of opportunity to be free from the pressures of urban life. To sell that dream, the developers bought Nature wholesale and sold it retail in the form of town lots, often at mass auctions. In 1853, they advertised 360 building lots at Bushwick, 600 lots in Brooklyn, 150 at Fort Hamilton, 500 at West Flushing, 400 at Masbeth, 950 at Newtown, 325 at East Newark, 723 at Clinton, 400 at Clinton, and more at Fordham, Morrisania, Yonkers, Jamaica, and other places. Their pitch was "buy yourself a home" at 10 to 40 percent down, the rest to be paid in three to five years. The developers of Laural Hill on Newtown Creek, for instance, promised that $80 to $100 a year for five years would enable anyone to enjoy the satisfactions of home ownership and to save on rent in a pleasant environment "freed from the noise, dirt and miasma of the city."[54]

Uniformly, the developers sold a residential environment, yet many could not resist adding the promise that their lands would rapidly increase in value and so were desirable investments. This was particularly so of some of the inner suburbs which were touted paradoxically not simply as refuges from the city but as incipient cities themselves. The developers of Laural Hill boasted both of the beautiful location of their village and of its omnibus, ferry, and railroad services which, combined with "its river advantages," guaranteed that it "must become a large manufacturing and commercial place"; essentially the same promise was used to promote land sales at East New York and other places. Buy a home—buy a profitable investment; that refrain heard so often in connection with city property indicated that the suburban frontier, like that of the West, was for Americans not only a place of new beginnings but also a place to repeat the same old mistakes with essentially the same consequences—in this case the spread of city congestion, noise, dirt and ugliness into green pastures.

The mass merchandising of the suburban dream had virtues as well as weaknesses. Though their rash geometry and rasher commercialism would deny the meaningful union of man and Nature provided for in Downing's carefully crafted world, the developers did provide a compromise between city and countryside that was far more accessible to members of the expanding urban middle class. Small cheap plots and small cheap houses combined with cheap speedy transportation to places of work were not the ingredients of the romantic suburb, but they meant a widespread diffusion of property ownership. Although the majority of the inhabitants of New York itself were to remain renters, the expansion of the metropolitan city, by progressively opening new lands for ownership, served to preserve and consolidate in an urban setting the American ideal of a nation of independent families, free to inhabit their own-and-owned individual worlds. On this suburban frontier, as one developer advertised, "EVERY FAMILY CAN HAVE A HOME," without losing his access to urban convenience and power. In this way, the development of the suburbs promised an open and opening world where men would be free not only to succeed but to spend the fruits of their success in the creation of a good life for themselves.[55]

The suburbs, then, were a realistic compromise between American ambitions and ideals suited to an urbanizing society, but like most compromises they left the question as to whether they represented the best of both the city and countryside or the worst. Certainly, the promise of individual independence was part illusion, for there could be no total independence in the metropolitan city. Worse, the suburban promise discouraged any sustained effort to grapple with the problems of an urbanizing world, to create a truly urban society. Like other frontiers, the suburbs were safety values for discontents, escapes from—rather than responses to—the crowded, dirty city.

Suburbia: Ideal and Real

FIGURE 14. (right, above) This view of Brooklyn was drawn by E. Whitefield in 1845. Two years earlier, Nathaniel Parker Willis had written regarding Brooklyn that "In twenty minutes from Wall Street . . . you may reach the elegant seclusion of a country town." Whitefield's view centers on the Fulton Ferry and, in the background, fashionable Brooklyn Heights. At the extreme left are the Brooklyn Navy Yard (hidden behind the buildings) and the still-open spaces of Williamsburgh, soon to be developed as a residential suburb for the middle and working classes. Brooklyn's waterfront on the extreme right was destined by 1860 to be developed as dock space to accommodate the expanding trade of New York Port.

Courtesy of the Prints Division, New York Public Library, Stokes Collection.

FIGURE 15. (right, center) The lithograph (1860) by Currier and Ives of New York Bay from Bay Ridge (extreme south Brooklyn) expresses a suburban ideal promoted by Andrew Jackson Downing, the landscape architect and early suburban planner. Spread out in the distance is the urbanizing region around New York harbor. To the right is New York itself, in view but remote from the neat, enclosed world of an affluent suburban family. The trees in the center of the view seem to divide the distant city from the house fashioned in the Gothic villa style popularized by Downing and his associate, Calvert Vaux.

Courtesy of the Museum of the City of New York.

FIGURE 16. (right, bottom) This lithograph (1861) of the village of Morrisania in southern Westchester County (now the Bronx) presents a suburban reality which both Downing and his successor, Frederick Law Olmsted, hoped to avoid by good planning. Morrisania was an affordable opportunity for New Yorkers to escape their congested city, but its railroad spur, lumber yard, crowded housing, and spindly trees omen its eventual absorption into Greater New York at the end of the century.

Courtesy of the Museum of the City of New York.

Like other frontiers, they meant that men could repeat old mistakes without apparent cost to themselves.

Downing recognized the fundamental issue: Would Americans settle down with themselves to work toward the permanent good life or would they continue their restless pursuit of new frontiers at the expense of wasted resources and societies. He placed his hopes chiefly in the urban rich and in the improvement of their suburban tastes. Their example, he thought, would set the tone for all of society: "He who gives to the public a more beautiful and tasteful model of a habitation than his neighbor, is a benefactor to the cause of morality, good order, and the improvement of society where he lives."[56] The worlds of urban wealth and urban culture, however, were far more complicated than Downing realized. In the metropolitan city, progress would not so easily fulfill the dream; society would not so readily resolve itself into a settled existence; the rich would not so willingly lead Americans to a good life for all.

Chapter 9

WEALTH

In MARCH 1848 (some 60 years after he had arrived in New York as a poor German immigrant boy), John Jacob Astor died. This "self-invented money-making machine," as the *New York Herald* called him, finally wore out at the age of 75, but not before he had made himself one of the richest men in the world. The fortune of $20 million or more which he bequeathed to his family put the Astors securely atop the new pyramid of wealth which had begun to overshadow the petty accumulations of simpler days. The 1840s had brought the invention of a new term, "millionaire," to describe men like Astor.[1] In 1845 there were perhaps ten New Yorkers who owned the $1 million or more in property needed to qualify for the title. Fifteen years later, according to Reuben Vose in his *The Rich Men of New York*, there were 115 millionaires. Some, like Astor, were self-invented money-makers. George Law, the son of a farmer, had worked his way to New York, become a

successful contractor, and then had won his millions in railroads, ferries, horsecar lines, steamshipping, banking, and
stock speculation. Cornelius Vanderbilt ruthlessly parlayed a
small stake in ferry boating into a fortune which eventually
overshadowed that of even the Astors.[2]

The poor boys who made good in the city of gold seemed
to prove that big opportunities awaited those with the strength
and ambition to seize them. Yet the emphasis on self-made
men, so common in the nineteenth century, obscured a deeper
and more complex reality, for the effect of plentiful opportunity was less to make some of the poor wealthy than to make
the rich even richer. Although there were many roads to riches,
most of them began with a place in the earlier merchant class,
whose members had acquired money, influence, and position
enough to seize the benefits created by the rapid expansion of
the city. Some acquired their place through marriage. Andrew
H. Mickle, the son of poor Irish parents, warmed the hearts of
those who believed in the rags-to-riches myth when he acquired
a small fortune from the sale of snuff, cigars, and chewing
tobacco before being elected Mayor of the city; but perhaps he
would not have gone very far, if he had not married the
daughter of his employer and thus become a partner in a
profitable tobacco business. Simeon Draper, one of the city's
wealthiest and most prestigious auctioneers, had the good sense
to marry a daughter of his employer, the great auctioneer John
Haggerty. Others were fortunate enough to find helpful patrons. William E. Dodge attempted to leave the impression that
his millions resulted from his early thrift, noting that he had
saved part of his meager salary as clerk "and when I started in
business that sum and my experience was all my capital," but
he also acknowledged that, in fact, those savings were supplemented by money from a retired merchant who wanted to set
his son up in business with Dodge. His marriage to a daughter
of Anson Phelps, the senior partner of Phelps, Dodge & Co.,
did nothing to deter his progress.[3]

Dodge also had one other advantage which gave him a quick
start on the road to success; he was the son of a merchant who
had gotten him his first job in New York. Most other men of

wealth also were lucky to have had fathers with money or influence or who, if they had little themselves, had brothers, cousins, or friends who held a key to the golden door. James Gore King was the son of the prominent Federalist leader Rufus King. George and Nathaniel L. Griswold descended from one of Connecticut's most prestigious families. Jonathan Goodhue was the son of a United States Senator. Robert B. Minturn's father was a large shipowner. Moses H. Grinnell, Minturn's influential partner, was the son of one wealthy merchant and the brother of two others. Many of the wealthiest New Yorkers ascended from established New York families which had accumulated small fortunes early in the century. Cornelius V. S. Roosevelt (grandfather of Theodore Roosevelt) was the son of a wealthy hardware and glass dealer. The super-wealthy Goelet, Rhinelander, and Schermerhorn families were founded by men who, like John Jacob Astor, had invested heavily in Manhattan lands. R. L. and A. Stuart, who made fortunes in sugar refining, owned their start to their father, a candy manufacturer. In sum, the overwhelming majority of New York's wealthiest persons in 1845 came from rich or at least decidedly advantaged backgrounds. Wealth generally brought more wealth. Of 15 men listed as worth $3 million or more by Vose in 1861, 12 had been ranked among the wealthiest in 1845.[4]

The seed money for this superwealth generally had come from some form of trade, but by the 1840s it had been planted in a variety of profitable and expanding fields. The most reliably lucrative was real estate, especially Manhattan land, which appreciated rapidly in value with the growth of trade and population. The Brevoorts prospered from their family farm located in the developing area worthwest of Washington Square. The father of the wealthy John H. Contoit had invested his profits from a Broadway ice cream shop in real estate. The father of the even wealthier James Lenox had invested his profits from trade and banking in Manhattan land. The list of those New Yorkers who had grown rich in property was a long one, including by the 1850s such prominent names as Beekman, Chesterman, Coddington, Crosby, Cutting, Delaplaine, Jones,

WEALTH

Livingston, Lorillard, Mott, Murray, Pearsall, Phelps, Post, Roosevelt, Schermerhorn, Van Rensselaer, and Whitney; but one name, Astor, decidedly topped the list.[5]

John Jacob Astor had blazed the trail others were to follow when early in the century he had recognized that the future expansion of the city would turn much of Manhattan into a goldmine. During the last 48 years of his life, he invested some $2 million in land, especially in what was later to become the midtown area of New York, much of which he got at bargain prices during the depression years after 1837. When he died, his property, which was yielding over $200,000 a year in rents, was worth ten times his investment and was rising in value. Had he, he was asked shortly before he died, invested too heavily in real estate? "Could I begin life again," answered the great man, "knowing what I now know, and had money to invest, I would buy every foot of land on the Island of Manhattan."[6]

His heirs, however, had little cause for regret. In his will, he bequeathed 100 lots below 14th Street to his daughter, Dorothea Astor Langdon. To his grandson, Charles Astor Bristed, he gave a house and 8 lots on Broadway, 9 lots on Eighth Avenue, 43 on Seventh Avenue, 8 lots on Avenue A, 22 lots in lower New York plus "my country seat at Hellgate." To three other grandsons went "all my lands lying between Bloomingdale-road, Hudson River, Forty-second and Fifty-first streets." Other heirs also received lots and houses, but the greater part of his estate went to his son, William B. Astor, who had already accumulated a fortune in land on his own. By 1860 William B. Astor's accumulated $25 million, by conservative estimate, was three times larger than the next largest property holding, that of Alexander T. Stewart, the lord of the department store; this did not include another $12 million, again a conservative figure, owned by ten other assorted Astors and their spouses.[7]

Even the Astors, however, invested in fields other than real estate. The rise of New York as the financial capital of the nation made banking an especially profitable if somewhat risky investment. When the powerful Bank of Commerce was organized in 1839, merchants such as James Boorman, Robert B.

Minturn, and Stephen Whitney subscribed heavily for its $100 shares, although the largest stockholder by far was the great mercantile banker James Gore King. Among those who served as directors of the bank before the Civil War were such prominent members of the merchant community as John Austin Stevens, Edwin D. Morgan (later Governor of New York State), James Brown (of Brown Brothers, the prominent international banking house), Samuel B. Ruggles, and Peter G. Stuyvesant. The older and even more prestigeous Bank of New York also was especially close to mercantile wealth, but the rosters of bank presidents, as well as directors, indicated that the money of the rich was widely invested. Among those who served as long-term presidents were such stalwarts as Shepherd Knapp (Merchant's Bank), John Q. Jones (Chemical Bank), George Newbold (Bank of America), John A. Stevens (Bank of Commerce) and Thomas Tileston (Phoenix Bank).[8]

The wealthy also invested heavily in the rapidly expanding insurance field. They had long experience with fire and marine insurance; by the 1840s their interests had broadened to meet the growing need, especially in urban areas, for life insurance. The list of directors of the New York Life Insurance and Trust Company read like a social register: James Kent, Gulian C. Verplanck, Peter Lorillard, Jonathan Goodhue, Stephen Whitney, Peter G, Stuyvesant, Gardner G. Howland, John Jacob Astor, and William B. Astor. When the Mutual Life Insurance Company was formed in 1843 conspicuous among its founders were James Brown, William H. Aspinwall, Robert B. Minturn, James Boorman, and Henry Brevoort. Their money was well invested, for the amount of life insurance in the United States rose some 16 times between 1840 and 1860. Such insurance companies provided much of the mortgage money required for the development of real estate in both the city and its suburbs.[9]

With the proliferation of corporations new frontiers of investment also appeared, in manufacturing and most especially in transportation. The Astors invested heavily in the monopolistic Delaware & Raritan Canal and the Camden & Amboy Railroad in New Jersey. William H. Aspinwall was the prime mover of the Pacific Railroad and Panama Steamship Company, intended to connect New York with gold-rich California. John Jay Phelps, a prominent merchant and land developer, was the first president of the Delaware, Lackawanna and Western Railroad. J. Phillips Phoenix, a prominent Whig politician and a director of the Howard Fire Insurance Company, was President of both the Auburn and Syracuse and the New Jersey railroads. By the 1850s, New York money was moving extensively into Midwestern railroads. in 1855, for instance, nearly a quarter of the $1 million in bonds issued by the Terre Haute and Alton Railroad was purchased by five New Yorkers, including Edwin D. Morgan and the sugar-refining Stuart brothers.[10]

Mercantile money planted in many fields—the situation was best summed up in the career of Philip Hone who, though far from being the wealthiest member of the merchant community, was certainly one of its most respected. Hone had accumulated a small fortune from his auction business. Although he retired in 1821 to devote his life to cultural, social, and public pursuits, he maintained an active interest in the business world, serving for a time as president of the American Exchange Bank and of the Bank For Savings. He was also the first president of the American Mutual Insurance Company, which he helped organize in 1843—and the last, for the company was forced into bankruptcy by the great fire of 1845. To balance this painful loss, Hone had substantial investments in the Delaware & Hudson Company, with its profitable coal mining and coal carrying business and in a prosperous textile mill.[11] Not all rich New Yorkers were as active—or as unlucky—as Hone, but the variety of investments was typical of the class. With the boom in commerce, banking, manufacturing, transportation, and land values during the 1850s, mercantile seed money grew into mighty fortunes. There were some risks, some losses, some failures; but the odds heavily favored the growth of wealth for those who had command not only over money but also over the talents of the lawyers, managers, accountants, and clerks needed to profit from a complex, modern urban economy.

There was little to deter the accumulation of wealth. Taxes

were low by later standards. There were no federal and state income taxes and local taxation was, despite complaints to the contrary, a light burden for the rich. Although state law required that property be assessed at true market value, property holdings were haphazardly underrated for tax purposes. Personal property, especially in stocks and bonds, was sometimes not assessed at all, either because it was hidden from view or because the owners were conveniently out of town during the summer assessment period.[12] In 1850, according to the Deputy Receiver of Taxes, the following sums were paid by men who ranked among the richest New Yorkers: William H. Aspinwall ($1962.39), Moses Grinnell ($682.50), and Robert B. Minturn ($1127) plus Grinnell, Minturn & Co. ($1740.33), Peter Goelet ($8968), Peter Lorillard ($13,306), and Stephen Whitney ($9398). Geolet, Lorillard and Whitney, at least, were millionaires, as was William B. Astor who paid $29,579.26 on property assessed at $2.6 million but probably worth ten times as much.[13]

Although this new class of millionaire was at least occasionally disturbing to democratic sensibilities, New Yorkers preferred to believe that death rather than taxes was the best defense against dangerous super-wealth, that the division of estates would, as John A. Dix put it in 1852, "dissolve the accumulations of wealth which are the fruits of successful enterprise. There are very few instances in which property remains in a family beyond the second or third generation."[14] In one way, Dix was right; great fortunes were fragmented among the second and third generations; accumulations under specific family names were slowed or reduced. Yet this process which affected the scale of individual fortunes did not prevent the development of a coherent class, whose rapidly accumulating collective wealth gave it a privileged place in New York society.

The tendency of wealth to associate with wealth was especially strong in the old merchant community, where ties of friendship and of family were readily formed, often as a matter of good business. Much of that earlier intimacy was preserved by the tendency of the children of the rich to marry into families much like their own—or better. John Jones Schermerhorn married Philip Hone's daughter, Mary. James M. Brown, of the bank-rich Brown family, married into the land-rich Post family. Intermarriage established a web of relationships among the Beekmans, Cuttings, DePeysters, Duers, Goodhues, Joneses, Kings, Lorillards, Schermerhorns, and other great families.

Many of these relationships centered on the Astor family. John Jacob Astor had married a poor relation of the Brevoort family; his half sister, Elizabeth, married John G. Wendel, who acquired a fortune in land. William B. Astor married the daughter of the prominent General John Armstrong (who himself had married into the Livingston family). One of his daughters married Sam Ward, Jr., whose father was part of Prime, Ward, King & Co. Another married Franklin Delano of the firm of Grinnell, Minturn & Co. A son, William, married Caroline Schermerhorn, who was destined to become the Queen of the Four Hundred. Another of John Jacob's grand-children, Charles Astor Bristed, married Laura Brevoort. Still another married the son of James Roosevelt and his first wife, Rebecca Howland.[15]

Marital ties were only some among many threads that bound the rich together. Often, they did business together; the Merchant's Exchange was their common meeting ground as were the boards of directors of banks, insurance companies, and railroads. More than occasionally, they were, or had been, partners.[16] They socialized together and vacationed together, participating in the great summer rush of the fashionable from sweltering New York to Saratoga and then, as Saratoga became *passé*, to Newport. They also tended to live together in the same general residential neighborhoods. Although they never settled as a group in one definite area, the northward movement of the city left them concentrated in an elite residential zone between Second and Sixth Avenues north of Houston Street. In 1845, more than half of the rich lived on just sixteen streets, nearly all of them in or near the Fifteenth Ward. James Brown moved in 1846 to University Place to be near James M. Brown and Stewart Brown who lived on nearby Waverly Place. George Griswold lived at 9 Washington Square, near Jacob Boorman at 13 and Gardner C. Howland at 15. James Lenox lived at

12th Street on Fifth Avenue, near his two brothers-in-law on 11th Street. A similar, though smaller and perhaps even more intimate, concentration of wealth had also developed across the East River in Brooklyn Heights.[17]

The rich also established a common institutional life for themselves in education, religion, culture, and politics. Often, they sent their sons and daughters to the same private schools and academies and, for higher education, to Spingler Institute at Union Square for young women and Columbia College for young men.[18] They had their own fashionable churches such as Trinity, the mother of New York Episcopal Churches, and Grace Church, where pews sold for as much as $1400 each. "The word of God," said Philip Hone acidly, "will cost the quality who worship in this splendid temple about three dollars every Sunday." There was the Unitarian Church of the Messiah (opposite Waverly Place at Broadway), the Congregational Church of the Puritans (at Union Square), and the First Presbyterian Church (on Fifth Avenue) where stylish Julia Gardner married President John Tyler in 1844.[19]

James Parton later said that the fashionable churches were designed "to produce a richly furnished, quietly adorned, dimly illuminated, ecclesiastical parlor, in which a few hundred ladies and gentlemen, attired in kindred taste, may sit perfectly at their ease, and see no object not in harmony with the scene around them." The poor were not deliberately excluded from partaking of this blend of God and Mammon—on the contrary, they were politely shown to seats—but the atmosphere made them uncomfortable: "Everything in and around the church seems to proclaim it a kind of exclusive ecclesiastical club, designed for the accommodation of persons of ten thousand a year, and upward."[20]

Even less likely were the rich to encounter anyone but themselves in the clubs which had become a conspicuous part of masculine social life by the 1840s. The grandest of them all was the Union Club, established by wealthy New Yorkers in 1836 as a place where they could socialize, read, and eat amid elegance and comfort for a $100 admission fee and $50 a year. Hardly less prestigeous and certainly more intellectual was the

Century Club formed in 1846 to promote both culture and good cheer among its members. "Its members," declared a student of club life in the mid-1850s, "represent almost every class, such as painters, journalists, brokers, auctioneers, engravers, dry-goods jobbers, judges, grocers, booksellers, . . . lawyers, and idlers. Smoking, drinking, and reading poetry are said to be favorite recreations." Despite its apparent openness, however, it was from the start essentially a gentleman's institution whose location on Clinton Place made it part of the elite society of the Fifteenth Ward. There were other organizations which supplied a more specialized social setting for the rich: The St. Nicholas Society, the New England Society, the New York Club (dissolved in the 1850s allegedly to get rid of some obnoxious members), the New York Yacht Club, and the Racket Club, described in 1846 by Philip Hone, one of its members, as having a "splendid new Club-House in Broadway."[21] The staid and the serious-minded had more purposeful meeting grounds. For those who were enchanted by the vanishing world of Knickerbocker New York, there was the New York Historical Society. For the art-loving, there were places as managers or trustees of the New York Gallery of Fine Arts, the National Academy, and the American Art Union. For those with musical interests, there was the Philharmonic Society. The benevolent found roles as directors, managers, and trustees of the Association for the Improvement of the Condition of the Poor, the Society for the Reformation of Juvenile Delinquents, the Public School Society, New York Hospital, medical dispensaries, and other organizations designed to improve the lot of the less fortunate. Scores of rich men divided up their time among a variety of organizations, although few could equal the record set by Philip Hone during his long career. Among his many duties, Hone was a trustee of the Clinton Hall Association (which maintained the Mercantile Library), a governor of New York Hospital, a trustee of the Bloomingdale Asylum, president of the Bank for Savings, vice president of the New York Historical Society, a trustee of Columbia College, and a vestryman at Trinity Church. Through such activities, the wealthy not only achieved individual satisfaction and influence but also added to the network of associations and relationships which gave them the coherence of a class.[22]

That network also extended into politics and government. From the rich came two Republican governors of New York State (John A. King and Edwin D. Morgan) and a variety of national and state legislators, but it was in their home city that their involvement was both most intense and, eventually, most frustrating. The merchant class and its business and professional allies experienced a steady erosion of their once strong place in the Common Council. Among the mayors before 1855, the role played by the rich was more definite. James Harper was a wealthy publisher; William F. Havemeyer was a rich sugar refiner; Andrew H. Mickle was a prosperous tobacco manufacturer and land owner; Caleb Woodhull was a wealthy lawyer whose brother was a partner in Woodhull and Minturn, commission and shipping merchants; Ambrose C. Kingsland was from a wealthy mercantile family.[23] The fact that Havemeyer and Mickle were Democrats while Woodhull and Kingsland were Whigs indicates that wealth was an influence within both of the major parties.

It was also true, however, that rich men played their most conspicuous role as candidates and as leaders of the Whig Party. Of some 600 wealthy men identified with party politics in 1845, perhaps as many as three-quarters were Whigs. The connection between wealth and Whiggery was especially pronounced in the Fifteenth Ward, which in the 1840s claimed the title of "Empire Ward" for its strong and persistent support of the party. From the Fifteenth came such prominent Whig officeholders as Mayor Mathew V. Brady, Henry E. Davies, and Erastus C. Benedict. When in 1849 Davies was given the Whig nomination for Corporation Counsel (he won his election), the *Evening Post* noted that there were complaints from Whigs elsewhere in the city stemming from "the extraordinary accumulation of official honors and emoluments in the Fifteenth Ward of this city. The United States District Attorney [J. Prescott Hall] is a resident of the Fifteenth Ward. The Fifteenth Ward furnishes the Naval Officer [Philip Hone]. We believe the Marshall of the Southern District of New York has his abode in the same favorite quarter of the aristocracy, but if he does not it is well known that General [President] Taylor went to the Fifteenth Ward for the Postmaster, Mr. Brady."[24]

The influence of the Empire Ward waned after 1850, as did the open influence wealth in the Whig Party and in politics generally. The politics of the 1850s became increasingly alien and uncomfortable, especially with the continued growth of the immigrant population and the rise of a new class of ambitious politicians, often of disreputable origins, who took control of the major party organizations. Yet the rich were not left defenseless. They could rely on the quiet workings of the law, for they were supported by some of the best legal minds in America. Henry E. Davies was a noted lawyer who repre-sented the Erie Railroad and other corporations; as a reward for his legal and political services he was appointed in 1855 to a seat on the State Supreme Court, where one of his rulings helped stem the banking collapse during the Panic of 1857. Ogden Hoffman, a talented criminal lawyer, and his brother Murray, a legal authority and judge of the Superior Court, were sons of the well-to-do Josiah Ogden Hoffman, also a judge on the Superior Court before his death in 1837. General Charles W. Sanford, who had studied law under Ogden Hoffman, was a successful railroad lawyer and, of equal importance to the rich, also was commander of the First Division of the state militia, which helped suppress the Astor Place riot and other major civil disorders.[25]

Although their pretensions to the status of an elite were weakened by the loss of political presence, the rich were discovering a consoling substitute in the form of a more subtle cultural and social power over the minds and imaginations of Americans. The growing dominance of the commercial me-tropolis raised hopes by 1850 that it might also make itself the cultural capital of the nation. What, asked *Harper's Monthly*, made London, Paris, Rome and Vienna each a metropolis? "It is the devotion of money to humane and permanent purposes— to the endowing of libraries, galleries, and institutions of every kind for the intellectual benefit of the population." Although the city was known far more for its successful pursuit of lucre than for its cultural tastes, the emergence of a wealthy class from the grubby pit of money-making raised the hope that at least some New Yorkers would use their money and their leisure for beautiful and humane causes. Through their patronage, they would draw to New York the best minds and talents in America and so make the city a home for literature, music, painting, and architecture. They would embellish their own lives and the life of their city; they would found institutions of culture open to all. And so would they make New York the metropolis which would radiate the light that would transform America—crude, boorish, uncivilized America so often mocked and condemned by Europeans—into a society of grace and beauty. The urban rich thus would find for themselves a permanent and justified role in democratic society as the heralds of cultural progress and founders of a high civilization.[26]

This hope was well suited to the efforts of the wealthy to find a secure place in their supposedly classless society. Rich men were not likely to find comfort in Dix's hope that their wealth would be dissipated among their descendents. What they required was some justification for permanent wealth which would distinguish it from an un-American, European-style aristocracy. How could permanent wealth be reconciled to democratic ideals? The broad answer was that the rich would serve the needs of the larger society by promoting the uplift of the mass of people, a process which would not only advance the cause of civilization but also bridge the gap which was opening between the wealthy and the rest of Americans.[27]

By the 1850s, indeed, there was reason to hope that the accumulation of urban wealth was making New York a cultural metropolis both in the depth of its commitment to beauty and the extent of its influence. There were many signs. The influence of Andrew Jackson Downing and of landscape architecture generally had borne fruit in the form of Central Park and the rising interest in the romantic suburb. The money, the style, and the needs of the rebuilding city had attracted a legion of architects who seemed capable of teaching the rich how to crystalize taste in marble and brownstone. Men such as Alexander Jackson Davis, James Renwick, Minard Lafever and Richard Upjohn had a broad influence through their designs for churches, public buildings, and homes, an influence further broadened when in 1857 the New York architects formed the American Institute of Architects both to improve professional standards and spread good taste throughout America.[28]

Boston continued to challenge New York as the literary capital of the nation, but there was little doubt that the metropolis was the art center. The annual spring exhibit of the National Academy had become for American painters the great event, the place to exhibit their works and to gain national recognition.[29] The National Academy, with its strong professional orientation, was overshadowed in the late 1840s and early 1850s, by the more popular American Art-Union. Through its *Bulletin*, the nation's first art magazine, and its distribution of original works and of reproductions, the Union created a mass market for American art, while its gallery on Broadway, open to the public without charge, set a precedent for later municipal art museums. Because it distributed art works by lot, it ran afoul of the state's anti-lottery laws and was abruptly dissolved in the mid-1850s, but it had served to strengthen the city's place as the unchallenged capital of American art. New York, with its private galleries and its wealthy art buyers such as Marshall O. Roberts and Alexander T. Stewart, had become the great artistic marketplace.[30]

The 1850s also sealed New York's supremacy as the center of musical culture. The previous decade had brought a rapid increase in the number of concerts by foreign performers, the Philharmonic Society, or by other organizations formed from the estimated 2000 musicians in the city. When the popular Norwegian violinist, Ole Bull, completed his performances in 1845, the *Tribune* expressed the hope, characteristic of the times, that music would serve "to educate the heart and mind of all men by inspiring the purer and gentler emotions, by substituting a sense of spiritual beauty in place of the lust of eye and the pride of life."[31] The influence and place of music in the metropolis, however, was more complex than this simple moralism would suggest. Although the purest of the arts flourished in the 1850s, stimulated by the growing presence of musical-minded Germans, the most noteworthy talisman of culture for the rich was that most exclusive and expensive form of musical drama, opera.

The opening of the Astor Place Opera House in 1847 inspired hope that opera, especially in its sophisticated Italian form, would receive the support of the wealthy both for its musical and social virtues. After attending a performance of *Lucrezia Borgia* at the new theater (located a few blocks from his home), Philip Hone expressed the hope that there "our young men may be initiated into the habits and forms of elegant social intercourse."[32] The experiment failed. Although the Opera House, according to the sneers of unsympathetic observers, saved the fashionable the trouble of walking and driving about to show themselves, the rich did not unite in support of the venture and it soon sank under the weight of its expensive productions. "Just think," declared a critic, "of the astounding fact that the curtain rises every night to the tune of over $300 expenses. Why this would sink the establishment if they had ten times the talent and double the audience." After five painful years of effort, disrupted by the great Astor Place Riot of 1849, the Opera House closed in 1852.[33]

Grand Opera (the term was used in the 1850s), however, was too precious to abandon, and in 1853 Moses H. Grinnell, Francis B. Cutting, and other wealthy men formed a corporation to build the Academy of Music at 14th Street and Irving Place. Even more than its predecessor, the Academy expressed the metropolitan ambitions of rich New Yorkers; not only was it the largest opera hall in the world (with 4000 seats) but it was also intended to be an educational institution, which would cultivate a popular taste for music. Early in 1855, after a first and less than successful year, its manager, Ole Bull, offered a $1000 prize for "the best Original Grand Opera by an American Composer, and upon a strictly American theme." No great American work was written nor did the opera achieve general popularity, though at one point the management cut the price of general admission to 25 cents. The Academy of

Music did survive, however, for the next thirty years as the grand institution of fashionable New York, until it was over-shadowed by the even richer and eventually more fashionable Metropolitan Opera.[34]

Music, Art, Literature—the growth of a wealthy, leisured class promised the birth of a metropolitan culture which would embrace every phase of the creative spirt. The travel of rich, young New Yorkers in Europe stimulated the ambition to make New York another London or Paris where beauty in its deepest sense would become the essence of society. In the early 1850s, William Henry Fry, perhaps American's first serious composer, observed in Paris how some American women were so impressed by Parisian culture that "they could not bear the mention of the Park, nor Washington Square," and asked: "Why do not artists sit on the Council? They can instruct politicians, check the career of ugliness, interrupt the dullness of routine, give a new birth, life and glory to Society." Artists did not sit on the Common Council, but there were signs that they had at least gained entrance into the councils of wealth. The Century Club offered a place where creators in all branches of culture could meet on equal terms with the rich. Later, John Durand, the son of a famous painter, was to call the Century a "local, moral institution" which, because of its capacity to assimilate the cultural diversity of the great metropolis, was also more national than any other association in America.[35]

The Century Club was one among many spots engraved on the cultural map of Uptown. By the mid-1850s, the eastern fringes of the Fifteenth Ward around Astor Place had become the "Athenian quarter" of the city. There were located New York's great libraries: The Astor Library and, in the old Astor Place Opera building, the Mercantile Library; nearby was the Society Library and the New York Historical Society. Nearby, too, were the Century Club, the National Academy of Design, and the Academy of Music.[36] Wealth and culture combined—thus was raised the prospect of a metropolitan culture which would call the talents of the nation to it and fuse them into a gleaming model of beauty and grace that would raise the tastes and so improve the collective life of all of America. It was a nice dream, but the realities of the metropolitan marketplace indicated that the glitter of the new wealth was not necessarily cultural gold.

Undoubtedly, wealth had begun to establish those great engines of culture which in the next century were to influence the tastes and thinking of Americans. Yet this development left unanswered the question as to what those engines should communicate. Was it to be a national culture which involved the collective experience of Americans, or was it to be a cosmopolitan culture derived essentially from Europe? Before 1850 especially, there were signs that New York was participating in the creation of a culture to which most Americans could relate. The popularity of landscape painting and landscape architecture, though both owed much to English inspiration, awakened in men like Downing the hope that the principles of taste guiding the development of society would be rooted in the American experience and environment. There were other hopeful signs—in the publication, for instance, of those distinctly different but classic expressions of the American spirit, Melville's *Moby Dick* (1851) and the first edition of Whitman's *Leaves of Grass* (1855).[37]

It was already evident by the 1850s, however, that the wealth of New York had chosen a different cultural destiny. Although the elements of national culture would survive, they were not to come to fruition in the metropolis. As the nation's great import center, New York was the natural entrance for European tastes, ideas, and fashions which gave it an increasingly cosmopolitan character. That character, however, would not have become the predominant influence on culture without the support of the rich. Even while wealth continued to patronize native artists and writers, at mid-century there was a significant increase in the tendency of the wealthy to identify their cultural and social aspirations with Europe. This was not new, for the social elite had long showed a leaning toward English ways and English literature, but the increased leisure and freedom of travel that came with the accumulation of wealth stimulated an appetite for continental culture. Having discovered the glories of Rome and Paris, the rich were less inclined to settle for the traditional and the familiar. The wealthy travelers returned home with new tastes for continental fashions, paintings, music, and architecture—and a new, if muddled, notion of what was beautiful.[38]

Any appreciation of beauty was better than no appreciation at all. For years, cultured New Yorkers had urged the need for an infusion of taste and imagination into mundane America. An indigenous American culture could not be built out of a void, but would depend heavily on the cultural inheritance from Europe. The essential question, however, was whether the rich in fact possessed any appreciation of European culture that could be translated into an influence for the aesthetic and moral improvement of American society. The question of an American culture—a Europeanized American culture—was overshadowed by the evident tendency of wealth to be concerned far less with encouraging a culture that would link them with the mass of Americans than with appropriating the cultural artifacts and tastes of Europe for use in a private world separated from the rest of society.

In the 1840s, social observers, with a mixture of awe, amusement, and concern, had begun to fix their attention on a comparatively small number of wealthy men and women who attempted to set the fashions and establish the tone of their society. At the very beginning of the decade, those observers were given a glimpse into the future when Henry Brevoort and his wife excited the interest and envy of the social world by giving a fancy costume ball at their new mansion on lower Fifth Avenue. There, some 500 people vied with each other to appear in the most lavish and spectacular dress. Philip Hone, who attended dressed as "Cardinal Wolsely [sic], in a great robe of scarlet merino," noted that the affair was the talk of the town "from the liberal minded gentleman who could discover no crime in an innocent and refined amusement of this kind" to the sneering New York *Herald*, one of whose reporters came to the ball dressed as a knight in armor. The French-educated Sam Ward praised "Mme. Brevoort" for introducing New York to a "European fete." Others had the bad manners to note that the glittering and expensive affair was held during a period of mounting poverty, but sensitivity to social problems was not a conspicuous trait among the fashion-loving rich.[39]

The wealthy themselves, especially men of the older generation, were not always comfortable in the strange new world which the fashion-makers were creating. As late as 1855, the *Tribune* could gleefully report that, when the "foreign custom" of announcing the names of entering guests was attempted at one grand ball, at least half-a-dozen times "the startled nominee, instead of hurrying toward the courteous and expectant hostess, incontinently turned upon his heels and fled." Fancy balls, however, became an established weapon in the rivalry among the fashionable rich to impress each other and to impress the larger society. In the Fifteenth Ward, the Schermerhorns gave one grand ball where the guests appeared dressed in the costumes of the period of Louis XV. "It was intended to be the greatest *affaire de luxe* New Yorkers had ever seen," wrote Ward McAllister later. "The lace and diamonds astonished society."[40]

What was apparent, at least, was that the rich were prepared to spend lavishly in order to embellish their lives, a boon for A. T. Stewart (whose department store offered cashmere shawls priced at $2000) and the fashionable jeweler, Charles L. Tiffany. "In happy America," said one observer, "every man and every woman is allowed to make money and grow rich and where's the use of wealth, if one can't spend it as he likes?" Why, indeed, not spend and spend heavily on jewels and clothes and furniture and works of art, if they were the appropriate tokens in the increasingly expensive game of fashion? In the mid-1840s, Lydia Maria Child reported that it was not unusual for the rich to spend $10,000 for one roomful of furniture as part of their efforts to achieve a "European style of living." A decade later, the *Tribune* reported that one New Yorker "proposes to adorn his very costly house with twenty pictures, at a thousand dollars each, to be painted by the first[-rate] Italian artists"—even though there were no first-rate Italian artists—and went on to complain that a vulgar cultural consumerism led some of the rich to "order so many pictures [from] their upholsterer or looking-glass maker—just as they would order home their marketing from the huckster."[41]

Many Americans were content to view the emergence of fashionable life, with all of its flaws, in a more favorable light. For its defenders, fashion was a civilizing discipline that encouraged refinement, developed taste, and restrained the most vulgar tendencies of new wealth. The doings of the "Upper Ten," as Nathaniel Parker Willis had tagged the trendsetters in the 1840s, was of as much interest to an awed public as those of the later fabled, fabulous, and fatuous Four Hundred. For some, the conspicuous and cosmopolitan style of the Upper Ten was a sign that New York had arrived as a metropolis. Europeans had long sneered at Americans for their provincialism and for their utilitarian disregard for the finer things of life. Now, the metropolis would show Europe that America, too, could produce a class which had raised itself about the vulgar necessities of life. How pleasing it was to discover that Thackeray had noticed the presence of the New York rich on the Continent in one of his short stories:

> They seem as rich as the Milor of old days; they crowd in European capitals; they have elbowed out the people of the old country from many hotels which we used to frequent; they adopt the French fashion of dressing rather than ours; and they grow handsomer beards than English beards. . . . The ladies seem to be as well-dressed as Parisians and as handsome. . . . They drive the finest carriages, they keep the grandest houses, they frequent the grandest company—and in a word, the Broadway swell had taken his station and asserted his dignity among the grandees of Europe.[42]

Certainly, New Yorkers could share the pride taken by the Reverend Charles E. Lester in Taylor's International Hotel, a "European Palace" with its restaurant designed to provide every luxury for fashionable women: "At all hours during the day superb equipages are seen before TAYLOR's door, breaking the monotony of a long day with a half-hour lounge for a delicate lunch. . . . TAYLOR has erected a temple of luxury worthy of its voteries. . . . water leaps from the great Fountain in the center of the Palace, and from the lofty ceilings the magic of light and shades of fresco flash their illusions of beauty." When in the 1850s Charles Astor Bristed critically portrayed the fashionable in *His Upper Ten Thousand*, originally published as a series of sketches in *Frazer's Magazine*, he was mindful of its effect in convincing Englishmen that America, far from being a land of healthy barbarians, had its own class of sophisticates like those of Europe, complete with the weaknesses of sophisticates.[43]

These European leanings, however, were also a source of much anxiety. In 1859, Amory Mayo, an Albany minister, attempted to sum up the meaning of the two previous decades of cultural development:

> In many wealthy and cultivated circles of our cities no one can mistake a sincere prejudice in favor of those ideas of man and society which are the soul of old world despotism. This idea of man proceeds logically to the European idea of refinement as associated with a permanent nobility of wealth, rank, or cultivation, and art as the finest luxury of an aristocracy rather than the idealization of a people's existence. This belief appears in the wholesale imitation of foreign society, amusements, and arts which . . . aims at building a little Europe in the cities of New York.[44]

It was easy to dismiss this and similar views as the alarms of provincials who did not understand the new metropolitan culture, but they were part of a deeper concern over the future of wealth in American society. The two decades before the Civil War brought concentrations of riches which could not readily be harmonized with the essential American doctrine of equality. The chief concern lay not with the existence of that wealth but with its relationship to the larger society. The rich could be justified, if they contributed to the general advancement of Americans. They might act as natural aristocrats of culture who promoted the growth of beauty and conveniences

[225]

which would benefit all Americans. They might also use their wealth to hasten the expansion of the economy and so multiply the opportunities available for all.

By their concern for aristocratic display, however, the rich threatened not only to divert the power of their wealth from the cause of progress but also to misdirect the energies and pervert the character of the people by the force of example. In a free and open society, without established classes and ranks, strivings for exclusiveness brought that conspicuous display of wealth which Edwin Chapin, minister and reformer, referred to as "a vulgar spirit of social rivalry blossoming in lace, brocade, gilding, and fresco." Wealth, in the hands of the fashionable, threatened to fortify those very weaknesses in the American social character which men like Downing hoped it would restrain. Conspicuous consumption, especially in the cause of exclusiveness, was a communicable disease, an incitement to the restless and relentless ambition which had kept Americans from settling down to perfect themselves and their society.[45]

Certainly, the rapid growth of conspicuous consumption and of an equally conspicuous social separation in the metropolis disturbed even the wealthy. One result was the beginnings of a long-term debate over the use of the single most important source of leisured wealth, urban land, an issue which forced itself on two of New York's most prestigious and influential institutions, Columbia College and the Episcopal Church. Both owned many lots which increased rapidly in value with the expansion of the city, and both were central institutions of fashionable society. It was therefore natural that they should become focal points for criticism and concern. One critic was Samuel B. Ruggles, the far-sighted land developer, friend of John Jacob Astor, Columbia trustee and staunch Episcopalian, who warned: "The very exuberance of our commercial property, our rank and rapid growth in wealth and luxury are scattering far and wide, the seeds of a deadly disease. The universal spirit of traffic, with its maddening love of gain and its insolent contempt for any intellectual greatness, artistic excellence, or moral worth, that does not yield a pecuniary return, are degrading and demoralizing the whole mass. . . . The virtue of our public men and public bodies is sinking."[46]

Ruggles publicly attacked Columbia in 1854 for its failure to work against this trend. The college was profiting from the increased value of its lands, the result not of its own efforts but of the labors of the community. It had, therefore, a responsibility to use its growing wealth wisely for the good of the community, which had the right to ask "why the College, surrounded by more than fifty thousand youths, of age suitable for college studies . . . teaches but one hundred and forty?" He urged that the college transform itself from a mediocre place for the sons of a few gentlemen into a major urban university which would train leaders to meet the problems of an increasingly unstable and divided society:

> No thoughtful man can look at the present elements of our society, without forebodings for the future. The utter feebleness of the sons of the rich, and their total inability to combat the misdirected education, the crude theories, that make perilous the growing power of the needy classes, become more and more apparent, with each succeeding generation. If our seats of learning will awake to their responsibilities and their work, they may greatly mitigate . . . these evils. If they can do no more, they may at least transmute the holders of wealth, bred only for ostentation or self-indulgence, into liberal and intelligent leaders, in every good and generous effort for the common welfare. Benevolence bids us teach the poor—but it will be a charity indeed to educate the rich.[47]

Ruggles carried his crusade to the public, with the support of George Templeton Strong (his son-in-law), Moses H. Grinnell, and the president of the college, Charles King. It was the opening gun in what was to be a long battle to convert the increasing wealth not simply of Columbia but of the rich in general into an effective and responsible influence on the new society. When King became president in 1849, he had raised the hope that he might provide enlightened, business-like leadership that would open the college to the larger world; and he did initiate a few of the many changes which eventually would convert the institution into a great university. But he proved to be a weak leader who barely budged the conservative majority of Columbia trustees. The biggest change under his administration came in 1857 when the college completed its move uptown from Park Place to 49th Street, a step which kept it close to the northward moving rich and committed its resources to an expensive building program. A new day was coming, but slowly: by 1857, the College had increased its enrollment from 140 to 154.[48]

The Columbia controversy was largely a spillover from a conflict which even earlier had forced its way into the sanctuaries of its distinguished sister institution, the Episcopal Church. In the 1840s, that church encountered the problem, which confronted Christianity generally, of adjusting itself to a changing urban society. The uptown movement forced it to invest heavily in new churches suited to the tastes of the rich, putting a great strain on its finances. At the same time, the uptown movement and the construction of new fashionable churches underscored and intensified the increasing separation of the rich and the poor, a trend troubling to both Christian and democratic sensibilities. In 1846, Rev. Stephen Olin, President of Wesleyan University, warned that an "anti-Christian" separation of classes was occurring throughout urban America: "Rich men, instead of associating themselves with their more humble fellow Christians, where their money as well as their influence and counsels are so much needed, usually combine to erect magnificent churches in which sittings are too expensive for any but people of fortune."[49]

Olin was condemning the failure of urban Protestantism generally, but the Episcopal Church, with its prominence, wealth, and strong institutional character, was a natural focus for criticism and concern. Moreover, its failings were publicized by a bitter conflict among the Episcopalians themselves over the nature and mission of their church. Of all religious entities in the United States, the Episcopal Diocese of New York, which embraced both the city and the eastern part of the state, seemed to have the strongest resources to meet the problems of the new urban age. The New York Diocese included both a high percentage of wealthy members and an extensive endowment in city lands. The lands, however, belonged not to the Diocese but to its most powerful parish church—great and proud Trinity. The Trinity estate, derived from a colonial grant, fanned out along lower Broadway from the Battery north to 14th Street in a vast array of lots on Greenwich, Varick, Hudson, Barrow, Hammersley, Chambers, and some 25 other streets in the most densely built-up areas of the city. Estimates as to their value varied wildly from Trinity's overly modest estimate of approximately $1.4 million to the equally overly inflated $15 million or more imagined by some critics. The $6 million figure furnished in 1855 by the agent of the Astor family for a state investigating committee was probably conservative, but in line with other property estimates of the times. Indisputably, Trinity possessed an immense urban estate which would grow rapidly in value.[50]

By its own standards, Trinity had been generous with its wealth, having provided financial assistance not only to churches in the city and upstate but also to the City Missionary Society which, before its termination in 1847, had ministered to the needs of the Episcopalian poor. It had, however, been even more generous to a few rich New Yorkers, to the detriment of its assistance program. As much of Trinity land was under long-term lease, revenues from rents, which had been set years before, were very low in comparison with the value of the land. This was a boon to Trinity leaseholders, especially to the Astors who paid $269 a year for some 350 lots on a lease that would not expire until 1866.[51] While its wealthy lessees prospered from its land, Trinity itself ran into financial difficulties in meeting its religious obligations. Having acquired a large debt to finance the construction of its new cathedral on Broadway, the Trinity vestry board, which controlled its properties, soon decided to make an almost equally heavy investment in Trinity Chapel on 25th Street to meet the needs of those parishioners who had moved uptown. Retrenchment seemed in order. Beginning in the mid-1840s, Trinity became more cautious with its religious gifts at a time when Episcopalian missionary efforts in the lower city were near collapse. The result was

WEALTH

quick and unfortunate: the demise of the Missionary Society and, within the space of a few years, the closing of three churches which had ministered especially to the poor, one of which, Zion Church at Five Points, was sold to the rival "Romanists." For a business corporation, retrenchment to assure payment of a debt was sound practice, but it left the church open to the charge that it had sacrificed the souls of the poor to the interests of the rich.[52] In 1846, a group of Episcopalians headed by Robert B. Minturn and Luther Bradish challenged Trinity's moral and legal right to its lands. Their challenge brought more than a decade of controversy in which Trinity's title to its land was challenged in the courts, investigated in the legislature, and debated in the press. Again and again, that title was upheld, although less out of sympathy for Trinity than out of a desire to defend existing property rights. The great wealth held by such religious corporations as Trinity was undemocratic and unchristian, said one judge, but to deny their legal right to ownership might "lead to scenes of fraud, corruption, foul injustice, and legal rapine, far worse in their consequences upon the peace, good order, and happiness of society than external war or domestic insurrection." The rights of property were saved, but not before the public was treated to the spectacle of a high-toned brawl over the use and abuse of wealth.[53]

Although the defenders of Trinity were partly right in charging that some of the challengers were influenced by no higher motive than to get a share of its property for themselves, men such as Minturn and Bradish were genuinely concerned over the failure of the church to respond to the challenge of the city. They believed that Trinity had failed to use its mounting wealth "to sustain the feeble, and to supply the destitute," and so not only had ignored its Christian duty but, in doing that, also threatened to isolate the Episcopal Church from the larger society.[54] Their concerns were amplified by William Augustus Muhlenberg, the rector of the Church of the Holy Communion and one of the most visionary ministers of his age.

Muhlenberg dreamed of a great Evangelical Catholic Church

which would unite all Protestants, rich and poor, into one Evangelical Community able to resist the physical, moral, and spiritual threat of the city, especially the twin perils of Romanism and secularism.[55] Toward that end, he succeeded in establishing St. Luke's Hospital, intended especially for the poor, in a tenement near his church in 1853. Five years later, with the support of Minturn and Murray Hoffman (both members of his congregation) and other wealthy Episcopalians, he was able to proclaim the opening of a new $200,000 hospital at 54th Street and Fifth Avenue.[56] Although Trinity had begrudgingly contributed the land for St. Luke's, it did little else to aid Muhlenberg's dream of an Evangelical Catholic Church which would save the bodies and the souls of the poor. In 1855, he complained that Trinity, while it had spent lavishly for the rich, had done virtually nothing to maintain Episcopal churches or an Episcopalian influence in the poor and crowded sections of the city.[57]

The debate stimulated much soul-searching among Episcopalians. In an effort to change its image and its ways, Trinity began to develop a master plan to make itself a positive influence on the poor inhabitants of the lower city: ministerial visits, sunday schools and industrial schools for their children, a relief bureau to meet their material wants, and free pews to meet their spiritual needs. To improve its financial position, in 1856 it sold St. John's Park, which it owned in connection with St. John's Chapel, for use as a railroad freight depot. In doing so, it gave up one of the few bits of park space in the lower city to expanding business, but the $400,000 which it received relaxed the constraints of its debts.[58]

Trinity's reawakened interest in missionary work was part of a more general awakening within the Episcopal Church which led to the revival of the Missionary Society in the 1860s. In 1856, William A. McVickar, who had been sent by the Church to investigate missionary activities in English cities, proposed that the Society be reestablished with its own bishop for the poor as part of a comprehensive effort which would include the establishment of church lodging-houses for the hopeless poor, houses of mercy to redeem the "fallen women of the town," and work with the inmates of charitable and penal institutions. Missionary work of this sort was essential, warned McVickar: "Our character, our existence as a church, seems wrapt up in it, and the course of action must set its seal upon us as a church that either cares for or neglects the poor."⁵⁹

Such concerns would evoke a wide variety of missionary and reform efforts in the next century, but they also marked the disappointment of Muhlenberg's hopes for a church which would unite rich and poor within one religious community. After the Civil War, James Parton would conclude his critical examination of the fashionable churches by suggesting that "the old conception of a Christian church, as the one place where all sorts and conditions of men came together to dwell upon considerations interesting to all equally, is not adapted to modern society. . . . It may be, that never again . . . will ignorant and learned, master and servant, rich and poor, feel themselves at home in the same church,"⁶⁰ Bridget, the maid, and Clarissa, her mistress, required different churches to meet their different needs—but suppose that the Bridgets of New York did not go to church at all?

The prospect that the poor would slip from under both the protection and constraints of religion posed a disturbing challenge to wealth. If the rich failed to use their power to bring Christianity to the poor, would they not only fail in their responsibilities but create conditions which would erode the foundations of their wealth? In 1856, William Jay, a prominent Episcopalian and jurist, noted this possibility when he attempted to persuade Trinity to endow at least 20 free churches for the poor: "Christianity is the only reformatory power, and the only safe basis of philanthropic action. Security for life and property can be attained only by the strong arm of authority or through the moral sense of the community."⁶¹

Some of the rich might occupy themselves with the fashionable news from Newport and Paris, but other New Yorkers, rich and not so rich, had cause to wonder whether society was not spinning out of control, whether the growing masses of the poor did not threaten their security and their property. Certainly, those who took the trouble to sample the opinion of

WEALTH

the city could not have failed to notice in the 1840s that the debate over the Trinity lands was accompanied by a more radical challenge to landed wealth raised by a small band of vociferous critics of the rich. The most vociferous of all was the politically ambitious, self-styled friend of the poor, Mike Walsh. Walsh, an Irish Protestant of uncertain background, blasted the rich in his aptly-named newspaper, the *Subterranean*, giving particular attention to his two pet evils, Trinity and John Jacob Astor. In 1845, he declared that Trinity's property, "enough to make every person in the United States comfortable and happy," should be confiscated for public use, and then followed this up by urging the city to take over St. John's Park on the grounds that it was an exclusive and privileged preserve from which the laboring class was excluded. Walsh demonstrated his contempt for Trinity's exclusiveness by climbing over the park's fence and walking on the forbidden ground.[62]

This contempt he extended to anyone who preached the cant that all was right with American society. In fact, society was going terribly wrong, because Americans had permitted capital to exploit labor: "Demagogues tell you that you are freemen. They lie; you are slaves. . . . No working man is free to obtain one-fourth of the proceeds of his own labor; every thing he buys, every step he turns, he is robbed indirectly by some worthless wealthy drone," most particularly by landlords who took a high and seemingly perpetual percentage of the workingman's earnings. As an example of this "legalized system of plunder," Walsh singled out Astor:

That you may form some conception of this outrageous and gigantic mode of robbery, I will just state that it would take thirty-five hundred men, working twenty years . . . three hundred days in each year, without being sick or out of employment an hour during the whole time, and getting a dollar a day without spending a cent, but living with their families on air like chamelions [sic], sleeping in the parks and going naked: Yes! 3,500 men working that length of time, living in that manner and receiving that much wages, it would take to *earn* what Mr. John Jacob Astor has *saved* from what the world calls "his industry."[63]

WEALTH

As Walsh's talents were for abuse rather than for thoughtful social criticism, he was often viewed as a libelous clown, a species of public entertainment who was not to be taken seriously. Yet he was elected in 1846 to the first of three terms as a state assemblyman from the Fourteenth Ward, immediately to the south of the wealthy Fifteenth.[64] Moreover, his attitude toward wealth was echoed in some of the public reaction to John Jacob Astor's death in 1848. The usual testimonials to the greatness of the deceased were, in Astor's case, accompanied by a few sour notes of open criticism. His chief public bequest of $400,000 to establish the Astor Library won praise, but it also raised awareness that the great bulk of his fortune went to his own family, leading the New York *Herald* to warn that the dead man had established the basis for a family dynasty. One-half of the Astor estate, said the *Herald*, actually belonged to the people of New York, for it was their labor which had given the Astor lands their value. Greeley's *Tribune*, after criticizing some of Astor's sharp dealings, noted that some radical reformers hoped to prevent speculative dealings in land by limiting the amount of land a person could own. Although the reformers did not propose the confiscation of the Astor estate, the did favor another way to harness more of that wealth for the public good: a direct national tax on his wealth in the belief that it was unjust and unwise for government, said Greeley, "to protect Mr. Astor's houses, lands, ships, stocks, etc., and yet exact no direct taxes from him according to his income."[65] This proposal won no cheers from conservatives. These were radical ideas, especially disturbing for a time which was attempting to find a place for the new concentrations of wealth in a democratic society. Although the overwhelming majority of respectable and influential men spurned such thoughts in favor of protecting property rights, who could be sure what the silent masses of the poor, the "subterraneans," were thinking? This was no idle question. Europe in 1848 was rocked by explosions of social radicalism far different from the political revolutions Americans had been accustomed to applaud. America had no such upheavals, no Communist Manifestos, but in 1849 New York was shocked by a major riot which had some disturbing, if ill-defined, overtones of class hostility to the rich.

The Astor Place Riot was a conflict of cultural as well as social styles involving a popular urban culture whose animus counterpointed that of the elite. While the Upper Ten were establishing the great cultural institution of Broadway and of the Fifteenth Ward for themselves, the Lower Hundred Thousand were flocking to their own institutions, especially on the nearby Bowery, which with its taverns, oyster saloons, and minstrel shows had become a popular haunt as well as workplace for the inhabitants of the lower wards. By the late 1840s, this unfashionable New York had crept north uncomfortably close to the Fifteenth Ward, especially in the form of Vauxhall Gardens, later described by the *Tribune* as a "cheap rendezvous for infamy . . . with its many-colored lamps—its bad music and worce [*sic*] ice-cream—its clowns, sawdust, serenauts, ballet-dancers, and other attractions too numerous to mention."[66] The style of the opera house and the style of Vauxhall Gardens were those of two increasingly distinct social worlds. Generally, those two worlds remained apart, but in 1849 they collided in the one cultural institution which embraced them both, the theater.

The trouble developed out of the notorious feud that had broken out between the noted English tragedian, William Macready, and the popular American actor, Edwin Forrest. Forrest's style of acting served better to please the plain people than the sophisticates. An ardent democrat and supporter of a national drama, he brought more enthusiasm and energy than finesse to his performances. "His gentlemen," said one New York critic, "are not such as Shakespeare drew; they are great roaring boys that cry like fat babies, and puff and blow like sledge men."[67] That style had little appeal to the fashionable ones who wished to rise above the crudities of American life. Nor did it please English audiences, as Forrest discovered when he was hissed and booed during a theatrical tour of England in 1845–46. Enraged by his English experience, Forrest blamed Macready for inciting the opposition and resolved to give the English actor a similar reception when

Macready toured the United States in 1848–49. Despite the latter's unwillingness to engage in a public quarrel, the affair excited a crescendo of popular interests and feelings which peaked in May 1849 when Macready closed his American tour by playing Macbeth at the fashionable Astor Place Opera House. Downtown, at the less fashionable Broadway Theatre, Forrest was also scheduled to play Macbeth. The stage was set for more than the Battle of Birnam Wood.[68]

The combination of Macready and the Opera House was an invitation for trouble. The Astor Place Opera was a focus of fashionable culture, a characteristic given further emphasis in February when the fashionable gathered there for a fancy ball. Even the presence of fashion had not wholly suppressed the tendency to disorder found in the downtown theaters. In November 1848, the Astor audience was given a double treat when during a performance of the opera *Norma*, the lead tenor, Benedetti, said some nasty words to the theater manager who, according to a *Tribune* reporter, "immediately laid down opera glass and hat, and planted a right-hander in the face of the handsome tenor. Benedetti then drew his sword and made a pass at the impressario, when they were separated and the performance went on." The news of the affair provoked a succeeding audience to twin storms of hoots and cheers when Benedetti appeared on the stage to sing in the same opera. This spectacle pleased George Templeton Strong who, in his diary, expressed hope for more of the same: "The present state of things gives a pleasing animation to an evening at the opera and greatly promotes the pecuniary health of the concern."[69] In May 1849 Strong had second thoughts about the desirability of "animation" at the opera house.

If a fashionable audience could hoot and hiss at an Italian tenor, then why could a less fashionable audience not hoot and hiss at an English actor? Unfortunately for Macready, the feud with Forrest became the focus of a controversy over culture in New York. Although the fashionable had begun to develop a taste for continental painting, architecture, and music, they also held firm to their traditional preference for English plays and English actors, which provoked the unprovable charge that theater managers were conspiring against American plays and actors. Provable or not, the charges fed the deep anglo-phobia of many New Yorkers. Most of the anglophobes were Irish, but they were joined by some natives who favored an exclusively American culture.[70]

The sleaziest member of this last group was Edward Z. C. Judson, better known as "Ned Buntline," a rabblerousing writer who mixed attacks on the British with sensational stories of murders and love affairs in his yellow journal, *Ned Buntline's Own.* In 1848, Buntline had attempted to organize an American movement against English immigrants and English influence. When he learned that Macready would soon appear at Astor Place, he issued a call for all good Americans to give the actor the same treatment Americans had given the British at Lexington. When on May 7 Macready appeared on the Astor stage, Buntline's militiamen supplemented the traditional hisses and boos with a shower of rotten eggs, potatoes, pennies, and chairs which finally forced this foreign Macbeth to retreat to his dressing room.[71]

The affair might have ended at this point, if Macready had given up and returned to England, as he was tempted to do; but he was persuaded to continue by such prominent New Yorkers' as Edward Sanford, Ogden Hoffman, Samuel B. Ruggles, Washington Irving, and Moses H. Grinnell, who issued a public letter in his support. The letter, which promised protection for him at the Astor, provoked a countermanifesto from the friends of Forrest and the enemies of English influence:

WORKINGMEN
SHALL
AMERICANS OR ENGLISH RULE
IN THIS CITY?

The crew of the English steamer has threatened all Americans who shall dare to express their opinion this night at the English Aristocratic Opera House!!

We advocate no violence, but a free expression of opinion to all public men!

WORKINGMEN! FREEMEN!!
STAND BY YOUR
LAWFUL RIGHTS.[72]

The rival manifestoes aroused great public interest in the confrontation. When Macready resumed on the night of May 10, the area around Astor Place was packed with people who had poured up Broadway and the Bowery. Protecting the Opera House were some 200 policemen supported by about 300 militiamen stationed nearby. Inside, the police were able to clear out the noisiest troublemakers, but their success only inflamed the crowd outside, some of whom began throwing bricks and paving stones. Near the end of the play, a mob tried to force its way into the theater, only to be turned back by the police. Macready's success in completing his performance further enraged the crowd which turned its anger against the police and the militia drawn up around the building. The Sheriff ordered the jeering crowd to disperse, but in the noise and darkness—most of the street lights in the area had been knocked out—apparently few people heard the order. The militia then fired a volley into the air, which only brought more hoots, jeers, and stones. Finally, the militiamen, some 40 to 50 of whom had been injured in the bombardment, on orders fired into the crowd, dispersing it in panic down the Bowery and Broadway and into neighboring side-streets. Twenty-two people died, including an old man waiting for a horsecar on the Bowery and an eight-year old boy.[73]

Later that night speakers in front of Vauxhall Gardens called for revenge. The next day a mass meeting in City Hall Park heard Mike Walsh condemn city authorities for murdering innocent citizens, and Isaiah Rynders, a political rabblerouser, give an inflammatory speech before urging his listeners *not* to burn down the Opera House or the home of the Mayor, Caleb Woodhull.[74] The same day threats were also made against the signers of the letter of support for Macready, some of whose homes were clustered at Union Square a few blocks north of Astor Place. In the evening, a vengeful mob did move uptown but were blocked south of the Opera House by a strong police and militia force supported by a detachment of regular infantry and by a thousand special constables appointed for that purpose. After throwing a few more paving stones, the mob retreated. The whole affair ended with the arrest of over 100 persons, including Ned Buntline, who was later sentenced to a year in the penitentiary for inciting the riot. After charging that both judge and jury in his trial had been bribed by "the millionaires of this city," Buntline went to jail. Later in life he would give violence a more acceptable form as one of the first authors of western novels.[75]

"The fact has been established," wrote Philip Hone on May 12, "that law and order can be maintained under a Republican form of government." Violence had been conquered—or had it? Not until 1857 did New York experience a riot as terrifying as that at Astor Place; yet the intervening years brought an ominous swelling of violence which could not be ignored. Certainly, there was reason to wonder whether the city had not developed an underlying culture of violence which threatened both life and property. Some New Yorkers attributed the trouble to radical economic defects in society, as did an anonymous author who saw the riot as a conflict between the rich and the poor: "Society, by an unjust distribution of the avails of industry, enables a few men to become rich, and consigns a great mass to hopeless poverty, with all its deprivations and degradations. . . . The only wonder is that more crimes are not committed against both property and life."[76] Such an analysis was pleasing to radicals, but to most Americans it seemed to be part of the problem. Few people disagreed when the *Literary World* declared that it was un-American "to disseminate the absurd and criminal notion of an hostility of castes in this country." Some, like the *Democratic Review*, did believe that the riot had developed out of hatred of what some rioters called the "codfish aristocracy." which had been further inflamed by the fact that the militia's officers were men from that class. Rather than conceding the reality of class differences, however, they concluded that hostility to the rich had been stirred up by "an insidious press."[77]

Violence, then, far from being a sign of an unjust society was, in America, the product of a defective morality. In a sermon on the riot, Henry W. Bellows, minister of the Unitarian Church of the Divine Unity, declared that in America there was "a most intimate connexion between the virtue and piety of the people and the safety and benignity of our Institutions," and went on to warn that the moral foundations of public order were beginning to deteriorate: "The day is coming, and, in parts of the country it has come, when the want of intelligence in many of our voters, and of Christian morality in others— will make wise men wish, as some now do, that a stronger government and less free institutions ruled the masses." Bellows was almost unchristianly violent in his denunciation of the rioters and of "the secret hatred of property and property-holders." with which they were associated.[78]

Most respectable folk agreed with Bellows that violence could be traced to the moral defects of the poor, but Horace Greeley's *Tribune* suggested that the trouble could be traced to the top as well as the bottom of society. In 1855, looking back over six years of violence, Greeley warned that the hope for "a virtuous and well-ordered community" was threatened by high-class as well as low-class scum who shared both an "almost unbridled lust for money" and a proneness toward violence, overt in the lower class, covert in the upper. The chief threat came from irresponsible wealth: "When we see the profligate manner in which this money is spent after it is once acquired; when we see the shameless ostentation which reigns in our dwellings and furniture; the boundless luxury which presides at our entertainments; the premature exposure of our young men to the contact of a vicious and rotten civilization . . . then we feel that our most urgent necessities are social rather than political, and that no reform but that which at the same time relieves us of profligacy and waste in the upper classes, will avail to relieve us also of the ruffianism in the lower."[79]

Corruption at the top—corruption at the bottom, some would see in that formulation the need to build a bridge between the rich and the poor, to build some semblance of community between them which would redeem each from its moral weaknesses, which would unite concentrated wealth and concentrated numbers in a new harmony of interests. Others, many others, preferred to believe that the trouble came chiefly from the bottom, that the poor had to be disciplined to accept the new society and wealth as just and natural. In either case, the end result was a redoubled effort to reach the poor, whether with policeman's club or Christian kindness. Out of the fashionable, materialistic, violent 1850s came the beginnings not only of the Gilded Age but also of a crusade to strengthen the moral and social order against an increasingly wicked city.

Chapter 10

PROGRESSIVE CITY
—WICKED CITY

As THE METROPOLIS GREW, so also grew the feeling that it had become two disturbingly different cities. One New York was the dynamic commercial center of progressive civilization. Its most enthusiastic spokesman was Henry W. Bellows, another of those many New Englanders who shaped the thinking of their adopted city. Minister of the prestigious Church of Divine Unity on Broadway, editor of the *Christian Enquirer* and a founder of the Century Club, Bellows was a member of small but influential intellectual establishment which was attempting to find a place for business enterprise in a Christian and democratic society.[1] Although he condemned the mere pursuit of money, he believed that wealth in the hands of energetic Christian businessmen was bringing moral and material progress for all. The privileged wealth of earlier aristocratic societies had resulted in a "vicious materialism," but modern commercial civilization under the lead of enlightened capitalists, assured a widespread dissemination of material comforts which would nourish morality and faith: "The whole tendency of rude, ill-furnished, indigent homes, is to make or perpetuate within them rude, graceless, and reckless inhabitants. The increase of comfort, beauty, convenience, and grace in the homes of Christendom is directly productive of the order, self-respect, dignity, and decency which are first conditions of moral sensibility and spiritual life."[2]

Similarly, Bellows believed that the new wealth produced by business enterprise was essentially democratic. Although the splendors of the fashionable rich were dazzling, they weighed little against the solid comforts and conveniences businessmen were making available for everyone. In a society committed to the ideal of mass production for a mass market, commercial progress would assure that all men would be equal in essential condition—if only all would join with businessmen as workers in the common commercial enterprise: "There is power and faculty enough in the world, were it all employed, to drive poverty, ignorance, crime, and every manner of defect into the sea. The world wants nothing but the awakened and occupied minds and hearts and hands it owns, to convert it into a paradise. Every idler is a criminal; a clog on the social wheels. . . . Let the appetite of the public be stimulated to desire every comfort, until he who produces nothing shall be universally regarded as a pest, and the worst of criminals."[3]

Bellows spoke for that business and bourgeois New York which, under the flush of the prosperous early 1850s, exulted in its growing power and technical genius. Although his words had little meaning for the fashion-loving rich, they fitted the outlook of New York's emerging middle class as well as of the hundreds of entrepreneurs, big and small, who were engaged in the business of a modernizing economy. The 1850s brought a remarkable expansion in the number and the scale of business enterprises in New York, and a comparable increase in the number of white-collar employees and professionals required to support increasingly complex business operations. In 1856, a city directory listed some 75 banks, 90 insurance companies, and a variety of mining, manufacturing, steamship, and railroad companies with their headquarters or offices in New York. Along with the expanding professions, public schools, and government, these businesses furnished new opportunities for white-collar work, especially for the 13,897 clerks, copyists, and accountants listed for the city by the state census of 1855.[4] All told, although class characteristics are as elusive as occupational statistics are vague, roughly 30 percent of the 215,000 employed New Yorkers in 1855 probably belonged to a broad middle class of small businessmen, professionals, clerks, salesmen, and the most skilled and highly paid wage earners.[5] Though still outnumbered by the poor and less skilled workers, this urban middle class had become a solid and significant part of commercial New York. It was these New Yorkers who had the greatest stake in Bellows' progressive civilization. Theirs was a city of work, respectability, morality, reliability, and comfort—of workshops, business offices, lecture halls, schools, churches, and stable families.

A vital part of this progressive city was its generally subdued majority, its women, who in 1855 constituted 53 percent of those between 15 and 40.[6] Observers gave a disproportionate and generally unfavorable attention to the two extremes of womanhood—the city's small but very conspicuous class of fashionable women and its more numerous but anonymous streetwalkers and brothel inmates. Between the pinnacle and the pit, however, the women's world had many shadings. The contemporary romantic ideal, an indignant repudiation of the corruption associated with both extremes, would confine the weaker sex to the role of domestic angel of happy hearth and home. Indeed, many upper and middle class women at least partially fulfilled that role as the wives-mothers-managers of their increasingly private and comfortable uptown households; but a combination of desire, necessity, and opportunity gave women of all classes a more varied part to play in the world. Many—unmarried, widowed, or deserted—were forced to take charge of their own lives and often to be breadwinners for dependents. Others, out of choice or ill luck, were childless or had only one child.[7] Moreover, the common practice even among families of settling into boarding houses (a practice encouraged by the city's chronic shortage of decent housing) meant that wives and mothers would play a role different from that set by the ideal. Whatever the particular lot of women, they were confronted by tempting opportunities furnished by a complex urban environment to lead varied and meaningful lives. Many sought and found larger work outside the household.

Some fulfilled the hope that the more spiritual sex would play a leading role in shaping a culture worthy of the metropolis. Anne Lynch Botta (she married an Italian scholar in 1855) with little money made her uptown home a weekly meeting place for artists, writers, and thinkers—for "the citizens of the kingdom of Mind," said one of her many friends, "instead of the kingdom of Mammon." The childless Mrs. Botta, who taught English at the Brooklyn Female Academy, managed her kingdom for a half-century after 1845, making it a cultural clearing house for two generations of American culture-makers. Horace Greeley, one of her frequent guests, supposedly called her the best woman that God ever made. Other women, too, made their presence known in the cultural world. An English woman, after observing some of the frequent dinner parties given by upper class New Yorkers in the 1850s, noted that "many of the ladies, had travelled in Europe, and had brought back highly cultivated tastes in art, and cosmopolitan ideas, which insensibly affect the circles in which they move." Such influences, although of questionable value in the development of an American culture, were vital elements in New York's increasingly cosmopolitan atmosphere. A few women, like Catherine Sedgwick, the author of numerous domestic novels, took advantage of the mass demand for literature created by literate city audiences to become professional writers and creative influences on popular culture, despite male sneers against "scribbling females."[8]

Many more women lent their time and talents to the world of reform, especially as the "directoresses," managers, agents, and teachers in a wide variety of benevolent societies. In 1853, they served as officers in at least 14 such societies; the Asylum for Friendless Boys alone employed the voluntary labor of more than 60 ladies as managers and trustees and as members of various committees. One of the most important organizations was the long-lived American Female Guardian Society, which in the 1850s not only supplied material assistance to the poor but ran both a home for friendless children and adults and an industrial school to train vagrant girls in employable skills.[9] Generally, women served, under male direction, as subalterns and soldiers in the armies of benevolence, but that service helped prepare some of them to challenge the limits men imposed on their lives. In 1853, the women of the New York Temperance Alliance met to hear, among other speakers, Susan B. Anthony declare that men were right in suspecting that "this Temperance demonstration is . . . another way of seeking Woman's Rights." The Guardian Society, for its part, was willing openly to condemn men for discriminating against women, especially in employment. Undoubtedly, the opportunities provided by the city for women to organize themselves in a meaningful way also served to prepare some of them to fight the long campaign for equality which lay ahead.[10]

The progressive city also provided opportunities for women to move up the vocational ladder, although with agonizing slowness. Education for girls beyond the elementary level seems to have improved significantly in the 1850s, although on a segregated basis. In 1855, for instance, the Board of Education opened a new girls school in the Fifteenth Ward which included a "Senior Grammar Department" to carry schooling to the high-school level. The Board could also note that between 1851 and 1856 it had doubled the number of evening schools for working girls and women to 14 schools, whose more than 4000 students studied a variety of essentially basic subjects, including bookkeeping, similar to those offered in the male schools. These advances undoubtedly inspired the move— unsuccessful before 1870—to establish a Free Academy for women, thereby ending what School Superintendent H. S. Randall in 1855 termed a "palpable discrimination" against females in higher education. If they were denied access to the

Free Academy however, ambitious young women were able to find a few alternatives such as the New York School of Design, founded privately in 1852 to open "a profitable career for women," whose training in wood engraving, designing and industrial art enabled some to find jobs as teachers of design and as wood engravers and colorers in New York's extensive printing industry."[11]

A few women found places for themselves in the professions. Dr. Elizabeth Blackwell in 1854 was able to establish, with the support of a few enlightened men like Horace Greeley, the New York Dispensary for Poor Women and Children, with herself as attending physician, in order "to give poor women an opportunity of consulting physicians of their own sex." By the early 1860s, she was able to open a teaching hospital where young women could complete their training as physicians. The uniqueness of her efforts, however, also served to demonstrate how nearly complete was the male domination of professions during this period.[12] The one exception was in teaching, where women heavily outnumbered men; they were more than three-quarters of the some 1000 teachers in the public schools by the mid-1850s. Although teaching was the only major break-through into a middle class occupation, women as designers, clerks, and in other ways were slowly acquiring new and significant roles, leading Freeman Hunt to conclude, regarding attempts to open jobs in retail stores for them, that their employment was "becoming more remunerative every year. . . . The enlargement of the sphere of woman's activity and use-fulness is a matter of public economy."[13]

The expanding economy of the progressive city indeed did furnish hope for productive roles outside the home, but except for the fortunate few that hope was the dim grey light of a distant dawn. Certainly, woman had cause to complain that their work was less remunerative to them than it was to men. The pay of female teachers was notoriously less than for their male counterparts, so much so that in 1849 even the Super-intendent of Schools considered the disparity "too great" and called for improvement. Fourteen years later, Virginia Penny in her pioneer study, *The Employments of Women*, noted that

[247]

while few "lady principals of the female departments" earned as much as $800 a year, many males with comparable responsibilities received $1500 in salary.[14] Penny's book, which deals largely with the 95,000 working women of New York and its surrounding counties, indicated that the great majority of females were treated as a convenient pool of cheap labor. Although some worked as sales clerks, as matrons and nurses in municipal institutions—and even as well-paid typesetters in the printing industry—the great majority were employed either as servants and domestics or as low-paid workers in light manufacturing. Women, nearly 25,000 of them, constituted over a quarter of the manufacturing work force in the city itself in 1860. Of these, more than half labored as seamstresses and "tailoresses" in the clothing industry, where they were not only poorly paid but were also subject to increasing competition both from the new sewing machine and from male immigrants. "The utility and profit of sewing machines," said Virginia Penny in 1863, "have to a great extent been usurped by Jew men." Like black people, working women often found that the upward mobility of white males was at their expense.[15]

Given their low wages and uncertainty of employment, it was not surprising that many women were driven by hard times either to the charity agencies or to prostitution. Life was likely to be especially grim for those who had to support themselves and their dependents. A sampling of the family heads and single inhabitants of the Fourteenth Ward in 1860, indicates that approximately 18 percent were women, some with large families. It was such situations that formed the stuff of so much sentimental literature, of stories of helpless women and children, of angels fallen from the sunlight into the shadows. Life, in fact, was frequently hard, but often it was less bleak and more complex than either literature or a simple reading of census figures would indicate. Some female family heads, for instance, were able to draw on their older children for support. Such was the case of Mary Rumiell, an Irish immigrant listed in the census schedules. Her family consisted of three daughters, ages 18 to 22, who worked in cloak-making, sewing, and the manufacture of parasols, and a 16-year-old son employed as a clerk. This example also suggests another consideration regarding aggregate statistics for working women in general: that many of them were girls who lived at home, where their wages helped to support the family. One such young woman was the 16-year-old seamstress daughter of Jacob Wolfe, a German capmaker, and the like-aged daughter of Edward Coe, a clerk, who despite her youth was listed as a school teacher.[16] Such cases tell a story not simply of human survival but of slow upward progress in the progressive city. Although the lives of the many are too complex to be told either by census figures or by case histories, it seems evident that reality for most women as for men lay in a broad grey world which, under the influence of expanding opportunities, stretched toward the light. In such a way were the majority of New Yorkers part of the dynamic metropolis with its promise of bourgeois progress.

Yet who could deny that at some point the grey deepened into darkness? Certainly, if the progressive city was much in evidence in the prosperous 1850s, so was its other, darker self, a city inhabited by the desperate and the deprived—by idlers, drunks, thieves, whores, and other clogs on the wheels of progress. This was a city dominated by the institutions of vice and dissipation, especially by the omnipresent drinking places—the liquor groceries, porter houses, taverns, and fancy saloons—with their attendant hordes of disreputable loungers, drunks, and fashionable sots. In 1849, there were 3814 licensed drinking establishments in the city; by 1852, there were 5780— to say nothing of the many places which illegally sold liquor. Except on those rare occasions when the Sunday closing laws were enforced, many remained open—to the outrage of those who wanted a quiet, orderly Sabbath. Such places spawned most of the petty public disorder which annoyed and disturbed respectable citizens; approximately one-half of the arrests made by the New York police between 1845 and 1850 were for public intoxication and other offenses directly related to drinking.[17]

Here, too, in this wicked city, were gambling houses and professional gamblers ready to take the money of the gullible. In 1846, the *Evening Post* noted that, besides an unknown number of petty gamblers, there were "public houses where women are employed to sing at night while the men congregate around the multitude of little tables placed in the saloon where they sip the intoxicating bowl, while they are initiated into the minor grades of gambling." The most lavish and seductive of such places generally were located in the Broadway area, where they could best catch the unwary out-of-towner, but none were above entrapping the New York merchant or the merchant's clerk. If there was luxurious seduction for the wealthy few, there was mass temptation for the poor in the form of lotteries and policy gambling, this last estimated by the *Tribune* in 1855 to be a $10,000 a day business. From such temptations, great and small, came financial ruin, embezzlement, and thievery; the *Tribune* warned that policy gambling "makes pilferers of one-half of the servants of the City."[18]

The popular theater seemed hardly less corrupting. Although there was some concern over the character of the plays, many of which were sentimental trash, the principal objection was to off-stage activities, for theaters were popular places of assignation. The opening of the new Broadway Theatre in 1847 provoked the *Tribune* to declare that theaters were "the ready and constant resort of simple youth from the country in quest of lewd women." It was only a short step from the theaters, with their infamous third tier where harlots and pimps were seated, to the brothel—in some cases literally a short step: When the National Theatre burned down in 1841, one of its falling walls half demolished, said George Templeton Strong, "a new and very magnificent temple of Venus," killing one of its inmates. The stage was slow to lose its association with prostitution. In 1857 *Harpers Weekly* complained that the construction of a theater in a respectable area invariably brought bagnios and saloons in its wake which destroyed "that quarter for any future decency of life."[19]

If the theater was a convenience especially for out-of-town visitors eager for sin, it could be a costly convenience, a painful discovery made by many visitors like Aaron Walk of Uniontown, Pennsylvania, who in 1856 complained to the police that he had been robbed of $600 by a girl he had met at the Bowery

Theatre. Despite such incidents, however, merchants, store-keepers, travellers, "raw country youth," and seamen continued to patronize the wicked city. Their desires made New York the capital of American prostitution. Estimates as to the number of prostitutes in the city varied from 6000 to 10,000.[20] Probably the most reliable estimate was made in 1858 by William Sanger, a New York physician, who calculated that there were nearly 6000 professionals plus another 1860 part-timers, mistresses, and other lost women, the whole of whom if marched up Broadway single-file "would reach from City Hall to Fortieth Street." The brothels of New York formed a multimillion dollar business which sustained itself by recruiting new talent from the ranks of country and immigrant girls. In the popular imagination, as the *Tribune* phrased it, "not the city only but the country for hundreds of miles is scoured by their emissaries, disguised as gentlemen and ladies, in search of fresh victims."[21]

Dr. Sanger concluded that prostitution had become a major problem for the entire metropolitan area: "Unlike the vice of a few years since, it no longer confines itself to secrecy and darkness, but boldly strides through our most thronged and elegant thoroughfares. . . . It is in your squares, and in your suburban retreats and summer resorts; it is in your theatres, your opera, your hotels; nay, it is even intruding itself into the private circles, and slowly but steadily extending the poison." He was concerned especially with the physical danger. As Resident Physician of the public institutions on Blackwell's Island, he had the dubious opportunity to observe the incidence of venereal diseases among the inmates. By determining the number of cases of venereal disease treated at public medical facilities and calculating the number of cases treated privately either by doctors or with patent medicines (such as "Red Drops" and "Unfortunate's Friend"), he concluded that in 1857 there were some 74,000 cases: "The city of New York contains, at this day, venereal infection sufficient to contaminate all the male population of the United States in a very short time."[22]

Dr. Sanger urged that prostitution be legalized and placed under medical supervision to guard the public health, but the idea found little public favor.[23] The middle class, especially, gave less thought to the perils of syphilis than to the danger that open vice would corrupt its children. "Is there not urgent demand for its repression," warned one New Yorker of prostitution, "when provocation to debauchery takes place in the open streets before the eyes of our rising youth of both sexes." Anxious citizens complained of the availability of pornographic literature and of other forms of lewdness, like a "model-artist exhibition" on Broadway where "gross signs were displayed, and men and boys stood at the door distributing prints of naked women to the immense throng of people" on the street. And so the city government was committed to an ineffectual effort to erase the ineradicable, to a policy of occasional sweeps against noisy streetwalkers and token raids on bawdyhouses. It was a policy guaranteed to foster a related civil vice, the corruption of magistrates and the police. In 1855, brothel and dance-hall keepers in the Fourth Ward became so incensed by the extortionate payoff demands of the police that they finally complained to the new Mayor, Fernando Wood.[24]

Public outrage was little more successful in suppressing another related problem which seemed less to be vice than outright crime, the crime of "baby killing." Illicit sex without effective contraceptives resulted in a demand in both the city and countryside for reliable abortionists. When in 1846 a young woman from a nearby village died as the result of an abortion executed in a house on Broome Street, the *Evening Post* complained that the city was overrun by abortionists like the Madames Restell and Costello: "The number of innocent babies thus sacrificed in the course of a year is truly frightful." Madame Costello was soon punished for her sinful service with six months in the state penitentiary. Madame Restell, however, was to have a long and profitable career, despite one effort to convict her for the death of a woman under her care (it was rumored that she had bought her acquittal for $100,000). The complaint made in 1846 regarding the immunity of this "murderess" would be repeated later: "She is still living in luxury, riding almost daily in an elegant carriage through our most public thoroughfares, supported by the price of blood." Such attacks gave wide publicity to her business—which was not difficult to locate, since she was listed in the city directory as "RESTELL MADAME, physician." No one knew the extent of abortion, but Dr. Sanger believed that it was widespread among prostitutes and, at the other extreme, fashionable women. Certainly, in the middle class imagination, it was a significant element in this other city of sin, corruption, dissipation, disease, and death.[25]

And of violence. The Astor Place Riot proved to be a prelude to a decade of disorder. In 1852, an "Old Resident" complained that "the increase of crime, the ferocity and frequency of assaults on private citizens at night in this city, and the undeniable imbecility and inefficiency of the police is creating great alarm in the decent and orderly portion of our inhabitants," many of whom were either buying "a couple of revolvers" or were moving to the suburbs; he himself was moving to Connecticut "where my person and property will be safe . . . and my anxiety for the safety of my children will be entirely removed." His claim was echoed by the New York Prison Association, which estimated that from 1848 through 1852, while crimes against property increased by 50 percent, convictions for crimes against persons increased by 129 percent, including a threefold increase in assaults to kill and a sixfold rise in murders. Others, too, noted an increase in shootings, stabbings, clubbings, and simple assaults, which were making New York one of the most dangerous cities in Christendom.[26]

Memories, like statistics, were short. Similar complaints had been made before—as they were to be made again; but police and newspaper reports served to convince New Yorkers that an organized culture of crime and violence was being formed among the drifters, pickpockets, thieves, thugs, and assorted riffraff of Europe and America who supported themselves on the earnings from prostitution and gambling and by thievery great and small. Much of their violence was directed among themselves, but it readily spilled into the streets and parks of the city. In 1850, the *Evening Post* complained that a gang of "killers" had one Sunday morning taken over City Hall Park and "went about stabbing and cutting several persons without the slightest provocation."[27] What made matters more threat-

[253]

ening was that this culture had spawned its own popular heroes, the most conspicuous being Bill Poole and John Morrisey, whose rivalry reached a murderous finale in 1855.

"Butcher Bill" Poole was the fighting hero of a westside gang of "roughs" who periodically terrorized the Ninth Ward. From his headquarters in his gambling and drinking place at Howard Street and Broadway, he used his muscle and popularity to support the Whig political cause in the city. Opposed to him was the popular Democrat hero of the Irish toughs in the "Bloody" Sixth Ward, John Morrisey, who worked out of his drinking and gambling house, the "Belle of the Union," on Leonard Street. The upsurge of nativism in the early 1850s intensified the feud between the two, for Poole became the popular champion of the "American" cause. In 1854 "Butcher Bill" beat Morrisey badly in a boxing and gouging match before their assembled partisans on Amos Street Dock. The feud reached a climax in February 1855 when some of Morrisey's men encountered Poole in the Stanwix house, a lavish new saloon on Broadway, and shot him at least four times. After lingering for nearly two weeks, the "American" champion died—a month before his thirty-second birthday. The murder did little to dim Morrisey's star; he went on to fortune and to two terms in Congress after the Civil War.[28]

Poole received a hero's funeral that would have done credit to Chicago seventy years later. Preceded by a 52-piece band and followed by a procession of some 2000 men, his body was conveyed down Broadway in an open hearse pulled by four white horses. An estimated 100,000 people from New York and surrounding areas gathered to watch the procession and to pay their last respects to an American hero. What did it all mean? The *Tribune* saw the murder as disturbing evidence of the growth of the wicked city:

> Bloody crimes like these are but the fruits of the hydra of vices which have been tolerated in our midst, and which, acting in an offensive and defensive alliance, constitute a fearful power in this city. So long as drunkeness, gambling, prostitution, prize fighting, and their associated evils continue, so long we shall

never be rid of the characters who constantly heap upon the city taxes and disgrace. The schools of vice are open, and hundreds are in training to take the places of those who now go to the grave or to prison.

As for Poole's funeral, Greeley noted with disgust that the public had given greater acclaim to a "notorious fighting character" than it had ever given to a genius, philanthropist, or other good man and warned that such a demonstration virtually invited thousands of young men "to prefer idleness, riot, vice, crime to labor, steadiness, respectability, and virtue— to turn their backs on heaven."[29]

New Yorkers did not agree on the causes of crime and corruption. Some emphasized the presence of a class of exploiting wealth and a class of exploited poor. More blamed the trouble on the inrush of degraded foreigners, or on the ever dangerous power of a great city to attract the criminal element from everywhere. Many condemned the failure of the police to arrest suspects and of the courts to convict them. A few, at least, believed that the influence of opponents of capital punishment and others who had "a morbid sympathy for all criminals" was an important cause of the breakdown of law and order; another few took the contrary view that much of the crime resulted from the overcrowding of penal institutions, which had turned them into schools for vice and crime.[30]

Whatever their beliefs, New Yorkers generally shared Greeley's fear that the progressive city was being overtaken by a corrupting atmosphere spewed out by its subterranean counterpart. Even those who sought refuge in the private worlds of uptown homes could not hide completely, for the culture of wickedness seemed responsible for the increase in city taxes which burdened their incomes as well as for the crime which endangered their persons and property. Moreover, it posed at least a distant threat to the moral character and thus to the future of their children. It was a contemporary cliché, especially in the native middle class, that a rural upbringing gave men the moral strength to cope with the perils of urban life. Henry Ward Beecher once said that every talented man ideally should have the opportunity both to acquire his character in the countryside and to develop his talents in the city. The cliché, however, was confronted by the growth in the number of city-bred children both of the middle class and of the poor. How could they be protected? How could they be redeemed?[31]

In answer, concerned New Yorkers resorted to a wide variety of institutions for the protection and expansion of the middle-class world. Most of these remedies had been developed early in the century, but the growth of the dangerous classes combined with the increase of wealth in the 1850s brought an intensification of organized effort against wickedness. Undoubtedly the most popular remedy was the public school. For some of its advocates, public education would provide children with access to the fundamental skills which later would enable them to take advantage of the expanding opportunities of a progressive civilization. It would, thus, eliminate corrupting artificial inequalities of wealth and advance the cause of middle-class society. "Universal education," said Joseph McKeen, County Superintendent of Education, in 1849, "would put an end to many unnatural and oppressive inequalities, in which some are raised to thrones without virtue, and others degraded to slavery without crime."[32]

Probably, most advocates were especially concerned with extending educational opportunities to the middle class, whose children could best avail themselves of these opportunities. More certainly, the schools were seen as necessary agencies of moral discipline which would shape the young of all classes into useful citizens. The school would at the least provide a moral refuge from the corrupting influences of the wicked city; more positively, it might discipline the children of the city to become constructive members of the urban community. The prevalent fear that the offspring of the immigrant poor were prospective recruits in the armies of wickedness gave special emphasis to the role of schools as acculturating agencies. "Common sympathy and security," warned McKeen, "require that the immigrant child be speedily qualified for citizenship. In order for this, they must be assimilated or identified with

[256]

us, and with our children, that we, as a nation, may stand a united and homogeneous people. . . . If we leave them uneducated, our sin of omission will bring upon us, as a community, the retributive effects of insecurity of life and property, and an increase of our already enormous taxes for prisons and poor houses. We strive therefore to educate and elevate every one."[33]

In a society deeply concerned about the preservation of moral and social order, these arguments provided powerful support for the efforts of public school administrators to create a unified system of urban education. Before the 1850s, public education was still in its formative stage. In 1845, at least 25 percent of registered school children were privately educated by a variety of 208 select, religious, and charitable schools. The rest of those attending schools were divided between two competing public systems. Although the Public School Society had been forced in the early 1840s to share its monopoly over public instruction with the newly created Board of Education, it continued to be a powerful influence throughout the decade; as late as 1850, eight years after the passage of the Maclay Act, it taught the majority of children educated at public expense. By that date, however, it had become obsolete, and in 1853 was forced into an extinguishing merger with the Board of Education. It had by one estimate educated 600,000 children and trained 1200 teachers during its 48 years of existence. In a real sense, death was its victory, for its managerial and teaching practices and personnel were absorbed into the consolidated public system.[34]

Despite the continued competition of private and parochial schools, the Board of Education had little trouble in proclaiming itself the guardian of popular education, a claim which it reinforced with an ambitious building program, distinguished by the construction of bigger and costlier schools than any the Public School Society might even have imagined a decade before. The large schools, built to hold one thousand or more pupils, were a natural outgrowth of the Board's philosophy and objectives, which could be reduced to the formula that

[257]

bigger and costlier equals better and cheaper. The new schools were, if nothing else, intended to be imposing emblems of the importance and dignity of public education.[35]

More significantly, their size, and the facilities size made possible, offered the hope that they would be microcosms of the middle-class world. They were to be comfortable and healthful places where the education of children would take place under the management of middle-class professionals in relative isolation from the contaminating influences of the surrounding society. Within this private educational world, the size of the student body made possible economies of scale which enabled the schoolmen to provide good education at low cost.[36] Size made possible the effective organization of the teaching staff so as to reduce instructional costs, especially by placing low-salaried and presumably low-quality teachers, chiefly women, under the supervision of experienced principal teachers, chiefly men. Size made possible the extensive teaching materials and the increase in the number of subjects which enriched education, especially at the post-primary grammar school level. It was also thought that large schools could provide the comfort, quality, and prestige needed to attract the children of the middle and upper classes, thus making them truly public institutions in which all classes would be united in true democratic community.[37]

Size also contributed to the moral mission of the schools, for it strengthened an informal but essential curriculum which emphasized behavior rather than knowledge. Large schools both required and provided the opportunity for mass uniformity of behavior: "In one of these great schools," said School Superintendent Henry S. Randall in 1855, "if well conducted, an *esprit de corps* is induced . . . a sort of intellectual momentum from the action in one direction of associated mind." In the schools, "associated mind" also became associated behavior under a system of discipline which required all students to be obedient, industrious, punctual, honest, neat, and clean. In 1852, Erastus C. Benedict, the recently reelected president of the Board, emphasized the virtues of discipline and order. The good teacher, he said, "finds it profitable and conducive to train and exercise his pupils together. Persons unskilled in the management of large schools, are liable to undervalue the use of mechanical movement and evolutions in concert. . . . A school trained in cooperative movements, is always easily controlled. The least touch of the bell, or signal from the hand, is enough to direct each class, and thus, the whole school. Simultaneous exercises are useful in the cultivation of habits of ready obedience, and greatly facilitate the movements of a school."[38]

Although the system was justified as a means of advancing learning, it readily became an end in itself. Mediocre students, especially the children of the poor, might learn little from the formal curriculum, but all could and should learn those habits which would make them good citizens. Within the protective confines of the schools, subject to the benign discipline of the system, the innocent victims of the vicious social environment of the wicked city would be redeemed and would be given the chance to become industrious, orderly, sober, time-conscious, moral, and contributing members of the progressive city. "Pass through room after room," observed a writer for *Putnam's Monthly*, "floor after floor, of the immense buildings they occupy, you find everywhere order, industry, animation, happiness. From the little toddlers that go gravely through the manual exercise of the infant school, chanting their pretty hymns and clapping their little fat hands, to the tall fair girl and the strong awkward boy of the highest rooms, all are busy, interested, hopeful."[39]

As important as it was, the informal curriculum perhaps was overemphasized both by advocates and critics of the system. Especially in its early years, the Board made a strong effort to expand educational opportunities beyond the primary levels emphasized by the character-builders. In 1847, it established a system of evening schools designed to provide an alternative to the theaters, saloons, and enforced idleness that led men and women down the path of crime and ruin. Between that date and 1856, the number of students registered for evening education grew steadily from less than 4000 to nearly 15,000.[40] At the same time, the Board rounded off its ambitious program by opening the Free Academy to provide free secondary and college education for the especially talented. The Free Academy was of special benefit to the middle class, but it also gave the talented sons of the working class at least some access to higher education; later, the door to higher education for them—and their sisters—opened wide when the Academy evolved into the great City University of New York. Despite their limitations, the evening schools and the Academy lent credence to the boast that the public system was "the common property of all classes of the community."[41]

The Board and its supporters could take pride in having created a powerful institution in harmony with a progressive and urbanizing age. They had succeeded in overcoming the notion that free education was charity education and so had made the schools one of the few institutions for community in the city, embracing, if not the rich, at least all the other classes of society. They had created a system which seemingly provided equal access to quality education for all children and so had founded a vital democratic institution which, though it might not eliminate all poverty in future America, might eliminate all *unjust* poverty. They had created a powerful and pervasive moral force which reinforced the habits of order, honesty, obedience to authority and the other virtues required by the progressive city. If they did not succeed in creating a system that could mold every child into a middle class citizen, they had at least established in the schools an environment which protected and encouraged those children of a middle-class character. At the very least, they offered a refuge from the morally and physically debilitating environment of the wicked city.[42]

The boasts of the schoolmen, however, were shadowed by their failure to reach many children of the poor. In the 1850s, the proportion of children, ages five to fifteen, who attended either public or private school may actually have declined. Certainly, this was the conclusion of William Sanger who estimated that between 1850 and 1856 the proportion fell from 76 to 66 percent. As school attendance figures were unreliable, New Yorkers were left free to guess that between 20,000 and

60,000 children were not in the schools. In 1856, School Superintendent H. S. Randall declared with some authority that at least 50,000 "are utterly unprovided with the means of education."[43] Even among those children whose registrations for school helped swell enrollment statistics, many attended too infrequently to get any real education—a reality that was built into the planning of the Board. In 1851, a school committee estimated that less than one-half of those pupils enrolled in schools actually were in attendance at any one time and, though it piously expressed the hope that attendance would increase, went on to use a 40 percent attendance figure to determine school building size, figuring that a building designed to accommodate 2000 pupils would meet the needs of 4500. The school figure was substantiated by later Board estimates: In 1852, of the enrolled children, 31 percent actually attended for less than four months in the year; in 1858, the figure was 38 percent.[44]

In the absence of any compulsory education law, many parents undoubtedly sent their children out to work at an early age; the young themselves, noted Superintendent Randall, were often seized by "the restless and uncontrolled desire . . . to plunge at the earliest possible period into the pursuits and to grasp the prizes of active life." There was a sharp falling off of the proportion of the young who attended public school after age nine; in 1851, only 8 percent of enrolled students were over 14 years old, a figure used to support recommendations that the Board give less attention to grammar schools for older children and more to primary schools especially in poor neighborhoods.[45] It is also probable, however, that whatever the level, the middle class ethos of the schools and the high value accorded both to the English language and to nonsectarian Protestantism alienated many children, and their parents, from public education. Intentionally or not, the schools served to weed out those children who would not or could not conform to such prevailing norms as neatness, punctuality, self-restraint, and proficiency in the English tongue. The failure to incorporate many of the children of the poor into the school system was thus an important element in the Board's early successes, for it not only lessened the demand for expensive school space in a cost-conscious city but also made it much easier to solve the problems of discipline and instruction raised by mass education.[46]

Supporters of the public system, however, preferred to treat the situation as a challenge to its most essential mission. The absence of children from the schools meant vicious parents who deliberately denied their sons and daughters the benefits of education; it meant exposure of the young to a corrupting home environment and to the dangerous culture of the wicked city. "There is a constant struggle," said George G. Foster, "going on between the tendency of the rising generation to seek the light and the influence of a degraded and besotted parentage to corrupt and depress it, whose results are visible in the wide-spread deterioration in public morals." As they consolidated their hold on education, the schoolmen recognized that the most dangerous competition came not from parochial or private schools but from the School of the Streets.[47]

One of the most troubling trends in the troubled 1850s was the conspicuous increase in the numbers of vagrant children, boys and girls without schools, jobs or, in many cases, homes. In 1850 Chief of Police George Matsell estimated that there were nearly 3000 vagrant children, concentrated in the lower city. Many supported themselves by scavenging or by selling fruits, nuts, newspapers or petty merchandise, keeping themselves and their parents—if they had any—alive on the leavings of the great commercial city. Often they won the begrudging respect of New Yorkers for their shrewdness and strength; but their independence made them a special threat, for they were potentially the most dangerous recruits of the wicked city: The future rioters, thugs, thieves, and prostitutes. "A great majority," warned Mayor Kingsland in 1852, "are apt pupils in the school of vice, licentiousness and theft, who, if permitted to grow up, will constitute a large portion of the inmates of our prisons."[48]

Many already were petty thieves who stole from stores and the docks; some graduated early into crime, often as professional pickpockets or junior members of adult gangs. In 1852, a grand jury declared that 80 percent of major felony complaints were against minors. Of some 16,000 criminals sent to City Prison in 1851, over 4000 were under 21 years old, 800 were younger than 15, and 175 were less than *ten* years of age. One New Yorker observed the next year that "almost every week there is the gloomy knell of some new execution through the land—generally of young men, once the street boys, the poor or neglected children of our great cities." Six years later came the unheralded birth in New York of one boy who would eventually achieve notoriety and death in the distant West under the name of Billy the Kid.[49]

Especially troubling was the fate of young girls, those who for a sentimental age should have been the tenderest flowers of youth. "No one can walk the length of Broadway," wrote George Templeton Strong in 1851, "without meeting some hideous troop of ragged girls, from twelve years old down, brutalized almost beyond redemption by premature vice, clad in the filthy refuse of the rag-picker's collections, obscene of speech, the stamp of childhood gone from their faces, hurrying along with harsh laughter and foulness on their lips . . . with thief written in their cunning eyes and whore on their depraved faces." Chief Matsell had already noted the existence of a class of girls, often neatly dressed and occasionally pretty, who used the disguise of petty merchandise sellers to "gain ready access to counting-rooms, offices, and other places, where in the secrecy and seclusion of a turned key, they submit for a miserable bribe of a few shillings to the most degrading familiarities." The girls, in particular, were a prod to the conscience of New York, a reminder of the failure of a great city to take care of its young.[50]

What could be done? One answer was to attempt to force the young vagrants into the public schools. As society was not ready to accept a universal attendance law requiring all children to be at school, concerned New Yorkers, headed by the Association for Improving the Condition of the Poor (AICP), persuaded the State to enact the Truancy Law of 1853. The law empowered the police to arrest any child, ages 5 to 14, found idle or truant in the streets. The parents or guardians of the child could procure his release only if they signed a written agreement to keep him at home or place him in a lawful occupation, and also to send him to school for at least four months a year until age 14. If they either refused or could not be found, the vagrant child was to be committed to a public institution designed to give him useful employment and educate him "in the elementary branches of an English education." As a solution to the truancy problem, the law was a failure. Few policemen were willing to arrest children simply for being idle, especially since the arrest might lead to the separation of parents and children; few parents were ready to be coerced into doing what they would not do voluntarily.[51] Probably, the proponents of the law neither expected nor wanted it to force the vagrants *en masse* into the schools, since this would have mixed bad children with good in the already crowded public system.

Rather, they wanted it as support for an effort, long in the making, to solve a problem beyond the mission of the public schools, a problem which society was coming to know as juvenile delinquency. As many of the vagrants had already been corrupted by the bad family life and bad associations of the wicked city, it seemed senseless to place them in the regular schools. In 1846 George G. Foster had complained that the schools too frequently served only to teach the children of the poor "to read licentious shilling novels, to calculate a game of seven-up or to forge a name at the bottom of a note—separated only for a few hours each day from vile and polluting associations." The public system could make little headway in rehabilitating children who spent the great part of the week in the school of the streets. For those who were already headed for a life of crime or vice, it seemed necessary to create a round-the-clock environment where, under public guardianship, they could be cleansed of their bad habits.[52]

Thomas L. Harris, a clergyman, said in 1850 that the best cure for "juvenile depravity" was a "home for children" where they would be reformed, educated, and taught a useful skill. Harris and the others gave little attention to the fact that the city already had a series of "homes" which, to one degree or another, received public money to take care of displaced children. Besides the various orphan asylums, the city-run Nursery connected with the Almshouse Department for years had provided food, clothing, shelter, and some education for pauper children. Like the inmates of other public institutions, however, such children were more housed than educated, subjected to the same crowding and the same inadequate supervision that characterized the other institutions even after they had been moved in the mid-1840s into new nursery buildings on Randall's Island.[53]

More directly committed to confronting the problem of delinquency was the privately managed New York House of Refuge, founded in 1824 by the Society for the Reformation of Juvenile Delinquents. By isolating delinquents behind walls from both the wicked city and, worse, adult prison life, its managers hoped to implant the habits of honesty, cleanliness, punctuality, self-discipline, and industry in their wayward charges. In 1857, they boasted that they had reformed 75 percent of the some 7000 delinquents who since 1825 had been subjected to their benevolent discipline. Aside from the dubious nature of such figures, however, it was evident that even in their eyes, they had encountered many incorrigibles who could not be reformed but simply restricted by prison routine. Moreover, the House of Refuge itself seemingly harbored corrupting associations which threatened to reinforce criminal tendencies. The place, said the superintendent of the city penitentiary in 1842, was a school for adult criminals: "It is as regular succession as the classes in a college, from the house of refuge to the penitentiary, and from the penitentiary to the State prison."[54]

Benevolent New York thus found it necessary to invent another institution which would isolate vagrant children from the contaminations not only of streets and prisons but the House of Refuge as well. Early in 1850, the AICP proposed a "House of Detention" for the "depraved, neglected and morally exposed children and youth in this city," as a way of striking at the roots of pauperism. The next year, it joined with other benevolent organizations to found the New York Juvenile

Asylum, a privately managed institution. The Asylum was especially intended to prevent disobedient and idle children from drifting into juvenile delinquency. Under a regimen of schooling, religious training, and work, so the managers hoped, their charges would soon learn the "self-discipline of body, mind, and heart" that would make it safe either to return them to society or, even better, to apprentice them to employers away from corrupting associations with friends, guardians, and parents. Supported by public funds, the Asylum soon became a major child-care institution which during the first 18 years of its existence accommodated over 15,000 children.[55]

Thus, by the mid-1850s, reformers believed they had created an effective supplement to the public school system. Under the Truancy Act, it seemed possible to impose a system of specialized moral education on vagrant children. Those who had not been contaminated by the wicked city could be channeled into the public schools. Those who were drifting toward delinquent behavior would be consigned to the Juvenile Asylum for redemption in a corrective moral environment. Juvenile delinquents would be forced to spend longer periods in the House of Refuge, where they would be reformed before they were released. Robert M. Hartley, head of the AICP, summed up these hopes when he said in regard to the juvenile system: "By assuming the place of a parent to its helpless children, and undertaking their training, it raises them from the degradation of their previous condition to one of equality with the other pupils of our public schools, while it saves such pupils from the dread of debasement by intercourse with them." The great mass of children in the city, thus, could be segregated into groups, each under the charge of men who had experience in dealing with that group. Experts, working in an institutional setting that kept out the corrupting influences of the outside world, would either convert potential members of the dangerous classes into safe citizens or determine who was too dangerous to be given the privileges of a free man.[56]

The idea was good. The results were good at least occasionally, if only in the sense that these institutions provided some food, shelter, and education for displaced children. The reformers, however, encountered the normal frustrations faced by those who attempt to provide mass solutions to mass problems. Like the schoolmen, they believed that a uniform system would enable them to carry out a mass modification of character at little expense for the community; their major selling point was that prevention and reform was cheaper than the police, prisons, and almshouses. Given the limited size of both the Asylum and the Refuge and the tendency of society to commit only the hardest cases to either, it was not surprising that the managers soon gave less thought to reform than to simply maintaining order.[57] At the same time, the reform schools succeeded in reaching only a small proportion of those who were to constitute the dangerous classes of the future. The great majority of vagrant and delinquent children were left in the streets—the same streets to which most of the graduates of the institutions would return. If the institutions failed to counter effectively the vicious culture of the subterranean city, if they themselves grew corrupt and corrupting, what then?

Few New Yorkers openly challenged these institutions, for they were at least isolating the troublesome young from the rest of society; but it seemed evident in the early 1850s that the juvenile apparatus needed at least one additional dimension if it was to succeed in saving society from its young. That was provided in 1854 by the establishment of the Children's Aid Society. Its founder, Charles Loring Brace, was still another of those Yankee-born ministers who discovered their mission in New York. Brace found his ministry not in a church but in the streets. Early, he concluded that Christianity, as practiced within most city churches, was a flabby influence against the materialism and indifference so strong in the great city. In 1849, he encountered a grim testimony to the ineffectuality of religion when he visited the paupers and diseased prostitutes confined to the Almshouse. Here, for him, were the results of the church's failure to inspire the fortunate to Christian kindness and charity: "The wrecks of the Soul; creatures cast out from every thing but God's mercy."[58]

Soon after, he left with his friend, Frederick Law Olmsted,

for Europe where he studied English and German efforts to cope with the juvenile problem—and also encountered Old-World tyranny when he was briefly imprisoned in Austria for his outspoken support of Hungarian freedom from Austrian rule. His European experiences strengthened his faith in the power of a progressive society to solve its problems. From Berlin in 1851, he wrote to a despairing Olmsted that his friend was wrong in assuming that "'Saints' were a dead species in America. . . . What nation is there where you could find a set of young persons growing up with the plans and theories and *aims* (I say not practice) of ours." To put his aims into practice, Brace returned to New York intent on devoting his life to the children of urban poor. He was to become one of the saints of the progressive city and to meet the need in New York for what Olmsted called "beautiful souls" to work against the materialist tendencies running so strong; another age would have called him a truly beautiful man.[59]

Brace combined a superb practical intelligence with his sense of mission. He recognized the necessity, in the money-conscious city, of appealing to the interests as well as the hearts of the Christian community. In 1854, he warned:

It should be remembered that there are no dangers to the value of property, or to the permanency of our institutions, so great as those from the existence of such a class of vagabond, ignorant, ungoverned children. This "dangerous class' has not begun to show itself, as it will in eight or ten years, when these boys and girls are matured. Those who are too negligent or too selfish to notice them as children, will be fully aware of them as men. They will vote—they will have the same rights as we ourselves, though they have grown up ignorant of moral principle as any savage or Indian. They will poison society. They will perhaps be embittered at the wealth and the luxuries they never share. Then let society beware, when the outcast, vicious, reckless multitude of New York boys, swarming now in every alley and low street, come to know their power and *use* it!

Like most native Americans, Brace attributed the increase in vice and crime to European immigration; unlike many, however, he did not blame the immigrants themselves. Rather, the initial disadvantages which burdened the most degraded of Europe's outcasts had become concentrated in the slums, where, isolated from American society, the immigrants were trapped in a vicious "community" whose influence encouraged vice, crime and rowdyism. From such "foul ulcers of the city . . . poisoned currents go out over the whole city and country, cursing with terrible disease, moral and physical, thousands who never saw or cared for the sources of the evil."[60]

For Brace, this wicked environment was an inescapable challenge. Although he shared the common belief that the moral environment of the rural village was superior to that of urban life, he also believed that the city was more likely to cope with its moral problems once it had been awakened to the challenge. In the village, the wicked or idle family was left alone with little chance of improvement. Urban areas, on the other hand, had the talent, money, and organization required to solve the moral problem, while the urban poor were not so isolated and were less likely to be "stamped in public repute with a bad name."[61]

Brace doubted that much could be done to reclaim the vicious adult poor, but he believed that most slum children could rise above their corrupt beginnings, if only society would come to their aid. They were not simply problems but "human beings, with warm hearts, and souls formed for an immortal destiny." Some, indeed, had been already corrupted either by bad heredity or bad environment—such were candidates for the asylum and penitentiary. The majority, however, could be redeemed by someone who accepted them as human beings. Though he recognized their flaws, Brace had great respect for the street children of the city. He admired, and at least occasionally romanticized, their virtues: Their shrewdness, toughness, self-respect, and independence—the character learned in the school of the streets which enabled them to survive even the blight of brutal, ne'er-do-well parents. In particular, he idealized the newsboys whose keenness of mind and sturdy independence made them worth saving as potentially "useful, active men for our community."[62]

[269]

The problem was how to reach the children of the street. The schoolmen and the managers of the asylums hoped to draw the children into their special worlds, but had limited success. Though he accepted the necessity of public schools for all and the asylums for some, Brace believed that the influence of reform had to be carried into the streets, if only because existing institutions in New York were not large enough to meet such a massive and growing problem. In the early 1850s, he joined a movement launched a few years before to hold street-corner "boy's meetings" to bring the gospel to the children of the lower city, one of the many signs of a reawakening of the urban missionary movement. Brace and many of the leaders of the effort, however, soon concluded that occasional Sunday forays into the slum would not counteract the influences of the wicked city. Moral reform, rather than being work for well-intended amateurs, required a full-time organized effort headed by paid professionals. In one sense, the Children's Aid Society was another one of the specialized and professionalized "systems" which reformers were establishing to deal with the complex problems of the city, but more than most it was designed to be a part of the human community.[63]

Like the AICP, Brace hoped to place visitors in every ward of the city, who would get to know the children and their problems. The visitor was to be a "friend to the vagrant child," an understanding friend who, on the basis of an appreciation of individual circumstance, would steer his charge in the appropriate direction. Some children could be directed into the established institutions of the city, especially the public schools and Sunday schools. Others required special agencies located in their own world, each of which would act as "a seed for reform." In his first Annual Report, Brace announced a plan to establish a lodging house for homeless newsboys, a place with books, religious services, and a sixpenny savings bank, where the boys would be gradually converted to good character. More ambitiously, he also planned to establish a series of "industrial schools," shaped to the particular needs of poor children, where street girls especially could learn useful skills and correct ways. Three years later, he could boast that the Society had established a lodging house for homeless girls, and five industrial schools for girls with paid teachers, one of which was especially intended for the German children of *Kleindeutscheland*. A home for newsboys had also been set up. By 1872, he reported that the Society maintained 5 lodging houses, 20 industrial schools, and 5 free reading rooms, intended to occupy the free time of children. The Society had come to the streets to stay.[64]

It had come to stay, however, in order that the children might leave. Brace did not intend to conquer the slum environment, nor did he plan to return his boys and girls to their old neighborhoods if he could do otherwise, for he recognized that the Society could not complete the reform of the street child so long as the child was exposed to the vicious influences of slum neighborhoods. Moreover, he believed—as did many of his fellow reformers—that there was little chance in New York of directing juveniles into a redeeming life of productive labor. Nearly everyone agreed that no man's character, certainly not that of the poor, was safe from corruption, unless he were engaged in disciplined, constructive work; nearly all could also agree that immigration resulted in a surplus of labor in the city. The primary aim of the Society, therefore, was to find homes and employment for city children in the countryside, where there seemed to be a virtually unlimited demand for labor. New York's problem, it was hoped, could be turned into a national asset which would accelerate the development of America's resources.[65]

Neither Brace's aims nor his means were new. Both the Almshouse and the House of Refuge had apprenticed children to city and rural families; the Juvenile Asylum in particular was founded on the hope that most of the children could be apprenticed to a master who would provide them with both a good home and the chance to acquire a useful skill.[66] It took the Society, however, to systematize the approach and to turn it into a powerful engine of reform.

Brace recognized that some children would not fit safely into the American household, while others required a period of training before they could be placed. He also had learned from the experience of earlier efforts of the need to be careful in choosing families; in 1850, The Almshouse Department had been condemned for its carelessness when five of its children died under the "care" of a foster mother. Brace therefore attempted to screen both children and families. Moreover, he was careful to retain legal guardianship of the children either for the Society or the natural parents, unless the employing families wished to adopt them. If the employers proved unwilling or unable to provide the child with decent care and with education, the child could be reclaimed. Conversely, as the Society advertised in a circular to farmers, "if the children are not satisfactory, they can be returned to our hands."[67]

This placing-out system was not entirely successful. Despite its efforts, the Society could not satisfy complaints that it was offering cheap labor to be exploited by farmers or that it was exporting depraved city youth to the innocent countryside. Moreover, it proved less able to place children in rural homes than Brace had hoped. Yet his work was one of the brightest features of the mid-nineteenth century. Although he was unable to raise all the money he needed for a full-time staff, he did succeed in winning widespread public support in the form of money and volunteer labor. The Society warmed the popular imagination, as the asylums could not, by offering a prospect more hopeful than reformatory walls, of children in Christian families amid "pure air, instead of the gases of sewers, trees and fields in place of narrow alleys." In an age when institutional trends often overran individualistic ideals, he succeeded in founding an organization on the principle that "no public charity can be for a moment equal in healthful influence to the humble home of an honest and kind-hearted man and woman."[68]

The principle was sentimental but effective. During its first forty years, the Children's Aid Society was to touch the lives of more than 200,000 children and to change significantly the destinies of the 90,000 who were placed outside the city. In 1872, Brace conceded that the Society had not eliminated the juvenile problem, but boasted with much truth that its existence made New York "the only large city in the world where there has been a comprehensive organization to deal with the sources of crime among children." He noted with pride that there had been a significant decline in the number of commitments of both boys and girls for crime since the late 1850s.[69]

As important as it was, Brace's organization was only one of many signs that a great wave of regeneration and reform had been developing for nearly a half century, the result chiefly of Protestant efforts to maintain New York as a Christian city. As it grew into a great commercial center, the metropolis had also become the capital of Protestant America. It was there each May that the great religious and benevolent societies such as the Bible Society, Home Missionary Society and Temperance Union met for their annual "anniversary" meetings. The leaders of local societies throughout the North came to select their national officers, make policy, listen to speeches, and also to have a good time. In 1849 *The Independent* complained that too many of those who attended the anniversaries "are more interested in seeing the sights of the city, in doing a little business, or in getting some taste and experience of city hospitality than in promoting the work of foreign missions." Despite such complaints, New York continued to be the place where the serious-minded as well as the frivolous centered their efforts to sustain what Edward Beecher, brother of Henry Ward Beecher, called the "great system of agencies which proposes to move the globe by the power of the word of God."[70]

Even while it was perfecting its efforts to save the world from the twin menace of infidelity and "Romanism," however, Protestantism found itself threatened by these enemies in New York itself. Although the most influential religious group in the city in 1855 were its estimated 118,000 Protestants, the traditional hegemony of Protestant churches was challenged by a combination of foreigners, degraded paupers, infidels, and Roman Catholics.[71] In fact, it looked as if New York were breaking into two hostile cities: The Uptown of Progress and Protestantism and the Lower City with its menacing hordes of immigrants and of the poor.

The acceleration of the uptown and suburban movement in

the decade after 1845 brought a rapid decline in the number of Protestants and their churches in the seven lower wards south of Canal Street. In 1855, the *Christian Advocate* listed 28 churches which had abandoned the area. There remained only 22 churches, four of which were Roman Catholic, to preserve a Christian influence over the some 180,000 people in the area. The equally rapid expansion of the wicked city in the same area served to convince many religious leaders that Protestant New York was seriously menaced by alien and immoral influences imported chiefly from Europe. Some, at least, believed that the battle between progress and wickedness in New York would decide the American future, for, in the words of one minister, the metropolis was "a city that is set on a hill," an influence for good or for evil that would penetrate even to the remotest districts of the nation.[72]

How to bridge the gap between the godly and the godless? The answer of the well-established City Tract Society was to intensify its missionary work. "There is a tendency and a temptation to provide a gospel for the rich in goodly sanctuaries, forgetting that Christ came to save the lowly," warned the Reverend Theodore L. Cuyler. "It is to counteract this tendency to pride and pomp . . . that this Society goes out on its mission of philanthropy. . . . Its city missionaries preach at the doors, in the garrets, underneath the ground, and to the outcast everywhere." In 1849 the Society reported that its 20 missionaries and 1160 part-time visitors were active in every part of the city, distributing tracts and Bibles, holding prayer meetings, and preaching the increasingly popular cause of temperance. Their particular aim was to induce the poor to attend church and especially to send their children to Sunday School.[73]

This work was reinforced by the even older interdenominational New York Sunday School Union, described by one of its supporters as "a preventive institution. It preserved children from a manhood of villainy and from an old age of desperation. . . . It was the recruiting and drilling agency of God's elect." In the 1850s, the Sunday School Union, through its missionary committee, gave increasing attention to reaching the tens-of-thousands of children who were assumed to be without religious instruction. By 1855, the Union employed 25 part-time missionaries to carry on a house-to-house campaign through "the darkest streets and alleys of the City" to persuade both the young and their parents to receive instruction in the gospel.[74]

Undoubtedly, many of these evangelists believed it was enough simply to bring the gospel to the heathen. As some missionaries soon recognized, however, the effort to save souls and establish Christian community demanded that they make themselves a persistent and meaningful presence in the lives of the poor. Therefore, they turned to the establishment of "mission stations" as a way of making religion a fixture in churchless slum areas. In turn, they often found it necessary to supplement preaching with at least some attention to the physical needs of the poor. This was especially the experience of the two well-publicized missions founded in the early 1850s to bring the Cross to the Five Points area of the Sixth Ward— a dismal world, said Charles Dickens, of "lanes and alleys paved with mud knee deep; underground chambers, where they dance and game. . . . ruined houses open to the street, whence, through wide gaps in the walls, other ruins loom upon the eye . . . hideous tenements, which take their name from robbery and murder."[75]

The Five Points Mission and its offshoot, the House of Industry, both fed and clothed bodies and ministered to the souls of the desperate inhabitants of the area. Rev. Lewis M. Pease, the founder of the House of Industry, attempted to make his mission an asylum from the corrupting influences of the Five Points, an island of purity which would serve the poor by providing jobs and training in its workshops for the un-employed, housing for the homeless, a free school for children, and food and clothing for all. Despite some rather unchristian hostility between the two missions, they played an important role in the lives of the Five Points poor for many years. Supplementing them by the late 1850s were the Gospel Union Mission and a special school established by the Children's Aid Society in the House of Industry for the growing number of

Italian children in the area. Not even four institutions could completely triumph over hardened sin, but they did work at least some social, moral, and physical regeneration of the most wicked environment in America.[76]

The Five Points missions were some of many signs which by the 1850s seemed to demonstrate the power of a vitalized Protestantism, working through both secular and religious means, to overcome the wicked city. By the end of the Civil War, there were 76 missions alone in New York, a pervasive benevolent network founded on the marriage of piety and social service. As the result of the efforts of a small number of committed Protestants, wealth was being harnessed to the task of converting the poor, especially the immigrant poor, into orderly, respectable, independent, and industrious Americans. New Yorkers could take pride in the vast array of organizations, associations, societies, asylums, schools, dispensaries and hospitals, and missions which they had created to heal what Brace called "the most ghastly wounds and diseases of society." If nothing else, they had made a pervasive apparatus to screen out and protect those of middle class character which contributed significantly to the work of the city in assimilating a diverse mass of rural poor people into the growing urban middle class.[77]

The 1850s, however, brought no conclusive victory over either poverty or wickedness. "We have evidence too strong to be either doubted or denied," warned the veteran missionary James M. Mathews, "that if the good among us are growing better, the bad are growing worse." Probably the wisest and strongest effort would not have conquered the subterranean city, if only because commercial New York attracted a vast rootless, floating population, much of which had already been apprenticed to the wicked life. The continued deluge of European immigrants after 1845 likewise assured the persistence of poverty and slums. On the other hand, defects in the Protestant crusade itself undoubtedly limited its successes and, indeed, might have widened the fissures in society which it hoped to close. Although its leaders made some notable efforts to improve the material condition of the poor, their main

[276]

objective was to change the characters and personalities of those whom they treated as problems to society. Thus, they did less to improve circumstances and provide jobs for the needy than to exhort weaklings and sinners to be good—an approach almost certain to antagonize many people, especially those who believed their poverty resulted not from defects of character but from a simple lack of money.[78]

The tendency of benevolent leaders to define the good in traditional Protestant terms especially left them open to some well-founded charges that they were hostile to the interests of the growing mass of non-Protestant immigrants. Although they generally refrained from attacking the Roman Church, they made no secret of their belief that Roman Catholicism was alien and inferior. The intensification of missionary efforts in immigrant areas raised Catholic opposition, which strengthened the Protestant conviction that Rome stood in the path of reform. The *Freeman's Journal*, for instance, charged that Rev. Pease tried to force Catholic children into his Five Points school against the wishes of their parents; Protestants countered with the charge that "Romanist bigots" compelled children to stay away from both mission and public schools. Without necessarily intending it, reformers and revivalists helped prepare the way for a resurgence of anti-Catholic nativism, especially in the form of the Know-Nothing Movement which mushroomed in 1853. By 1854, the nativists, with their pledge to bring the Bible back into the schools and to oust Catholics and foreigners from public office, had become a political force to be reckoned with.[79]

Nativism withered away after 1856, but not before it had intensified Catholic leaders' fears that Protestants were conspiring to destroy their faith. The conflict between the two great Christian churches had its positive side. Mutual suspicions and hostilities tended to reinforce the commitment of the faithful to both religions in a secularizing city, while the competition undoubtedly intensified the efforts of each to meet the needs of the young, the sick, and the unfortunate. Hostility to Protestant-dominated institutions stimulated Catholic efforts to establish their own schools, hospitals, and orphanages. In

[277]

The Streets of New York (1850)

FIGURE 17. (at right) This map, taken from a street guide published in 1850, shares the inadequacies of most street maps of the period, especially a blurring of many street names. It does, however, serve to display some of the special characteristics of mid-century New York. In 1850, business activity was still heavily concentrated in the First Ward below Liberty Street, but the commercial city had also spread north into an area which 20 years earlier had been the center of New York's social and institutional life. Note City Hall and its Park (the white triangle), Columbia College (the building in the white block at the head of Park Place), St. Paul's Chapel (On the left side of Broadway below the tip of the Park), and New York Hospital (On the left side of Broadway two blocks north of the Park). With the spread of commerce, the well-to-do had already moved out of the area uptown to new residential areas centering on Washington Square and Astor Place (top center) or to Brooklyn Heights (lower right corner). The location of the Fourth and Sixth wards north and east of the expanding commercial area and oriented toward the South Street docks (where most immigrants landed before the mid-1850s) best explains why these wards became the poorest and most socially depressed in the city. Note the Five Points slum area at the intersection of Orange, Cross, and Anthony streets northeast of City Hall. Note also the route of the Harlem Railroad from the bottom of Centre Street (to the right of City Hall) to Broome Street and thence uptown on the Bowery.

The street pattern of the lower city explain why, with the expansion of business activity, there were increasing jams in the movement of merchandise. As the old city was oriented toward South Street, little provision had been made for the movement of goods or people crosstown, between the East River and the rapidly expanding Hudson River waterfront. Perhaps the highlight of this increasingly irrational street pattern is Pearl Street which, beginning at the Battery, forms a crude semi-circle with its other end on Broadway above City Hall. Upper Pearl Street, however, did help ameliorate the effects of the failure to also make adequate provision for movement of traffic between downtown and uptown. Note how, in the areas east of Broadway, the north-south streets bend eastward in conformity with the early orientation of commerce toward the East River and also with the expansion of the East Side residential areas. On the West Side, three streets (West, Washington, and Greenwich) did provide direct access to uptown, but they divurged from the main north-south axis of development along Broadway and better served Greenwich Village (upper left corner) than the rest of the city. Little wonder that lower Broadway, the main access not only to uptown but to the East Side through Chatham Street, had became a major traffic problem by the 1850s.

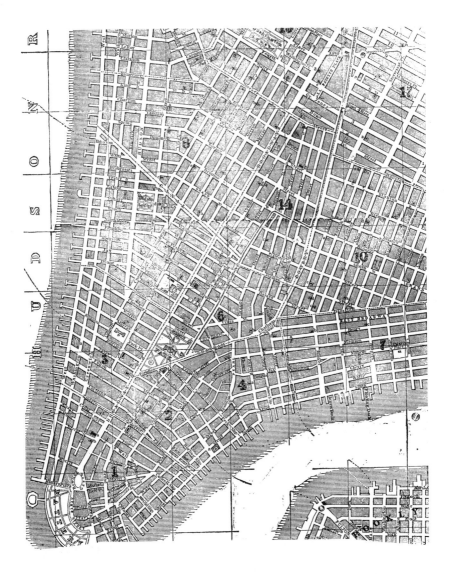

such ways, the Catholic Church with its more meager resources supplemented the Protestant social effort, for it too served to succor the needy, to educate the children, to inculcate morality, and generally to transform a heterogeneous mass of rural poor into respectable members of the urban middle class.[80] Yet the reality was conflict as well as competition. It was tragic that two powerful religious institutions, with much in common, each with a dream of Christian community, should enter into a long period of mutual antagonism which embittered both sides and assured that in the great city citizens would be strangers.

The tendency of Protestant reformers to widen rather than close the gap which separated them fron New York's growing Catholic population was matched by their failure to strike at the heart of the materialism and the violence which troubled their dream of a benevolent Christian city. Although they could claim to have saved the future through their successes in redeeming women and children and in strengthening the middle class household, even the most optimistic reformers recognized that they had not penetrated the two powerful extremes which dominated the public world of New York. One was the intensely masculine society of the subterranean city with its drinking places, fighting gangs, and growing influence in politics. The other was commercial and fashionable New York with its dedication to the getting and spending of money. The early 1850s strengthened both extremes, if for no other reason than it brought a burst of prosperity that weakened those memories of depressed times which earlier had chastened the exuberant worldliness of the city. While prosperity did aid the reformers by providing them with the money which they needed to perfect their engines of redemption, simultaneously it brought an intensification of the social tensions, violence, materialism, and corruption which threatened the moral order. Certainly, the hopes for an Age of Benevolence were dimmed by the spectacular emergence of a competing Age of Gold.

Chapter 11

THE AGE OF GOLD

IN 1849 NEW YORK entered the Age of Gold. The news of the California gold discoveries in 1848 had reached the city late in the year, stimulating dreams of wealth and adventure even in the cautious imaginations of the merchant community. "Gold! Gold!" wrote Philip Hone in January 1849. "The California fever is increasing in violence; thousands are going, among whom are many young men of our best families." Even earlier, the *Tribune* predicted that the gold rush would withdraw from New York and other crowded cities "thousands of people ready and willing to work, but who can find nothing to do." Certainly, both New York city and state did more than their share to plant, in the words of the *Tribune*, "another mighty Anglo-American empire" on the shores of the Pacific. In 1860, about one-fifth of the adult population of California had been born in New York state.[1]

During the first year of the gold rush, the city sent out some

[281]

of its very best sons with names like Schermerhorn, Beekman, Spofford, Ward, Livingston, Le Roy, Emmett, Ruggles, and Knapp. Along with them, New York sent its organizational skills. In February, members of the New York Union Mining Company set sail for the land of gold, soon to be followed by some "thirty enterprising young men, from the best families of our city," who formed the New York Excelsior Trading and Mining Association headed by ex-Congressman Moses G. Leonard. While progressive New York contributed more than its share of talents to the development of California, its wicked other self also provided a fair quota of the thieves, gamblers, and toughs who made early San Francisco a hell for the respectable. The various vigilance committees, organized in the California city with the help of New Yorkers, repaid this debt in kind by running some of the troublemakers out of town.[2]

The close ties between these Atlantic and Pacific cities was a consequence of New York's predominance in the California trade. Eastern gold-seekers recognized the difficulty of reaching California by land. In March 1849 Porter and Robjohn advertised that their "Aerial Locomotive" would soon be ready to fly to the land of gold, the expected travel time being two to five days. Their advertisement was premature; two years later, the Aerial Locomotive, a huge steam-powered balloon, remained unfinished at Robjohn's shop near Hoboken. More practical-minded New Yorkers focused their hopes on a variety of projects for a Transcontinental railroad, including a proposed $100 million company to build a line from New York to San Francisco.[3] During the gold rush, however, easterners had to depend on ocean shipping, particularly on the steamers run by the Pacific Mail Company, organized in 1847 by William H. Aspinwall and other prominent New Yorkers to carry the mails from New York to the Pacific coast via the Isthmus of Panama. The Company, in its first decade, carried some 175,000 passengers to California and brought back $200 million in gold, aided by a railroad which Aspinwall and his New York associates had managed to complete across the Isthmus in 1855.[4] By that year, the Pacific Mail steamers were only some among many sailing and steam vessels which made New York the focal point of the California traffic either by way of Central America or Cape Horn. To handle the increasing flow of gold and other valuables by sea, expressmen and bankers organized Wells, Fargo & Co. at New York in 1852. Wells, Fargo soon began to buy up the local express and stage lines in California, which expedited the gold traffic and made the company a financial power in the West.[5]

From the beginning, the gold rush jolted the city out of its sluggish recovery from the depression which followed the panic of 1837. The demands of the eastern Forty-Niners who thronged to the port created an instant demand for clothes, tools, and provisions—and whisky, rifles, pistols, and bowie knives—which New York merchants rushed to meet. One dealer in India Rubber goods offered "to California the best Gold Washer extent. A blind man, washing with either hands or feet, may wash out $5,000 worth of gold a day. This is no puff."[6] The demand for gold washers and similar paraphernalia, however, had less effect than the trade soon generated by the spectacular increase of population in California. During the early 1850s, the new state was a lucrative export market for virtually everything commercial New York had to offer; butter exports alone, said the *Tribune*, engrossed "an enormous" amount of New York capital. An even greater shock to the sluggish economy was furnished by the unprecedented flood of gold into New York from San Francisco, over $175 million worth for the years 1851 through 1854 alone.[7]

Gold! Gold! The deluge produced by the California and then by comparable Australian gold strikes affected the psychology of the entire commercial world. In 1852, the *Scientific American* declared that "gold is beginning to be counted by tons. . . . Surely this is the age of gold." More money, more credit, more investment, more production, more consumption, more exchange—commercial New York was caught up in a giddy upward spiral.[8] In the years 1851 through 1853, there were 27 new banks created, more than doubling the number existent in 1849. Prosperity increased the sales of ready-made clothing, to the great benefit of the New York garment industry.[9] It also brought the golden age of New York shipbuilding and of ancillary industries, especially the building of engines for the growing number of steamers. A steady increase in the value of exports and imports was capped in 1854 by a spectacular surge to levels more than double those of 1849; ship tonnage engaged between foreign ports and New York increased by more than 60 percent during the same period. Prosperity—it was great, especially for the larger merchants, manufacturers, and money men. The burgeoning of the economy, however, placed a great strain on New York's facilities, especially on its public space.[10]

The rapid expansion of waterborne commerce overburdened New York's inadequate port facilities, particularly its woeful piers and wharves which, complained one critic, looked as if the city fathers were striving to nullify Manhattan's natural advantages.[11] Even more, the new prosperity threatened to choke the equally inadequate system of narrow and crooked streets in the lower city. A correspondent for the *London Times* wrote that "the throng and rush of traffic in the business part of New York is astonishing even for London. . . . There is a perpetual jam and lock of vehicles for nearly two miles along the chief thoroughfare; the traffic is outgrowing the capacity of the streets to admit it, and as the busiest part of the city is also the narrowest . . . it is a puzzle to devise any plan to relieve the pressure." Although the narrowness of the lower city was chiefly responsible for this crush, the correspondent also blamed the careless, "provincial" business practices for needlessly choking the streets. Having failed to develop a system of warehouses to store imports near the docks, merchants had the goods hauled through the streets to their places of business for storage; when the goods were sold, they had to be hauled back through the streets for shipment. Moreover, this process obstructed the flow of traffic which it had helped create; boxes, bales, and packing cases were left on streets and sidewalks until they were stored away; goods when sold, frequently had to be repacked, with much of the packing being done on the public walks: "Casks are hooped and cases nailed in the paths of men."[12]

Prosperity also multiplied the number of small manufacturers, craftsmen and retailers who crowded the available space of the lower city. The 1850s brought the construction of buildings especially designed to accommodate the needs of light manufacturing, but, whether in new buildings or old, the makers of goods found themselves crowded together, often cheek by jowl with the sellers of goods. A fire which in 1853 ravaged five buildings around one corner of Nassau and Fulton streets burned out a diversity of businessmen: A clothier, wood engraver, job-printer, lithographer, three publishers, and manufacturers of surgical instruments, military ornaments, and jewelry. This concentrated mixture of business was largely the result of the dependence of small businessmen on the external economies provided by the commercial city, the rental space, credit facilities, transportation facilities, and customers concentrated there; whatever the advantages for business, however, it added to the number of carts, wagons, barrows, boxes, bales, barrels, and people jamming the streets and sidewalks on business days.[13]

Thriving business attracted other businesses, but it also accelerated the flight of the upper and middle classes from the lower city either uptown or to the suburbs. The burgeoning class of commuters, in turn, further complicated the downtown rush and crush. Ferry boats from New Jersey and Brooklyn disgorged thousands of passengers each morning; the wagons and hacks associated with the ferry traffic helped jam the streets. Even more troublesome were the horsedrawn omnibuses required to haul masses of commuters first downtown and then back uptown six days a week. By the late 1840s omnibuses had become a big business, and an essential part of the emerging system of mass transportation. In 1846, 10 companies ran a total of 255 licensed stages; seven years later 22 companies operated 683 stages, a million-dollar business which transported more than 100,000 people a day.[14]

The jouncing, often painfully overcrowded omnibuses were a vital part of the city's internal economy. When in 1848 a $60,000 fire destroyed most of the stages and horses used by Kipp & Brown on their busy West Side lines, downtown merchants and city officials rushed to help get the stages rolling again. In 1850, Thomas Kettell, the editor of the *Democratic Review*, noted that the expanded lines and reduced fares of the "omnibus system" enabled more and more New Yorkers to remove their homes from the cramped environment of the lower city, a double blessing in that it established a healthier and more comfortable residential environment uptown while providing additional downtown space for expanding business.[15]

If the omnibuses served to promote essential efficiency, they also made a particularly noticeable contribution to the traffic congestion which threatened to choke the lower city. The fan-like system which provided stage service every five minutes during the day on the uptown avenues came to a focus on Broadway below City Hall. "You pick your teeth on the Astor House steps," wrote George G. Foster, "and see, on an average, fifteen omnibuses pass each way, every minute, and for the greater part of the day, all full." Omnibus drivers hurried their horses down the avenues to merge into a sea of other vehicles, also attracted by Broadway's character as the city's fashionable shopping street and as the most convenient route to downtown business and ferries. Add to these the traffic on Broadway's busy cross streets, introduce the numerous obstructions presented by the haphazard city, and the result was a situation where, said one observer, "carts and omnibuses are daily at a deadlock for half an hour together." One irate commuter complained that he had been virtually imprisoned for 20 minutes on a deadlocked omnibus; he could not disembark because he was afraid that he might get run over in the passing traffic. In a city which had taken as its article of faith the adage that "time is money," such delays were intolerable.[16]

Even the most patient citizen had reason to complain that the city had failed to develop the street system demanded by its two major traffic problems. One was the need for an efficient crosstown route to accommodate the increasingly heavy freight and passenger traffic between the east and west sides. The East River and Hudson River waterfronts each handled a share of trade and passenger service, but the first was oriented toward Long Island Sound and New England, while the second faced north and west. With the exception of

Fulton Street, the street system of the lower city seemed designed to frustrate rather than expedite the transfer of goods and people from one waterfront to the other. Beginning in the mid-1840s, New York debated a proposal to continue Canal Street, which angled south from the Hudson River to Centre Street, through to the East River docks. The proponents of the scheme argued that it would remove some traffic from Broadway as well as facilitate movement across the city. In 1848, a group of prominent East Side propertyholders offered to pay for the work themselves. It was not until the mid-1850s, however, that the city actually began work on the much-overdue project. By that time, the upward progress of the city and the continued growth of commerce generated new pressures for more crosstown routes which, again, the city was slow to meet. In 1857, Mayor Wood complained that in the area below Fulton Street, with one partial exception (Liberty Street) "there is almost an entire absence of facility for the transportation of merchandise from one side of the city to the other."[17]

The north-south movement of traffic in the lower city was served little better, for the municipal government was equally slow to develop the alternative uptown routes needed to divert vehicles from overburdened Broadway below City Hall Park. In 1848, a committee of Aldermen recommended that Church Street on the West Side be widened and extended so as to make it "another Broadway." Nothing was done. More successful was an effort to extend the Bowery. In 1854 a group of East Side propertyowners and businessmen, claiming to represent $12 million in property, asked the city to extend the Bowery from Chatham Square to Franklin Square so as to give downtown Pearl Street direct access to an uptown route. Their arguments were compelling: The new thoroughfare would not only ease the pressure on Broadway (which received Bowery traffic by way of Chatham Street) but open the way for the business development of a large portion of the Fourth Ward, where real estate, as if defying the law of gravity, had not grown in value. The fact that the Bowery extension and the expected business development would displace many of the poor inhabitants of the Fourth Ward weighed little against the interests of $12 million in property. The project was started the next year.[18] One Bowery, however, did not make another Broadway; the need for a comprehensive system of streets and avenues to relieve New York's great show-and-shopping street remained unfulfilled despite fears that downtown congestion would eventually depreciate Broadway property values.

The 1850s did bring a major reorganization of the city's system of transportation, but the result was far less a masterful solution to the underlying problems of the city than a patch-work response to the varied pressures and opportunities of growth. A masterful response to any fundamental problem was too much to expect from the chief guardian of public space, the Common Council. Whatever its defects as a mirror of the popular will, the Council traditionally was sensitive to the voice of private property. When decisions for the widening and extending of streets affected millions of dollars in property often for ill as well as good, the municipal legislature tended to act cautiously unless they had the clear support of business-men and real estate owners.[19] Yet the growth of the city, even in the sluggish days before the gold rush, demanded action. How to facilitate the flow of crosstown and uptown traffic? How to resolve downtown congestion? How, especially, to please businessmen, propertyowners, and taxpayers? These questions, which even Solomons and saints would find difficult to answer, confronted the 40 largely unpaid, part-time Ald-ermen and Assistant Aldermen, themselves chiefly lawyers and small businessmen associated with the prevailing culture of private gain.

It was not surprising, therefore, that the most important decision made by the Council involved not the reordering of the public streets but their use by private enterprise for private profit. While the congested state of the lower city posed a problem for the harried legislators, it promised profits to those businessmen who could devise an effective means of moving masses of people. What could convey more people more quickly and quietly than the cumbersome omnibuses? In 1846, John Randel, Jr. proposed that passenger cars, pulled by an endless rope, be run on an elevated railroad over Broadway. Even earlier, the Council briefly considered a plan for a railroad under Broadway, an idea that was revived in 1852 by a New Yorker in the even more grandiose form of "two under-ground Railroads" which would run the entire length of Manhattan Island.²⁰ These ideas appealed to the advanced imagination of an age which could devise telegraphs and "Aerial Locomotives," but they had little influence in a city which wanted quick solutions that would not damage business or propertied interests. When the solution came, it arrived in a more plodding form, but, plodding or not, it ushered in a new era both for transportation and for politics.

The answer already existed in the shape of the New York and Harlem Railroad, whose horsedrawn cars had since the 1830s carried hundreds of thousands of passengers from the area north of City Hall uptown by way of the Bowery and Fourth Avenue to Yorkville and beyond.²¹ The steady growth of commuter traffic encouraged others to adapt the horsecar railroad for use in downtown areas below the limits of Harlem service. As early as 1844, the Common Council received two proposals to lay a railroad through Broadway, one for a city-owned line whose profits would be used to pay the municipal debt. Two years later, a group of businessmen interested in developing the West Side applied for permission to construct a city railroad through Hudson Street and Eighth Avenue. These proposals were uniformly rejected by the Common Council, chiefly because they threatened the interests of the omnibus companies, which had much influence on members of the council. In 1849 the *Evening Post* complained that the Eighth Avenue Railroad plan had been annually defeated by the opposition of three West Side omnibus lines, even though it was backed by "a majority of householders along the line, and by other parties representing thirty millions of capital."²²

The arguments in favor of the horsecars, however, were too strong to be denied for long: They were quieter and faster than the omnibuses—and bigger, for a horse could draw a much heavier load on rails than on the rough pavements of New York. By moving more people faster with fewer vehicles, they would lessen traffic congestion, especially on Broadway.

They would, thus, increase surrounding property values, while at the same time reducing the need to widen and repave streets—a matter of growing concern both for the city and for property owners. One other advantage was less often noted but was perhaps even more compelling: There were big profits to be made from an efficient system of mass transportation, especially in a city with so few private conveyances.[23] In crowded, congested New York, there was as much gold in the public streets as there was in California—for those businessmen who could get public permission to use them.

In 1851, Erastus C. Benedict, a farsighted, former Whig member of the Common Council from the Fifteenth Ward, attempted to reconcile the rival interests. Metropolitan New York, he said, had become a society of interrelated parts, each of which depended for its survival on an efficient system of transportation. His experience on the Council had convinced him that the omnibusmen had fallen into "an attitude hostile to the public interest," because they believed that omnibuses and horsecars were incompatable.[24] In order to substitute harmony for conflict, Benedict urged the Council to pass a comprehensive ordinance incorporating all forms of transportation into one coherent metropolitan system.

To relieve lower Broadway of the congestion caused by the uptown omnibuses, all stages serving that street would be barred under his plan from running north of City Hall Park. In compensation for the loss of their uptown business, the omnibus lines would be granted new crosstown routes in the lower city, particularly for the convenience of passengers on the Brooklyn and New Jersey ferries; Benedict noted that there was not one such route in the downtown area, even though ferry and steamboat landings were clustered there. To meet uptown commuter needs, his plan provided for a horsecar line on Broadway north of City Hall and five similar lines from the same general area on either side of Broadway, forming a system in which virtually every uptown resident would be within two blocks of one of the lines. In addition, the Harlem and Hudson River railroads would be permitted to extend their tracks as far south as the Park in exchange for more frequent horsedrawn service uptown to 42nd Street and beyond. This plan, said Benedict, would make the Park the point "convenient to the centre business, from which conveyances radiate in every direction, so that passengers can never fail to find some conveyance ready to take them near their destination, any moment of the day."[25]

Under such a system, Broadway would be decongested, conveyances would be accessible for all, and "the city will be everywhere alive with public conveyances, in which we may ride a mile for one, two, or three cents in every direction . . . and then the public conveyance, like the streets, will be used by every one." As a result, the uptown movement would be accelerated, downtown would be cleared for commercial expansion, New Yorkers would have access to a healthy residential environment, property values would increase, tax revenues would rise, and both omnibus and railroad companies would profit from the anticipated fourfold increase in travel on their lines.[26]

Benedict's effort to harmonize the conflicting interests of the expanding city, however, had little chance against the limited vision and even more limited options of the Common Council. In the beginning, the Council made some effort to guide the development of the new system. In 1850, a special committee of Aldermen reported a general railroad plan which provided for two horsecar lines beginning near the Battery, one to serve the West Side and the other the East Side of the city as far north as the Harlem River. The whole system, some 32 miles of main and branch lines, would have expanded uptown service and indirectly diminished the pressures on Broadway, but the Committee made little effort either to resolve the downtown traffic problem or to harmonize the omnibus and railroad interests. It was inevitable that the omnibus companies would condemn the plan as ruinous to their business. As an alternative, omnibus owners proposed that city government construct its own rail system which would be rented out for use by specially equipped omnibuses at one cent per passenger carried.[27]

The omnibus plan provoked debate in the Council over public ownership. Proponents of the plan argued that the government, which had successfully developed both streets and a Croton water system, certainly was capable of laying out an effective rail system. They emphasized the importance of maintaining public control over the public streets, especially as a source of revenue; an Alderman estimated that the scheme would yield $300,000 a year to the city, while assuring low fares for the public and adequate profits for the omnibus companies. The omnibusmen, anxious to put their own operations in the best light, introduced a note of prophecy when they warned that to turn mass transit over to the railroad companies would "result in such a combination of capital and profits as to enable them to exert a powerful influence over the interests of the city."[28]

Such arguments, however, had little weight in the Board of Aldermen. The Special Committee on Railroads identified the idea of public ownership with a few "well-meaning persons of small forethought" and went on to assert that public construction would double the costs of laying the rail lines "owing to the entire absence of a system of responsibility that private enterprise alone can arrange and insist upon." After charging that the omnibus companies had conspired to keep their rates high and service poor, at the expense of workingmen, the Committee predicted that in less than a year after private railroads were completed "many hundreds of neat little cottages will spring up all over the unoccupied acres in the upper wards, affording residences and homesteads to many thousands of mechanics, clerks, and laborers."[29]

The pretty pictures painted by both sides, however, could not conceal the conflict among rival interests for control of the increasingly lucrative mass transit business. Confronted with a growing traffic problem, the Council was obliged to make an agonizing choice between competing forms of business enterprise. In 1850, it refused to act in favor of the railroads, but that was the last victory for the omnibuses. The logjam broke during the next year, in part—perhaps largely—because some of the more influential omnibusmen joined the opposition. Were they simply yielding to progress? Or were they associating, as rumor suggested, with railroadmen in order that the railroads would buy them out for more than their omnibus operations were worth? Whatever their reasons, such West Side omnibus partnerships as Kipp & Brown and O'Keefe & Duryea figured prominently among the beneficiaries when in July 1851 the Council granted two companies the right to lay rails from the City Hall area through the streets to and up, respectively, Sixth and Eighth avenues as far north as the Harlem River.[30] The next year brought what the *Evening Post* called "a very deluge of railroad projects," some of them inspired by East Side omnibus operators. The Council responded by granting charters for a new West Side line on Ninth Avenue and for lines on Second and Third avenues, the last to a combination of omnibus owners and prominent Democratic politicians.[31]

Thus, in two short years, the once-laggard Common Council established the general outlines of the transportation system which was to dominate the city for the next half century. Confronted by the reality of five street railroads, some of the omnibus companies quickly sold their horses and equipment to their competitors; the Third Avenue line reportedly spent $400,000 to buy out five omnibus operations. The rest of the omnibusmen attempted to adjust to the new situation. After first trying to undercut the new competition by reducing rates, they concentrated their operations on the uptown and crosstown streets not served by the horse car lines. Though the omnibus business ceased to grow, it remained a vital part of the transit system for many years, bolstered by its continued possession of the most lucrative of all the streets, Broadway.[32]

As for the railroads, eventually they pushed their lines farther south as well as north to the Harlem. The Third Avenue line celebrated its progress uptown as far as Yorkville in 1856 by opening a new $100,000 terminal building at 65th Street. The previous year, the Second Avenue Company received a reward for its rapid progress uptown to 61st Street and beyond when the Council authorized it to bridge the Harlem in anticipation of an extension of its service into southern Westchester. By 1856 the railroad companies had laid nearly 23 miles of track in the city. With their five-cent fares (the maximum permitted under their charters), they quickly built a mass commuter traffic; in 1857, the brightly colored, rumbling horsecars carried over 23 million passengers. One New Yorker could boast that in developing the horsecar the city had created an "American institution" which later was adapted to the needs of that model for urban America, London.[33]

By the mid-1850s, the combination of omnibus and horsecar formed a system of mass transit for the expanding, crowded city. A guidebook in 1857 reported that the system carried more than 50 million passengers a year, "collecting small change" to the amount of $2 million. What's more, that system was becoming the basis for the future expansion of metropolitan New York. The Second Avenue and other Manhattan railroads eventually connected with transportation lines in southern Westchester County, which later would become the Bronx. Moreover, the East River ferries provided a connection between the New York lines and Brooklyn's extensive system of horsecars and omnibuses. In 1859, the *Economist* predicted the day would soon come when a tunnel under the East River "would permit the New York City railroads to connect with the Brooklyn railroads, allowing the population to circulate freely as much upon Long Island as northerly upon Manhattan Island," and went on to note that the prospect to easy commuting on the New York lines had encouraged speculators in New Jersey real estate to dream of establishing a ferry across the Hudson at 100th Street to encourage the settlement of their properties.[34]

Although they contributed to the beginnings of the future metropolitan system, the greatest effect of the street railroads was to hasten the development of upper Manhattan. Able in the same half-hour's time to cover four miles to the omnibus's three, the horsecars expanded the limits of the old city to 59th Street and beyond. In 1856, the *Tribune* declared that the city railroads had become one of the necessities of city life and noted how the Third Avenue line affected a broad area around 30th Street: "Up until the present year there were large open spaces of ground in the vicinity of the old Phelps mansion; but the piles of building now arising around it will soon obliterate all appearance of its ever having been a country residence. It will be in the heart of the city. The families that will next year occupy the hundreds of buildings there, will be within half an hour and five cents cost of the City Hall." By opening up residential territory uptown, the new transit system slowed the migration of taxpayers to neighboring suburbs, to the great benefit of the revenue-hungry city government.[35] By accelerating the movement of residents out of the lower city, it opened new territory for commercial development and so helped prevent downtown New York from choking on its own congestion. As Erastus Benedict had hoped, the combined system of omnibuses and horsecars promoted the growth of a more efficient city of specialized but interdependent parts.

Yet the new system was a mixed blessing for New York. New Yorkers had first gloried in the smooth and spacious superiority of the horsecars over the old jouncing omnibuses, but soon they began lamenting the overcrowded cars and erratic schedules. They had dreamed of low fares that would enable them to abandon the crowded residences of the lower city, but they soon learned that five-cent rides were not cheap on an income of four or five dollars a week.[36] They had hoped that the passage of horsecars by their doors would increase the value of their homes, but they learned that mass transit and mass movement could bring with them mass blight.[37] And they had been willing to believe that the horsecars would free them from the power of the omnibus companies—only to learn the truth of the omnibusmen's prophecy in 1850 that a greater, more menacing power would rise. Seven years later, Mayor Wood warned: "It sometimes occurs that incorporated companies become more powerful than the laws or the authority of those who execute them. It is feared that some of the companies owning and conducting the city railroads have reached this high degree of assumption."[38]

Certainly, the city in giving the street railroad a quasi-monopoly of the public streets, with their ready-made rights of way and the ready-made business of a concentrated population, gave life to profitable and powerful corporations far larger than the partnerships of omnibusmen. The scale of investment and of anticipated profits dramatically increased; the Third Avenue company, the largest, was capitalized at over a million dollars. The extensive cost of laying track and providing horse-powered cars was inflated by the desire of the incorporators to get rich as quickly as possible. Although they employed light rails and enjoyed the use of a public right of way, the city's railroads cost, on the average, more than $120,000 per mile (the figure was $50,000 in Boston) to build, nearly three times as much as the average cost of the steam railroads in the state of New York, and as one observer estimated, five times more than they should have cost. This extravagance, said the *Railway Times*, included the cost of buying up municipal legislators, although an even heavier expense resulted from the need to buy out competing omnibus lines.[39]

Probably the greatest excess resulted from the new and profitable art of stock-watering. The anticipated returns from public franchises enabled the incorporators to sell over $4 million worth of stocks and bonds at great profit for themselves. Henry Varnum Poor, an expert on railroad finance, noted a further advantage of overcapitalization: as profits were estimated on the basis of capital rather than the actual cost of the roads, the companies were able to silence public demands for fare reductions by pleading low profits when in fact they were making enormous gains; practically, it meant that the railroadmen were able to siphon off most of the benefits the public should have derived from the lower costs of rail transportation: "The success of these roads is a remarkable illustration of . . . the manner in which the right to build them has been exercised, of the entire impunity with which the grossest outrages on the public are perpetrated in the city of New York."[40]

By establishing the opportunities to make such profits, the Common Council gave life to the corporate demons which were for decades to plague New York. Public franchises were even better than gold mines; they promised to grow more valuable over time. The rapidly growing need for mass transit increased the businessmen's stake in the public streets. In 1860, the right to run street cars on Broadway was valued at $3 million. Big stakes meant big power to persuade and big money to bribe the public officials responsible for granting franchises or for enforcing their provisions.⁴¹ Thus, the early horsecar franchises marked the beginning of the pattern of corporate abuse and political corruption so troubling to the nation and the city after the Civil War. Political corruption, corporate power, big wealth, social cleavages and tensions—in retrospect, it is evident that the Age of Gold ushered in a new era in New York which made the peculations and social troubles of the period before 1850 look like the emblems of innocence.

The beginnings of the new era came quietly in November 1851, when New Yorkers voted on a wide variety of state and local candidates. "The fact that there were *thirteen* different ballots to be deposited by each voter," complained the *Tribune*, "rendered the process of voting exceedingly tedious"—so tedious that many men did not vote at all. There was, however, at least one influence to guide the bewildered voter: A wide-spread dissatisfaction with the Whig-dominated Common Council, which had disappointed the hopes for reform raised by the Charter of 1849.⁴² Citizens were particularly unhappy with the President of the Board of Aldermen, one Morgan Morgans of the Seventh Ward, who discreetly chose not to run for reelection. In his place, the Seventh Ward Whigs nominated the Assistant Alderman, John B. Webb. As their challenger, the Democrats nominated a small businessman and popular foreman of the Americus Fire Engine Company, William Marcy Tweed, who had lost a listless race to Webb the year before. This time, helped by the presence of a Temperance candidate, Joel Blackman, who polled 206, mostly Whig, votes, Tweed won by 48 votes. The Seventh was one of ten wards in which independent candidates split the Whig vote. City-wide, the Democrats won 15 of the 20 seats on the Board of Aldermen.⁴³

What did this nondescript election mean? For the *Tribune*, it meant the repudiation of a Council which had proven itself "inefficient, prodigal and unworthy." For Tweed it meant a great deal more. Although he left no papers, no record of his thoughts, it seems evident that election meant opportunity.

THE AGE OF GOLD

The brawny Tweed was a popular local hero as the courageous foreman of the "Big Six," the familiar name of the Americus Fire Company. As a 28-year-old brush manufacturer and chairmaker, however, the ambitious Tweed was lost in the roar of the downtown city, one of thousands of striving small businessmen.[44] The young man had achieved more success than most, yet that success was small when measured in terms of the Age of Gold. Political power offered more. Tweed had been involved in politics long enough to recognize that government often did favors for the influential. He must also have been aware of the growing importance of the Common Council as a source of valuable grants to businessmen. The late 1840s had brought rumors of payoffs to Aldermen for ferry franchises; conveniently, the new Alderman was placed on the Ferries Committee—as well as Repairs and Supplies, which could do favors for small contractors. The conflict between the stagemen and advocates of the horsecars educated him in the value of railroad franchises; in 1852 one of the recipients of the Second Avenue franchise granted by Tweed's Council was his father-in-law and ex-employer, Joseph C. Skaden.[45]

As a businessman as well as fireman, he had made some influential friends. He owned two stores, at 240 and 357 Pearl Street, in 1852; undoubtedly, he knew the proprietor of the porterhouse at 340 Pearl, Jacob Oakley, who also had been elected in 1851 as Alderman from the Eighth Ward. Probably, he also knew the Alderman from the Sixth Ward and proprietor of the livery stable at 470 Pearl, Thomas J. Barr; Barr's nephew, Peter Barr Sweeny, was rumored to have helped persuade the previous Council to grant the Eighth Avenue franchise, an appropriate beginning for one of the members of the later alleged Tweed Ring. Nor was it improbable that Tweed knew the newly elected Aldermen from the Second, Thirteenth, and Seventeenth Wards, all in business at nearby Fulton Market: Dudley Haley, fishmonger; John Pearsall, fruit vendor, and William H. Cornell, butcher. Pearsall was to serve with Tweed on the Ferries Committee, with Tweed and Haley on Repairs and Supplies, and with Haley and Cornell on the Markets Committee.[46]

It was all one happy family—one which perhaps already knew what it wanted when the Common Council was first organized for business early in 1852. Most of the new Aldermen had not served on that Board before, although several had been Assistants in the previous Council. Virtually none of them came from the class of lawyers and merchants who had once dominated the Council; few had any notion of the old ideal of disinterested public service that had made membership on the boards a matter of unsalaried honor. They were mostly small businessmen—a tobacconist, a saloonkeeper, a chairmaker, a stonecutter, a saddler, three marketmen, four dealers in lime, timber and ice—who had stood silently on the margins of the business world watching their "betters" get rich.[47] Having long been aware that previous Councils had, at least occasionally, given and taken favors, they saw nothing particularly unnatural or immoral about getting their cut of the municipal pie. They arrived at the right time. The booming, congested city demanded a wide variety of municipal improvements: Schools had to be built, dock facilities upgraded, sewer and water pipes laid, markets improved, streets cleaned, paved, and widened, avenues extended and, above all, the traffic problem unsnarled. After more than a decade of cautious administration, it was time for a great spurt in municipal activity, without much regard for the traditional complaints of taxpayers.

From the moment it organized, the new Council displayed an unprecedented initiative and ruthlessness. Early in January 1852, the Aldermen, as an act allegedly of entrenchment and reform, voted to suspend several of the projects approved by the previous council, "for the purpose," charged the *Tribune*, "of seizing upon several contracts for their hungry partisans." Next came an effort to seize control of patronage, particularly in the City Inspector's Department; in March, the same newspaper reported that "the party facitiously termed '*Our Folks*' . . . walked over the Mayor's veto, turned the Deputy City Inspector out of office, and seized upon the entire business of inspecting cesspools and appointing night scavengers." Almost from the first, the Council attracted a swarm of favor-seekers, asking for jobs, for contracts and for franchises. The *Tribune's* city reporter complained that at times he and other newsmen were crowded out of their places near the Aldermen's table by crowds of "lobby members"; at one meeting, "there were thirty or forty men inside the bar, roosting on the backs of Aldermen's chairs, and crowding the Reporters with the most impudent freedom."[48]

Despite the crowds, the Council showed a marvelous ability to pass ordinances and resolutions with dispatch—and also to spend money. In September, the minority complained of "the imprudent and hasty manner in which legislative proceedings are conducted and important measures adopted by the Common Council—often upon simple resolution." By then it was apparent that the restraints embodied in the Charter of 1849 on legislative spending had broken down. During the year, expenditures for lamps and gas increased by nearly 45 percent, for street cleaning by 70 percent and for the purchase of real estate by 400 percent. In his annual report for 1852, the conservative City Comptroller, A. C. Flagg, warned that city spending was approaching "the aggregate annual expenditures, for the ordinary support of government, of the thirty one states of the Union." Despite Flagg's warning, expenditures continued to rise. During Tweed's two years on the Board of Aldermen, they totaled nearly $8.5 million, some 37 percent more than during the previous two years. As a result, the taxrate, which had fallen during the two earlier years, increased by over 25 percent.[49]

The Council showed an equal propensity to use and abuse public property. Not satisfied with simply leasing out city-owned piers at giveaway rents to their favorites, the Aldermen attempted to sell off most of the city's most profitable dock properties on the same terms. Although they were blocked by a judicial injunction, they did succeed in selling the Gansevoort Market property on the Hudson River, perhaps the most valuable single piece of real estate in the city, for much less than it was worth, allegedly pocketing between $45,000 and $75,000 for themselves.[50]

Most lucrative of all were the franchises so desired by businessmen. The Board of Aldermen overrode the Mayor's veto in order to grant the Wall Street ferry franchise to one of their favorites, Jacob Sharp, for some $5000 less in ferry rents than other applicants for the franchise had been willing to pay to the city; the next year, the Council cut Sharp's rent from its original $20,000 a year to $5000. Aware of a possible political ambush by the still powerful omnibus men, the Aldermen were more hesitant about the granting of railroad franchises. In the summer of 1852, however, they stepped into the troubled waters by attempting to transfer the Eighth Avenue franchise from its original grantees to another group; the move was blocked by the Mayor and the courts, but the Council emerged, so it was charged, $40,000 richer in bribes from both groups. After waiting until the local and national elections had been held in November, they opened the gates by approving franchises for Second and Third avenues on terms unfavorable to the city.[51]

They also passed one other railroad franchise, for Broadway. Here, however, they were taught a painful lesson in the dangers of intervening in the interests of the merchant elite. Broadway was attractive but poisoned fruit for the Council. For years, the crowded, busy street had posed a double problem for the city: the concentrated mass of omnibuses and other vehicles both created a traffic tangle and also broke down the pavements, requiring expensive repairs. A street railroad seemed to be an ideal solution, for it would eliminate hundreds of heavy, noisy omnibuses. It was ideal for capitalists as well, since the crowds promised tremendous profits for the company which got the right to lay rails in the street; one New Yorker estimated the annual receipts of such a railroad at $1 million a year. It was no surprise, then, when in July 1852 a group headed by Jacob Sharp applied for the Broadway grant.[52]

It was no surprise, either, that his application should raise a storm. The experienced Sharp was prepared to quiet the opposition of the omnibusmen by buying out their interests in Broadway, but he could not buy off the major Broadway shops and their rich patrons, who feared that a street railroad would ruin *their* street. Headed by A. T. Stewart, the millionaire owner of the great department store, Broadway businessmen rallied to attack Sharp's scheme as ruinous to property values and, worse, to the character of New York's proudest street. The opposition made one point that appealed to the romantic side of New Yorkers, when they noted that the congested condition, so troubling to the city fathers was very much a part of Broadway's character:

> The more noise, the more confusion, the greater the crowd, the better the lookers on and crowders seem to like it, and the world from the match-boy to the gentlemen of leisure, resort there to see the confusion, the uproar, and the sights while all enjoy it alike. The din, this driving, this omnibus-thunder, this squeezing, this jamming, crowding, and at times smashing, is the exhilerating music which charms the multitude and draws its thousands within the whirl. This is Broadway—this *makes* Broadway. Take from it those elements, the charm is gone.[53]

Walt Whitman could hardly have said it better, but such an ode to congestion was not likely to have much influence either on the Council or its constituents. The opposition, therefore, maneuvered on to more practical grounds when the nature of the proposed grant to Sharp and his Manhattan Railroad Company became known in November. The defenders of the grant pointed out that it provided for a combined system of horsecars and omnibuses which would solve the mass transit problem. The plan would eliminate the troublesome omnibuses from Broadway and relocate them on new crosstown routes to be established on Canal Street and other important streets farther north; transfer privileges would enable a rider to use the combined system for five cent, the fare set by the grant for the next ten years. David Dudley Field, the lawyer for the Manhattan Company, called it "one great trunk line through the center of the island, with branches to the shore on both sides." Sharp himself defended the plan as a "comprehensive scheme of intercommunication between the different parts of the island" which would bring every New Yorker within two blocks of a public conveyance.[54]

What the opposition noted, however, was not the comprehensive trunk system, but the meager financial return to the city. For the use of the most valuable public space in the city, Sharp agreed to pay an annual license fee of $20 per car, about $2000 as a whole for each of the next ten years, after which the fee could be renegotiated. The *Evening Post*, which favored a Broadway railroad, condemned the proposal for failing either to provide an adequate return to the city or to assure the lowest possible fare for the riding public; others blasted the grant as an outright steal of a public right worth millions.[55]

The details of the proposed grant evoked a shower of competing offers. Thomas E. Davies and other prominent landowners promised to pay the city $10,000 a year for 10 years on a five-cent fare or to charge a three-cent fare. William McMurray and others offered a lump sum of $100,000 on a five-cent fare. Watts Sherman, et al. promised the city one cent of every five-cent fare collected. Perhaps the most lucrative offer came from A. T. Stewart, who was willing to pay a license fee of $1000 per car and to charge a three-cent fare.[56] If nothing else, the offers served to sharpen the criticisms of the Council. The Aldermen justified their refusal to abandon the Sharp grant on the grounds that the competing proposals either were insincere maneuvers to head off any grant at all or were less satisfactory than their comprehensive plan. Perhaps, for once, they were right; A. T. Stewart spent the rest of his life and a rumored half-million dollars to block any railroad in front of his store.[57]

Much of the public, however, preferred to believe that the Broadway grant was the biggest steal of the "Forty Thieves." In November, the *Evening Post* reported the rumor that "a secret financial committee" dominated the Council: "We have heard strange stories of large sums divided by this committee among a portion of their associates in the two boards, about the time certain ferry privileges and railroad grants were conferred; of extensive investments making and made by members of both boards." The record of the Council and the fact that Alderman Barr's nephew, Peter Barr Sweeny, was one of the grantees suggest that public suspicions were justified, although no charge of bribery or conflict of interest was proven in the Broadway case.[58]

Whether for motives good or foul, the Council stubbornly persisted in its intentions. In December, it approved the Broadway grant, provoking both an expected veto from Mayor Kingsland and a judicial injunction against the scheme. The Mayor's veto, which could be overriden by a simple majority, was easily overcome, but the Council could not overcome the judiciary. By defying the injunction, the majority brought upon themselves convictions for contempt of court and $200 fines.[59] More trouble followed. In February 1853, a Grand Jury investigation uncovered sufficient evidence of bribery in some of the Council's decisions to indict two Aldermen; it might have uncovered more if the Court of General Sessions had not refused to compel a witness to answer whether he had bribed members of the Council. Two members of the three-man court which made the decision were Aldermen, a fact which strengthened the cry for charter reform to limit the responsibilities and powers of the Council.[60]

Even worse, the tide of politics, so strong in their favor two years before, had turned against the Aldermen. Yet none of this deterred them from making one last effort at the end of 1853 to revive the grant to Sharp; only the expiration of their two-year terms of office prevented them from continuing the attempt. Despite the fines, indictments, and charges against them, they retired as free and perhaps wealthy men. In February 1853, the *Times* had declared that, if it were not for the laws governing libel, it would "publish the names of individual Aldermen who . . . declared that they spent some thousands of dollars securing their election, and must make it up by being paid for their services. We know members of the Common Council who were not worth a thousand dollars in the world when they entered that body—who have done no business since, except in connection with it—and who are now worth twenty to fifty thousand dollars." But there was no proof. The *Tribune* might note that nine of the Aldermen had become owners of nearly a thousand shares of stock in the new Central Bank; Tweed owned 120 and Cornell 300 shares. But there was insufficient proof of wrongdoing.[61]

The new Board of Aldermen elected in November 1853

contained none of those who had made the Council, in the words of the *Tribune*, "the most debased, corrupt and disgraceful body of men ever invested with legislative power, at least in this country." The great majority of the "Forty Thieves" returned to the obscurity from which they had come.[62] Tweed, however, had only begun his career. In 1852, while only halfway through his term as Alderman, he was elected to the House of Representatives, where he served two unhappy years yawning through national issues in which he had little interest. In 1855, he returned home, again to run for Alderman, only to be defeated and to lose control over the Democratic political organization in his own ward. These political humiliations were partially assuaged by financial success. In the mid-1850s, Moses Y. Beach listed Tweed as worth a $100,000 and described him as living "in elegant style in Rutger's Place." Tweed was too much the politician and too ambitious, however, to be satisfied with modest success. Having served his political apprenticeship, he began in the late 1850s to lay the foundations for his "Ring," whose alleged corruptions after the Civil War involving millions of dollars made the Forty Thieves look like schoolboys.[63]

Both the Forty Thieves and the Tweed Ring were byproducts of the Age of Gold as well as of the rapid growth of the city. Prosperity brought a wave of public materialism which in 1853 led John A. Dix to lament: "A luxurious and extravagant people cannot maintain a simple and frugal government. . . . Private profusion comes first, next corporate recklessness and extravagance and last of all public corruption." The *Evening Post* complained a year later of the "extraordinary increase of defalcations, embezzlements, frauds, and robberies committed by men in places of trust."[64] Although the new metropolis did not invent human corruption, the nature of its prosperity weakened public morals in both the business and political worlds. The boom brought a jump in the scale of wealth for which society was morally unprepared. The near doubling of the assessed value of real and personal property from some $254 million to nearly $487 million between 1848 and 1855 combined with the California gold strikes to reinflame the get-rich-quick enthusiasms that earlier had been dampened by memories of the Panic of 1837. Expectations were further inflated by the rapid growth in the scale of public life, expressed in the expansion of governmental activity as well as the size and complexity of business enterprise. In particular, the revolution in transportation raised the scale both of operations and of anticipations, since the steamships, railroads, and horse-car lines required extensive capital and excited high expectations for profit; where once commercial partnerships dealt in thousands of dollars, now corporations could deal in millions.

The growing importance of the corporate form of business enterprise, with its anonymous stockholders and distant directors, especially attracted the attentions of get-rich-quick enthusiasts. In the early 1850s, the New York capitalists who controlled the Illinois Central Railroad reportedly issued a million dollars in stock to themselves. In 1854, Robert Schuyler, of the prestigeous Schuyler family, was discovered to have issued 20,000 shares of spurious stocks in the New Haven Railroad of which he was president. During the same year, it was rumored that the managers of the Erie Railroad had manipulated the stock of that railroad to their advantage. No wonder that Freeman Hunt, the moral guardian of the old merchant community, should warn that, while in the past a man could be trusted to keep his word, it is now necessary "to deal with every man and woman, so far as business is concerned, as if they were rogues."[65] Such lessons were not ignored by the Daniel Drews and the Jay Goulds (they would later be known as "Robber Barons") who were gradually working their way up in the business world. Nor were they lost on the Tweeds and other public servants, who had become the guardians of public space and public power worth millions to private interests like the horsecar lines.

The apparent collapse of public morals, which threatened both the moral base of society and the interests of the propertied and investing classes, caused much concern. No less disturbing was the increase in social tensions brought by the Age of Gold. The new prosperity, the growth of the city in population and in industry, and the emergence of metropolitan society had especially benefited the upper and middle classes.

THE AGE OF GOLD

Those with property and with money to invest were first in line to receive the fruits of progress. The personal prosperity of that fortunate minority was reflected in the expanding uptown areas, especially in the lavish display of Fifth Avenue and in the increasing comfort of middle class households.[66] Progress, however, was not so kind to the majority who lived below 14th Street.

The expansion of trade, manufacturing, and the construction industry in the early 1850s created new employment opportunities not only for the unskilled poor but also for skilled and semi-skilled workers. The working man, however, faced increasing competition for jobs from immigrants who were often willing to work for lower wages. To make matters worse, food prices, which had remained stable in the years around 1850, began a steady climb after 1852, particularly in 1854 when a combination of domestic drought, foreign crop failures, and the demands of the Crimean War brought an alarming increase in the price of such basic foods as potatoes, flour, and meat. Worse still, the rapid increase in property values which benefited the fortunate minority translated into burdensome increases in the city's already high rents. In 1853, even before the big increases of the following year, the *Times* estimated that it took $600 a year to support a workingman's family of four in moderate circumstances, this at a time when housepainters were paid $2 and skilled ship-carpenters $2.50 for each day of labor.[67]

Inflation brought a wave of strikes unseen since the years before the Panic of 1837. In 1853, coopers, printers, horsecar drivers, hotel waiters, housepainters, and other workers struck for higher wages. "High wages has been the cry of the month," reported the editor of *Harper's Monthly* in the summer. "It is reasonable and natural, that in view of the splendid trappings of our growing houses, and our metropolitan hotels, that the gas-fitters, and cordwainers and ladies' shoemakers, and saloon-servants should hold out their hands for their share of the excess." The strikers' actions were motivated less by the desire to get more than to protect what they had from the gnawings of inflation. There were more strikes in 1854, but before the end of the year such activity was confronted by a short yet ominously sharp break in the new prosperity.[68]

During the summer, public confidence in the financial world was weakened by a decline of stock prices and by several failures on Wall Street. The largest was Robert Schuyler's, which led to the discovery of his worthless stock issues. By October, New York was approaching a crisis of confidence. In that month, the *Times* reported a variety of "ugly and very unfavorable developments," including defalcations in the Ocean and Knickerbocker banks, forgeries on a number of city banks carried out "by a gang of forgers from the western frontier," a run on savings banks, and an oyster panic started by rumors that several well-known New Yorkers had contracted cholera from eating the sea food. Looking back on the summer and fall, the commercial columnist for the *Times* called 1854 a year of disaster, especially conspicuous for the frauds, by "the gross betrayal of official trust," which plagued the creditors and stockholders of corporations. The causes of the approaching crisis were many, the most important being a sharp decline of imports in the fall, but especially notable were the troubles that afflicted the shipping industry, which had especially profited from the Age of Gold.[69]

Early in October 1854 the *Arctic*, one of the great new steamers of the trans-Atlantic Collins line, the pride of New York, sank. When New Yorkers learned the details of the sinking, they were horrified. The ship had gone down quickly after colliding with a French steamer, abandoned by a panic-stricken crew who had fled in the lifeboats, leaving nearly two hundred passengers to drown. Among the casualities were three members of the family of E. K. Collins, the owner of the line, and seven members of the family of James Brown, a prominent banker. The disaster not only shook the city's faith in the Collins line but provided a symbolic end to the golden age of New York shipbuilding. By 1854 the great stimulus to shipbuilding from the California gold discoveries had exhausted itself, while the rising costs of labor and materials placed shipbuilders at a disadvantage before foreign, especially English, competition. That became evident early in November with the default of one of the largest shipbuilding firms, J. A. Westervelt & Co.; Jacob A. Westervelt had been elected Mayor in 1852 to do battle against the Forty Thieves.[70]

By the end of the month, it was apparent that the whole economy was in trouble as mercantile firms and banks failed, factories and shipyards suspended operations, and the building boom stopped. Two days before Christmas, the *Citizen* reported that the city was shrouded in gloom: "You will see loungers at the corners of the streets, men, skillful and willing to work, but without employment, and having hunger and fearful forebodings of the future pictured in their wan faces." It was perhaps but a grim accident that the Broadway Theatre presented *The Beggars Opera* at this time.

What followed was one of the hardest and most terrifying winters ever experienced by New York. The *Tribune* noted that poverty and idleness had always characterized the city, "but this winter, unlike any of the fifteen preceeding it, has seen thousands of able and generally industrious men and women reduced to distress and beggary by the sudden and wholesale failure of their accustomed work." While unemployment rose and wages fell, the cost of necessities remained obstinately high; the price of flour reached an 18-year high early in 1855.[71] To compound the misery, in February the city was struck by a snow storm and a cold wave which drove the temperature down to −10°F (−23°C). By then, the system of charities had begun to collapse under the strain posed by the thousands of newly unemployed. The AICP warned that in January it had nearly exhausted its treasury to succor some 50,000 needy people, three times the number relieved during the same month in 1854, and issued a humiliating plea to the municipal Almshouse department to increase its spending for outdoor relief: "It is too late for remedial schemes. Defer, and thousands suffer."[72]

The general sense of crisis was heightened by evident signs of resentment among many of New York's workingmen. Caught between inflated prices and the wage-cutting of desperate employers, some of those who still had jobs attempted to resist reductions in their pay. The longshoremen went on strike in January, only to encounter strikebreakers, some of them recent immigrants furnished by the Emigration Commission. After the police broke up an effort by the strikers to prevent the unloading of a ship on the East River, the longshoremen voted to accept their employers' terms.[73] More frightening to anxious conservatives was the behavior of some of the unemployed. Thousands of them gathered in mass meetings to demand relief and jobs—and to listen to the speeches attacking "speculators" for allegedly holding up food prices, while workingmen were starving. "Walking through the crowd," said a newspaper reporter of one meeting, "one could have heard muttered threats and execrations against the wealthy, and some of the more inconsiderate of the mob said they would have money ... or blood would be spilled." Conservatives feared the worst. In January 1855, George Templeton Strong reported the rumor, unfounded, "that a Socialist mob was sacking the Schiff mansion in the Fifth Avenue, where was a great ball and mass meeting of the aristocracy."[74]

Contrary to such fears, workers sought not revolution but jobs. In mid-January, a mass meeting at the Washington Parade Ground approved a resolution calling on city authorities to raise sufficient revenue "for the immediate employment of such numbers of unemployed workingmen as may be deemed necessary." The resolution was vague as to the nature of work relief, but one speaker at the meeting proposed that the city appropriate up to $1 million to employ the jobless in building dwellings for workingmen. The meeting also called on city, state and national governments to cooperate in providing both the land and the money needed to establish many of the unemployed as independent farmers.[75]

Although such proposals were rejected by most influential New Yorkers, they did win the attention of the wealthy reformer Peter Cooper, who in an open letter to Mayor Wood proposed that the city either provide land for the unemployed or put them to work quarrying marble for the construction of new and substantial docks and piers to replace the city's shabby waterfront facilities. The *Times* agreed that the city should begin a public works program to employ the jobless at good wages, although it denounced the members of the mass meeting as a "miscellaneous crowd of alien chartists, communists and agrarians." Horace Greeley's *Tribune*, which had long been concerned with the plight of the unemployed, now attempted to state the fundamental problem: "As cities expand, and life becomes more and more artificial, and human relations more complicated, the necessity for a practical solution becomes every day more urgent. To give the needy work instead of Alms—to let him live on the proceeds of his own labor."[76]

Perhaps if massive unemployment had persisted through 1855, the city would have been forced to find a practical solution to the problem; but the storm passed as quickly as it had come. The crisis, though locally severe, had not disrupted most of the rest of the country; with the spring there came the traditional upswing in business orders from the hinterland, accompanied by a blessed flow of gold, that restored much of the shattered confidence of business. Foreign trade, which had been upset the previous year by events in Europe, recovered in the summer to reach a new high in 1856. Although neither New York shipbuilding nor shipping were to regain their previous vitality, general prosperity returned sufficiently for the advantaged to forget the fearsome winter of 1854–55. But the essential problems remained. The price of necessities, after briefly faltering, resumed its upward climb in the face of a much weakened and chastened labor movement. The deterioration in public morals resumed, as did the growth of the social gap separating conspicuous affluence and poverty. In 1856 Freeman Hunt warned that "If there is any symptom of another commercial crisis in the United States, similar to that of 1837, it is to be found in the really wicked personal extravagance, which at present forms the most prominent social feature of our Eastern cities. Such ruinous wastefulness has always hitherto been among the immediate antecedents of great revulsions, serving both as index and a cause of coming disaster."[77] Hunt's was the voice of a more cautious past, and it was ignored in an era of dazzling progress; but he was right. The whirlwind of 1854–55 proved to be the omen of the more general and prolonged storm which broke with the Panic of 1857.

The prosperity of the early 1850s had not created new problems. Poverty, social tensions, lapses in public morals, the inability of government to meet the physical needs of the growing city—these and other problems could be found in the more sluggish 1840s. The new era, however, had so substantially increased their scale as to make them conspicuous elements of a new era which dawned in the 1850s. These were the problems, this was the era, which was to dominate the horizon of an urbanizing America for at least the next half century. Just as the Forty Thieves were the immediate ancestors of the Tweed Ring, so were the omnibus and horsecar men the forerunners of the great business Titans and terrors of the future; so, too, was the Crisis of 1854–55 a dark prophecy of the great "social earthquakes" which periodically were to shake urban America after the Civil War.

The growing scale of these problems and the growing complexity and artificiality of human relations (to use the *Tribune's* terms) gave government important new responsibilities. Government itself, however, had become a problem, especially in the eyes of taxpayers and native-born citizens. What in the 1840s had been a troublesome neighbor for them became in the 1850s a contemptible but terrible giant—and yet a necessary giant to be redeemed and tamed. The apparent collapse in public morals, in particular, seemed to demand a mighty effort to reform municipal government, but such efforts encountered one persistent reality: while government was an agent of public purpose, it was even more a political creature entangled in New York's complexly rampant politics.

Chapter 12

THE TROUBLE
WITH POLITICS

BY THE 1850s, New York had become a metropolis, a great
organization of powers and skills that strengthened its commercial and cultural dominance of the nation while making it
a major presence in world society. It was, said the *Times* in
1854, the purest product of the "perfecting skill, magnificent
commerce and boundless enterprise" of the progressive age.
As the newest of the world's great cities, its uninhibited
intelligence and energy gave it unprecedented mastery of the
new material agencies of progress, of the railroads, steamships,
factories, and business organizations which sustained the development of modern civilization. With equal pride, *Putnam's*
predicted that the "Metropolitan City of New York," the
concentrated diversity of Manhattan and associated suburbs,

would soon become the world's greatest city in a century where progress was synonymous with the growth of great cities: *"The most perfect organization of which human society* (outside of the family) *is capable is a well-ordered city."*[1] Metropolis, model of human industrial organization, a well-ordered society, agent of business and bourgeois progress—the ideal New York excited hope and pride, but it also served to highlight the fundamental failures of the real city as a human community.

Certainly, no one in the early 1850s could mistake New York for a well-ordered community. Disorder seemed to dominate public space, in marked contrast to well-ordered enterprises and middle-class households of the progressive age. Especially was it evident in the noisy streets and alleys of the lower city. The *Times*, so hopeful regarding the commercial metropolis, noted some examples: A "dull vapor of corrupting odors that hung like an unembodied vengence over our devoted roofs. We have seen a good many European cities . . . , but we must candidly confess that at the present moment New York transcends them all for aggregated, unadulterated and overpowering filth"; a Sunday night on Broadway, "a perfect hell of Drunkiness. A howling, staggering Pandemonium of brutalized men"; a wave of fires in late 1853 and early 1854 which destroyed some $10 million in property; and, most prominently, a steady, frightening increase of crime.[2]

Many New Yorkers agreed that their city was a fearful place. Walt Whitman advised visitors not to wander in the streets or parks at night, since "New York is one of the most crime-haunted and dangerous cities in Christendom. There are hundreds—thousands—of infernal rascals in our floating population." *Harpers Weekly* observed that no one knew exactly what the nature and extent of crime was in the city, but this did not deter New Yorkers from gravely discussing the question "whether it is not necessary to carry sword-canes, dirks, bowie-knives, and revolvers to protect us free citizens from the assaults of other free citizens."[3] Crime statistics, although they rather inaccurately recorded arrests rather than the real number of crimes, seemed to prove that criminal activity was increasing much faster than population, especially in what the

THE TROUBLE WITH POLITICS

New York Prison Association called the "highest crimes," such as assaults with intent to kill and murders. A more modern society might not be especially disturbed by the 56 murders in 1852, but the figure was an outrage for a society which had recorded only nine murders five years before. "There *was* a time," declared the *Times* in 1854, "when the process of murder was carried on in-doors by the silent means of poisons and strangling. These days are past and stabbing and shooting are in vogue in the public streets."[4]

The anxiety over crime was part of an even broader concern over the apparent deterioration of civic discipline and civic order. In thirty years, said *Harpers Weekly* in 1857, "what was then a decent and orderly town of moderate size, has been converted into a hugh semi-barbarous metropolis—one half as luxurious and artistic as Paris, the other half as savage as Cairo or Constantinople—not well-governed nor ill-governed, but simply not governed at all."[5] The spokesmen for the progressive city at least dimly recognized that progress itself was indirectly a cause of the problem. The growing commercial city had attracted substantial hordes of newcomers who had to be absorbed into a modernizing urban society. In the decade after 1845 the population of New York had grown by at least 70 percent, while its foreign-born population had increased by over 140 percent. It is possible that the 629,000 inhabitants reported by the state census of 1855 served to underestimate the growth of the prosperous early 1850s, if only because the figure did not include the city's substantial floating population of sailors, businessmen, and ne'er-do-wells who were likely to escape the censustakers. Many new inhabitants were young adults, the most restless and rootless part of any population; in 1860, nearly 22 percent of white New Yorkers were of ages 20 to 30, as compared to 18 percent of white Americans generally.[6]

No unprejudiced observer blamed the trouble exclusively on the newcomers, but available statistics indicated that crime and related forms of disorder were in some way associated with the great mass of the uprooted and unassimilated migrants, especially the great majority who had come from Europe. Of the

27,000 persons reported as convicted of crimes throughout the United States in 1850, more than half were foreign-born, although the foreign-born constituted only one-eighth of the population; similarly, more than three-quarters of those arrested for crimes in the city in 1859 were born in Europe.[7] That the immigrant poor were especially likely to be arrested for such minor offenses as vagrancy and drunkenness modified but did not overturn the conclusion that the city was threatened from within by a substantial part of its population which was either indifferent to or hostile to civic order.

The city attempted to train its young for safe, sound citizenship through its schools, asylums, benevolent associations, and tract societies; each of these were themselves models of the well-ordered city, especially as they became increasingly professionalized and bureaucratic during the 1850s. There remained, however, those who would not or could not practice civic restraint. For them, by the early 1850s, there was a large body of ordinances and regulations designed both to prevent crime and to restrain behavior in the interests of order: sanitary regulations to prevent the accumulation of disease-engendering filth; traffic regulations to prevent dangerous driving and the obstruction of streets and sidewalks; fire regulations to prevent the outbreak of conflagrations in the crowded lower city; liquor regulations to prevent Sunday drinking and to control the number of drinking places. Despite the laws, however, New Yorkers continued to dump their garbage in public places, to block the public streets, to burn themselves and their neighbors out of their homes, and to get roaring and often belligerently drunk on Sundays—all with such monotonous regularity as to suggest that the presence of laws served as much to encourage disrespect for law as to control human behavior.

It took no sage to remind those who favored a well-ordered society that even the best of laws, if not enforced, were no laws at all. Long before the 1850s, New Yorkers had complained that the city was lax in law enforcement. By the mid-1840s, many had concluded that the enforcement system of marshals, constables, and nightwatchmen inherited from simpler days was too inept and ill-disciplined to maintain order. Some believed that only a professional police force, a disciplined urban army, could maintain order in an increasingly fragmented society. "So long as we have one division of the people," said one anxious citizen, "rich and powerful affluent and ostentatious, and another numerous division wretchedly poor and dependent, as in the case of New York, profligacy, crime and debauchery, immorality, and gross corruption will be there, and hence the necessity (as in London) of a civic ARMY, a numerous Municipal Police."[8]

In 1845, after several years of discussions, the Democrats established a professional force of 800 salaried policemen intended to consolidate in one system a variety of law enforcement functions. The new force took the place of 100 marshals, 18 street inspectors, 54 fire wardens, 18 health wardens, 50 Sunday police, an assortment of other officials, as well as some 1200 nightwatchmen. New York quickly came to depend for most of its law enforcement on this increasingly professional and also increasingly expensive system.[9] During its first nine years, the New York Police made over 310,000 arrests, mostly for such minor offenses as drunkenness and disorderly conduct but also for crimes ranging from petty larceny (nearly 29,000) and grand larceny (more than 5300) to assault with intent to kill (1333) to murder (248).[10]

Yet not even the defenders of the new system could effectively refute the charges made by critics, often on the basis of police reports, that the force had neither suppressed the brothels, gambling establishments, dives, and Sunday drinking so fruitful of petty crimes and not so petty violence, nor apprehended many of the thieves, burglars, incendiaries, thugs, rioters, rowdies, and murders who threatened lives and property. Even the long-term Chief of Police, George W. Matsell, confessed that during the first half of 1852 crimes of violence had so increased that citizens were afraid to venture out of their homes after dark, a situation which he blamed on the too prevalent carelessness, indolence, and cowardice of his force.[11] Although it is impossible to prove that the police had failed to prevent an increase in crime, there is no doubt that they failed to dispel the public apprehension that crime—especially crimes of violence—had increased faster than the city's population.

Defenders of the system argued that the force could not meet public expectations, because it was expected to do too much with too little. In 1853 New York's "Civic Army" consisted of 1003 men to maintain order in a lawless city of more than 600,000 people. Omitting police officers, there were some 900 policemen, of whom, complained Chief Matsell, 178 were detailed to such special duties as enforcing the regulations governing pawnshops and public conveyances. Of the remaining 725 men responsible for preventing crime, only half were available for night duty, so that each man had to patrol between 9 and 15 city blocks. By 1856 the force had grown to nearly 1200 men but the city had also grown in both population and territory. In 1856 Mayor Wood charged that whereas London had one policeman for every 351 inhabitants, New York had to make do with one for every 812.[12]

Law-abiding New Yorkers agreed that policemen were not sufficiently in evidence in the city, but most blamed that problem on a lack of discipline and dedication caused by a radical imperfection in the original system. Contrary to the hopes for a disciplined civic army, the original police had been shaped by traditional American fears of a standing military force removed from popular control. Policemen were not required to wear uniforms in deference to the popular hostility against what was considered the uniformed lackeys of despotic governments; their only identification was a star-shaped copper badge. Nor were they furnished with any weapons. Even more destructive of the hopes for a disciplined force was the fact that, under the original law, policemen were appointed for two-year terms by the Aldermen and Assistant Aldermen of the wards in which they were expected both to serve and to live.[13]

These provisions kept the police close to the people, but even more they assured that the system would be tangled up with ward politics. Each policeman was forced to serve two masters. One, the police hierarchy, had the most immediate influence over his daily professional role, but the other, the Alderman and his allies, had the greater ultimate authority. As early as 1846 Mayor Havemeyer urged that policemen be given four year terms to free them from "connexion with the cliques and factions which disgrace our party," noting that in several wards anxiety about their jobs had driven some of the police to take an active part in politics. Even more seriously, the situation tended to discourage arrests of the Alderman's friends and political supporters, a major cause of the failure to enforce the laws against Sunday drinking and unlicensed drinking places. That political leaders were interested in saving their friends from jail was made clear to even the most dim-witted "copper" when Aldermen used their judicial powers to discharge some of those who had been taken into custody.[14]

In the summer of 1852, during the reign of the "Forty Thieves," law-enforcement almost broke down altogether as the practice of making discharges reached critical proportions. Because of political interference, complained one New Yorker, less than 500 of the more than 2000 men arrested for street fighting and disorderly conduct had been punished: "Our Aldermen are frequently at the same work. These men, they reason, are men of nerve, they are useful at elections, they must be taken care of." The *Tribune* listed some 90 discharges made by the various Aldermen (in comparison with some of his colleagues, Tweed was a minor offender); this figure did not include the even greater number of offenders who were released by the Aldermen before they were booked at the police stations. Little wonder that in the summer of 1852 fear of rowdyism discouraged citizens from using the streets at night. The following years, the *Times* made a complaint to be repeated many times in the future: "We lavish money upon City Prisons; increase the number of our City Courts; and crime increases in vastly more than equal ratio. Hundreds escape punishment after having been brought before our Courts; and thousands of those whose hands and hearts are stained with many crimes, have not been brought even within the presence of a judge."[15]

The police system was not the only public institution to feel the withering breath of politics. Critics complained of a collapse of civic discipline in the Fire Department, which, unlike the salaried police, remained a volunteer organization headed by a small number of paid officials. In 1850, Alfred Carson, the Chief Engineer of the Department, complained that the Aldermen had not only intervened to prevent the punishment of gangs who had attacked his men on their way to a fire but had impaired discipline in the department by refusing to punish Tweed's Americus Company for attacking Hose Company No. 31. The Committee on the Fire Department of the Common Council had originally reported in favor of suspending the company and ousting Tweed as its foreman; the report, which might have nipped Tweed's political career in the bud, was altered before it was finally approved so as to provide for a short suspension of the foreman—the work, charged Carson, of Tweed's friends on the Council. Two years later, Carson complained that the Council again had interfered with discipline by reinstating firemen who had been expelled for fighting with other firemen. In the midst of a wave of destructive fires in 1854, some New Yorkers complained that firemen had plundered private property during a fire and extorted money from owners of burning buildings. Why? One fireman charged that, while most of his colleagues were honest men, "during the past two or three years there have been *men of the worst character smuggled into the Fire Department for base party purposes.*"[16]

Elsewhere, too, critics noted a slackness in the discipline and dedication required to run the machinery of a modern urban society. The sanitary reformer, John H. Griscom, declared in 1852 that the city had spent millions to bring a river of water to its citizens and to construct a sewerage system for the disposal of wastes, but the net result was a city filthier and more unhealthy than ever. The largely nonpolitical Croton Aqueduct Department was not to blame, said Griscom for it had efficiently managed the water and sewerage systems; the fault lay with the lax enforcement of the sanitary laws, especially in the failure of the politically appointed health wardens to perform their duty as protectors of public health. In the same year, the *Scientific American* complained that, despite the frequent and terrifying explosions of steam boilers in America, the city was making no effort to control the use of steam: "The streets of New York are pent-up volcanoes; huge high pressure steam boilers are in continued blast beneath our pavements, in the cellars of our public buildings, etc., and these boilers are of such a character that explosions may be often apprehended." Others, too, noted the growing contrast between modern efficiency and governmental deficiency, between expectations of a well-ordered public household and what seemed to be the increasingly anachronistic and anarchistic character of municipal affairs.[17]

In general, the public authority responsible for enforcing or instilling civic discipline was failing in its duties; worse, it seemed to have allied itself with the very lawlessness and license it was supposed to control. "When a Government becomes rotten," warned the *Tribune*, "when our rulers become corrupt, every valuable interest drifts from its moorings. We are exposed to constant perils. Our security is endangered. Property, the public order, are all placed in jeopardy."[18] Government, responsible for controlling the pent-up social volcanoes of city life, seemed instead to be encouraging the growth of violence and disorder. Who was responsible? By the 1850s, municipal government had evolved into a bewilderingly complex organization of elective and appointive officials, but it was not difficult to trace most of the trouble to one source, the Common Council.

The Charter of 1849, intended to control the spending propensities and other wayward habits of the people's representatives, had obviously failed. In the eyes of reformers, Tweed and his fellow Aldermen in 1852–53 committed virtually every conceivable sin against the public good. They had undermined discipline in the various city departments. They had encouraged lawlessness and disorder. They had misused city property. They had threatened to violate fashionable Broadway with a street railroad. They had given away railroad and ferry franchises, worth millions, to their friends and favorites. Even worse, they had committed the outrage of dramatically increasing spending and taxes during their two years in office. Appropriations from taxes for city purposes increased by 70 percent, from $2,765,000 in 1851 to $4,836,-000 in 1853, while the tax rate jumped by one-third from 91 cents per $100 of assessed value in 1851 to $1.23 per $100.[19]

The critics preferred to ignore the fact that, on a per capita basis, both taxes and indebtedness in New York were less than they were in Boston, still probably the best-managed city in the United States.[20] Nor did they listen to Tweed when on the last day of his term he spoke out in defense of himself and his colleagues. He said that nearly one-half of the appropriations made by the Board in 1853 were for purposes beyond the control of the Council, especially for the Almshouse establishment and for the public schools, each of whose budgets were determined by independent boards. In any case, what was so wrong with the level of expenditures? "I ask the people if a city such as ours, daily receiving an immense population of the idle, degenerate, vicious, and good from all parts of the world, could be governed at less expense?"[21]

Perhaps Tweed was close to the truth. Certainly, the obscurities of city budgets and the mysteries of city needs made definitive judgments virtually impossible. For the critics, however, the rising tax rate was an obvious sign that government, far from being the protector of good citizens, was becoming their oppressor. The city, declared one reformer, would have had 200,000 more people if high taxes and resulting high rents had not driven mechanics, merchants, and other productive citizens to the suburbs. If the good were driven out of the city, then who would rule? For anxious citizens, the answer seemed all too terribly clear. Already the government was falling under the control of the subterranean mass whose interests were in disorder, corruption, and high taxes. In 1848, Mayor Havemeyer had warned that increasing expenditures tended to perpetuate themselves: "The disposition of the enormous patronage consequent upon the expenditure of a million and a half dollars . . . create an interest in favor of expenditure."[22] Six years later, expenditure was three times as great.

The excesses of the Forty Thieves revived the interest in reform which had flagged after the Charter of 1849. In

The Trouble with Politics

September 1852 William E. Dodge, John Harper, Stephen Whitney, and other prominent New Yorkers (including Daniel Drew, who had as yet to carve out his career as a manipulator of railroads) formed the nonpartisan City Reform League to rally the public against "a complete network" of corruption which had gained control of city government. Despite efforts of its leaders to create a counter-network of ward reform organizations, the League had little effect, although its endorsements may have contributed to the victories in the November elections of two reform Democrats, Jacob A. Westervelt for Mayor and Azariah C. Flagg for City Comptroller; Flagg's budget-cutting genius as State Comptroller in the 1840s had already made him a hero of tax-conscious property owners.[23] The work of reform, however, had only begun. Spurred on by the Broadway Railroad battle, reform-minded businessmen and property holders attempted in 1853 to devise permanent ways of frustrating the forces of corruption.

Most reformers believed that the chief problem was the fragmentation of power and responsibility which had resulted from the haphazard growth of government; this increasing fragmentation both encouraged carelessness and corruption and discouraged able men from seeking office. Generally, reformers favored a clear-cut separation of powers modeled on the national government: A strong executive, an independent judiciary, and a legislature restricted to legislative matters. They hoped especially to lop off the troublesome tentacles of the Common Council by excluding it from the executive province of law enforcement and from the judicial function of interpreting the law. Even more, they wanted to curb the spending propensities of the Council without violating the strong democratic feelings of the times. To do so, they hoped to give the Mayor a presidential-style veto and also to model the Council along the lines of Congress by making its two boards representative of two distinctly different constituencies. The Aldermen and Assistant Aldermen, having been elected by the same voters in the same wards, tended to work—and conspire—together rather than to restrain each other.[24]

In March 1853, reform leaders launched their drive to

[323]

reorganize government in a mass meeting at Metropolitan Hall under the chairmanship of Peter Cooper. The meeting endorsed a list of reforms, presented by Henry J. Raymond of the *Times*, which it called on the State Legislature to embody in a new charter for the city.[25] While the charter approved by the legislature in 1853 did not satisfy all reform hopes, it was enough for reformers to champion as a much needed modernization of city government: "The City, by a growth unexampled in all previous history, has outgrown its form of government. The Charter, as it now stands, was adapted for an inconsiderable population and locality. It was suited to a people who were homogeneous. . . . The vast duties now to be performed, attendant upon our advance in number, wealth, and extent—and the avidity with which selfish and interested individuals seize upon the immense patronage of the City— call for a careful division of duties, and for the interposition of checks and safeguards upon their performance." As the Charter had to be approved by the voters in a popular referendum scheduled for early June, its advocates gave much attention to building popular support for it through a series of local and citywide meetings. They succeeded. With nearly half of the city's voters participating, the reform proposal was approved by 10 to 1.[26]

The new Charter provided for a major reorganization of municipal government. It strengthened the Mayor by giving him the presidential-style veto, and it weakened the power of the Aldermen to meddle in enforcement matters by removing them as judges of city courts and by denying them the right to appoint policemen. To further remove law enforcement from the influence of ward politics, the police were put under the authority of a Board of Commissioners consisting of the Mayor, City Recorder, and City Judge, all of whom were elected on a citywide basis. To make the Council both less spendthrift and more democratic, it was restructured into two distinct boards. The old Board of Aldermen was retained essentially as it was, although its members were to be elected for two-year terms on a staggered basis with odd-numbered wards voting in even-numbered years; as a check on ward politics, a new board of sixty Councilmen was created, each member to be elected annually from districts equal in population. To prevent the recurrence of the corrupt practices associated with the Forty Thieves, the Charter required that all leases and sales of public property and franchises, including ferry grants, and all contracts for work worth more than $250 be subject to public bidding, while it also provided stiff penalties for anyone who attempted to bribe a member of the council and any member who accepted a bribe.[27]

Although it retained the cumbersome ten executive departments established in 1849, the Charter was a significant step forward in the modernization of municipal administration, especially in the police department. By shifting power and responsibility over law enforcement from the Council to the Board of Commissioners, it provided the basis for a unity of policy and also opened the way for supplementary legislation in 1853 which attempted to insulate policemen from ward politics by assuring them permanent tenure on good behavior. The early hopes for the establishment of a disciplined civic army came even closer to realization in the fall of 1853 when Mayor Westervelt ordered the police into uniforms; with uniforms, said the *Evening Post*, the police were more likely to "watch society, and society will watch them."[28]

The new Commissioners and Chief Matsell soon could boast of a 40 percent increase in the number of arrests during the first half of 1854. The New York Prison Association, which included such reform notables as Dr. John H. Griscom and Peter Cooper, expressed the belief that these figures and an estimated 20,000 persons committed to prison during the year proved conclusively that the now vigilant police were winning the battle against crime; the wording of its report provides an insight into the reform mentality: "The laws of statistics presuppose the element of administrative efficiency to be uniform and positive. If this be fickle and variable, but little reliance can be placed on the deductions from the figures. With a lax police, therefore, there might be an actual increase of crime, while the number of commitments and consequently of convictions would lead a casual observer to infer a decrease. . . .

During the year named there was a marked and continuing improvement in the police, which satisfactorily accounts for the increased number of 'guests.'"[29]

If the elimination of political influence and the establishment of internal discipline could assure efficiency in the Police Department, it seemed logical to conclude that they would work as well in other departments. In 1856, the reformer Myndert Van Schaick, the President of the Croton Aqueduct Department, noted that his department had improved efficiency by adopting the principle that "no man is removed who tells the truth and faithfully performs his duty."[30] Thus did reformers begin to grope their way toward a bureaucratic system of administration insulated from politics. The growing size and expense of the municipal departments both required and furnished the opportunity for the creation of administrative bureaucracies staffed by experts and manned by civil servants dedicated to municipal interests.

These early efforts, however, were made in an intensely political city, where the elective principle seemingly had run wild, where not only mayors and aldermen but school boards, the governors of the Almshouse, the heads of the municipal departments, and city judges were selected by popular vote. At least occasionally, the results were good, as in the election of Comptroller A. C. Flagg, a champion of honest and frugal government, but the occasional good produced by election roulette offered little hope for the uniform administrative efficiency of which reform leaders had begun to dream. Though they might prefer to tinker with the governmental machine, they were forced to recognize that the success of any governmental organization they could devise depended on the men elected to manage it. Though they might hope to exclude the increasingly dirty and complex world of "politics" from their own, they had reluctantly to acknowledge the importance of politics. How to elect good men? To answer that question, reformers had to confront the subterranean facts of government in New York.[31]

The most unyielding, unpalatable, and ultimately most frustrating fact was that politics meant not only the election but the nomination of candidates. Tweed once reportedly said that he was willing to concede control over the elections to anyone who wanted it provided he could control the nominating process; his remark pointed up a fundamental weakness of the American political system. Governments and elections were public and subject to public law, but the nominating process was left to the rules and regulations of political parties, which had no official standing. Ostensibly to give the rank-and-file an influence over party policies and candidates, both Whigs and Democrats had devised jerry-built systems of primary meetings and conventions which in practice often served less to express than to confound the popular will.

The Democratic organization had become especially dependent on local primaries. These meetings, held in taverns, hotels, and other popular places of resort for the male electorate, nominated local ward candidates and also selected delegates to the various party conventions which made the nominations for the more important city, state, and national offices. They also determined, directly and indirectly, who was to fill places in the hierarchy of party leadership culminating in the Democratic General Committee which made, or at least tried to make, policy for the city party. By the early 1850s the primary system had become as complex and confusing as the general elections. In 1852, besides making nominations for ward offices, the various Democratic primary meetings selected delegates to six different conventions to nominate candidates for state offices, mayor, county offices, the city departments, city judge, and for Congress.[32]

For more than a decade, the system had been falling into disrepute. In 1843 Democrats charged that a Street Inspector had used the men he employed on the public payroll to pack primary meetings in favor of himself and his allies. By the mid-1840s primary elections in some of the lower wards had become the proving grounds for virtually every kind of election corruption. A bitter primary fight between the Alderman of the Sixth Ward and a challenger, for instance, featured illicit voters, repeaters, ballot-box stuffing, and intimidation which climaxed in a battle of clubs and brickbats typical of the politics of the "Bloody Sixth." Few primaries were as violent as this, but the system in general, for many reformers, seemed to be little more than a device by which "wire-pullers" and political hacks secretly manipulated the nominating process.[33]

Little was done, however, to reform the primaries beyond urging good citizens to take control of them away from corrupt manipulators—a difficult assignment for several major reasons: first many citizens were too busy or too indifferent to attend the meetings; second, the primaries frequently were held in August and early September when many respectable folk were out of town on vacation; third, even if they were able to participate, they were often discouraged from doing so by clusters of bullies at the entrance to the place where the primary was held; fourth, if they succeeded in getting in, they discovered that they lacked the experience needed to upset the prearranged nominations of the "wire-pullers;" fifth, the presence of substantial numbers of the unwashed poor, especially in the lower wards, made primary gatherings about as socially attractive for the respectable as leper colonies.[34]

By the early 1850s, reformers complained that the primary system had fallen under the control of place-seekers and rowdies. In 1852, the *Tribune* charged that the Democratic leadership was attempting to rig the election of delegates to the various party nominating conventions with the help of "a dozen of beastly ruffians in each ward, hired to do the voting and knockdown any one who should presume to interfere with the play." The attempt raised strong resistance from rival Democrats. In the First Ward, rowdies kept down the primary vote, while, elsewhere, local political rivalries led to brawls in at least nine wards. Greeley's *Tribune* had little reason to gloat over the troubles of the Democrats, for the same kind of canker appeared in the Whig primaries, as its editor recognized; the year before, Greeley had been shouted down at an Eighth Ward meeting by Bill Poole and his fellow musclemen who had chosen the Whig party for their gymnastics. In fact, reformers complained that corruption in the primaries was acquiring an even more ominous bipartisan character. "Till within two or three years past," said the Municipal Reform

Committee in 1854, "primary elections were under the control of whigs and democrats, in their respective parties—but it is now known that there are organized bands of unprincipled and reckless men who sell out their services to aspirants for place, without regard to party association." This corrupt and corrupting disruption of the nominating process was to haunt the efforts both of reformers and of party leaders to create a meaningful, manageable political order.[35]

The chief consequence seemed to be the corruption and disorder associated with the Forty Thieves. Ambitious men had to pay good money to be nominated and elected to office. "It takes an Alderman from three to eight thousand dollars to be elected," said *The Day-Book*, "and it is generally understood that this money is to be got back somehow." Such a situation was hardly unnatural in a city and an age when so many ambitious men gave their attentions to making their investments pay. Aside from its costs to the taxpayers, however, the political situation threatened a breakdown in public order. The growing importance of money in politics meant the growth in government of private interest at the expense of public interest. More frightening because more definite, the growing dependence of politicians on rowdies and ruffians was weakening public control over the lawless and disorderly. The lawless, warned the reformers, "reason, and they reason well, that if they can create the Magistry, they can overawe it, and control it." Corruption in the primaries led straight to the reign of "Rum and Rowdyism" which seemed to have settled on the city in 1852.[36]

It was much easier for the reformers to identify the disease than to prescribe the cure. The *Tribune* suggested a system for the registration of primary voters. The Metropolitan Hall meeting urged both parties to adopt the practice of "voluntary and spontaneous nominations" which prevailed in rural areas. Other reformers proposed that the city elections be moved from November back to April on the grounds that the fall elections required primaries in the late summer when many respectable citizens were out of the city on vacations.[37] None of these proposed reforms was affected. How to select and elect good men? The reformers agreed on two propositions: (1) That the primary systems of both parties were corrupt. (2) That so long as city politics were mingled with state and national politics, New Yorkers would vote for bad municipal candidates in order to assure the state and national victories of their parties. If partisan politics had thus become a convenient screen for local corruption, then, it seemed logical to conclude, as did the *Times*, that New York needed a "Reform Party" which would make city affairs a separate and distinct issue. Reform leaders, however, were reluctant to commit themselves to a separate party, leading the *Tribune* to charge in August 1853 that some leaders were ready to betray the reform cause in order not to jeopardize expected nominations from the regular parties. Even if honest men were nominated in the regular primaries, it warned, they would be indebted to the "piebald mob of rum-crazed rowdies and ruffians" who determined primary decisions.[38]

Undoubtedly recognizing that an independent reform party would fail to win power in the intensely partisan city, the reformers made no effort to create a separate political organization in preparation for the fall elections in 1853. Instead, the General Reform Committee appointed by the Metropolitan Hall meeting issued a call for the creation of reform associations in the various wards to select candidates for the Common Council "without reference to National or State politics." In such a way, the reformers could nominate candidates without having to commit themselves to the dirty business either of formal primaries or organized election effort. They were both helped and hindered by the fact that the crudities of the Forty Thieves had made reform politically fashionable. In the silk-stocking Fifteenth Ward and in its middle-class neighbor, the Ninth Ward, they had little trouble in nominating their own local candidates. In most of the other wards, however, the situation was confused by the fact that one or both of the regular parties nominated good men themselves. As a result, most of the candidates endorsed by the reformers had also been selected in regular party primaries.[39]

The *Times* proclaimed the election result in 1853 a "complete triumph of the reform ticket," but, though an obvious repudiation of the Forty Thieves, the election was by no means a repudiation of partisanship. Although 14 of the 22 new Aldermen were identified as reformers, all but two had also run as the nominees of the regular parties. Perhaps the enthusiasm of the Whig-oriented *Times* was influenced by partisan bias, since a close reading of the results suggests that the real winners were the Whigs who, benefiting from the rampant factionalism of the Democrats, won a majority on the Board of Aldermen; a close reading of the situation in the sixty-man Board of Councilmen suggests nothing except that no one group had effective control. Any doubts as to the health of party feelings were quenched when the new Council met to organize in January of 1854. The Aldermen lent little comfort to reformers when they chose as their president a regular Whig over one of the candidates endorsed at Metropolitan Hall. The Councilmen won the rebuke of the *Times* by taking 47 ballots, "two days and some thousands of dollars" to elect a presiding officer.[40]

Under the circumstances, the Council was bound to disappoint reform hopes for energetic but thrifty government. In one sense, it did nothing to block the spirit of reform. It did not grant questionable franchises. It did not interfere with the newly energized police system, and it did not interfere with the efforts of Comptroller Flagg to impose a frugal administration on the city. Yet, though it provided relief from the excesses of the previous Council, it failed to give reform a constructive direction, or even to hold down spending. It temporarily reduced the tax rate, but only by, as the Forty Thieves had done, appropriating more money than had been provided for in the city budget; the deficit helped raise taxes in 1855 to a new high. Chiefly because of the mounting costs of schools and the police, total taxes in 1854 and 1855 were actually 25 percent higher than they had been during Tweed's two years as Alderman. Even before these failings became fully apparent, the Reform Committee publicly repudiated the Council with the assertion that the majority of its members were "party men" rather than reformers.[41]

[331]

THE TROUBLE WITH POLITICS

Still hopeful, the Reform Committee tried again in 1854, when voters would elect half of the Aldermen, all of the Councilmen, and, most important of all, a mayor. By then reformers were beginning to recognize the necessity of strong executive leadership to override the division of authority inherited from the Charter of 1849. As their champion, the Reform Committee chose Wilson G. Hunt, a Democrat and prominent businessman whom the *Evening Post* presented as another DeWitt Clinton. "Great cities," the Committee told New Yorkers, "are not necessarily 'great sores' on the body politic, and they only become so as good citizens abandon their political duties." Unfortunately, the times were not ripe for another DeWitt Clinton, or for reform in general, if only because 1854 was one of the most chaotic years in the history of American politics. The normal complexities of the political situation in New York were further complicated by the factionalization of both the Whig and Democratic parties under the impact of the slavery issue and of resurgent nativism. It was characteristic that Hunt should have been nominated both by the reformers and by part of the "Hard-Shell" faction of the Democrats; among the committee chosen to convey the news of this last nomination to the candidate were two reminders of the "Forty Thieves." Thomas J. Barr and Peter Barr Sweeny.[42]

In the election, the reform ticket was lost among a crowd of competing tickets. When voters went to the polls, they encountered a gambler's delight: Four candidates for Mayor, five for City Judge, three for District Attorney, five for Commissioner of Streets and Lamps, a multitude of candidates for various other offices—to say nothing of an array of candidates for Aldermen and Councilmen listed on one or more of five party tickets. Whoever won in this unhappy election, it was apparent that reform had lost. Wilson G. Hunt, the reform hero, was defeated handily by Fernando Wood, the only one of the mayoralty candidates not to run as a reformer. It was true that the Reform Committee had endorsed the victorious candidate for District Attorney, the smoothly intellectual A. Oakey Hall, but the next decade proved that even wins could be losses; as

THE TROUBLE WITH POLITICS

District Attorney and then as Mayor in the 1860s, Hall played a crucial role in the triumphs of the Tweed Ring.[43]

Perhaps New York *was* a "great sore" on the body politic. After two years of reform effort, municipal government seemed no better. Although the reformers did not give up, the future of reform proved to be very much like its past: A short, partial victory and then defeat; an improvement in the machinery of government but never enough good men and not enough time to perfect the work. By the 1850s, city government was well on its way to becoming, for its critics, the greatest failure in American life, especially when compared with the other agencies of the progressive age. While businessmen built the great railroads and steamships, while the agents of benevolence built the great engines of moral regeneration, government blundered from one mistake and sin to another, in the process undermining public faith in itself as an instrument of public purpose. When Colonel John Devoe attempted to explain the causes of the degeneration of his beloved market system, he noted one great consequence of the decline in public faith: "If a movement for public accommodation is suggested, out comes the conservative or opposition press to show that what would legitimately cost 150,000 dollars would, if conducted by these inefficient officers, cost the city 250 or 300,000."[44] Progressive private enterprise, so experience seemed to indicate, would do well what government could only do badly.

Reformers placed the blame not on government itself, which even in their eyes had its uses, but on "politics," which had failed to provide the good men required for public office. At the end of 1853, an editor of *Harpers Monthly* attempted to explain the causes of and suggest a cure for the political corruption he saw at work on all levels of American government. He traced the problem back to one cause: the influence of "politicians by trade," who had debased government and politics by acting on the principle that public office was a reward for party service; as a result, officeholders had come to see their positions less as places of public trust than opportunities for private gain. The editor concluded that the only solution was to teach the next generation that there was a glory higher than politics: "The strong temptation which comes from political influence, and the strong desire for public favor through which it is obtained must be abated by the substitution of something better and higher."[45] Undoubtedly, he hoped to encourage young men to venture into politics with the public good in mind, but his kind of reasoning tended to reinforce the inclination of the progressive city to see politics as bad, as disreputable, as something to be avoided. If politics were only a dirty and grubby means to higher things, then was it surprising that a growing number of young men should avoid it altogether in favor of business, literature, and the world of fashion?

It did not occur to reform-minded New Yorkers that their disappointments in part resulted from their failure to develop a model of political life appropriate to New York. They wanted to make government another agency of the progressive age. Public power, with maximum efficiency and minimum expense, was to provide the services and enforce the discipline required for the maintenance of the great city. Ideally, politics was simply the convenient and rational means for the selection of men needed to manage a rational government. Ideally, too, political decisions should be made on the rule that the public interest was synonymous with the interests of taxpaying, property-holding, respectable citizens. Such a model was logical and appealing to the uptown world of the city's "better" citizens, especially those who had become increasingly preoccupied with the private life of the home and with the specialized and time-consuming opportunities afforded by the metropolis in business, cultural, social, and benevolent affairs.

Political life in New York, however, was neither simple nor especially rational. Reformers called on all good citizens to work for the public interest, but in the heterogeneous city there was no clearly defined public interest with which everyone could identify. Reform government, with its emphasis on efficiency, did not appeal to the great majority of people who were not taxpayers and who were not part of the uptown world. Moreover, the politics which the reformers hoped to

exclude from government in the interests of thrift and efficiency was, for many others, more real and vital than government itself. Far from being simply the means to elect able men
to office, it had a variety of other purposes for the thousands
of humble people who did not share in the power, profit, and
glory of the progressive city. For them, politics was protection
against government; it was an avenue to success; it was a source
of identity; it was perhaps especially a way to express feelings
and to find satisfaction of anxieties and resentments.

Thus, reformers had difficulty making headway against
"politics," especially as practiced by Tammany Hall, even under
the best of circumstances. To make matters worse, reform was
seriously disrupted in the mid-1850s by the competition of
another movement against the existing disorder of politics.
This new movement was less rational and less respectable, but
it was more successful in winning both attention and votes,
especially from those citizens to whom reformers appealed for
support. The competitor was nativism which, a decade after
the rise and fall of the American Republican Party, reappeared
in political form.

Anti-immigrant and anti-Catholic feelings among Protestant
New Yorkers intensified in the early 1850s for several reasons.
The continued influx of the European poor seemed to account
for the growing social problems of the city; simple logic and
simple observation suggested that poverty, crime, drunkenness
and disorder had resulted from the great glut of dispossessed
and demoralized newcomers. Moreover, the open hostility of
the Catholic hierarchy to the public schools and to Protestant
benevolent work intensified the disposition of many Protestants
to see the Roman Church as an alien presence which stood in
the way of efforts to solve the social problems created by
immigration.[46] The same logic led many New Yorkers to
conclude that Catholic foreigners were largely responsible for
the degeneration of both politics and government. The day
had not yet arrived when corrupt politics could be closely
identified with Irish politicians (most prominent political figures were still native Protestants like Tweed), but by the 1850s
Irish Catholics were becoming conspicuous in ward politics as

politicians and election rowdies. It was not difficult for the fearful to conjure up the future: a Catholic Church which stood in the way of the Americanization of immigrants; the growth of an alien and disorderly population; the corruption of the public agencies required to maintain order; the reign of alien politicians, policymakers, and troublemakers.[47]

A look at the composition of the electorate seemed to confirm these fears. In 1855, there were nearly 89,000 legal voters in New York, nearly half of whom were naturalized citizens. Although the number of voters had grown by some 25,000 since 1845, the proportion of inhabitants who could vote declined from 17 to 14 percent, because of the great mass of as yet unnaturalized immigrants who had poured into the city after 1850. Only the Fifteenth Ward and the neighboring Ninth were secure for native rule. Already, naturalized citizens were the majority of voters in nine wards of the city; it would not be long before the vast pool of soon-to-be naturalized newcomers would provide foreign majorities in at least five other wards—especially since it was the practice of Tammany Hall to promote the mass naturalization of immigrants before election time in order to manufacture new voters for the Democratic cause.[48]

New York had become a foreign city. A population which had been over 60 percent native-born in 1845 was more than half foreign-born a decade later. If the newcomers were disruptive competitors for political power, they also competed for jobs and business opportunities. *Harpers Monthly*, on the basis of the census of 1850, noted the positive influence of immigration in promoting the development of a native middle class: "The vast influx of foreign population has tended to elevate the occupations of our native working classes, by relieving them of the humbler forms of labor."[49] While un-doubtedly many natives did rise on the class scale, many others—petty businessmen, skilled workers, and especially laborers—suffered from foreign competition. The growth of a pool of cheap labor encouraged the development of sweat-shop operations, often run by foreigners, which undercut native workmen and working women. As early as 1845, the

Tribune noted that native cabinent-makers were suffering from the competition of cheap furniture sold in auction shops and "mostly made by Germans, who work rapidly, badly and almost for nothing." Similar troubles damaged other skilled trades such as tailoring and shoemaking, leading George Foster to charge that immigrant labor enabled the "sweater" to rise, while taking jobs from the hands of "educated and thoroughly-trained journeymen."[50]

The age of Gold caused further frustrations for many natives. While prosperity brought wealth and a chance for a comfortable uptown life, it also brought a rising cost of living which bore down heavily on the less successful. It was as if progress, distorted by immigration, were driving a wedge into the native population, raising some and depressing others down to the level of the foreigners. In 1856, Thomas R. Whitney, in his *A Defence of the American Policy*, attempted to speak for the "American Mechanic." Once, the mechanic had been a proud citizen, the equal of all in his moral, political, and social standing, able to maintain a decent home and a respectable life. Because of the competition of cheap foreign labor, however, many "have been alienated from their home, their comforts, their ambition!" Moreover, the presence of cheap, degraded labor was promoting a caste system in the United States not only by creating an aristocracy of wealth but by undermining the dignity of labor, creating a distinction "between intellectual labor and mere drudgery . . . which forms the basis of caste, and encourages an aristocratic anti-republican sentiment."[51]

For many New Yorkers, it looked as if the world had been stolen from them, not only by the foreigners themselves but by the organizations which benefited from their presence: the Romanist hierarchy, the political clubs and voting blocs, the sweatshops and the large business concerns—all were part of a conspiracy, the more frightening because it could not be proven. If the native American faced secret conspiracies and combinations, it seemed obvious that he needed a secret organization of his own, invisible to the wirepullers and manipulators. In 1853, nativists formed the Order of the Star-

Spangled Banner, soon to be given the more mysterious name, the "Know-Nothings," apparently by E. Z. C. Judson, the "Ned Buntline" of the Astor Place Riot. The new movement spread rapidly throughout the city, particularly because it seemed to meet the need of anxious individuals for a sense of place and power. Its secret meetings, rituals, signs, distress calls, and handshakes fostered the feeling of belonging to an important organization.[52]

By 1854, the Know-Nothings were strong enough to launch a separate political party under the leadership of James W. Barker, a small businessman and advocate of temperance. In the spring, they created an action organization, the Order of Free and Accepted Americans—better known as the "Wide Awakes"—whose members soon made themselves noticed in the streets by their distinctive white felt hats and by their willingness to "mix it up" with Irish Catholics. Know-Nothing-ism had become a popular political movement which made no secret of its objectives: the elimination of all foreigners and Roman Catholics from public office, the establishment of a 21-year naturalization period for all aliens, the deportation of foreign paupers and criminals, Bible-reading in the public schools, and the preservation of Protestant domination in all areas of public life. It presented itself as the party of honesty and order. One of its leaders, who claimed to have been twice elected to office and then defeated by vote fraud, declared that "our party is the only one that pays its debts, don't drink bad liquor, don't vote but once at a time, don't carry ballots to crowd into the ballot'box while two of the inspectors are off to get a drink; but are quiet, honorable and peaceful."[53]

The Know-Nothing party came close to electing James Barker as Mayor in 1854. Barker, running in a four-man race, won pluralities in eight wards scattered throughout the city, while losing most of the heavily immigrant wards to Fernando Wood and the upper class Fifteenth Ward to Hunt, the reform candidate. Although his 18,607 votes left him over 1500 votes behind Wood, they put him more than 3000 ahead of the reform candidate. This near-victory seemed to foretell a glorious future for Know-Nothingism, and indeed by 1856 it had become a major influence in national as well as state politics. Time soon indicated, however, that it had missed its golden opportunity to win power in the city. In 1856, its candidate for Mayor, Isaac O. Barker (a cousin of James), polled more than 23,000 votes but still ran a poor second to Fernando Wood, who temporarily had the support of a united Democratic organization. After that, the movement disintegrated rapidly, pulled apart by internal conflicts over its leadership and over the slavery issue. Later nativist movements, too, would learn the perils of an open venture into politics.[54]

For many native citizens, Know-Nothingism seemed an appropriate response to the deeply disturbing social and political trends of an urbanizing society, but it had the misfortune to antagonize one of the two powerful social extremes in New York without attracting the other. If it did nothing else, Nativism served to drive naturalized citizens into politics, usually on the side of the Democratic party, in defense of their interests as new Americans. The *Citizen*, a newspaper sympathetic to the Irish cause, said in 1854 that while it was wrong for new citizens to vote as a bloc, the nativists left them little choice but to unite against all those who proposed or even tolerated their exclusion from public life.[55] At the other extreme, the nativists failed to convince men of political and social standing that the foreign menace was serious enough for them to abandon other issues. If only because they were better protected against the stresses of changing times, most members of the native upper class, though they might resent foreigners as the source of the city's woes, clung to the hope that the newcomers would eventually be, in the words of Robert M. Hartley, "thoroughly Americanized and fused with the body of the people."[56] For such men, the factionalism enflamed by Know-Nothingism threatened further to disrupt the good order required by a progressive society if it were to complete its assimilating work.

In the progressive city, indeed, there was hope that an expanding economy, the benevolent agencies, and the public schools would eventually make citizens of all but the most resistant of strangers. Even the rowdiest of foreigners, predicted *Harpers Weekly* in 1858, would "be absorbed, partly in the rural districts and partly in the penitentiaries, and then New York will be orderly."[57] The future would largely justify the hopes for assimilation if not for order. The hopeful, however, seemed to have overlooked what may well have been the most successful means of assimilating the alien population into American life. This was none of the agencies of the progressive city, but that which reformers condemned as hostile to their model of public life—the annoyingly intrusive politics and political culture of the subterranean city.

Chapter 13

TAMMANY'S CITY

THE LIVES OF THE GREAT are told in books; the lives of the humble in statistics. In 1847, G. W. Peck, in his "The Physiognomy of Cities" written for the *American Whig Review*, attempted to describe New York as it would look from a balloon:

> Here beneath are thousands and thousands as insensible to all this beauty of nature as though they had no instinct but to build cities and live in them. By far the greater part traverse these dark and narrow grooves, or toil in darker cavities beneath these slated roofs. . . . The substance of the earth is perforated for many miles with pipes and holes running in all directions, and its natural surface honeycombed like an old worm-eaten log by labors of the city building insect, whose nature it is to crowd together in as large numbers as possible, and keep in continual struggle and commotion. . . . He *must* assemble in crowds, build cities and live in them, and he does; and what is most singular is, that though gregarious considered at large, in

the individual there is no created thing more solitary and more disposed to prey on its own kind.[1]

Who were these city-building insects? Preferring easy answers, the progressive uptowners and reformers, in their balloons at the top of society, were inclined to view city people as two sharply defined extremes: The affluent and the poor, the virtuous and the vicious, skydwellers and subterraneans. But the true picture was more subtle and complex: it included a broad middle ground of workers and strivers, arrayed across a social continuum that stretched upward from the shadows of the subterranean city to the golden glow of Fifth Avenue.

In 1855, if there were untold numbers of the degraded and vicious poor along with thousands of ill-paid laborers, seam-stresses, and servants, there were also some 50,000 skilled and semi-skilled workers listed in the census: bakers, blacksmiths, boatmakers, butchers, cabinet-makers, carpenters, coopers, machinists, masons, painters, tailors, tinsmiths, and others.[2] Some of these, as independent craftsmen, small manufacturers, and shopkeepers, also belonged to a broad class of petty enterprisers outside the world of Wall Street and Broadway. Although the occupational categories used in the census were too crude for precise judgment, it is probable that between 30,000 and 40,000 New Yorkers, approximately one-quarter of the male adult population, were engaged in some form of individualistic enterprise that would qualify them, if only marginally, as entrepreneurs. The city's concentrated popula-tion and its trade generated a vast array of business roles: grocers, drinkinghouse proprietors, boardinghouse keepers, peddlers, druggists, restaurant operators, brewers, clothiers, contractors, carters, hackmen, expressmen, and dealers in cattle, horses, fruit, milk, oysters, fish, ice, coal, lumber, stone, and books.[3]

Perhaps only the magnificent eye of Walt Whitman was capable of perceiving the totality of the city-building insect, and then only by translating a list of occupations and activities into a great hymn to the equality of man:

TAMMANY'S CITY

The daily routine of your own or any man's life—the
  shop, yard, store, or factory;
These show all near you by day and night—workmen
  whoever you are, your daily life![4]

Certainly, few uptowners and reformers gave much attention to this vast middle society of work and business; yet it was essential to the life and character of the city—and to its politics. Reformers had little understanding of the strange political world which confronted them in the 1850s. For them, it was a world of rum and rowdyism—of corrupting politicians and degraded, vicious people—intrinsically and perversely hostile to good government. It was, however, a much more complex world that included the many workers and strivers, who could not or would not identify their interests and ambitions with the politics favored by downtown businessmen and large property-owners. Although it comprised men of all party persuasions, it was the special province of the Democratic Party and, most especially, of Democratic Tammany Hall.

Just as the progressive business city had its Wall Street and Broadway, so did Tammany's city have its great street of trade and fashion in the Bowery which ran north only a few blocks east of Broadway from Chatham Square to (at this time) Union Square. Especially on the lower Bowery, which separated the Sixth and Fourteenth Wards on the west from the Tenth Ward on the east, there was a marvelous jumble of human activity. One New Yorker counted some 240 different trades on the street: Saddleries, stove shops, stage offices, clothiers, druggists, jewelers, candy and peanut vendors, pawnshops, junk shops, and no less than 27 oyster stands and 52 taverns. Generally business was done on a small scale: "There are no great plate-glass windows, no gorgeous jeweler's shops, no overpowering furniture establishments." Trade, manufacturing, and residences were jammed together. A fire which broke out in a building between Grand and Hester streets in 1855 burned out three clothing stores, a carpet warehouse, a millinery shop, and a chair factory along with several residents.[5]

Like Broadway, the Bowery was a place for people to congregate, but, unlike its fashionable neighbor, it was far less a stage for success than a refuge from failure. Cornelius Mathews, the author of two rather undistinguished studies of New York life, wrote that "the Bowery is very much haunted by broken merchants, gentlemen under indictment," and others in shabby suits unwilling to encounter their ex-peers. Even more, however, it was a place to enjoy, to dream, and to shine for the inhabitants of the surrounding wards, especially of the Seventh, Tenth, and Thirteenth Wards which made up most of the Lower East Side, strange territory for the fashionable people of Broadway: "When from time to time," said Mathews, "some wild adventurous Broadway gentlemen takes a cab, and allows himself to be carried by a most desperate driver thither: he comes back, it is said, with hair on end." Whereas the progressive city had its eyes on Europe and America, the Lower East Side was a closed and insular world, most of whose inhabitants worked, shopped, and played close to where they lived. By the end of the 1840s, it had become a subculture with a style of life very different from that of Broadway and Fifth Avenue.[6]

If Broadway was home to that ultimate in fashion, the Dandy, the Bowery could boast of an equally conspicuous and bizarre representative of its culture, the B'hoy. Generally a young worker, the Bowery Boy summed up the male virtues of his society in the form of an aggressive and muscular individualism. Rough, boisterous, pugnacious, and irreverent, yet good humored, frank, and loyal to his friends, contemptuous of hypocrisy and hostile to "aristocracy," he seemed an original American type, a primitive democrat for those who, like Whitman, saw his positive side. George G. Foster declared that the B'hoy was part of an American type which included "the Hoosier of the Mississippi, the trapper of the Rocky Mountains, and the gold-hunter of California." One look at the dress and manner of the B'hoy was enough to distinguish him from the Broadway dandy. Dressed in blazing colors, often fireman's red, a cheek bulging with a quid of chewing tobacco, a swing to his walk (when not leaning against a lamp post), the B'hoy was a deliberately constructed picture of masculine power.[7]

He and his flashily dressed g'hal were only the most conspicuous members of the crowds that flocked to the Bowery in the evenings and on Sundays, drawn by the drinking places, "museums," music hall, theaters, restaurants, and the rich human vitality that enlivened the street: A place for shopper's bargains by day, a place for excitement, pleasure, and dreams by night. Bowery audiences liked their entertainments sweetly sentimental or brawnily violent. Whitman described the audiences of the Old Bowery Theater as "the best average of American-born mechanics" aroused to full masculine emotion by the power and magnetism of Edwin Forrest or Junius Brutus Booth. A later observer of Bowery theatergoers was less kind. "Q. K. Philander Doesticks" said that they demanded maximum violence from stage battles and deaths, often forcing the too subtle actor to repeat an unsuccessful death with the right number of jerks, spasms, and groans. For them, "a tragedy hero is a milksop, unless he rescues some forelorn maiden from an impregnable castle, carries her down a forty-foot ladder in his arms, holds her with one hand, while with the other he annihilates a score or so of pursuers." In the 1840s and early 1850s, the legendary hero of the Bowery stage was Mose Humphrey, a super B'hoy and urban Paul Bunyan, a giant who uprooted lampposts as weapons in his triumphs over his evil enemies and who carried street cars for blocks in one hand.[8]

Respectable uptowners viewed the Bowery with a mixture of fascination, amusement, and concern. The advocates of a well-ordered community had special reasons to fear and resent it for its ill-disciplined character. Undoubtedly, when they urged the need for good, inexpensive amusements to keep the young and the poor out of places of vice, they had the cheap theaters, music halls, barrooms, beer halls, and hotels of the Bowery in mind. Although the street escaped the reputation for degraded vice and violence of the nearby Five Points, its rowdy character was amply advertised by the Bowery Boys (who were not synonymous with the B'hoys) and their associated gangs, a largely native American bloc of pugnacious young toughs with whom Butcher Bill Poole was allied before he died. Although reputedly less vicious than their enemies, the Dead Rabbits, Plug Uglies, and other largely Irish gangs of the Five Points area, the Bowery Boys seemed to be part of a pervasive culture of violence which had burst out in the great Astor Place Riot.[9]

The society surrounding the Bowery did have a high regard for muscular aggressiveness. It was an intensely masculine society, respectful of physical power, which proved hospitable to fighters even of the most brutal sort. After a savage brawl between Orville "Awful" Gardner and William "Dublin Tricks" Hastings, the latter swore out a complaint claiming that Gardner was indeed awful, that "he was violently assaulted and beaten by Orville Gardner, who struck depondent with his fist, knocked him down, and then threw himself upon deponent's body, seized deponent's left ear between his teeth, and felioniously bit a large piece entirely out of the lower part of his ear, thereby maiming and permanently disfiguring him." To the outrage and disgust of respectable New Yorkers, violence had become a popular sport in the form of prizefighting. These "brutal Exhibitions" were trebly repugnant to the advocates of a well-ordered community, because they generally took place on Sunday and were associated with gambling, drinking, and with the failure to enforce the law. Despite the fact that prizefights were illegal, pugilists continued to beat each other into bloody messes before crowds of "rowdies and vagabonds."[10]

The rowdies and the fighting men, indeed, were often no better than drunken thugs. Yet the advocates of order ignored some significant realities of the Metropolis, among them the fact that the city attracted a sizable number of men of unusual physical vitality and strength, often intelligent and ambitious men who were dissatisfied with the limited opportunities of both rural society and urban slums. A century later, many would find their way into organized professional sports where their peculiar talents would be appreciated, but in the 1850s organized sport was still in its infancy. Only the Germans had established adequate channels for the physically talented in the form of their *Turnverein*, gymnastics societies that were intimately related to the rest of German social life.[11]

The most generally sanctioned and profitable form of physical endeavor was with one's fists. Proven fighting ability was admired on the Bowery and elsewhere in the city. John Morrissey won a place in society and a start in politics when as a young newcomer from Troy, New York, he walked into one of the toughest places in the Five Points and announced that he could beat anyone there. He was promptly mobbed and beaten up, but he had made his mark. After a brief but well-publicized career as a prizefighter, he opened a gambling house and a saloon, which led, in turn, to a political career. William "Butcher Bill" Poole, before his murder in 1855, had risen from a young butcher at Washington Market to fighting man to saloon-keeper to head of a Whig political club.[12]

Such men were heroes to a great many New Yorkers who desperately wanted heroic champions. The uptown movement, the influx of immigrants, and the sheer mass of life in the metropolis had widened the gap between the lower classes and the social and business leadership. For the poor, the great men of wealth and social influence might well have been creatures from another planet. Mike Walsh, the self-proclaimed defender of the common man, graphically expressed the resentment and frustration created by this situation when he told an audience: "Why if one of you want to light your segar in the street you will pass twenty well dressed loafers, with lighted segars in their mouths, without asking for a light, for fear of a refusal which you are not independent enough to resent, and wait until you find some chap as shabbily dressed as yourself." The age proclaimed equality among all men; reality proclaimed otherwise. The contrast between Fifth Avenue and dingy streets of the lower city proclaimed that men were not equal, and so did the fact that the well-to-do left the city in the summer for Newport and Saratoga, leaving the "nobodies" to swelter in the August heat. In such a situation, it was natural that frustrated and resentful men should consider the fighters and the fighting gangs as their local champions to confront the great outside world, should give Bill Poole a hero's funeral, and should follow the lead of their champions in the sleazy depths of ward politics.[13]

That reformers condemned the fighters as lawless and the ward politicians as corrupters of government made little impression. For many New Yorkers, especially those of the lower city, both law and government were things of the other planet, rarely useful and often threatening. The law did not protect the helpless laborers and servant girls from being exploited by their employers, nor did it protect the poor from the exorbitant rents of grasping landlords. On the other hand, it did back landlords who turned their tenants out in the street for nonpayment of rent; it did make homeless poverty, in the form of vagrancy, a crime, and it did, through the Truancy Act, threaten to take children away from their parents.[14]

The dangers of the law were illustrated by the growing demands for legal restraints on drinking. "Ought law to conform to public sentiment," asked Horace Greeley at the World's Temperance Convention in 1853, "or ought law be based upon essential righteousness, and then challenge a public sentiment to act in conformity therewith?" He had no doubts. If he and other temperance men could not get laws to close the "rum-holes" which had caused much of the crime and misery of the city, they demanded at the least the enforcement of the laws requiring that drinking places be closed on Sunday. Mike Walsh reminded them that the saloons were a necessary evil for a city which had failed to meet the human need for excitement and healthy play: "So long as it is looked upon as indecent, if not criminal for persons to run, sing, dance, and skylark in the public streets and squares, so long will the greater mass of the poorer portion of people, who have scarcely room enough to turn around in, continue to seek excitement and amusement in public places." Temperance men often did recognize that need, but, while they talked ineffectually about coffee-shops and reading rooms for the working classes, they bent most of their efforts to closing the saloon, often the workingman's only social club, on the workman's only day of rest.[15]

The Sunday closing laws were an obvious threat both to the

workingman's social life and to the business hopes of the drinking-house proprietor, whose future might depend on the willingness or unwillingness of the police to enforce the law. Nor were the vendors of whisky and rum the only petty entrepreneurs to feel the chill of law. The hackmen, who like the tavernkeepers were required to have public licenses, faced a variety of ordinances limiting their fares and regulating their mode of operation, desirable regulations from the point of view of uptowners, but irritants or worse for the intensely competitive hackmen. In 1854, the public cart and wagonmen, many of whom were Irishmen, were reminded by the city that they were required to have city licenses, and that they could not get a license unless they were American citizens. In similar ways did street peddlers and vendors face the threat of laws limiting or prohibiting their businesses as public nuisances. The *Tribune*, for instance, called on the city to take action against the vendors of cheap candy and ice cream and against "the pestilent fellows with fish horns, wagons and baskets who are constantly ringing door bells, or bawling into open windows."[16]

Resentment of specific laws did not lead to hostility to all rules, but it bred skepticism regarding the sacredness of law. If reformers exalted the law and condemned politics as a corrupting nuisance, many other New Yorkers reversed the formula. Law was a possible danger, the courts a distant horror, while the local politician was close, familiar, and accessible. The Aldermen who used their power as magistrates to free their constituents from the hand of the law released not only the lawless (as reformers tended to emphasize) but the innocent, although not so often as to keep a grand jury from charging in 1849 that 743 people were illegally confined in the penitentiary.[17] If only crudely, politics served as a protective medium between the New Yorker and a government which, as an individual, he could not control. It served an essential purpose in mitigating the effect of laws made in the interests of the affluent, influential, and "respectable" at the top of society without regard for the motley needs of tens of thousands of people at the bottom.

Among those who benefited were the helpless and the weak, but largely only as a byproduct of politics. By 1850 a rough specialization of function had developed. The benevolent societies, the almshouse, and the prisons had the chief responsibility for the truly helpless and hopeless. Politics was designed for the useful, the able, and the ambitious; for petty entrepreneurs with interests to protect such as the hackmen, saloon-keepers, and operators of slaughterhouses; and even more for those many men who for a variety of reasons could not or would not fit readily into the world of work and business.

As both critics and defenders could agree, popular politics emphasized not the enactment of good laws but the acquisition of place and of power. The ambition to achieve public office was the fuel which fired political energies and the glue which held, if only weakly, masses of diverse individuals together in some common purpose. The possession of office meant a livelihood and also influence, identity, esteem, and a meaningful place in society. Many offices in local government that seemed mean and undignified to uptowners were, for those at the bottom, steps upward in the world, opportunities worth fighting for and worth defending. It was probably inevitable that, in a city where private interest was so naked and so strong, the line between public interest and private possession should be blurred. Upper-class reformers defined public office as a public trust, somehow insulated from the private world of individual interest; but this was an unnatural distinction for those who had committed themselves and their energies to politics. Office was a reward for service to the victorious party or political faction. In 1847, soon after the Whigs won the city elections, the *Evening Post* noted that City Hall was crowded "with men clustered together in small parties, or reclining thoughtfully against the wall. . . . Nearly all these men are seeking for office, and hence the anxious looks and care-worn countenances that many of them exhibit."[18]

The range of patronage opportunities was almost as great as the range of human talents and ambitions involved in the political world: there were city, county, state, and federal offices; there were elected positions and appointed positions—

positions paying fees, daily wages, or annual salaries; there were places for day laborers, street sweepers, and bell-ringers; clerks, policemen, and health wardens; assessors and commissioners of deeds; aldermen and assemblymen; judges, heads of departments, and the mayor.[19] The patronage pyramid (and, as a result, city politics) was distorted by the presence at its top of a dazzling array of federal offices. As the nation's chief port of entry, New York was second only to Washington, D.C., as a national patronage center. The juiciest plums were to be found in the Custom House, located in a "Grecian temple" on Wall Street. It contained a small empire of nearly 700 federal employees ranging from the Chief Collector (his salary was $6400 a year) to nightwatchmen ($1.50 per night)—lucrative positions at a time when workingmen were fortunate to make $500 a year. As the Democratic party controlled the national government for all but four of the years between 1845 and 1860, these prizes generally went to deserving Democrats. The presence of this mass of Federal patronage in New York firmly tied local politics to National politics, thus defeating the hopes of reformers for a city-party devoted exclusively to municipal problems.[20]

If patronage prizes were numerous, the number of aspirants for them was greater, great enough to assure intense party, and also intra-party, conflict. Between 1840 and 1854, New York politics was dominated by the rivalry between the Whig and Democratic parties. Although the Whigs were the weaker of the two, they were strong contenders for power in the city, until the collapse of the national party in 1854–55. Supported by most of New York's wealthy men and by their allies in the middle and working classes, the Whig organization was able to elect three of its candidates for mayor between 1847 and 1851 (Brady, Woodhull, and Kingsland) and to rival the Democrats for control of the Common Council. Dominant in the elite Fifteenth Ward, the Whigs were also able to win a wide following in most of the wards of the city, especially in the heavily commercial districts at the tip of the island and in residential areas west of Broadway.[21]

The Whigs, however, were handicapped by their strengths.

Much of the party's appeal lay in its character as the advocate of the respectable native-born upper and middle classes. Despite the efforts of a few spokesmen like Greeley, it repelled many of the Germans and nearly all of the Irish who flooded into the city after 1845. In 1854, it was shattered not only by the controversy over slavery but also by the simultaneous eruptions of reform, nativism, and temperance. By 1856, there was no Whig party and no party capable of taking its place. The new Republican party, though it inherited some of the old Whig support in the Fifteenth Ward and elsewhere, proved to be a weak contender for power without the support of substantial numbers of dissatisfied Democrats.[22]

The future belonged to the Democratic party. It was strong in every part of the city outside of the Whig Fifteenth Ward, but the key to its growing power lay in the Sixth and Fourteenth wards, between Broadway and the Bowery, and in the wards of the Lower East Side, areas where it was particularly successful in organizing the foreign-born vote; by 1855 naturalized voters outnumbered native-born voters 3 to 2 in the eight wards east of Broadway.[23] Although party leaders were generally native-born Protestants, they worked actively to win and to hold the allegiance of immigrants, especially the Irish. In 1848, Greeley's *Tribune* complained that newcomers "are met as they land on our shores with assurances that the party termed Democratic is the embodiment of what they desire—is the party of Liberty. . . . They do not support the party because of the measures which divide it from the Whigs, but they support the measures because of the party. They become a class, and their votes cast almost solid, defeat the Whigs." Despite Greeley's warning that bloc voting encouraged nativism among the Whigs, the great majority of immigrants continued to support the Democratic organization as the party of liberty and opportunity.[24]

Although political opportunities for immigrants were generally limited to minor offices and minor positions of ward leadership, the Democratic party had by the 1840s established an open and egalitarian character inviting to ambitious men who might otherwise have been alienated from the political and social life of the city. In this strength, however, lay a major weakness, for the competition for place and power among the ambitious made the party as much a battleground as a political organization. The intense competition in the world of Democratic politics encouraged practices which gave it a disreputable character in the eyes of respectable citizens regardless of party.

The opportunities for conflict were especially inviting at the base of the party structure, in the primary elections. Ideally, the ward primaries were exercises in local popular democracy. Practically, however, the system created many invitingly open doors for the politically active and ambitious. As the primary meetings were generally poorly attended, it was comparatively easy for a few insiders to manipulate the nominating process. For the same reason, however, the primaries were open to organized attacks from ambitious outsiders with sufficient presumption and backing to challenge those in control. The man able to organize a small bloc of active voters, such as the members of one of the many (84 in 1845) volunteer fire companies, was a major force in any ward.[25] As the number of ambitious men grew faster than the number of political offices, it was inevitable that conflict would intensify, especially since it was encouraged by feuds within the state and national party.

In 1846, for instance, the heavily Democratic Fourth Ward was shaken by a battle over the nomination of an Alderman. When the incumbent, a wine merchant by the name of Divver, was renominated, he was challenged by the friends of the Assistant Alderman, George H. Purser, an English-born druggist. Charging that violence and intimidation had been used to nominate Divver, they held their own primary, nominated Purser, and issued a call for "Sailors, Mechanics, Stevadors, Long-shore-men, and Laborers to the Rescue." With the support of the Fourth Ward Jefferson Association, the druggist defeated the wine merchant (supported by the Fourth Ward Jackson Association), only to be himself challenged at the next election by a new contender; Purser won this next election by a meager seven votes. As the Fourth was the strongest Democratic ward in the city, even a split did not defeat the party. Elsewhere, the Democrats were not so lucky. In 1847, the Democratic organization was rent by similar conflicts in eight other wards; the result was political disaster, as the Whigs won the city elections.[26]

Conflict had its positive side. Competition excited popular interest and involvement, drawing into politics hundreds of otherwise marginal men as voters and, more significantly, as members of the innumerable nominating committee, ward committees, "safety committees," ratifying meetings, and protest meetings that enlivened the nominating process. In a city where so many men were powerless and alone, the primary system provided a place for those who needed and demanded a sense of self-importance. In a city where so many were isolated in their neighborhoods from the larger city, the primary was, like the local election, a meaningful, touchable link with the outside world. Yet the primaries were often a rotten training ground, where the next generation of politicians received their apprenticeship in the use of those practices and attitudes which were to corrupt city politics for decades. As competition for nominations intensified, manipulation, muscle, and money became increasingly important—and so, as the behavior of Forty Thieves attested, did the disposition to "make politics pay."[27]

Theoretically, fraud in city elections was punishable as a public offense, although the absence of a voter-registration law made illegal voting difficult to stop.[28] In the party primaries, there was not even the meager restraint of public law, for primary fraud was a private matter subject to the will of the party leadership. In the long run, self-interest alone demanded the elimination of practices which embarrassed even the party faithful and antagonized respectable voters. To win citywide elections, the Democratic organization needed the support of the *Evening ʾost*, the major Democratic newspaper in the city and an enemy of primary fraud; and it needed respectable businessmen to head its ticket, men such as its successful mayoralty candidates, Havemeyer, Mickle, and Westervelt. In the short run, however, the party leadership proved unable and unwilling to enforce honesty and order, because it was itself a reflection of the disorder at the base of the party.

Superficially, the Democratic organization was more centralized than its Whig rival. By the 1840s, it had become a convenience for both friends and enemies to associate the party with Tammany Hall, but this was glib political shorthand which obscured the lack of unity and cohesion at the top of the organization. Essentially, there were two Tammanys. One was the Tammany Society which, as its name indicated, was a "venerable" social organization (founded in 1787) with a select membership. It was perhaps this fraternal character which enabled New Yorkers to ignore the bizarre fact that the major party of the nation's biggest and most sophisticated city was associated with a society named after an Indian and organized along the lines of an Indian tribe. At the very time that the metropolis had begun to grope its way toward bureaucratic organization, politics became increasingly associated with an order headed by Sachems, Sagamores, and Wiskinkies.[29]

Yet perhaps it was this very anachronistic character which gave the Society its almost magic appeal to faithful Democrats. Although the rank and file of the party generally were not members, they did have access to its Hall for both social and political functions. The annual Tammany Ball was the social event of the year for those who would not be permitted even to serve at the grand affairs of the Astors and Schemerhorns. Mike Walsh recognized one reason for Tammany's popularity: "The gloomy, churlish, money-worshipping, all-pervading spirit of the age has swept all the poetry of life out of the poor man's sphere. . . . No wonder, then, that thousands of poor men flock to Old Tammany and the neighboring houses on such occasions to get a taste of the equality which they hear so much preached, but, never save there, see even partially practiced."[30]

The magic and poetry of social Tammany did not carry over to its political side. Political policy for the party was determined not by the Society but by the Democratic General Committee, an unwieldy body composed of three representatives from each ward. Ideally, it should have been able to maintain order in the primary system, but since its membership was chosen annually through that same system, the Committee itself was shaken by the tempests of local politics. When it did make a rare effort to supervise the local primaries, it provoked cries of interference and "wire-pulling" from those who stood to lose from its interference. Although it might fall under the temporary dominance of shifting cliques of ward leaders, no strong authority emerged to assure the enforcement of a coherent party policy.[31]

The best prospects for stability lay in the overlap between the General Committee and the Tammany Society. The Society had strong political influence, if only because it was the owner of Tammany Hall, the site of the most important Democratic political meetings. As the owner, it could deny the Hall, and so such legitimacy as there was, to a clique or faction that had become obnoxious to the Tammany membership. Moreover, some Tammany members had political power independent of their position in the Society. In theory, it was possible for a few strong members of the Society to dominate the party organization. In practice, however, no men were able to acquire the power needed to put the Democratic house in order. As a result, the party organization deteriorated steadily after 1845. If at the bottom the party was weakened by conflict within the wards, it was torn apart at the top by national discord centered on the slavery issue. By the early 1850s, both the city and state organization had split into two factions, the "Hard-Shells" and the "Soft-Shells," neither of which had a clearcut position regarding slavery, both of which had a clearcut ambition to get as many federal and state offices as possible.[32]

The battle between the two sides swirled up and down the organization from the wards to the Tammany Society. The "Softs" maintained control of the Society itself, chiefly by appointing a host of new members, including—for the first time—a significant number of Irishmen. They could not, however, win a clearcut victory over their rivals. In 1852, the two sides temporarily buried their tomahawks and united to elect Westervelt as Mayor by a large majority over the Whig candidate, in part to demonstrate their ability to aid in the election of the national party's candidate for the presidency, Franklin Pierce; four years out of power on the national level had sharpened their appetites for federal offices.[33]

With the election out of the way, they again fell to fighting over patronage matters. By early 1853, the party was further split by the appearance of two contending General Committees, one headed by Daniel Delevan, the other by Thomas J. Barr. Confronted by two committees claiming the legitimate right to use Tammany Hall, the Tammany Society was forced to step openly into politics by conferring legitimacy on the Delevan committee, backed by the Softs. The Society appealed for party unity: "This city, by its size and metropolitan character, exercises an important influence throughout the country; and it is essential to the best interests of the democratic party that it should be the home, not only of sound, but also vigorous and harmonious democracy."[34] Vigorous, yes; sound and harmonious, no. The Hards persisted in their opposition, and then in 1854 the simultaneous eruption of nativism, reform, and the slavery issue threatened to disintegrate the party.

This apparently meaningless factionalism actually had a significant effect on municipal affairs. It meant the near collapse of responsible authority within the city's majority party. It meant the disintegration of that organization which had most successfully given a diversity of marginal groups a sense of place and of power. More, it meant the weakening of effective and responsible authority of any kind to manage the affairs of the city. Reformers could gloat that "the discipline of party is shaken," but they could not provide a substitute for it. Neither nativism nor reform could persuade a majority to accept their cause; neither could unify a socially fragmented city. Nor could they unify the city government. The Charter of 1853, while it had strengthened the Mayor, had not eliminated the awkward fragmentation of power and responsibility inherited from the past. During the summer of 1854, in the face of the threat of a cholera epidemic, the *Evening Post* asked: "Who is responsible for the present filthy and pestilential condition of our streets? Is it Mayor Westervelt, who is at the head of the police department, or is it either [sic] of the other eight mayors who are heads of other executive departments, or are the eighty members of the Common Council to have charge of the matter?"[35]

Who could govern such a fragmented government? Who

could govern the fragmented city? Certainly it was not the honest but weak Mayor Westervelt. In simpler days, said the *Post*, Westervelt's weak leadership would have been tolerable, but the metropolis now required a strong man to fill an office which had become more important than that of the governor of the state: "He has more responsibility, more patronage, more business to transact, more perplexing questions of a practical nature to decide." Other New Yorkers could agree that the city required a new type of executive leader of "honesty, capacity and firmness" to save it from a complete breakdown of the governing process.[36] It was not long before they were confronted by a new leader of capacity and firmness, who had been nurtured by the competitive politics of the Democratic party. Few of them, however, were long pleased with the change, for the leader was Fernando Wood, probably the most controversial mayor the city ever would have.

The fragmentation of authority in politics and government was an invitation for a strong leader with sufficient talent and ruthlessness to seize power. Wood was that man. A dapper, almost prissy figure, he could, said one observer, easily have been mistaken for a missionary or moral reformer "were it not for that pitiless eye and those closely compressed lips." A later critic summed up Wood's character when he called him a "brilliant desperado."[37] By the 1850s he had proven his toughness through a rather shady career in business and politics which took him a long distance away from his Quaker background.

He was the son of a Philadelphia merchant who had failed and had eventually settled in New York, where he recovered sufficiently to send Fernando to a private school for several years. In 1832, young Wood, then 20 years old, went into business for himself as the owner of a "Wine and Segar" shop. This first business failed within three years, but Wood bounced back as the owner of a combination grocery and grog-shop near the waterfront. Within a few years, he had acquired three small ships and had begun to establish himself as a merchant shipper.[38]

Business success gave Wood the time and influence he

[358]

needed to cultivate his growing political ambitions. In 1839, three years after joining the Tammany Society, he was elected Chairman of the Democratic Young Men's Committee, whose secretary was young Richard B. Connolly, the later "Slippery Dick" Connolly of the Tweed Ring. That success soon led to his election to Congress in 1840, despite some well-publicized Whig charges that earlier he had cheated a local bank, the first of several allegations of business dishonesty that were to haunt his political career.[39] Like Tweed later, Wood served only one term in the House of Representatives, being defeated for renomination in 1842, another victim of the city's political instability. Throughout the rest of the 1840s, he concentrated on his thriving business as a merchant-shipper, striking wealth in the lucrative gold-rush trade in 1849. Having invested heavily in land both in New York and in San Francisco, he was able by 1850 to devote his full time to politics.[40]

For years, Wood had been busy cultivating political support for himself, especially among the immigrants of the lower city, so that it was no surprise when he was nominated as the Democratic candidate for mayor in 1850. The election, however, was a personal disaster. His enemies publicized the fact that he had been sued by his brother-in-law, Edward E. Marvine, for fraud in a joint business venture in the California trade. "Fernando Wood," Philip Hone grumbled, "instead of occupying the mayor's seat, ought to be on the rolls of the State Prison." Despite his denial of the charge, ex-Mayors Havemeyer and Mickle, two influential Democratic merchants, refused to support him in the election, and he was easily defeated by Ambrose Kingsland. The *Evening Post* declared that Wood had "grossly overrated the influence of party organization, and as grossly underrated the importance of unimpeachable personal integrity," and went on to blame him for having caused the defeat of almost the entire Democratic ticket.[41] The charge was unfair, since 1850 was not a Democratic year (the Whigs won heavily in the state as well as in the city) but Wood was twice impeached as a business cheat and as a political liability.

Such a reputation would have sunk the career of a lesser

man and might have defeated anyone during a period of political stability. Neither the man nor the times, however, were ordinary. In 1853, Wood allied himself with the Softs in their successful struggle to maintain control of Tammany Hall. Having made a special effort to win the support of the Irish, who were becoming an influence in Tammany politics, he easily won the Soft nomination for mayor in 1854. That was expected; what was not expected was his nomination also by the Hards, over the opposition of their own leaders. How he was able to carry out this coup is unclear, but it seems likely that he had quietly influenced the Hard primaries to select delegates favorable to him. Whatever the reasons, the Hard Convention selected him by a narrow majority, after Tweed refused to stand for the nomination. As Wood was to discover again and again, however, even the strongest and shrewdest political strategist could not overcome the divisions within the Democratic organization. He acted less to unite the party than to split the Hards. Part of that faction supported him, but the rest bolted under their leaders (including Tweed, who was becoming Wood's most formidable enemy) and eventually nominated Wilson G. Hunt, the reform candidate.[42]

The decision of the Hards to support Hunt kept the number of mayorality candidates in 1854 down to a mildly confusing four: a Whig; Barker, the Know-Nothing; Wood; and Hunt, the Democratic–Reform fusion candidate. The respectable press and most respectable citizens agreed that anyone was to be preferred to Wood. He was associated with Rum and Rowdyism; his questionable business dealings again were dredged up; he was accused of being a secret member of the Know-Nothing order and thus a hypocrite in his professions of support for the immigrant. Anyone but Wood— the trouble was that the opposition could not unite on anyone. Although both Hunt and Barker cut into Democratic Strength, Wood was elected with slightly over 20,000 votes, about one-third of the total vote, his victory clinched by an overwhelming majority in the Sixth Ward. Undoubtedly, he owed his election to the immigrant vote, especially to the Irish and to the immigrant press which, according to the *Tribune*, "warmly" supported him.[43]

The Know-Nothings challenged the results, charging fraudulent voting. After investigating the matter, however, the Board of County Election Canvassers decided that it was "not authorized by law to investigate questions of fraud and illegality." Wood had climbed to the top, but there was only chaos there—for the election had yielded an even more badly fragmented government than before. The city had a Soft Mayor, a Hard Recorder, a Know-Nothing Commissioner of Streets, a Whig City Judge and a Whig District Attorney, while the Common Council was splintered among Softs, Hards, Know-Nothings, Whigs, and Reformers. What could Wood do? What would he do? After the election, the *Tribune* predicted that the new Mayor would work hard to dispel the shadows around his reputation: "On the whole we believe he will do better than a majority of those we have seen serving as Mayors have done, for he has more force of character and will not content himself with naively sitting two or three hours per day in his office and signing such papers as are handed up to him."[44] The *Tribune* was at least half right. Wood proved to be a forceful mayor. In attempting to provide the strong executive leadership which many had demanded, however, he soon made himself a fearful presence in politics who was to set in motion developments which were to haunt the city for decades.

TEMPERANCE, BUT NO MAINE-LAW.

The Troubled City I

FIGURE 18. (left, above) This lithograph (dated 1853 but possibly later) of the Gem Saloon at the corner of Broadway and Worth Street seems to satirize the slogan, "Temperance, But No Maine Law," favored by opponents of prohibition like Fernando Wood. A close look at this scene indicates that the artist, A. Fay, has made some effort to populate the ornate saloon with a variety of sins. The thin man with his hat on who is engaged in shaking hands at the center of this view is reputed to be Wood himself, soon to be, first, New York's "model mayor" and, then, the target of reformers because of his convoluted course regarding prohibition and other moral issues.

Courtesy of the Museum of the City of New York.

FIGURE 19. (left, below) *Leslie's Illustrated* published this view of Tammany Hall as it looked shortly before the election of 1856 in which Fernando Wood won reelection as mayor over a bitter but divided opposition. Soon after this election, reformers appealed to the state legislature to reorganize both the city's government and its police system. The result in 1857 was a new city charter for New York, state intervention in its affairs, and a conflict over the control of its police which led to Wood's temporary political downfall to the advantage of William M. Tweed.

Courtesy of the New York Public Library.

Chapter 14

TYRANNY, TAMMANY, AND THE STATE

IN 1854 ELIZABETH SCHUYLER HAMILTON died at the age of 96, a half-century after her husband was killed by Aaron Burr. She had seen the once tight little city grow into a sprawling metropolis, a vast and tangled outgrowth of the contradictory wills of Hamilton and of his assassin. New York had become, as Hamilton had dreamed, the heart and mind of a dynamic, capitalistic nation; what once had been a city of petty merchants had become the base for great bankers, wholesale merchants, brokers, railroadmen—the builders of a modern economy. But it was also very much Burr's city. In his happier days before the fateful duel, Burr had been an important influence in converting Tammany from a fraternal society into a political organization. His New York was a city which, with the age of mass politics, had become a sprawling democratic world of many groups and many interests. In half a century, New York had become two mismatched cities, one preoccupied with exploiting a continent, the other with finding places for a heterogeneous population of strangers and citizens. How to govern such a world? That was the question which fascinated and tantalized Fernando Wood:

> Our city is a great empire—great in its extent—great in its population; great in its wealth; great in its commerce; great in its splendor; great in its pretensions to religious sanctity; great in the quantity of vice, destitution, and wretchedness which pervades its streets, and great in the variety of its social classes and the national characteristics of the world combined into one community, all living under the same laws and dependent upon the same system of government.

In a city governed by personal ambitions, the result of such diversity was a jumble of individualisms, a multitude of competing interests. While reformers in their uptown worlds spoke as if there was naturally a public will to be rallied for the public good, Wood declared that there "is no such thing as *one* public mind; where there is not *one*, a *single* public mind, it is almost impossible that the decrees or wishes of government can be generally understood or made acceptable."[1] How to govern such a city?

A less thoughtful man would not have asked the question; a less ambitious one would not have attempted to answer it. Why Wood made the attempt probably will never be known. Even more than Tweed, he was a secretive man who left no record of his thoughts and feelings. Perhaps he was, as his enemies claimed, simply a creature of avarice, greedy for wealth and power. Perhaps, as some reformers hoped, he was a man of pride who hoped to overcome his disreputable past by championing civic good. Perhaps, beneath his cool exterior, he was a romantic, influenced by the example of Louis Napoleon who, in the years after 1852, fashioned a splendid empire from the disordered politics of France. Whatever the reason, he identified himself with the proposition that only the concentration of power and responsibility in one man could bring efficiency and order. He may not, as reported later, have eulogized "a splendid despotism," but he did adopt as his model "a strong executive head with nerve, integrity, will, courage, and capacity, and an abundant authority of law, with wide spread discretion in which to exercise it."[2]

Both his friends and enemies could agree that he was a man of forceful character. There was reason, however, to doubt that even a forceful man could find sufficient authority in the mayor's office to manage the fragmented city, for the chief executive was not even master of his own executive house; authority was scattered among nine independently elected executive heads over whom he had little control. When he took office on the first day of 1855, Wood complained that earlier efforts to solve the city's problems by tinkering with its charter had been doubly wrong; such efforts had produced "a complicated, many-headed, ill-shaped monster" of a government as well as "an uncaring spirit in the people who, by continued application to State legislation, have been taught to look to foreign remedies for domestic abuses." He called for government reorganization to give the Mayor the same unified executive powers and responsibilities held by the President of the United States, that "one-man power, which history teaches is the least dangerous, and the most positive for good."[3]

The new Mayor blamed the fragmentation of authority for the "startling increase" in taxes of 250 percent over the previous decade. Although convinced that only a strong executive could effectively curb city spending, he did urge the Common Council to devise some system of restraint and accountability which would at least keep city officials from spending more money than had been appropriated to them. He also proposed the consolidation in one department of the various powers over the streets (then held by six of the departments, besides several outside Commissioners, Inspectors, Surveyors, Appraisers, and other temporary agents) in order to deflate the ballooning costs of street management and improvement associated with the Age of Gold. To reduce taxes on real estate, he asked for a new effort to tax both undisclosed personal property and the street railroads. Most of the rest of his program repeated the well-intentioned wishes of earlier mayors, for the reduction of congestion on Broadway, the reconstruction of municipal dock facilities, and cleaner streets.[4]

His administration, however, proved to be different from any that had gone before. When Wood assumed office, he was confronted by the winter of desperate unemployment which followed the Panic of 1854. Rather than ignoring the problem, he invited attention to it, digressing in his inaugural from a call for economy in government to declare that, if high taxes were to be continued, more revenue should be devoted to relief of the jobless. He followed that with a lecture on the responsibilities of capital: "Do not let us be ungrateful as well as inhuman. Do not let it be said that labor, which produces every thing, gets nothing and dies of hunger in our midst, while capital, which produces nothing, gets every thing, and pampers in luxury and plenty." If only because the depression was short, Wood did very little to provide public work relief, but he was soon able to consolidate his reputation as a friend of the working poor in a way which perhaps he had not anticipated.[5]

Late in January, he notified New Yorkers that his office had opened a Complaint Book for all matters under municipal jurisdiction: "The Mayor will entertain, and, so far as the laws give him power, take cognizance of charges preferred by responsible parties for violation of the ordinances and dereliction of duty upon the part of any person holding office under the City Government." Apparently, he intended to rally citizen assistance behind his effort to give authority to the law. The Complaint Book, however, also drew to the mayor's office a crowd of people with grievances against other private citizens, particularly employers and landlords. "The impression seems to prevail," said the *Tribune*, "that the Mayor has power to redress all wrongs." Wood and his assistants were confronted with the previously unnoticed problems of those who had found no support in the law: the worker cheated by his employer; the man defrauded of his property; even married

[367]

couples burdened by "the most delicate cases of domestic difficulty." Wood attracted much favorable attention when he intervened on the side of a seamstress who claimed that she had been cheated by her employer, a shirt-seller. Calling the offender to his office, the Mayor ordered him to pay the seamstress for her work and lashed out at all such exploitation of poor working girls.[6]

Wood did very little actually to improve the material condition of the working poor, but the interest shown by his administration in their welfare was sufficiently unique to strengthen his position with the lower classes. Even his general failure to solve their problems served to demonstrate his need for greater power and authority. "If there is one quality more than another that the people admire in a public officer," he wrote in 1856, "it is firmness of purpose and a consistency of official conduct."[7] Whether intended or not, his policies gave him a strong popular base for the exercise of firmness and consistency, removed from the vagaries of Tammany politics. Popular support, however, was not enough for the exercise of authority. If only to get the reorganization of government needed to strengthen his power, he had to win support from the rich and the respectable. At the start of his administration, he set out to demonstrate to them the advantages of effective authority.

Even a cursory reading of the newspapers in 1854 was enough to convince him that the upper and middle classes were deeply concerned not only by rising taxes but also by the apparent collapse of public order. Hardly had he been elected before the *Tribune* instructed him on his future duties: "The Mayor and Chief of Police of this City ought to break up the infamous dens of Gambling and Lewdness. . . . By his course with regard to these social evils, we shall judge Fernando Wood, forgetting all that has been said to his prejudice in the past." For the new Mayor, the police were a natural and congenial instrument. Although he was only one member of the three-man Police Commission, he moved quickly to establish his dominance over the force. On his first day in office, he issued a general order that policemen report to him all unlicensed saloons, drinking places kept open on Sunday, houses of prostitution, gambling houses, public nuisances, and every violation of law: "It is my duty to see the laws faithfully executed. . . . You are to be the eyes through which the theater of my duties is to be observed." He closed his directive with the warning: "You have now a determined Chief Officer, who will not be indifferent to a single dereliction of duty."[8] It was probably to assure the vigilance of his thousand sets of eyes, often sleepy in the past, that he instituted the Complaint Book, which made citizens watchmen over enforcement agencies.

Wood persuaded the other commissioners to give him exclusive authority over all cases of policemen charged with neglect of duty and other infractions of police regulations. Armed with this power to dismiss or to suspend, he set out to reorganize his civic army. A telegraph network connecting the various station houses with the office of Chief Matsell was begun. The Surgical Bureau in the department was reorganized so as to reduce the number of man-hours lost to the force either through legitimate sickness or through malingering. Above all, he tried to create a disciplined force loyal to him, proud of its work, and free from the entanglements in ward politics which had hampered it in the past. Five months after he took command, he had his men parade in City Hall Park. New Yorkers were impressed with the military precision with which the marchers executed their parade drills, a marked contrast with the generally slipshod manner of the earlier police. "The value of such a visible exponent of the huge power wielded by the Mayor," declared the *Tribune* hopefully, "capable of being quickly concentrated by the magical telegraph wires on any given part of the city is a terrible warning to . . . the ruffianism which has so long beset our city."[9]

As the dynamic leader of a quasi-military force, Wood appealed to those who respected either a strong tribal chief or an efficient bureaucrat. From the beginning, he attempted to demonstrate that one-man power would, as he had promised, be "most positive for good." The police were to be the instrument through which he hoped to tame a city of free-wheeling individuals into a well-ordered community: they were to help him force laggard street cleaners and health inspectors to make a clean and healthy city; they were to protect the poor against short-weighting by cheating shopkeepers; and especially they were to maintain public order.[10]

Wood won enthusiastic support from the respectable when early in January he launched a crusade to close the saloons on Sunday. Backing his effort with the threat to revoke the licenses of uncooperative saloonkeepers, he was able to boast by the end of the month that of the 2800 saloons which had violated the Sabbath before his administration began only 26 remained open.[11] In February, he also launched a drive to clean out gamblers and prostitutes from their traditional haunts along lower Broadway; the elimination of the prostitutes, it was hoped, would not only remedy a dangerous social evil but destroy the chief source of livelihood for the many rowdies who were believed to be their "fancy men." "Never has any municipal Hercules awakened brighter hopes in the bosoms of all good citizens," enthused a New Yorker when the police arrested a number of Broadway gambling house and brothel keepers who had operated openly in the past.[12]

The wearied observer of similar crusades in the past and in the future might be skeptical. Even at his busiest, the Mayor could not completely clean the Augean stable. Some saloons remained open on Sundays, especially in the Fourth and Sixth Wards (where Wood had his greatest political strength), whose Aldermen openly defied the Mayor's decrees. Even when licensed saloons did shut down, unlicensed places, in growing numbers, continued to provide Sunday refreshment. Many of the street-walkers arrested during police sweeps of the Broadway area soon won their freedom on the grounds that they had been illegally arrested; anyway, some of the enthusiasm for that part of the crusade vanished when citizens discovered that the drive was scattering prostitutes into previously respectable areas.[13]

The police raised complaints that they had arrested good women as well as bad and that they had neglected to inform those whom they had seized of their legal rights. George Templeton Strong, a conservative-minded lawyer, had praised

Wood as a "Civic Hero" in February, but soon he became disgusted with the Mayor's apparent disregard for law: "He becomes the more popular for his courage in taking the responsibility of action unsupported by precedent and statute. So rise dictators in degenerate commonwealths." The *Times*, too, expressed concern over the popular disposition to ignore the safeguards of government in favor of concentrating power in the hands of the Mayor.[14]

Whatever its limitations, however, Wood's crusade was a good show, an effective demonstration of the virtues of one-man power. The failures? They demonstrated Wood's primary point that he needed more power to complete his work. The *Times, Tribune* and other newspapers supported his call for the consolidation of the executive power in his hands. The editor of *Harpers Monthly* praised him as a man who actually was fulfilling the traditional promise to establish municipal order and declared that "for many years there has not been so popular a magistrate, nor one that better deserved popularity." As the "Model Mayor" of the metropolis, Wood's fame spread into the hinterland; in April, the Governor of Ohio informed him that he was the most popular man west of the Alleghenies and that all the women in Ohio were in love with him.[15]

Wood's reputation as a champion of virtue served him well when he resisted what was soon to be the greatest threat to his authority—interference from the state government. Frustrated by their failures to redeem the wicked city, reformers, temperance men, and taxpayers had come increasingly to look for assistance from Albany. From the beginning, the Mayor kept an anxious eye on the capital, where the legislature was considering a bill to reorganize the police department. Since it would have placed the police under a new five-man board elected by the people, the bill posed a direct threat to Wood's authority: "The whole theory of my views of Executive Government of every character, is *one head*," he wrote in a public letter. "I am satisfied that no good Government can exist in a city like this, containing so many thousands of the turbulent, the vicious, and the indolent, without a Chief Officer with necessary power to see to the faithful execution of the laws."[16]

Supported by his reputation as a champion of good order, he was able to rally the rich and the respectable to his side. Late in March, Peter Cooper, Robert B. Minturn, William F. Havemeyer, and a long list of other prominent New Yorkers issued a call for a mass meeting to protest the bill as threatening to throw the police system "into the hands of packed primary meetings and corrupt political committees." The meeting was a triumph for the man who but a few years before had been virtually drummed out of the merchant community. As one of Wood's supporters boasted, the representatives of more than $50 million in property attended to praise him for bringing government, in the words of the President of the Chamber of Commerce, "from chaotic mismanagement to harmonious efficiency." Faced with such a powerful protest, the legislature dropped the bill, despite one legislator's warning that Wood was attempting to convert the police into "a mammoth political machine."[17]

The Mayor had fended off one threat to his authority, but he could not defeat another that was to undermine his reputation as a champion of order and to throw him back into the dark and bloody ground of Tammany politics. For several years, radical temperance men had called on the state to enact a law prohibiting the sale of intoxicating liquors, a law they believed would wipe out the great source of crime and misery in one stroke. Unfortunately for the great majority in the city who opposed prohibition, the state elections in 1854 had seriously weakened the two-party system in favor of a coalition of nativists and temperance men which won temporary control of the state government. Wood did his best to derail the prohibitionist movement. Late in January, backed by his success in enforcing Sunday closing, he told the legislature that existing laws were sufficient, if enforced, to control intemperance and warned that the disposition to pass new laws to deal with old evils was self-defeating: "This mistake has been productive of continued and never ending legislation upon all subjects, until the books are so full of laws, that none, but the most astute and studious lawyer can tell what is, and what is not the law." The prohibitionists, however, had already convinced themselves that Wood's program, no matter how sincere, would neither eliminate saloons nor prevent drunkeness. Encouraged by Greeley's *Tribune*, which had a wide circulation throughout the state, the legislature passed the Prohibitory Law in April, scheduling it to take full effect on the Fourth of July, the day that New Yorkers had traditionally celebrated with the greatest abandon.[18]

The timing of prohibition was only a small part of its offensive character. The Prohibitory Act was a bad law. To begin with, it was anti-city: It prohibited the sale of any domestically produced intoxicating liquor as a beverage and even forbade the possession of intoxicants in stores, boarding houses, and places of amusement; but it made exceptions favorable to the rural regions by permitting the sale of cider and wine. It was harsh: The penalty for a first offense was $50, while any public official guilty of neglect in enforcing the law faced a possible $500 fine and six months in jail; worse, a person arrested for public drunkeness was not only to be fined $10 but kept in jail until he was ready to testify as to the source of the intoxicant. And it was a legal horror: aside from some doubts as to whether it clearly empowered the Mayor to enforce prohibition, the act left ample opportunities for confusion by prohibiting only the sale of domestic liquors; the exemption of imported liquors (to avoid constitutional conflict with federal power) posed few problems for rural areas, but it was bound to cause trouble in the great commercial metropolis.[19]

For Wood, the Prohibitory Act was politically ruinous. He had staked his career on proving his personal ability to enforce the law, yet here was a law that in the city was virtually unenforcible. Successful authority required consistency of enforcement, but authority also required that he maintain the political influence he had built up as the champion of the popular interest. The act was particularly offensive to those Democratic wards which had elected him in 1854. It was not long before both his friends and enemies in Tammany Hall joined with the liquor dealers to rally popular protest to the act; among the many Democratic politicians who headed the protest was that earlier beneficiary of temperance politics,

Tweed. Caught between protests against and support for the act, Wood was bound to lose some of the authority which he had been carefully accumulating.[20]

His first response was the expected pious promise to uphold the new law, but he moved quickly to disassociate himself from it. In preparation for the fateful Fourth, the act prohibited the issuance of new liquor licenses after May 1. Wood ingeneously twisted this provision into an illustration of the danger of piling new law on old law by declaring, on the advice of District Attorney A. Oakey Hall, that it effectively annulled all previous restrictions on the sale of liquor. The crusade against Sunday drinking ground to a halt, the victim—as Wood preferred to have it—of state interference.[21] From May 1 to July 4 there would be the glow of unrestricted drinking, but after that would come the gloom of prohibition, unless the Mayor found legal grounds for refusing to enforce it.

Conveniently, the act provided several escapes. As it exempted imported liquor, Wood warned the police that they faced possible legal action against them if they interfered with the sale of the imported stuff. His colleague on the Police Commission, Recorder James Smith, did his part by informing a grand jury that they had no right to indict anyone for violating the act. By the end of June, the Mayor and his legal advisors had convinced themselves that the Prohibitory Act was unconstitutional, as indeed it was later determined to be. By the Fourth of July, they had effectively nullified it in the city. Perhaps the chief effect of prohibition was to diminish the number of arrests for public intoxication, as the police were reluctant to submit drunks to the harsh and humiliating penalties of the law.[22]

In simple political terms, Wood gained more than he lost by his stand. He did antagonize the well-organized and vocal temperance lobby, but it had little weight in city politics when compared to the great many New Yorkers, particularly Irishmen and Germans, who applauded the Mayor for championing their rights. Moreover, he managed to maintain some support among the small but prestigious, group of municipal reformers. In November 1855, a year after his election, a reform meeting approved of a resolution praising him for his "manly, dignified, honest and able administration," this almost with the same breath used to praise the sainted budget cutter, A. C. Flagg, whom the reformers had renominated for Comptroller. Significantly, however, the resolution provoked a number of hisses from some members of the meeting. Although the Prohibitory Act may not have been costly in terms of raw political support, it did break the charmed circle, the aura of authority, which the Mayor had built up during his first months in office. His stand on the act, while probably necessary to prevent it from completely demoralizing the police, weakened his effort to establish himself as the faultless leader of the force. Far worse, it left him vulnerable to attack by proponents of the act and by his political enemies inside and outside the Democratic party.[23]

In June 1855 the Common Council, which had been unusually cooperative during the first months of the Wood administration, began to take on an aggressive character, beginning with a nativist effort to ferret out foreigners from the police force. When the Mayor refused to cooperate, the Aldermen launched an investigation of his claim that he had exclusive power over the police system.[24] A more damaging attack came over his disposal of the *Joseph Walker*, a ship which had sunk at its pier the previous December. In May, Wood, as head of the Health Board, proclaimed the vessel a menace to public health and granted a contract to Walter R. Jones to remove it. At least one New York newspaper attacked the grant as illegal, furnishing grounds for the Alderman to investigate the matter. Their investigation proved nothing except that some of the Aldermen were out to give, in the words of one, "Fernando the First" trouble for his handling of police matters, but it raised public suspicions that, though he had not benefited personally from the Jones contract, he was slipping back to the devious practices of his disreputable past.[25]

Thus, by the end of July, the erosion of Wood's authority was well underway. The Mayor, however, refused to give up. Early in 1856, he began his second year in office by associating himself with the hope for a new and better metropolis. New York, he said, was rapidly achieving its destiny as "the mighty metropolis" of America, but, in contrast to private enterprise, public effort had not kept step with progress, owing to misgovernment, corruption, and "an entire want of intelligence in public affairs, and proper attention to the further development of the resources we possess." In compensation for past failure, he offered a comprehensive program to modernize the city and provide for the well-being of its citizens.[26]

To improve public health, he supplemented the usual demands for clean streets with a call for housing legislation prohibiting unhealthy accommodations and for the establishment of a corps of sanitary police to enforce health regulations. To improve the food supply, he urged the abolition of the market system in favor of private enterprise in food retailing, or, if that could not be done, then the development of a great "market avenue" 200 feet wide to run north from 14th Street in order to bring the markets within easy reach of the uptown population. To assure an adequate water supply, he advocated an expansion of the Croton System to meet the needs of future millions and the installation of water meters in all homes so as to discourage the chronic wastefulness of New Yorkers. To improve the efficiency of the Port of New York and to enhance the city's image, he proposed that its shamefully delapidated dock facilities be replaced by durable stone docks and piers, suggesting—in harmony with the scheme proposed by Peter Cooper the year before—that they be built by "the labor of the poor who are supported more or less by the City alms in periods of great distress."[27]

He gave particular attention to promoting the rapid development of the upper island so as to provide a decent residential environment for New Yorkers. Recognizing the importance of transportation for uptown development, he promised to compel the street railroads to improve their service. He emphasized the need to revamp the city's ponderous and costly system of public street development which had delayed street openings and raised the cost of residential land; his system would provide for a single, unified commission to develop the streets, while allowing private land developers to open streets and lay sewers at their own expense. To assure adequate space for "healthful recreation, pure air, and rural beauty" for the millions of people whom he expected soon to inhabit the Island, he fought for the rapid development of Central Park and vetoed a decision of the Common Council to reduce the Park's size.[28]

In July 1856, he proposed a reorganization of the city's still primitive system of higher education, beginning with an increase in the number of free academies to provide advanced schooling for women as well as men. To cap this enlarged educational pyramid, he conceived of a great municipal university which would train teachers for the academies and would, in conjunction with the libraries and museums to be associated with it, attract scholars in every discipline: "New York, now our commercial emporium, would thus become the great seat of learning and arts, and would like Paris and other European cities, attract multitudes by the charms of its all-pervading refinement."[29]

For the Mayor, the university would be "the crowning work of our generation." For the Common Council to which his proposal was addressed, however, the scheme was the crowing audacity of an ambitious politician. It was denounced by one Alderman as "an electioneering document . . . meant for buncombe to influence the rural districts" in support of his rumored bid to become governor. Undoubtedly, Wood was driven by ambition, but the political design behind his program escaped the limited imaginations of the Aldermen. He was careful to borrow the elements of his program from some of the leading minds of the Progressive City, from Dr. John H. Griscom (who in 1855 had made another unsuccessful bid to be elected City Inspector), from Peter Cooper, from Samuel B. Ruggles, from Henry B. Tappan (who had suggested a municipal university in 1855), and even from A. C. Flagg. By associating himself with their ideas, Wood made a strong appeal to the social and cultural elite of the city, whose support was essential if he were going to strengthen his authority. In proposing his program, he was careful to emphasize that it could not be achieved unless the municipal charter were revised to give him the unified executive power he had long wanted. Given the power, he would make a new city: "Then will a New

Yorker be proud of his citizenship in this metropolis . . . for he can say with Paul of Tarsus, 'I am a citizen of no mean city.' "[30]

Wood's quest for authority could succeed only if he identified himself with the larger interests of the city and disassociated himself from the slippery world of politics. He succeeded in doing neither. By the middle of July, he was enveloped in a whirlpool of local, state, and national politics. When he began his two-year term in 1855, the Mayor had proposed that city elections be held in the spring so as to separate local matters from those of the state and nation.[31] Nothing was done, and so in 1856 he found himself, as an expected candidate for reelection, ensnarled in one of the most complex presidential campaigns on record. Three national parties started early in 1856 to build support for their candidates. The Democrats nominated James Buchanan. He faced a strong challenge from the popular John C. Fremont, nominee of the new Republican party. The situation was complicated by the presence of a remnant of the political chaos from which the Republicans had emerged: the nativist American party, which nominated ex-President (July 1850–March 1853) Millard Fillmore, an upstate New Yorker. For all three parties, New York State was of crucial importance, and the key to the state was the city with its influential newspapers, mass electorate, and federal patronage.

Inevitably, the highly publicized Mayor became a central figure in state and national politics. The nativists, having been denied effective power by Wood's victory in 1854, were especially anxious to undermine him. As early as April, according to some of his supporters, they attempted to undercut him as a possible candidate for governor by launching a "regular crusade against him—making charges as to his police appointments and removals which they know to be false." In July, some of them published a notice in the city's newspapers suggesting that one of their number would make an excellent Mayor to redeem the city "from villainey and dishonor." The Republicans, too, attacked Wood's credibility. When in May, the *Richmond Enquirer* praised the Mayor for bringing order and security to the city, the *Tribune*, which was both Republican and prohibitionist, countered with the charge that, since his failure to enforce Prohibition, Wood had allied himself with liquor dealers and other agents of disorder: "Gambling, lotteries, policy-playing, brothels, and every form of public or social vice, were never more active and brazen than now," while there were an average of two murders a week in the city.[32]

Wood was vulnerable to attack. Certainly, he had not been able to still public apprehension over crime and disorder, which—if they had gotten no worse—were not perceptibly better. Nor was he able to restrict municipal expenditures. During his first two years in office, annual appropriations increased by 42 percent and the tax rate by over 30 percent, an increase more spectacular even than that during the days of the Forty Thieves; the $7 million spent from tax money in 1856 made their first budget look almost modestly old-fashioned. Most of this increase was beyond Wood's control, resulting from inflation, a substantial rise in appropriations to meet state taxes (which more than doubled), an equally substantial increase in Almshouse expenditures necessitated by the depression in 1855, an increase in spending by the Board of Education, the interest on the new debt acquired to purchase land for Central Park, and a budget deficit which could be traced back to the "reform" government of 1854. Spending for the police, the department over which Wood had the most control, increased by less than 1 percent; as these were inflationary years, this may help explain why Wood's guardians of civic order made, by one count, 14 percent fewer arrests in 1856 than in the previous year.[33]

The Mayor had little control over the politically fragmented and strongly partisan Common Council. No more did he control the Board of Education, which ran up a substantial deficit, forcing it to ask for the first million-dollar appropriation in its history. Nor did he control the nativist Street Commissioner, Joseph Ebling, who made a public menace and disgrace of himself by completely exhausting his street-cleaning money in August, near the beginning of the cholera season. It was easy, however, to blame the dynamic and disreputable Wood for these and for the many other afflictions of government. At best, he disappointed the hopes which he had raised for a strong executive solution to New York's troubles. By the summer of 1856, *Harper's Monthly*, one of his staunchest advocates, had abandoned its faith in his ability to bring order to the individualistic and privatistic city. The Municipal Hercules had failed.[34]

Hercules, however, had not fallen, for he remained a potent force in the increasingly tumultuous politics of the city, the champion of many men including not a few very respectable citizens. Early in September, some 100 prominent New Yorkers issued a public letter urging Wood to stand for reelection in the hope that the legislature would soon give him the executive power needed "to complete the various improvements in the municipal administration which you have initiated during your present administration." Among the signers were Brown Brothers, Goodhue and Company, William B. Astor, Fletcher Harper (one of the Harper brothers), and the still respectable Daniel Drew. Whether Wood had prompted them to issue the letter is unclear. Equally unclear was their motive, although probably they believed his candidacy would help Democrats defeat the Republican national ticket in 1856 and so prevent the threatened secession of the South, a catastrophe for the city's trade.[35] Whatever the motives, their letter enabled Wood to initiate his campaign for renomination by restating his favorite theme that only the absence of effective power had kept him from doing the good which he had promised.

Support from a portion of the elite was nice, but the Mayor needed far more than their praise if he were to win renomination in the rough and rambunctious world of Democratic politics. Although Wood had made some effort to unite the party behind him, the character of his politics proved more successful in uniting its leaders against him. His emphasis on one-man rule and the concentration of power was not in harmony with the localism and competive individualism which characterize Tammany politics. The Mayor proved to be a political lone wolf who seemed more disposed to monopolize patronage than to share it among his fellow Democrats. It was natural that Wood should attempt to strengthen his personal power and to avoid committing himself to the entangling web of politics. It was equally natural for other Democratic leaders to suspect him of having created a personal political machine designed to destroy their power and to place the whole organization under his despotic rule. Even before he announced for renomination, he had raised the opposition, open or covert, of most of the Tammany leadership, including Elijah Purdy, a long-time power in the Democratic organization, and such rising powers as Tweed and Sweeny. The opposition controlled two centers of Democratic power, the Tammany Society and the Custom House.[36]

If Wood had united most of the leadership against him, he was nonetheless a power sufficient to overwhelm their opposition to his renomination. He had strong support among the rank-and-file, especially among the Irish who loved him for his opposition to prohibition and for his willingness to appoint Irishmen to public office, especially to the Police Department; the bitter attack of nativists on his appointment of foreigners to the force only amplified his achievement in Irish eyes.[37] More, he had his police force to counter the organized political band that operated out of the Custom House. And he had himself, one of the shrewdest and most decisive political tacticians in the history of New York politics.

According to his enemies, Wood succeeded in manipulating the Democratic General Committee into appointing primary election inspectors favorable to him; the inspectors then manipulated the primaries, with the assistance of Wood's police, into selecting the right delegates to the Mayoralty Nominating Convention; those opponents who were not eliminated by this process allegedly were kept from attending the convention by Wood's musclemen, backed by the police.[38] Whatever the truth of these charges, Wood was easily renominated at the convention; probably he would have won in an honest primary, but honest primaries were not an outstanding feature of Democratic politics. Although most of the Tammany leadership swallowed this bitter pill in the interest of party unity, those most hostile to the Mayor bolted and nominated James S. Libby, a hotel-keeper and President of the Sixth Avenue Railroad.[39]

TYRANNY, TAMMANY, AND THE STATE

The campaign which followed in the autumn of 1856 was embittered by this intraparty feud as well as by the three-party rivalry for presidential votes. The most poisonous and personal attack on Wood came in the form of a pamphlet, *A Biography of Fernando Wood. A History of the Forgeries, Perjuries, and Other Crimes of our 'Model Mayor,'* ironically dedicated to those merchants who had urged the Mayor to stand for reelection. The author, apparently one Abijah Ingraham, disinterred all the ghosts: Wood's troubles with a bank in the 1830s; his apparent cheating of Marvine; his supposed secret membership in the Know-Nothing organization; his handling of the *Joseph Walker* affair; and his alleged manipulation of the primaries through a secret association pledged to advance his power.[40]

The author also added a new ghost which would haunt Wood for much of the rest of his career, this in a concluding accusation that his subject was an "artful knave" of Napoleonic proportions whose "great desire to be Mayor of this city grew out of a supposition that the office would make him acquainted with all the schemes resorted to by the bold and lawless to plunder the community." As the Mayor had seized the power he desired, then he must be responsible for the manifold corruptions which threatened government and society. Although the logic was as shaky as the charge, it was in harmony with the paramount theme of the campaign that Wood was, as the *Tribune* phrased it, a "bold, bad man" who had prostituted his office to his insatiable quest for power. There were no records or hearings, and of course no tapes, to document such charges; nonetheless, they intensified suspicions that Wood was a potential tyrant who would use his one-man authority only to build more power for himself. Tyranny, said the *Tribune's* city reporter, was as natural to Wood as lying was to a lottery swindler.[41]

Much of the concern, real and pretended, focused on Wood's handling of the police force. His alleged use of the police in the primaries led to further charges that he had made the force his private partisan army to control the election. Late in October, an anonymous "policeman" claimed that Wood had ordered all of the police in the lower wards to contribute between $25 to $50 depending on rank for use in his campaign: "I paid my $25 without a whimper to save my head."[42] Shortly before the election came a more serious and better publicized charge made by Wood's two colleagues on the Police Commission, the Recorder and the City Judge, that he had not only levied assessments on the policemen but had furloughed some of them so that they could electioneer on his behalf. These allegations were not wholly above suspicion, since the Recorder, James M. Smith, was an anti-Wood Democrat, while the City Judge, Elisha Capron, was running for reelection on the Republican ticket. But, whatever their accuracy, they were to have dire consequences in the future.[43]

They had, however, little effect on the election. Although Wood's opponents might agree that he should be defeated, they could not agree on a candidate to oppose him. The Republicans nominated Anthony J. Bleecker, the wealthy auctioneer, as Mayor; the Americans chose Isaac O. Barker, a cousin of their previous candidate, while the Municipal Reformers insisted on running their own nominee, Judge James Whiting. Barker, Bleecker, Libby, or Whiting—which one should be supported against Wood? The mildly Republican *Times* settled for a "plague-on-all-your houses" position that came close to expressing a preference for Wood. If the Mayor would only forgo his notorious ambitions, declared the editor, he would be the man to elect, for he had shown vigor and energy in administering his office. As for the others, their failure to unite against him indicated that "the Government of this great Metropolis is to continue to be the mere appendage of political partisanship—a makeweight in the scale of political parties—something for partisans to fight over."[44] The partisan rivalries of the anti-Democratic parties cancelled out the factionalism within the Democratic organization.

Although the opposition polled more votes than ever before in 1856, they were swamped by a flood of Democratic votes, resulting in part from the excitement of the presidential election and in part from the unusual activity of the Tammany naturalization mill, which turned out over 14,000 new citizens in 1856. In the Mayoral race, the anti-Wood candidates got nearly 60 percent of the votes, but the Mayor was nonetheless reelected, with a 9000-vote plurality over his nearest opponent, Barker. The Reform candidate Whiting, came in last with about one-tenth of Wood's 32,480 votes. To complete their triumph, the Democrats, benefiting from a landslide in the city for their presidential candidate, Buchanan, won control of the Common Council for the first time since the Forty Thieves.[45]

Victory in 1856, however, only assured disaster in 1857. While the Democrats had strengthened their position in the city and its metropolitan area, the Republicans had swept much of the rest of the state; the chaos of the mid-1850s was resolving itself into the classic Republican upstate and Democratic downstate antinomy which has dominated New York State politics ever since. The Republicans won the governorship and control of the state legislature, giving them the opportunity to intervene in the affairs of the increasingly foreign, Democratic, and politically important metropolis. All that they needed was encouragement to act, and they received plenty of that. A week after the election, Elisha Capron, the defeated Republican City Judge, warned the state that it must drastically remodel the police system, to destroy Wood's power over the police "which, in many emergencies likely at any time to arise, he would wield with tremendous force to promote his own purposes."[46] Other New Yorkers, too, looked to Albany: Health reformers for a state agency to replace sluggish street inspectors and health wardens; temperance men for state action to suppress demon alcohol; conservatives who were for state restraints on the corruption and extravagance which they believed had unnaturally inflated taxes. All agreed that the state must intervene to lift decision-making and administration in the city out of the mire of its "politics." The Republican *Courier and Enquirer*, for instance, declared that the power of nominating and electing city officials was "in the worst and not the best element" of society and proposed the creation of a state-appointed Board of Commissioners, independent of politics, to decide on all appointments and removals of city officers and to approve or veto all expenditures from taxes.[47]

In his annual message to the Common Council early in 1857,

Wood repeated his warning that only the consolidation of power in the executive would prevent the further degeneration of civic administration and order. He urged the Council to submit a proposal for a new charter along his lines to the state legislature in order to head off what he called "the contemplated transfer of the government of this city . . . to Albany," adding querulously that if the state carried through on its scheme to weaken his powers he would resign and let his enemies run the city onto the rocks. The Council did prepare a new charter strengthening the Mayor, but there was little chance that anything designed to aid Wood would be acceptable in Albany. The much publicized ex-Model Mayor had now become the symbol of all that was wrong in the city. The *Times* put it accurately when it asserted that justly or not "personal and political hostility to Mayor Wood constitutes the main obstacle to the universal demand for a new charter."[48] Over Wood's ineffectual protests, a great glacier of legislation had begun to move south from Albany by the late winter, threatening to chill either, depending on the perspective, corruption or popular liberty in the city.

In 1853, during a debate over a proposal to require state approval of city railroad franchises, one upstate legislator had declared that "the time has come when it is to be settled whether New York City is an empire—a community by itself." Four years later, the legislature gave its answer when in April it completed its package of restrictive measures. On the positive side, it did substantially revise the City Charter so as to give the Mayor authority to appoint the heads of the Street, Croton Aquaduct, and City Inspector's departments; these replaced five independently elected departments which since 1849 had been outside the Mayor's control. In this and other ways, the revisions furthered the differentiation of function and consolidation of authority long required for efficient and reasonable government.[49]

The new Charter, however, was a travesty of Wood's plan for a concentration of executive power, especially in its provisions regarding the Corporation Council and the Comptroller (the two officials most actively hostile to Wood in 1856), both of whom were elected independently and for terms longer than the two years accorded the Mayor. The attention lavished on the Comptroller's domain, the Department of Finance, indicated his central importance in the eyes of state and city reformers. He was made the guardian of municipal real estate, the auditor of city accounts, the watchdog over disbursements, and the collector of all taxes and other revenues. In case this powerful post fell to corrupt politicians, the Governor was empowered to remove the Comptroller for cause. As an extra safeguard, the saintly and safe A. C. Flagg was permitted to finish out the three-year term to which he had been narrowly elected in 1855. The Mayor, in contrast, had to stand for reelection in December 1857, the new time set for city elections, as did the Common Council, which also was subjected to forced reorganization. The new Charter exuded the growing upstate mistrust and resentment of city politics. Unlike the revisions of 1849 and 1853, it was not submitted to the people of New York for their approval or rejection.[50]

Moreover, it was only the least offensive part of the state's effort to undercut the wicked politics of the wicked city. A new Excise Law required expensive licenses to serve liquor; the licenses cost from $50 to $300 each and were to be granted only to persons of good moral character on petition of 30 respectable "freeholders." Another law reorganized the New York County Board of Supervisors so as to make it a more effective check on city government; it replaced the Mayor, Recorder, and Aldermen, who previously had sat as Supervisors, with an annually elected board so structured as to assure the minority Republicans half of its seats. The legislature also created several state administrative agencies: A new Harbor Commission to regulate New York Harbor, a Central Park Commission to preside over the development of the park, and even a commission to manage the construction of a new city hall. In theory, at least, the state would appoint good and able men as commissioners who would manage the people's affairs wisely without interference from the people's representatives.[51]

The same theory governed the state's imposition of the Metropolitan Police Act, which merged the police of New York,

Kings, Richmond (Staten Island), and Westchester counties into one force under the control of five state-appointed commissioners (three of whom were to be from New York), with the Mayors of New York and Brooklyn as *ex-officio* members. The Metropolitan Police would be responsible for enforcing all laws, state and local, throughout the metropolitan district. Although the act deprived New York of direct control of its police, the city was required to provide the major part of the money required by the Commission.[52] The new law, modeled on English legislation creating the London Metropolitan Police, was based on the assumption that New York was too important to be left in the hands of New Yorkers. The committee which drafted the act noted that the city and surrounding areas were fast merging into one metropolitan "community" of 1.5 million people, constituting the most important commercial section in North America. As such, it was to be protected from crime and disorder in the interest of all Americans:

> Public peace and security of person and property in Brooklyn, New York and their enormous suburban villages have been of late injuriously affected. Murders have increased and an inattention from police authorities accompanied these fatal circumstances. Highway robberies have multiplied. The escaped convicts of other states, cities and countries and foreign lands have been allowed to congregate together and agree upon schemes of plunder. Citizens from the interior have been afraid to venture towards the great commercial metropolis of the continent in consequence of these things.[53]

The new Charter and the new commissions made 1857 one of the most important years for reform in municipal history. For years, reformers had demanded the separation of administration from the political influence of the subterranean city. Wood's policy of one-man rule, for a time, had offered the hope of separation without radical political change, but the Mayor himself had become a creature of subterranean politics. Even *Harper's Weekly*, a strong critic of state intervention, admitted that some radical change was necessary: "The truth is, that the misgovernment or no-government . . . must inevitably force upon the minds of our people the fact that cities of the size of ours, and composed as our cities are, can not be governed on the pure republican plan of frequent elections and universal suffrage, unless some new check or element of discipline is introduced." The legislation of 1857 laid the foundations for modern bureaucratic administration designed to administer the law impersonally without regard for political considerations. The police, park, and harbor commissioners, along with the bureau chiefs in the various city executive departments, would be remote from ward primaries and aldermen; the taxpayer's money would be safely spent; patronage politics would be denied its sustenance, and—something pleasing to both nativists and reformers—the city would be protected from the influence of an increasingly foreign electorate.[54]

The system, however, was radically imperfect. The reorganization of government proved to be a reorganization of chaos, for it brought a new fragmentation of power and responsibility among the city government, the Board of Supervisors, and an increasing number of independent state commissions to manage the harbor, the police, the parks, the fire department, the asylums and prisons and public health. When in 1866 James Parton decided to investigate the government of New York, he naïvely tried to find it at City Hall: "It proved not to be there. To keep the whole city from falling prey to the monster, it has been gradually cut to pieces, and scattered over the island. . . . Was there ever such a hodgepodge of a government before in the world?" Neither did the new system eliminate the influence of politics from government. Certainly, it did far less to destroy ward politics than to force a reorganization and realignment of political forces. Designed to eliminate partisanship from government, it became itself an issue of partisan politics in the state as well as in the city.[55]

The fact that a Republican legislature had passed the new laws convinced many New Yorkers that the aim was not so much reform as a Republican conquest of the city's patronage, money, and power. When Governor King (brother of James Gore King, the merchant-banker) appointed a largely Repub-

lican Metropolitan Police Commission, the *Times* complained
that he had spoiled it as a solution to the police problem: "The
mass of our people will see in the change only an adroit trick
by which the Police Department ceases to be the tool of one
party, only to become the tool of another." In response, the
Democratic party strengthened its image as the defender of
home rule and popular self-government. In May, Democratic
leaders held a mass meeting in City Hall Park to protest every
phase of the Republican program as insulting, partisan, and
despotic; among the various officers of the meeting—the
Patrick Henrys and Sam Adamses who rose to fight against
alien tyranny—was William Marcy Tweed, who thirteen years
later would allegedly spend some $600,000 in bribes to get the
state out of city affairs.[56]

"New York City," said the *Democratic Review*, "is really and
truly the grand school and hot-bed of American democracy."
The real motive of the reformers, it warned, was to protect
wealth against the rising influence of urban democracy. In
rural areas, the rich had pervasive influence over the people,
but in the city "we see every day multitudes of poor men
becoming rich, and rich men becoming poor; we see every day
poor men controlling the opinion and managing the business
and affairs of the rich: Consequently, although riches may
confer temporary importance, they fail to create a sense of
awe, or even of respect." Although the *Review* exaggerated the
power and opportunities available to the common man, it was
by no means wrong in asserting that local politics was a refuge
and an instrument of the ambitious poor. The Democratic
party might grow corrupt, sometimes egregiously so, but it did
not lose its character in the city as the champion of practical
democracy, which met the real needs of the great many people
whom the advantaged classes either ignored or viewed as the
troublesome scum of society.[57]

Popular government versus elitism—the theme was a good
one; but it was immensely complicated by the presence of
Fernando Wood. By April 1857 the Mayor had lost control of
the situation. Not only had he been unable to prevent the state
from reducing his formal powers, but he was routed by the

Tammany leadership in the battle for control of the Democratic party organization. In late April, he lost the last round in the battle when the Tammany Society rejected his slate of Sachems in favor of a reform slate headed by Elijah Purdy, Samuel J. Tilden, and Peter B. Sweeny.[58] Even worse, his struggles against both the state and Tammany attracted a swarm of accusations against him from his respectable and not-so-respectable enemies. perhaps the most personally damaging attacks came from his foes within the Democratic party, from Recorder Smith (who hinted that Wood had used his authority as Police Commissioner to obstruct justice) and most especially from the anonymous "A Bird in the Bush," who published a lengthy exposé of the Mayor's alleged misbehavior just before the crucial election at Tammany. Essentially, "A Bird" updated Abajah Ingraham's charge in 1856 that the Mayor had successfully conspired to gain control of the nominating process, thus concentrating "all the municipal patronage in his own hand." The final conclusion was self-evident: While Wood was hypocritically bemoaning his inability to prevent misgovernment, he was actually exercising a tyrannical power for corrupt purposes.[59]

Wood, the advocate of one-man rule, was learning that when things go wrong all the blame is placed on the one man. By May, government seemed to have sunk to a new low. Comptroller Flagg announced that since the opening of the year the city had been overdrawing on its accounts, spending a half million dollars more than it had received. More, there seemed to be a further collapse of law and order. Even the *Times*, which a few months before had mocked the nervousness of the *Tribune*, declared that in the previous twelve months there had been a "terrible increase of crime. . . . only to be accounted for under a system when the police force is perverted from its proper calling and made the political machine that it notoriously has been and still is."[60] In the absence of reliable information, it was impossible to prove that there had been either an increase or decrease in crime generally, but there was a widespread belief that violence and disorder had grown to frightening proportions. The next months would supply support for that belief.

Wood intensified this sense of anxiety through his efforts to keep himself in power. Given the circumstances, a more conservative and less ambitious Mayor might have resigned in protest against state interference, as Wood had indeed threatened to do. The *Tribune*'s "Bold, bad man," however, was not inclined to retreat. Whether he resigned or acquiesced, he would lose his distinctive power and fall to the rank of a mere Tammany politician. He therefore decided to fight for the principal instrument of his authority, the police. Even before the legislature passed the Police Bill, he had begun to replace captains of questionable loyalty with men he could trust to support him in the fight; the fact that two of his appointees were saloonkeepers seemed to clinch the increasingly popular notion that he had allied himself with the forces of disorder. When the Bill was approved, he applied for a judical injunction to forestall the new law until he had fully tested its constitutionality or, so some suspected, at least until he had used the force to win reelection in December. The courts, however, refused to issue a permanent injunction. Although the Common Council supplied him with the money needed to challenge the constitutionality of the act, Wood was left to face a painful dilemma during the crucial weeks before a final judicial determination could be expected: either he had to capitulate and turn his municipal force over to the new Metropolitan Police Commission or he had to defy both the Commission and the law.[61] He chose defiance, the Commission chose to implement the law, and so New York was furnished with the makings of a police war between Wood's Municipals and the new Metropolitans.

The conflict began as a comic opera. In the Fifth Ward, when Captain Daniel Carpenter showed signs of disloyalty to the Mayor, he was dismissed for insubordination and replaced by Daniel D. Horrigan. Carpenter soon reappeared at the Ward Station House as a captain of the Metropolitans and attempted to take command. The ward police refused to accept him, but he was persistent; an onlooker saw him sitting stubbornly at the captain's desk side-by-side with Horrigan. Persistence paid, for Carpenter was soon appointed a Deputy Superintendent of the Metropolitans. The two-headed police provided much entertainment. A story was circulated that the two rival policemen had fallen into a fight over a prisoner whom both claimed to have arrested. Essentially, however, the war was a serious war of attrition destined to end in tragedy. The attrition was on the Municipals' side. By early June, about a third of the old force had joined the Metropolitans, motivated by a respect for the new law or by a desire for pay; Comptroller Flagg had refused to release the money needed for their salaries. Supported by the Common Council, Wood held on, appointing new men to fill the places of the departing policemen.[62]

Open war came in mid June, precipitated by an unexpected event, the death of Street Commissioner Joseph Taylor. The Street Department was rich in patronage, too rich for either Governor King or Mayor Wood to leave alone. The Governor appointed, without legal authority as it was later determined, Daniel D. Conover to the vacant post; Wood appointed Charles Develin, who was approved by the Council, allegedly after he agreed to divide up the patronage among the Aldermen.[63] Two police forces and two Street Commissioners—the inevitable occurred when Conover came to City Hall to stake out his claim to the office. He was thrown out, whereupon he persuaded Recorder Smith to order Wood's arrest for inciting a riot. When a Metropolitan attempted the arrest in the Mayor's office, he too was thrown out by some of the Municipals. Smith's response was to issue another arrest warrant, this one to be conveyed by a force of some 200 Metropolitans under the command of the County Coroner, F. W. Perry. By the time this force reached City Hall, a large crowd had gathered in the Park. The Metropolitans pushed their way through, only to be met at the City Hall steps by a large force of Municipals massed there to protect the Mayor. They were attacked by the Municipals in front and by rowdies in the rear. Clubbed and punched from all sides, the outnumbered Metropolitans finally retreated, after 20 or more of their force had been injured. In response, the Coroner called for ten regiments of the state militia to assist in making the arrest. Although they helped overawe the mob, none of the militia was needed to seize Wood. Soon after the police riot, Recorder Smith issued still another arrest warrant, this one to the County Sheriff who walked unmolested into City Hall, met a polite reception from Wood, and equally politely took the Mayor into custody.[64]

"Civic Rebellion," cried the *Times* in an editorial condemning Wood as a disgrace to the city. The Mayor issued a proclamation, addressed to the people, denouncing the "usurpers" of municipal rights for having tried to "take life in an effort to degrade you through my person," but the words were empty bombast. The man who 18 months before had started out to build respect for his authority now was able to escape jail only be raising $50,000 in bail money. Early in July, the New York State Court of Appeals dashed his last hopes when it ruled that the Metropolitan Police Act was constitutional and thus effectually abolished the Municipal Police. Almost immediately, Wood quietly disbanded his force and the police war was over—but not the most violent of its consequences.[65]

On the Fourth of July, New York celebrated national independence with one of the bloodiest riots in its history. It began when the "Dead Rabbits," a largely Irish fighting gang and supporters of Wood, attacked some Metropolitan policemen on the Bowery, forcing them to flee for their lives. The Rabbits then launched an assault on a saloon associated with their traditional foes, the Bowery Boys. By the end of the day, open war had broken out between the two gangs and their allies. Perhaps as many as a thousand men and boys rioted through the streets of the Lower East Side, clubbing, knifing, and shooting. When the Metropolitans intervened, they were attacked and forced to retreat, bombarded by bricks and stones rained down on them from roofs of tenements. "AWFUL RIOTS AND BLOODSHED," reported the *Tribune* in bold captions, "BARRICADES IN THE STREETS—CIVIL WAR IN THE BLOODY SIXTH—TEN KILLED AND EIGHTY WOUNDED—THE HOSPITALS OVERFLOWING."[66]

The Metropolitans finally restored order on the evening of

July 5, supported by two militia regiments; but the affair left much bitterness. At one meeting called to protest state intervention, a speaker proposed that the city and its metropolitan counties be made into a separate state. A new conflict soon broke out in the Seventeenth Ward between the Metropolitans and a largely German crowd. That, too, was ended, but this time with open German complaints of "criminal violence" by the police.[67] The hatred of the new police survived, to erupt in an even more terrible form six years later in the Civil War draft riots.

By the summer of 1857 the once-model Mayor had become a source of civic shame and outrage. The *Times* declared that Wood had failed not so much because he lacked power, but because his activities had convinced the public that his apparent concern for public good was simply a screen for his personal ambitions. To make his plight worse, Tammany was able to disassociate itself from its now disreputable enemy and to proclaim that it had reformed the internal organization of the party, the key ingredient being newly formed ward associations which if they did not guarantee an honest election of members of the General Committee at least minimized Wood's chances of regaining control of the committee. Seemingly, "His Honor Fernando I" was finished. Yet in October the Tammany organization accepted his renomination for Mayor by an overwhelming majority. By then, two facts had become clear: That Wood was still a hero to many Democratic voters, and that he had resolved to run for reelection with or without Tammany support. Anxious to maintain party unity for the state elections in November, the party leadership decided to endorse him at least until that time.[68]

Soon after his renomination, the Mayor committed a final outrage in the eyes of anxious New Yorkers. By mid-October the great commercial city was paralyzed by the Panic of 1857, an even more violent economic whirlwind than the one that had afflicted it during Wood's first month in office. This collapse threw some 30,000 or more men and women out of work, leading the *Times* to express the wish that New York be governed by a Louis Napoleon who would put the unemployed to work rebuilding the city into a second Paris. The next day, in a special message to the Common Council, the Mayor urged an acceleration of existing public works projects so as to provide employment for several thousand of the unemployed, with the workers to be paid largely in flour, cornmeal, and potatoes to be purchased by the city. "If the present want of employment continues," he warned, "many must rely upon either public or private charity, and I fear that not a few will resort to violence and force rather than submit to either of these precarious and humiliating dependences." He then repeated the statement he had made nearly three years before: "Truly may it be said that in New York those who produce every thing get nothing, and those who produce nothing get everything."[69]

This Napoleon had spoken like Karl Marx. The *Times* was not pleased with Wood's proposal and even less pleased with his rhetoric. In an editorial darkly entitled "1848 and 1857," it declared that "Mr. Wood raises the banner of the most fiery communism." Others agreed, especially when in early November radical workingmen held "work and bread" demonstrations to protest the failure of the Council to act on Wood's suggestions. George Templeton Strong denounced him as a demagogue who had excited "the *canaille* of the city" to thoughts of insurrection. Robert M. Hartley declared that Wood's "Communistic notions" had stirred up unjustified bitterness among workers when they should have been taught "to bear with manliness what they must bear."[70] Demagogue! Communist!— the man who had once hoped to win support from the progressive city for his authority now was completely identified with the subterranean city, a creature of darkness against the city of light.

Early in November the Democrats won the state and county elections; elected as District Attorney was Wood's old enemy, Peter B. Sweeny. Although Tammany leaders did not openly repudiate Wood, some of them worked secretly with conservative and reform-minded members of the party to defeat him in the upcoming city election. They joined with Republicans and Municipal Reformers to run Daniel F. Tiemann, a Democrat, respected politician, and wealthy paint manufacturer, against the Mayor. Freed from the divisive influence of state and national politics and fearful of the Mayor's apparent radicalism, Wood's opponents were finally able to unite against him. The Republican *Tribune* called for an all-out campaign against the "cool villain" who sat in City Hall and fanned the flames of radicalism. Even then, however, they feared that he might carry the December election, since he was the over-whelming favorite of foreign-born voters, increased by 6000 or more by the reactivated Tammany naturalization mill.[71] On December 1, New Yorkers cast 84,105 votes in a generally honest and peaceful election. It was a record number, over a third more votes than in 1855. Wood carried the heavily German and Irish wards on the East side, but he barely won in Tweed's Seventh Ward and lost Elijah Purdy's Tenth. In these and other wards, enough Democrats voted against Wood to defeat him, the final tally being 43,216 to 40,889. The Democrats won control of both boards of the Common Council and elected their half of the Board of Supervisors, among whom were Purdy and Tweed.[72]

Who had won? Certainly, it was not the "People's Party" which had elected Tiemann, for it soon broke apart; nor was it Tiemann, for after a mediocre term as Mayor he was denied renomination by his party. The real winner was Tweed who, now that Wood was effectively denied control of Tammany Hall, used his post on the Board of Supervisors to launch his conquest of the Tammany organization. As for Wood, he bounced back one more time. In 1859, he again ran for Mayor as the candidate of his own organization, "Mozart Hall," and won a narrow victory over a divided opposition. Early in 1861, he made a last gesture of defiance at both New York State and the Republican party when he suggested that it might be desirable if the city seceded from the Union, and made itself the free and self-governing "Republic of New York." Despite this last offense against respectable society, he was nearly reelected in 1861, but this was his last hurrah as Mayor of New York. Faced by the increasing power of Tweed and his asso-ciates in Tammany Hall, he permitted himself to be eased upstairs to Congress in 1863 where he served, with only one break (1865–67) and with some distinction, until his death in 1881.[73]

Wood attempted to unite the city by building an effective authority, in himself, which could act in the civic interest. In pursuit of that goal, he offered to assume the burden of government—an appealing offer for the many citizens who wanted the freedom to pursue their private interests, but one which antagonized those many other New Yorkers, inside and outside of Tammany, who treated politics as a matter of private interest threatened by Wood's "tyranny." He failed as others were to fail in the future. The more realistic and less egocentric Tweed temporarily solved the problem by buying the support of virtually everyone in sight, but his gigantic scheme of corruption proved to be too expensive and he too fell when the finances of the city threatened to collapse under the mountainous debt he accumulated.[74] Wood went to Congress, Tweed to jail—neither was able to tame the diverse and intense individualism of the metropolis; neither one-man authority nor massive corruption worked, anymore than the pieties of reform worked.

Was New York, then, an ungovernable city? Perhaps the best answer was that the metropolis was actually governed well in terms of the real interests of its citizens. Complain though they did about their taxes and the mismanagement of their public affairs, few New Yorkers would deny that during the reign of the Woods and the Tweeds New York prospered more than any other city in the world. Municipal government did nothing well, but it did many things required by the expanding metropolis. In the two decades after 1840, it laid a water and sewerage system, extended and reorganized the street system, rebuilt its docks and markets, began a modern park system, expanded its charitable and prison facilities, established a public school system, and created a professional police force. During these same decades, the municipal corporation also underwent a painful internal reorganization necessitated both by its new responsibilities and by the changing political society of the expanding city. Even the failures of government frequently served to meet human needs. The politics so ardently con-

VIEW FROM THE "DEAD RABBIT" BARRICADE IN BAYARD STREET, TAKEN AT THE HEIGHT OF THE BATTLE BY OUR OWN ARTIST, WHO, AS SPECTATOR, WAS PRESENT AT THE FIGHT.

The Troubled City II

FIGURE 20. (left, above) This woodcut published in *Leslie's Illustrated* catches some of the ferocity of the great riot of 1857 which climaxed a decade of disorder in New York. The result of a long-term feud between two street gangs, the "Dead Rabbits" and the "Bowery Boys," as well as of much popular resentment against a new state-imposed police force, the riot raged through much of lower New York for two days before it was suppressed with the aid of the state militia.

Courtesy of the New York Public Library.

FIGURE 21. (left, below) James H. Cafferty and Charles Rosenberg painted this scene of the Panic on Wall Street at 2:30, October 13, 1857, when New York banks announced that they were suspending specie payments, precipitating a final plunge into depths of a financial panic and economic depression which had begun in August. The crowd in the foreground is in front of the Merchant's Exchange (extreme left) and includes a number of prominent New Yorkers. Although the key identifying these men has been lost, the crowd includes Cornelius Vanderbilt (apparently the man with the folded umbrella at the extreme right), Jacob Little (a prominent speculator who, with his light coat and stunned expression, forms the center of the scene), and the managing editor of the New York *Herald*, Frederic Hudson (apparently the man with the mostache at the left). The bearded man immediately to the right of Hudson may be Horace Greeley, editor of the *Tribune*, who months before had warned New Yorkers of the gathering financial storm. A comparison of the buildings in this scene with those in the earlier view of Wall Street (1850) indicates a significant upward thrust in construction, toward the skyscrapers of the twentieth century.

Courtesy of the Museum of the City of New York.

demned by reformers as a great leech on the neck of respectable citizenry was, in another perspective, a protector of many subterraneans who might otherwise have been lost in the city. If government failed to satisfy all completely, it did succeed in providing some satisfaction for most of the interests in a diversifying and strongly individualistic society.

What seemed to many sensitive observers to be a social and political breakdown was actually part of an awkward but essential reorganization of a city into a complex, modern metropolis. That reorganization was governed chiefly by the essential needs and ambitions of a free and varied people. From politicians to bankers, rowdies to writers, what New Yorkers wanted most was an environment of maximum opportunity to pursue their private goals. No great leader and no great dream governed the development of the city—only lesser men and lesser dreams. In this haphazard way, New Yorkers thus built a metropolis, not a Rome or Paris of grace and charm, but a great economic and cultural center for a free, dynamic, and rapidly changing nation.

Chapter 15

METROPOLIS

NEW YORK WAS THE FAIR-HAIRED CHILD of the progressive nineteenth century. Marred though it was by poverty, corruption, dirt, disease, and disorder, it was the undoubted prodigy of prodigious times and a prodigious nation, not merely a fast growing city but a vital force in the modernization of both Europe and America. The metropolis was the special beneficiary and the special cause of one of the most spectacular spurts of wealth in American history; by one estimate, national wealth increased by nearly 90 percent between 1850 and 1857.[1] These seven golden years brought a marked acceleration of trade resulting especially from the California gold discoveries and from the increasing use of steamships and railroads. American foreign trade, for instance, more than doubled in value. As the nation's great commercial center, the new metropolis experienced the pressures as well as the benefits of rapid expansion. "Look at that city," said ex-President John

Tyler, "and see her extending streets, her palatial mercantile establishments, with her vast congregation of vessels at her docks bursting forth like a crab from the shell, and expanding itself until it covers the adjacent shores of the beautiful roadstead and rivers with cities and villages."[2]

Much of the expansion centered on New York harbor, the great focal point of the water and rail routes which linked the industrializing nations of Western Europe with the rapidly developing American West. The growing needs of shipping brought the construction of new dock facilities on Manhattan Island and especially on the Brooklyn and New Jersey shores of the harbor. In 1853, for instance, the Morris Canal Company planned a million dollar development of the Jersey City waterfront to meet the increasing demand for dock space.[3] By the mid-1850s, the expanding demands of shipping and the expansion of the cities threatened to collide. The filling in of waterfront lands and the extension of piers, especially on the New York and Brooklyn sides of the East River, caused, said Charles King, "no little alarm" among merchants that encroachments on the upper harbor might soon seriously interfere with shipping.[4] Concern was deep enough to evoke an early effort at tristate cooperation when in 1855 the governors of New York, New Jersey, and Connecticut came to the city to investigate the matter.

Governor Dutton of Connecticut noted an increasingly significant dimension of the port when he said that the threatened choking up of the harbor endangered not only commerce and agriculture but also the substantial manufacturing interests of his state.[5] By the 1850s, the harbor had become the center of one of the world's greatest industrial regions in the form of a loosely organized and highly diversified conglomeration of manufacturing facilities in the eleven counties of the tristate region that had direct access to the mouth of the Hudson by canal, river, or railroad. In 1860 the eleven-county area produced, in value, 14 percent of all manufactures in the United States, most of the production being located in a few major cities. Among American cities, New York ranked first in the value of its manufactures, Brooklyn 5th, Newark 6th, Jersey

City 29th, Paterson 31st, Bridgeport, Connecticut 37th, and Yonkers 60th.[6] Some 154,000 persons, a tenth of the total population of the region, were employed in these and smaller centers in making a great variety of products: especially clothing, hats, and shoes for the prospering domestic market but also such things as sewing machines (in Bridgeport), locomotives (at Paterson), and carriages in Union County, New Jersey.[7] Some products were made and sold independent of New York City, but most relied on the shipping, merchandising, and credit facilities of the metropolis.

By the 1850s, the rough outlines of a metropolitan economy had appeared. The extension of railroads and other improvements in transportation, by providing easy access to New York and its port, encouraged some decentralization of manufacturing outside the city. In the late 1840s industrial developers founded Elizabethport and Lodi in New Jersey and Mott Haven in southern Westchester County for manufacturing purposes. In 1855 the developers of an unspecified location near New York promised to give manufacturers one lot of ground "for every twelve hands employed in a flourishing village within three miles of the city, with steamboat, railroad, and omnibus communication every half hour during the day."[8] Decentralization, however, was overshadowed by the rapid growth of the major centers, often at the expense of the village retailers and craftsmen who had served the more isolated local rural markets of the past. "A country Tailor" warned in 1849 that the large cities were swallowing up the small towns and complained that competition from the ready-made clothing industry of the major urban centers was "casting many an honest hardworking man and woman out of employment, or drawing them to the city, by taking their work there."[9]

New York City was, unquestionably, the dominant industrial center for the region. Between 1840 and 1860, investment in manufacturing there had increased by nearly 550 percent; between 1855 and 1860, the value of its industrial product grew by 60 percent, an increase greater even than that of its fast-growing neighbor, Brooklyn. In 1860, it had more than half of the manufacturing capital, work force, and product of the whole region.[10] The city was especially hospitable to light manufacturing of a highly varied sort. The reconstruction of the city in the 1850s included the erection of many buildings designed for light industry. Their owners advertised: "Workshops to let cheap"—"Wide stairs, easy access to floors; hoist wheel with every convenience"—"Well lighted rooms"—"Rooms to let with Steam Power"—"Excellent location for Printers, Bookbinders, Carvers, Gilders, Jewelers, Silversmiths, Piano Makers, or any other light manufacturing business." Available space, a ready supply of labor, and convenient access to transportation, wholesale, and credit facilities made New York an ideal site for the small manufacturer. In 1860 more than 4300 establishments made a wide variety of common and specialty items like soaps, cigars, jewelry, shoes, furniture, umbrellas, envelopes, telescopes, wigs, billard cues, and playing cards. Some firms crafted their wares for a limited market; 33 firms, including that of Henry Steinway, made pianos. Others used mass production techniques; William H. Beebe in 1848 made 30,000 silk hats a year by dividing his labor force into eight sets of workers, each committed to a distinct phase of hat manufacture.[11]

Some forms of manufacturing were conspicuous for their large scale. By 1860, New York had become the nation's great sugar refining center. Fourteen firms employed the most up-to-date machinery to convert more than 200 million pounds of crude sugar, imported mostly from the West Indies and Brazil, into a nearly $20 million product sufficient to meet half of the rapidly growing domestic demand for sweets. *Hunt's Merchants Magazine*, eager for examples of American industrial superiority, declared proudly in 1856 that "an important branch of industry has been transferred to this from other countries; and already the importation of foreign refined sugars has almost entirely ceased."[12]

The city was also an important machine- and engine-building center. Using iron either imported from Great Britain or shipped from more than a score of furnaces and forges in the Hudson Valley and in New Jersey, some forty firms made steam engines for use in manufacturing as well as in the river and ocean steamships built in the New York yards. The largest, the Novelty Iron Works on the East River, employed more than 1000 men to make engines, marine hardware, sugar refining machinery, and assorted other iron products. In 1851, one New Yorker described it as being an efficiently organized modern firm, "having . . . its gradations of rank, its established usages, its written laws, its police, its finances, its records, its rewards, and its penalties." In value of product, the city produced nearly 10 percent of the nation's machinery in 1860.[13]

Two industries had a particularly great influence on the character and future of New York—garment-making and printing. By the early 1850s, the city had established itself as the major supplier of the nation's clothing. It had long been the great market for fabrics of all sorts, especially for those imported from Great Britain and the Continent. Besides the materials, New York clothiers had ready access to wholesalers and retailers in the West and especially the South. More, they could draw on a vast pool of cheap and frequently experienced labor, continually increased by foreign immigration. The New York Chamber of Commerce estimated that in 1855 nearly 32,000 men and women in New York and its surrounding counties worked in the clothing trade. In the outlying counties, many were employed by clothiers in nearby production centers, especially Newark, while others labored at home to produce clothing for New York wholesalers. Production, however, was heavily concentrated on Manhattan Island and became more so in the 1850s, in part because the growing use of the sewing machine encouraged employers to organize unskilled sewers in what later were to be called sweatshops. Although some of the clothing was custom-made on special order, most workers produced "ready-mades" for sale in a mass market.[14]

The industry was loosely organized and intensely competitive. At the top were a few large wholesalers who employed a mass labor force in an integrated, efficiently organized system of production; the largest, Hanford and Brother, claimed to have over 4000 workers engaged in the various phases of production and sales. The major producers often purchased

[405]

their fabrics straight from the mills, thus saving the expense of middlemen. Below were an uncounted number of petty manufacturers who sold their product through wholesalers. The openness of the industry at the bottom enabled many immigrants to begin their climb to wealth, but it also intensified the exploitation of garment workers, especially woman sewers who were paid as little as 25 cents for a full day's work. Efficient organization, competition, the exploitation of labor, the use of machinery, and New York's commercial advantages served in the 1850s to consolidate the city's position as the nation's clothing center. Although much of their product was crude and inexpensive, clothiers also catered to style-conscious Americans. Chiefly by adapting English and Continental styles to American conditions, they made themselves the directors of men's fashions in the United States. One observer charged that clothiers deliberately changed their styles and even hired men to "parade" the new styles on Broadway so as to make everything else look out of date.[15]

Another industry gave the Metropolis an even stronger influence over Americans. In 1860 the city did 30 percent of the nation's printing and publishing, most of it in the Second and Fourth Wards of the lower city. The industry employed over 5000 printers, bookbinders, engravers, type-founders and others needed to meet the growing hunger for printed words and pictures. Some printers did small-scale job printing of the varied letterheads and circulars required by commercial firms. In contrast, John A. Gray of Cliff Street advertised his business as "the very largest and most comprehensive general newspaper, book, and job printing office on this continent . . . where every conceivable variety of work is done . . . from a Mammoth Poster or Colored Showbill, to the handsomest, cheapest or smallest circular, card, or label, plain or fancy. Where Books, Magazines, and Pamphlets are stereotyped, electrotypes, illustrated, printed and bound. . . . Where sixty of the standard periodicals of this city have originated." Even so large a printer as Gray, however, was cast in the shadows by the various publishers of newspapers, magazines, and books.[16]

New York was a newspaper town in a newspaper-reading

age. As the commercial metropolis and center of the import trade, it far surpassed any other American city in providing the advertising and access to European news required for successful newspaper ventures. In 1849, it was home to 88 newspapers with an aggregate issue of over 62 million a year. Eight years later, there were 104 newspapers with 78 million issues. The majority were weeklies, a highly varied lot of religious, ethnic, political, sensationalist, family, and trade papers. Included among them were the *Scientific American* and Henry Varnum Poor's *American Railroad Journal*, both important sources of the technical information and the encouragement required for the rapid industrial development of the United States.[17]

Even with the addition in the 1850s of such popular newspapers as *Harper's Weekly* and Robert Bonner's spicy *New York Ledger*, the weeklies were overshadowed in prestige and influence by New York's great daily newspapers: well-established and rather old-fashioned journals like the *Courier and Enquirer* and the *Journal of Commerce*, respected organs of opinion such as the *Evening Post*, the *Tribune*, and the *Times*, and the popular, freewheeling *Herald* and the *Sun*. Availing themselves of the revolutionary improvement in printing technology, particularly Richard Hoe's cylinder press, the major newspapers by the 1850s had become big businesses, often producing newspapers at one to two cents a copy for a mass reading public. In 1861 the five major newspapers had a total daily circulation of almost 250,000. The New York papers circulated widely through the nation, benefiting from reduced postal rates and the improvement of transportation.[18]

An even wider influence was exercised by the city's many monthly magazines. In 1849 there were 54 monthlies with some 500,000 readers. Some of these died within a few years, but their places were quickly filled; during the prosperous mid-1850s, 30 of the 93 periodicals established in the United States were founded at New York. They often appealed to specialized and occasionally eccentric audiences. Fowler and Wells advertised that subscribers could receive their *Phrenological Journal* and their *Water Cure Journal* along with the weekly

Life Illustrated—all for three dollars a year. New York was the home of several farm journals, including the influential *American Agriculturist*, which was located in the city, because, as its editor explained, "more Farmers and Planters resort here than to any other city of the Union." For those with commercial interests, the city provided Freeman Hunt's solid and serious *Merchant's Magazine*. For liberal Democrats, it published the *Democratic Review*; for Whigs, in the late 1840s and early 1850's, the *American Review*. For those interested in cultural and social matters, there was a wide variety of literary magazines, including the brilliant but short-lived *Putnam's* and the enduring *Harpers Monthly*, which in 1860 claimed a circulation of 200,000.[19]

This concentration of print made New York the great national focus of literary and artistic endeavor. Although newspapers and magazines continued their established practice of clipping from foreign periodicals and pirating from foreign authors, the creation of a mass market for the printed word also increased the demand for native writers. Few authors could hope to receive as much as the $30,000 paid to Henry Ward Beecher when the *Ledger* serialized his novel, *Norwood*, but they could at least dream of more modest rewards for their talents which would assure them, as Bayard Taylor put it, "more time for study and scribbling." *Putnam's*, founded on the policy of buying only original works by American authors, intensified the writer's hope of living by his pen when it was begun in 1854. That venture proved premature, but the increasing demand for original material for the popular weeklies and monthlies did enable the metropolis to attract and hold an increasing class of professional writers, critics, and literary men like Bayard Taylor and Thomas Bailey Aldrich, who were to influence the later development of American literature.[20]

By the 1850s New York had also consolidated its position as the nation's great supplier of books. Many were imported from foreign publishers, but the trend was toward the publication of American authors. In preparation for the spring trade in 1855, the following publishers advertised their wares: Bunce & Brother (seven books including Ann S. Stephens' best-selling novel, *Fashion and Famine*), J. C. Derby (*The Hen Fever* by George

P. Biernsham), H. Long & Brothers (*The Life and Beauties of Fanny Fern*, "An authentic history" of the best-selling author), Dangiel Burgess & Co. (*The Speller and Definer's Manual*), Stringer & Townsend ("Sam Slick's" *Nature and Human Nature*), Miller, Orton & Mulligan (upstate publishers who announced their move to the city in their advertisement for their series of "Popular Biographies"), Fowler and Wells (*Three Hours School A Day—A Talk With Parents*, which condemned the excessive length of the school day), and Garrett & Co. (*The Mountain Outlaw . . . A Tale of Love and Wild Adventure*).[21]

Other publishers were names long familiar to American readers: D. Appleton & Company, John Wiley, Charles Scribner and G. P. Putnam. All were overshadowed, however, by the great firm of Harper & Brothers. The four Harper brothers (the oldest, James, had been elected Mayor in 1844) took the lead in promoting the mass production of inexpensive books for Americans. In 1842, $65 bought all 150 volumes of Harper's Family Library, which was advertised as exclusively a library of useful knowledge, without fiction and with nothing that might corrupt the morals of children. By the early 1850s, the mammoth Harper book factory located near Franklin Square was printing hundreds of works a year under the house label. In 1853, it turned out 733 works, nearly 400 of which were original books by American authors; someone estimated that it produced, on the average, 25 volume per minute. That plant was destroyed in December of 1853 by a spectacular million-dollar fire, but in less than two years the brothers opened an even more efficient plant based on the latest industrial principles.[22]

Like sugar refining and like much of the clothing industry, book publishing was becoming a large scale enterprise which produced in volume for a mass market. In 1860, New York's seventeen book printing firms manufactured more than $3 million worth of school, nonfiction, and fiction books. In this and other ways, the book industry was a microcosm of the new commercial and industrial America which was emerging in and around New York and other major cities. The improvement of both transportation and commercial facilities and the growing affluence of Americans was creating a mass market which encouraged businessmen to organize their operations for volume production. The new industrial organizations improved efficiency and reduced prices, which stimulated consumption. The larger the production and the larger the market, however, the larger loomed the need of assuring the sale of the product. The Harper book factory was sustained by a sales organization involving over a thousand volunteer booksellers supplemented by itinerant clergymen and other travelers willing to vend Harper books throughout the nation. In a similar way, clothing wholesalers resorted to paid "drummers," first to contact out-of-town buyers during their stay in New York hotels, later to go direct to inland towns to drum up business.[23]

Advertising, too, became increasingly important. According to Moses Y. Beach, the Harpers gave much attention to publicizing their books, going so far as to employ literary men "to write notices and puffs for the more important newspapers and magazines which they have either directly or indirectly subsidized to their interest." More puffery was done openly; one publisher advertised *The Life and Beauties of Fanny Fern* under the heading, "All the World will Read this Book." George Palmer Putnam noted that, while in the 1830s advertising was of little consequence, thirty years later it had become a major expense for publishers, which "frequently adds one-half to the cost of a book." In the 1850s, advertising was still closely associated with the vending of quack medicines, but it had become sufficiently respectable and important for the first of the professional advertising agencies to appear.[24]

The first grand practitioner of the advertiser's art was Volney B. Palmer, who billed himself as "the Morse of commercial intercourse." Palmer opened his first office in Philadelphia and later established branches in New York and Boston; some of the New York's earliest advertising men were his proteges. In the 1850s, he proclaimed advertising the new art and science which would revolutionize the world of trade: "The work is but begun—the mighty system is but partially in operation. But the day will come when a man will as readily think of walking without feet . . . as of success without advertising." By

1856, he was warning darkly that those who did not advertise faced ruin, because they had thrown away the most reliable means of making themselves known to consumers in the increasingly competitive and anonymous marketplace. Even if there were no competition, advertising would be necessary, for it was the best way to stimulate people to buy what otherwise they would feel no need to buy. By stimulating consumption and accelerating the flow of trade, the new business art would be a mighty agent of progress:

> In stimulating the industrial energies and unlocking capital, it is both a cooperator and connecting link to leading influences, aiding them to act more efficiently in the physical, social and political movements which distinguish our nation and age. And it cannot be doubted that in effecting an intelligent and reliable communication between producers and consumers, it is making itself felt in that widespread confidence of the future which is extending facilities for the exchange of commodities encompassing the entire country and intersecting its commercial marts by railroad and telegraph.[25]

It was an appropriate expression for the Age of Gold.

Despite Palmer's enthusiasm for his new craft, however, it was not advertising but banking which made the new age go and grow. The gold discoveries marked the beginning of a great expansion of money and credit needed for the purchase, sale, and shipment of goods. In the six years after 1849, the number of banks in the city more than doubled; the mid-1850s brought a complementary wave of expansion as existing banks increased their capital in response to the growing demand for credit. During the decade, the metropolis forged far ahead of its nearest banking rival, Boston, more than doubling its banking capital while Boston's hardly grew at all. New York bankers further strengthened their position when in 1853 they formed the New York Clearing House Association to coordinate and rationalize banking transactions among themselves, one manifestation of a broader movement during the age to control competition; New York publishers formed an association in 1855 to regulate their trade, while New Yorkers took the lead in organizing "conventions" of railroad executives to end a wave of rate-cutting which threatened their industry.[26] Wall Street could proclaim itself not merely the financial center of the nation but a world center second only to the great mistress of money, London.

Money attracted money. The high interest rates paid by New York banks drew deposits not only from the thrifty but from foreign investors and especially from domestic banks throughout much of the United States. By one estimate, deposits increased by more than 70 percent between 1854 and 1857. More deposits meant more money for bankers to lend. Directly and indirectly, Wall Street provided the credit used by Americans to purchase the imports which flowed through New York. It also advanced the money required to move the rapidly increasing product of the interior to the seaboard for consumption in the cities or for export. As money was offered on more convenient terms at New York than elsewhere, people flocked there to transact their business. Moreover, the sale of public and corporate securities through the New York Stock Exchange and by private New York bankers made Wall Street the great source of capital for the expansion of manufacturing and, especially, the extension of canals and railroads.[27]

In 1854, the *Times* declared proudly that the city had so sharpened its skill in the management of money that it used every thousand dollars ten times more effectively than mankind had ever used it in the past. Three years later that same newspaper said that the enormous expansion of credit which had taken place in the interim was a natural and necessary element of a new era of human progress. Credit was the soul of modern commerce, a great inspiring power founded on man's growing confidence in his ability to control his material destiny: "In proportion as ships sail more swiftly, as mails arrive more regularly, as men travel more securely, as markets are more easy of attainment; in proportion, in short, as obstacles opposed by nature and bad laws to the growth of civilization are overcome, in exactly the same proportion does the disposition to trust increase." Railroads, steamships, and the telegraph—the great agencies of steam and lightning—

had both accelerated and regularized trade; Wall Street was regularizing and accelerating the use of credit, making it the power to move the world. Who could doubt that the credit system, under the management of enlightened businessmen, would bring rapid and steady progress for America?[28]

Horace Greeley's *Tribune* could doubt. In the summer of 1857, it said that Wall Street had acted more out of delusion than wisdom when it handled the financing of what was proving to be an overbuilt and excessively expensive railroad system. How could it be said that Wall Streeters had acted shrewdly when railroad leaders were forced to combine "for the relief of their long suffering stockholders." Nor had New York bankers and merchants acted wisely when, through their all-too liberal granting of credit, they encouraged Americans to build a mountain of debts to pay for foreign merchandise. The United States was becoming more a nation of consumers than of producers, paying its debts to European manufacturers and merchants through the sale of railroad securities and the export of gold. Prosperity built on such grounds could not last much longer. The *Herald*, too, warned that Americans were headed for an economic collapse even more catastrophic than that of 1837: "Government spoilations, public defaulters, paper bubbles of all descriptions . . . millions of dollars, made or borrowed, expended in fine homes and gaudy furniture; hundreds of thousands in the silly rivalries of fashionable parvenues in silks, laces, diamonds and every variety of costly frippery are only a few among the many crying evils of the day. The worst of all these evils is the moral pestilence of luxurious exemption from honest labor, which is infecting all classes of society."[29]

The *Times* ridiculed such "croakers," yet even it agreed that many merchants had dangerously overextended credit to in-land buyers. In fact, New York had grown rich by encouraging the consumption of foreign merchandise. Between 1849 and 1858, the United States imported $365 million more than it exported; most of the imported goods came through the metropolis. To balance its accounts, the nation had exported railroad stocks and bonds and over $250 million in California

gold—most of it through New York. In the process of expanding its railroads and its appetites, the nation had built a
scaffolding of indebtedness which rested on public confidence
in the commercial future. That confidence was much shakier
than the *Times* pretended it was. The price of railroad stocks
on the Exchange had for several years been depressed and
unstable, their value made even more dubious by their role as
the favorite playthings of speculators. In the spring and
summer of 1857, merchants found it difficult to collect debts
owed them in the Middle West, although neither this nor the
troubles on the Exchange discouraged New York bankers from
extending new loans, which reached an all-time high early in
August.[30]

By that time, some observers had begun to count the costs
of the national buying spree. In "A Warning to Merchants,"
Harper's Weekly noted that in the previous seven months imports
had reached record levels. The nation was blessed with an
unusually abundant harvest, but it had become evident that
Europe, the major market for American breadstuffs, also
enjoyed the same blessing. How would Americans pay? The
question became more than an abstract one when in mid-
August western businessmen, who had temporarily placed their
surplus funds on deposit in New York banks, began to call the
money home in order to finance the movement of crops. In
turn, the banks began to call in their loans, especially money
lent for stock market speculation. On August 23, stock prices
fell sharply. The next day the New York branch of the Ohio
Life Insurance and Trust Company, which had invested heavily
in railroad stocks, suspended payments. August 25 brought
what the *Times* reluctantly called a "pretty good stampede in
Wall Street" and the suspension of two financial firms: "The
Foundations of financial confidence appear to have been
knocked from under the Stock and Money markets by the
force of an indiscriminate and unreasoning distrust."[31]

Distrust soon became outright panic. The great agencies of
progress suddenly seemed to turn malevolent. Expected gold
shipments from California were delayed at the very time when
the city was forced to make an unusually heavy specie shipment

to England; in September came the news that the steamer *Central America* had sunk with a million and a half dollars of California gold aboard. Credit, that marvelous force for expansion, suddenly became onerous debt as anxious creditors rushed to collect their due. The telegraph which, through its lightning speed, had promised to regularize trade throughout the nation now spread the panic with that same lightning speed. Westerners anxiously called in their deposits; New York merchants demanded payment. The New York Clearing House Association, instituted to expedite transactions among banks, with equal efficiency forced a general contraction of bank credits. And so the mounting financial tremors knocked the props of confidence out from under the golden age.[32]

George Templeton Strong, who remembered the troubled times after the Panic of 1837, concluded at the end of September that the public had lost all confidence "in the solvency of our merchant princes" and went on grimly to gloat over the plight of those businessmen who had embraced the Age of Gold: "They are fighting hard for the grand, ugly house in Fifth Avenue; for the gold and damask sofas and curtains that are shrouded in dingy coverings, save on the one night of every third year when they are unveiled to adorn the social martyrdom of five hundred perspiring friends." Struggle they did, often without success:

> Rushing around the corners,
> Chasing every friend.
> Plunging into bank—
> Nothing there to lend—
> Piteously begging
> Of every man you meet.

Panic and more panic—in October Strong concluded that the crisis was more acute than that in 1837. By the middle of the month, a run on the banks forced them to suspend specie payments. More than 160 important business firms failed in one week; businesses closed and construction stopped, throwing thousands of men and women out of work; the AICP reported that during three ugly months some 41,000 homeless and jobless poor were forced to seek shelter in police stations. "We were," wrote Robert M. Hartley, "now brought to realize something of the distress which, at times, has often been experienced in European cities."[33]

Like a great earthquake, the panic convulsed the city and the nation, only to pass away as quickly as it had come. By December, confidence was beginning to return, bolstered by unusually large shipments of gold to the city, by a large cotton crop which could be profitably exported, and perhaps also by the defeat of Mayor Wood for reelection. On December 12, the banks resumed specie payments and by January 1858 the city was on its way to recovery.[34] The Panic, however, had put a temporary close to the Age of Gold. Under its chastening influence, the rampant materialism of prosperous times was swamped by a great religious revival in late 1857 and early 1858. Where the year before in both homes and offices New Yorkers had worshipped the golden calf, now they knelt in Christian prayer. Briefly, the revival gave the city a quiet and orderly Sabbath at least partly free from the Sunday business, theaters, concerts, and drunks that had so badly stained the character of this metropolis of a still largely Protestant America. The great religious tide receded almost as quickly as the panic, but the chastening lesson was not quickly forgotten.[35]

Although the economic consequences of the collapse were less severe than those of the Panic of 1837, commercial New York was hurt by the uneven recovery of the larger economy on which it depended. The panic hardly touched the cotton producing South, but other areas were less fortunate, especially the Middle West where wheat and corn prices remained low until the Civil War. Railroads were further weakened by the crash and by the slow recovery of trade. The slide in American shipping which had begun in 1855 accelerated when the maritime world encountered a surplus of ships after 1857. Even the number of passengers, especially immigrants, arriving at the Port of New York recovered only slowly from a sharp decline in 1857–58; the number of arrivals in the three years after the panic was one-third less than in the three years before.[36]

METROPOLIS

Despite such troubles, however, it was evident that New York had passed its final test as a commercial metropolis. In 1858, one New Yorker declared that the city had emerged from every financial crisis in a stronger position than its most immediate rival. Philadelphia and Boston had fallen farther behind as the result of earlier panics, now it was the turn of London, the mistress of the world's money: "The time will ere long arrive, when New York, and not London, will become the financial center, not only of the New World, but also to a great extent, of the Old World." Such hopes were premature, but no one could doubt that New York was rapidly achieving its destiny as the world's greatest commercial city. Nor could anyone doubt that it was and would long be the major influence on the development of American society. George Francis Train in 1857 called it "the locomotive of these United States" which pulled the rest of the nation faster and faster into the future— "twenty miles an hour—thirty—forty," and striving for fifty until the collapse.[37]

With the assistance of steam power and electric power and the power of credit, the Metropolis had become the dominant center of the rapidly urbanizing region around New York Harbor, the consolidating and energizing force for a dozen cities and a hundred towns: Brooklyn, Flatbush, Flushing, Jamaica, Bridgeport, New Rochelle, Morrisania, Yonkers, Hackensack, Paterson, Lodi, Union, Hoboken, Jersey City, Orange, Plainfield, and others. In 1856, the *Tribune* noted how fast the city's presence had grown: "Out of town, which a few years ago meant above Canal-Street, now means across the river or the bay, far down by the sea-shore, or in the fast receding forests of adjoining counties." New York's streets, said Ralph Waldo Emerson, were "stretching out toward Philadelphia until they touch it, and northward until they touch New Haven, Hartford, Springfield, Worcester, and Boston." Its commercial and cultural influence extended north and west along the railroads and canals and southward by sea and by land. By 1860, New York was in direct contact by rail and telegraph with every major city of the North. By then, it had become the dynamo of the emerging urban system of cities and towns in the Northeast and Middle West which was working a fundamental change in American life.[38]

The significance of this broad ranging influence was best measured in its own state. In the thirty years before 1860, New York State underwent a series of changes that foreshadowed developments nationally in the late nineteenth and early twentieth centuries. By the 1850s, the urban system had established its supremacy over rural society. After 1830, the major cities had grown rapidly. The populations of both New York City and Albany more than doubled, while Rochester increased four times and Buffalo five. Strings of infant cities had appeared along the canals and railroad lines: Amsterdam, Utica, Rome, Oneida, Syracuse, Auburn, Seneca Falls, Geneva, and Canadaigua—all, said Fredrika Bremer in 1850, were "pretty, all increasing, all abounding in lovely houses and gardens," worlds apart from New York City, yet also extensions of the Metropolis. Bayard Taylor, in one of his novels set in the 1850s, describes the fictitious town of Tiberius which, having been connected to the outside world by a branch of the New York Central Railroad, considered itself quite metropolitan. The Tiberians took special pleasure in their business district, modeled as much as possible on that of New York, where "houses were jammed together as compactly as possible, and huge brick blocks, with cornices and window-caps of cast-iron, staring up pompously between one-story buildings of wood, saying to the country people, on market: 'Behold, a city!'"[39]

The Tiberiuses grew much faster than the rural population of the state. In fact, the 1840s had brought population declines in some of the rural townships (80 declined between 1840 and 1850) and in those rural villages which were losing their marketing functions to the larger towns. The decline seems to have accelerated in the early 1850s, leading the *Times* to predict that shortly there would be "deserted villages enough" to provide all the material needed for melancholy poetry. In 1857, Franklin B. Hough, the Superintendent of the State Census, noted this trend and concluded that agricultural areas quickly reached their limits of growth and opportunity, leading part of their populations to move either to the rural west or to the cities. Hough also noted that there was a "centralization of our population" which especially favored New York City and its associated cities and suburbs: "The influence which its wealth, its institutions, and its press exert upon the nation at large, are but the beginnings of other and still weightier influences which it is destined to exert upon the fortunes of the general commonwealth." The United States census of 1860 tended to confirm Hough's conclusion. During the 1850s, the city and its great suburb Brooklyn grew faster than any other major city in the state, with the exception of Buffalo. This growth, sustained by the inpouring of immigrants, was in the late nineteenth century to move the statistical population center of the state not ever westward but seemingly ever southward in the direction of New York Harbor.[40]

While the 1850s brought a general awareness of the urbanizing trend, few New Yorkers attempted to comprehend its social meaning. The most impressive exception was a transplanted New Englander, Amory D. Mayo, a Unitarian minister in Albany. In his book *Symbols of the Capital* (1859), he attempted to explore the implications of the new urban system for American society by treating New York State as "the best mirror in which we can behold the reflection of our present progress." Mayo was able to observe the decline of rural society from his vantage point at Albany and to make some astute observations regarding the urban tendency. Although he shared the common view that the countryside ideally was the real America of virtue, beauty, comfort, freedom, and personal independence, he also was careful to reject the "sentimental Arcadian view" held by many dissatisfied city people. The countryside was not simply a charming landscape but a society with some important drawbacks—especially a monotony of life which "stupifies rather than deepens character." Because of its weaknesses, rural society was open to the worst kind of urban influence, especially to the luxurious materialism of cities which was "inflaming young men with the aspiration to exchange the honor of health and independence at home for slavery and effeminancy in the town; and changing the good old race of country women into feeble imitations of the fashion plates who sigh among the groves and gardens of the Hudson for the splendors of Broadway millenery and the exhausting pleasures of a city career."[41]

Mayo's attitude toward the cities was decidedly ambivalent. He recognized that they were exciting and necessary places which would inevitably attract the ambitious and the talented, for the city at its best was the source of human progress:

> Doubtless, a city is a large labor-saving machine, where the greatest amount of spiritual energy can be directed to a given point with the least waste of material resources. . . . This is the great charm of the city to the leaders of every realm of life. Here, too, the tendencies of classes, the needs of crowds, and the secrets of public and wide-ranging influence over men, are best to be learned. And the town is a great workshop, filled with the best tools in the shape of organized forces and institutions. Labor and business are systematized, society can be taken by the handle, literature classified, and education and art in every branch assigned to its peculiar department. The caucus, the convention, the city church, the philanthropic institution, are the finest implements to do the work they represent.

Cities were necessary exchange points which served efficiently to organize not only rural production but the talents, dreams, moral sentiments, and finest aspirations of rural folk.[42]

The trouble was that these virtues attracted too many people, especially those who lacked the abilities to contribute to, or benefit from, urban life. Cities, thus, were burdened with an excess of people whose destiny it was either to become "an unknown cog in a social machinery" or to be drawn into a whirlpool of competition which destroyed the weak and warped the characters of the strong. To keep such people where they belonged, Mayo proposed a wide-ranging reform of rural life so as to improve the health, expand the leisure time, refine the manners, and extend the education of country folk. As the basis for his ideal society, Mayo placed his faith in the expanding technology of the century—especially in farm machinery, railroads, and the telegraph—which would assure that every rural community would have the advantages of a civilized and republican life. Woven through his book was a vision of an America of comfortable farms, prosperous villages, and great cities—an ideal blend of the natural and the urbane: "Our long green valleys, threaded by the railroad, open their arms to the weary citizen; our thousand inland cities and villages can become as many centers of taste and virtue."[43]

That dream, however, led back to the great metropolis at the mouth of the Hudson, and to trouble. Regarding New York, Mayo's ambivalence was heavily shaded by anxiety. He was awed by its power and also by its sublime beauty as a monument of human achievement. He recognized that it was an essential center for the exchange of both goods and ideas. Yet he also saw it as a threat to American life, not only as a corruptor of human character but also as the home of three threats to the national society. One resulted from the failure of those who dominated the urban system "to manage the involved machinery they have set up on this continent" with sufficient wisdom to avoid such economic catastrophes as the Panic of 1857: "Our commercial system explodes, and faith between man and man departs, and the nation, like Tantalus, sees its own abundance hanging as in mockery above its reach, while it wildly talks of starvation." Another was an emerging oligarchy of businessmen who, benefiting from the "subtle invading power of the gigantic corporations," threatened to elevate money and property above the rights of man. The third was a modern barbarism arising from the great masses of the poor who had crowded into the city, there possibly to fall under the control of political demagogues like Fernando Wood. Such a city, Mayo warned, must be kept under the control of the people of the state in order to assure that it did not threaten Christian and Republican America. Eventually, he hoped, much of New York's population and power would be safely dispersed throughout the system of smaller cities and towns that seemed to be developing as part of the urban trend.[44] In spite of his faith in the long-run tendencies of a progressive civilization, however, there were deep shadows in his book expressive of the developing dark side of the nineteenth century, with its threatening bands of exploitive capitalists and political bosses, of troubles soon to come to America—troubles which in some form had already come to the Metropolis.

New York did much to justify Mayo's concern. Its concentrations of wealth, its fatuous fashions, its masses of unplaced aliens, its poor, its corruptions, its politics, its government, its dirt, disease, and disorder—all seemed to make it an alien presence threatening to the ideal America of happiness and virtue. It seems evident, however, that it was the victim as well as the villain, the effect as well as the cause of deep changes which were transforming and disrupting the world around it. After 1815, a great wave of modernization had risen in the North Atlantic world which had an especially strong effect on the British Isles and on the Northeastern United States. As the metropolis of the western Atlantic, New York fell heir not only to the benefits but also to the troubles of social and economic change. Between 1840 and 1858, the North Atlantic economy had completed one of those tidal cycles from bad times to good which so frequently disrupted progress in the nineteenth century. The depression of the early 1840s had temporarily slowed the economic growth of the city and had deepened its social and political problems; the prosperous years of the Age of Gold, while they favored New York's headlong rush for commercial dominance, also intensified and multiplied its troubles in both government and society. In good times especially, the metropolis was confronted by the pressing and bewildering tasks of housing, feeding, moving, governing, assisting, employing, and assimilating a heterogeneous mass of people drawn to it from other places and other lands. This mass supplied much of the talent, skill, and muscle needed by the city, but it also posed in concentrated form many of the vexing social questions which had begun to haunt a modernizing world. As Nature bestowed its blessings on commercial New York, so did social and economic change present its troubles, which the metropolis had to confront with little help and much interference from outside.

Although these external influences were strong and perhaps decisive, the character of New York itself helped shape its ambiguous destiny. The most remarkable characteristic of this competitive city of citizens and strangers was its cosmopolitan individualism, its freedom from the restraints of a narrow and definite social character. More than any other American place, it provided a large measure of that liberty, so prized by modern persons, for each individual to develop in his own way toward his own ends. In its seemingly infinite diversity, the new metropolis was a world apart from much vaunted rural America, whose limiting social character often made men so used to social conformity that, in the words of Henry Ward Beecher, "they cease to know how much each man is the echo of the other." Little wonder that, though the road to the city was often seen as the road to ruin, ambitious and exceptional young men and women should continue to flock to the metropolis.[45]

New Yorkers themselves often complained that this freedom enabled the strangers in their midst to develop the worst side of human nature; the *Tribune* said, almost with pride, that no place could show "a better assortment" of thieves, prostitutes and murderers. It had, in the opinion of some observers, encouraged many foreign immigrants, who had been kept peaceful in their native lands by Old World despotism, to turn to crime and violence. In the eyes of others, this same freedom had diminished civic spirit and commitment to the benefit of the me-first, ruthless, and dim-sighted individualism so evident in public places. Certainly, there was much evidence to support the view held by many citizens of the progressive city that institutional restraints like the police and the school were needed to control a freedom which seemingly had run wild: Disorder, crime, corruption in business and politics, municipal mismanagement, and other forms of scrofulous behavior which served to convince many Americans that their metropolis was a wicked, dangerous and unAmerican place.[46]

Freedom, however, also provided opportunities for men and women to develop their talents and expand their energies in the interests of society as well as themselves. Mike Walsh perhaps exaggerated when he said that it took more "genius" to cross a street in Manhattan than to act as the justice of the peace of a rural county, but few would deny that experience in the crowded, dynamic city could hone individualism to a sharpness of mind unsurpassed elsewhere. Freedom, necessity, and opportunity encouraged specialization, the fine-tuning of skills, with the result that New York became a vast metropolitan assemblage of the human energy and specialized talents required for the progress of modern society. This power for progress was haphazardly and wastefully organized, but the evident interdependence of people in the crowded city often served to guide their self-interests into cooperative effort. The American Metropolis, said Fitz-Hugh Ludlow, "will not let a man harden inside his own epidermis. He must affect and be affected by multitudinous varieties of temperament, race, character. . . . Professionally he may be a specialist, but in New York his specialty must be only the axis around which are grouped encyclopaedic learning, faultless skill, and catholic intuition."[47] Although this description applied only to a select few business and professional men, it was also expressive of a weaker but wider disposition of New Yorkers to relate their awakened self-interests to some more general good.

Cosmopolitan and commercial New York was especially successful in organizing men for the great ventures in trade, transportation, and finance so vital for economic progress. The more fragmented and insular social city, however, also had its successes. Both need and opportunity led many New Yorkers to organize themselves—or to be organized—in highly varied, often conflicting, but generally meaningful forms of social involvement. The benevolent societies, the churches, the schools, and even the city's sputtering reform movements were powerful antidotes to civic anemia and passivity. Others found their involvement in the much condemned and dubious politics of the city, in a system of political clubs, primaries, and elections whose haphazard character engaged many men who otherwise would have been lost and alienated. Divisive though they frequently were, the manifold ways in which New Yorkers organized themselves served both to humanize the seemingly impersonal metropolis and, in combination with the institutions of the progressive city, to maintain a basic order in society. That order was imperfect, but it sufficed. Like a circus clown teetering on a tightwire, New York staggered along the path of progress, veering toward chaos and anarchy but never falling, able not simply to survive but to thrive. Despite its corruptions and disorders, observed one writer in 1858, it had "during the past ten years thriven . . . far more than any other city in the world."[48]

In fact, the city had "thriven" so fast and so much that it had little time to perfect itself. Certainly, it lacked the grace and charm of the great European cities, which benefited both from their well-established traditions and their positions as capitals of their nations. New York may have been the only metropolis in the world which received no assistance from its national government either to maintain or to embellish itself. While London had its British Museum and Paris its Louvre, New York had only its federal Custom House and Post Office. Men like Henry Tappan and Fernando Wood might dream of capping their materialistic metropolis with a crown of culture similar to those adorning the European capitals, but circumstances decreed that New York would long fail to equal the intellectual and artistic attainments of London and Paris or even the literary attainments of its defeated commercial rival, Boston. Yet the American metropolis by the late 1850s could boast of its "Athenian Quarter," whose cluster of libraries (most notably the Astor Library) housed the greatest collection of books in North America. In this same general area around Astor Place could also be found New York University, the Academy of Music, and the newly opened Cooper Union, "a great People's College." All had been created by the city's private wealth and enterprise. Despite its undue fascination with the fashions and furbelows of Europe, wealthy New York was awakening to its cultural duties, preparing itself for that time after the Civil War when it would establish such mighty engines of culture as the Metropolitan Museum of Art and would make Columbia College into a great university.[49]

The nation's great marketplace was poor soil to develop a high civilization, but no one could deny its vitality and many-faceted power. In a generation, New York had transformed itself from a large mercantile city with an extensive but ill-defined hinterland into a world metropolis. The new metropolis at the mouth of the Hudson had by 1860 become a vast and complicated society whose variety and complexity was beyond human vocabularly to describe and beyond human mind to comprehend. Although it included a wide range of human existence, New York was best known in its extremes, as a city capable of shedding the most brilliant light and casting the deepest shadows. Perhaps no place in the world evoked such extremes of love and hate, often in the same person. In its slums, dirt, materialism, violence, congestion, rush, politics, and municipal mismanagement, it could depress, degrade, and offend the human spirit. In its wealth, intelligence, power, opportunities, freedom, and in the seemingly endless wonders of its streets, it could exalt, exhilarate and, occasionally, even charm strangers and citizens alike. The new metropolis was radically imperfect, but its imperfections were those of a masterwork of collective human effort and a masterful presence in the world.

In the two decades after 1840, New York had to transform, expand, reorganize, and in other ways prepare itself to play a vital role in the development of America and of the North Atlantic world. It had created a downtown business district capable of handling a mounting volume of foreign and domestic trade. It had organized the capital and skill required to maintain and stimulate a developing national economy. Its port and financial district had become the dynamic center of a great metropolitan area of suburbs and industrial satellites which supported one of the greatest aggregations of population in the world. In its freedom, its growth, its jobs and its many-sided society, it provided opportunities for thousands of men and women to perfect their skills and to achieve great ambitions. Through its benevolence, its schools, its employment opportunities, and even its admittedly shabby political system, it opened the way to a better life to masses of rural pool people, especially to the depressed and uprooted poor of Europe. In a generation, it had built the material foundations for a modern city able to sustain the lives of millions: It had built a food and fuel supply system, a water and sewerage system, a great urban park, a stock of housing for all classes, and a system of streets, street railways, and ferries. Despite its crime, corruptions, slums, and the hundred other evils catalogued by its critical visitors and impatient citizens, New York did not disappoint the hopes of Fernando Wood that it become "no mean city." It was an imperfect success, perhaps even a magnificent failure, but for more good than ill the transformation of the Atlantic port city into the new metropolis was a spectacular fact and essential element in the progress of the United States and of the North Atlantic world.

APPENDIX

I Mayors of New York, 1840–60

Elected for One-Year Terms:
Isaac Varian (D), 1840–41
Robert H. Morris (D), 1841–44
James Harper (A.R.P.), 1844–45
William F. Havemeyer (D), 1845–46
Andrew H. Mickle (D), 1846–47
William V. Brady (W), 1847–48
William F. Havemeyer (D), 1848–49
Caleb S. Woodhull (W), 1849–50

Elected for Two-Year Terms:
Ambrose C. Kingsland (W), 1851–52
Jacob A. Westervelt (D), 1853–54
Fernando Wood (D), 1855–57*
Daniel Tiemann (Reform D), 1858–59
Fernando Wood (D), 1860–61

* Wood's second term was cut short by the Charter of 1857.

II Municipal Finance

Year	Assessed Property Value	Appropriations from Taxes (Excluding state	Tax Rate[a]	Debt
	($millions)	taxes)	(Per $100)	(Funded)
1836	310	$1,085,130	$.36	
1840	252	$1,354,835	$.53	$10,725,385
1845	240	$2,096,191	$.88($.87)	
1850	286	$3,100,749	$1.14	$12,204,176
1853	414	$4,836,269	$1.23($1.17)	
1855	487	$5,372,204	$1.20	$15,024,418
1857	521	$7,171,482	$1.56($1.38)	
1860	577	$8,789,100	$1.69	$18,901,440
1875	1,100	$32,367,744	$2.94	$116,733,824

SOURCES: Durand, *Finances*, 372–73 and Disturnell, *New York*, 86
    a. Includes state taxes collected as part of the city property tax; state taxes are excluded from the tax rate figures in the parentheses.

APPENDIX

III Comparative Taxes and Debts (four cities)

	New York	Boston	Philadelphia	Baltimore
Tax Rate (1854)	$1.20	$.77	$1.80	$1.33
Debt (per capita, 1854)	$19.92	$48.62	$39.74	$58.36

SOURCE: *Hunt's*, 33(1855), 93, 719

IV Immigration

	Immigrant Arrivals[a] (1847–54)	Foreign-Born Population[b] 1850	Foreign-Born Population[b] 1860	Percent Male (1860) U.S.	Percent Male (1860) N.Y.	Death Rate[c] (per 1,000)
Total	1,796,000	235,733	383,717	53.9	47.9	17.8
Irish	848,000	133,730	203,746			25.3
German	686,000	56,141	119,984			14.5

SOURCES: Albion, *New York Port*, 418. Rosenwaike, *Population*, 41–2. *Eighth Census* (1860): *Mortality*, lix, lvii–lviii.

a. Arrivals at New York only; figures have been rounded to the nearest thousand.

b. In New York; the foreign-born constituted 45.7 percent of the city's population in 1850 and 47.1 percent in 1860. New York had 10.5 percent of the foreign-born inhabitants of the United States in 1850 and 9.3 percent in 1860

c. In 1850

V City Growth

City	1840	1850	1860	Increase, 1840–60 (Percent)
New York	312,710	515,547	813,669	160
Brooklyn	47,613	138,883	279,122	483[a]
Newark	17,290	38,894	71,941	316
Jersey City	3,072	6,856	29,226	866
Philadelphia	258,037	408,762	565,529	115[a]
Baltimore	102,313	169,054	212,418	108
Boston	93,383	136,881	177,840	90
	(124,037)	(208,972)	(288,735)	(132)[b]

SOURCES: *Fifteenth Census* (1930): *Population*, 486, 498, 711, 746. Rosenwaike, *Population*, 32. Taylor, *Mass Transportation*, 127.

a. The figures for Brooklyn and Philadelphia include populations of adjacent areas which were annexed to these cities in the 1850s.

b. The population of Boston and its nearby suburbs.

APPENDIX

VI Mortality, 1859–61[a] (Deaths per 1,000)

Ages	New York (Male/Female)	Philadelphia	U.S. (White population)
0–1[b]	257(281/234)	188.9	
1–4[b]	64.5(69.4/59.5)	48.4	34.3(0–4)
5–9	10.2(10.3/10)	13	6.6
10–14	3.9(4.0/3.8)	3.9	4.4
15–19	6.2(6.3/6.0)	5.9	5.8
All ages[c]	27.3	21.8	13.7

SOURCES: *Eighth Census* (1860): *Mortality*, 280, 522. Duffy, *Public Health*, 578–79. Ewer, *Public Health*, 16–17.

a. Annual death rate. The average annual death rate (1821–63) for whites: New York (31.3), Philadelphia (23.2), and the average of eleven cities (27.5).

b. Duffy estimates average mortality for ages 0–4 in New York at 85.5 for 1840–44, 165.8 for 1850–54, and 140.7 for 1855–59.

c. In 1861, F. C. Ewer, an authority on public health, estimated mortality in New York at 25 in 1840 and 36.6 in 1855. He also gives these death rates for 1857: New York (37), Boston (24.7) and London (25).

VII Foreign Trade

Year	Imports[a] ($millions)	Exports[a] ($millions)	Tonnage (Percentage of U.S.)[b] (Thousands of tons)
1840	60(57.9)[c]	34(25.6)[c]	545(25)
1845	70	36	579(19.7)
1850	111(59.8)[c]	52(30.5)[c]	1,145(26)
1855	164	113	1,735(25.8)
1857	236(64.7)[c]	134(38.52)[c]	2,035(28)
1860	248(68.5)[c]	145(36.2)[c]	1,973(23.8)

SOURCES: Albion, *New York Port*, 390–92. Chamber of Commerce, *Report* (1858), 11.

a. The imports and exports of New York State.

b. Entered from foreign ports.

c. New York's percentage of U.S. imports and exports for the preceeding decade or period including the year noted (1860 for that year only).

APPENDIX

VIII Population and Property—By Wards (1840–55)

Ward	Population		Gain	Density[a]	Property Values[b]		Foreign-Born[c]
	1840	1855	(percent)		1841	1856	(percent)
Business							
1	10,629	13,486	27	87	59	101	68(46)
2	6,394	3,249	−49	64	17	28	61(36)
3	11,581	7,909	−31	78	18	35	48(29)
	28,604	24,644	−14		94	164	
East Side							
4	15,770	22,895	45	194	10.6	11.0	70(46)
6	17,198	25,562	48.5	198	9.8	11.0	70(42)
7	22,982	34,422	50	103	16.0	16.4	51(34)
10	29,026[d]	26,378	?(26)	135	6.9	9.4	51(13)
11	17,052	52,979	211[c]	142	4.0	8.0	56(18)
13	18,517	26,597	43	229	4.6	5.7	47(19)
17	18,619	59,548	220[c]	95	11.0	21.6	58(25)
	139,164[d]	248,381	78		62.9	83.1	
West Side							
5	19,159	21,617	13	105	11.0	17.0	48(23)
8	29,073	34,052	17	124	13.5	19.0	44(21)
9[f]	24,795	39,982	61	89	10.0	16.9	34(20)
	73,027	95,651	31		34.5	52.9	
Middle							
14	20,235	24,754	22	156	8.7	12.9	57(36)
15[g]	17,755	24,046	35	61	23	49	41(26)
	37,990	48,800	26		31.7	61.9	
Uptown[h]							
	33,925 (11%)	212,328 (34%)	530		26.5	152.3	45

SOURCES: Population from the *Sixth Census* (1840), *State Census* (1855), and Holly, *Description*, 13. Population density from *Hunt's*, 27(1852), 412. Property values from Beach, *Wealth* (4th ed.), 24, and Boyd, *Tax-Book*. Foreign-born percentages from Ernst, *Immigrant Life*, 193.

a. Thousands per square mile in 1850.

b. Assessed value, in millions of dollars, of combined real and personal property.

c. Percentage for 1855. Irish percentages in parentheses. The Tenth and Eleventh wards were heavily German in 1855.

d. This census figure may be inflated; the population of the Tenth Ward in 1845 was 20,913, and without any apparent change in ward boundaries to explain the seemingly sharp drop in population. The figure in the parentheses is the percentage gain between 1845 and 1855.

e. The Eleventh Ward was the "Dry-Dock" ward, which benefited from the expansion of shipbuilding. The Seventeenth Ward (Tompkins Square) was sufficiently removed from commercial activity to be a desirable residential area.

f. Greenwich Village

g. Washington Square and lower Fifth Avenue.

h. The wards above 14th Street. In 1840: Wards 12 and 16. In 1855: Wards 12, 16, 18, 19, 21 and 22. Uptown percentages of whole city population in parentheses.

IX The New York Metropolitan Area, 1840–1860

Counties	Population (thousands)			Increase (%)	Manufactures in 1860 Value	Employ-
Core[a]	*1840*	*1850*	*1860*	*(1840–60)*	*($million)*	*ment*
New York	312.7	515.5	813.7	160	159.1	89,754
Kings	46.6	138.9	279.0	483	34.2	12,758
Hudson, N.J.	9.5	21.8	63.0	568	6.8	3,310
	368.8	676.2	1155.7	212	200.1	105,822
	(63)[b]	(71)	(72)		(76)	(70)
Fringe[a]						
Queens	30.3	36.8	57.4	90	5.3	2,264
Richmond	11.0	15.0	25.5	130	1.6	990
Westchester	48.7	58.3	99.5	106	5.9	6,083
Bergen, N.J.	13.2	14.7	22.3	69	1.2	933
	103.2	124.8	204.7	98	14.0	10,270
Satellite[a]						
Essex, N.J.	44.6	74.0	100.6	128	27.9	21,820
Passaic	16.7	22.6	29.6	78	6.3	5,092
Union[c]			28.6	—	3.9	3,533
Fairfield, Ct.	49.9	59.8	77.5	55	11.5	6,017
	111.2	156.4	236.3	113.5	49.6	36,462
Metro. Total	583.2	957.4	1596.7	172	264.7	152,554
	(3.4)[d]	(4.15)	(5.0)		(14)	(14.7)

SOURCES: *Sixth* (1840), *Seventh* (1850) and *Eighth* (1860) censuses.

a. Kings and Hudson counties are included with New York in the core, because they were closely related, especially through the agency of the steam ferry, to New York City. Fringe counties were those which, lacking any notable strengths, were destined to be drawn into a strong dependent relationship with New York as the city grew; Queens, Richmond, and southern Westchester (later Bronx County) would along with Kings eventually become part of consolidated New York. Satellite counties, because of their distance from the city and their relative economic strength, enjoyed a semi-independent position but were nonetheless dependent on the financial and commercial services furnished by New York and its port. It is noteworthy that the population of the satellite counties grew more slowly (52 percent) in the 1850s than did that of the core (71 percent) or the fringe (78 percent).

b. Figures in the parentheses are the core's percentage of the total metropolitan area.

c. Union county was created in the 1850s.

d. Figures in the parentheses are the metropolitan area's percentage of the whole United States.

NOTES

Abbreviations
The following are used after the first source citation.

Trib.—Tribune
E.P.—Evening Post
B. of Ald., *Docs.*—Board
  of Aldermen, *Documents*
AICP—Association for Improving
  the Condition of the Poor
B. of Ed. *Docs.*—Board
  of Education, *Documents*
C.A.S.—Children's Aid Society

Chapter 1: Commercial New York

1. The best single source regarding the development of New York as a commercial city is Robert C. Albion's classic *The Rise of New York Port*, [1815–1860]. Trade and shipping figures are derived from Albion's tables of statistics, pp. 389, 390–91, 394–95.

1. COMMERCIAL NEW YORK

The Chamber of Commerce of New York estimated that between 1831 and 1840 New York handled an average of 58 percent of United States imports and 26 percent of exports; the percentages for 1841–50 were 60 and 30.5 *Report* (1858), 11. For descriptions of New York during this period see especially Bayrd Still, *Mirror for Gotham: New York as Seen by Contemporaries*, chs. 5–6. The quotation in the first paragraph is from *The Knickerbocker Magazine*, 32 (1848), 375–76.

2. Philip Hone, *Diary, 1828–1851*, Allan Nevins, ed., pp. 127–28, 202. *Harbinger*, 6(1847–48), 67.

3. Still, *Mirror*, pp. 117–18,123. *American Penny Magazine*, 1(1845), 177–78. Charles Dickens, *American Notes*, p. 100. Joel Ross, *What I Saw in New York*, p. 179.

4. Hone, *Diary*, pp. 418–19, 422, 759, 764–65. Joseph J. Gurney, *A Journey to North America* (Norwich, Eng. 1841; repr. 1973), p. 134.

5. I.N.P. Stokes, *The Iconography of Manhattan Island, 1498–1909*, 3, 623. Talbot Hamlin, *Greek Revival Architecture in America*, pp. 153–54. New York *Mirror*, June 27, 1840. *Broadway Journal*, 1(1845), 76, 168. [George G. Foster], *New York in Slices*, p. 18. Hone, *Diary*, 574.

6. Albion, *New York Port*, 16–37. [D. Curry], *New York: Historical Sketch of the Rise and Progress of the Metropolitan City of America*, pp. 331–33.

7. The economy of the Northeast is yet to be given the scholarly study it deserves, but it seems evident that, while each of the major cities of this section continued to be the dominant economic force within its own region, considerable specialization and interdependence had developed among them by the 1840s. New York served as the major nexus of the system which made this possible, playing an important role, for instance, in the sale and distribution of Massachusetts textiles, Pennsylvania manufactures, and Maryland tobacco, while furnishing these states with imported goods from Europe. In 1852, *Banker's Magazine* said that "It is fully conceded that New York is now the grand center of commercial and monetary movement in this country. . . . Both Boston and Philadelphia assume the conditions of the New York market as a criterion for themselves." Quoted in Albert O. Greef, *The Commercial Paper House in the United States*, pp. 20–21n. In 1854, the New York *Evening Post* boasted that the merchants of Boston, Philadelphia and Baltimore bought most of their European supplies through New York and went on to say regarding these cities that New York "is continually augmenting its prosperity by absorbing and withdrawing their former peculiar business," citing as an example the shift in the tea trade from Boston to the city. Aug. 19, 1854. Of its three rivals, Boston posed the strongest challenge to New York's key role as the importing and financial center of the Northeast. Although a definitive study of these matters has yet to be written, two superb books are helpful here: Albion, *New York Port*, especially ch. 7 and Diane Lindstrom, *Economic Development in the Philadelphia Region, 1810–1850*, especially pp. 8–19, 53–63, 74–91, 183–85, 213n. Also see Glenn Porter, ed., *Regional Economic History: The Mid-Atlantic Area Since 1700* (Preceedings of a Conference Sponsored by the Eleutherian Mills-Hagley Foundation, Wilmington, Del., 1976). Allen Pred says that New York also enjoyed an "informational hegemony" both nationally and within the coastal Northeast, *Urban Growth and the Circulation of Information: The United States System of Cities, 1790–1840*, pp. 5, 23, 31, 71–73, 86, 141, 158–60.

8. Albion, *New York Port*, ch. 6. Harold D. Woodman, *King Cotton and His Retainers, 1800–1925*, pp. 171–73. In the first two months of 1843, New York exported over 47,000 bales of cotton; approximately the same amount was exported in the same

1. COMMERCIAL NEW YORK

period of 1844. Much of the cotton had been sent to New York to cover loans to the South. *Hunt's Merchant Magazine*, 10(1844), 372.

9. Albion, *New York Port*, 12–13, 59, 63. Benjamin Chinitz, *Freight and the Metropolis*, pp. 9–10.

10. Albert Gallatin, *Writings*, Henry Adams, ed., 2:560–61, 569, 581. Norman S. Buck, *The Development and Organization of Anglo-American Trade, 1800–1850*, pp. 155, 160–61. Fred M. Jones, *Middlemen in the Domestic Trade of the United States, 1800–1860*, pp. 17–18. Also, Ralph W. Hidy's definitive study, *The House of Baring in American Trade*, esp. pp. 246, 301, 346–48, 359–60.

11. Albion, *New York Port*, pp. 236, 248–50. See also one of the editions of Moses Y. Beech's unreliable but unavoidable directory of wealth published in the 1840s and 1850s under a variety of titles. The sixth edition, *Wealth and Biography of the Wealthy Citizens of New York City* (1845) is reprinted in Henry W. Lanier, *A Century of Banking in New York*. Of the 223 men whose origins are mentioned in the sixth edition, 61 came from New England; this understates the Yankee presence, since it does not include those born of New England parents in New York, city or state. The quotation is from the *Independent*, Dec. 28, 1848.

12. *Hunt's*, 1(1839), 2; 2(1840), 9–26; 10(1843), 70–71.

13. National merchandise imports increased from $95,885,000 in 1831 to $176,-579,000 in 1836 at a time when New York was increasing its hold on the import trade. U. S. Bureau of Census, *Historical Statistics of the United States, Colonial Times to 1950* (Washington, D.C., 1960), p. 538. George Templeton Strong, *Diary*, Allan Nevins and M. H. Thomas, eds. (N.Y.: Macmillan, 1952), 1, pp. 131, 152, 299.

14. Hone, *Diary*, pp. 467, 574. Hidy, *Baring*, pp. 303, 340. The most notorious case involved Edward Nicol, Secretary of the New York Life and Trust Company, who was short some $250,000 in his accounts, money allegedly lost "in lottery gambling, women, and real estate speculation." *Brother Jonathan*, 4(1843), 60, 90. Also, *Hunt's*, 10(1844), 274; 11;(1844), 75. *Tribune*, Jan. 2, Feb. 9, 1842.

15. *Weekly Journal of Commerce*, Aug. 20, Sep. 3, 1840; Feb. 11, Sep. 10, Nov. 25, 1841. Nathan Miller, *The Enterprise of a Free People*, pp. 230–31. Hone, *Diary*, pp. 518–19. *Hunt's*, 33 (1855), 53. In value, imports at New York, 1841–44, averaged 19 percent lower than they had been in the previous four years; the averages were, respectively $62 million and $76.5 million. Total exports declined only slightly, but cotton exports from southern ports, from which New York derived substantial benefits, declined some 13 percent in value. Computed from tables in Albion, *New York Port*, pp. 90–92. Peter Temin says that there was a severe deflation in prices in 1839–1843—which accounts for some of this reduction; but he also notes a real decline in imports and European investments and purchases of cotton, all of which adversely affected New York. *The Jacksonian Economy*, pp. 155–65.

16. Between 1841 and 1843, the assessed value of real estate declined some $22 million (nearly 14 percent), while the value of personal property remained stable. In the next five years, real estate rose in value, but most of this increase was cancelled out by a decline in personal property, so that by 1848 total assessed property values were only 1 percent more than in 1841. New York City Common Council, *Manual* (1853), 169. *Hunt's*, 25(1851), 227. In 1842, the Treasurer of New York's Bank for Savings explained that the bank had been forced to reduce its loans, because many of its depositors "in consequence of the extreme depression of business and the difficulty of procuring employment in this city are daily withdrawing their deposits and

emigrating to the Western States." John Oothout to A. C. Flagg, April 6, 1842. A. C. Flagg Papers, New York Public Library.

17. In 1845, J. E. Bloomfield estimated that between 1841 and 1844, combined property values in Boston increased by 22 percent, while they fell in New York by 7 percent. In 1847, New York's values were still slightly less than in 1841, while Boston's were 55 percent higher. *Hunt's*, 13(1845), 261; 19(1848), 638. *Banker's Magazine*, 4(1849–50), 570. For the entire decade of the 1840s, Boston's population increased by nearly 47 percent, from 93,383 to 136,881, while New York's increased by 65 percent, from 312,710 to 525,547, much of its increase coming from a substantial rise in foreign immigration after 1845. United States, *Fifteenth Census (1930): Population*, 498,746.

18. *Weekly Journal of Commerce*, April 30, June 11, Oct. 22, 1840. *United States and Democratic Review*, 10(1841), 598–99. *Brother Jonathan*, 1(1842), 101.

19. The *Tribune* in 1842 estimated that only 12 miles of railroad track actually terminated at New York: "If we estimate all the Railroads that terminate in the vicinity . . . she can even then boast of 287 miles!—440 behind Boston; 22 behind Baltimore; 132 behind Philadelphia. . . . But none of the roads that terminate in the vicinity of the city are at all times and on all occasions accessible." April 2, 1842.

20. Hone, *Diary*, pp. 477,646. Hidy, *Baring*, pp. 272, 295, 362, 372. Walter B. Smith and Arthur H. Cole, *Fluctuations in American Business, 1790–1860* (Cambridge: Harvard University Press, 1935), p. 42.

21. *Hunt's*, 12(1845), 278, 370, 470, 476. Hone, *Diary*, pp. 685, 749, 784, 794. *Trib.* Sept. 9, 1844; April 23, Nov. 6, 1847. The average number of days for navigation, 1844–46, was 278 on the Hudson and 223 on the Erie Canal. In 1847, it was 262 and 214 respectively. *Hunt's* 34(1856), 245.

22. Edward Hungerford, *Men of Erie*, pp. 69–73, 89–91. *Trib.* June 7, 28, 1845; April 11, 1846; Jan. 8, 22, 23, 1847. *Evening Post*, Jan. 2, 20, 1847; Oct. 9, 1851. In 1852, the New York and Harlem was pushed North to a junction with Boston's Western Railroad. This plus the completion of the New York and New Haven in 1849 strengthened New York's access to Western and Southern New England at Boston's expense. Edward C. Kirkland, *Men, Cities and Transportation: A Study in New England History, 1820–1900*, 1, 225–27, 247, 253, 260. In 1868, Henry Flint indicated that New York had nine railroad trunk lines to the West, while Philadelphia and Baltimore had two each, and Boston only one. *The Railroads of the United States* (Philadelphia, 1868), pp. 46–50. Also, Balthasar H. Meyer, *History of Transportation in the United States Before 1860*, pp. 364–65, 382–83.

23. D. C. North, "Sources of Productivity Change in Ocean Shipping, 1600–1850," in Robert W. Fogel and Stanley E. Engerman, eds., *The Reinterpretation of American Economic History*, pp. 168–73. Winthrop L. Marvin, *The American Merchant Marine*, pp. 242–50. Erastus C. Benedict, *New York and the City Travel*, p. 5. *Weekly Journal of Commerce*, Oct. 6, 1840. Albion, *New York Port*, 405.

24. Curry, *New-York*, pp. 330–35. *Hunt's*, 27(1852), 249, 317; 31(1854), 508. Lewis Atherton, *The Southern Country Store*, pp. 57–61, 86n. By the mid-1850s, New York had succeeded in diverting most of the western grain trade from the Mississippi River to its system of canals and railroads. John G. Clark, *The Grain Trade in the Old Northwest*, pp. 120, 140, 142, 193. In 1860, New York and its satellite areas produced approximately 14 percent of American Manufactures in value; in this same year, it handled 68 percent of all U.S. imports. *United States Eighth Census (1860): Manufactures*, 38, 331–411. Albion, *New York Port*, 391.

25. Chamber of Commerce, *Report* (1858), 8. *Banker's Magazine*, 3(1848-49), 149–50;

2. Strangers and Citizens

5(1850–51), 87–88, 692–94. Margaret Myers, *The New York Money Market, Vol.* 1: *Origins and Development*, pp. 103–18. Alfred D. Chandler, Jr., *Henry Varnum Poor*, pp. 76–77, 93–96. Hidy, *Baring*, 386, 413–14. Vincent Carosso, *Investment Banking in America*, pp. 10–12. In the late 1850s, the Philadelphia Board of Trade complained that New York had through its loans for the movement of the product of the interior to the seaboard further strengthened its commercial dominance: "Money had been advanced upon it in the West, by New York merchants, and to that port it must go, although it may pass directly through our streets and by our doors, in the cars of our own Pennsylvania Railroad Company." G. W. Baker, *Review of the Commercial Progress of the Cities of New-York & Philadelphia*, p. 50.

26. *Independent*, May 2, 1850. James F. Beard, Jr. "The First History of Greater New York," pp. 113, 127–28.

27. *Congressional Globe*, 31st Cong., 2nd Sess., pp. 395–96, 400, 417.

28. Freeman Hunt, *Work and Wealth*, pp. 72, 134, 144, 217. *Hunt's*, 5(1842), 26. In 1851, *Hunt's* warned that changes in business were outrunning the "outward form and resemblance of our great commercial markets" 25(1851), 201–2. For a thorough discussion of the growing concern over the reliability of the clerks employed by businessmen see Allan S. Horlick, *Boys and Merchant Princes: The Social Control of Young Men in New York* pp. 12–14, 149–50, 226–27.

29. *Trib.*, July 6, 1842; May 1, 1846. *E.P.*, March 23, 1855.

30. A rough indication of this situation can be found in New York's per capita wealth (based on assessed property values), which declined from $806 to $555 between 1840 and 1850, while Boston's rose from $961 to $1,297. *Hunt's*, 27(1852). In 1856, per capita property in New York was slightly more than $800; population was approximately 630,000, while real and personal property was assessed at $509,344,000. Between 1845 and 1855, the foreign-born population of the city more than doubled. Ira Rosenwaike, *Population History of New York City*, p. 42.

Chapter 2: Strangers and Citizens

1. Census schedules, Seventh Census (1850), Fourteenth Ward. The census-takers in both 1850 and 1860 listed sex, age, occupation, and place of birth for each inhabitant, along with some very elementary information regarding education and property ownership.

2. The Census of 1850 reported that 234,843 inhabitants (56 percent of the total) were born in New York State. It does not indicate how many of these were born outside of New York County, but the state census of 1855 reported about 11 percent. In 1850, then, approximately 210,000 New Yorkers were born in the city and 25,000 elsewhere in the state. Of the rest, 17,500 were born in New England 13,000 in New Jersey, 12,000 elsewhere in the United States, 134,000 in Ireland, 56,000 in Germany, 31,000 in Great Britain, and 13,000 elsewhere in the world. Rosenwaike, *Population History*, p. 42.

3. *Tribune*, March 27, 1855.

4. William J. Bromwell, *History of Immigration to the United States*, pp. 105–65. Robert* Ernst, *Immigrant Life in New York City, 1825–63*, pp. 61–62. In 1845, pp. 236, 569

2. STRANGERS AND CITIZENS

inhabitants of New York were native-born; 134,656 were foreign-born. In 1855, the figures were 307,444 and 322,460. Rosenwaike, *Population*, p. 42.

5. *Banker's Magazine*, 4(1849–50), 1035–36. Hunt's, 21(1849), 657–58. Terry Coleman, *Going to America*, p. 40. Hidy, *Baring*, p. 401.

6. Bromwell, *Immigration*, pp. 106–30, 134–66. Stephen Byrne, *Irish Emigration to the United States*, p. 19. *Hunt's*, 35(1856), 38, 254, 630. In 1856, the Superintendent of Immigration estimated that 141,625 immigrants brought in $9,642,104 in cash. *Ibid.*, 36(1857), 360.

7. Some New Yorkers believed that their city had become a giant filter for the nation which purified the migratory mass while retaining the dregs. This sense of burden was heightened by the suspicion that some European Nations were dumping part of their criminal and pauper classes on the city. Friedrich Kapp, *Immigration and the Commissioners of Emigration*, pp. 157–58. Board of Aldermen, *Documents*, 15(1849–50), 96–97. Samuel Halliday, *The Lost and Found, or Life Among the Poor*, p. 184. Ernst, *Immigrant Life*, p. 201.

8. For a favorable view of "Kleindeutschland" see Bayrd Still, *Mirror*, pp. 161–63. In 1855, Germans were 29 percent of the foreign population of the city and 7 percent of the foreign inmates of the Almshouse. Ernst, *Immigrant Life*, pp. 6–62, 201. In both words and action, Germans were conspicuous opponents of prohibitionism; see, for instance, *Trib.*, May 24, July 13, 1855.

9. Ernst, *Immigrant Life*, pp. 74–80; 214–17. Jay P. Dolan, *The Immigrant Church*, ch. 4. Albert B. Faust, *The German Element in the United States*. George C. D. Odell, *Annals of the New York Stage* 6:398, 414, 485. Even in some of their less acceptable behavior, Germans often made a favorable impression when compared with the Irish. The *Tribune*, for instance, noted that their Sunday drinking was temperate and orderly, while a drunken person was almost certain to be of "Celtic or Anglo-Saxon origin." July 13, 1855.

10. Ernst, *Immigrant Life*, p. 201. Halliday, *Lost*, pp. 183–84. The New York Association for Improving the Condition of the Poor (AICP) estimated that between 1854 and 1860, 69 percent of those whom it aided were Irish and 11 percent German, while 69 percent of the inmates of the Almshouse were Irish and 10 percent German. Of those arrested by the police in 1859, 55 percent were Irish, 10 percent German, and 23 percent native-born, many of whom probably were the children of immigrants. *Annual Report* (1860), 48, 49, 55. A high proportion of the arrests were made for vagrancy. In June 1843, for instance, 416 of 542 inmates in the city's prisons had been arrested for that offense; 213 of these were Irish. B. of Ald., *Documents*, 10(1843–44), 922–51.

11. For a discussion of the stereotyping of the Irish, see Robert S. Pickett *House of Refuge*, p. 16. Contrast the *Tribune's* favorable view of Germans (note 9) with its accounts of: (a) "A disgraceful fracas" among Irishmen who fell to fighting among themselves over the question as to where to take the body of a dead friend, and (b) An Irishman who was killed by a brick thrown by his wife to protect herself from his drunken brutality. May 30, 1842; Sep. 22, 1845.

12. Edward M. Levine, *The Irish and Irish Politicians*, pp. 27–34, 58. Between 1841 and 1851, more than 70 percent of the 491,278 single-room cabins which housed the Irish poor were destroyed, chiefly as a result of the consolidation movement. *Eighth Census (1860): Mortality*, p. iv.

13. Coleman, *Going*, esp. pp. 169–88. Kapp. *Immigration*, pp. 23, 27, 35, 37, 159.

14. During the peak years of Irish immigration (1840–60) some 70 percent of all

2. STRANGERS AND CITIZENS

immigrants were classified either as farmers or laborers. D. C. North, "Capital Formation in the United States During the Early Period of Industrialization," in Fogel and Engerman, *Reinterpretation*, p. 279. The Irish were the least likely to have the money needed to establish themselves as farmers and thus the most likely to remain in New York.

15. The Irish were strong in every job category in which Negroes were conspicuous except those of barber and hairdresser. Ernst, *Immigrant Life*, pp. 214–17. In 1850, James Fenimore Cooper wrote: "The germans [sic] are driving the irish from the field. Even the groceries are passing into the hands of the Germans and beer is supplanting whiskey. Cooper, *Letters and Journals*, James Franklin Beard, ed. (Cambridge: Harvard University Press, 1960–68), 6, 237.

16. In 1860, there was a slight preponderance of males among the native-born in New York City. In contrast, while foreign-born males were in the majority nationally, they were in the minority in the city; German males outnumbered females, but Irish females were far more numerous than males (117,120 females and 86,580 males). It is probable that there was an especially great number of young Irish women between ages 15 and 30, which would explain why, in the city's population as a whole, young women substantially outnumbered young men. *Eighth Census (1860): Population*, pp. 345, 609.

17. The Irish deathrate in 1850 was 25.3 per thousand and the German rate was 14.5. Rosenwaike, *Population*, p. 41. Estimated mortality for immigrant males, 1856–64, was 24 percent greater than among females, although an undercounting of males probably exaggerated the difference. *Eighth Census (1860): Mortality*, pp. lix, 279.

18. Charles Loring Brace, *The Dangerous Classes of New York*, pp. 41–42. Carl Wittke, *The Irish in America*, pp. 42, 67–68. Pickett, *House of Refuge*, pp. 11–13.

19. The New York State Emigration Commission, established in 1847, provided much temporary aid for the newly arrived, but this did not benefit those many Irish immigrants who had arrived before that time. Kapp. *Immigration*, p. 236.

20. Census figures, which are given by wards, indicate that the Irish settled almost everywhere in the city. In 1855, when the Irish constituted 28.2 percent of New York's population, their percentages in 16 of the city's 22 wards ranged from 25.4 to 46. Only in four wards were they less than 20 percent of the population; significantly, in three of these wards, the German percentage (from 22.6 to 33.6) was more than in the city at large (15.7). Both groups were small in the Ninth Ward, which had the highest proportion of the native-born. These figures are supplied by Ernst, *Immigrant Life*, p. 193, on the basis of the State Census of 1855. The State Census of 1845 indicates that this pattern had already formed ten years earlier.

A sampling of census schedules suggests that there was some tendency among the Irish to concentrate in small districts or in clusters of dwellings. One group of eight buildings in the Fourteenth Ward, for instance, housed 44 families, 37 of which were headed by persons of Irish birth, along with 40 single boarders (33 Irish) and 59 children (53 in families headed by an Irish man or woman). Two nearby buildings contained only native-born inhabitants. Census Schedules, Fourteenth Ward (1850), dwellings #43–52. Another sampling of the same ward in 1860 indicates a similar situation. It is possible, then, that the Irish suffered from the worst of two possible situations, being partly segregated from the native population, yet too widely scattered for them to develop the group advantages of immigrant colonies like Kleindeutschland. For another view, see Dolan, *Immigrant Church*, especially chs. 2 and 3.

21. Charles L. Brace said that "the Emigrant is released from the social inspection

[441]

and judgment to which he has been subjected at home, and the tie of church and priesthood is weakened." *Dangerous Classes*, p. 35. Pickett, *House of Refuge*, p. 9. Wittke, *Irish*, pp. 67–68. John T. Smith, *The Catholic Church in New York*, 1, 143.

22. Quoted in Henry A. Brann, *Most Reverend John Hughes*, p. 132. Although he did not succeed to the full dignity of Bishop until 1842, Hughes as coadjutor-bishop administered the affairs of the New York Diocese from 1838 on. He advised Irish immigrants that, while as individuals they might love Ireland, "in your social and political relations you must become merged in the country of your adoption." John R. G. Hassard, *Life of the Most Reverend John Hughes, D.D.*, p. 312.

23. John Hughes, *Complete Works*, Lawrence Kehoe, ed., 1, 257. Hassard, *Hughes*, p. 227. Brann, *Hughes*, pp. 88–89. Ernst, *Immigrant Life*, pp. 137, 141.

24. Hassard, *Hughes*, pp. 258, 351. Francis E. Lane, *American Charities and the Child of the Immigrant*, pp. 105–8. J. R. Bayley, *A Brief Sketch of the History of the Catholic Church on the Island of New York*, pp. 122–27. James Grant Wilson, ed., *The Memorial History of New York*, 4, 643–44. *Trib.*, Oct. 21, 1854.

25. Smith, *Catholic Church*, 1, 99, 115. Hughes, *Works*, 1, 61, 93–4, 182, 529.

26. In 1840, there were 23,177 pupils in the city's primary schools, 9690 of whom were educated at "public charge." In 1845, there was 78 common schools with an average attendance of 23,203, and 208 private and select schools with 8354. *Sixth Census* (1840), p. 23. New York State, *Census of 1845*, pp. 29ff. The early history of the Public School Society is ably discussed by Diane Ravitch, *The Great School Wars: New York City, 1805–1973*, chs. 1–3.

27. Hughes, *Works*, 1, 58–60, 93–94. Harold A. Buetow, *Of Singular Benefit: The Story of Catholic Education in the United States*, p. 139. B. of Ald., *Docs.*, 6(1839–40), 295. Also, Carl F. Kaestle, *The Evolution of an Urban School System: New York City, 1750–1850*, pp. 151–58. Ravitch, *School Wars*, pp. 33–57. Glyndon G. Van Deusen, "Seward and the School Question Reconsidered," *Journal of American History*, 52(1965), 314.

28. Charles I. Foster, *An Errand of Mercy: The Evangelical United Front 1790–1837*, pp. 121–22, 125, 138, 145, 174, 186–87. Clifford S. Griffin, *Their Brothers' Keepers: Moral Stewardship in the United States, 1800–1866*, pp. 31, 63. Paul Boyer, *Urban Masses and Moral Order in the United States*, pp. 17, 25–27. The 1830s had already brought troubles for the benevolent societies, especially in the forms of growing sectarianism within Protestantism and of the decline of financial support after the Panic of 1837. Foster, *Errand*, pp. 253–73. Griffin, *Brothers' Keepers*, pp. 31, 63.

29. Edward M. Connors, *Church-State Relationships in the State of New York*, pp. 19–23. Stephen Allen, *Memoirs*. John C. Travis, ed., pp. 192–93. Allen was an influential trustee of the Society. B. of Ald., *Docs.*, 7(1840–41), 327, 333. *Trib.*, Sept. 16, Oct. 30, 1841.

30. The Society received public support from a tax on city property. The Common Council restricted the Society's ability to respond to the needs of the growing city by limiting the amount provided by the tax to that collected in 1831 when the tax was instituted. Thomas Boese, *Public Education in the City of New York*, pp. 64–65. Conners, *Church-State*, 18. B. of Ald., *Docs.*, 7(1840–41), 313, 333. The quotation is from *Arcturus*, 2(1841–2), 330-34.

31. Allen, *Memoirs*, 193. *E.P.*, Oct. 20, 1840; Jan. 20, 1841.

32. B. of Ald., *Docs.*, 7(1840–41), 295. Jerome Diffley, "Catholic Reaction to American Public Education, 1792–1852," pp. 194, 274, 283. Connor, *Church-State*, p. 59. In 1853, Hughes's secretary, James R. Bayley, wrote that, while the public schools were "administered with as much impartiality and fairness, as could be expected," the

2. STRANGERS AND CITIZENS

exclusion of religious instruction was "most fatal to the morals and religious principles of our children," Bayley, *Catholic Church*, p. 113. Also, see Hassard, *Hughes*, pp. 240–41. Hughes, *Works*, 1, 58–59. For a more detailed treatment of this situation, see Ravitch, *School Wars*, esp. pp. 44–57.

33. For the political side of the school controversy, see Connor, *Church-State*, pp. 28–40ff. Ira M. Leonard, "New York City Politics, 1841–44: Nativism and Reform," pp. 98–141, 154–94. Allen, *Memoirs*, pp. 195–97. Boese, *Public Education*, pp. 66ff. Ravitch, *School Wars*, pp. 58–82.

34. *Ibid.*, p. 67. B. of Ald., *Docs.*, 10(1843–44), 1321–23. Kaestle, *Urban School*, p. 152. State Supt. of Common Schools, *Annual Report* (Albany, 1845), pp. 236–38. *Trib.*, Dec. 24, 1844; Feb. 14, July 23, Aug. 6, Oct. 24, Nov. 28, 1845.

35. In 1853, the American and Foreign Christian Union charged that "Rome seeks to gain possession of as large a portion as possible of the education of youth in this country. . . . She now opposes the public schools, and calls them godless. A few years ago she opposed them as sectarian because the Bible was read in them." *E.P.*, May 10, 1853. The AICP estimated that three-quarters of those who asked for charity were Roman Catholics. *Annual Report* (1852), p. 25.

36. Lane, *American Charities*, pp. 55–56. Bayley, *Catholic Church*, p. 113. Connors, *Church-State*, pp. 48–49.

37. B. of Ald., *Docs.*, 7(1840–41), 562–63. Although nativism grew from native roots, hostility to the Catholic Irish was intensified by the presence of English and Irish Protestants who brought that hostility from the British Isles. Rowland T. Berthoff, *British Immigrants in Industrial America, 1790–1950*. Smith, *Catholic Church*, 1, 97, 125–28.

38. *Trib.*, July 23, 1842. Market butchers, who had to pay for licenses and stalls in the city's markets, complained of competition from "persons of all description and occupation, many of whom are not even citizens," who openly violated the market laws. Thomas F. DeVoe, *The Market Book*, p. 584. AICP, *Annual Report* (1852), 22.

39. For some examples of concern over disorder, see *E.P.*, Aug. 15, 1840; *New York Review*, 6(1840), 499; *Trib.*, Aug. 27, 1841, Sept. 7, 1843, March 13–14, 1844.

40. Thomas Ritter to James Harper, May 25, [1844], James Harper Papers, New York Historical Society.

41. There were frequent complaints of election frauds and irregularities, including the illegal voting of aliens and inmates of the penitentiary. Hone, *Diary*, p. 655. *Trib.*, April 20, 25, May 6, Aug. 1, Sep. 27, 1842. *Brother Jonathan*, 3(1842), 525. *E.P.*, April 12, 1841.

42. Ira M. Leonard, "The Rise and Fall of the American Republican Party," pp. 163–64. Levine, *The Irish*, pp. 37, 112–16. Louis D. Scisco, *Political Nativism in New York State* (N.Y.: Columbia University Press, 1901), 39–40. *Trib.*, Aug. 24, 1844.

43. Leonard, *Politics*, p. 209; *Rise and Fall*, p. 15. When in 1842, a Fourth Ward meeting nominated James Harper for School Commissioner, it declared "That we feel a native pride in being called American citizens, and that notwithstanding partizans have done for foreigners what they would not do for us, still we believe the day will come when the community" would condemn the Maclay Act; it also warned that Hughes's success "has shown a power which is most alarming, a power which, if not counteracted by the Protestant community, will most assuredly at some day overthrow and destroy this once happy Republic." *Trib.*, May 25, 1842. Also, Strong, *Diary*, 1, 204–5.

44. Leonard, *Rise and Fall*, pp. 164–65.

45. In January 1842, a meeting at Military Hall proposed the 21-year naturalization

requirement and asserted that existing requirements were not sufficient to protect Americans "from the dangers of foreign influence." *Trib.*, Jan. 15, 1842. The American Republican Party Declaration of Principles, adopted in June 1843, resolved that all unnaturalized foreigners "be empowered . . . to hold and convey real estate and enjoy all the Privileges of citizenship except the election franchise." Harper Papers, New York Historical Society. See also: General Executive Committee of the American Republican Party, *The Crisis. An Appeal to Our Countrymen* (N.Y., 1844), pp. 6–8; Hone, *Diary*, p. 677, and *Trib.*, Jan. 11, 1844.

46. C. and E. W. Brainerd, eds., *The New England Society Orations*, 1, 315.

47. Leonard, *Rise and Fall*, pp. 171–72. Scisco, *Nativism*, pp. 44–46. Of the 17 men who had served as Aldermen in 1843, only six stood for reelection and only one was elected. Common Council, *Manual* (1844/45), 159–60, 279–84. One Democrat estimated that more than 3000 Democrats supported Harper as the best hope for municipal reform and added: "I find that many citizens of *foreign birth* have been electioneering for the *native* ticket—some of our greatest apostles—anticipating defeat . . . discreetly avoided a contest by not being . . . nominated." A. Warren to Charles P. Daly, April 10, 1844. C. P. Daly Papers, New York Public Library. The 48,950 votes cast in this election were some 4000 more than in 1843. The vote by election districts can be found in the *Trib.*, Oct. 30, 1844.

48. Benson J. Lossing, *History of New York City*, 2, 493, 493–94n. J. C. Derby, *Fifty Years Among Authors, Books, and Publishers*, pp. 96, 107. Draft of speech, n.d., Harper Papers, New York Historical Society.

49. J. Henry Harper, pp. 39–40.

50. *Working Man's Advocate*, May 8, 1844. *Trib.*, May 29, June 1, 21, July 23, 1844.

51. Leonard, *Rise and Fall*, p. 177. *Trib.*, June 1, 5, 1844. *Working Man's Advocate*, June 1, 8, 29, 1844.

52. *Trib.*, July 4, 1844. A self-designated "friend of temperance, and a member of the 'law and order' party" urged Harper to close one place described in an enclosed clipping from a temperance newspaper as serving liquor, "while a distinguished professor, with black moustaches, will preside at the piano; and a 'lady in black' (with arms bare and bosom nearly so) will accompany herself upon the harp." H. H. Denison to Harper, Jan. 25, 1845. Harper Papers.

53. *Trib.*, Dec. 24, 1844; Jan. 28, Feb. 12, 27, April 1, May 14, 1845.

54. Leonard, *Rise and Fall*, pp. 179–81. *Trib.*, Nov. 1, Dec. 9, 1844; Jan. 20, 1845. The Council petitioned the state legislature for support in altering the Federal naturalization law, after the Alderman had eliminated a proposal that all voters be required to speak English. *Ibid.*, Nov. 19, 26, Dec. 3, 1844. As early as February 1844, Representative Hamilton Fish had presented a petition signed by an estimated 10,000 New Yorkers for an alteration of the law. *Cong. Globe*, 28th Cong., 1 sess., p. 295. Ray A. Billington, *The Protestant Crusade* (N.Y., 1938), pp. 205–8.

55. Leonard, *Rise and Fall*, pp. 183–88. *Trib.*, Nov. 9, 12, 1844; March 10, April 5, 1845. Thomas R. Whitney, *A Defence of American Policy*, p. 255.

56. Scisco, *Nativism*, pp. 54–61. Harper polled 7025 fewer votes than in 1844, while the two regular parties increased their vote by a total of 5400. In 12 of the 17 wards, Harper's loses were greater than the combined gains of the regular parties. The nativists also lost the school board elections in June. *Trib.*, April 18, June 5, 1845. American Republic party leaders attempted to affect an alliance with the Whigs, but their hopes were dashed when Judge Robert Taylor, the leading contender for the Whig nomination for mayor in 1846, rejected a nomination from the nativists. Taylor

3. THE TROUBLE WITH GOVERNMENT

noted in his diary that, while he approved of nativist efforts to end the illegal naturalization of aliens, he "deemed many of their notions, and their violent abuse of foreigners very offensive." Robert Taylor, mss. Autobiography and Diary, New York Public Library, pp. 12,14, 17. Beginning in 1845, Horace Greeley and other Whig spokesmen disassociated themselves from nativism and made an appeal for votes from foreign-born citizens. *Trib.*, March 19, 31, 1845; Nov. 30, 1847; June 6, Nov. 15, 1848.

57. Hone, *Diary*, pp. 508, 655. For a similar view expressed two years earlier, see Strong, *Diary*, 1, 94.

58. Scisco, *Nativism*, p. 253. *Trib.*, June 7, 1844.

59. Hughes, *Works*, 1, 462. Hughes claimed credit for restraining Roman Catholics from retaliatory attacks on nativists, but he also warned that "if a single Catholic church were burned in New York, the city would become a second Moscow." Hassard, *Hughes*, pp. 273–76. Lydia M. Child, though she believed that the Irish were responsible for much of the political corruption in New York, concluded that the nativist crusade had caused an "ungenerous strife" and a consequent "spirit of clanship" among the Irish. Child, *Letters from New York: Second Series*, pp. 165–66.

60. The author of an article, "The World of New York," said that "It is . . . desirable that every nation should possess one city in which every interest of man and society is adequately represented and cared for," one city whose impartiality would serve to convince Americans generally that there were worthy viewpoints and tastes other than their own. *Putnam's Magazine* (July 1856), 108–9.

61. Curry, *New-York*, pp. 300–21. He asserted that "in New England the consolidation of society has, to a great degree destroyed individuality of character, while in New-York the social mass is but an aggregation of persons, each complete in his own individual integrity. *Ibid.*, p. 318.

62. Thomas B. Gunn, *The Physiology of New York Boarding Houses* p. 12.

63. Brother Jonathan, 4(1843), 469. *Harbinger*, 1(1845), 170. Also, Gunn, *Physiology*, p. 210–11.

Chapter 3: The Trouble with Government

1. *Trib.*, Oct. 20, Dec. 24, 1842. The new state tax (for repayment of the state debt) averaged over $200,000 for the city in the 1840s; by 1857, it was $1,328,000. See notes 7 and 11.

2. A summary of the police functions and powers of the Municipal Corporation can be found in B. of Ald., *Docs.*, 10(1843–44), 696–785. Murray Hoffman, *A Treatise upon the Estate and Rights of the Corporation of the City of New York*, p. vii. In 1844. city-owned land comprised about 1450 acres, or nearly 12 percent of the acreage of Manhattan. George Black, *The History of Municipal Ownership of Land on Manhattan to 1844*, p. 62n.

3. B. of Ald., *Docs.*, 6(1839–40), 685–87. The New York *American* charged that some members of the Common Council were pushing a scheme to require that all steamboats from New England dock uptown in order to promote the development of, and increase land values in, upper Manhattan. *American*, April 14, 1843.

4. B. of Ald., *Docs.*, 10(1843–44), 786–92. Many of these officials and employees were not paid directly out of the city treasury. The 1661 firemen, for instance, were volunteers who received special privileges such as exemption from militia duty but no

3. THE TROUBLE WITH GOVERNMENT

pay. The majority of those who did receive pay worked on a per diem basis; this included the 1193 watchmen and sweepers. The best paid among the comparatively few salaried officials were the Mayor ($3000), the Recorder, and the Street Commissioner ($2500 each). For lists of city employees see the annual Common Council Manual.

5. *Broadway Journal*, 1(1845), 243. *Trib.*, Aug. 26, Sep. 17, 1842; March 13, July 31, 1846; Dec. 15, 1848. *Brother Jonathan*, 6(1843), 43.

6. Leonard, *Politics*, p. 34. Gross budget expenditures rose from $1,605,742 in 1840 to $3,368,163 in 1850 to $9,785,056 in 1860, from $5.13 per capita in 1840 to $12.14 in 1860. Edward D. Durand, *The Finances of New York City*, pp. 376–77.

7. The tax rate rose from 51¢ to 80¢. This increase is attributable to several almost simultaneous needs: (1) to pay off a floating debt contracted before 1840; (2) to pay the interest on the new Croton water debt; (3) to provide for a new state mill tax which the city had to collect; (4) to finance the new public school system established under the Maclay Act. William T. E. Hardenbrook, *Financial New York*, pp. 334–37. B. of Ald., *Docs.*, 12(1845–46), 8.

8. B. of Ald., *Docs.*, 6(1839–40), 73. By later, post-Tweed, standards neither taxes nor the debt were heavy. In 1875, the assessed value of New York property was slightly more than four times that in 1840, but taxes were 20 times as great, while the debt was more than 10 times as large. John Disturnell, *New York as It Was and as It Is* (N.Y., 1876), p. 86.

9. While spending for the police increased by 60 percent between 1840 and 1850, expenditures for public education increased four times. Durand, *Finances*, pp. 376–77. In 1844, the tax committee of the nativist Board of Aldermen complained that the school tax had more than doubled during the year and suggested that the school system was too burdensome to continue. B. of Ald., *Docs.*, 11(1844–45), 226.

10. The costs of major civic improvements such as new streets were borne not by taxpayers but by those property holders who benefited from the improvements. In 1844, Mayor Harper, after claiming that some citizens had been "ruined" by assessments for ill-considered city improvements, said that "heavy assessments have been laid and collected, years ago, for the opening of streets and avenues which remain unpaved to this day." He suggested that no street project requiring assessments be initiated without the consent of the majority of property holders who would be assessed for the project. B. of Ald. *Docs.*, 11(1844–45), 13. Durand, *Finances*, pp. 372–73. For a full discussion of this matter, see Victor Rosewater, *Special Assessments: A Study of Municipal Finance*, esp. pp. 29–34.

11. To make matters worse, 1842 brought the imposition of the new state mill tax which the city had to collect. Between 1842 and 1848, this tax averaged about $205,000 a year. In 1849, the Board of Assistant Aldermen protested that the city was paying a disproportionate share of the total tax, because some counties in the state assessed their property at a much lower rate than in New York; it also asserted that the city's heavy burden of government "should entitle her to support from the state, instead of being called upon to bear more than her proportion of the state taxes." *Trib.*, Oct. 12, 1848; Feb. 21, 1849.

12. Durand, *Finances*, pp. 372–73. It is probable that tax assessors, who were elected in the various wards, reacted to discontent over taxes and to the depression by assessing property at an excessively low rate. In 1850 Mayor Woodhull charged that property was assessed at only one-half or two-thirds of its real value. B. of Ald., *Docs.*,

17(1850–51), 5. It is doubtful, however, that anyone actually knew what the "real" value actually was.

13. E. Hale, in the fourth of a series of articles on New York for *Hunt's*, estimated the per capita tax for New York at $3.61 and for Boston at $7.09 in 1845. The per capita debts of both Boston and Philadelphia were approximately twice that of New York. *Hunt's*, 27(1852), 687–90; 33(1855), 93.

14. B. of Ald., *Docs.*, 11(1844–45), 226–27; 15(1848–49), 29. *Trib.*, Oct. 8, 1847. In 1843, the Finance Committee of the Board of Aldermen complained that much personal property in the city was owned by nonresidents who benefited from city services but paid no taxes: "It has been a subject of common reproach that persons thus situated have built up neighboring villages and thus reduced the value of taxable property in the city." *Docs.*, 9(1842–43), 805–7.

15. *Trib.*, June 2, 1846. In 1842, William Gibson, an owner of New York real estate who lived in New Jersey, suggested that the city tax professional men and merchants and other tradesmen specifically on their occupations. To Charles Osborn, Sept. 16, 1842, Osborn Papers, New York Public Library.

16. *Trib.*, Jan. 21, 1847. Also, *Proceedings of a Meeting in Favor of Municipal Reform . . . March 22, 1844* (N.Y., 1844, p. 23.

17. In the early 1840s, the Whigs were more inclined than Democrats to favor the withdrawal of government from such matters as street cleaning and market regulation, because they believed that the resultant patronage had helped keep the Democrats in power. *American*, March 30, 1843. *Trib.*, Oct. 26, 1841; March 11, 23, 1842; Jan. 6, 14, 17, 21, 1843. Reformers in both parties, however, tended to favor a reduction of the government's involvement in matters they believed could better be handled by private enterprise. William P. Havemeyer, a Democrat, supported the contract system of street cleaning. B. of Ald., *Docs.*, 12(1845–46), 14; 13(1847–48), 20.

18. *Ibid.*, 10(1843–44), 589–90, 607. Mayor Morris in 1841 said that the city should own no property not required for its needs and should not be a landlord that collected rents from private individuals. This was before the Collector of City Revenue was accused in 1842 of having kept for himself some $60,000 in rents which should have gone to the city. *Ibid.*, 8(1841–42), 4. Black, *Municipal Ownership*, pp. 63–64, 75–79. A few New Yorkers believed that the government should retain its lands as a source of future revenue. *E.P.*, Feb. 12, 1840. *Democratic Review*, 42(1858), 426.

19. B. of Ald., *Docs.*, 10(1843–44), 11; 13(1846–47), 15; 15(1848–49), 20.

20. In January 1845, for instance, the city auctioned off, among other properties, 313 lots on Fifth and Sixth avenues, Broadway, and 36th, 37th, 39th, 40th, 42nd, and 43rd streets. One group of lots on 35th and 36th streets near Sixth Avenue sold for from $300 to $675 each; 60 percent of the sale price could remain on mortage for five years at 6 percent. *Trib.*, Jan. 20, 24, 1845. The quotation is from a biographical sketch of Daniel F. Tiemann who earlier, as an Aldermen, had proposed that the city, instead of selling its lots, lease them on condition that they be improved at once. *Democratic Review*, 42(1858), 426. Tiemann's proposal was based on the dubious assumption that city property would be managed for public good rather than private gain. In 1843, city lots located north of 42nd Street were renting for $1500 a year, although they were valued at $839,000. Peter Cooper rented 55 lots between 31st and 33rd streets for $35 a year. B. of Ald., *Docs.*, 10(1843–44), 384–85. Also, Black, *Municipal Ownership*, pp. 75–79. Cleveland Rodgers, *New York Plans for the Future*, p. 48.

21. B. of Ald., *Docs.*, 7(1840–41), 927–28. Rich presented the minority report of the

3. THE TROUBLE WITH GOVERNMENT

Committee on Laws. He proposed that the Council ask the state legislature for the right to establish a fixed compensation for council members. He also asserted that there were few political leaders in the city capable of protecting it from increasing state interference and warned: "The time may come and it is probably not far distant, when it will become the imperative duty of our city to assume the position of a sovereign and independent state." *Ibid.*, 930. See ch. 15 of this work.

22. *Ibid.*, pp. 927–28.

23. On the basis of the rather vague occupational identification made in city directories: The majority (24) of some 42 Aldermen and Assistant Aldermen in 1841 and 1842 whose occupations could be identified were either small businessmen (such as grocers and coal and hardware dealers) or mechanics (including a shipjoiner, carpenter, printer, sailmaker, hatter, and tailor); there were also 11 attorneys. The Council in 1845–46 had eight mechanics and craftsmen, four grocers, three lawyers, two merchants and a sprinkling of other occupations, but most noteworthy is that seven members were listed simply as holders of government office. *Longworth's New York City Directory* (1841). *Doggett's New York City Directory* (1843 and 1846).

24. Of 34 members of the 1842–43 Council, only 17 had served in 1840–41. In the next Council, 17 members of the 1842–43 Council were returned, eight of whom had also served in 1840–41. Of the Board of Aldermen elected in 1846, 14 of the 17 members had served in the previous Council, but only four had more than one year of experience. Common Council, *Manual* (1847), 194–96. *Doggett's* (1843, 1845–46). *Longworth's* (1841).

25. *Trib.*, May 30, 1843.

26. B. of Aid., *Docs.*, 7(1840–41), 927.

27. *Trib.*, April 11, 1843.

28. *Ibid.*, Dec. 24, 1842.

29. *Obituary Addresses on the . . . Death of the Hon. Robert M. Morris* (N.Y., 1855), pp. 4–6, 16–17. Leonard, *Politics*, pp. 4, 74.

30. B. of Aid., *Docs.*, 8(1841–42), 4–5.

31. Leonard, *Politics*, p. 243, and *Rise and Fall*, p. 155. *Trib.*, July 20, 1842.

32. Leonard, *Politics*, pp. 243–48, and *Rise and Fall*, p. 155. *Trib.*, June 1, 1842.

33. The Whig Council abolished the compulsory inspection of firewood, weighing of coal, and measuring of grain—an act popular with merchants—but the inspection system was revived by the next Council. Leonard, *Politics*, pp. 273–74, 290. *Trib.*, March 21, April 23, 24, May 3, July 20, Sept. 8, Nov. 22, Dec. 13, 14, 21, 24, 1842; March 14, June 28, 30, July 25, 29, 1843.

34. The *Tribune* claimed that the Whigs had been defeated by illegal voting. April 13, 15, 1843. *Brother Jonathan*, however, said that, while there were election frauds on both sides, the Whigs lost, because tax increases "combined with the unfortunate street-sweeping contract, no doubt had a great effect in prejudicing the tax-payers against the party in power." 4(1843), 435, 439.

35. B. of Aid., *Docs.*, 10(1843–44), 6–11. Leonard, *Rise and Fall*, pp. 159–61.

36. Morris said that once executive departments were created it would not be necessary for the Council "to meet oftener than once a month . . . which, of itself, would save great expense to the city." B. of Aid., *Docs.*, 10(1843–44), 16–18.

37. *Ibid.*, pp. 214–19. Morris said of his proposal: "All executive officers are elected by the people and immediately responsible to them for faithful performance of their duty. The Police would be perfectly effective; each Ward, being guarded both day and

3. THE TROUBLE WITH GOVERNMENT

night by citizens of the ward, would be known; suspicious places would be marked, and a stranger appearing at an unusual hour would be looked to." *Ibid.*, pp. 218–19.

38. Although the Maclay Act created a central Board of Education, it also authorized every ward to elect its own school officials who would make decisions governing the ward schools. Kaestle, *Urban School*, pp. 157–66.

39. Leonard, *Rise and Fall*, pp. 159–61. *Trib.*, March 14, 31, 1844. The *Tribune* expressed a widespread belief that the Council's reluctance to abandon its control over patronage stemmed from the involvement of party leaders with national politics when it complained of "little knots of ward politicians" who "assume control over and parcel out the most important interests or urgent necessities of the City, but with an ostensible view to the interest of this or that candidate for President." July 29, 1843.

40. B. of Aid., *Docs.*, 12(1845–46), 19–24. Howard B. Furer, "The Public Career of William Frederick Havemeyer," pp. 32–33.

41. The *Tribune* complained that both the number of city officials and the amount of expenditures had doubled over the previous few years. Feb. 11, 1846. Before the end of February, the Council sent a committee to Albany to urge the legislature to pass a bill for a new city charter. Regarding the expected increase in taxes, an anxious Democrat wrote: "It is exceedingly important . . . that the bill should be passed promptly. . . . If something is not done to relieve the public mind from the apprehension of still further inflictions, a change will be effected in the administration of the city." John Ewer to S. J. Tilden, Tilden Papers, New York Public Library.

42. B. of Aid., *Docs.*, 12(1845–46), 505–8. *Trib.*, Feb. 6, 13, 20, 26, March 7, 1846.

43. *Trib.*, Feb. 26, 1846. *E.P.*, Feb. 26, 27, March 7, 1846.

44. *Trib.*, Feb. 26, 1846. Isaac V. Fowler, an influential Democrat, wrote that "there is strong feeling in favor of the election of heads of departments. . . . The *boys* go for it as it increases the chance for spoils." To S. J. Tilden; March 10; 1846; also Charles B. Davis to Tilden, March 3, 1846. Tilden Papers, New York Public Library.

45. *Trib.*, June 2, July 15, 29, 1846. Almost one-third of the delegates were present or past members of the Common Council.

46. The proposed charter also provided for the annual election of the Mayor, a police department headed by the Mayor, and yearly salaries of $400 for Aldermen and $250 for Assistant Aldermen (the latter were to represent constituencies of 10,000 people each, while Aldermen would continue to represent the much larger wards). It also required that any law increasing the funded debt of the city be submitted to the people for their approval and prohibited the sale of any property, right, privilege, or franchise belonging to the city except by public auction, a provision which might have prevented the "boodle" scandals of the early 1850s. Previously, some Democrats had proposed that the Council not have the power "to grant the use of the public streets for railroad purposes, without first submitting it to the People." *E.P.*, May 29, Oct. 25, 28, 1846.

47. *Ibid.*, Nov. 7, 1846. *Trib.*, Nov. 24, 1846. Fewer than one-half of those who voted for the state constitution and about one-third of those who voted on candidates for the state assembly cast ballots on the charter question. The vote on the legislative provisions of the charter was 5870 for and 7159 against.

48. *E.P.*, May 11, 1847.

49. *Ibid.*, Nov. 24, Dec. 1, 1846. *Trib.*, Jan. 15, 18, 1847. Stephen Allen, who voted against the charter, wrote that the voters rejected it, because it "contained most of the objectionable provisions of that prepared by the Common Council, such as paying the

members a salary. . . . No restraint was laid on the Common Council in the matter of borrowing money on corporation bonds; taxes on real estate when assessed was [sic] final, allowing no appeal for errors of judgment. It interferes with the courts, a matter always under the control of the legislature." *Memoirs*, p. 222. The chief reason for the defeat of the charter, however, may simply be the effect of the overwhelming vote in the city against the new state constitution, in part motivated by a proposed provision to eliminate suffrage discriminations against Negroes.

50. *Trib.*, Jan. 20, 21, 1847.

51. Durand, *Finances*, pp. 67–70. In 1853, William A. Brewer declared that the growing corruption and extravagance of the early 1850s resulted not from matters directly affecting taxpayers but from the mismanagement of other sources of revenue such as ferry franchises: "What is to be thought of a political corporation which, charged with the duty of protecting the interests of all citizens, bestows upon a few plethoric ferry-companies, incomes sufficiently ample to build churches, found hospitals, and educate swarms of ragged children." After asserting that "*Private property managed by political corporations is always mismanaged,*" Brewer urged that city property be removed from the Council's control and, whenever possible, sold. Brewer, *A Few Thoughts for Tax Payers and voters in the City of New York*, pp. 14–15, 23.

52. In March 1849, "A Tax Payer" claimed that, even without formal salary, Aldermen were amply compensated in the form of pay received for their work in associated offices such as County Supervisor and Judge of the Court of Sessions as well as in the form of the material benefits of their positions like free food and drink in connection with their meetings. *Trib.*, March 17, 20, 1849.

53. The charter amendments were reported in the *Tribune*, March 30, 1849. The executive provisions can be found in Thomas H. Reed and Paul Webbink, *Documents Illustrative of American Municipal Government*, pp. 106–9.

54. *Trib.*, Nov. 4, 5, 1851. *E.P.*, Oct. 5, 1851.

55. *Trib.*, Feb. 3, 1849.

56. *Putnam's Monthly*, 3(1854), 244. In 1854, New York's tax rate ($1.20) was lower than that of both Philadelphia ($1.80) and Baltimore ($1.33). Its per capita debt was also much lower than in these two cities and in Boston as well. *Hunt's*, 33(1855), 93, 719.

Chapter 4: Poverty

1. *E.P.*, Dec. 16, 1846. *Trib.*, March 31, 1847.

2. *E.P.*, March 3, 1843. The *Tribune* declared that "the City is deformed with Beggary, which sits haggard and blear-eyed, at the corners, or reels weak and tottering along the walk." Oct. 21, 1848.

3. *Ibid.*, Nov. 14, 1848.

4. *Independent*, April 12, May 3, 1849.

5. *Trib.*, Jan. 28, 1845. Prime added up all those listed as receiving aid from public and private sources (155,614) and then assumed that 50,000 were listed only once as receiving aid, while the rest were listed on an average of four times each, i.e., the remaining 105,614 actually represented about 25,000 recipients of relief. Prime, *Life in New York*, pp. 209–11.

4. POVERTY

6. *Trib.*, July 9, 1845. *Working Man's Advocate*, Aug. 3, 1844.

7. Census Schedules (1850): Fourteenth Ward. Although no ward could typify so diverse a city, the fourteenth was as representative as any ward in the city. Much of the real estate was owned by petty businessmen and craftsmen, probably in connection with their work, but it is noteworthy that nearly one-third of the 125 owners had $10,000 or more in real estate. Of some 1500 families in one large section of the ward, only 44 were real estate owners.

8. *Trib.*, Oct. 1, 1845; Jan. 5, Oct. 28, 1847. Horace Greeley said that winter distress was intensified by the movement of farm laborers, dismissed after harvest time, to the city, where some found jobs, while "the rest live on the good-nature of relatives, landlords, or grocers, so long as they can, and then make their choice between roguery and beggary." Writing in the late 1860s, he noted that the expansion of the railroad system and of manufacturing had increased winter employment. Greeley, *Recollections of a Busy Life*, p. 144.

9. *Trib.*, July 14, 1843, March 7, July 9, 1845. In 1863, an estimated 95,000 women earned a living in New York and vicinity. Virginia Penny, *The Employments of Women*, p. vii. *E.P.*, Jan. 22, 1846. George G. Foster said that a seamstress was fortunate to earn 75¢ to $2.00 for a six-day week. *New York in Slices*, p. 53. A persistent complaint among sewing women was that employers demanded free samples of their work and also often refused to pay for garments on the grounds that the work was unsatisfactory. The *Independent* charged that "this is the habitual practice of some wholesale dealers. . . . they get large quantities of work done by poor sewing girls for nothing." March 7, 1850.

10. *E.P.*, Dec. 8, 1840. *Trib.*, March 7, 1845. Penny, *Employments*, p. 105. Penny noted that an increasing number of retailers were employing saleswomen in order to cut costs. She also said, however, that there was always a surplus of women seeking employment, especially as seamstresses, many of whom had been thrown out of work after the mid-1850s by the introduction of the sewing machine. *Ibid.*, pp. 106, 308–10, 351.

11. *E.P.*, March 27, Nov. 18, 1854. *Putnam's*, 9(1857), 222. *Trib.*, Jan. 28, July 30, 1845. Foster, *Slices*, p. 53.

12. *E.P.*, Feb. 15, 21, 1840. The *Tribune* charged in 1845 that women had to pay $3 to $4.50 a month for dirty, unhealthy rooms, leaving them little money for clothing, fuel, and food. Aug. 12, 1845. In the late 1840s, monthly rents ranged from $4 to $10 for two rooms. Douglas T. Miller, *Jacksonian Aristocracy*, p. 135.

13. *Trib.*, July 9, 1845; Aug. 10, 1846.

14. *Ibid.*, Jan. 14, 15, 1842; Nov. 30, 1843; Dec. 2, 24, 25, 1845.

15. *Putnam's*, 1(1853), 673–86. For other lists of benevolent institutions, see Edward Ruggles, *A Picture of New York* (N.Y., 1846), pp. 37–49. O. L. Holley, *A Description of the City of New York* (N.Y., 1847), pp. 27–47.

16. Common Council, *Manual* (1843/44), 252; (1844/45), 171–73. B. of Ald., *Docs.*, 10 (1843–44), 920–21. *Trib.*, April 3, 1846, Oct. 2, 1847. The *Tribune* said that 916 of the 1379 prisoners on Blackwell's Island had been convicted of vagrancy. Oct. 7, 1845.

17. Ruggles, *Picture*, 108. *Trib.*, Jan. 17, 1843. Charles Dickens, *American Notes*, p. 114.

18. B. of Ald., *Docs.*, 9(1842–43), 708; 15(1848–49), 87. *Trib.*, Jan. 1, 30, 1847. City Inspector, *Annual Report* (1854), 221.

19. B. of Ald., *Docs.*, 6(1839–40), 654–55, 664. *American*, Feb. 14, 1843. *Trib.*, April 3, 1846; May 12, 1847; Jan. 1, 1848; Feb. 14, 1849. *E.P.*, Feb. 16, 1849. Total spending

4. POVERTY

for the Almshouse Department increased from $179,000 in 1840 to $255,275 in 1844 to $343,037. Of the $400,000 spent in 1848, $111,376 went for the Almshouse and for the Colored Home, $39,992 for Bellevue Hospital, $42,260 for the Nursery, and $32,660 for the Lunatic Asylum. Additional money was spent for outdoor relief. B. of Ald., *Docs.*, 15(1848–49), 5–6. The weekly average of inmates in the Almshouse, Bellevue Hospital and the Nursery was 2563 in 1845 and 4695 in 1848. Common Council, *Manual* (1845/46), 191; (1849), 219.

20. B. of Ald., *Docs.*, 15(1848–49), 87. *E.P.*, March 24, 1841.

21. Kapp, *Immigration*, 236. *Hunt's*, 21(1849), 29–30. *Trib.*, Jan. 1, 1847; May 24, 1855. In 1844, a committee of the nativist Board of Aldermen, after complaining of "alien paupers," declared that "it is clearly within the ability and duty of the Federal Government to remedy this evil," but it did not say how. B. of Ald., *Docs.*, 9(1844–45), 157.

22. *Trib.*, Jan. 30, 1847.

23. *Arcturus*, 1(1840–41), 310. The author, probably J. M. Van Cott, preposed that outdoor relief be abolished and that a workhouse be established where all paupers would be confined until cured of their moral "disease." *Ibid.*, pp. 307–9.

24. B. of Ald., *Docs.*, 8(1841–42), 6–7.

25. *Ibid.*, p. 7. For a thorough discussion of the almshouse as a remedy for pauperism, see David J. Rothman, *The Discovery of the Asylum*, ch. 8, esp. pp. 188–90.

26. Greeley, *Recollections*, pp. 145, 198–99. *Trib.*, June 3, 21, July 13, 29, 1841; Jan. 17, Feb. 17, 22, 26, Nov. 30, Dec. 1, 4, 15, 1843.

27. *Ibid.*, Feb. 17, 1843. B. of Ald., *Docs.*, 9(1842–43), 703.

28. *Ibid.*, pp. 215–16, 1013, 1394–95; 10(1843–44), 250–53. Some Aldermen evidently hoped that by moving the almshouse farther from the city they could discourage the poor from seeking public aid.

29 *Ibid.*, 11(1844–45), 126, 157–65. *E.P.*, June 24, 1846.

30. *Knickerbocker Magazine*, 25(June 1845). *E.P.*, Aug. 6, 1846. B. of Ald., *Docs.*, 13(1846–47), 133.

31. *Trib.*, May 30, 1845.

32. B. of Ald., *Docs.*, 13(1846–47), 132–43. *E.P.*, Nov. 3, 1846. The *Post* reported happily that the use of pauper labor on Randall's Island had discouraged applications for public relief. June 24, 1846.

33. *Ibid.*, Feb. 16, 1849. Commissioner Leonard complained in March 1849 regarding outdoor relief that "much of our distribution of money and fuel is done through entreaty and representation of members of the Common Council." B. of Ald., *Docs.*, 15(1848–49), 52.

34. Dickens, *American Notes*, pp. 113–14.

35. The Board was given the powers over poor relief previously held by the Almshouse Commissioner, the Common Council and the County Board of Supervisors. The Board of Supervisors was required to raise the money needed by the Almshouse Department through a tax on real and personal property, thus eliminating the Department's previous financial dependence on the Common Council. Curry, *New York*, p. 244. *Trib.*, April 4, 10, 1849.

36. B. of Ald., *Docs.*, 15(1848–49), 87, 1061. *Trib.*, March 7, 1848. *Democratic Review*, 40(1857), 445–51. *E.P.*, Nov. 2, 1850. The Board was responsible for The Almshouse, Bellevue Hospital, the Penitentiary Hospital, the Small-Pox Hospital, the Colored Home, the Nursery on Randall's Island, the Workhouse, the Penitentiary, and the city

4. POVERTY

prisons on Centre Street and at Jefferson and Essex Markets, as well as for outdoor relief. *Ibid.*, May 24, 1852.

37. Between 1853 and 1856, expenditures rose from $385,000 to $925,000. B. of Ald., *Docs.*, 23(1856), 11–13.

38. In September 1853, only 297 of the 5500 inmates in city institutions were employed in the Workhouse; in March of 1855, a time when many able-bodied poor were unemployed as a result of the Panic of 1854–55, 969 of 6892 inmates were in the Workhouse. In 1854, of some 10,000 persons who received outdoor relief from the Department, over 6000 were children; probably many of the adults were elderly "pensioners." *E.P.*, Sept. 14, 1853; Feb. 20, 1854. *Trib.*, March 29, 1855.

39. The Superintendent of the Workhouse was prohibited from employing convicts and paupers in competition with free labor. Of the total of 1668 persons "admitted" to the Workhouse in 1853, approximately 70 percent were employed as laborers. *E.P.*, Nov. 4, 1850; Jan. 26, 1854.

40. Rothman, *Asylum*, pp. 196–98, 202–5, 292–94.

41. *Trib.*, July 18, 1843.

42. Children's Aid Society, *Report* (1855), 35; (1856), 4–5; (1857), 4, 6, 24. *Trib.*, Dec. 20, 1844. Rev. Edwin Chapin declared in 1854 that "the children of the Poor create an appeal to *prudential* considerations. They form a large proportion of those groups known in every city as 'The Dangerous classes' for they will develop somehow." Chapin, *Humanity in the City*, p. 196.

43. Carroll Rosenberg, *Religion and the Rise of the American City*, pp. 77, 84, 188–89. John H. Griscom, *Memoir of John Griscom*, pp. 158–60.

44. See lists of officers printed in the AICP annual reports. Brown, Dodge, Lenox and Wetmore were founders of the Presbyterian Hospital. Minturn was a founder of St. Luke's Hospital and a member of the Emigration Commission; Boorman was also a member of the Commission. James Brown's cousin, Stewart, was a manager of the AICP, a member of the American Bible Society, a manager of the Foreign and Domestic Missionary Society (Episcopalian), and a founder of the New York YMCA. Wilson, *Memorial History*, 3, 436, 4, 441. Kapp, *Immigration*, pp. 224–25. Brown, *Hundred Years*, pp. 6, 314. Boorman and Griswold lived on Washington Square; James Brown on nearby University Place; Stewart Brown on Waverly Place, and both Lenox and Minturn lived on Fifth Avenue near 12th Street. *Doggett's Directory* (1847–48). Erastus Benedict, another prominent officer of the AICP, also lived in the Fifteenth Ward.

45. Isaac S. Hartley, *Memorial of Robert Milhaum Hartley*, pp. 162–78. Rosenberg, *Religion*, pp. 256–60. Robert H. Bremner, *From the Depths: The Discovery of Poverty in the United States*, pp. 35–37. Frank D. Watson, *The Charity Organization Movement in the United States*, pp. 79–81.

46. AICP, *Annual Report* (1846–, p. 15. *Trib.*, Dec. 7, 1844.

47. *E.P.*, Feb. 14, 1840.

48. AICP, *Annual Report* (1845), pp. 13–14, 16–17; (1847), p. 12; (1853), pp. 21–22.

49. *Ibid.*, (1846), p. 20; (1847), p. 12; (1848), pp. 13–14, 23; (1849), p. 18; (1851), pp. 20–21; (1852), p. 42; (1853), p. 36. *American Whig Review*, 7(1848), 420–23.

50. AICP, *Annual Report* (1845), pp. 17–18ff; (1847), p. 13. The number of visitors grew from 297 in 1845 to 337 in 1853; these served all of New York south of 86th Street. Of the visitors, six were physicians in 1845 and 23 in 1853. See the lists of visitors in the reports for 1845 and 1853.

4. POVERTY

51. *Ibid.*, (1845), p. 18.

52. *Ibid.*, (1845), pp. 21, 28, (1849), pp. 15–20; (1850), p. 20; (1852), pp. 18–19; (1860), p. 32. *E.P.*, Dec. 1, 1846. R. E. and M. W. Pumphrey, eds., *The Heritage of American Social Work*, pp. 106–9.

53. AICP, *Annual Report* (1845), pp. 16–17, 21, 26–29; (1846), p. 19; (1847), p. 25. *American Whig Review*, 7(1848), 424.

54. AICP, *Annual Report* (1847), pp. 18–19; (1848), p. 20.

55. See membership lists in the various annual reports. In 1845, some 3000 subscribers contributed a total of $16,693 to the AICP.

56. J. F. Richmond, *New York and Its Institutions*, pp. 500ff. Stokes, *Iconography*, 5, 1778–79. AICP, *Annual Report* (1851), pp. 19–22; (1852), pp. 38–40; (1853), p. 23; (1859), pp. 58–59; (1860), p. 66.

57. Richmond, *New York*, p. 506.

58. Between November 1, 1852 and November 1, 1853, for instance, the AICP spent $29,692 to relieve 24,606 persons and, in 1855–56, approximately $50,000 on 43,516 persons, this last an index of the bad times in 1854–55. AICP, *Annual Report* (1853), p. 33; (1856), p. 56. In contrast, the city in 1855 spent $121,861 to provide outdoor relief for 85,136 persons. David M. Schneider, *The History of Public Welfare in New York State*, p. 272.

59. AICP, *Annual Report* (1848), pp. 13–14.

60. *Ibid.*, (1850), p. 23; (1851), p. 18. In 1854, Hartley declared that, if poverty had increased as rapidly as population in New York, the AICP would have had to relieve 9272 families instead of the 5468 actually assisted. *Ibid.*, (1853), pp. 28–29.

61. *Day-Book*, Feb. 23, 1852. Schneider, *Public Welfare*, p. 271. Rosenberg, *Religion*, pp. 238–39. AICP, *Annual Report* (1852), p. 16.

62. *Ibid.*, pp. 16–17.

63. *Ibid.*, pp. 17, 28, 35–36; (1850), pp. 24–27; (1851), p. 18; (1852), pp. 26–27. Rosenberg, *Religion*, pp. 209–19, 235–36. Bremner, *From the Depths*, p. 38.

64. Schneider, *Public Welfare*, pp. 270–71. Hartley's logic led to the conclusion that the city should be stripped of all "attractions" for the able-bodied poor. AICP, *Annual Report* (1849), p. 18; (1850), p. 27. *Trib.*, Feb. 1, 1855.

65. AICP, *Annual Report* (1858), pp. 47–58. Schneider, *Public Welfare*, p. 276n. As early as 1847, the Emigration Commission had established an employment office intended to find jobs in the interior. In the mid-1850s, the American and Foreign Emigrant Protective and Employment Society engaged in a similar venture. In 1855, the Society advertised that at its office "male servants, farm and other laborers, mechanics, female domestics newly arrived, and children to be bound out can always be obtained." *Trib.*, March 20, 1855. Ernst, *Immigrant Life*, p. 65.

66. For another view of the response to urban poverty see Boyer, *Urban Masses*, esp. pp. 72–92.

Chapter 5: A Rich and Growing City

1. The subject of this chapter is discussed in colorful detail in Charles Lockwood, *Manhattan Moves Uptown*. The quotation is from *Putnam's*, 3(1854), 242.

2. *American Penny Magazine*, 1(1845), 178. *Harbinger*, 6(1847–48), 67.

5. A Rich and Growing City

3. *American Whig Review*, 6(1847), 240.

4. Hone, *Diary*, pp. 729–30.

5. *Trib.*, Sept. 17, 1846. Foster, *Slices*, p. 11. Dickens, *American Notes*, p. 100. Cornelius Mathews, *A Pen-And-Ink Panorama of New York City*, pp. 35–37.

6. *Trib.*, April 5, 1843; Sept. 13, 1844; Sept. 17, 1846. *E.P.*, Dec. 22, 1846.

7. *Trib.*, Nov. 15, 1845.

8. John Crawford Brown, "Early Days of the Department Stores," pp. 98–107.

9. *E.P.*, Sept. 21, 22, 1856.

10. Harry E. Ressiguie, "A. T. Stewart's Marble Palace—The Cradle of the Department Store," pp. 132–58. Philip Hone, who called the store "one of the 'wonders' of the western world," said that A. T. Stewart and Co. was "the largest importers by every vessel from France and England." *Diary*, pp. 902, 913.

11. Jefferson Williamson, *The American Hotel*, pp. 44–46. *Putnam's* 1(1853), 359–65. Depew, *Hundred Years*, 1, 151–55. Hamlin, *Greek Revival*, p. 152. *E.P.*, Feb. 21, 1840. *Harbinger*, 7(1848), 158–59. In 1852, of New York's 57 hotels, 27 were located on Broadway. *Doggett's Directory* (1852–53), 46–49.

12. *Trib.*, Sept. 19, 1848. *E.P.*, March 4, 1853. The *Evening Post* declared that "as the people of the United States are sovereigns, it is no more than fitting that they should lodge and eat in edifices worthy of their royal pretensions . . . in the amount of domestic comfort they are capable of furnishing their inmates . . . owing to the many and vast improvements in cooking, heating, ventilating, bathing, washing clothes." Aug. 21, 1852.

13. *Ibid.*, Nov. 9, 1854. *Trib.*, April 14, 1855. *Hunt's*, 28(1853), 58.

14. *Putnam's*, 1(1853), 360–63. Meryle R. Evans, "Knickerbocker Hotels and Restaurants, 1800–1850," pp. 400–1. The *Tribune*., said that a "philanthropist" had introduced the cafeteria to New York, "thus economising the time and money of his customers." Sept. 24, 1846.

15. *Trib.*, Feb. 7, 1855. Wilson, *Memorial History*, 3, 370. Herbert Asbury, *The Gangs of New York*, pp. 87–88.

16. *American*, March 22, 1843. *Weekly Journal of Commerce*, June 7, 1849. Hone, *Diary*, 913. For an urban geographer's generalized view of the organization of specialized business districts, see David Ward, *Cities and Immigrants*, pp. 5, 85–102.

17. *Putnam's*, 1(1853), 356–58. *Trib.*, May 21, 1849. *Literary World*, 7(1850), 175. In 1850, some New Yorkers planned to raise $450,000 to "erect a *first class Hotel*, with say, six stories adapted to the wholesale dry goods business, underneath it," and to widen adjoining Whitehall Street to facilitate the flow of traffic. *Weekly Journal of Commerce*, June 7, 1849.

18. *Putnam's*, 1(1853), 125–29. [Isaac C. Kendall], *The Growth of New York*, p. 35. *Trib.*, May 3, 1847; May 3, 1855.

19. *Ibid.*, *Putnam's*, 1(1853), 128. *E.P.*, Aug. 21, 1847. The population in the Third Ward fell from 11,581 in 1840 to 7909, about 60 percent male, in 1855. By 1850, the ward had the lowest population density in the city, with the exception of the Second and Fifteenth Wards. *Hunt's*, 27(1852), 412; 31(1854), 489. State *Census* (1855).

20. The *Evening Post* also proposed that Anthony Street be widened as a way of eliminating the notorious slum at Five Points. Stokes, *Iconography*, 1792, 1796.

21. *American*, March 22, 1843. Of the three wards at the tip of Manhattan (the First, Second and Third), only the First gained population between 1825 and 1850 and that, said an observer, solely because it had become "a dépôt for poor emigrants." *Hunt's*, 27(1852), 313.

5. A Rich and Growing City

22. Strong, *Diary*, 1, 150, 294, 355, 363.

23. Henry James, *Washington Square*, p. 25.

24. Rosenwaike, *Population*, p. 48.

25. Stokes, *Iconography*, 3, 527, 675n, 676. Kendall, *Growth*, p. 11. *Hunt's*, 27(1852), 313–14.

26. Frederick Law Olmsted and Lewis Mumford were the two most prominent critics of the 1811 plan. *The Knickerbocker Magazine* noted an earlier critic in the form of a "worthy proprietor" of some westside property who "declined the de-'grading' system which had brought the thoroughfares of New-York to a dead level; and when the Comissioners were 'sinking' streets in all the squares around him, he built a massive wall to protect the home of his fathers and his 'native soil.'" 33(1849), 185.

27. James Frost, "The Art of Building," no. 6, *American Repertory*, 1(1840).

28. D. G. Brinton Thompson, *Ruggles of New York*, pp. 61–65, 71–72. Samuel B. Ruggles, *Memorial . . . on the Social and Fiscal Importance of Open Squares*, pp. 10–11. Charles King, *Progress of the City of New York*, pp. 61–65.

29. Edgar Allan Poe, *Doings of Gotham*, pp. 25–26, 41.

30. Benedict, *City Travel*, 3. Augustine E. Costello, *Our Firemen*, pp. 338–40. In 1852, a committee of Aldermen said that the assessment of unimproved uptown property "at from one-third to one-half its known value" slowed the development of streets, since by law the city could require land owners to pay no more than one-half the assessed value of their lands for street improvements. B. of Ald., *Docs.*, 19(1852), 1484.

31. *Trib.*, April 7, 9, 1849. Stokes, *Iconography*, 3, 675–76. George R. Taylor, "The Beginnings of Mass Transportation in Urban America," in James F. Richardson, ed., *The American City*, 129. Thomas Adams, et al., *Population, Land Values and Government*, p. 53.

32. Charles Astor Bristed, The *Upper Ten Thousand*, p. 41. The interests of the Astor family were not entirely in harmony with those of builders, if we can believe Matthew Hale Smith who, after the Civil War, wrote that in the upper part of the city "hundreds of lots can be seen enclosed by delapidated fences, disfigured by rocks and waste material, or occupied as gardens; mostly corner lots. These are eligibly located, many of them surrounded by a fashionable population. They give an untidy and bankrupt appearance to the upper part of the city. Mr. [William B.] Astor owns most of the corner lots. He will sell the centre lots, but keep the corners for a rise. . . . He knows that no parties can improve the centre of the block without benefitting the corners." Smith, *Sunshine and Shadow*, p. 188.

33. *E.P.*, Jan. 12, 1846. Edward Mack, *Peter Cooper*, p. 179. *Hunt's*, 28(1853), 593–94. Samuel Halliday, something of an expert on housing, said in 1859 that "the class of houses in a neighborhood has much more to do in fixing the price of building lots than the geographical position of the lots." Halliday, *Lost and Found*, p. 196. As their advertisements attest, city builders made it a point of including the latest conveniences such as central heating, gas lighting, and interior plumbing.

34. Kendall, *Growth*, p. 23.

35. Citizens Association of New York Upon the Sanitary Condition of the City, *Report of the Council of Hygiene and Public Health* (N.Y., 1866, repr. 1970), p. 23. Issachar Cozzens, Jr., *Geological History of Manhattan*, pp. 27–28.

36. *E.P.*, April 17, 1854; also, June 19, 1852; Oct. 24, 1853. Stokes, *Iconography*, 5, 1861.

37. The river wards were the Third, Fourth, Fifth, Seventh, Eighth, Eleventh and Thirteenth with 200,471 inhabitants and $14,252,879 in personal property ($71 per

5. A Rich and Growing City

capita). The interior and middle-island wards were the Fifteenth, Sixteenth, Seventeenth, Eighteenth and Twenty-First with 180,840 people and $60,602,900 in personal property ($335). If the personal property of the First Ward (where over one-third of all personal property in the city was located, since it contained the headquarters of most of the city's corporations) is omitted from the total of personal property in New York, the percentage of total personal held in these two sets of wards was, respectively, 15 percent and 54 percent. William H. Boyd, *New York City Tax-Book*. State *Census* (1855), p. 8.

38. Bristed, *Upper Ten*, p. 17. *Weekly Journal of Commerce*, June 17, 1849.

39. Henry C. Brown, *Fifth Avenue: Old and New*, pp. 36, 51. Mary Booth, *History of the City of New York*, pp. 786–88. [Columbia University], *A History of Columbia University*, p. 130. Stokes, *Iconography*, 5, 1865–66. *Trib.*, March 7, May 5, June 11, 1855.

40. E.P., Aug. 14, 1850; Dec. 23, 1852.

41. Advertisement of A. J. Bleecker, who said that the nearby Harlem Railroad made the area convenient "for persons doing business down town, or for the working man or mechanic." Bleecker sold one group of lots for $135 each, 75 percent of which could be on bond and mortgage for five years at 6 percent. *E.P.*, May 17, 21, 1852.

42. Citizens Association, *Public Health*, pp. 325–30, 346. In 1855, one resident of Yorkville said that the majority of the population there "is made up from the middle class. . . . We have a large sprinkling of builders, mastermasons, carpenters, etc.: we have merchants and brokers, who do business 'down-town'; printers, book-binders, bookkeepers, clerks, journey-men of every trade whose daily work is performed 'down-town' have their abodes here." *Trib.*, March 10, 1855.

43. Kendall, *Growth*, pp. 23–25.

44. Citizens Association, *Public Health*, pp. 118–24.

46. Halliday, *Lost and Found*, p. 196.

46. Citizens Association, *Public Health*, p. 220. See also pp. 275–76.

47. Thompson, *Ruggles*, pp. 63–64. Stokes, *Iconography*, 3, 702–5. *Literary World*, 8(1851), 32. Charles King said that Ruggles' heavy financial loses during the depression, 1837–43, prevented him from carrying through a plan to develop all his properties around Union Square and Gramercy Park "along one line." King, *Progress*, p. 65.

48. Bristed, *Upper Ten*, p. 17.

49. *Trib.*, May 30, 1845. *E.P.*, Jan. 14, 1846. Hone, *Diary*, pp. 855, 894. Strong, *Diary*, 1, 302. *Valentine's Manual for 1916–17*, 16, 87–89. Brown, *Fifth Avenue*, pp. 27, 36, 58. "Clinton," *The Value of Real Estate in the City of New York*, p. 3.

50. Scoville, *Merchants*, 1, 133–34. *Trib.*, July 26, 1855.

51. *Trib.*, Sept. 6, 1848.

52. *Hunt's*, 28(1853), 593–94. *Citizen*, Aug. 26, 1854. In 1855, one realtor offered 23 "first-class houses with all the modern improvements" for sale at prices ranging from $6500 for a house on 45th Street to one for $17,000 on E. 31st Street. *Trib.*, Jan. 20, March 10, 1855.

53. *Putnam's*, 3(1854), 233, 244–45. Bristed, *Upper Ten*, pp. 42–43.

54. *Harper's Weekly*, 1(1857), 810. *Democratic Review*, 31(1852), 254.

55. A southern visitor in the 1850s described his walk down the avenues: "Look to the right or left, and you see row after row of three or four story tenements—all faced with omnipresent brown stone, and characterized by an undeviating style of steps leading from the sidewalks to the front door. . . . It is wearisome to behold such and endless succession of houses so closely resembling each other." Quoted in Stokes, *Iconography*, 5, 1811.

5. A RICH AND GROWING CITY

56. *Putnam's*, 3(1854), 22. By 1858, the built-up area had moved north as far as 42nd Street on the East Side (Yorkville was still a distinct community) and to nearly 50th Street on the West Side, while on Fifth Avenue it had moved up to 40th Street. Adams, *Population*, p. 53. Hunt's predicted that in 1878 New York's population would be 1.3 million "which will involve the occupation of Manhattan Island to Harlem River." 19(1848), 632. The actual population in 1880 was 1,206,000.

57. Henry P. Tappan, *The Growth of Cities* (N.Y., 1855), pp. 15, 33.

58. *Ibid.*, pp. 29–32.

59. *Ibid.*, pp. 29–36.

Chapter 6: Manhattan Survival Machine

1. Nelson A. Blake, *Water for the Cities*, pp. 164–70. Hone, *Diary*, p. 625. Stokes, *Iconography*, 3, 638.

2. *Trib.*, June 22, 1842. Hone, *Diary*, pp. 678, 740.

3. Allen, *Memoirs*, pp. 166–67. Cozzens, *Geological History*, pp. 38–39.

4. *Hunt's*, 12(1845), 65. Curry, *New-York*, p. 231.

5. *Independent*, Feb. 14, 1849. B. of Ald., *Docs.*, 12(1845–46), 129.

6. Chester Jones, *The Economic History of the Anthracite-Tidewater Canals*, pp. 98–99, 113–15, 122, 141. Chamber of Commerce, *Report* (1858), 83. The Delaware and Hudson Canal, of which Philip Hone had long been a director, expanded its capacity from about 20,000 tons in the early 1840s to more than a million tons by 1855. Jim Shaughnessy, *Delaware & Hudson*, pp. 3, 6–9, 17.

7. James M. Fitch, *American Building*, *1*, 116–7. By 1850, of 15,007 street lamps in the city, 8144 were gas lights, most of them located either downtown or in the better residential neighborhoods. *Trib.*, Feb. 10, 1853. *Times*, Oct. 1, 1856.

8. Fitch, *Building*, pp. 110–11. *Democratic Review*, 33(1853–54), 261–62.

9. John Duffy, *A History of Public Health in New York City*, p. 398. Stokes, *Iconography*, 5, 1777, 1785. *Trib.*, Aug. 7, Sept. 29, 1842. *Independent*, Feb. 15, 1849. B. of Ald., *Docs.*, 15(1848–49), 362. Joel Ross, *What I Saw In New York*, p. 41.

10. Marcuse, *New York*, p. 59. In 1848 citizens complained that the gashouse located in the Canal Street area was a public nuisance. *Trib.*, Sept. 5, 1848.

11. Fitz-Hugh Ludlow estimated that in 1863 New York consumed 1,908,671 barrels of flour, 2,276,257 bushels of wheat, 8,540,490 bushels of corn and 209,279 barrels of pork. *Atlantic Monthly*, 15(1865), 85. *Hunt's*, 6(1841), 185.

12. *Eighth Census* (1860): *Miscellaneous*, p. 326. Meyer, *Transportation*, p. 326. *Hunt's*, 27(1852), 249. B. of Ald., *Docs.*, 7(1840–41), 139. The *Tribune* said, in support of aid for the Erie Railroad, that "there is no northern city upon the sea-board, the markets of which are so poorly supplied and wherein the prices are higher than our own." April 2, 1844. In 1850, it was estimated that, in comparison with wagons, railroads increased the area of supply nine times or more. *Democratic Review*, 17(1850), 151.

13. Paul Henlein, *Cattle Kingdom in the Ohio Valley*, pp. 65, 116–18. *Trib.*, May 24, 1848. *Eighth Census* (1860): *Agriculture*, p. cxxxi.

14. *E.P.*, Dec. 27, 1853. *Hunt's*, 30(1854), 752; 33(1855), 117; 35(1856), 505. *Trib.*,

6. Manhattan Survival Machine

Dec. 25, 1854; May 24, 1855. Solon Robinson, *Selected Writings*, 2, 318. *Atlantic Monthly*, 15(1865), 83.

15. *Citizen*, Nov. 4, 1854. In 1855, New York State granted legal recognition to property rights in sea-bottom land used for raising oysters. Ralph H. Gabriel, *The Evolution of Long Island*, p. 97. *Trib.*, May 22, 1855. *Times*, Oct. 27, 1854.

16. The value of market-garden produce in New York, Kings, Queens, Westchester, Richmond, Bergen, Essex, Hudson and Passaic counties increased from a total of $320,000 in 1840 to $2,620,000 in 1860. *Sixth Census (1840): Compendium*, pp. 131–32. *Eighth Census (1860): Agriculture*, pp. 98–99.

17. Andrew Jackson Downing, *Rural Essays*, pp. 78, 388. Danhof, *Agriculture*, pp. 21, 30–31, 35, 44–45. Ulysses P. Hedrick, *A History of Horticulture in America to* 1860, pp. 230, 239–41. John T. Cunningham, *Garden State*, pp. 133–34 and *This is New Jersey*, pp. 84–85. Herbert G. Schmidt, *Agriculture in New Jersey*, pp. 184–85.

18. *Hunt's*, 28(1853), 684–85, 689. *E.P.*, Nov. 17, 1852. Ellis, *Landlords and Farmers*, pp. 206–8. Joel E. Ross, a physician, wrote in 1851 that impure milk was "fed to children by thousands and millions of quarts every season, and diarrhea, cholera morbus, cholera infantum, scrofula . . . etc. follow in its train." *What I Saw*, p. 244.

19. *Hunt's*, 28(1853), 685–88. North-Western Dispensary, *Second Annual Report* (N.Y., 1854), p. 9. *E.P.*, Sept. 27, 1852.

20. *Ibid.*, Aug. 31, Sept. 6, Oct. 19, 1852. *Hunt's*, 28(1853), 684. Ross, *What I Saw*, p. 244.

21. Duffy, *Public Health*, pp. 428–35. Hunt's, 28(1853), 689. *E.P.*, Sept. 6, 27, Oct. 19, Nov. 9, 1852; March 30, 1853. *Trib.*, March 31, 1853.

22. *Literary World*, 7(1850), 115–16. Stokes, *Iconography*, 3, 958–59.

23. DeVoe, *Market Book*, pp. 441–49. *Subterranean*, July 18, 1846. Robinson, *Writings*, 2, 505. Cornelius Mathews, *Big Abel and the Little Manhattan*, p. 33.

24. Duffy, *Public Health*, p. 420. DeVoe, *Market Book*, pp. 532–33, 536. In 1845, the *Tribune* said that formerly butcher stalls in the markets were auctioned off for from $500 to $1,000 each, with yearly rents of $50 to $150. Nov. 8, 1845. By law, the deputy clerks of the markets were to "examine all articles . . . which they may expect to be unwholesome, stale, disease, etc.," and "to exclude all persons engaged in combinations to raise the price of provisions." B. of Ald., *Docs.*, (1843), 747–48.

25. DeVoe, *Market Book*, pp. 430–34, 472–73, 476–78, 486. *Trib.*, Sept. 6, 1848. *E.P.*, April 12, 1853.

26. Robinson, *Writings*, 2, 444–46, 504–5. *Harbinger*, 7(1848), 14. *E.P.*, Aug. 12, 1852. DeVoe, *Market Book*, pp. 442–45, 512–15.

27. *Ibid.*, pp. 364, 563, 576, 580. Thomas DeVoe himself was a butcher at Jefferson Market along with five other DeVoes. In 1850, the *Evening Post* noted that Clinton Market, a mile north of Washington Market, "has received many additions, undergone several alterations and presents, in its cleanly appearance, a strong contrast to the delapidated and filthy condition of Washington Market and the surrounding localities." *E.P.*, Aug. 5, 1850.

28. Robinson, *Writings*, 2, 507. DeVoe, *Market Book*, p. 366.

29. DeVoe, *Ibid.*, pp. 532–33, 536–37. Duffy, *Public Health*, p. 424. This committee, one member of which was Peter Cooper, also reported against a repeal of the market laws "as there are many advantages obtained by having several stalls together, both as to the variety furnished, and the security from imposition, by the competition between butchers, and the contrast between their meats." *E.P.*, Feb. 24, 1841.

6. MANHATTAN SURVIVAL MACHINE

30. *Trib.*, May 9, 1849. *E.P.*, April 12, 1853. DeVoe, *Market Book*, p. 369. Stokes, *Iconography*, 3, 958–99. Board of Assistant Aldermen, *Docs.*, (1849), 18–19. In 1851, some 370 marketmen opposed a proposal to completely rebuild Washington Market on the grounds that it would disrupt their business and also would be a useless expense, "as it is evident that in a very few years a market further up town will be required by the wants of our citizens . . . and at which period the proposed market would be deserted." *Ibid.* (1851), pp. 344–45.

31. The Democratic *Evening Post* condemned the market butchers for charging "monopoly prices" (Dec. 9, 1840), while the Whig *Tribune* declared: "It is a well-known fact that our citizens generally pay about twice as much for their fruits and vegetables" as a result of forestalling at the markets (July 8, 1843).

32. DeVoe, *Market Book*, pp. 454, 514, 570. Duffy, *Public Health*, pp. 422–24. *E.P.*, Jan. 11, 1841. Mayor Westervelt said that "in a city like New York, the residents of every section should have equal accommodations from public markets," but added the significant qualification, "if any are established or maintained." *Ibid.*, Jan. 3, 1853.

33. *Ibid.*, May 16, 1854. B. of Ald., *Docs.*, 21(1854), 647–50, 668–69. Mayor Kingsland declared that unless the markets could be made a source of revenue they should be sold. *E.P.*, Jan. 5, 1852.

34. *E.P.*, March 23, Sept. 11, 1854. Duffy, *Public Health*, pp. 425–26. Junius H. Browne, *The Great Metropolis* p. 408.

35. B. of Ald., *Docs.*, 13(1846–47), 82–83. *E.P.*, Sept. 9, 1852; Feb. 3, 1854.

36. Edward Wegmann, *The Water Supply of the City of New York* (N.Y., 1896), 64. *Hunt's*, 25(1851), 709. *E.P.*, July 20, 1852. B. of Ald., *Docs.*, 17(1850), 33–34. King, *Progress*, p. 55. New Yorkers were taxed for water on the basis of the size of the building served; in 1850, the tax was $8.00 for an ordinary two-story house. Ross, *What I Saw*, p. 41.

37. Solon Robinson, *How to Live* (N.Y., 1874), pp. 299–300, 340.

38. *Francis's New Guide to the Cities of New York and Brooklyn* (N.Y., 1857), p. 124.

39. Duffy, *Public Health*, pp. 376–78, 385.

40. Downing, *Rural Essays*, pp. 391, 394–95.

41. *Trib.*, March 9, 1853; Jan. 18, March 10, 21, 1855.

42. B. of Ald., *Docs.*, 7(1840–41), 117. *Trib.*, June 20, 1942. Hedrick, *Agriculture*, p. 348. Schmidt, *Agriculture*, p. 132.

43. Poe, *Doings of Gotham*, p. 31. *E.P.*, April 6, 1852; April 11, 1854. Actually, the city did receive some revenue from the sale of manure ($45,000 in 1845, for instance), but revenues declined in approximate ratio with the growth in the size of the manure heaps in the streets; in 1857, they fell to nothing. Hardenbrook, *Financial New York*, pp. 336, 342. Regarding nightsoil, Dr. John H. Griscom said in 1842: "The raw material for the manufacture of Poudrette is found only in large cities in sufficient abundance to justify the manufacture; and in this, the largest city of this hemisphere, it is almost wholly wasted. Had all the Poudrette that has been heedlessly cast to the fishes from our wharves been distributed over the neighboring farms, a double crop would long ago have been gathered from the already fertile earth." B. of Ald. *Docs.*, 8(1841–42), 168.

44. Duffy, *Public Health*, pp. 405–11. King, *Progress*, p. 56. *American Repertory*, 1(1840), 413–14. *New York Mirror*, Sept. 17, Dec. 24, 1842. *Hunt's*, 12(1845), 53–65. B. of A., *Docs.*, 15(1848–49), 897.

45. *Ibid.*, 8(1841–42), 163–67.

6. MANHATTAN SURVIVAL MACHINE

46. *Ibid.*, 11(1844–45), 128, 132, 221, 676–77. *Trib.*, Dec. 31, 1844. *Hunt's*, 25(1851), 710.

47. Duffy, *Public Health*, pp. 415–16. Anne S. Loop, *History and Development of Sewage Treatment in New York City* (N.Y., 1964), 14. *E.P.*, Aug. 19, 1851. B. of Ald., *Docs.*, 23(1856–57), 56. In 1849, the state created the Croton Aqueduct Department and gave it responsibility for the sewage system. *Ibid.*, 15(1848–49), 380–81, 1052–53.

48. AICP, *Report* (1859), p. 50. Duffy, *Public Health*, pp. 411, 415. Edgar W. Martin, *The Standard of Living in 1860*, p. 112. The *Tribune* complained that "in all the old streets, where sewers have been put down at such trouble and expense, we do not believe one house in ten is connected with the sewers." Nov. 29, 1854.

49. *E.P.*, Sept. 3, 1847. Citizens Association, *Public Health*, pp. 145–46.

50. *Ibid.*, p. 145. *E.P.*, Aug. 14, 1852. AICP, *Report* (1859), pp. 52–53. Loop, *Sewage Treatment*, p. 17.

51. Strong, *Diary*, 2, 178. *E.P.*, Aug. 14, 1846; July 15, 29, 1854. *Independent*, May 30, 1850. Duffy, *Public Health*, pp. 444–46, 588.

52. *Weekly Journal of Commerce*, Nov. 12, 1857. City Inspector, *Annual Report* (1853), pp. 209–10; (1854), pp. 206–7; (1856), pp. 139. Duffy, *Public Health*, pp. 434–36, 578–79. *Hunt's*, 27 (1852), 129.

53. The City Inspector in 1853 estimated the death rate for every state and federal census year between 1805 and 1850. *Annual Report* (1852), pp. 209–10. The AICP supplied rates for 1840, 1845, 1850, 1855 and 1857. *Report* (1859), p. 26. Duffy, *Public Health*, pp. 575–77. The *Scientific American* reported an estimate of one death per 24 persons in 1852. 8(1852–53), 298. The AICP estimated that in 1857 the death rate was 1 per 27.17 persons in New York; 1 per 40 in London; 1 per 35.7 in Paris; 1 per 36.2 in Philadelphia, and 1 per 40 in Boston. *Report* (1859), p. 26. Also, see F. C. Ewer, *Public Health of the City of New York*, pp. 16–17. Martin, *Standard of Living*, p. 246. *Hunt's* 30(1854), 529; 32(1855), 259. The estimated death rate for the United States in 1859–60 was 1 per 79; for New York State, it was 1 per 82. *Eighth Census (1860): Mortality*, pp. xli, 280, 522. In 1850, the City Inspector estimated, in support of his contention that New York was actually a healthy city, that over the previous ten years the death rate was 1 per 36 in New York and 1 per 21 in the major European cities. B. of Ald., *Docs.*, 18(1851–52), 468. Adna F. Weber later estimated that in 1856–65 there were 32.19 deaths per 1,000 (1 per 31) in New York City; in 1886–95, there were 25.18 per 1,000 (1 per 39.6). *The Growth of Cities in the Nineteenth Century*, p. 356.

54. City Inspector, *Annual Report* (1856), p. 5. In 1854, 17,979 births and 28,568 deaths were recorded; probably, however, many births were not reported. *Ibid.*, (1854). *E.P.*, Aug. 25, 1853. Rosenwaike, *Population*, pp. 37–38. Duffy, *Public Health*, pp. 315, 577.

55. James J. Walsh, *History of Medicine in New York*, 1, 250–51. John H. Griscom, *The Sanitary Condition of the Laboring Population of New York*, pp. 12–13, 22–23, 39.

56. Duffy, *Public Health*, pp. 304–5, 451–58, 472, 507–10. John W. Francis, *New York during the Last Half Century*, pp. 195n–196n. In a complaint that New York had too many doctors, the American Medical Association estimated that the city had some 800 physicians, excluding quacks, and concluded that there was one physician for every 375 New Yorkers, after deducting the number given free treatment at dispensaries and hospitals, but it used the population in 1845 to arrive at this ratio. *Literary World*, 6(1850), 202. Dispensary services included diagnosis, prescriptions, and vaccinations, generally at the dispensary but also at the patient's home. By 1853, there were

6. MANHATTAN SURVIVAL MACHINE

four dispensaries: The New York at Centre and Franklin streets, the Northern at Waverly Place and Christopher Street, the Eastern at Ludlow Street and Essex Market Place, and the DeMilt, established by the AICP in 1851 to meet the needs of the uptown poor, at Second Avenue and 23rd Street. In 1854, the New York Dispensary for Women and Children was opened on the East Side, with Dr. Elizabeth Blackwell as attending physician. By 1871, the DeMilt Dispensary alone had treated 464,596 patients. Undoubtedly, treatment was limited if only by a shortage of funds. In 1855, Dr. Franklin Tuthill estimated that the average cost per patient for dispensary services was 16½¢, "a sum for which one could not get even a second-class doctor to look at his tongue." Curry, *New-York*, p. 247. Richmond, *New York*, p. 521. *E.P.*, April 24, 1852; April 1, 5, 1853. *Trib.*, March 2, 1855.

57. Thomas K. Downing, a City Inspector in the early 1850s, gave particular emphasis to immigration as the source of the high death rate. He also argued that the many transients in the city, some of whom had been attracted by "the celebrity of our medical and surgical institutions," contributed to an inflated death rate. Although neither Downing nor his successor, George W. Morton, ignored the need for improved sanitation, they took the position that New York actually was no more unhealthy than other cities or rural areas, that it was, in the words of Morton, "one of the healthiest cities in the world." City Inspector, *Annual Report* (1852), pp. 195–96, 202; (1853), pp. 201–2, 215; (1854), p. 221; (1856), pp. 188, 195. In 1850, City Inspector A. W. White argued that the migration of many of New York's healthiest and most affluent citizens to suburbs also distorted the meaning of the death rate. Rosenwaike, *Population*, p. 37.

Such arguments had their point. Defective sanitation was largely responsible for the high (by modern standards) mortality rate in New York and elsewhere in the nineteenth century, but the city's *exceptionally* high rate probably resulted less from its undoubted filth and congestion than from its position as the nation's chief point of entry. Not only were mortality statistics distorted by the presence of large numbers of transients in New York but the port city was unusually susceptible to diseases of foreign origin. The fact that many immigrants settled in the city may not have significantly affected the death rate, since an unusually high percentage of them were in their prime (between 15 and 40). The rate, however, was increased substantially by the disproportionate number of deaths among their children, the result of their parents' poverty and difficulty in adjusting to New York's crowded situation. In 1857, D. Meredith Reese, M.D., estimated that 40 percent of all deaths in the city over the previous 50 years were of children under five years of age *Weekly Journal of Commerce*, Nov. 12, 1857); in the previous two years, 1855–56, near the end of a decade of rising immigration, children under five accounted for 61 percent of all deaths (*Ibid.*, Jan. 8, 1857). In 1861, some 88 percent of deaths among children were the sons and daughters of the foreign born (Duffy, *Public Health*, p. 536).

58. Duffy, *Public Health*, p. 447–58. Charles Rosenberg notes that there was widespread disagreement nationally regarding the causes of cholera. Charles E. Rosenberg, *The Cholera Years* (Chicago: University of Chicago Press, 1962), 164n, 171.

59. John H. Griscom, *Sanitary Legislation, Past and Future*, pp. 9–10. Griscom excluded from his figure the approximately 50,000 victims of consumption during this period, many of whom, he claimed, could have been saved by better sanitation. In 1857, Dr. John W. Francis blamed improper sanitation for 25 to 30 percent of deaths. Francis, *New York*, p. 197.

60. Griscom, *Sanitary Legislation*, pp. 4, 9, 18–20 and *Sanitary Condition*, p. 5. Charles

7. THE USE OF URBAN SPACE

E. and Caroll S. Rosenberg, "Pietism and the Origins of the American Public Health Movement . . . ," pp. 22–24.

Chapter 7: The Use of Urban Space

1. Duffy, *Public Health*, pp. 297–302, 309–19, 496–97.
2. *Ibid.*, p. 302. Rosenberg, *Pietism*, p. 19–20.
3. Duffy, *Public Health*, pp. 303–4. *Trib.*, March 8, 1843.
4. Duffy, *Public Health*, p. 306. Griscom, *Sanitary Condition*, pp. 2–3. Initially, Griscom submitted his proposal to the Common Council, but a committee of that body advised that "they do not think it proper at this time, to go into such a measure." Griscom, *Ibid.*, preface. The sneer was provoked by a petition from New York physicians for the removal of Eli Leavett as City Inspector on the grounds that he was ignorant of medical science. Whatever his merits, Leavett submitted a report which, like Griscom's, criticized the existing housing situation. *Trib.*, July 24, 1844; May 13, 1845. Also see James Ford, et al., *Slums and Housing*, 1, 108–11.
5. Griscom, *Sanitary Condition*, pp. 1, 8, 11–13. Rosenberg, *Pietism*, p. 24.
6. Griscom, *Sanitary Condition*, pp. ;6, 12–13. "Men's passions are kept in check," said Griscom, "by the restrictions of the society by which they live. Remove these checks—take from the individuals the moral atmosphere in which they move, and their evil passions will rise." *Ibid.*, p. 25.
7. *Ibid.*, pp. 2, 7, 22–23, 43–50. Rosenberg, *Pietism*, p. 22.
8. Griscom, *Sanitary Condition*, p. 26.
9. *Ibid.*, p. 48. Ford, *Slums and Housing*, 1, 103. *Trib.*, March 3, 1843. City Inspector Eli Leavett repeated this hope in 1845 but urged philanthropists to build "many hundreds of dwellings" for one or two families. *Trib.*, May 13, 1845.
10. AICP, *Report* (1847), pp. 22–24. Ford, *Slums and Housing*, 1, 112–13; 2, 879. *Trib.*, Feb. 1, 1849.
11. Ford, *Slums and Housing*, 1, 127. *Trib.*, Feb. 15, 1853. As early as 1847, the *Democratic Review* reported that several "men who have for years devoted their leisure moments to benevolent purposes" planned to build four-story tenements, each of which were to have eight apartments of three rooms with "the necessary conveniences of fire and water"; rents were to be "no higher than the prices paid for the damp, unwholesome hovels the lower class at present inhabit." 20(1847), 281.
12. AICP, *Report* (1853), pp. 26–27.
13. Stokes, *Iconography*, 5, 1856–60. Ford, *Slums and Housing*, 2, 878. The original tenents were black families, selected because black people usually had the worst accommodations. AICP, *Report* (1856), pp. 46–47. Roy Lubove, "The New York Association for Improving the Condition of the Poor: The Formative Years," *New York Historical Society Quarterly*, 43 (1959), 322.
14. Ford, *Slums and Housing*, 1, 103. *Independent*, Feb. 7, 1850.
15. City Inspectors frequently complained about their lack of authority to force health improvements in existing housing. The Metropolitan Police Act of 1857 provided for sanitary police with power to compel the cleansing of filthy tenements,

but it was only with the creation of the Metropolitan Health Commission in 1866 that a sustained effort began to improve health conditions. Although as early as 1846, the *Tribune* had advocated legislation to govern the construction of new housing to assure adequate light and air, it was not until after the Civil War that the state enacted its first (inadequate) housing law. Ford, *Slums and Housing*, 1, 127–41. Duffy, *Public Health*, p. 529. *Trib.*, April 30, 1846; Aug. 1, 1849. AICP, *Report* (1853), p. 27.

16. *Trib.*, Feb. 7, 1853.

17. AICP, *Report of the Committee on the Sanitary Condition of the Laboring Classes* (N.Y., 1853), pp. 9–13.

18. Ford, *Slums and Housing*, 1, 25, 131–34.

19. Ernst, *Immigrant Life*, 192–93. *Hunt's*, 27(1852), 412–14. *Independent*, May 9, 1850.

20. Citizens Association, *Public Health*, pp. 43–64, 73–82. In 1850, there were an estimated 2626 dwellings in the two wards; in 1860, there were 2403. *Hunt's*, 27(1852), 414. *Eighth Census (1860): Mortality*, p. 339.

21. *Trib.*, July 13, 1852. *E.P.*, Aug. 9, 1853. Ernst, *Immigrant Life*, 197. As early as 1845, the City Inspector reported: "The prevailing practice which is becoming every year, more general, of building houses for the poorer classes of our population so as to cover the whole or nearly the whole area of ground, and thus crowding a large number of families together in a space which is not sufficient for one, doubtless has a tendency to increase the mortality of the city." B. of Ald., *Docs.*, 11(1844–45), 580.

22. *Literary World*, 1(1847), 247. State Census (1855), p. 8.

23. *Hunt's*, 27(1852), 412; 33(1855), 378. Citizens Association, *Public Health*, pp. 74–75, 132. Halliday, *Lost and Found* pp. 193–96.

24. *Ibid.*, p. 192. *Trib.*, Feb. 10, 1853.

25. *Harbinger*, 6(1847–48), 148. *Democratic Review*, 31(1852), 254; 33(1853–54), 22–24. *Trib.*, Aug. 1, 1853. *Times*, Nov. 9, 1853. "Clinton," *Real Estate*, pp. 4–6.

26. *Trib.*, Feb. 17, 18, 24, 1848. *Harbinger*, 6(1847–48), 142; 8(1848), 28. Ernst, *Immigrant Life*, p. 50.

27. *Harbinger*, 6(1847–48), 148, 156. *Trib.*, May 4, 15, 16, 23, July 17, 1848; May 21, June 12, 1849.

28. *Ibid.*, Feb. 14, 17, March 3, 1852. *Trow's New York City Directory* (1852–53), pp. 19–22.

29. *Hunt* 26(1852), 594; 27(1852), 215. "Report of the Special Committee on Building Associations in the City of New York," New York State Assembly, *Documents*, 79th sess. (1856), pp. 1–3, 9. *Trow's Directory* (1856–57) listed 46 building associations (pp. 24–25).

30. *Harbinger*, 6(1847–48), 148. *Democratic Review*, 31(1852), 254. *Trib.*, Feb. 10, March 24, Aug. 1, 1853.

31. Christopher Tunnard, *The City of Man*, pp. 115–21. It was perhaps with the Astors in mind that the Rev. Peter Stryker in 1866 declared that the "tenant houses . . . are a standing reproach against our rich men who ought for the sake of humanity, to be using their surplus funds in erecting cheap and comfortable residence for the poor." Lucy Kavaler, *The Astors*, pp. 63–64. In 1867, James Parton concluded a generally favorable essay on the Astors by expressing the hope that either William B. Astor or his heirs would devote part of their vast wealth to building a "new order of tenement houses" that would provide decent accommodations for the working classes. James Parton, *Famous Americans of Recent Times*, p. 473.

32. Walt Whitman, *New York Dissected*, pp. 92–101. Everard M. Upjohn, *Richard*

7. THE USE OF URBAN SPACE

Upjohn: Architect and Churchmen, p. 164. See also, Allan Nevins, *The Evening Post*, p. 367.

33. *Citizen*, Aug. 26, 1854. Undoubtedly, interest in housing construction was dampened by the apparently widespread belief that high land values and high taxes made housing a poor investment, unless it were constructed for the well-to-do. The *Democratic Review*, for instance, said that "the price of lots has become so enormous that no man can afford to erect a house on one," unless it rented for $1500 or more a year. 33(1853–54), 24. Two years later, "Z," in a public letter defending high rents, charged that city tax practices discriminated against real estate and claimed that the average return on rental property over the previous thirty years was only 5 percent; he complained that the city assessed lands at their speculative rather than at their much lower real values. *Trib.*, March 1, 1855. In 1848, one landlord decided not to buy more property, because "the taxes in the city are so enormous that a man is actually better off by getting 4 percent in stocks than 7 or 8 percent on property." D. Binsse to F. H. Osborn, Dec. 29, 1848, Osborn Papers, New York Public Library.

34. *Hunt's*, 25(1851), 136. *Independent*, Jan. 17, 1850.

35. *Independent*, Oct. 17, 1850. *Hunt's*, 22(1850), 421. *Trib.*, Feb. 10, 1853.

36. *Trib.*, Feb. 21, 1853. *Hunt's*, 25(1851), 136; 33(1855), 378.

37. Hone, *Diary*, p. 919. Ross, *What I Saw*, p. 37. The average number of families per dwelling in the Eleventh Ward was the highest in the city in 1854, while the Seventeenth (which included some well-to-do areas) ranked sixth highest behind the Fourth, Sixth, First, and Twentieth. *Hunt's*, 33(1855), 378. AICP, *Report* (1859), pp. 37–39.

38. Hone, *Diary*, pp. 740–43. *Trib.*, April 1, 1842; July 21, 1845. *Weekly Journal of Commerce*, Jan. 30, 1840. Common Council, *Manual* (1848), 110.

39. *Hunt's* 35(1856), 290–301. In early 1840, investigators estimated that 54 of 105 fires "were occasioned by incendiarism." *E.P.*, Feb. 13, 1840. The frequent demands for fireproof construction in the lower city led the state in 1849 to enact a law requiring the use of fireproof materials in the wall of all buildings constructed south of 32nd Street, but this did not prevent builders from using inflammable materials within those walls. Costello, *Our Firemen*, p. 113. *Hunt's* 35(1856), 199.

40. *Trib.*, May 3, 1855. By rough estimate, the *number* of dwellings in the four business wards (First, Second, Third and Fourteenth) declined from 3800 in 1850 to 2800 in 1860. *Hunt's*, 27(1852), 414. *Eighth Census* (1860): *Mortality*, p. 339.

41. In contrast, London built 64,000 new houses for some 325,000 additional people and Baltimore 13,000 for 70,000. *Banker's Magazine*, 4(1849–50), 1034–35, 1038. *Hunt's*, 22(1850), 420. *Independent*, Dec. 20, 1849. *E.P.*, April 29, 1852. In 1846, the *Post* estimated that the number of dwelling houses "compared with the number of inhabitants, falls short of what it was four years ago, by twelve hundred." Stokes, *Iconography*, 5, 1797. Of course, the size as well as the number of dwelling-houses determined the actual amount of living space, but, in an age where five-story buildings were considered tall, only an intense crowding of people could explain how in the Fourteenth Ward 40 families could be housed on a 25 by 100 foot lot, while another 48 families could occupy a 50 by 75 foot lot. *Weekly Journal of Commerce*, Sept. 16, 1856.

42. *Subterranean*, Feb. 13, 1847. B. of Ald., *Docs.*, 23(1856), 29.

43. *Weekly Journal of Commerce*, June 14, 1849.

44. *Trib.*, Sep. 21, 1848. *Hunt's*, 25(1851), 706.

45. *New York Mirror*, May 15, 1841. *Knickerbocker Magazine*, 21(1843), 349; 27(1846), 177. *Harbinger*, 1(1845), 134.

7. THE USE OF URBAN SPACE

46. *Harper's Monthly*, 13(1856), 272–73.

47. William Bridges, *Map of the City of New-York and Island of Manhattan; with Explanatory Remarks and References* (N.Y., 1811), pp. 7, 24–30. Stokes, *Iconography*, 5, 1457. Kendall, *Growth*, pp. 35–42. Henry James, "A Review of Earlier Planning Efforts in New York and Its Environs," in Harold M. Lewis, *Physical Conditions and Public Services* (N.Y.: Regional Plan of New York, 1924), p. 68. Ford, *Slums and Housing*, 1, 259–60.

48. James, "Earlier Planning," 156, 161–62, 178.

49. *American Repertory*, 1(1840), 339–40, 412–16. Charles King, *Chamber of Commerce*, p. 108. *Hunt's*, 30(1854), 647. DeVoe, *Market Book*, p. 447.

50. Duffy, *Public Health*, pp. 380–86. When the Common Council received a petition against some cow stables in the Sixteenth Ward, the owners of the stables threatened "political vengence" if the Council acted on the petition. For years, the efforts to remove slaughterhouses from the lower city had encountered resistance from the city's many butchers (they claimed to be 1600 strong in 1850). As late as 1866, a health inspector complained that there were six large slaughterhouses in the Fourteenth Ward, the heart of the city, which threatened not only public health but also the business interests of Broadway and the Bowery. *Independent*, Jan. 10, 1850. *E.P.*, Sept. 2, 1850; Sept. 9, 1852. Citizens Association, *Public Health*, pp. 86–87.

51. *New York Mirror*, Nov. 7, 1840. The reduction in park acreage resulted largely from the abandonment of the 240-acre parade ground provided for in the original plan.

52. Black, *Municipal Ownership*, pp. 53, 62, 81, and map xvi, appendix. John W. Reps. "Public Land, Urban Development, and the American Planning Tradition," in Marion Clawson, ed., *Modernizing Urban Land Policy*, pp. 36–39. In 1846, Mayor Mickle did urge the Common Council to reserve such lands as would be required for public health in the future, but he emphasized the need for a "speedy disposition of the city property, that private enterprise by its improvement may make it contribute largely on the subject of annual taxation." B. of Ald., *Docs.*, 13(1846–47), 9.

53. *Banker's Magazine*, 4(1849–50), 1038. Curry, *New-York*, pp. 217–20.

54. *Trib.*, Nov. 22, Dec. 16, 1848. *Literary World*, 3(1848), 814. Board of Assistant Aldermen, *Docs.* (1848), 119–23.

55. *E.P.*, Aug. 5, 1851; July 17, 1852; May 3, 1853; April 15, 1854. *Weekly Journal of Commerce*, June 7, 1849. Smith, *Sunshine and Shadow*, p. 78.

56. *Artist* (1843), p. 53. *E.P.*, Oct. 12, 1852; Nov. 29, 1854.

57. *E.P.*, June 17, Nov. 27, 1852. The *Tribune*, in advocating the planting of trees in developing uptown areas, said that "for three or four miles along Third avenue there is nothing but mortar, bricks and blasted rocks, while it is quite bare of trees or shadow." July 3, 1845.

57. *New York Mirror*, July 23, 1842. *Knickerbocker Magzine*, 28(1846), 253. *Democratic Review*, 22(1848), 476. B. of Ald., *Docs.*, 17(1850–51), 13.

59. *Trib.*, May 3, 1855 (also see note 78). *Literary World*, 1(1847), 271.

60. Ford, *Slums and Housing*, 1, 128. The *Express* article was quoted in the *Literary World*, 5(1849), 13.

61. Lossing, *New York*, 2, 607. Frederick Law Olmsted, *Walks and Talks of an American Farmer in England*, pp. 52–54, 225. George Bancroft said, regarding the necessity of public parks: "Think what will be the condition in the morals, the health, and the enjoyment of the public, where there shall be no spot set apart where you can look out upon the face of nature and be freed from being suffocated with dust." *E.P.*, Jan. 26,

7. THE USE OF URBAN SPACE

1853. New Yorkers were also influenced by the presence of Greenwood Cemetery in Brooklyn. Opened in 1842, this park for the dead and for the living of the metropolis covered more than 300 acres traversed by 15 miles of ways, described as winding "in every direction through valleys and along hill-sides, skirting sylvan lakes, and leading through miniature groves of ancient forest trees." Curry, *New-York*, pp. 298–99.

62. Nevins, *Evening Post*, 193–96. Stokes, *Iconography*, 5, 1785. Bryant argued that Jones' Wood was especially needed by the people of the East Side, who were too far removed to take advantage of the pleasure grounds at Hoboken, but he also predicted that the park would take the place of the Hoboken grounds as those grounds passed into "the occupation of individuals." *E.P.*, July 6, 1850; March 18, 1854.

63. *Trib.*, June 8, 1847. *E.P.*, July 6, 1850. Wilson, *Memorial History*, 6, 555.

64. Downing, *Rural Essays*, pp. 81, 141–43.

65. *Ibid.*, pp. 149–51. *Literary World*, 9(1851), 123-24.

66. *E.P.*, July 10, 1851. DeVoe, *Market Book*, p. 552. Smith, *Sunshine and Shadow*, pp. 359–60. B. of Ald., *Docs.*, 18(1851–52), 1466.

67. *Ibid.*, pp. 1468–73. Egbert L. Viele, "Topography of New-York and Its Park System," in Wilson, *Memorial History*, 4, 556–57. "Report of Select Committee . . . [on] Central Park," New York State Senate, *Documents* (1861), no. 18, 7–8.

68. Bristed, *Upper Ten*, 17. B. of Ald., *Docs.*, 18(1851–52), 1474–75. Charles Haswell, *Reminiscences of an Octogenarian*, p. 468. King, *Chamber of Commerce*, p. 137. Philip L. White, *The Beekmans of New York*, pp. 610–11. Nevins, *Evening Post*, p. 199.

69. *E.P.*, Sept. 20, 1853; Jan. 31, April 4, 1854. B. of Ald., *Docs.*, 18(1851–52), 1467.

70. Board of Councilmen, *Docs.* (1854), pp. 486–91. Durant, *Finances*, p. 100.

71. Frederick Law Olmsted, Jr. and Theodora Kimball, *Frederick Law Olmsted, Landscape Architect, 1822–1903*, p. 2, 30. Stokes, *Iconography*, 5, 1860–63. *Trib.*, March 27, 1855. B. of Ald., *Docs.*, (1856), 73. For a short but insightful discussion of Olmsted's thinking regarding parks and cities, see Thomas Bender, *Toward an Urban Vision*, pp. 162–81.

72. Olmsted and Kimball, *Olmsted*, 2, 37–49, 181. A sensitive and comprehensive study of Olmsted is Laura Wood Roper, *FLO: A Biography of Frederick Law Olmsted*. Also, Albert Fein, *Frederick Law Olmsted and the American Environmental Tradition*.

73. Kendall, *Growth*, pp. 34–39.

74. Olmsted and Kimball, *Olmsted*, 2, 43–47, 248–51. *Harper's Weekly*, 1(1857), 757. "Report of Select Committee . . . [on] Central Park" (1861), pp. 10–11, 39, 47–48. In 1866, an health inspector said that previously the central part of the island was an especially unhealthy spot: "Beautiful country-seats were deserted, and fever held entire control." But the Park, in combination with street development, had "changed the whole face of the country both in a sanitary and topographical point of view." Citizens Association, *Public Health*, p. 93.

75. *Report of Select Committee* (1861), pp. 17–19. Samuel B. Ruggles, *Memorial*, p. 12, and *Letters on Rapid Transit* (N.Y., 1875), pp. 11–12. Olmsted and Kimball, *Olmsted*, 2, 173, 270. Kendall, *Growth*, pp. 27–28. "Clinton," *Real Estate*, pp. 1–3.

76. *Harper's Weekly*, 1(1857), 757.

77. Roper, *FLO*, pp. 136–37. Olmsted and Kimball, *Olmsted*, pp. 56–61, 170–71, 269–70.

78. In 1854, Olmsted urged his longtime friend, Charles Loring Brace, to "get up parks, gardens, music, dancing schools, reunions which will be so attractive as to force

into contact the good and the bad, the gentlemanly and the rowdy. And the state ought to assist these sorts of things as it does schools and Agricultural societies." Roper, *FLO*, pp. 82, 93–94.

79. Junius H. Browne, *The Great Metropolis*, p. 122.

80. In 1859, George Templeton Strong predicted that by 1900 the Park would be "a lovely place. . . . Perhaps the city itself will perish before then, by growing too big to live under faulty institutions corruptly administered." *Diary*, 2, 454. Lewis Mumford saw the Park as a reaction to the increasing dirt, disorder, and misery of the muddled nineteenth-century industrial city. *Roots of Contemporary Architecture*, pp. 102–7.

Chapter 8: Escape to Suburbia

1. Lewis Masquerier, *Sociology: or the Reconstruction of Society, Government and Property*, pp. 17–18. The most intense and quotable anti-city rhetoric was generated by radical reformers who were dissatisfied with the general direction of American social development. The National Land Reformers and the Fourierists were especially prone to depict the city as the disturbing result of a defective society. For example, "Tocsin," writing in the Fourierist *Harbinger*, warned that the growth of cities evidenced "the ascendancy of a monied oligarchy and a commercial feudality—of the increase of crime, and the degradation of the laboring classes." 1(1845), 328.

2. *American Repertory*, 3(1841), 111. *Democratic Review*, 13(1843), 205; 23(1848), 30. *Hunt's*, 17(1847), 324. *Trib.*, Oct. 2, 1845. *Harbinger*, 1(1845), 328.

3. Walt Whitman, *Specimen Days*, p. 268.

4. Ross, *What I Saw*, p. 136. *Hunt's* 28(1853), 251. *Trib.*, April 19, 1849.

5. In 1840, the populations of New York City, the Northeast and the United States respectively were 312,710, 6,762,082 and 17,069,453. In 1860, they were 813,669, 10,594,268 and 31,443,321. *Fifteenth Census (1930), 1: Population*, 11, 746. In 1855, the *Tribune* said that the 1850s showed: "1st. A centralization of population in the City of New York. 2d. A fair but not remarkable increase in the other commercial towns [of New York State]. 3d. A considerable decrease of the agricultural population of the State." July 27, 1855. In 1850, there were 42,909 New Yorkers born in the United States outside of New York State; to these are added another 26,000 people who are assumed to have been born in the State but outside of the City (as was true of approximately 11 percent of native-born New Yorkers reported in the state census of 1855. Rosenwaike, *Population*, p. 42).

6. *Hunt's*, 17(1847), 324.

7. Ross, *What I Saw*, pp. 136, 163, 182. *Harper's Monthly*, 11(1855), 272. "C.D." in the *Trib.*, July 2, 1852; also, April 19, 1849.

8. Greeley, *Recollections*, pp. 147–50, and *Hints Toward Reform*, p. 317. Greeley's *Tribune* said in 1855 that there was little demand for farm labor during the winter months: "It is in part from a plethora of laborers dismissed in November by the farmers of Long Island, New-Jersey, etc., that our city is now suffering. If our farmers really fertilized the soil they cultivate instead of skinning it, they *would* employ a great deal more labor in winter than they do." Four days later, however, the *Tribune* published an article by Frederick Law Olmsted which concluded that there was a

8. ESCAPE TO SUBURBIA

strong demand for agricultural labor and urged the city to help subsidize the removal of the unemployed to rural areas. Jan. 25, 29, 1855.

9. Masquerier, *Sociology*, pp. 94–95. *The Radical*, 1(1841), 6–8, 21.

10. *Working Man's Advocate*, March 16, April 6, 1844. John R. Commons, et al., eds., *A Documentary History of American Industrial Society* (N.Y., 1910; repr., New York: Russell and Russell, 1958), 7, 293–301, 338.

11. The thinking of other land reformers can be found in: Masquerier, *Sociology*, pp. 13, 18, 95–97, 107, 123–26. Thomas A. Devyr, *The Odd Book of the Nineteenth Century*, pp. viii-ix, 39–41. *American Whig Review*, 15(1852), 551. Also, Mike Walsh's *Subterranean*, July 25, Dec. 19, 1846; March 27, 1847.

12. *Harper's Monthly*, 11(1855), 272.

13. Curry, *New-York*, pp. 337–38. In 1851, a minister called for the establishment of more churches in the suburbs to assure that the "families of the merchant and artisan" who settled there would not stray from Christianity. William Bannard, *A Discourse on the Moral Aspect and Destitution of the City of New York*, pp. 22–23.

14. *Putnam's*, 5(1855), 259–60. The reference may be to the Westcott Express Company which in 1857 employed some 40 men and 20 wagons to deliver parcels and baggage between New York and Brooklyn, Williamsburg, Jersey City, and Hoboken. A. L. Stimson, *History of the Express Companies*, pp. 197–99. Even earlier, James Fenimore Cooper had recognized the growing metropolitan unity of the areas of New York and New Jersey around New York Harbor. James F. Beard, Jr., "The First History of Greater New York. Unknown Portions of Fenimore Cooper's Last Work," *New-York Historical Society Quarterly*, 37(1953), 119–33.

15. Adams, *Population*, p. 68. Kings County grew from 47,613 in 1840 to 279,124; Hudson from 9483 to 62,717, and Essex from 30,789 to 98,877. Also, see Taylor, *Mass Transportation*, pp. 127–29.

16. Alexander, McLean, *History of Jersey City*, 1, 56. Cunningham, *New Jersey*, pp. 95–98. John E. Bebout and Ronald J. Grele, *Where Cities Meet: The Urbanization of New Jersey*, pp. 26–32. Daniel Van Winkle, *History of the Municipalities of Hudson County*, 1, 288–89. Curry, *New York*, p. 293.

17. *Eighth Census (1860): Manufacturers*, pp. 336–38. The largest concentration was in and around Newark. *Ibid.: Population*, pp. xxxi-xxxii. *E.P.*, July 31, 1851.

18. *Hunt's*, 34(1856), 382–83. Rosenwaike, *Population*, p. 31. Wilson, *Memorial History*, 4, 21–23. Curry, *New-York*, pp. 285–91. The *Evening Post* attributed the rapid growth of Williamsburgh "to the increased facilities presented for communication between the two cities within the last two or three years, and also the cheaper rates of houses." Dec. 23, 1852.

19. *Eighth Census (1860): Manufactures*, pp. 374, 384–85. *Democratic Review*, 23(1848), 278–79. Benedict, *City Travel*, p. 3. Edward Pessen, "A Social and Economic Portrait of Jacksonian Brooklyn," p. 332. *E.P.*, Nov. 17, 1854.

20. Henry I. Hazelton, *The Boroughs of Brooklyn and Queens*, 3 1186–87, 1194–1208. Pessen, *Jacksonian Brooklyn*, p. 332. Clay Lancaster, *New York's First Suburb: Old Brooklyn Heights*, pp. 122, 130, 161. *Brother Jonathan*, 4(1843), 499.

21. Henry Ward Beecher, *Star Papers: or Experiences of Art and Nature*, pp. 211–14.

22. In 1855, while 2556 natives of Kings County resided in New York, 30,101 natives of New York lived in Kings; there was a total net loss of 34,416 people to Kings, Queens, Westchester, and Richmond counties as of 1855. The net loss to New Jersey, as of 1860, was 25,631. Rosenwaike, *Population*, pp. 42, 65–66. In 1855, *Putnam's*

8. ESCAPE TO SUBURBIA

estimated that about 70,000 residents of surrounding suburbs were "exclusively a New York City population." 5(1855), 261.

23. Benedict, *City Travel*, p. 1. Wilson, *Memorial History*, 4, 23. Robinson, *Selected Writings*, 2, 437. Martin, *Standard of Living*, p. 315..

24. *E.P.*, March 30, June 9, 10, 11, 1840. Hone, *Diary*, p. 618. In 1856, a state assembly committee said that Staten Island was "one of the suburbs of the City of New York, a sort of outer ward . . . inhabited by merchants and others doing business in New York city." New York State Assembly, *Documents*, 80th sess. (1856–57), no. 64, p. 1.

25. In 1848, a new ferry company estimated that it would probably spend $150,000 to provide service to Williamsburgh. *Trib.*, Sept. 13, 1848; Jan. 17, 1849. The Union Ferry consolidation soon provoked cries of "extortion" and "monopoly" when the company raised the fare to Brooklyn from one cent to two. *E.P.*, Dec. 5, 1853; Aug. 4, 16, 1854. The Jersey City ferries were aligned with the railroads that terminated at that city. In 1857, the New Jersey Railroad built a new depot so designed as to permit passengers to walk between trains and ferries without being exposed to the weather. *Times*, July 24, 1857. *Trib.*, July 28, 1857.

26. *Ibid.*, Sept. 13, Nov. 24, 1848; April 26, 1849. Cunningham, *New Jersey*, p. 98. Henry R. Stiles, *History of the City of Brooklyn* (Brooklyn, 1870), 3, 564.

27. *E.P.*, March 23, 1853. *Trib.*, Feb. 19, 1853. Gabriel, *Long Island*, pp. 149–51. In 1846, there were also 12 stage lines between New York and outlying villages in Manhattan, Long Island and New Jersey. Stokes, *Iconography*, 3, 657.

28. Bebout and Grele. *Where Cities Meet*, p. 26. One seller of lots at Bergen Heights advertised that "a charter has been granted for a horse-car railroad from the ferry to Bergen Point." *Trib.*, May 7, 1855. *Dinsmore's Thirty Miles Around New York*, pp. 16–20.

29. Hazelton, *Brooklyn and Queens*, 1, 390–92. *Dinsmore's*, p. 22. Henry V. Poor, *History of the Railroads and Canals of the United States*, p. 254. In 1852, an advertiser of Jamaica lots claimed that the town was only 20 minutes from New York, but a resident of Jamaica, in complaining of the poor services provided by the railroad, said that it took an hour to get to Brooklyn, without counting in the ferry time to New York. *E.P.*, Nov. 28, 1852. *Day Book*, June 9, 1852.

30. Taylor, *Mass Transportation*, p. 141. Hungerford, *Men and Iron*, pp. 151–52. John H. Morrison, *History of American Steam Navigation*, p. 165. J. Thomas Scharf, *History of Westchester County*, 1, 482. *Literary World*, 9(1851), 231. F. H. Stow, *The Capitalist's Guide and Railway Annual*, pp. 111, 466.

31. *Trib.*, May 1, 1853. Greeley, *Recollections*, p. 296.

32. Taylor, *Mass Transportation*, p. 141. *Dinsmore's*, p. 12. "Wall Street" complained in 1849 that, because of poor service and high fares on the railroad, "from the beautiful and healthy village of White Plains there are only two or three commuters and until you reach Harlem they are few and far between." *Trib.*, Feb. 27, 1849.

33. Yearly commutation rates were $45 to Bronxville and White Plains and $50 to Kensico and Croton Falls. Hungerford, *Men and Iron*, p. 131. There were at least seven protest meetings of commuters in southern Westchester at Morrisania in the summer of 1854. One speaker, after urging his fellows to tear up the Harlem tracks if the company did not comply with their demands, complained that "they look upon us as a set of mechanics who have very little influence and little money." Another warned that if the fare increases were permitted, "our property will become lessened in value, and we shall find it very difficult to dispose of it under such circumstances." *E.P.*, July 10, 12, 14, 19, 24, Aug. 1, 1854. There were more such meetings early in

8. Escape to Suburbia

1855. *Trib.*, Jan. 6, 17, Feb. 8, 1855. There were also meetings in 1855 on Staten Island and in Hoboken against increases in ferry rates. The Hoboken meeting decided to try to place control of the ferries in the hands of the Hoboken city council. *Ibid.*, May 24, 1855.

34. In 1854, a commuter spokesman estimated that 3000 daily commuters used the Harlem line. *E.P.*, July 19, 1854. Total passenger traffic on the Harlem rose from approximately 1 million in 1840 to 3.5 million in 1859. Taylor, *Mass Transportation*, pp. 141–43. The population of the Town of West Farms (which included such places as Fordham, William's Bridge, Tremont, Mount Eden, and, before 1856, Morrisania) rose from 4436 in 1850 to 12,436 in 1855. Between 1850 and 1860, the population of all Westchester increased by nearly 75 percent. Scharf, *Westchester*, 1, 836. Rosenwaike, *Population*, p. 52.

35. *Putnam's* 5(1855), 260–61.

36. AICP, *Report* (1850), p. 21. Halliday, *Lost and Found*, p. 203. Benedict, *City Travel*, p. 3.

37. B of Ald., *Proceedings* (1842), 333. *Democratic Review*, 42(1858), 426–27. *E.P.*, April 8, 1854. Jacob Judd, "A Tale of Two Cities," pp. 24–28. In 1850, Mayor Woodhull charged that, because of New York's failure to facilitate travel to upper Manhattan, "thousands . . . have sought residences out of the city." B. of Ald., *Docs.*, 17(1850–51), 11. The flight of wealth to the suburbs encouraged agitation in the 1840s for the taxation of the property of nonresidences and also for the consolidation of Brooklyn with New York. Early in 1849, the Common Council passed a resolution to initiate discussions with Brooklyn for consolidation, a proposal which impressed the *Tribune's* city reporter as promising "amicable and permanent settlement of the troublesome ferry question, the supplying of Brooklyn with Croton water, and the payment by our New-York merchants who live there, of a fair proportion of the city taxes." Mayor Havemeyer vetoed this decision on the grounds that consolidation would create new problems of government and encourage the migration of New Yorkers to Brooklyn. In 1850, a consolidation plan was defeated in the State Senate. *Trib.*, Dec. 1, 1848; Jan. 30, 1849. Furer, *Havemeyer*, pp. 155–57. In 1854, encouraged by the consolidation of Philadelphia and its suburbs, a member of the Board of Councilmen proposed the annexation of Brooklyn, Williamsburgh, Bushwick, Newtown, and possibly other towns. Hopes for consolidation were further stimulated by proposals to join New York and Brooklyn either with a bridge over, or an iron tunnel under, the East River. *E.P.*, April 4, 1854. Stokes, *Iconography*, 5, 1867. These hopes, however, were not realized until the creation of Greater New York in 1898.

38. *Trib.*, June 11, 1849. *E.P.*, March 1, 1852. Brace, *Dangerous Classes*, 58–59. Also, *Harbinger*, 4(1847), 64, and *Hunt's*, 26(1852), 110.

39. *E.P.*, Nov. 4, 1854; also, Jan. 7, 1853. Dix, *New York*, pp. 11–13.

40. For Downing's life and character, see George W. Curtis's introductory memoir in Downing, *Rural Essays*, pp. xi-l. For a general appraisal of Downing's work and influence, see John William Ward, "The Politics of Design," pp. 54–67, 79. In her *The Homes of the New World*, Fredrika Bremer, a Swedish author, frequently refers to Downing with whom she was highly impressed.

41. Downing, *Rural Essays*, pp. 16–17, 56, 110–11. Downing wrote: "The love of country is inseparably connected with the love of home. Whatever, therefore leads man to assemble the comforts and elegancies of life around his habitation, tends to increase local attachments and render domestic life more delightful; thus not only augmenting his own enjoyment, but strengthening his patriotism and making him a

8. ESCAPE TO SUBURBIA

better citizen." Downing, *A Treatise on the Theory and Practice of Landscape Gardening*, 6th ed., p. ix.

42. *Rural Essays*, pp. 112, 125, 130, 136, 172. One suburban commuter recounted some of his trials, including a late arrival home to a cold dinner and an evening of home repairs, and complained: "The inability to get to a meeting or a lecture—to a place of amusement, or to do a little shopping are tolerable; but to be half a day in getting to and from business is a bore." *Times*, Jan. 26, 1854.

43. *Ibid.*, p. 228. *Landscape Gardening*, pp. 318–19, 352, 362. John William Ward notes that Downing's thinking was shaped by eighteenth-century associationist psychology, which still prevailed in America. A cultivated landscape and the rural Gothic architecture favored by Downing would, because of their subjective associations in the minds of beholders, have a tranquilizing effect which would counterbalance (Downing's words) "the too great bustle and excitement of our commercial cities." Ward, *Design*, p. 61. Also see Neil Harris, *The Artist in American Society*, pp. 210–14.

44. Downing, *Rural Essays*, p. xxxiii.

45. *Ibid.*, pp. 229–32, 237–40, 242. Downing's essay "On the Improvement of Country Villages" was reprinted in *Literary World*, 6(1850), 639–40.

46. *Rural Essays*, pp. 241–42. Downing may have been influenced by the formation in 1846 of a company in England to develop healthy, tasteful and efficiently arranged suburban villages for the London middle class. *Scientific American*, 2(1846–47), 307.

47. Downing, *Landscape Gardening*, p. ivc. John O. Simonds said in his Appreciation to the 1967 edition that the monument had "been removed from the path of construction and is in storage." *Ibid.*

48. *Harper's Monthly*, 7(1853), 130; 11(1855), 765. Don Gifford, ed., *The Literature of American Architecture*, pp. 246–47. Gifford also reprints selections from Downing's *Architecture of Country Houses* and from *Rural Essays*.

49. Tunnard, *City of Man*, pp. 183–86. Downing, *Landscape Gardening*, pp. 568–71. *Crayon*, 4(1857), 248.

50. Downing, *Rural Essays*, p. 238. *Landscape Gardening*, pp. 22–35. Downing said that Americans, being of English stock, had a natural love of rural life, which had been temporarily subordinated to the enterprise and movement required to develop the New World: "In the older states as wealth has accumulated . . . , a return to those simple and fascinating enjoyments in country life and rural pursuits is witnessed on every side." *Ibid.*, p. viii.

51. Pierre M. Irving, *The Life and Letters of Washington Irving*, 3, 67, 87. *Knickerbocker Magazine*, 33(1849), 413. *Literary World*, 9(1851), 231. *Harper's Monthly*, 7(1853), 129.

52. Poe, *Doings of Gotham*, pp. 59–60, 65. Strong, *Diary*, 2, 423. After viewing the villas at Birkenhead, a suburb of Liverpool, Frederick Law Olmsted said that "they can never look so shabby and desolate and dreary, as will nine-tenths of the buildings of the same denomination now errecting about New York, almost as soon as they lose the raw cheerless imposterlike airs which seem inseparable from their newness." Olmsted, *Walks and Talks*, p. 56. In 1849, the *Tribune* urged that steps be taken to preserve the natural beauty of Hoboken from suburban developers. Six years later, noting that the place had become a favorite pleasure ground of New York's working classes, it observed that "the march of improvement has cut many of the broad lawns and miniature forests into streets and house lots, and the entire appearance of the present Hoboken reminds one but little of the Hoboken of our childhood." *Trib.*, April 28, 1849; July 13, 1855. In 1865, Andrew H. Green warned that "several villages have within the last twenty years, been projected in Westchester by the owners of farms,

9. WEALTH

which already embarrass the question of future improvements, and unless the difficulties are soon met by the adoption of a general plan, these embarrassments will have increased, and become so fixed that no generation will be found bold enough to grapple with and remedy them." John Foord, *The Life and Public Service of Andrew Haswell Green*, pp. 281, 290. Green was probably referring to that part of Westchester which later became the Bronx.

53. See, for instance, the advertisements of land sales in the *Evening Post*, March 2, 1852 (Fordham), Sept. 15 (Newton), Oct. 19–20 (Bergen Hill and East Newark), Oct. 26 (West Flushing), Nov. 28 (Fort Hamilton), 1853. *Day-Book*, Aug. 31, 1852.

54. See advertisements in the *Evening Post*, Feb. 24 (Clinton, N.J.), Aug. 5 (Fort Hamilton and East New York), Sept. 19 (Bushwick), Oct. 15 (Morrisania), Oct. 29 (East New York), 1853. *Citizen*, Aug. 26, 1854. Not all suburbs were established by private developers. In the early 1850s, a number of building associations were created ostensibly to enable working men and others to buy and develop suburban land. The Petersville Homestead Association, for instance, boasted that it had acquired lands "unrivaled for beauty" near New Rochelle; the price of four city lots for members was $75. *Trib.*, Aug. 1, 1853; July 2, 1855. The most successful were the Industrial Home Associations, founded in 1850, which established Mount Vernon, N.Y. Association No. 1, intended to enable workers to escape the control of land monopolists, claimed over a thousand members, and was able to raise $75,000 to buy a 370-acre tract along the New Haven Railroad line. Otto Hufeland, *Early Mount Vernon*, pp. 14–21. Other suburbs were initially established in connection with industrial enterprises. Edward Kellogg of New York, for instance, promoted Elizabethport, N.J., as a manufacturing village. Moses Y. Beach, *Wealthy Citizens*, p. 43. Lodi, N.J., developed around a calico print works, apparently as a company town. *Trib.*, June 21, 1849. In New York, Jordan L. Mott moved his stove works from Tarrytown to Morrisania and there established the village of Mott Haven. J. Leander Bishop, *A History of American Manufactures from 1608 to 1860*, 2, 577–78. See also the advertisement for an unnamed manufacturing village, probably Mott Haven, in which the developer offered to give manufacturers one lot for every 12 hands employed in the village and also to provide loans for the construction of buildings. *Trib.*, Jan. 17, 1855.

55. *E.P.*, Aug. 5, 1855. Some developers emphasized both the proximity of their villages to New York and the view prospective residents would have of the city and its harbor. See the advertisements in the *Tribune*, Feb. 17, 1852 (Brooklyn) and May 9, 1855 (Bergen Heights). Also the *Citizen*, Aug. 26, 1854 (Laurel Hill).

56. Downing, *Rural Essays*, p. 212.

Chapter 9: Wealth

1. Kenneth W. Porter, *John Jacob Astor*, 2, 939, 1121.

2. Edward Pessen lists nine persons and one estate with property assessed at $500,000 or more in 1845. *Riches, Class, and Power Before the Civil War*, p. 323. As property generally was underassessed, it is likely that all were worth a million or more. *Ibid.*, p. 19. Reuben Vose, *The Rich Men of New York*. Browne, *Great Metropolis*, p. 642.

3. William Armstrong, *The Aristocracy of New York* (N.Y., 1848), p. 25. Scoville, *Merchants*, 1, 115, 142–43. William E. Dodge, "A Great Merchant's Recollections," p. 150, 173, 182ⁿ

[473]

9. WEALTH

4. Pessen, *Riches*, pp. 100–5, 323. *E.P.*, June 6, 1854.

5. Pessen, *Riches*, pp. 46–71, 103–4. Henry Hall, *America's Successful Men*, 1, 394. The power of money was illustrated after the Panic of 1837 by the widespread foreclosures on loans made to land buyers during the land boom of the mid-1830s. One observer said that "there has been a gradual concentration of property into the hands of the lenders. Each successive year has found the quantity acquired by foreclosure larger than the amount sold." *Hunt's*, 11(1844). 260. The most active forecloser was John Jacob Astor. Kaveler, *Astors*, p. 32.

6. Porter, *Astor*, 2, 912–40. Arthur Pound, *The Golden Earth*, 270–84.

7. *Trib.*, April 5, 1848. Porter, *Astor*, 2, 1260–96. Vose, *Rich Men*.

8. Hardenbrook, *Financial New York*, pp. 228–51. Allan Nevins, *History of the Bank of New York and Trust Company*, pp. iii–iv. *Banker's Magazine*, 2(1847–48), 776; 5(1850–51), 12.

9. Nevins, *Bank of New York*, pp. v–vi. Shepard B. Clough, *A Century of American Life Insurance*, pp. 31–40, 100–2.

10. Porter, *Astor*, 2, 1002. George R. Taylor, *Transportation Revolution*, p. 51. Scoville, *Merchants*, 1, 311. Hardenbrook, *Financial New York*, p. 300. *Trib.*, Jan. 16, March 21, 1855.

11. Hone, *Diary*, pp. viii–xiv, 369, 678, 740, 751.

12. Pessen, *Riches*, pp. 14–15. John C. Schwab, *History of the New York Property Tax*, 5, 72–73. B. of Ald., *Docs.* (1848), 29. *Hunt's*, 22(1850), 659.

13. *Trib.*, June 3, 1848. William A. Darling, *List of Persons, Copartnerships, and Corporations Who Were Taxed*, pp. 5, 8, 34, 36, 54, 59, 93. The *Times* claimed that the property owned by five leading property owners and assessed at $5 million was actually worth at least 10 times that much. March 10, 1857.

14. *E.P.*, Jan. 7, 1853. *Trib.*, March 1, 1853. Also see Pessen, *Riches*, pp. 31–45, 130–50. Lance E. Davis, et al., *American Economic Growth*, pp. 30–38, 53–54. Douglas T. Miller, *Jacksonian Aristocracy*.

15. Pessen, *Riches*, pp. 211–14. Kaveler, *Astors*, pp. 8, 17, 28, 53. Dixon Wecter, *The Saga of American Society* (N.Y.: Scribner, 1937), pp. 110, 115, 333. Hone, *Diary*, p. 81. Kouwenhoven, *Partners*, pp. 82–83.

16. For instance: The wealthy Moses Taylor had been a business associate of the Astors; Albert W. Woodhull, the brother of the Mayor, had been a partner of Moses H. Grinnel; Shepherd Knapp had been a partner of Gideon Lee; Abram S. Hewitt was not only Peter Cooper's son-in-law but was also the partner of Cooper's son, Edward, in the Trenton Iron Company. Beach, *Wealthy Citizens*, p. 8. Hall, *Successful Men*, 1, 372. Scoville, *Merchants*, 1, 25. Allan Nevins, *Abram S. Hewitt*, p. 83, 146.

17. Pessen, *Riches*, pp. 177, 182. Kouwenhoven, *Partners*, pp. 82–83. *Doggett's New York City Directory* (1847–48).

18. The following schools were all located between Union Square and 37th Street and between Lexington and Sixth avenues in 1856: The French Institute for Young Gentlemen; Mrs. Benedict's Boarding and Day-School for Young Ladies; Mrs. Gibson's Boarding and Day School for Young Ladies; Madison Square Collegiate Institute; The Select Classical, English and Mathematical School (to prepare young men for Columbia College). Nine other private schools were also located there. *Trib.*, advertisements, Oct. 3, 1856. Other wealthy children went to boarding school and academies outside the city.

19. Hone, *Diary*, pp. 130, 396, 398, 754. Brown, *Fifth Avenue*, pp. 35–36.

9. WEALTH

20. Parton, *Famous Americans*, pp. 349–50.

21. Pessen, *Riches*, pp. 225–30, and "Phillip Hone's Set: The Social World of the New York Elite," pp. 289–95. Wecter, *Saga*, pp. 262–63. Wilson, *New York*, 3, 234–35, 243–44. Browne, *Great Metropolis*, pp. 443–47. *Trib.*, May 2, 1855.

22. Pessen, *Riches*, pp. 258–75, 294. Hone, *Diary*, pp. xiii–xiv.

23. Pessen, *Riches*, pp. 284–87. Scoville, *Merchants*, 1, 142–43. Beach, *Wealthy Citizens*, pp. 32. In 1856, assessed value of property: James Harper ($95,000), William F. Havemeyer ($102,000), A. C. Kingsland ($73,000), C. S. Woodhull ($52,700), A. H. Mickle ($114,000). Boyd, *Tax-Book*.

24. Gatell, *Money and Party*, pp. 243–49. *E.P.*, Oct. 30, 1849. Between 1838 and 1858, the Fifteenth Ward voted consistently Whig, Republican, or nativist. *Tribune Almanac* (1838–58). It was alleged that Davis realized $100,000 in legal fees from the city during his three years as Corporation Counsel. *Times*, Oct. 10, 1856.

25. David M. McAdam, et al., eds., *History of the Bench and Bar of New York*, 1, 292–93, 468–69. Hone, *Diary*, pp. xxv, 348, 875. Hardenbrook, *Financial New York*, p. 223.

26. *Harper's Monthly*, 11(1854), 122, 260; 15(1857), 128. *Putnam's*, 8(1856), 108–12.

27. Henry Ward Beecher was a successful popularizer of the gospel of cultural philanthropy. See his *Star Papers*, pp. 295–99, and also William C. McLoughlin, *The Meaning of Henry Ward Beecher*, pp. 101–2, 112–29.

28. Jacob Landy, *The Architecture of Minard Lafever*, p. 50. Upjohn, *Upjohn*, pp. 159–63. Mumford, *Roots*, p. 58. *Brother Jonathan*, 5(1843), 61–62, 92. *Democratic Review*, 21(1847), 393–94.

29. For the New York art world see Harris, *Artist in American Society*, pp. 110–22, 254–82. Eliot Clark, *History of the National Academy of Design*, pp. 60–68. John Durand, *The Life and Times of A. B. Durand*, pp. 44, 125–30, 141. James T. Flexner, *That Wilder Image*, pp. 105–9. James T. Callow, *Kindred Spirits: Knickerbocker Writers and American Artists*, pp. 13, 29, 33–35, 94–97, 102–16. *Literary World*, 1(1847), 517.

30. Harris, *Artist in American Society*, pp. 105, 262–63, 280–1, 300. Flexner, *Wilder Image*, pp. 111–16. Lillian B. Miller, *Patrons and Patriotism*, pp. 143, 156–57. *Literary World*, 3(1848), 852–53. George Inness, who began his career as a painter in Newark, attracted the attention of a wealthy New York auctioneer, Ogden Haggerty, who sent him to Italy and France in the early 1850s to further his study of art. George Inness, Jr., *Life, Art, and Letters of George Inness*, p. 24.

31. *Trib.*, Oct. 7 (supplement), Nov. 28, 1845. *Democratic Review*, 20(1847), 373. In 1852, William Henry Fry, America's first serious composer and critic, gave a series of lectures intended to deepen the understanding of music among New Yorkers. Neither his lectures nor his music, however, won a popular hearing. William T. Upton, *William Henry Fry*, pp. 123, 134–38.

32. Hone, *Diary*, p. 837. Henry E. Krehbiel, *Chapters of Opera*, pp. 43–52. Wilson, *New York*, 4, 177, *Trib.*, Jan. 5, May 7, 1847. *Democratic Review*, 20(1847), 280; 21(1847), 281–82, 273, 564.

33. Krehbiel, *Opera*, pp. 47–52. *Democratic Review*, 22(1848), 88–89, 473, 568–69; 42(1858), 403–4.

34. Krehbiel, *Opera*, pp. 65–67. *E.P.*, May 9, Dec. 3, 1853; Sept. 26, Oct. 2, 3, 5, 1854. *Trib.*, Nov. 14, 1854; Jan. 16, 1855. The editor of *Harper's Monthly* doubted that opera would succeed in New York, because he believed that Americans were not a musical people. He conceded that "Ethiopian minstrels" were popular but denied that this was either American or music: "The crowds that throng to Christy's and Wood's

do not prove that there is in the American people a love of music which will make the Italian opera a permanent fact among us." 8(1854), 695–96.

35. Upton, *Fry*, p. 56. John Durand, *Prehistoric Notes of the Century Club*, p. 12.

36. Wilson, *New York*, 4, 79–82, 101–10, 364. Charles E. Lester, *Glances at the Metropolis*, p. 197–99.

37. Harris, *Artist in American Society*, p. 300. Flexner, *Wilder Image*, pp. xi–xii, 16, 31, 111, 116. Durand, *Durand*, p. 217. Miller, *Patrons*, p. 143. On Nov. 8, 1853, the *Times* supported efforts to establish a "Metropolitan Museum" around Dr. Henry Abbott's collection of Egyptian antiquities. Central Park, the libraries, and the museums were extensions of the world the rich were creating for themselves—open to the public but on the philanthropists' terms. Daniel M. Fox says that the philanthropists who founded the art museums after the Civil War "did not believe the country had a national art treasure worthy of Museum exhibition." *Engines of Culture*, p. 3.

38. Upton, *Fry*, p. 60. In the 1850s, Ward McAllister, later the chamberlain of Mrs. Astor's Four Hundred, established himself in a villa in southern France, where he might have stayed, if he had not been "called home by the stupidity of an agent, who was unable to treat with my old friend, Commodore Vanderbilt, for an extension of his lease on our dock property." McAllister, *Society as I Have Found It*, p. 77.

39. Hone, *Diary*, pp. 461–65. Miller, *Jacksonian Aristocracy*, p. 166. Maude H. Elliott, *Uncle Sam Ward and His Circle*, p. 203.

40. *Trib.*, March 12, 1855. McAllister, *Society*, pp. 14–15.

41. Miller, *Jacksonian Aristocracy*, pp. 168–69. F. Saunders, *New-York in a Nutshell* (N.Y. 1853), p. 102. Ross, *What I Saw*, p. 155. Child, *Letters, Second Series*, p. 279. *Trib.*, Jan. 30, 1855; Oct. 14, 1856. *E.P.*, Jan. 27, 1854. *Democratic Review*, 22(1848), 379.

42. McAllister, *Society*, pp. 156–62. Bayard Taylor, *Hannah Thurston*, p. 134. *Literary World*, 8(1851), 134. N. P. Willis, in a much-publicized lecture on fashion at the Tabernacle in 1844, attempted, said a listener, to refine and exalt "fashion into a power—the talisman of a self-sustaining, unprivileged aristocracy." *Trib.*, June 12, 1844. Henry A. Beers, *Nathaniel Parker Willis*, p. 341.

43. Lester, *Glances*, p. 103. Bristed, *Upper Ten*, pp. 5–6, 9.

44. Amory D. Mayo, *Symbols of the Capital; or Civilization in New York*, p. 227. For more regarding Mayo, see ch. 15 of this work.

45. Chapin, *Humanity in the City*, pp. 71–77. "Extraordinary aggregations of wealth," said John A. Dix, "unless rightly employed, are never desirable. When they are the ministers of luxury and extravagance, they misdirect industry, pervert the public taste, and endanger the purity of society and the safety of government." *E.P.*, Jan. 7, 1853. Also, George G. Foster, *New York Naked*, pp. 40, 47. Hunt, *Worth and Wealth*, pp. 182–83. *Literary World*, 6(1850), 413–14.

46. Thompson, *Ruggles*, pp. 85–86. Samuel B. Ruggles, *Writings and Speeches*, p. 16.

47. Thompson, *Ruggles*, pp. 75, 78, 82, 85–87. Ruggles, *Writings*, pp. 13–16.

48. Strong, *Diary*, p. 168. Columbia University, *Columbia*, pp. 123–25, 130, 135. Horace Coon, *Columbia*, pp. 73–77.

49. Morgan Dix, ed. *A History of the Parish of Trinity*, 4, 262–63, 304, 320–26, 392–93. Wilson, *New York*, 4, 629–30. *Trib.*, March 11, 1846.

50. New York State Senate, *Documents* (1846), no. 86, pp. 9–29; *Report of the Select Committee to Whom was referred the Report of Trinity Church* (1855), pp. 9–10; *Documents*, no. 46, p. 62. New York State Assembly, *Documents* (1854), no. 130, pp. 7–21. *E.P.*, April 3, 1854. Poe, *Doings of Gotham*, p. 41. Matthew Hale Smith in 1868 claimed that

9. WEALTH

Trinity's property was worth between $50 and $100 million. Smith, *Sunshine and Shadow*. pp. 122, 278.

51. Dix, *Trinity*, 4, 302–11. William Berrian, *Facts Against Fancy*, pp. 19–21. New York State Senate, *Documents* (1846), no. 86, pp. 9–21. New York State Assembly, *Documents* (1854), no. 130, pp. 23–26. In 1856, William Jay estimated the gross income from Trinity's 938 lots at $89,486, and then declared that when the Burr and other long-term leases expired "Peppercorns will be exchanged for thousands of dollars, and five dollar rents will rise to as many hundreds." Jay, *A Letter to the Rev. William Berrian*, pp. 5–7.

52. Dix, *Trinity*, 4, 322–26, 359–61, 392–93. *Report of the Select Committee* (1855), pp. 20–21. Faced with the collapse of the Mission Society, Trinity offered to continue its annual contribution to the Society but apparently only if other Episcopal churches also made contributions to the Society. Rosenberg, *Religion*, pp. 147–50. When Trinity rejected his plea for additional aid for St. Jude's, a free church for the laboring poor, the Rector of St. Jude's, Henry Dana Ward, wrote in disgust that "all the great churches are full of the wealthy. The poor are left to their freedom"; he soon gave up what he considered to be a hopeless ministry. Ward, Mss. diary, May 31, 1852–Jan. 23, 1853, New York Public Library.

53. Dix, *Trinity*, 4, 266–72. *Memorial . . . Praying the Repeal or Amendment of an Act . . . Passed January 25, 1814* (N.Y., 1846), pp. 49ff. *E.P.*, Jan. 21, 23, Feb. 2, 1846. *Trib.*, Jan. 16, 18, 1846. Wilson, *New York*, 4, 205–6. Trinity's title was also challenged from outside the church. In 1848, Clinton Roosevelt urged the State Attorney General to begin forfeiture proceedings to reclaim Trinity land for the state, arguing that Trinity had no legal title to the land, the "resumption" of which would "pay the debts of the city and state, and relieve the citizens from taxation." *E.P.*, March 16, 1848. Trinity's title was again attacked in 1854 by Rutger B. Miller and others who claimed that they had proof that the lands belonged to the State and offered to bring a suit of ejectment against Trinity provided they received one-quarter of the recovery. William H. DeLancey, *The Title, Parish Rights and Property of Trinity Church*, pp. 6–7.

54. L. Bradish, et al., *A Statement and Declaration of Views*, p. 5–6. After the publication of this statement, Robert B. Minturn wrote to Bradish: "If I rightly remember the able and satisfactory report which you prepared for our committee no reference is made to the short coming of Trinity Church in failing to apply her . . . trust fund to providing free church accommodations for the poor of the city—it is for this sin chiefly that I am enlisted against her." Dec. 27, 1846. Luther Bradish Papers, New-York Historical Society.

55. Anne Ayres, *The Life and Work of William Augustus Muhlenberg*, pp. 177, 181–82, 196, 226–27, 261. William W. Newton, *Dr. Muhlenberg*, pp. 157, 187–88, 204–7. James Addison, *The Episcopal Church in the United States*, pp. 164–69, 177–78, 185.

56. Ayres, *Muhlenberg*, pp. 205, 209, 214, 218, 256, 277, 311. Dix, *Trinity*, 4, 367–69. Wilson, *New York*, 4, 438–40. Richmond, *New York*, pp. 367–70. In 1849, Roman Catholics opened St. Vincent's and in 1855 Mount Sinai was established as Jews Hospital. Duffy, *Public Health*, p. 504.

57. New York State Senate, *Documents* (1857), no. 46, pp. 114–15. Disappointed in his hopes for a united Evangelical Church, Muhlenberg later transferred his dreams to St. Johnland, a model "Christian Industrial Community" he founded on Long Island after the Civil War; he hoped that it would be the first of many "cities of refuge" for the working poor from the physical and especially the moral devastation

9. WEALTH

of great cities like New York. Ayres, *Muhlenberg*, pp. 398–425, 435–38, 466. Newton, *Muhlenberg*, pp. 210–17.

58. Dix, *Trinity*, 4, 393, 419, 423–24, 440–45, 458. Also, Strong, *Diary*, 2, 325–26.

59. William A. McVickar, *City Missions*, pp. 5–6, 9–10, 16–26. E. C. Chorley, ed., *Quarter of A Millennium*, pp. 73–74.

60. Parton, *Famous Americans*, p. 355. Jay, *Letter*, pp. 17–19. *Times*, Jan. 11, 1854.

61. Jay, *Letter*, pp. 17–19.

62. *Subterranean*, July 19, 1845; July 11, 1846. *Working Man's Advocate*, April 27, 1844; Jan. 18, 1845.

63. *Subterranean*, Sept. 6, 13, 1845; June 20, July 18, 1846. *Young America*, Jan. 17, 1846.

64. Robert Ernst, "The One and Only Mike Walsh," pp. 43–65. Wittke, *Irish in America*, pp. 109–10.

65. Sigmund Diamond, *The Reputation of the American Business Man*, p. 23, 30, 33, 39–40. *Trib.*, March 30, 1848. *Subterranean*, April 24, 1847.

66. *Trib.*, April 3, 1855. Cornelius Mathews wrote in 1853: "Some have expressed a belief that the people of that whole section of the city lying east of Broadway are composed of different material from the settlers about Fifth Avenue and Union Square; that they are an essentially distinct and inferior race." *Pen-and-Ink*, pp. 124–30. Alvin F. Harlow, *Old Bowery Days*, pp. 218–31.

67. George C. D. Odell, *Annals of the New York Stage*, 5, 261. Richard Moody, *Edwin Forrest*, pp. 220, 252, 257. *Trib.*, March 12, 20, 1855.

68. Odell, *Annals*, pp. 387–88, 426, 482. Moody, *Forrest*, pp. 230, 252, 257. *Literary World*, 1(1847), 234; 3(1848), 877–78.

69. *Trib.*, Nov. 30, Dec. 2, 1848; Feb. 21, 1849. Strong, *Diary*, 1, 336.

70. *E.P.*, Aug. 26, Sept. 1, 1847.

71. Jay Monaghan, *The Great Rascal*, pp. 162, 169–70, 172, 174–75. Joel T. Headley, *The Great Riots of New York*, pp. 114–19. Moody, *Forrest*, pp. 269–71.

72. Monaghan, *Great Rascal*, p. 176. Headley, *Riots*, p. 120. Moody, *Forrest*, p. 273. Wilson, *New York*, 3, 432. Hone, *Diary*, p. 877.

73. *Ibid.*, 877–78. Strong, *Diary*, 1, 352. *Trib.*, May 11, 12, 1849.

74. Moody, *Forrest*, pp. 279–80. *E.P.*, May 12, 1849. *Trib.*, May 12, 1849.

75. Monaghan, *Great Rascal*, p. 187. Thompson, *Ruggles*, p. 11–13. Strong, *Diary*, 1, 352–53. *Literary World*, 5(1849), 300. *Independent*, Oct. 4, 1849. Scrapbook G. C. P. Daly Papers, New York Public Library, 9–34ff.

76. Hone, *Diary*, p. 878. *Account of the Terrific and Fatal Riot* (N.Y., 1849), 19, 32.

77. *Literary World*, 4(1849), 438; 5(1849), 129. *Democratic Review* (1849), 482–83. *Independent*, May 17, Oct. 11, 1849. Judge C. P. Daly, in his charge to the Grand Jury investigating the riot, declared that the affair had grown out of the growing disposition in New York "to substitute force and violence" for law. The *Weekly Herald* attributed this growing disrespect for law to the influence of "Socialism—Fourierite socialism—mixed with infidelity, folly, and abstractions of all kinds." Scrapbook G. C. P. Daly Papers, New York Public Library. The *Tribune*, which had preached the Fourierite doctrine, provided perhaps the simplest and most valid explanation when it said that there was a natural tendency for ruffians to congregate in large cities; it also mentioned, however, the influence of an inflammatory press as a cause of the riot. *Trib.*, May 15, 1849.

78. Henry W. Bellows, *A Sermon Occasioned by the Late Riot in New York*, pp. 11, 13–14.

79. *Trib.*, March 12, 1855.

10. PROGRESSIVE CITY—WICKED CITY

Chapter 10: Progressive City—Wicked City

1. *National Cyclopedia of American Biography*, 3, 261. Strong, *Diary*, 2, 300, 335, 386, 396–97.

2. Henry W. Bellows, *The Christian Merchant . . . Discourse on . . . the Death of Jonathan Goodhue*, pp. 6–9, and *The Leger and the Lexicon: or, Business and Literature*, pp. 18–23, 31. Bellows turned the prevailing concern over the threat materialism posed to Christian faith and morals into a defense of the Christian businessman as a hero of his age who had survived the "trial by gold." Directly challenged by the demon of materialism as they were, the virtues of the merchant were hard-won and real: "They do not exist by the forebearance of circumstances. They are not passive graces. They need to be positive, active, aggressive quantities." Businessmen constituted a democratic elite, superior not so much to the people (from whom it was convenient to assume they had come) as to both politicians and the fashionable. *Christian Merchant*, pp. 6–7, 11, 14–15.

3. Henry W. Bellows, *The Moral Significance of the Crystal Palace*, pp. 5, 12–19. Bellows argued for the necessity and reality of class harmony in America. The merchant and financier, by making the exchange of goods possible, benefited all producers from large manufacturers down to working men. All good Americans belonged to the same general class: "All honest men are laborers here, because we recognize no class above or below the dignity of labor, and few can afford to despise its generous and stimulating rewards," *Leger and Lexicon*, pp. 21–23.

4. New York State *Census* (1845), 2, 29ff. *Eighth Census (1860): Manufactures*, pp. 379–85. William H. Boyd in 1856 listed 50 corporations in New York with property assessed at $500,000 of more in his *Tax-Book*. New York State *Census* (1855), p. 180. *Harper's Monthly* noted that during the early 1850s there was a "great increase in those departments of labor which require more than a consuming degree of intelligence and skill." 10(1854), 343. Stephen Thernstrom says that beginning in the 1850s there was a distinct loosening of the occupational structure in Boston and other cities (none of them New York) and a consequent increase of both upward and downward mobility. *The Other Bostonians: Poverty and Progress in the American Metropolis*, pp. 233–35. Probably New York—because of its relatively loose social structure and its size, complexity, and rapid growth—experienced the same situation at a somewhat earlier time, although there as elsewhere the exceptional prosperity and economic development of the 1850s were the major factor in "opening" the occupational structure. Unfortunately, no systematic study of occupations and mobility comparable to Thernstrom's has been made for New York during this period.

5. The New York State *Census* (1855) presents detailed occupational statistics for each county (pp. 178–95) which make it possible to devise rough estimates regarding those New Yorkers who, possibly, were part of a middle class. My figures (rounded to the nearest hundreth) by general occupational category are: Arts and Letters, including actors, artists and musicians (1900); clerks, copyists and accountants (13,900); Professions (7300); small business (approximately 20,000), and skilled workers (approximately 20,000). Total middle class (63,100). These figures are "guesstimates" intended to illustrate the point and are not to be cited. Occupational statistics for the unskilled are somewhat more solid. Unskilled workers—notably servants (the biggest category, 31,740, in the census), laborers, sailors, and seamstresses—totalled 76,900; note that the unskilled occupations included a high percentage of women, whereas those of the

10. PROGRESSIVE CITY—WICKED CITY

middle class were heavily dominated by men. Probably, some 70,000 other New Yorkers belonged to a vague working class of the semi-skilled.

The whole matter of class and occupation, however, is so badly confused that it is probably impossible to achieve a precise determination of the real situation. The state census of 1855, while unusually detailed regarding occupations, is of dubious service here, in part because its occupational categories are vaguely defined. It classifies, for instance, 12,609 New Yorkers as "tailors" but makes no distinction between those who had the requisite skills to qualify as masters of this trade and those who were apprentices, helpers, or otherwise below the skilled level. The biggest problems are in determining the number of small businessmen. At the upper extreme of this category, the census enumerated 6001 "merchants" (down from the some 8000 "merchants" given in the census of 1845), an upper-class occupation, but likely many were actually small businessmen. Also, it is impossible to determine how many of those listed in the various trades, such as the 2856 bakers and the 6,745 "boot and shoe makers and dealers," had independent businesses although *Rodes' Business Directory* (1853/54) furnishes some help in listing approximately 550 bakers and 880 boot and shoe makers.

There are also problems aside from those associated with the vagueness of census figures. The character of class, especially when related to occupation, is especially elusive. One might, for instance, classify New York's 442 saloonkeepers, 442 (yes, the figure is the same) brewers and distillers, and 619 wine and liquor dealers as small businessmen (as indeed they are so classified in chapter 13 of this work), but, ignoring the fact that the threat of state imposed prohibition at this time produced an underestimate of the number engaged in the liquor business, one hesitates to call them "middle class" as the term is used in my chapter 10. More problems appear when one attempts to classify the whole population (nonworking as well as working) on the basis of occupational status. It is possible, for example, that the proportion of middle class families was higher than the percentage of middle class occupations would indicate, since proportionately far more women and children of this class than that of the lower classes would not have been employed and so not enumerated occupationally. However, it is also possible that many poor people were not enumerated in this or any other way because they were simply not "found" by the censustakers. Probably, this was especially the case in 1855, since the winter of 1854–55 had brought a short but sharp decline in employment opportunities for many lower class people.

Although I am awed by the statistical ingenuity of cliometricians, I am not impressed by the result of much of their work. Selma Berrol, using the manuscript census schedules for the Eighteenth and Twenty-First Wards, estimates that 40.8 percent of the population of these uptown wards was middle class. This figure is not inconsistent with my estimate for the whole city, since the two wards were undoubtedly more middle class than the whole. She achieves this figure, however, by classifying 31 percent of the population as "skilled" workers and including all of these in the middle class. As "skilled" workers constitute three-quarters of the middle class as defined by Dr. Berrol, her estimates are open to question on the grounds indicated above. It should be noted that this estimate is only the lesser part of an otherwise excellent article on education. Selma Berrol, "Who Went to School in Mid-Nineteenth Century New York? An Essay in the New Urban History," in Irwin Yellowitz, ed., *Essays in the History of New York City* (Port Washington, N.Y.: Kennikat Press, 1978), pp. 48 and 59–60, n. 12.

10. PROGRESSIVE CITY—WICKED CITY

Carl F. Kaestle, in his study of New York schools before 1850, has attempted to use the census of 1855 to determine the occupational structure of the city. Although he does not attempt to determine the class structure as such, it is worth noting that he estimates that 41.2 percent of employed New Yorkers were skilled workers, while—using his estimates—the percentages in the middle class categories of clerical, proprietary, and professional totalled 18.8 percent, a decline from the 20.3 percent estimated for 1796. The chief difficulty here is posed by his large and amorphous category of skilled workers. See his *The Evolution of an Urban School System*, pp. 102–3. Also Ernst, *Immigrant Life*, pp. 206–12.

6. State census (1855), p. 8. F. B. Hough, Superintendent of the state census, called attention to this situation in 1857, noting that New York County had a greater proportion of women than any other county in the state with the exception of neighboring Kings County. The key difference was in the age group 15–20, where women heavily out-numbered men in the city while men were more numerous in the state as a whole. *Trib.*, July 3, 1857. The percentage of young women in the age group, 15–25, was slightly more than 57 in 1855, approximately the same proportion as existed five years later, in the age group, 20–30. *Eighth Census: Population*, pp. 322–23.

Hough attributed this disparity to the westward migration of young men. A sampling of children in the Fifteenth Ward in 1840, however, suggests the need for another explanation. Of 113 children, ages 0–5, in this sample, 52 percent were male, yet of 139 children, ages 5–15 (who would be ages 20–30 in 1855), males constituted only 29 percent of the total. In another small sample in the neighboring Fourteenth Ward (1840), there were 24 males of 47 children, 0–5, and 24 males of 61 children, 5–15. These samples are too small to prove anything, but they do raise the possibility that there was an unusually high mortality rate among male infants during this period. U.S. Census Schedules (1840): Fourteenth and Fifteenth Wards.

7. A sampling of 112 couples of child-rearing age in the Fourteenth Ward in 1860 indicates that 10 percent had no children while another 23 percent had only one. *Ibid.*, (1860). See also note 16 below.

8. Vincenzo Botta, ed., *Memoir of Anne C. L. Botta*, pp. 6, 56, 85, 175–6, 185. Anne M. Dolan, "The Literary Salon in New York," pp. 82–99. Robert E. Riegel, *American Woman*, pp. 160–75. Isabella Bird, *The Englishwoman in America*. Foreword and notes by Andrew H. Clark (Madison: University of Wisconsin Press, 1966), 372. For Catherine Sedgwick, see E. K. Spann, *Ideals and Politics*, pp. 85–91, 143–44.

9. The Common Council *Manual* (1853, pp. 231–51) lists the officers of the various societies. *Trib.*, May 9, July 19, 1855. A similar but even older organization was the New York Female Assistance Society.

10. *Ibid.*, March 8, 1853. For women's assertiveness, see Barbara Berg, *The Remembered Gate: Origins of American Feminism*, esp. pp. 154–55, 170–71, 174–75, 182–83, 204–05.

11. *Trib.*, Feb. 2, March 1, 1855, May 15, 21, 1856. *E.P.*, Oct. 18, 1854. New York Board of Education, *Documents* (1855), Report of the Evening School Committee, pp. 7–14 and Appendix, pp. 16, 19. Riegel, *Women*, p. 191. Virginia Penny, *The Employments of Women*, pp. 89–94.

12. Berg, *Remembered Gate*, pp. 237–39. *Trib.*, March 2, 1855. Penny, *Employments*, pp. 27–29. Riegel, *Women*, pp. 178–79.

13. In 1853, more than 750 women were teachers, mostly in the primary level and in the girls department on the grammar school level, but many also taught in the boys

department. Common Council, *Manual*, pp. 215–25. In 1868, 2030 of the 2206 teachers were women. Ravitch, *School Wars*, p. 103. Hunt, *Worth and Wealth*, pp. 499–500.

14. County Superintendent of Schools, "Report," in New York State Assembly, *Documents* (1849), no. 50, p. 130. Penny, *Employments*, pp. 38–39.

15. Penny, *Employments*, pp. vii, x. Penny said that "on most of the avenues in New York, Merchants do not sell as much, nor receive such profits as on Broadway, and employ women because they can get them cheaper." *Ibid.*, pp. 129, 309, 318. The proportion of women employed in the clothing industry fell, by one estimate, from 64 percent in 1860 to only 47 percent in 1900. Edith H. Altbach, *Women in America*, p. 54. Women typesetters, although well-paid by the standards of the day, were subject to strong discrimination from men, not only because they were women but also because many had originally been hired in the 1850s as strikebreakers. Ellen Carol DuBois, *Feminism and Suffrage*, pp. 129–30.

16. Census Schedules (1860): Fourteenth Ward. The sample consists of the first household name on every third page of the schedules, a total of 144 persons of whom 27 were women.

17. B. of Ald., *Docs.* 15(1848–49), 1109. *Trib.*, Jan. 1, 1853. The 1852 figure is for license renewals. In April 1849, the Chief of Police estimated that there were 729 unlicensed drinking places, making a total of 4567 drinking places. Of 144,364 arrests from July 1845 to December 1850, 36,675 were for intoxication, 29,190 for intoxication and disorderly conduct, 20,252 for disorderly conduct, and 13,896 for assault and battery. B. of Ald., *Docs.*, 18(1851–52), 554–55. In 1853, the New York Prison Association claimed that since 1848 imprisonments for disorderly conduct, "in almost every instance the result of rum," had increased 278 percent, while imprisonments for intoxication had grown by 75 percent. *Trib.*, March 17, 1853.

18. *Ibid.*, Feb. 1, 27, 1855. *E.P.*, July 20, Oct. 19, 1846.

19. *Trib.*, Sept. 11, 1843; Aug. 16, 1844; Sept. 19, 1845; Sept. 30, 1847. Strong, *Diary*, 1, 162. *Harper's Weekly*, 1(1857), 65–66.

20. *Trib.*, May 10, 16, 1856. In 1846, the Chief of Police estimated that there were some 1000 houses of prostitution with nearly 7000 inmates in New York. In the same year, two Aldermen claimed that there were 10,000 prostitutes, or nearly one in seven women between ages 16 and 36. *E.P.*, Nov. 18, 1846. *Trib.*, March 14, 1844; March 21, 1846 (supplement). Prime, *New York*, p. 165.

21. William W. Sanger, *The History of Prostitution*, pp. 451–59, 580, 586–60. This work was written in 1858. Sanger, Resident Physician for the public institutions on Blackwell's Island, asked New York's prostitutes to answer a questionnaire relating to their profession. He assumed that the 2000 respondents represented two-fifths of the professional prostitutes in the city; to these he added another 500 to 1000 whom he believed had been driven to full time prostitution by the depression of 1857–58. *Ibid.*, p. 34. The *Tribune* made its charge in connection with the disappearance of a young women teacher. It later reported the rumor that she had joined a company of "Model Artists" bound for New Orleans; the "Model Artists" seem to have been early strip-teasers. Nov. 17, 18, 1848.

22. Sanger, *Prostitution*, pp. 29, 593–99, 645.

23. *Ibid.*, pp. 642–43, 652–53, 662, 672. C. J. Warner to Charles P. Daly, Oct. 13, 1853 and Scrapbook G, 66–71, C. P. Daly Papers, New York Public Library.

24. *Trib.*, March 14, 22, 1855; Oct. 20, 1856. When a court ruled that the arrest of 30 streetwalkers for vagrancy was illegal, the *Times* declared: "So far as public morals

are concerned there can be but one feeling in this matter—that Broadway and our other quiet thoroughfares must not be permitted any longer to be used as the mart to advertise the most shameless immorality." April 2, 1855. Such complaints did little to remove prostitution from the Broadway area. In 1866, it was estimated that there were 108 brothels west of Broadway between Spring and Houston Streets, generally of the "most respectable class" intended for out-of-town occupants of the hotels. Citizens Association, *Public Health*, p. 67.

25. Sanger, *Prostitution*, pp. 478–79, 483. Browne, *Great Metropolis*, p. 583. *Trow's New York City Directory* (1856/57). Edward Van Every, *Sins of New York*, pp. 98–104. *E.P.*, Jan. 29, Feb. 4, 12, 17, 1846. *Trib.*, Aug. 20, 1856.

26. *Trib.*, July 10, 1852. *E.P.*, Oct. 11, 1851; March 1, April 11, 1853. Between July 1845 and December 1853, the police made 160 arrests for murder and 1061 arrests for assaults with intent to kill; 96 of the arrests for murder and 571 of those for assault with intent were made between 1850 and 1853. Augustine E. Costello, *Our Police Protectors*, pp. 116, 131. In 1854, there were 88 arrests for murder and 272 for assault with intent to kill. B. of Ald., *Docs.*, 22(1855), 6–8.

27. Strong, *Diary*, 2, 99. Children's Air Society, *Annual Report* (1858), p. 8, *E.P.*, July 9, Aug. 5, 1850, Dec. 28, 1853.

28. *Trib.*, March 10, 12, 1855. Asbury, *Gangs of New York*, p. 99. Van Every, *Sins*, pp. 73–86.

29. *Ibid.*, pp. 87–89. *Trib.*, March 10, 12, 1855. For those who attributed crimes of violence to immigrants, Greeley pointed out that, while Morrisey was Irish, Poole was American born.

30. For examples of these analyses, see, in order, *Democratic Review*, 33(1853–54), 210. *Harper's Monthly*, 3(1851), 557. Stokes, *Iconography*, 5, 1845. *Trib.*, July 1, 1852. Bristed, *Upper Ten*, p. 34. *E.P.*, March 19, 1846.

31. Prime, *New York*, p. 4. *Hunt's*, 24(1851), 150. Pickett, *House of Refuge*, pp. 90, 103, 108, 187. Thomas L. Harris, *Juvenile Depravity and Crime in Our City*, p. 11. *Trib.*, March 10, 1855.

32. County Superintendent of Schools, *Report* in New York State Assembly, *Documents* (1849), no. 50, pp. 137–38.

33. Kaestle, *Urban School*, pp. 111–16, 141–42. *Trib.*, Jan. 1, March 14, 1855. *Harper's Monthly*, 7(1853), 271.

34. New York State *Census* (1845), 2, 29:5. Average attendance for private and select schools was 8354 and for common schools, 23,203. Boese gave the average common school attendance as 24,134. In 1850, average attendance in Board of Education Schools was 18,717 and in those of the Public School Society, 19,292. Boese, *Public Education*, 74n. The whole number (i.e., those students registered in the schools) reported for 1844 was 57,236 for the common schools and 24,500 for private, charity, and church schools. The County Superintendent attributed the disporportion between the average attendance (22,784 in common schools) and the whole number to truancy and to the registration of many pupils in more than one school during the year. State Superintendent of Schools, *Annual Report* (Albany, 1845), pp. 243–44.

35. Boese, *Public Education*, p. 76. *E.P.*, April 29, June 3, 1852. E. C. Benedict, President of the Board, used the opening of Ward School 29 to defend the building of expensive schools: "I believe it is our duty to be liberal in a matter of such great moment as the cause of education, for in no way can we better command the attention of the community than by making the school houses attractive to the public eye and conspicuous among the public buildings of the city." *E.P.*, Sept. 7, 1852. It is worth

noting that this policy survived New York's greatest school disaster when in 1851 49 children in Ward School 26 (with 1841 pupils) died as a result of a panic caused when the pupils thought, wrongly, that the building was on fire. *Ibid.*, Nov. 21, 1851.

36. *Times*, April 24, 1855. In 1851, the Board estimated that the average cost per pupil was $6.87, adding pridefully that the average cost *per inhabitant* was one-third that of Boston. Board of Education *Documents* (1850–52), no. 7, pp. 5–6. Luther Bradish, speaking for the Board, not only amplified this contention but also asserted that the cost per student in large schools was some $2.00 (12 percent) less than in small schools. *Ibid.*, no. 9, pp. 9–10, 23–24.

37. Kaestle, *Urban School*, p. 177. *E.P.*, May 26, 1852; Jan. 8, 1853. B. of Ed., *Docs.* (1850–52), no. 10, pp. 8–9; (1856), no. 19, p. 3. In 1849, the County Superintendent, in arguing for higher salaries to attract good teachers, said that of the 720 teachers in the common schools, 554 were women. In 1854, the Board attempted to classify teachers for salary purposes; annual salaries ranged from $1500 for male principals and $600 for female principals to $250 and $150 respectively for male and female third assistants. In general, the trend was toward administrative centralization, a trend which undermined the decentralization originally established in 1842 by the Maclay Act. Boese, *Public Education*, pp. 86–88. New York State Assembly, *Docs.* (1849), no. 50, pp. 47, 130–36. *Trib.*, Dec. 23, 1848; Jan. 22, 1849; Feb. 3, 1853; Nov. 16, 1854. Also Kaestle, *Urban School*, pp. 177–84. B. of Ed., *Docs.* (1855), appendix 35–36.

38. Kaestle, *Urban School*, p. 112–17. David B. Tyack, *The One Best System*, pp. 50–52. *E.P.*, Jan. 8, 1853. B. of Ed., *Docs.* (1850–52), no. 1, p. 20; (1855), appendix, 9.

39. *Putnam's*, 2(1853), 4.

40. Boese, *Public Education*, 141. *E.P.*, Jan. 23, 1847; Dec. 5, 1850; Sept. 10, 1851; Oct. 18, 1854. *Trib.*, Jan. 29, 1847; July 1, 11, Nov. 29, 1848; Jan. 4, 1856. B. of Ed., *Docs.* (1850–52), no. 8, pp. 1–7, 13; (1856), "Report on Evening Schools," p. 13.

41. S. Willis Rudy, *The College of the City of New York*, pp. 10–33, 66. Wilson, *New York*, 4, 607–9. Curry, *New York*, pp. 271–75. Strong, *Diary*, 1, 295. *Literary World*, 7(1850), 114; 8(1851), 349. In 1853, the Free Academy reported the occupations of the fathers of its students: Merchants (67), cartmen (48), carpenters (44), lawyers (32), clerks (31), physicians (25), grocers (24), masons (15) and clergymen (15). *E.P.*, Dec. 26, 1853. In 1855, the *Tribune* complained that the Academy gave too much emphasis to classical studies at the expense of more practical ones: "Instead of a High-School as might naturally crown our excellent Common-School organization, the Free Academy is but a College." Feb. 19, 1855. Five years earlier, E. C. Benedict, President of the Board, had denounced such views as absurd and warned that "this institution should not be vulgarized and degraded to exclude those who must then be driven elsewhere," asserting that it was "inequality and injustice" to exclude "men of wealth and leisure" and others interested in scholarly or professional training. "An Address Delivered at the First Anniversary of the Free Academy," B. of Ed., *Docs.* (1850–52), 17–24. In 1855, City Superintendent H. S. Randall condemned the exclusion of women from higher education as "palpable discrimination," and proposed that either a Free Academy for women be established or that the present one be abolished. *Ibid.*, (1855), appendix, 19. The Board tabled a motion to establish an academy for women early in 1855. *Trib.*, March 1, 1855.

42. Kaestle, *Urban School*, p. 93. New York Assembly, *Docs.* (1849), no. 50, p. 46. B. of Ed., *Docs.* (1855), no. 1, p. 9. *Putnam's*, 2(1853), 4. *Trib.*, June 13, 1849; Jan. 11, March 14, 1855. It should be noted that the period before the Civil War was a time of educational reform and enthusiasm. After the war, education in New York and elsewhere became increasingly rigid, routinized, and mediocre as educators lost some

10. PROGRESSIVE CITY—WICKED CITY

of their earlier confidence in their mission. See Ravitch, *School Wars*, pp. 100–104, 112–15, and the conclusions of Michael Katz, *The Irony of Early School Reform: Educational Innovation in Mid-Nineteenth Century Massachusetts*, pp. 213–17.

43. Sanger, *Prostitution*, pp. 471–72. Average attendance in the public schools alone increased from 40,055 in 1850 to 58,505 in 1860 (about 40 percent); the number of children ages 5–15, increased by nearly 60 percent during the same period. Between 1855 and 1860, while public school attendance increased by about 24 percent (11,178), the school-age population increased by 40 percent (46,174). According to Jay Dolan, Catholic-school enrollments increased by only 2000 between 1853 and 1860; it seems evident that neither parochial nor private schools absorbed more than a small part of the school-age population not in the public schools. B. of Ed., *Docs.* (1856), no. 21, p. 7; appendix, 17. *Seventh Census (1850)*, p. 117. *Eighth Census (1860): Population*, pp. 322–23. Dolan, *Immigrant Church*, p. 106. Neither the census nor school statistics are sufficiently reliable to support a definitive judgment; see Rosenwaike, *Population*, pp. 45–48.

Despite its failings, New York may have been more successful in providing access to public education than many other American cities. In 1860, for instance, while New York City's 153,032 school enrollments constituted approximately 19 percent of the whole population of the city, St. Louis's 12,166 enrollments made up only 7 percent of the population of St. Louis. Selwyn K. Troen, *The Public and the Schools*, p. 34.

44. B. of Ed., *Docs.* (1850–52), no. 10, pp. 12–13. *E.P.*, Jan. 29, June 17, 1852. Superintendent of Public Instruction, *Annual Report* (1858), p. 46. Probably, the Board's preference for "respectable" locations for its buildings contributed to the overcrowding of slum schools noted by Boese in 1867. *Public Education*, p. 133.

45. B. of Ed., *Docs.* (1856), appendix, 16; (1850–52), 34; no. 1, p. 5.

46. Carl F. Kaestle says that socioeconomic factors discouraged school attendance among the poor as well as the rich but warns against assuming that the schools were "simply a middle-class institution." Kaestle, *Urban School*, p. 111. Certainly, the schoolmen did attempt to get the children of the poor into the schools (Superintendent Randall, for instance, in 1856 urged improvements in teaching and a reduction in school hours to five as ways of attracting the poor. B. of Ed., *Docs.* [1856], appendix, 19–23). Selma Berrol, in her study of Grammar School no. 14, says that the middle class was proportionately overrepresented in this school chiefly because of the underrepresentation of the upper class; the lower classes, with 44.1 percent of the eligible population in the service area contributed 41.5 percent of students in the school. Aside from the difficulties involved in accurately determining social classifications (see note 5 above), however, this school may not have typified the general school situation. She notes, moreover, that the sons of lower class parents were greatly underrepresented among graduates from the school. *Who Went to School*, pp. 48–57. In any case, there is little doubt that the schools encouraged those who were of middle-class *character* (as distinct from economic background) and discouraged those who were not.

47. Foster, *New York Naked*, pp. 121, 136. *Trib.*, Oct. 7, 1846.

48. *Independent*, Jan. 24, 1850. *E.P.*, Jan. 5, 1852.

49. Robert H. Bremner, et al., eds., *Children and Youth in America: A Documentary History* (Cambridge: Harvard University Press, 1971), 1, 417. C. A. S., *Annual Report*, 10. *E.P.*, Feb. 25, 1854. In Boston in 1856, approximately 16 percent of those arrested were minors. Lane, *Policing*, p. 230. More than a century later, 8.4 percent of all arrests made in all the United States were of children 15 or younger. Parsl, *Criminal Justice*, p. 482. Note that the imprisonment figure used in the text does not include the

children (130 in 1852) sentenced to New York's Juvenile House of Refuge. Common Council, *Manual*, (1857), pp. 146–47.

Despite the high death rate among children, the increase during the 1850s in the population between 5 and 15 (55 percent) was only slightly less than the increase in the general population (58 percent). Undoubtedly, migration to the city added substantially to the school-age and late teenage population. By comparing the number in an age group in 1850 with the number in an age group ten years older in 1860, it is possible to determine, if only crudely, the increase resulting from migration. For the age group 0–5 years, in 1850 the increase from outside by 1860 was slightly less than 10 percent, a substantial underestimate of the increase, since this age group had the highest death-rate; for ages 5–10, the increase was about 36 percent; for ages 10–20, it was a noteworthy 90 percent, which suggests that while the growth of the school-age population was substantial, it was exceeded by migration into the city in the 1850s of those in their late teens and early 20s, an instant "youth explosion" which may account for the increase in crime and violent behavior during that decade. *Seventh Census* (1850), pp. 88–89. *Eighth Census* (1860): *Population*, pp. 322–23.

50. Strong, *Diary*, 2, 57. *Independent*, Jan. 24, 1850.

51. Bremner, *Children and Youth*, 1, 466–67. Lane, *American Charities*, p. 60. Boese, *Public Education*, pp. 126–28. E.P., April 14, 1854.

52. *Trib.*, Oct. 7, 1846. *Independent*, Feb. 14, 1850. Harris, *Juvenile Depravity*, pp. 9, 13. AICP, *Report* (1853), pp. 24–25. Bremner, *Children and Youth*, 1, 466–67. Rosenberg, *Religion*, 217 and n.

53. Harris, *Juvenile Depravity*, p. 13. Homer Folks, *The Care of Destitute, Neglected and Delinquent Children*, pp. 19–22, 75–77. Duffy, *Public Health*, pp. 485–88. *Trib.*, Jan. 19, 1843, May 26, 27, 1848. E.P., Dec. 22, 1846.

54. Pickett, *House of Refuge*, esp. pp. 90, 102–3, 118, 122, 173, 176, 181, 187. Schneider, *Public Welfare*, pp. 325–28. Robert M. Mennel, *Thorns and Thistles*, pp. 11–15, 18–31. Griscom, *Griscom*, pp. 196–98. *Knickerbocker Magazine*, 19(1842), 600. E.P., Nov. 26; Feb. 9, 1854. Child, *Letters, First Series*, p. 210. In 1854, the House of Refuge moved into a new and larger building which the Juvenile Society hoped would enable them to segregate the young and comparatively innocent from hardened delinquents. Bradford K. Pierce, *A Half-Century with Juvenile Delinquents*, pp. 165–66, and *Times*, Nov. 25, 1854.

55. Mennel, *Thorns & Thistles*, pp. 35–45, 62. Schneider, *Public Welfare*, pp. 329–30. Richmond, *New York*, pp. 329–32. George P. Jacoby, *Catholic Child Care in the Nineteenth Century*, pp. 65–69. The act incorporating the Juvenile Asylum can be found in Murray Hoffman, *A Digest of Charters*, 2, 152–63.

56. Rothman, *Asylum*, pp. 206–10ff. Pickett, *House of Refuge*, pp. 102, 176. Jacoby, *Catholic Child Care*, p. 31. AICP, *Report* (1853), pp. 24–25, 69–70.

57. Lane, *American Charities*, pp. 61–62. Rothman, *Asylum*, pp. 210–36, 257–64. Pickett, *House of Refuge*, p. 112. Jacoby, *Catholic Child Care*, p. 47. *Independent*, Feb. 7, 1850. In 1872, J. F. Richmond wrote regarding the Juvenile Asylum: "The correctives applied are mainly moral, the rod being rarely employed; but the hundreds of unruly boys received annually make more and more necessary the erection of a high enclosure around the premises." Richmond, *New York*, p. 331.

58. Emma Brace, *The Life of Charles Loring Brace*, pp. 70, 76–77. Miriam Z. Langsam, *Children West*, pp. 5–7. Bremner, *From the Depths*, p. 38.

59. Brace, *Brace*, pp. 109–14, 154, 181.

60. C.A.S., Annual Report (1854), pp. 4–5, 13–14; (1856), pp. 4–5; (1857), p. 6. Brace, *Dangerous Classes*, pp. 321–22.

10. PROGRESSIVE CITY—WICKED CITY

61. *Ibid.*, 48–50. Brace did say that "the isolation or selfishness which is almost a necessity in city life" removed the poor "from the good influence of those who would aid them," but he believed that the city potentially had the will and power to override that isolation. C.A.S., *Annual Report* (1855), pp. 3–5.

62. Langsam, *Children West*, p. 19. Brace, *Dangerous Classes*, pp. 98–99. C.A.S., *Annual Report* (1854), pp. 11–12, 19–20; (1855), pp. 4, 9, 15, 17.

63. Langsam, *Children West*, pp. 7, 15. Brace, *Dangerous Classes*, pp. 137, 368–72. C.A.S., *Annual Report* (1856), p. 7. *E.P.*, March 2, 1853; Feb. 25, 1854.

64. Bremner, *From the Depths*, p. 39. Brace, *Dangerous Classes*, pp. 96, 101, 104, 132–33, 146, 148–50, 154, 174, 179–80, 433. *E.P.*, Feb. 25, 1854. C.A.S., *Annual Report* (1856), pp. 7–8, 13–19; (1858), pp. 17–20. Brace called the industrial schools "a connecting link more and more in our artificial society, necessary, between the lowest poor and the rich, between the fortunate and unfortunate." *Ibid.* (1857), p. 14.

65. Langsam, *Children West*, pp. 13–19. Brace, *Dangerous Classes*, p. 92. C.A.S., *Annual Report* (1856), pp. 7–8. In 1872, Brace said that the trades taught to boys in the reformatories generally required some capital and were overcrowded anyway, while boys who learned farming "are sure in the country, of the best occupation which a laboring man can have." He was probably influenced here by the earlier disappointment of his hopes of establishing self-supporting workshops for his children; such workshops failed to survive competition from skilled labor and, often, machinery. "Philanthropy," he concluded, "will never cut down the expenses of production as will individual self-interest." Brace, *Dangerous Classes*, pp. 96, 400.

66. Mennel, *Thorns and Thistles*, pp. 35–45, 62. Jacoby, *Catholic Child Care*, p. 68. Folks, *Destitute Children*, pp. 20–22. *Trib.*, Sept. 26, 1848. *Independendent*, Aug. 30, 1849.

67. Brace, *Dangerous Classes*, p. 309. Schneider, *Public Welfare*, p. 333. Langsam, *Children West*, p. 18–24. C.A.S., *Annual Report* (1856), p. 10. In 1857, the *Times* proposed that the placing-out system, in modified form, be used to remove unemployed and underemployed adult immigrants from the city. July 23, 1857.

68. Brace, *Dangerous Classes*, pp. 433, 435–36.

69. Langsam, *Children West*, pp. 19, 25–29, 35. Lossing, *New York*, 2, 640. Brace, *Dangerous Classes*, pp. 433, 435–36.

70. *Independent*, May 10, Sept. 20, 1849. *Democratic Review*, 22(1848), 572. During one week, for instance, at least ten major missionary and benevolent organizations held their anniversaries in New York along with a variety of other organizations such as the American Baptist Historical Society, the New York Prison Association, and the New York Sunday School Union. *Trib.*, May 5, 7, 8, 9, 1855. The new Bible House built in the early 1850s by the American Bible Society housed the offices of several missionary and benevolent societies as well as an extensive printing department for the Bible Society. *Ibid.*, March 28, 1853.

71. Rosenwaike, *Population*, p. 53. By one count, there were 238 Protestant churches, 24 Roman Catholic churches, and 16 Jewish synagogues. *Francis's New Guide to the Cities of New-York and Brooklyn* (N.Y., 1857), p. 102.

72. *Trib.*, Feb. 19, 1855. *E.P.*, Nov. 12, 1854. J. M. Mathews, *Recollections of Persons and Events* (N.Y., 1865), pp. 271–79. Bannard, *Discourse*, pp. 5–8.

73. Rosenberg, *Religion*, pp. 193–95. *Independent*, Oct. 4, 1849. *Trib.*, Dec. 22, 1848. *E.P.*, Dec. 16, 1846; Sept. 21, 1853.

74. Kaestle, *Urban School*, pp. 121–26. *Trib.*, May 9, July 20, 1855. The Sunday School Union Claimed 196 schools in New York, but most of these were connected with established congregations; only one-third were "Mission Schools." Early in 1856, "Franklin" accused the Union of overstating its missionary successes and went on to

condemn the "benevolent rascality" of certain individuals who had established bogus schools not to save souls but to raise money for themselves from contributions. *Ibid.*, Jan. 25, 30, Feb. 2, 4, 1856. In that year, the Union itself estimated that some 60,000 children had not been reached by the schools and complained that "it is strange that men who are loudmouthed in praise should overlook this most essential and economical of reforms." *Ibid.*, May 7, 1856. Earlier, "some benevolent persons" estimated that 4000 teachers were needed to meet the "emergency" presented by the existence of 55,000 children in the lower seven wards of the city who were without Sunday School instruction. *E.P.*, Nov. 20, 1854.

75. Dickens, *American Notes*, pp. 108–10. Furer, *Havemeyer*, pp. 58–59. *E.P.*, Jan. 30, 1846. Foster, *Slices*, p. 23. For some of the many descriptions of the Five Points, see Asbury, *Gangs of New York*, pp. 9–10. Ford, *Slums and Housing*, 1, 91–93. Ross, *What I Saw*, pp. 103–4. *Harbinger*, 6(1847–48), 68. Child, *Letters, First Series*, pp. 26–27. The area had a widespread reputation for vice that attracted outsiders. In 1846, Alexander Hart of Massachusetts brought his sons to the Five Points, was enticed into a brothel, and there was robbed. *E.P.*, March 2, 1846. Another visitor from Massachusetts was Richard Henry Dana, Jr.; see his *Journal*, 1, 119–22, 232–33.

76. Ladies of the Mission, *The Old Brewery and the New Mission House at the Five Points*, pp. 21, 36–40, 46–50, 76–83, 98–102, 225–34, 302–3. Caroll S. Rosenberg, "Protestants and Five Pointers," pp. 333–48. Rosenberg, *Religion*, pp. 227–34. Timothy Smith, *Revivalism and Social Reform*, pp. 169–70. Lossing, *New York*, 2, 627–34. *Harper's Weekly*, 2(1858), 753–54. Richmond, *New York*, pp. 481–85. Brace, *Dangerous Classes*, pp. 197–200. Smith, *Sunshine and Shadow*, pp. 208–11. In 1859, the AICP declared that the Sixth Ward "appears to have improved in salubrity" in large part because of "the excellent charitable institutions occupying the once notorious 'Five Points' which with faithful missionary labor, have done much for its social and moral renovation." *Report* (1859), p. 37. In 1869, Junius Browne said that "the Five Points is bad enough now . . . , but compared to what it was twenty years ago . . . , it is an abode of purity and peace." Browne, *Great Metropolis*, p. 523.

77. Ladies, *Old Brewery*, pp. 46–47. Richmond, *New York*, pp. 334–40, 497–505. Lossing, *New York*, 2, 688–99. Smith, *Revivalism*, pp. 172–76.

78. J. M. Mathews, *Fifty Years in New York* (N.Y., 1858), p. 32. Rosenberg, *Religion*, pp. 198–99. *Trib.*, Feb. 2, 1856. Strong, *Diary*, 2, 56–57, 149. In 1866, the American Female Guardian Society claimed that 125,000 children in the city were "unreached and uncared for, as far as moral and religious training is concerned." Rosenberg, *Religion*, p. 171.

79. Brace, *Dangerous Classes*, pp. 154–55. Scisco, *Nativism*, pp. 85–166, 176, 203–9. *Times*, Oct. 13, 1853. *E.P.*, Jan. 21, Feb. 7, May 22, May 29, Oct. 30, 1854.

80. Dolan, *Immigrant Church*, pp. 100–1, 117–32, 157–58, 167–69.

Chapter 11: The Age of Gold

1. Hone, *Diary*, p. 867. *Trib.*, Dec. 11, 1848. In 1860, 28,654, of the 155,759 Californians born outside of that state had been born in New York State, more than the combined contribution of the next most significant states, Missouri and Massachusetts. *Eighth Census (1860): Mortality*, p. lxi.

11. THE AGE OF GOLD

2. *Trib.*, Jan. 8, 12, 30, Feb. 26, April 25, 1849. *E.P.*, Feb. 17, 1849. Franke Soulé, et al., *The Annals of San Francisco*, pp. 192, 556, 574–75, 618, 620. In 1856, the *Tribune* warned that, as a result of the work of the San Francisco Vigilance Committee, "it is expected that a large number of vagabonds who have been expelled from San Francisco will come to this city." Shortly after, one of the members of the committee, who had returned to live in Jersey City, was beaten up on a New York street by friends of some of those whom the Committee had expelled. *Trib.*, July 2, 30, 1856. Also see Peter R. Decker, *Fortunes and Failures*, pp. 3–25. Some San Franciscans charged that eastern Democratic politicians, ousted from federal office by the Whigs in 1849, had introduced "the New York system of politics to the West coast city." *Ibid.*, p. 127.

3. *Trib.*, March 12, 1849. *Scientific American*, 6 (1850–51), 368. *E.P.*, Jan. 28, Dec. 15, 1853. *Harper's Monthly*, 6 (1853), 550. In the spring of 1849, the Frémont Association, headed by the prominent Democratic politician, Isaac Fowler, had attempted an overland journey from Galveston, Texas but turned back; one of its members advised New Yorkers not to take any overland route because of the shortage of water and forage. *Trib.*, March 5, June 8, 1849.

4. Robert R. Russel, *Improvement of Communication with the Pacific Coast*, pp. 56–61. Marvin, *Merchant Marine*, pp. 244–45, 254. *Trib.*, June 29, 1849; Feb. 5, 1855.

5. Stimson, *Express*, pp. 112–13, 180–83. Edward Hungerford, *Wells Fargo*, pp. 6, 12, 15, 32. In 1852, Wells Fargo advertised that "by an arrangement with the Pacific Mail Steamship Company, in consideration of our freight being sent by their line, precedence is given our Express Freight over all others, on mail steamers from Panama to San Francisco." *E.P.*, July 19, 1852.

6. *Trib.*, Jan. 30, 31, Feb. 7, 1849. *Bankers Magazine*, 3(1848–49), 528, 587.

7. *Harper's Weekly*, 1(1857), 338. *Trib.*, July 17, 1856. *Hunt's*, 25(1851), 241; 28(1852), 494; 32(1855), 487.

8. *Scientific American*, 7(1851–52), 410. Smith and Cole, *Fluctuations*, p. 90. Hidy, *Baring*, pp. 391–93. Henry Varnum Poor said that the influx of gold psychologically weaned the New York merchant community from its earlier concern over the export of specie and so encouraged the purchase of imports. Chandler, *Poor*, p. 84. *Harper's Weekly*, 1(1857), 338. Between 1850 and 1857, the United States imported a total of $335.3 million more than it exported, excluding specie exports which were $275.7 million more than imports. Smith and Cole, *Fluctuations*, p. 129.

9. Lanier, *Century of Banking*, 212. Egal Feldman, "New York's Men's Clothing Trade," pp. 9–12, 123–31.

10. John H. Morrison, *History of New York Ship Yards* (N.Y.: W. F. Sametz, 1909), pp. 149–52. Marvin, *Merchant Marine*, p. 261. Albion, *New York Port*, pp. 390–403. *Trib.*, Aug. 4, 1856.

11. *Scientific American*, 10(1854–55), 357. Fernando Wood, *Communication . . . to the Common Council . . . Feb. 4th 1856* (N.Y., 1856), pp. 11–14. The city spent over a million dollars on the repair and construction of piers and slips from 1850 through 1854, but public resistance to such spending, opposition to increases in municipal pier rents, and the conversion of waterfront facilities to uses other than commerce prevented New York from catching up with its needs. See the Controller's report, *Trib.*, Feb. 22, 1855.

12. *Trib.*, Oct. 9, 1856. *Hunt's*, 25(1851), 263.

13. *E.P.*, Oct. 31, 1853. *Trib.*, Dec. 6, 1848; Jan. 20, March 20, 1855.

14. Taylor, *Mass Transportation*, pp. 136–37. *Trib.*, Jan. 22, April 18, 1846; Nov. 25, 1847; Oct. 2, 1848. *Doggett's Directory* (1852/53), p. 52.

15. *Trib.*, May 29, 30, 31, 1848. *Democratic Review*, 17(1850), 148–49.

11. THE AGE OF GOLD

16. Foster, *Slices*, 65. *Trib.*, July 12, 1848. *E.P.*, Nov. 2, 1850. *Literary World*, 2(1848), 458. *Putnam's*, 3(1854), 242. Stokes, *Iconography*, 5, 1794, 1814.

17. *Trib.*, May 2, 1845; May 3, 4, 1847; Feb. 1, 15, May 6, 1848; Jan. 1, 1853. *E.P.*, July 13, 1852; Jan. 31, 1854. *Times*, Feb. 1, 1853. B. of Ald., *Docs.* (1850), 1167–69; (1854), 141. The *Tribune* said, regarding a proposal to extend Chambers Street, that the Fourth Ward, "with such a vast amount of manufacturing, shipping, and other business as it contains, has not one single street that leads to the North [Hudson] River, nor is there any tolerable way of getting from the center of the ward to any point on the opposite side of town." July 13, 1855.

18. *Ibid.*, Jan. 11, May 5, 1848; Feb. 1, 1855. *E.P.*, Feb. 26, Dec. 10, 13, 14, 27, 1853; May 19, 20, June 3, 1854.

19. *Trib.*, Feb. 2, Dec. 5, 1848. *E.P.*, March 16, 1854. In 1854, Trinity Church successfully opposed a proposal to improve the access of the lower West Side to the rest of the city by extending Albany Street through the Trinity graveyeard; one advocate of the proposal complained that the obstructionism of that church had long been "a withering blight" upon the property of nearby areas. *Ibid.*, Jan. 17, 18, Feb. 27, 28, March 3, 4, 7, 8, 30, May 9, 1854. *Trib.*, Feb. 3, 1853; Dec. 22, 1854. William Curtis Neys, *The Argument . . . in the Matter of Extending Albany Street* (N.Y., 1854). B. of Ald., *Docs.* (1854), 631–37. The natural cautiousness of property owners regarding street changes that might adversely affect their interests was strengthened by the fact that public improvements of this sort were financed out of assessments on adjoining property. Especially in the 1840s, street improvements were inhibited by memories of the abuses of the assessment system during the boom years before the Panic of 1837. The Common Council was further inhibited by the fear of running afoul of the courts which, on matters of improvement, were inclined to protect the interests of property. Rosewater, *Special Assessments*, pp. v, 13, 28–34ff. Durand, Finance, 32, 58–59. *E.P.*, Jan. 15, Aug. 5, 1846.

20. Stokes, *Iconography*, 3, 699. *Trib.*, July 9, 1845; March 25, 1846; Oct. 11, 1848; Aug. 27, 1852. *E.P.*, Oct. 24, 1849; March 7, April 19, 1854. *Scientific American*, 9(1853–54), 33, 82, 112, 152. *Hunt's*, 31(1854), 72–73.

21. Harry J. Carmen, *Street Surface Railway Franchises of New York City*, pp. 17–27. Stokes, *Iconography*, 3, 657. Meyer, *Transportation*, p. 363. Between September 1839 and September 1840, 605,000 passengers paid to ride the Harlem line from City Hall to 15th Street, another 43,000 to Yorkville and 357,000 more to the town of Harlem. *Trib.*, Oct. 16, 1841.

22. *Trib.*, Oct. 1, 30, 1844; Oct. 23, Nov. 28, 1845; May 15, 1849. *E.P.*, May 1, 1849.

23. Taylor, *Mass Transportation*, pp. 145–46. *Scientific American*, 5(1849–50), 101; 8(1852–53), 293. The proponent of the scheme for an elevated line on Broadway estimated that, on the basis of a 5 cent fare, it would yield a 30 percent return on a $2 million investment. *Trib.*, Oct. 11, 1848.

24. Benedict, *City Travel*, pp. 1, 6–7.

25. *Ibid.*, p. 8–12.

26. *Ibid.*, p. 7–14.

27. B. of Ald., *Docs.* (1850), 700–5, 776–77. *Literary World*, 6(1850), 620. *E.P.*, July 9, 1850.

28. B. of Ald., *Docs.* (1850), 775–77, 991–93.

29. *Ibid.*, pp. 972, 987, 1090.

30. Carmen, *Street Surface Railway*, pp. 41–47. Taylor, *Mass Transportation*. pp. 145–47. *E.P.*, Aug. 1, 1851; Aug. 27, 1852. The failure of the new companies to begin

11. THE AGE OF GOLD

laying their tracks at the time specified in their charters excited suspicions that the omnibusmen among the grantees were more interested in forestalling than in building railroads. In 1852, the Common Council attempted to transfer the Eighth Avenue grant to another company, but this was blocked by Mayor Kingsland. In 1852, both companies hurried their lines into operation to meet charter requirements; the Sixth Avenue Company was to complete its line to 42nd Street before the end of the year, the Eighth Avenue to 51st Street. *E.P.*, Aug. 1, Oct. 3, Nov. 7, 1851; June 8, 18, 23, July 9, 24, Aug. 7, 11, 12, 16, 27, Sept. 1, 1852. *Trib.*, Nov. 13, 1851; Sept. 1, 1852.

31. Carmen, *Street Surface Railway*, pp. 55–61, 72. *E.P.*, Nov. 16, 26, 1852. Among the Third Avenue grantees were Myndert Van Schaick, unsuccessful candidate for mayor in 1849, and Elijah Purdy, Grand Sachem of Tammany Hall. The franchises granted in 1852 were much like those granted the previous year, but they omitted two significant provisions in the earlier grants, one requiring the consent of the Council for any change of ownership and the other giving the city the right to buy the railroad after it had been put into operation; these two omissions and the fact that the grants were made in perpetuity strengthened the character of the franchises as private property, to be bought and sold as such, even though they involved the public streets. Some kind of public control characterized all the franchises, especially in the form of provisions determining the scheduling of street cars, prescribing the way that tracks were to be laid and maintained, and restricting fares to five cents. As with the omnibuses, each car was to be annually licensed by the Mayor at a fee set by the Common Council. D. T. Valentine, ed. *Ordinances of the Mayor, Aldermen and the Commonalty of the City of New York* (N.Y., 1859), pp. 534–42.

32. *E.P.*, Sept. 6, 1852; March 10, May 23, June 5, 1854. In 1854, under a new state law authorizing the stagemen to incorporate, most of the remaining omnibus companies were consolidated into two corporations, the New York Consolidated Stage Company and the Knickerbocker Company. *Trib.*, Nov. 16, 1854.

33. *E.P.*, Oct. 10, Nov. 18, 1853; June 5, July 31, 1854. *Trib.*, May 31, 1856. Poor. *History of Railroads*, pp. 225, 267–71. *Scientific American*, 14(1858–59), 104.

34. *Francis's New Guide* (1857), p. 98. Taylor, *Mass Transportation*, p. 145. The article from the *Economist* was reprinted in the *Railroad Record*, 7(1859–60), 104.

35. Kendall, *Growth*, p. 48. *Trib.*, Nov. 10, 1856. *E.P.*, Feb. 14, 1853; April 5, 1854.

36. Taylor, *Mass Transportation*, pp. 150–51. Critics asserted that the railroads could have charged 3 cents, rather than 5, and still made a profit, a contention disputed by the *Tribune* which declared that most of the critics were uptowners who should have been grateful for receiving a five to six mile ride for 5 cents. In 1854, the Common Council tabled a motion that the Comptroller ascertain the value of the Sixth and Eighth Avenue railroads with the view toward determining whether they could make profits with a 3 cent fare. *Trib.*, March 1, 16, 27, May 15, 1855. *E.P.*, Jan. 10, 1854.

37. Charles Astor Bristed claimed that the horsecars had killed off the development of Second Avenue as "a first class thoroughfare" and went on to note the effect of the railroads on much of residential Brooklyn: "Mile after mile, there is not a street . . . which any person having once seen, would stop to look at a second time. The only impression the place makes on you is a desire to get through it as quickly as possible." Bristed, *A Few Words of Warning . . . on the Consequences of a Railroad in Fifth Avenue*, pp. 11–12, 17–18n. *Trib.*, March 1, May 22, 1855; July 10, 1856. There were also complaints that the railroad companies were delaying uptown development by refusing to extend their rails into the less profitable upper island. *Ibid.*, March 2, 1855. "Clinton," *Real Estate*, p. 10.

11. THE AGE OF GOLD

38. Wood, *Communication* . . . *1857*, p. 18.

39. Taylor, *Mass Transportation*, p. 141, B. of Ald., *Docs.* (1854), 364–72. New York State Senate, *Docs.* (1855), no. 35, pp. 493–94. The *Railroad Record* contended that "the enormous cost of the New York roads is undoubtedly a deception, but they pay a handsome dividend on that large cost," a dividend which earlier it had estimated ranged from 3 to 5 percent per quarter. 3(1855–56), 306; 6(1858–59), 441.

40. Poor, *History of Railroads*, pp. 267–71. *Railroad Record*, 7(1859–60), 104.

41. New York Board of Councilmen, *Remonstrance and Protest Against the Passing of the Bills Now Before the Legislature* (N.Y., 1860), pp. 7–9.

42. *Trib.*, Jan. 7, Nov. 5, 7, 1851. *E.P.*, July 12, Oct. 7, 15, 1851; Sept. 28, 1852. *Times*, Nov. 5, 1851.

43. Dennis T. Lynch, *"Boss" Tweed*, pp. 59–66. The Seventh was one of ten wards in which the Whig vote was split by temperance men and other dissidents. *Trib.*, Nov. 8, 1851. *Times*, Oct. 22, 28, Nov. 1, 4, 6, 1851.

44. Matthew P. Breen, *Thirty Years of New York Politics*, pp. 45–47. Alexander B. Callow, Jr., *The Tweed Ring*, pp. 5–7.

45. *Trib.*, Oct. 4, 1848, June 19, 20, 25, 1849. On Jan. 1, 1851, the *Tribune* blasted a new city contract with the New-York Gas-Light Company, passed by the Council but vetoed by the Mayor, as "the most barefaced job that the annals of our Corporation, so fruitfull of venality, can attest." Lynch indentifies Skaden as Tweed's business mentor and father-in-law (*Tweed*, pp. 38–39), but ignores his relationship with the Second Avenue company; Carmen, *Street Surface Railway*, lists Skaden (p. 55) as one of the grantees but apparently was unaware of his relationship to Tweed.

46. *Doggett's* (1852–53), pp. 17–18. Sweeny was identified as Barr's nephew by the *Tribune*, Jan. 11, 1856. In 1854, he was a director of the New-York Consolidated Stage Company. *Times*, Nov. 6, 1854.

47. *Doggett's* (1852–53), pp. 17–18. Regarding the matter of pay, the *Tribune*, said that the Aldermen, in addition to their $4 daily expense allowances, were paid for their work as judges of the courts of Special Sessions and of General Sessions, as Excise Commissioners, and as County Supervisors; it estimated that total pay for each Alderman ranged from $15 to $50 per working day. March 12, 1852.

48. *Trib.*, Feb. 5, 7, 13, March 16, 1852.

49. Durand, *Finances*, pp. 372–73. Hardenbrook, *Financial New York*, pp. 339–40. By Durand's calculation, the tax rate was $1.14 per $100 valuation in 1850, $.92 in 1851 (there was a substantial increase in assessed values), $.97 in 1852, and $1.23 in 1853. Assessed property values increased by some 40 percent between 1850 and 1853. *E.P.*, Sept. 15, 16, 1852; Feb. 15, 1853. *Trib.*, Jan. 1, 1853.

50. Lynch, *Tweed*, pp. 76–79. *E.P.*, Dec. 29, 1852; Feb. 15, 1853. The *Tribune*, under the heading "How the City is Robbed," charged that in 1852 the Council had rented a city-owned tract of land to an unspecified individual for $610 a year for 21 years, when the tract might have brought five times as much, thus depriving the city of some $60,000 in revenues. March 1, 1853.

51. Lynch, *Tweed*, pp. 76–77. Carmen, *Street Surface Railway*, pp. 47–48, 54–72. *E.P.*, May 25, June 17, 1852; Nov. 2, 1853. *Trib.*, July 9, 10, 23, 27, Aug. 7, 1852. When the Council debated the resolution to reduce the Wall Street Ferry rent, one Alderman informed his colleagues of "what they already knew, that other means than persuasion were resorted to by agents of the Company in order to get the grant." *Times*, Oct. 24, 1853.

52. *E.P.*, Jan. 5, Feb. 17, 1852. *Day-Book*, Feb. 11, Aug. 1, 1852. "Report of the

11. THE AGE OF GOLD

Majority on the Broadway Railroad," New York State Assembly, *Documents* (1856), no. 168, pp. 5–6. The estimate as to annual receipts was found in a memorandum regarding the Broadway Railroad in the Daniel Sickles Papers, New York Historical Society.

53. *E.P.*, July 17, 1852. The *Tribune*, under the heading "Another Railroad Job on Hand—Lookout for Tricks," noted that a quarrel had broken out among the Aldermen as to what committee should consider the proposal; finally, it was assigned to a special committee. A city reporter warned that "Tax-payers and other sufferers would do well to watch this scheme," but, after further investigation, he concluded that the Broadway proposal was the work of honest, responsible men. *Trib.*, July 17, 19, Aug. 2, 9, 1852. Probably much of the controversy within the Board resulted from the hostility of the still powerful omnibus interests. Early in 1853, "Civis," who defended the Council against charges of bribery, asserted that the "friends" of the Broadway project on the Council had "announced to the applicants for the grant their unalterable purpose not to make the grant unless the omnibus owners were compensated, and the cross lines provided to carry passengers to either side of the island . . . for a single fare." *Times*, Feb. 23, 28, 1853. Before the opposition convened a mass meeting of protest in early September, the project had been debated extensively in the press. *E.P.*, July 26, Aug. 18, 20, 25, Sept. 7, 8, 1852.

54. *Ibid.*, Nov. 11, 1852; Jan. 23, 25, Feb. 22, 1853. State Assembly, *Documents* (1856), no. 168, pp. 6–15.

55. *E.P.*, Nov. 18, 1852. Alderman Sylvester Ward of the fashionable Fifteenth Ward, where many of the opponents of the project lived, charged that it involved an "immense monopoly amounting substantially to a gift of $200,000 per annum from the city treasury." A few days later, the *Post* claimed that in the previous two years the Council had given away railroad grants which might have been made to yield at least $600,000 in revenues a year to the city. *Ibid.*, Nov. 20, 23, 1852.

56. Carmen, *Street Surface Railway*, pp. 78–80. *E.P.*, Nov. 20, Dec. 20, 28, 1852.

57. *Ibid.*, Dec. 1, 1852; Jan. 25, 1853. *Times*, Feb. 23, 1853. Breen, *Thirty Years*, p. 99. Probably, the rival proposals were intended to lay the basis for a taxpayer suit against the project; certainly, the grant was stopped by just such a suit initiated by at least one of its opponents, Thomas E. Davies. *E.P.*, Dec. 28, 1852.

58. *Ibid.*, Nov. 23, 1852. Sweeny was listed as an associate of the Manhattan Company in an injunction granted by Judge Roosevelt of the Supreme Court. *Trib.*, Jan. 5, 1853. At this time, he was a partner in the law firm of Willard, Sweeny and Anderson, which specialized in handling litigation involving railway franchises and other municipal grants. One of his partners was Henry H. Anderson who had worked in the law office of Henry Davies, a prominent Whig who, as Corporation Counsel in the early 1850s, had been responsible for most of the legal work in preparing contracts and franchises. McAdam, *Bench and Bar*, 2, 16–17.

59. Carmen, *Street Surface Railway*, pp. 78–80. *E.P.*, Dec. 20, 28, 1852. The injunction was upheld by justices of both the State Supreme and Superior courts, in part on the grounds that taxpayers had been injured by the apparent giveaway of such a valuable franchise, in part because the Council had violated the city charter by making a perpetual grant of the right to use a public street. This last ruling was made by Judge Duer of the Superior Court, who also declared that he could not rule against the grant on grounds of corruption, because he had no evidence of corruption. *Ibid.*, Jan. 29, Feb. 7, April 2, Aug. 25, 1853. *Times*, Nov. 28, 1853.

60. One of the members of the Third Avenue Company testified that he thought

an agent of the company had paid Tweed $3000 to get the Third Avenue grant through the Board of Aldermen. Carmen, *Street Surface Railway*, pp. 47–48. The Grand Jury charged that "enormous sums of money have been expended for and towards the procurement of railroad grants in this city," but it went on to complain that the "voluntary absence" of key witnesses left it without direct testimony on the matter. *Times*, Feb. 26, 1853.

61. *Times*, Feb. 26, 1853. *E.P.*, April 21, 1853.

62. *Trib.*, June 1, 1853.

63. Callow, *Tweed Ring*, pp. 15–16, 163–70, 177–78, 181, 279–98. Beach, *Wealthy Citizens* (1855), p. 73. The net bonded debt of the city was $13,978,564 in 1848 and $14,010,737 in 1855; it was $73,373,522 in 1870. Durand, *Finance*, pp. 374–75. The Democratic Council in 1852 may have been attempting to avoid the fate of its Whig predecessor which, said the *Evening Post*, had borrowed $1 million so as "to keep down taxation for the time being without diminishing the amount of money to be expended." Sept. 23, 1854.

64. Dix, *New York*, p. 8. *E.P.*, Nov. 24, 1854. *Times*, Feb. 16, 1853.

65. Chandler, *Poor*, pp. 100, 113. Strong, *Diary*, 2, 178. *E.P.*, Aug. 15, 1854. Hunt, *Worth and Wealth*, pp. 72, 144, 482, 484. In 1856, the *Herald* moralized on the case of Charles B. Huntington, a broker who had forged drafts of nearly $500,000 on various firms: "Our merchants make their money easy and throw it away foolishly.... They trust all their affairs to confidential clerks, agents, factors, brokers; and it is no wonder that these men dazzled by the display of their employers, should yield to temptation." Reprinted in *Trib.*, Oct. 25, 1856.

66. Not all uptowners were happy with the boom. George Templeton Strong, who had little property, feared the effects of inflation on his hopes for a comfortable life. *Diary*, 2, 69, 122, 132.

67. Miller, *Jacksonian Aristocracy*, p. 180. Rosenberg, *Religion*, p. 166. Arthur Cole, *Wholesale Commodity Prices in the United States*, p. 137. Hidy, *Baring*, p. 437. Whitney, *American Policy*, pp. 308–11. *Harper's Monthly*, 10(1855), 343. *Hunt's*, 33(1855), 337. *Trib.*, March 1, 10, 1853. *E.P.*, Jan. 30, March 17, Sept. 19, 1854. *Times*, Feb. 1, 4, 16, Nov. 10, 1853. The *Times* budget (reprinted in Martin, *Standard of Living*, 395) was inspired by Mayor Westervelt's complaint that the $600 a year salaries paid to policemen was more than the wages earned by skilled mechanics. The budget provided $100 a year for rent for a four room apartment "on the third floor, in a part of the city where the streets are swept every six months." Subsequently, the *Times* declared regarding working men: "Rents are enormous; provisions are very high.... Nothing they have to buy grows cheaper, yet there are plenty who will step into their places." Nov. 8, 10, 1853.

68. *Times*, March 12, 1853. *E.P.*, March 4, April 30, Aug. 2, 12, 27, 29, 30, Sept. 16, 19, 1853; March 31, April 1, June 14, 1854. *Harper's Monthly*, 8(1853), 129. Commons, *American Industrial Society*, 8, 336–43.

69. Strong, *Diary*, 2, 178–81. *Times*, Oct. 20, 23, 25, 26, 28, 30, 1854; Jan. 1, 1855. *Trib.*, Feb. 20, July 11, 1855.

70. Strong, *Diary*, 2, 186–92. Morrison, *Ship Yards*, 153–55. *Times*, Oct. 28, Nov. 6, 1854. *E.P.*, Nov. 6, 1854.

71. *Citizen*, Dec. 23, 1854. *E.P.*, Nov. 28, 1854. *Trib.*, Dec. 23, 1854; Jan. 16, 29, Feb. 3, March 9, May 15, 1855. AICP, *Report* (1856), 17.

72. Rosenberg, *Religion*, p. 237. *Trib.*, Jan. 15, Feb. 8, 20, 1855. The Five Points Mission also announced that it had nearly exhausted its funds. *Trib.*, Feb. 16, 1855.

12. THE TROUBLE WITH POLITICS

73. *Ibid.*, Jan. 13, 16, 17, 18, 19, 20, 25, March 7, 27, 1855. The Emigration Commission had set up an "Intelligence Office and Labor Exchange" which advertised that persons seeking labor "can have their orders filled" at that office; it is probable that the office also supplied strikebreakers to the interior. In February, for instance, it sent 50 men to the Pennsylvania coal country, aided by the railroads which "generously made a reduction of the fare to the society." *Ibid.*, Jan. 29, Feb. 21, 1855.

74. *Ibid.*, Dec. 23, 1854; Jan. 10, 16, 1855. Strong, *Diary*, 2, 209.

75. *Trib.*, Jan. 16, 23, Feb. 5, 1855.

76. *Ibid.*, Jan. 6, Feb. 8, 1855. *Times*, Jan. 17, 1855.

77. *Trib.*, May 8, July 9, 11, 12, 1855; Oct. 11, 1856. *Hunt's*, 34(1856), 77, 583. *Harper's Weekly*, 1(1857), 308. In 1857, W. O. Bourne declared that the "last four years have been full of sorrow and disorder for laborers of the union—the fluctuating demand for labor, the reverses of trade, the very high and apparently increasing articles of consumption," and said that the working men of New York were uniting to preserve "Democracy from a cursed corruption and transition into a hateful oligarchy of delegated power." Address of the Iron Platform Association, May 28, 1857, W. O. Bourne Papers, New York Historical Society. Miller, *Jacksonian Aristocracy*, pp. 147–49. Hunt, *Worth and Wealth*, p. 482.

Chapter 12: The Trouble with Politics

1. *Times*, Aug. 5, 1854. *Putnam's*, 5(1855), 254, 258–59.

2. *Times*, Sept. 3, Oct. 4, 21, 1853; Jan. 9, 1854.

3. Whitman, *New York*, p. 140. *Harper's Weekly*, 1(1857), 65.

4. *Trib.*, March 3, 1853. *Times*, Jan. 2, 28, 1854. B. of Ald., *Docs.*, 21(1854), 332.

5. *Harper's Weekly*, 1(1857), 225.

6. Rosenwaike, *Population*, p. 42. *Eighth Census (1860): Population*, pp. 322–23. 592–93. Cities Census Committee, *Population of the City of New York, 1890–1930* (N.Y., 1932), p. 299. State *Census* (1855), 8. The *Times* casually estimated the population at "Three-quarters of a million." Jan. 2, 1854. An unknown number of immigrants returned to Europe as a result of the hard times in 1854–55.

7. *Times*, Sept. 24, 1853. Ernst, *Immigrant Life*, p. 58. *Harper's Weekly*, 2(1858), 723. Halliday estimated that nearly 80 percent of the 251,344 persons committed to City Prison in previous years were foreigners. *Lost and Found*, p. 184.

8. James F. Richardson, *New York Police, Colonial Times to 1901*, pp. 44–50. Costello, *Police*, pp. 103–5. *Trib.*, March 13, 14, 20, 1844. "Roger Sherman" in *Ibid.*, April 7, 1847. An especially insightful study of the character and purpose of the nineteenth-century police is Wilbur R. Miller, *Cops and Bobbies: Police Authority in New York and London, 1830–1870*.

9. Costello, *Police*, p. 106. Expenditures for police increased from $270,000 in 1844 to $614,000 in 1853. Hardenbrook, *Financial New York*, pp. 339–40.

10. B. of Ald., *Docs.*, 13(1846–47), 502; 22(1855), no. 14, pp. 6–8. *E.P.*, May 14, 1847.

11. *E.P.*, Sept. 3, 1850; April 26, May 10, 1852; March 17, 1853. B. of Ald. *Docs.*, 18(1851), 1034–35.

12. THE TROUBLE WITH POLITICS

12. *E.P.*, March 17, 1853. Richardson, *New York Police*, pp. 51–53, 140–41.

13. *Ibid.*, 49–61. Raymond Fosdick, *American Police Systems*, p. 68.

14. Furer, *Havemeyer*, pp. 112–14. Havemeyer to Samuel J. Tilden, April 22, 1846. Tilden Papers, New York Public Library.

15. *Trib.*, July 1, 8, 16, 1852. *E.P.*, June 5, July 2, 1852. In August, Mayor Kingsland intervened by ordering all Police Captains not to discharge prisoners on the authority of the Aldermen; the District Attorney had declared such discharges illegal. *Ibid.*, Aug. 30, 31, 1852. *Times*, Aug. 20, 1853.

16. Costello, *Our Firemen*, p. 119. B. of Ald., *Docs.*, 17(1850), 934, 945–48, 1015–19. *E.P.*, July 2, 1852. *Times*, Jan. 30, 1853.

17. Duffy, *Public Health*, pp. 310–11. *Trib.*, July 13, 1852. The commissioners of the Croton Department were elected, but the charter of 1849 gave them unusually long (by current standards) five-year terms in office. The *Times* complained that "King Death" was "begotten by the New-York City Government, out of Miasma, who is the daughter of corruption." Sept. 3, 1853. *Scientific American*, 8(1852–53), 61.

18. *Trib.*, Jan. 3, 1853.

19. Durand, *Finances*, pp. 372–73. Hardenbrook, *Financial New York*, pp. 337–40. Common Council, *Manual* (1853), 169. B. of Ald., *Docs.*, 23(1856), 11–13. *E.P.*, Sept. 15, 1852; Feb. 15, 1853. These figures do not include money collected for state taxes nor do they include all money actually received and spent by the city on its various accounts. The Comptroller estimated total receipts, including those for the Sinking Fund to redeem the city's debts and from assessments for public improvements, at $10,849,168 in 1853. *Times*, Feb. 7, 1854.

20. In 1855, a Mr. Walsh of Philadelphia estimated the per capita tax in 1854 as $10.60 for New York, $12.63 for Cincinnati and $15.25 for Boston. *Hunt's*, 33(1855), 719. It has been estimated that in 1860 taxes were $10.52 per capita in New York and about $20 in Boston. Martin, *Standard of Living*, p. 279. It should be noted, however, that the city, with approximately 20 percent of the population of New York State, paid one-half of all property taxes (state and local) collected in that state in 1857. The city's taxes in 1860, per capita, were roughly four times those paid in the rest of the state. John C. Schwab. *History of the New York Property Tax*, pp. 81–83.

21. *Times*, Jan. 2, 1854. Tweed also charged that the Comptroller, the economy-minded A. C. Flagg, had deliberately underestimated expenditures for the next year (1854). Whether deliberate or not, spending from taxes did exceed the Comptroller's estimates by about 10 percent. Durand, *Finances*, p. 89.

22. *E.P.*, Feb. 15, 1853. *Trib.*, March 7, 1853. *Banker's Magazine*, 2(1847–48), 753.

23. *Trib.*, Nov. 1, 1852. *E.P.*, Sept. 24, Oct. 5, 30, 1852. The League also nominated Dr. John H. Griscom for City Inspector, but Griscom, running against the candidates of the two major parties, finished third, 28,000 votes behind the winner. *Ibid.*, Dec. 3, 1852.

24. *E.P.*, March 5, 1853. *Trib.*, March 5, 1853. *Times*, Feb. 28, 1853.

25. *E.P.*, March 7, 1853. *Trib.*, March 7, 1853.

26. *Trib.*, May 11, June 3, 6, 7, 8, 1853. *E.P.*, April 13, June 8, 1853.

27. The amended charter was reported in full by the *Tribune*, March 31, 1853 and in the *Post*, April 13, 1853. It is summarized in Jerome Mushkat, *Tammany: The Evolution of a Political Machine*, p. 276.

28. Richardson, *New York Police*, 65, 78–81. B. of Ald., *Docs.*, 21(1854), 324, 328–29. *E.P.*, Oct. 13, Nov. 16, 1853. *Times*, Jan. 4, 1854.

12. The Trouble with Politics

29. *E.P.*, Sept. 12, 1854. *Trib.*, May 12, 1855.

30. B. of Ald., *Docs.*, 23(1856), No. 2, 22.

31. In supporting the Metropolitan Hall meeting, the *Tribune* urged all good citizens to rally to the cause of reform, charging that "some of them have not even voted half the times; others have barely voted, leaving to the contract-jobbers, office-seekers, grog-shop keepers and hireling rowdies the substantial control of our elections." March 5, 1853.

32. Polling places in each ward were open in primary elections from sunrise to sunset to all Democratic voters whose names were on the poll lists from the previous election. Election inspectors normally were appointed in each ward by ward committees. As the committees also made up slates of delegates and nominees to be approved by the primary meetings, the men who controlled the committees had great influence over local party matters. The committees themselves were annually elected by the Democratic voters of the wards. Leonard, *Politics*, pp. 35–36. *E.P.*, Sept. 5, 14, 24, 26, Nov. 14, 1846; Aug. 18, 21, 30, 1852.

33. *Proceedings of a Number of Democratic Citizens of the Eighth Ward in Opposition to the Secret Clique System* (N.Y., 1843), pp. 2–4. *E.P.*, Sept. 14, Oct. 27, 28, Nov. 14, Dec. 1, 4, 1846; March 24, 31, 1847; May 14, 17, 22, 1852. *Trib.*, April 27, 1846; April 12, 15, 1848.

34. James W. Gerard, a reformer, described the experience he and his friends had in attending an Eighteenth Ward primary held in a "corner groggery." Innocently, they voted along with the rest to permit the chairman of the meeting to select a committee for the purpose of reporting a list of nominees: "I smelt no rat all the time, till the chair gave the list of nominees to the Committee, and then we found out the list was made up of would-be contractors, policemen, and ragamuffin politicians." When Gerard and his friends objected to this procedure, they were outvoted. *Times*, March 7, 1853. Also see Breen, *Thirty Years*, p. 43.

35. *Trib.*, July 30, Aug. 2, 27, 1852. *Day-Book*, Sept. 24, 2852. *E.P.*, Oct. 28, 1851, Oct. 28, 1854. Zane Miller notes the existence of a comparable problem in Cincinnati in the 1880s. *Boss Cox's Cincinnati*, p. 72.

36. *Day-Book*, July 17, 1852. *Times*, Feb. 26, 1853. *Trib.*, July 1, 1852; Aug. 2, 1853. *E.P.*, June 5, 1852.

37. *Ibid.*, Feb. 5, 1853; Oct. 28, 1854. *Times*, March 7, 1853; Nov. 2, 1854. *Trib.*, March 7, 1853.

38. *Times*, Sept. 27, 1853. *Trib.*, Aug. 2, 1853.

39. *Times*, Sept. 29, Oct. 1, 5, 6, 13, 15, 19, Nov. 1, 8, 1853. *E.P.*, Oct. 13, 15, 17, 31, Nov. 1, 1853.

40. *E.P.*, Nov. 10, 12, 1853. *Times*, Nov. 9, 10, 1853; Jan. 2, 6, 11, 1854.

41. Durand, *Finances*, pp. 89, 372–73. *Times*, Nov. 2, Dec. 9, 1854. *E.P.*, June 7, 9, Sept. 23, 1854.

42. *E.P.*, Oct. 28, Nov. 6, 1854. *Times*, Oct. 27, Nov. 2, 6, 1854. Henry J. Raymond's *Times* declared that "there are in reality but two important issues to be decided;—all the others have been dragged into the contest under false pretenses. . . . *Slavery Extension* and the *Liquor Traffic*." The *Times* was tepid in its support of reform, even though its editor was a member of the Reform Committee, perhaps because Raymond was running for Lieutenant Governor on the Whig and Temperance tickets. Oct. 26, Nov. 4, 7, 1854.

43. *Ibid.*, Nov. 1, 7, 10, 14, 1854. *Trib.*, Nov. 9, 14, 1854. *E.P.*, Oct. 13, 1854. A

12. THE TROUBLE WITH POLITICS

combination of Whigs and reformers formed the majority in both houses of the Common Council. *E.P.*, Nov. 9, 1854.

44. DeVoe, *Market Book*, pp. 454–55. William Brewer in 1853, in urging the city to sell off its markets, piers and unneeded lands, declared that *"private property managed by political corporations is always mismanaged."* By private, Brewer seems to have meant all revenue-producing property. *A Few Thoughts*, pp. 14–32. In 1854, Comptroller Flagg proposed that market properties and franchises be leased at public auction and the management of them be put "in the hands of businessmen on the same footing with other business interests." *Trib.*, Feb. 22, 1855.

45. *Harper's Monthly*, 8(1853–54), 125–26, 411–14.

46. Ira M. Leonard and Robert D. Parmet, *American Nativism*, pp. 85–88. Whitney, *American Policy*, p. 277. In the fall of 1853, a controversy erupted over Roman Catholic charges that the Five Points House of Industry, a Protestant mission, was interfering with the efforts of immigrant parents to educate their children in their faith. Soon after, the New York Bible Society complained that it had encountered Catholic interference in its efforts to encourage Bible reading, even of the Catholic Douay Bible. *Times*, Oct. 4, 13, 22, Nov. 22, 1853.

47. Leonard and Parmet, *Nativism*, p. 90. *Times*, Aug. 10, 30, Nov. 10, Dec. 6, 1854. *E.P.*, Aug. 22, 1954. Colonel Ephram L. Snow, a Whig temperance man and later a Know-Nothing, charged that a Whig convention had withdrawn a nomination for the Assembly, which it had initially offered him, because it did "not desire to offend the groggery keepers of our district by presenting a Whig for their suffrage who has dared to declare against Intemperance." *Trib.*, Oct. 28, 1852.

48. State *Census* (1855), p. 8. *Trib.*, July 3, 1857. In 1844, Gansevoort Melville wrote: "Tammany Hall a perfect jam from 8 A.M. till after midnight. Naturalization going on among our friends to an immense extent. On Saturday 260—all *Democrats*—read their papers." Jay Leyda, *The Meville Log*, 1, p. 188. For the same matter, see *Arcturus*, 1(1840–41), 54, and *E.P.*, Oct. 10, 1851. In 1853, a month before the elections, there were numerous meetings of Germans against Sunday restrictions. *Times*, Oct. 19, 24, 1853.

49. *Trib.*, Jan. 31, 1855. *Harper's Monthly*, 10(1854–55), 343.

50. Foster, *New York Naked*, pp. 118, 138. Wittke, *Irish in America*, p. 217. *Trib.*, Nov. 11, 1845. Rosenberg, *Religion*, p. 166. Ernst, *Immigrant Life*, pp. 214–17.

51. Whitney, *American Policy*, pp. 307–12.

52. Scisco, *Nativism*, pp. 85–88, 103–5. Leonard and Parmet, *Nativism*, p. 91.

53. Scisco, *Nativism*, pp. 85–86, 136, 141, 173–76. In 1855, a meeting of nativists adopted an address declaring that their movement intended to: (1) Eliminate "from popular use every foreign language;" (2) Print all public documents in English alone; (3) Require that all schools use English; (4) Disband all military companies "founded on and developing foreign sympathy;" (5) "Purify and ennoble the elective franchise, etc." The address was presented by Cornelius Mathews, a long-time literary nationalist. *Trib.*, June 5, 1855.

54. Scisco, *Nativism*, pp. 206–24. *Trib.*, Nov. 11, 1854.

55. *Citizen*, Oct. 28, 1854.

56. Hartley, *Hartley*, pp. 359–60. At least two New York newspapers agreed that the Roman Church and the immigrants deserved the nativist rebuke, but then concluded that the exclusionary tendencies of the nativists were both un-American and unnecessary. *E.P.*, Aug. 16, 1854. *Times*, Dec. 6, 1854.

57. *Harper's Weekly*, 2(1858), 723.

13. TAMMANY'S CITY

Chapter 13: Tammany's City

1. *American Whig Review*, 6(1847), 234.

2. State *Census* (1855), pp. 178–95. The ten largest groups of semi-skilled and skilled workers were: (1) Tailors, 12,609 (as many of these were largely unskilled sewers, I have arbitrarily halved the number in computing the total number of semi-skilled and skilled workers); (2) Carpenters, 6901; (3) Boot and shoemakers and dealers, 6745; (4) Masons, plasterers, bricklayers, etc., 3634; (5) Painters, glaziers and varnishers, 3400; (6) Bakers, 2865; (6) Blacksmiths, 2611; (8) Cabinet-makers and dealers, 2606; (9) Printers, 1901; (10) Stone and marble polishers, 1755. See also Ernst, *Immigrant Life*, pp. 214–17.

3. State *Census* (1855), pp. 178–95. The total is in line with Doggett's estimate in 1843 that about 6 percent of the populations of major cities and towns in the United States were businessmen. The *Eighth Census (1860): Manufactures* reported 4375 manufacturing establishments in the city.

4. Whitman's "Carol of Occupations," written in 1855.

5. Harlow, *Old Bowery Days*, pp. 218–19. Mathews, *Pen-and-Ink*, pp. 126–27. *Trib.*, Jan. 19, 1855.

6. Mathews, *Pen-and-Ink*, p. 136, and *Big Abel*, p. 73.

7. Harlow, *Old Bowery Days*, pp. 188–97. Mathews, *Pen-and-Ink*, pp. 88–89, 132. Foster, *New York by Gas-Light*, pp. 101–7. Bobo, *Glimpses*, pp. 161–65.

8. Whitman, *Complete Prose*, p. 442. Harlow, *Old Bowery Days*, pp. 211–12. Odell, *Annals*, 5, 363, 372–74. *Trib.*, March 12, 1855.

9. Harlow, *Old Bowery Days*, pp. 187–88. Asbury, *Gangs of New York*, pp. 28–30. Hone, *Diary*, p. 434.

10. *Times*, Sept. 28, 1853, Oct. 17, 1853. *E.P.*, Aug. 25, 1854. *Trib.*, Oct. 8, 20, 1856; July 1, 1857.

11. The best discussion of the role of sports in urban life during this period is Dale A. Somers, *The Rise of Sports in New Orleans*, part I. New York pugilists and other sporting figures were prominent in the New Orleans sporting scene. *Ibid.*, pp. 49–50, 55–58, 61. There were some organized sporting events in New York: For baseball, see *Trib.*, May 26, July 7, 18, 21, 1855. For foot-racing, see *E.P.*, July 29, Aug. 4, 8, 10, 12, 17, 1854. For the *Turnverein*, see *Trib.*, June 8, 21, 1852; May 13, 1856.

12. Coleman, *Going to America*, pp. 187–88. Breen, *Thirty Years*, p. 529. *Trib.*, March 10, 12, 1855.

13. *Subterranean*, Nov. 15, 1845. Soon after Poole's death, DeWitt and Davenport published *The Life of William Poole, with a Full Account of the Terrible Affray In Which He Received His Death-Wound. His last words, "I Die a True American" . . . Phrenological Character . . . By Messrs. Fowler and Wells, Examination of his Heart by Edward H. Dixon Etc.*

14. *Subterranean*, Jan. 23, Feb. 13, 1847. *Trib.*, Aug. 7, 1841. In 1854, the *Post* complained that the Truancy Act was "a dead letter," and said that when the police initially enforced the act, "many Irish fathers and mothers came to the Hall of Justice and got their children released on condition that they would take care of them and send them to school." *E.P.*, Oct. 19, 1854.

15. *Times*, Sept. 2, 1853. *Subterranean*, July 11, 1846. In 1841, Greeley proposed the establishment of "a Ward House in each ward, with a Lecture-Room, a Library, and every intellectual attraction and aid for the great body of the People. . . . Such a building, however humble, would form a point of union, an intellectual centre." He

soon added, however, that to take full advantage of such centers, the people would first have to be freed from the burden of poverty. *Trib.*, July 12, 29, 1841.

16. *E.P.*, July 3, 18, 1851; Sept. 14, 20, 1854. *Trib.*, Jan. 13, 1846; Feb. 7, May 1, 1855. Among the irritants to small retailers was the suppression by the police in 1855 of sandwichboard advertising. Some temperance schemes were plainly intended to drive the small drinking-house proprietors out of business. In 1853, "many of our prominent citizens," urged the Mayor to deny grocers licenses to sell liquor and to raise the price of liquor licenses from $10 to $50. *Ibid.*, July 17, 1855. *E.P.*, April 30, 1853.

17. *Trib.*, Dec. 30, 1845. *Independent*, Feb. 15, 1849.

18. *E.P.*, May 22, 1847. In 1849, the *Tribune*, in urging good and able men to stand for the Common Council, said that "we know our greatest obstacle to better government has hitherto been the obstinate refusal of the fittest men to serve in such a thankless, annoying and unpaid position." Feb. 3, 1849.

19. The yearly Common Council *Manuals* listed positions and those who held them. Also see B. of Ald., *Docs.*, 23(1856), 13, 20, 27.

20. "Report of the Secretary of Treasury" (1849), U.S. Senate, *Documents*, 31st Cong., 1 sess., pp. 322–44, 363–70. *Tribune [Whig] Almanac* (1849), pp. 24–25. Other important federal officials were the Postmaster, District Attorney, and Marshal.

21. The Common Council *Manuals* give the vote by ward for mayoralty candidates. In six mayoralty elections, 1841–1843 and 1846–1848 (1844 and 1845 were confused by the American Republican party), Whig candidates carried the First Ward four times and the Second, five (these two wards formed the tip of Manhattan), the Third Ward all six times and the Fifth, four times (these wards were west of Broadway and south of Canal Street) and the Fifteenth, all six times; the Whigs were also strong in the West Side Ninth Ward.

22. In 1857, after the disappearance of the Whig organization, the *Tribune* said that the Republicans and nativist parties were strongest in the Eighth, Ninth, Fifteenth, and Sixteenth wards, all west of Broadway. *Trib.*, July 1, 1857. In these wards, native-born voters outnumbered foreign-born voters 2 to 1 (14,566 to 7,345). State *Census* (1855), p. 8. Per-capita property in 1854 in these four wards was about $670, more than double the figure ($312) for the predominantly Democratic wards east of Broadway. These figures are based on assessed values as reported in *Hunt's*, 31(1854), 489. They exclude the Eighteenth Ward east of Broadway and north of 14th Street, a ward which, chiefly because of the concentration of wealth around Union Square, rivaled the Fifteenth as the wealthiest in the city outside of the predominantly commercial wards at the tip of the island.

23. In seven mayoralty elections in 1841–1843 and 1845–1848, Democrats carried the Fourth, Sixth, Fourteenth, and Sixteenth wards seven times each; all but the Sixteenth were on the East Side, as were the Seventh (carried but twice), the Tenth (five), the Eleventh (five), the Thirteenth (six), and the Seventeenth (six). In five elections for the Board of Aldermen, 1841–43 and 1847–48, the Democrats were especially strong in the Fourth (four victories), Sixth (four), Tenth (five), Eleventh (four), Thirteenth (five). In the eight East Side wards in 1855, there were 19,954 foreign-born and 13,733 native-born voters, about 47 percent of the foreign-born and 30 percent of the native-born voters in the city. State *Census* (1855), p. 8.

24. *Trib.*, Nov. 15, 1848. Ernst, *Immigrant Life*, pp 166–67.

25. Leonard, *Politics*, p. 35. *Secret Clique System* (1843), pp 2–4. *E.P.*, April 2, 3, 8, 11, 1841; Jan. 31, Sept. 5, 14, 24, 26, Nov. 14, Dec. 4, 1846; April 14, 1847 (meeting

notices, public letters and editorials). Much of the controversy centered on the first step in the primary process—the selections of persons to be nominated. Generally, this was done by a committee dominated by those who controlled the ward; then, the slate was submitted for approval by the rank-and-file in primary meetings. Those who contested the slate had to stand against the power of the ward organization. Although most complaints were about Democratic primaries, the Whigs, too, had their problems. In 1854, for instance, the "Independent Whigs" of the Thirteenth Ward condemned the primary system as "a fraud and a swindle" designed by and for "tricky demagogues and mercenary politicians." *Trib.*, Nov. 4, 1854.

26. *E.P.*, Jan. 14, March 30, April 2, 4, Dec. 1, 2, 1846; April 14, 16, 1847.

27. In 1846, Mike Walsh complained that it was impossible for a man to get elected "unless he is himself of ample means and spends it freely with a certain prospect of regaining it fifty fold in case of success—or basely sells himself to corrupt and wealthy men." In early 1851, the *Post* charged that agents of steamship companies seeking federal mail subsidies were spending money "freely" in the primaries and nominating conventions to assure the election of Congressmen favorable to subsidies. *E.P.*, Oct. 8, 1851.

28. *Trib.*, April 27, Sept. 27, Nov. 23, 1846. In 1843, the *Tribune* claimed that as it was possible for men to vote illegally in many of the city's 75 election districts "a few hundred determined villains may easily cast *ten* thousand votes at an election." April 27, 1843; June 25, 1846. In 1840, the Whig-controlled state legislature enacted a registry law for New York City, but this was replaced in 1842 by a system of election inspectors, three for each ward, to be selected by the Common Council. In 1842, three men including George Matsell (later Chief of Police) were arrested for allegedly voting vagrants from the Almshouse, but they were acquitted by a court. *Trib.*, April 20, 25, 1842. *Brother Jonathan*, 3(1842), 525.

29. Mushkat, *Tammany*, pp. 1–2, 8–9. The Society determined its own membership; it elected its officers annually.

30. *E.P.*, Dec. 21, 1853. *Subterranean*, Oct. 25, 1845.

31. Mushkat, *Tammany*, pp. 209, 228. In 1847, the General Committee refused a petition to overturn the nomination of George Purser in the Fourth Ward; the previous year, it had refused to act on a similar petition from Purser's supporters. In 1852, the Committee divided sharply over the question as to whether the ward committees should appoint the inspectors to supervise ward primaries. It initially appointed the inspectors in 1852 but, when it encountered resistance to this "centralization," decided to permit the ward committees to replace two of the three inspectors which it had appointed for each ward. *E.P.*, Feb. 22, 1841; March 28, 1846; Aug. 18, 21, 1852. *Trib.*, June 3, 1847.

32. Mushkat, *Tammany*, pp. 233–64, 66. Gustavus Myers, *The History of Tammany Hall*, pp. 143–48.

33. Mushkat, *Tammany*, pp. 264–66. Myers, *Tammany*, p. 33. *Democratic Review*, 40(1857), 518–20. *E.P.*, Jan. 9, 1854. In early 1853, a Democrat complained that after four years of Whig management of the Custom House there remained only 62 Democrats among the 625 persons employed there. *Ibid.*, March 10, 1853.

34. Mushkat, *Tammany*, pp. 269–74. *E.P.*, Jan. 21, Feb. 10, 14, 1853. *Times*, Sept. 3, 1853.

35. *E.P.*, June 12, 1854.

36. *Ibid.*, Sept. 6, 1854.

37. Leonard Chalmers, "Fernando Wood and Tammany Hall: The First Phase," p.

13. Tammany's City

380. Browne, *Great Metropolis*, p. 627. *Harper's Weekly* published an excellent engraving of a photograph of Wood taken by Matthew Brady in its Dec. 12, 1857 issue.

38. Samuel A. Pleasants, *Fernando Wood of New York*, pp. 11–17. Donald MacLeod, *Biography of Hon. Fernando Wood*, pp. 40–46.

39. *E.P.*, June 11, 1840. Wood was charged with using money which mistakenly had been put in his account and refusing to return it. Wood's side of the matter was presented in *Ibid.*, Nov. 2, 27, 1840.

40. MacLeod, *Wood*, pp 58–59. Pleasants, *Wood*, pp. 24–27. In his 1855 edition of *Wealthy Citizens*, Beach estimated Wood's wealth at $200,000. In 1861, Reuben Vose listed Wood as worth $500,000. Wood was challenged for renomination in 1842. When the rivalry threatened to split the party, he and his rival were both dropped in favor of another candidate. Leonard, *Politics*, pp. 263–64.

41. Pleasants, *Wood*, pp. 30–32. Ernst, *Immigrant Life*, p. 289. Hone, *Diary*, p. 925. *E.P.*, Nov. 4, 6, 7, 9, 1850. *Trib.*, Nov. 6, 1854. Wood allegedly inflated bills of sale to convince Malverne that he had invested more in the venture than he acutally had.

42. Pleasants in his biography says that Wood manipulated the Hard primaries through the General Committee (p. 46), thereby attributing Wood's alleged tactics in an entirely different situation in 1856 to 1854. Mushkat asserts that Wood "packed the Hard meeting with hired thugs who then intimidated the startled delegates into selecting him" (*Tammany*, p. 284). These assertions seem unfounded. The Hard primaries, like those of the Softs, were unusually peaceful. It was not until the Hards met to make their nomination that their leaders awoke to the fact that, as the *Post* put it, "Fernando Wood had more friends present than was thought wholesome for Hard Shell democracy." The *Post* charged that Wood had packed the convention but makes no mention of hired thugs. Wood had been a leading advocate of a fusion of the two factions, so it is not unlikely that he had considerable support from Hards who were sick of intraparty conflict. He won the nomination with 33 of the 61 votes cast at the convention. *E.P.*, Sept. 15, 27, 29, Oct. 4, Oct. 10, 13, 21, 1854. *Times*, Aug. 30, Oct. 3, 4, 1854.

43. Strong, *Diary*, 2, 195–96. *E.P.*, Oct. 27, 28, 31, Nov. 1, 4, 6, 8, 11, 1854. *Trib.*, Nov. 3, 6, 11, 14, 1854. *Times*, Nov. 7, 10, 1854. *Citizen*, Nov. 18, 1854.

44. *Trib.*, Nov. 9, 11, 13, 14, 15, 17, 1854. *E.P.*, Nov. 9, 16, 1854.

Chapter 14: Tyranny, Tammany, and the State

1. *New York Daily News*, Nov. 29, 1859, clipping in Genet Scrap Book, New York Public Library. "Donald MacLeod," *Wood*, pp. 14–15. The quotations are taken from a long speech, as reported in the *News*, which Wood gave in 1859 at Mozart Hall (his version of Tammany). Some of these same passages, however, were used earlier in 1856 by "MacLeod" in a campaign biography of Wood. It may be that Wood was the actual author of this biography. In a later biography, Samuel A. Pleasants does not refer to this speech, but he does quote a passage from Wood's annual message in 1860 in which the Mayor makes the same general argument for executive authority. *Wood*, p. 102.

2. MacLead, *Wood*, pp. 14–15. Bristed, *A Few Words of Warning*, p. 26.

14. TYRANNY, TAMMANY, AND THE STATE

3. MacLeod, *Wood*, 157–62. B. of Ald., *Docs.*, 23(1856), no. 1, pp. 13–14. *Trib.*, Jan. 3, 4, 1855. *Times*, Jan. 3, 1855.

4. MacLeod, *Wood*, pp. 163, 170–81. *Trib.*, Jan. 12, 1855.

5. MacLeod, *Wood*, pp. 163–64. *Times*, Jan. 3, 1855. *Trib.*, Jan. 5, 6, 11, 23, 1855. He did recommend that the Common Council adopt Peter Cooper's plan to employ the jobless in quarrying stone for the construction of new piers to improve docking facilities. *Times*, Feb. 9, 1855.

6. *Trib.*, Jan. 23, Feb. 14, 26, 1855; Jan. 16, 1856. *Times*, Feb. 3, 6, 1855.

7. Wood to Gov. M. H. Clark, April 29, 1856. Wood Miscellaneous Papers, New York Public Library.

8. *Trib.*, Nov. 15, 1854; Jan. 3, 1855. *Times*, Jan. 3, 1855.

9. James F. Richardson, "Mayor Fernando Wood and the New York Police," pp. 8. Fosdick, *Police Systems*, pp. 69–70. *Trib.*, Jan. 12, Feb. 23, March 1, 30, May 28, July 11, 1855; July 18, 1856. B. of Ald., *Docs.*, 23(1856), no. 10, pp. 33–38.

10. MacLeod, *Wood*, pp. 212–14. *Trib.*, Feb. 9, 12, March 7, 1855.

11. *Trib.*, Jan. 15, 18, 19, 22, 25, 29, 31, Feb. 9, 20, 1855.

12. *Ibid.*, Feb. 1, March 23, 28, 29, 30, April 3, May 23, 1855.

13. *Ibid.*, Jan. 18, 25, 30, 31, Feb. 9, 21, April 3, 1855. *Times*, Feb. 6, 1855.

14. *Trib.*, April 3, May 21, 1855. *Times*, April 9, 1855. Strong, *Diary*, 2, 212, 218. The *Tribune*, though it praised Wood's messages in January, did express uneasiness regarding the Mayor's avowed intention "to exercise doubtful powers in the administration of his office." Jan. 13, 1853.

15. *Times*, April 2, 1855. *Harper's Monthly*, 10(1855), 553; 11(1855), 123. *Trib.*, Feb. 16, March 8, April 14, 1855.

16. Richardson, *Wood*, pp. 9–10. *E.P.*, March 22, 27, 1854. *Trib.*, Feb. 16, 1853; Feb. 22, March 12, 1855. *Times*, April 6, 1855.

17. MacLeod, *Wood*, pp. 219–20. *Trib.*, March 13, 15, 20, 21, 22, April 4, 6, 1855.

18. *Ibid.*, Jan. 29, April 7, 9, 17, 1855.

19. *Ibid.*, April 7, 1855.

20. *Times*, April 20, 25, 28, 1855. An estimated 10,000 people signed the call for a mass meeting of protest. *Trib.*, July 2, 3, 1855.

21. *Ibid.*, May 1, 4, 1855. *Times*, April 28, 30, 1855. The police, however, continued to make arrests for selling liquor without a license. *Trib.*, May 11, 1855.

22. Pleasants, *Wood*, pp. 54–55. Richardson, *Wood*, p. 20. Chalmers, *Wood*, p. 587. *Trib.*, May 7, July 9, 12, 16, 23, 1855; May 9, 1856. *Times*, July 4, 9, 1855. *Harper's Monthly*, 11(1855), 399, 688.

23. *Times*, Nov. 2, 1855. The *Times* charged that the failure of the Mayor to push for the conviction of the proprietors of gambling houses was chiefly responsible for the failure even to bring them to trial. Oct. 26, 1855. The *Tribune* claimed that, while Wood had publicly instructed the Police to enforce the acceptable provisions of the Prohibitory Law, he had not *really* instructed them to do so. July 9, 1855.

24. Richardson, *Wood*, pp. 11–12. MacLeod, *Wood*, pp. 234–35. *Trib.*, June 7, July 3, 4 6, 1855.

25. Pleasants, *Wood*, pp. 56–57. *Trib.*, July 12, 14, 19, 24, 1855. *Times*, July 10, 19, 20, 21, 24, 27, Oct. 26, 1855.

26. B. of Ald., *Docs.*, 23(1856), no. 1, pp. 13–15; no. 10, p. 29. *Trib.*, Jan. 8, 1856. *Times*, Jan. 8, 1855.

27. *Ibid.*, Feb. 5, 1856. B. of Ald., *Docs.*, 23(1856), no. 10, pp. 27–52. Wood, *Communication . . . Feb. 4, 1856*, 11–15, 22–24, 45–46, 55–56.

14. TYRANNY, TAMMANY, AND THE STATE

28. *Ibid.*, pp. 27–29, 36–40. B. of Ald., *Docs.*, 23(1856), no. 10, pp. 27–31, 73. MacLeod, *Wood*, pp. 189, 308–9. *Times*, Dec. 27, 1856.

29. *Ibid.*, July 8, 1856. B. of Ald., *Docs.*, 23(1856), no. 31, pp. 7–9.

30. *Times*, July 8, 1856. *Trib.*, Jan. 8, 1856.

31. In a public letter to a state legislator, Wood said that a return to spring elections was essential to the city's welfare, because under the existing system: (1) the number of candidates was so great as to confuse the voter; (2) local issues were overshadowed at election time by state and national issues; (3) state and national interests served to disrupt city elections: "The power derived from the patronage of the Central Government in this City overwhelms all other political considerations." *Trib.*, Feb. 19, 1855.

32. *Ibid.*, May 14, July 21, 26, 1856. *Day-Book*, April 24, May 5, 1856. *Times*, July 11, 1856.

33. Durand, *Finances*, pp. 372–73. Hardenbrook, *Financial New York*, p. 340. Wood, *Communication . . . Feb. 4, 1856*, pp. 4–5. B. of Ald., *Docs.*, 23(1856), no. 34, pp. 11–38. *Trib.*, Oct. 8, 1856. *Times*, Jan. 22, 23, 1857. There were 36,224 arrests in 1852, 52,815 in 1855, and 45,287 in 1856. Costello, *Police*, p. 144. Comptroller Flagg said that more than one half of the increase in expenditure was beyond the control of the Common Council. *Times*, Sept. 4, 1856.

34. *Trib.*, Aug. 9, Nov. 13, 14, 1856. *Day-Book*, May 8, 1856. *Times*, July 3, 19, Aug. 2, 9, Oct. 10, 1856. *Harper's Monthly*, 13(1856), 703. Ebling was charged with demanding a bribe from Smith, Seckel and Company who planned, with Wood's endorsement, to use street sweeping machines; he was brought to trial early in 1856 but escaped punishment when his jury split nine to three for conviction. *Trib.*, Jan. 31, May 8, July 23, 24, 1855; Jan. 26, 28, 1856.

35. *Times*, Sept. 3, 1856. Mushkat, *Tammany*, p. 297. Lucy Kavaler claims that Astor and other landlords were "rewarded with low tax assessments and additional waterfront rights" after Wood's reelection, but gives no supporting evidence. *Astors*, p. 65. It is likely that Wood's proposals early in 1856 for the rapid development of uptown areas did have a strong appeal for large landowners like the Astors.

36. Mushkat, *Tammany*, pp. 289–93, 296–97. Chalmers, *Wood*, p. 389. William C. Gover, *The Tammany Hall Democracy*, pp. 34–38.

37. *Day-Book*, May 5, 1856. Richardson, *Wood*, pp. 12–17. In 1855, Alderman Briggs of the Thirteenth Ward, a nativist intent on ferreting out foreigners from government, charged that Wood had appointed Frank O'Keefe as a police lieutenant and Simeon O'Keefe as a deputy to a city official. Since David O'Keefe and David O'Keefe, Jr. also held public office, said Briggs, it only seemed logical to urge Wood to appoint Mrs. O'Keefe as a police matron. *Trib.*, June 6, 1855. According to Chief Matsell, about 27 percent of the police force was of Irish birth in 1855; Irish policemen outnumbered native-born members of the force in the First, Fourth, Sixth, and Fourteenth wards, all heavily Irish and pro-Wood. *Ibid.*, March 20, 1855.

38. *Ibid.*, Oct. 8, 9, 1856. *Times*, April 16, 1857. [Tammany Society], *Statement of the Majority . . . Feb. 14, 1857* (N.Y., 1857), pp. 10–11. Gustave Myers elaborated on these charges (*Tammany*, p. 176) as does Mushkat (*Tammany*, pp. 297–98). The best account is Chalmers, *Wood*, pp. 390–92.

39. *Ibid.*, pp. 392–93. *Times*, Sept. 16, 21, 1856. *Trib.*, Oct. 4, 9, 1856.

40. [Abijah Ingraham], *A Biography of Fernando Wood* (n.p., n.d.), pp. 2–31. Although this pamphlet is published without the author's name, it ends with a copy of a purported agreement, signed by an "Abijah Ingraham," with Wood not to publish

[504]

these charges, supposedly "the production of various pens," in exchange for $500. According to Ingraham, he took the money and published the pamphlet anyway. *Ibid.*, p. 32.

41. *Ibid.*, pp. 30–31. *Trib.*, Oct. 14, 15, 18, 1856. In a long public letter written after Wood's renomination, Peter B. Sweeny and S. Y. Savage, as secretaries of the anti-Wood Central Committee, charged that Wood had so manipulated the primaries as to give him control over "every nomination for office from Mayor to constable, including Congressmen, members of the Legislature, City officials, Aldermen," etc., and went on to assert that it was Wood, not Libby, who had the support of the Custom House. *Times*, Sept. 27, 1856.

42. *Trib.*, Oct. 18, 20, 31, 1856. Richardson, *Wood*, p. 23.

43. *Times*, Jan. 1, Oct. 28, 31, 1856. *Trib.*, Oct. 21, 31, 1856. Richardson, *Wood*, p. 23.

44. *Trib.*, Oct. 10, 14, 28, 30, 1856. *Times*, Oct. 13, 23, Nov. 3, 1856.

45. Chalmers, *Wood*, pp. 393, 400. *Trib.*, Oct. 27, Nov. 8, 11, 1856. *Times*, Nov. 5, 6, 1856. Buchanan also had substantial pluralities in Kings and Richmond counties and in Bergen County, New Jersey. He was narrowly defeated by Frémont in Westchester and Hudson counties and by Fillmore in Queens. *Ibid.*, Nov. 6, 7, 1856.

46. *Trib.*, Nov. 12, 13, 1856.

47. *Times*, Jan. 24, 1857. In the late winter, a committee of the Academy of Medicine, with Dr. John H. Griscom as its leading member, urged the state to create a Metropolitan Health Commission to eliminate politics from matters of public health. *Ibid.*, March 28, 1857. Duffy, *Public Health*, p. 554.

48. Wood, *Communication . . . Jan. 5, 1857* (N.Y., 1857), 3–13. *Times*, Jan. 6., 1857.

49. *Trib.*, Jan. 24, 1853. In the State Assembly, every Democrat voted against the new charter and all but three Republicans voted for it. *Times*, March 27, 1857.

50. Hoffman, *Digest of the Charters, Statutes and Ordinances*, 1, 43–45, 120–39, 185–92, 212–35, 306. Valentine, *Ordinances*, pp. 9–22. New York State Assembly, *Documents* (1857), nos. 125 and 126. Durand, *Finances*, p. 77. In the hope of disrupting the old system of politics which had ruled the Board of Aldermen, the wards were eliminated in favor of 17 aldermanic districts which, especially in the lower city, overlapped the old ward boundaries. The First District, for instance, included portions of the Second and Third wards as well as all of the First Ward. A new Board of Councilmen, reduced to 24 members, was to be elected from the city's four state senatorial districts, six from each district. The *Times* said that this redistricting would end the system of "rotten boroughs" which had given the lower city undue influence in the Common Council. Wood, however, charged that the new districts had been gerrymandered to the benefit of the minority Republican party. *Times*, April 13, May 7, 1857.

51. Durand, *Finances*, pp. 66, 78. *Harper's Monthly*, 15(1857), 117. *Times*, March 17, April 10, 18, May 28, 1857. *Trib.*, July 4, 1857. Dean Richmond, Chairman of the State Democratic Committee, wrote to S. J. Tilden that the promoters of the police bill were willing to "give our friends the selection of one half the commissioners if we get our Senators to help get it through—they want to breakup the present organization but do not want the responsibility for doing it alone. . . . It will give a large patronage to our friends." April 2, 1857, Tilden Papers, New York Public Library.

52. The Metropolitan Police Law can be found in Reed and Webbink, *Documents*, pp. 222–25. *Times*, April 18, 1857. Also see Richardson, *Wood*, pp. 29–30, and Fosdick, *Police Systems*, pp. 83–85. The *Times*, which initially had opposed the idea of a state commission on the grounds that the state constitution prohibited state appointment of

14. TYRANNY, TAMMANY, AND THE STATE

local officials, supported the new law as providing for a "State Police" removed from the constitutional prohibition. Feb. 28, March 24, 1857.

53. New York State Assembly, *Documents* (1857), no. 127, pp. 2–5. *Times*, March 24, 1857.

54. *Harper's Weekly*, 1(1857), 225. In 1867, the Citizens Association, headed by Peter Cooper, defended state-appointed commissions on the grounds that New York was a metropolis of vital importance to the whole state, adding that the "foreign vote" in the city was 80,000, while the native vote was only 52, 000. Reed and Webbink, *Documents*, pp. 114–22.

55. Quoted in Mandelbaum, *Boss Tweed's New York*, pp. 50–51.

56. *Times*, April 16, May 1, 13, 1857. *Harper's Weekly*, 1(1857), 194. *Proceedings . . . of the Young Men's Democratic Union Club* (N.Y., 1857), pp. 9–10, 30. *Democratic Review*, 40(1857), 67-78.

57. *Democratic Review* pp. 207–9. The *Times* agreed that local self-government was essential: "We look to it for the growth of public spirit, for the habit of self-government, for the virtue of independence, for reverence, for forming and for the spread of sound morality, and the culture of self-restraints." It concluded, however, that self-government in New York had only brought corruption and recklessness which required a centralization of power: "Most of the objects of a city administration are far better carried out . . . by a vigorous and arbitrary police system than by a representative assembly." May 7, 1857.

58. Mushkat, *Tammany*, pp. 300–7. Leonard Chalmers, "Tammany Hall, Fernando Wood, and the Struggle to Control New York City," pp. 7–9.

59. *Times*, April 18, 20, 22, 1857. The *Times* set the stage for this attack in a lengthy editorial, "Our Municipal Horizon," in which it referred to a "civic conspiracy," "ever vigilant and omnipresent system of espionage," and "drilled and disciplined army," and concluded that "our political liberty has been suppressed, our municipal treasury depleted, our city made the scoff of all mankind." All of this was developed out of Recorder Smith's charges that Wood had tyrannically misused his power over the police. April 8, 11, 14, 1857.

60. *Ibid.*, April 30, May 7, 8, 12, 1857.

61. Richardson, *Wood*, pp. 29–38. *Weekly Journal of Commerce*, April 30, 1857. *Times*, April 13, 16, 21, 23, 30, 1857.

62. Richardson, *Wood*, p. 34. *Harper's Weekly*, 1(1857), 289, 338. *Times*, May 19, 20, 21, 22, 26, 27, June 8, 1857.

63. *Ibid.*, June 10, 11, 19, 1857. Furer, *Havemeyer*, p. 195. Strong, *Diary*, 2, 342. Gustavus Myers says that Wood sold the office to Develin for $50,000 (*Tammany*, 182). "Civis," writing in the *Tribune*, charged that the Street Department in the past had inflated assessments for public works by padding its payrolls, and concluded by saying that it was understandable that the Mayor and the Governor would struggle over the department, since it was a valuable prize. *Trib.*, July 3, 1857.

64. Costello, *Police*, pp. 141–42. Pleasants, *Wood*, pp. 78–80. Strong, *Diary*, 2, 343–45. *Times*, June 17, 19, 1857.

65. *Ibid.*, June 17, 19, 1857. *Trib.*, July 3, 4, 1857.

66. *Ibid.*, July 6, 1857. *Harper's Weekly*, 1(1857), 434, 438. Strong, *Diary*, 2, 346–50. Headley, *Great Riots*, pp. 131–34. Asbury, *Gangs of New York*, pp. 112–17.

67. *Trib.*, July 14, 18, 1857. *Times*, July 10, 13, 15, 1857. Significantly the Germans charged that the police used guns as well as clubs against a crowd which had gathered on Avenue A. *Ibid.*, July 21, 23, 1857.

15. METROPOLIS

68. Mushkat, *Tammany*, pp. 306–8. Chalmers, *Tammany*, pp. 12–13. *Times*, Sept. 4, Oct. 16, 19, 22, 1857. The ward associations, like the Tammany Society, were restricted, new members being admitted by a majority vote of existing members. Membership in each association was limited to those who were legal voters in the ward. The associations chose five delegates each to the General Committee. *Ibid.*, June 13, 1857.

69. *Ibid.*, Oct. 9, 21, 23, 1857. Chalmers, *Tammany*, p. 13. Stokes, *Iconography*, 5, 1870.

70. *Times*, Oct. 27, 1857. *Trib.*, Oct. 23, 26, Nov. 10, 11, 12, 1857. Strong, *Diary*, 2, 370. AICP, *Report* (1858–, p. 19. *Harper's Weekly*, 1(1857), 799. The Superintendent of the Metropolitan Police recommended that ten policemen in each ward be armed with revolvers "for the suppression of riots." When the state decided to build a new armory at 35th Street and Seventh Avenue, General Sandford expressed satisfaction that this arsenal was more than a mile closer to City Hall than the former one. Near the end of November, there were rumors of plans to seize the arsenals as part of "an organized crusade against law and order." *Weekly Journal of Commerce*, Nov. 5, 12, 26, 18f;57.

71. Mushkat, *Tammany*, p. 309. Furer, *Havemeyer*, p. 194. Chalmers, *Tammany*, pp. 15–16. *Democratic Review*, 42(1858), 427–36. *Trib.*, Nov. 4, 6, 12, 28, 30, Dec. 2, 1857. *Weekly Journal of Commerce*, Nov. 26, 1857.

72. *Ibid.*, Dec. 3, 1857. *Times*, Dec. 2, 3, 1857. *Harper's Weekly*, 1(1857), 786. Strong, *Diary*, 2, 374–75. Tiemann carried all of the lower West Side and all but one of the wards above 14th Street. He ran up an impressive 2847-vote majority in the heavily native and strongly nativist Ninth Ward, more than enough to make his citywide majority.

73. Furer, *Havemeyer*, pp. 197–98. Mushkat, *Tammany*, pp. 336–49. Pleasants, *Wood*, pp. 100, 113–16, 131, 134–36.

74. Callow, *Tweed Ring*, pp. 3–10. Mandelbaum, *Boss Tweed's New York*, pp. 46–58, 75–82, 86. In 1874, Wood, reacting against the growing disreputability of politics, asserted that the greatest danger to free government in the United States was the "want of respect for authority—the lack of reverence, so to speak, for the public acts of those who make and enforce the laws." Quoted in *Ibid.*, p. 48.

Chapter 15: Metropolis

1. According to Horatio Burchard in 1881, national wealth increased from $7135 million in 1850 to $13,318 million in 1857. By a later estimate (1938), realized private income increased from $2326 million in 1849 to $4098 million in 1859. U.S. Bureau of Census, *Historical Statistics of the United States, 1789–1945* (Washington, D.C., 1949), pp. 9, 14.

2. Miles of railroad track in operation increased from 7365 in 1849 to 24,503 in 1857. During this same period, exports grew from $145,756,000 to $362,961,000 and imports from $147,857,000 to $360,890,000 (includes specie; net export of specie in 1857 was nearly $57 million). The total tonnage entered at American ports rose from 2,429,000 to 4,843,000 tons. *Ibid.*, 200, 215, 244–45. *Democratic Review*, 40(1857), 303.

3. Stiles, *Brooklyn*, 3, 574. *Trib.*, May 6, 1853.

4. King, *Chamber of Commerce*, p. 108. *E.P.*, Feb. 3, 1854. *Trib.*, Jan. 17, 1856. A committee of Aldermen charged that the first Harbor Commission had attempted to

15. Metropolis

limit the filling in of the Manhattan side of the East River in order to promote the growth of Brooklyn at New York's expense. B. of Ald., *Docs.*, 23(1856), no. 45, pp. 1–9, 52.

5. *Trib.*, Feb. 5, 1855.

6. *Eighth Census (1860): Manufactures*, pp. 38, 331, 336, 338, 343, 346, 384, 394, 396, 409. Total value of manufactures in the eleven-county area was $265 million; total for the nation was $1,886 million. Philadelphia ranked first in capital invested and employment in manufacturing, but New York was far ahead in product value, chiefly because of the concentration of sugar refining and the clothing industry there. *Ibid.*: *Mortality*, pp. xviii–xix. Also see Allan R. Pred, *The Spatial Dynamics of U.S. Urban-Industrial Growth*, p. 20. Chamber of Commerce, *Report* (1858), pp. 160–66.

7. *Eighth Census (1860): Manufactures*, pp. 37–38ff. Cunningham, *New Jersey*, 125. Depew, *Hundred Years*, 2, 340.

8. Beach, *Wealthy Citizens* (1845), p. 16. Bishop, *Manufactures*, 2, 577–78. *Trib.*, June 21, 1849; Jan. 17, 1855.

9. *Ibid.*, June 16, 1849. *Democratic Review*, 27 (1850), 150–51. Rolla M. Tryon, *Household Manufactures in the United States*, pp. 306–7, 316.

10. *Sixth Census (1840): Compendium. Eight Census (1860): Manufacturing*, p. 384. Chamber of Commerce, *Report* (1858), 19–20.

11. *Eighth Census (1860): Manufactures)*, pp. 379–85. Bishop, *Manufactures*, 3, 121–22, 147, 1973. Depew, *Hundred Years*, 2, 510. *Trib.*, March 30, 1848. A fire which raged through the upper part of the Harlem Railroad depot on Centre Street drove out a maker of Daguerrian apparatus, a gutta percha producer, an optician and telescope maker, an ivory turner, an envelope manufacturer, and several other small manufacturers. *Trib.*, May 2, 1856.

12. Victor S. Clark, *History of Manufactures in the United States*, 1, 494. Chamber of Commerce, *Report* (1858), p. 18. Bishop, *Manufactures*, 3, 121, 150–1, 153. *Hunt's*, 35(1856), 500–2.

13. Albion, *New York Port*, pp. 149–50. Bishop, *Manufactures*, 3, 123–31. Ross, *What I Saw*, pp. 202–6. *Harper's Monthly*, 2(1851), 724. A fire which in 1853 destroyed the Empire Iron Works on East 23rd Street also damaged another iron works, an iron foundry, an agricultural implements factory, and manufactuers of razor strops, daguerreotype plates, boiler coverings, textile machinery, and brass knob mountings. *Times*, Nov. 18, 1853.

14. *Eight Census (1860): Manufactures*, pp. lx–lxxxvii. Chamber of Commerce, *Report* (1858), pp. 38–39. Feldman, *Men's Clothing Trade*, pp. 12–16, 214. Jesse E. Pope, *The Clothing Industry in New York*, pp. 12–14.

15. Pope, *Clothing Industry*, pp. 20–35. Feldman, *Men's Clothing*, pp. 44–46, 58–60, 83–84, 140–41, 211–14, 237–39. Penny, *Employments of Women*, pp. 111–14. *Hunt's*, 20(1849), 116. Chamber of Commerce, *Report* (1858), p. 38.

16. *Eighth Census (1860): Manufactures*, pp. cxxxiii, 380–84. *Trib.*, April 3, 1855.

17. *Hunt's*, 20(1849), 103. *Scientific American*, 13(1857–58), 294. Frank L. Mott, *A History of American Magazines, 1850–1865* pp. 10, 34–38. Chandler, *Poor*, pp. 21–22, 38, 47. Depew, *Hundred Years*, 1, 176–77.

18. James M. Lee, *History of American Journalism*, p. 284. Augustus Maverick, *Henry J. Raymond and the New York Press*, pp. 95, 101–2. Frank O'Brien, *The Story of the Sun*, pp. 108, 1917, 212. Parton, *Famous Americans*, p. 266.

19. Frank L. Mott, *A History of American Magazines, 1741–1850*, pp. 376, 377, 379, 517–18, 805–9; Mott, *Magazines, 1850–1865*, pp. 11, 19, 31, 390, 420–27. *Trib.*, March 3, 1855. *Hunt's*, 20(1849), 103.

15. METROPOLIS

20. Mott, *Magazines, 1850–1865*, pp. 20–26, 349–53, 362, 426. J. C. Derby, *Fifty Years Among Authors, Books and Publishers*, pp. 46, 181, 203, 229–31, 445.

21. *Eighth Census (1860): Manufactures*, pp. 380–84. S. G. Goodrich estimated the value of the New York book trade at $6 million and that of Philadelphia and Boston combined at $5.9 million. *Trib.*, March 16, 17, 1855.

22. Depew, *Hundred Years*, 1, 310–12. Hellmut Lehmann-Haupt, *The Book in America*, p. 72. Henry W. Boynton, *Annals of American Bookselling*, pp. 166–81. Harper, *The House of Harper*, pp. 90–96. *Hunt's*, 5(1842), 97. *E.P.*, Dec. 12, 1853.

23. *Eighth Census (1860): Manufactures*, pp. 380–84. Beach, *Wealthy Citizens* (1845), p. 13. Grant Overton, *Portrait of A Publisher*, pp. 44–45. Feldman, *Men's Clothing*, pp. 27–28. Publishers disposed of their books through semiannual trade sales which attracted booksellers from throughout the nation. Because of the growing competition and friction within the industry, they established the New York Publishers Association in 1855 to regulate the trade sales and other aspects of bookselling. Derby, *Fifty Years*, pp. 36–37. Lehmann-Haupt, *Book*, pp. 132, 246–47. *Times*, July 12, 1855.

24. Beach, *Wealthy Citizens* (1845), p. 13. George Haven Putnam, *George Palmer Putnam*, p. 22. *Trib.*, March 2, 1855.

25. Mott, *Magazines, 1850–65*, pp. 17–18. Depew, *Hundred Years*, 1, 70. Palmer advertised himself and his trade in the press. See especially the *Tribune*, July 9, 1852; Feb. 8, 1855; Oct. 11, 25, 1856.

26. *Eighth Census (1860: Mortality*, pp. 292–93. Lanier, *Century of Banking*, pp. 212–17. Myers, *Money Market*, 1, 89–94. *Trib.*, July 21, 1855; Oct. 17, 1856.

27. Myers, *Money Market*, 1, 93, 126–31, 173, 208. Otto C. Lightner, *The History of Business Depressions*, p. 145. Schultz and Caine, *Financial Development*, p. 239. James K. Medbery, *Men and Mysteries of Wall Street* pp. 6–8. James S. Gibbons, *The Banks of New York*, p. 173. Chandler, *Poor*, pp. 75–109, 312 n15. G. W. Baker, *A Review of the Commerical Progress of the Cities of New-York and Philadelphia* p. 50.

28. *Times*, Aug. 5, 1854; April 16, 1857.

29. *Trib.*, July 6, Aug. 10, 19, 1857. The *Herald* as quoted in Lowitt, *Dodge*, p. 95.

30. Smith and Cole, *Fluctuations*, pp. 104, 122, 129, 135, 184. Schultz and Caine, *Financial Development*, pp. 266–67. H. M. Hyndman, *Commercial Crisis of the Nineteenth Century*, pp. 73–74. *Hunt's*, 37(1857), 70–71. *Democratic Review*, 40(1857), 393. *Times*, July 23, Aug. 3, 5, 13, 1857.

31. Hidy, *Baring*, pp. 456–57. Samual Rezneck, *Business Depressions and Financial Panics*, pp. 103–5. *Harper's Weekly*, 1(1857), 530, 562. *Times*, July 23, Aug. 13, 20, 24, 25, 26, 1857. By August 27, the *Times* was urging prominent men to calm the public mind, "for our present dilemma is not a difficulty—but a panic."

32. Hidy, *Baring*, p. 457. Gibbons, *Banks of New York*, pp. 346–66. D. Morier Evans, *The History of the Commerical Crisis*, pp. 34, 123. Strong *Diary*, 2, 352–53.

33. Strong, *Diary*, 2, 355–65. *Harper's Weekly*, 1(1857), 678. Rezneck, *Business Depressions*, pp. 114–24. *Scientific American*, 13(1857–58), 37, 45, 85. AICP, *Report* (1858), pp. 18, 22, 29. *Trib.*, Oct. 14, 15, 16, 1857.

34. Smith and Cole, *Fluctuations*, pp. 124, 133. Brown, *Hundred Years*, pp. 102–3. *Harper's Weekly*, 1(1857), 754. *Hunt's*, 37(1857), 711. Strong, *Diary*, 2, 376, 408–9. *Scientific American*, 13(1857–58), 118, 141.

35. Griffin, *Brothers' Keepers*, pp. 237–39. Spring, *Reminiscences*, 2, 144–47. Mathews, *Fifty Years*, pp. 29–34. *Harper's Monthly*, 16(1858), 839–40.

36. Hidy, *Baring*, pp. 464–66. Evans, *Commercial Crisis*, pp. 111–16. Albion, *New York Port*, p. 418. The combined index of trade, as compiled by Smith and Cole, fell from 106 in 1856 to 93 in 1858. *Fluctuations*, p. 104.

15. METROPOLIS

37. Evans, *Commercial Crisis*, p. 114. George Francis Train, *Young America in Wall Street*, p. xi. Joseph B. Bishop, *A Chronicle of One Hundred & Fifty Years*, p. 60.

38. *Trib.*, 24, 1856. Emerson is quoted in Michael H. Cowan, *City of the West*, p. 53. Kendall, *Growth*, pp. 11–17.

39. *Fifteenth Census 1930*, Vol. 1: *Population*, pp. 744–48. Bremer, *Homes*, 1, 574, 576. Bayard Taylor, *Hannah Thurston* p. 129. *Harper's Monthly*, 8(1853–54), 267.

40. Ellis, *Landlords and Farmers*, pp. 163, 172, 219–20, 222. Kendall, *Growth*, pp. 6–11. *Times*, July 30, 1855. Bureau of Census, *Statistical Atlas of the United States* (Washington, D.C., 1914), plate 128. Hough's observations were given in a paper delivered before the American Geographical Society. *Trib.*, July 3, 1857.

41. A. D. Mayo, *Symbols of the Capital*, pp. iii, 14–18, 20, 45.

42. *Ibid.*, pp. 43, 46–47.

43. *Ibid.*, pp. 11–13, 19–30, 49–51.

44. *Ibid.*, pp. 10–13, 44, 114–15, 198. Mayo hoped that the urban poor and "thousands of middlemen" could be removed to rural and small town America, but he also concluded that cities "will be the huge receptacles for all varieties of humanity, and represent the worst as surely as the best in our American character." *Ibid.*, pp. 53, 55.

45. McLoughlin, *Beecher*, p. 106. The quintessential New Yorker resembled the "metropolitan man" whom Georg Simmel, the German sociologist, believed characterized a modernizing Europe in the nineteenth century. For a thoughtful view of New York's character, see Bayrd Still, "The Essence of New York City," pp. 420–23.

46. *Trib.*, Aug. 5, 1857. The advocates of a strong police especially argued the need for force to restrain immigrants until they had accepted the responsibilities of freedom. Miller, *Cops and Bobbies*, p. 143.

47. The *Literary World* attributed the remark regarding city "genius" to James T. Brady (6[1850], 522), but the *Evening Post* (Sept. 2, 1850) reported Brady's speech in which he quotes Walsh as making the comment. Fitz-Hugh Ludlow, "The American Metropolis," *Atlantic Monthly*, 15(1865), 87.

48. *Harper's Weekly*, 2(1858), 723.

49. Isaac Kendall said in 1865 that the European cities "owe much of their grandeur to government expenditures. New York can show proportionately more as the result of private and individual expenditure." *Growth of New York*, p. 14. For descriptions of the "Athenian Quarter" see Wilson, *New York*, 4, 80–109, and Lester, *Glances*, p. 199. New York's cultural responsibilities as a metropolis were much discussed in the 1850's; see, for instance, Tappan, *Growth of Cities*, pp. 19–24, 32–36; *Harper's Monthly*, 9(1854), 122 and 15(1857), 128. The *Times* (Nov. 8, 1853) reported a proposal to establish a Metropolitan Museum of Art, Antiquity and Natural History with the comment that New York had nothing to compare with the great museums of European cities. Also see Daniel M. Fox, *Engines of Culture*, pp. 3–11.

BIBLIOGRAPHY

Manuscripts

NEW YORK PUBLIC LIBRARY
Daly, Charles P. Papers and Scrapbooks.
Flagg, A. C. Papers.
Osborn, Charles F. Letters.
Taylor, Robert. Autobiography and Diary (1846–47).
Tilden, Samuel J. Letters.
Ward, Henry Dana. Diary (1850–53).
Wood, Fernando. Miscellaneous Papers.

NEW-YORK HISTORICAL SOCIETY
Bourne, William O. Papers
Bradish, Luther. Papers.
Harper, James. Miscellaneous Papers.

ON MICROFILM (BUREAU OF THE CENSUS)
Census Schedules (1840, 1850, 1860), New York County, Fourteenth and
    Fifteenth Wards.

BIBLIOGRAPHY

Printed Documents

Address of the Committee to Promote the Passage of a Metropolitan Health Bill (1865).

American Republican Party. *The Crisis! An Appeal to Our Countrymen.* New York, 1844.

Bremner, Robert H., et. al., eds. *Children and Youth in America: A Documentary History.* 2 vols. Cambridge: Harvard University Press, 1970.

Chamber of Commerce of the State of New York. *Annual Report* (1858). New York, 1859.

Children's Aid Society. *Annual Reports* (1854–63). Reprint: New York, 1971.

Citizens Association of New York. *Sanitary Condition of the City, Report of the Council of Hygiene and Public Health.* New York, 1866, repr. 1970.

Commons, John R., et. al., eds. *A Documentary History of American Industrial Society.* 10 vols. New York: A. H. Clark, 1910, repr. 1958.

Harper, James. *Annual Message.* New York, 1844.

Havemeyer, William F. *Message . . . in Relation to the Police.* New York, 1845.

Memorial . . . Praying the Repeal or Amendment of an Act . . . Passed January 25, 1814. New York, 1846.

Northern Dispensary. *Annual Report* (1854).

North-Western Dispensary. *Annual Report* (1854).

New York Association for Improving the Condition of the Poor. *Annual Reports* (1845–60). Also *Annual Reports* (1845–53). Reprint: New York, 1971.

New York City. Board of Aldermen. *Documents* (1839/40–1856).

———— *Report of the Special Committee on Parks.* New York, 1852.

—— Board of Assistant Aldermen. *Majority and Minority Reports . . . in Relation to Rebuilding Washington Market.* New York, 1851.

———— *Minority Report of the Special Committee, to whom was referred the petition for the enlargement of the Battery.* New York, 1849.

—— Board of Councilmen. *Remonstrance and Protest Against the Passing of the Bills now before the Legislature to Establish Railroads in the City.* New York, 1860.

—— Board of Education. *Documents* (1850–52, 1855–56).

—— —— *Report* (1849).

—— Board of Health. *Report of the Proceedings of the Sanitary Committee.* New York, 1849.

—— City Inspector. *Annual Reports* (1852–54, 1856–57).

—— Common Council. *Manuals* (1843/44–49, 1853, 1857).

—— Mayor. *Annual Messages* (1840, 1843–51, 1854, 1857–58).

New York County. Superintendent of Common Schools. *Annual Report* (1849).

New York State. *Census* (1845) (1855).

—— Assembly. *Journal* (1847–48).

—— —— *Documents* (1849, 1854, 1856–57).

CITY DIRECTORIES

—— Senate. *Communication of the Rector, Church-Wardens and Vestrymen of Trinity Church . . . to the Senate of New York.* 1846.
—— —— *Documents* (1861).
—— —— *Report of the Select Committee Appointed to Examine into the Condition, Affairs and Progress of the New York Central Park.* Albany, 1861.
—— —— *Report of the Select Committee on the Report of Trinity Church Made in 1855.* Albany, 1857.
—— —— *Report of the Select Committee to Whom was referred the Report of Trinity Church.* Albany, 1855.
—— —— *Testimony Taken Before the Senate Committee in the Matter of Trinity Church.* Albany, 1857.
—— Superintendent of Common Schools. *Annual Report.* Albany, 1845.
—— Superintendent of Public Instruction. *Annual Report.* Albany, 1855.
Proceedings of a Meeting in Favor of Municipal Reform held at Tammany Hall on . . . March 22, 1844. New York, 1844.
Proceedings of the Meeting of Young Men's Democratic Union Club . . . October 6, 1857. New York, 1857.
Proceedings of a Number of Democratic Citizens of the Eighth Ward in Opposition to the Secret Clique System. New York, 1843.
Statement of the Majority of the Grand Council of the Tammany Society . . . February 14, 1857. New York, 1857.
United States. *Sixth Census* (1840): *Inhabitants* and *Compendium.*
—— *Seventh Census* (1850).
—— *Eighth Census* (1860): *Population. Manufactures. Mortality and Miscellaneous.*
—— *Fifteenth Census* (1930): *Population.*
—— Bureau of Census. *Historical Statistics of the United States, 1789–1945.* Washington, D.C., 1949.
—— Congress. *Congressional Globe*: 28th Cong., 1 sess. (1843–44) and 31st Cong., 1st and 2nd sess. (1849–51).
—— Secretary of the Treasury. "Report . . . December 24, 1849," in U.S. Senate. *Documents*, 31st Cong., 1st sess., 4, no. 2.
Valentine, David T., ed. *Ordinances of the Mayor, Aldermen and Commonalty of the City of New York.* New York, 1859.
Wood, Fernando. *Communication . . . February 4, 1856.* New York, 1856.
—— *Communication . . . February 18, 1857.* New York, 1857.

City Directories and Guidebooks

Appleton's New York City and Vicinity Guide. New York, 1849.
Dinsmore's Thirty Miles Around New York. New York, 1857.
Disturnell, John. *New York As It Was and As It Is.* New York, 1876.

BIBLIOGRAPHY

Doggett's New York City Directory (1842/43–43/44, 1845/46, 1847/48, 1850/51, 1852/53).
Francis's New Guide to the Cities of New-York and Brooklyn and the Vicinity. New York, 1854 and 1857.
Holley, O. L. *A Description of the City of New York with a Brief Account of the Cities, Villages and Places of Resort within Thirty Miles.* New York, 1857.
Longworth's . . . City Directory. New York, 1841.
New-York As It Is. New York, 1840.
Phelps, Humphrey. *What to See and How to See It.* New York, 1857.
Rode's New York City Directory (1851/52, 1853/54–1854/55).
Ruggles, Edward. *A Picture of New York.* New York, 1846.
Saunders, F. *New-York in a Nutshell.* New York, 1853.
Trow's New York City Directory (1852/53–53/54, 1855/56–57/58).

Newspapers and Periodicals

The American Repertory of Arts, Sciences and Manufactures (1840–42).
American Whig Review (1845–52).
Artist: A Monthly Lady's Book (1842–43).
Bankers' Magazine (1847–51).
The Broadway Journal (1845–46).
Brother Jonathan (1842–43).
The Citizen (1854).
The Crayon (1855–57).
The Harbinger (1845–49).
Harper's Monthly (1851–58).
Harper's Weekly (1857–58).
Hunt's Merchant's Magazine and Commercial Review (1839–58).
Independent (1849–50).
Knickerbocker Magazine (1840–49).
The Literary World: A Journal of Science, Literature, and Art (1847–51).
Methodist Quarterly Review (1841–50).
New York American for the Country (1843).
New York Day-Book (1852–1856).
New York Evening Post (1840–50, 1852, 1854).
New-York Mirror (1840–42).
New York Review (1840–42).
New York Times (1851–57).
New York Tribune (1841–57).
Putnam's Magazine (1853–56).
Railroad Record (1853–60).
Scientific American (1845–59).

ARTICLES

Subterranean (1845–47).
United States Magazine and Democratic Review [*Democratic Review*] (1840–58).
Weekly Journal of Commerce (1840–41, 1849, 1856–57).
Working Man's Advocate (1841–44).
Young America (1845–46).

Articles

In the *New York Historical Society Quarterly*:
Arrington, Joseph E. "Otis A. Bullard's Moving Panorama of New York City." 44(1960), 309–35.
Beard, James F., Jr. "The First History of Greater New York. Unknown Portions of Fenimore Cooper's Last Work." 37(1953), 109–145.
Chalmers, Leonard. "Fernando Wood and Tammany Hall: The First Phase." 52(1968), 379–402.
—— "Tammany Hall, Fernando Wood, and the Struggle to Control New York City, 1857–1859." 53(1969), 7–33.
Ernst, Robert. "The One and Only Mike Walsh." 36(1952), 43–65.
Evans, Meryle R. "Knickerbocker Hotels and Restaurants, 1800–1850." 36(1952), 377–409.
Leonard, Ira M. "The Rise and Fall of the American Republican Party in New York City, 1843–45." 50(1966), 151–92.
Lockwood, Charles. "The Bond Street Area." 56(1972), 309–20.
Lubove, Roy. "The New York Association for Improving the Condition of the Poor: The Formative Years." 43(1959), 307–27.
Parsons, John E., ed. "Nine Cousins in the California Gold Rush." 47(1963), 349–97.
Pessen, Edward. "Philip Hone's Set: The Social World of the New York City Elite in the 'Age of Egalitarianism.'" 56(1972), 285–300.
—— "A Social and Economic Portrait of Jacksonian Brooklyn." 55(1971), 318–53.
—— "The Wealthiest New Yorkers of the Jacksonian Era: A New List." 54(1970), 145–72.
Resseguie, Harry E. "A. T. Stewart's Marble Palace—The Cradle of the Department Store." 48(1964), 131–62.
Richardson, James F. "Mayor Fernando Wood and the New York Police Force, 1855–57." 50(1966), 5–40.
Rosenberg, Carroll S. "Protestants and Five Pointers: The Five Points House of Industry." 48(1964), 327–47.
Still, Bayrd, "The Essence of New York City." 43(1959), 401–23.
In *Valentine's Manual of Old New York*, Henry Collins Brown, ed. New York, 1920–22:

BIBLIOGRAPHY

Brown, Henry Collins. "The North River." No. 6, n.s. (1922), 41–86.
Brown, John Crawford. "Early Days of the Department Stores." No. 5, n.s. (1921), 97–148.
Dodge, William E. "A Great Merchant's Recollections of Old New York, 1818–1880." No. 5, n.s. (1921), 149–82.
Giergerich, L. A. "Reminiscences of the Eleventh Ward." No. 5, n.s. (1921), 211–19.
Havens, Catherine E. "Diary of a Little Girl in Old New York, 1849–1850." No. 4, n.s. (1920), 1–49.
Mendoza, Aaron. "Some Associations of Old Ann Street, 1720–1920." No. 4, n.s. (1920), 263–303.
In other sources:
Berrol, Selma. "Who Went to School in Mid-Nineteenth Century New York? An Essay in the New Urban History." *Essays in the History of New York City*, Irwin Yellowitwitz, ed. Port Washington, N.Y.: Kennikat Press, 1978, 43–60.
Ellis, David M. "New York and the Western Trade, 1850–1910." *New York History*, 33(1952), 379–396.
Gatell, Frank O. "Money and Party in Jacksonian America: A Quantitative Look at New York City's Men of Quality." *Political Science Quarterly*, 82(1967), 235–52.
Hirsch, Leo H., Jr. "The Negro and New York, 1783 to 1860." *Journal of Negro History*, 16(1931), 382–473.
Judd, Jacob. "A Tale of Two Cities: Brooklyn and New York, 1834–1855." *Journal of Long Island History*, 3(1963), 19–33.
Pessen, Edward. "The Marital Theory and Practice of the Antebellum Urban Elite." *New York History*, 53(1972), 389–410.
Rezneck, Samuel. "The Social History of An American Depression, 1837–1843." *American Historical Review*, 40(1934–35), 662–87.
Rosenberg, Charles E. and Carroll S. "Pietism and the Origins of the American Public Health Movement: A Note on John H. Griscom and Robert M. Hartley." *Journal of the History of Medicine and Allied Sciences*, 23(1968).
Taylor, George R. "American Urban Growth Preceding the Railway Age." *Journal of Economic History*, 27(1967), 308–39.
—— "The Beginnings of Mass Transportation in Urban America," *The American City: Historical Studies*, James F. Richardson, ed. Waltham, Mass.: Xerox College Publishing, 1972. Originally published in *The Smithsonian Journal of History*, 1(Summer 1966), 35–50 and 2(Autumn 1966), 31–54.
Ward, John William. "The Politics of Design." *Who Designs America*, L. B. Holland ed. Garden City, N.Y.: Doubleday, 1965.
Williamson, Jeffrey G. "Antebellum Urbanization in the American Northeast." *Journal of Economic History*, 25(1965), 592–608.
Wyatt-Brown, Bertram. "God and Dun & Bradstreet, 1841–1851." *Business History Review*, 40(1966), 432–50.

BOOKS, PAMPHLETS AND DISSERTATIONS

Books, Pamphlets and Dissertations

Account of the Terrific and Fatal Riot at the New-York Astor Place Opera House. New York, 1849.

Adams, Thomas, Harold M. Lewis and Theodore T. McCrosky. *Population, Land Values and Government* (vol. 2 of the *Regional Survey of New York*). New York: Regional Plan of New York, 1929.

Addison, James T. *The Episcopal Church in the United States, 1789–1931.* New York: Scribner, 1931.

Albion, Robert G. *The Rise of New York Port.* New York: Scribner, 1939; repr., 1970.

Allen, Stephen. *Memoirs,* John G. Travis, ed. Typescript, New York Public Library.

Almond, Gabriel. "Plutocracy and Politics in New York City." Ph.D. diss., University of Chicago, 1938.

Altbach, Edith H. *Women in America.* Lexington, Mass.: D. C. Heath, 1974.

Andrews, Wayne. *Architecture, Ambition and Americans.* New York: Harper, 1955.

Asbury, Herbert. *The Gangs of New York.* New York: Knopf, 1929.

Atherton, Lewis. *The Pioneer Merchant in Mid-America.* Columbia: University of Missouri Press, 1939.

——— *The Southern Country Store.* Baton Rouge: Louisiana State University Press, 1949, repr. 1969.

Ayres, Anne. *The Life and Works of William Augustus Muhlenberg.* New York, 1881.

Armstrong, William. *The Aristocracy of New York.* New York, 1848.

Baker, G. W. *A Review of the Commercial Progress of the Cities of New-York & Philadelphia.* Philadelphia, 1859.

Bannard, William. *A Discourse on the Moral Aspect and Destitution of the City of New York.* New York, 1851.

Bates, William W. *American Marine: The Shipping Question in History and Politics.* Boston and New York, 1893.

Bayley, J. R. *A Brief Sketch of the History of the Catholic Church on the Island of New York.* New York, 1853.

Beach, Moses Y. *The Wealthy Citizens of New York* (title varies). 4th ed. (1842), 6th ed. (1845), 13th ed. (1855).

Bebout, John E. and Ronald J. Grele. *Where Cities Meet: The Urbanization of New Jersey.* Princeton, N.J.: Van Nostrand, 1964.

Beecher, Henry Ward. *Star Papers; or Experiences of Art and Nature.* New York, 1855, repr. 1972.

Beers, Henry A. *Nathaniel Parker Willis.* Boston, 1888.

Belden, E. Porter. *New-York: Past, Present, and Future.* New York, 1849.

Bell, John. *Report on the Importance and Economy of Sanitary Measures to Cities.* New York, 1859.

Bellows, Anna L. *Recollections of Henry Whitney Bellows.* Boston, 1897.

BIBLIOGRAPHY

Bellows, Henry W. *Address . . . in Behalf of the United States Inebriate Asylum.* New York, 1855.
—— *The Christian Merchant . . . Discourse on Occasion of the Death of Jonathan Goodhue.* New York, 1848.
—— *The Leger and the Lexicon: or, Business and Literature.* Cambridge, Mass., 1853.
—— *The Moral Significance of the Crystal Palace.* New York, 1853.
—— *A Sermon Occasioned by the Late Riot.* New York, 1849.
Bender, Thomas. *Toward an Urban Vision.* Lexington: University Press of Kentucky, 1975.
Benedict, Erastus C. *New York and the City Travel: Omnibus and Railroad. What Should Be Done.* New York, 1851.
Benson, Lee. *Merchants, Farmers, & Railroads: Railroad Regulation and New York Politics, 1850–1887.* Cambridge: Harvard University Press, 1953.
Berg, Barbara. *This Remembered Gate: Origins of American Feminism.* New York; Oxford University Press, 1978.
Berrian, William. *Facts Against Fancy.* New York, 1855.
Berthoff, Rowland T. *British Immigrants in Industrial America, 1790–1850.* Cambridge: Harvard University Press, 1953.
Bidwell, Percy W. and John I. Falconer. *History of Agriculture in the Northern United States, 1620–1860.* New York: P. Smith, 1925, repr. 1941.
Bishop, J. Leander. *A History of American Manufactures from 1608 to 1860.* 3 vols. Philadelphia, 1868, repr. 1966.
Bishop, Joseph B. *A Chronicle of One Hundred and Fifty Years: The Chamber of Commerce of the State of New York, 1768–1918.* New York: Scribner, 1918.
Black, George A. *The History of Municipal Ownership of Land on Manhattan to . . . 1844.* New York, 1891.
Blake, Nelson M. *Water for the Cities.* Syracuse, N.Y.: Syracuse University Press, 1956.
[Bobo, William M.] *Glimpses of New-York. By a South Carolinian.* Charleston, S.C., 1852.
Boese, Thomas. *Public Education in the City of New York.* New York, 1869.
Bogen, Jules I. *The Anthracite Railroads.* New York: Ronald Press, 1927.
Booth, Mary L. *History of the City of New York.* New York, 1859.
Botta, Vincenzo, ed. *Memoir of Anne C. L. Botta.* New York, 1893.
Boyd, William H. *New York City Tax-Book.* New York, 1857.
Boyer, Paul. *Urban Masses and Moral Order in America, 1820–1920.* Cambridge: Harvard University Press, 1978.
Boynton, Henry W. *Annals of American Bookselling, 1638–1850.* New York: Wiley, 1932.
Brace, Charles Loring. *The Dangerous Classes of New York.* New York, 1872.
Brace, Emma. *The Life of Charles Loring Brace.* New York, 1894.
Bradish, Luther, et al. *A Statement and Declaration of Views.* New York, 1846.
Brainerd, Cephas and Eveline W., eds. *The New England Society Orations.* 2 vols. New York: Century Co., 1901.

BOOKS, PAMPHLETS AND DISSERTATIONS

Brann, Henry A. *Most Reverend John Hughes, First Archbishop of New York.* New York, 1892.

Breen, Matthew P. *Thirty Years of New York Politics Up-To-Date.* New York, 1899.

Bremner, Robert H. *From the Depths: The Discovery of Poverty in the United States.* New York: New York University Press, 1956.

[Brewer, William A.] *A Few Thoughts for the Tax Payers and Voters in the City of New York.* New York, 1853.

Bridges, William. *Map of the City of New-York and Island; with Explanatory Remarks,* New York, 1811.

[Briggs, Charles F.] *Bankrupt Stories.* New York 1843.

Bristed, Charles Astor. *A Few Words of Warning to New Yorkers on the Consequences of a Railroad in Fifth Avenue.* New York, 1863.

—— *The Upper Ten Thousand: Sketches of American Society.* New York, 1852.

Bromwell, William J. *History of Immigration to the United States.* New York, 1856, repr. 1969.

Brown, Henry Collins. *Fifth Avenue: Old and New, 1824–1924.* New York: The Fifth Avenue Association, 1924.

Brown, John C. *A Hundred Years of Merchant Banking.* New York: Private printing, 1909.

Browne, Junius Henri. *The Great Metropolis: A Mirror of New York.* Hartford, Conn., 1869.

Buck, Norman S. *The Development of the Organization of Anglo-American Trade, 1800–1850.* New Haven, Conn.: Yale University Press, 1925; repr. Hamden, Conn.: Shoe String Press, 1969.

Buetow, Harold A. *Of Singular Benefit: The Story of Catholic Education.* New York: The Macmillan Co., 1970.

Byrne, Stephen. *Irish Emigration to the United States.* New York, 1873; repr. New York: Appleton, 1969.

Callow, Alexander B., Jr. *The Tweed Ring.* New York: Oxford University Press, 1966.

Callow, James T. *Kindred Spirits: Knickerbocker Writers and American Artists, 1807–1855.* Chapel Hill, N.C.: University of North Carolina Press, 1967.

Carmen, Harry J. *The Street Surface Railway Franchises of New York City.* New York: Columbia University Press, 1919.

Carosso, Vincent P. *Investment Banking in America: A History.* Cambridge: Harvard University Press, 1970.

Casey, Robert J. and W. A. S. Douglas. *The Lackawanna Story.* New York: McGraw-Hill, 1951.

Chandler, Alfred D., Jr. *Henry Varnum Poor: Business Editor, Analyst and Reformer.* Cambridge: Harvard University Press, 1956.

Chapin, Edwin H. *Humanity in the City.* New York, 1854.

—— *Moral Aspects of City Life.* New York, 1854.

Child, L. Maria. *Letters from New York.* 3rd ed. New York, 1845.

—— *Letters from New York. Second Series.* New York, 1845.

BIBLIOGRAPHY

Chinitz, Benjamin. *Freight and the Metropolis*. Cambridge: Harvard University Press, 1960.

Chorley, E. Clowes, ed. *Quarter of a Millennium: Trinity Church in the City of New York, 1697–1947*. Philadelphia: Church Historical Society, 1947.

Clark, Eliot. *History of the National Academy of Design, 1825–1953*. New York: Columbia University Press, 1954.

Clark, John G. *The Grain Trade in the Old Northwest*. Urbana: University of Illinois Press, 1966.

Clark, Victor S. *History of Manufactures in the United States*. Rev. ed. 3 vols. New York: McGraw-Hill, 1929.

Clawson, Marion, ed. *Modernizing Urban Land Policy*. Baltimore: Johns Hopkins University Press, 1973.

Cleveland, Frederick A. and Fred W. Powell. *Railroad Promotion and Capitalization in the United States*. New York: Longmans, 1909, repr. 1966.

"Clinton." *The Value of Real Estate in the City of New York*. N.p., n.d.

Clough, Shepard B. *A Century of Life Insurance: A History of the Mutual Life Insurance Company of New York, 1843–1943*. New York: Columbia University Press, 1946.

Cochran, Thomas C. *Business in American Life*. New York: McGraw-Hill, 1972.

——*Railroad Leaders, 1845–1890*. Cambridge: Harvard University press, 1953.

Cole, Arthur H. *Wholesale Commodity Prices in the United States, 1700–1861*. Cambridge: Harvard University Press, 1938.

Coleman, Terry. *Going to America*. New York: Doubleday, 1972.

[Columbia University]. *A History of Columbia University*. New York: Lemcke, 1904.

Condit, Carl W. *American Building: Material and Techniques from the First Colonial Settlements to the Present*. Chicago: University of Chicago Press, 1968.

Connors, Edward M. *Church-State Relationships in Education in the State of New York*. Washington, D.C.: Catholic University of America Press, 1951.

Coon, Horace. *Columbia, Colossus on the Hudson*. New York: Dutton, 1947.

Costello, Augustine E. *Our Firemen: A History of the New York Fire Departments*. New York, 1887.

—— *Our Police Protectors: History of the New York Police*. 2nd ed. N.p., 1885.

Cowan, Michael H. *City of the West: Emerson, America, and Urban Metaphor*. New Haven, Conn.: Yale University Press, 1967.

Cozzens, Issachar, Jr. *Geological History of Manhattan*. New York, 1843.

Cummings, Richard O. *The American Ice Harvests*. Berkeley and Los Angeles: University of California Press, 1949.

Cunningham, John T. *Garden State: The Story of Agriculture in New Jersey*. New Brunswick, N.J.: Rutgers University Press, 1955.

—— *Made in New Jersey: The Industrial Story of a State*. New Brunswick, N.J.: Rutgers University Press, 1954.

—— *This is New Jersey*. New Brunswick, N.J.: Rutgers University Press, 1968.

[Curry, D.] *New-York: Historical Sketch of the Rise and Progress of the Metropolitan City of America. By a New Yorker*. New York, 1853.

BOOKS, PAMPHLETS AND DISSERTATIONS

Dana, Richard Henry, Jr. *Journal.* R. F. Lucid, ed. 3 vols. Cambridge: Harvard University Press, 1968.

Danhof, Clarence. *Change in Agriculture: The Northern United States, 1820–1870.* Cambridge: Harvard University Press, 1969.

Darling, William A. *List of Persons, Co-partnerships, and Corporations Who Were Taxed on Seventeen Thousand Five Hundred Dollars and Upward in the City of New York in 1850.* New York, 1851.

Davies, Pearl J. *Real Estate in America.* Washington, D.C.: Public Affairs Press, 1958.

Davis, Lance E. et al. *American Economic Growth.* New York: Harper and Row, 1972.

De Bow, J. D. B. *Statistical View of the United States.* Washington, D.C., 1854.

Decker, Peter R. *Fortunes and Failures: White-Collar Mobility in Nineteenth-Century San Francisco.* Cambridge: Harvard University Press, 1978.

DeLancey, William H. *The Title, Parish Rights and Property of Trinity Church.* Utica, N.Y., 1857.

Depew, Chauncey M., ed. *1795–1895: One Hundred Years of American Commerce.* 2 vols., New York, 1895.

Derby, J. C. *Fifty Years Among Authors, Books and Publishers.* Hartford, Conn., 1884.

DeVoe, Thomas F. *The Market Book.* New York, 1862, repr. 1969.

Devyr, Thomas A. *The Odd Book of the Nineteenth Century . . . A Personal Record of Reform—Chiefly Land Reform.* Greenpoint, N.Y., 1882.

Diamond, Sigmund. *The Reputation of the American Businessman.* Cambridge: Harvard University Press, 1955.

Dickens, Charles. *American Notes.* Introduction by Christopher Lasch. Greenwich, Conn., 1961.

Diffley, Jerome E. "Catholic Reaction to American Public Education, 1792–1852." Ph.D diss., University of Notre Dame, 1959.

Dix, Morgan, ed. *A History of the Parish of Trinity Church.* 4 parts. New York: Putnam, 1906.

—— *Memoir of John Adams Dix.* 2 vols. New York, 1883.

Dodge, William E. *Old New York.* New York, 1880.

Dolan, Anne M. "The Literary Salon in New York, 1830–1860." Ph.D. diss., Columbia University, 1957.

Dolan, Jay P. *The Immigrant Church: New York's Irish and German Catholics, 1815–1865.* Baltimore: Johns Hopkins University press, 1975.

Domett, Henry W. *A History of the Bank of New York, 1784–1884.* 3rd ed. Cambridge, Mass.: Riverside Press, 1902.

Downing, Andrew Jackson, *Rural Essays.* George W. Curtis, ed. New York, 1853.

—— *A Treatise on the Theory and Practice of Landscape Gardening.* 6th ed. (1859). Reprint with appreciation by John O. Simonds, Jr. New York: Funk & Wagnalls, 1967.

DuBois, Ellen Carrol. *Feminism and Suffrage: The Emergence of an Independent*

BIBLIOGRAPHY

Women's Movement in America, 1848–1869. Ithaca, N.Y.: Cornell University Press, 1978.

Duffy, John. *A History of Public Health in New York City, 1625–1886.* New York: Russell Sage Foundation, 1968.

Durand, Edward D. *The Finances of New York City.* New York, 1898.

Durand, John. *The Life and Times of A. B. Durand.* New York, 1894, repr. 1970.

—— *Prehistoric Notes of the Century Club.* N.p., 1882.

Early, James. *Romanticism and American Architecture.* New York: A. S. Barnes, 1965.

Ellet, Elizabeth F. L. *Queens of American Society.* New York, 1867.

Elliott, Maude H. *Uncle Sam Ward and His Circle.* New York: Macmillan, 1938.

Ellis, David M. *Landlords and Farmers in the Hudson-Mohawk Region, 1790–1850.* New York: Octagon Books, 1967; reprint of 1946 edition.

Ernst, Robert. *Immigrant Life in New York City, 1825–1863.* New York: King's Crown Press, 1949.

Evans, D. Morier. *The History of the Commercial Crisis, 1857–58.* London, 1859.

Ewer, F. C. *Public Health of the City of New York.* New York, 1861.

Faust, Albert B. *The German Element in the United States.* 2 vols. Boston and New York: Houghton Mifflin, 1909.

Fein, Albert. *Frederick Law Olmsted and the American Environmental Tradition.* New York: Braziller, 1972.

Feldman, Egal, "New York's Men's Clothing Trade, 1800 to 1861." Ph.D. diss., University of Pennsylvania, 1957.

Fitch, James M. *American Building. 1: The Historical Forces that Shaped It.* 2d ed. Boston and Cambridge: Houghton Mifflin, 1966.

Flexner, James T. *That Wilder Image.* Boston: Bonanza Books, 1962.

Fogel, Robert W. and Stanley L. Engerman, eds. *The Reinterpretation of American Economic History.* New York: Harper, 1971.

Folks, Homer. *The Care of Destitute, Neglected and Delinquent Children.* New York: Macmillan, 1902.

Foord, John. *The Life and Public Services of Andrew Haswell Green.* Garden City, N.Y.: Doubleday, Page, 1913.

Ford, James, et al. *Slums and Housing with Special Reference to New York City.* 2 vols. Cambridge: Harvard University Press, 1936.

Forsyth, David P. *The Business Press in America.* Philadelphia and New York: Chilton Books, 1964.

Fosdick, Raymond B. *American Police Systems.* New York: The Century Co., 1921.

Foster, Charles I. *An Errand of Mercy: The Evangelical United Front, 1790–1837.* Chapel Hill: University of North Carolina Press, 1960.

[Foster, George G.] *New York by Gas-Light.* New York, 1850.

—— *New York Naked.* N.p., n.d.

—— *New York in Slices.* New York, 1849.

Books, Pamphlets and Dissertations

Fox, Daniel M. *Engines of Culture: Philanthropy and Art Museums*. Madison: University of Wisconsin Press, 1963.

Francis, John W. *New York during the Last Half Century*. New York, 1857.

Furer, Howard B. "The Public Career of William Frederick Havemeyer." Ph.D. diss., New York University, 1963.

Gallatin, Albert. *Writings*. Henry Adams, ed. 3 vols. Philadelphia, 1879.

Gabriel, Ralph H. *The Evolution of Long Island*. New Haven, Conn.: Yale University Press, 1921.

Gerard, James W. *The Impress of Nationalities upon the City of New York*. New York, 1883.

Gibbons, James S. *The Banks of New York, Their Dealers, The Clearing House, and the Panic of 1857*. New York, 1859; repr. Westport, Conn.: Greenwood Press, 1968.

Gifford, Don, ed. *The Literature of American Architecture*. New York: Dutton, 1966.

Gourlay, Robert F. *Plans for Beautifying New York and Improving the City of Boston*. Boston, 1844.

Gover, William C. *Tammany Hall Democracy*. New York, 1875.

Gras, N. S. B. *Business and Capitalism*. New York: Crofts, 1939.

Greef, Albert O. *The Commercial Paper House in the United States*. Cambridge: Harvard University Press, 1938.

Greeley, Horace. *Hints Toward Reforms*. New York, 1850.

—— *Recollections of a Busy Life*. New York, 1868.

Greenleaf, Jonathan. *A History of the Churches of All Denominations in the City of New York*. New York, 1846.

Greenslet, Ferris. *The Life of Thomas Bailey Aldrich*. Boston and New York: Houghton Mifflin, 1908.

Griffin, Clifford S. *Their Brothers' Keepers Moral Stewardship in the United States, 1800–1865*. New Brunswick, N.J.: Rutgers University Press, 1960.

Griscom, John H. *Memoir of John Griscom*. New York, 1859.

—— *The Sanitary Condition of the Laboring Population of New York*. New York, 1845.

—— *Sanitary Legislation, Past and Future*. New York, 1861.

Gunn, Thomas B. *The Physiology of New York Boarding-Houses*. New York, 1857.

Gurney, Joseph J. *A Journey to North America*. Norwich, Eng., 1841, repr. 1973.

Hall, Henry, ed. *America's Successful Men of Affairs*. 2 vols. New York, 1895.

Halliday, Samuel. *The Lost and Found, or, Life Among the Poor*. New York, 1859.

Hamlin, Talbot F. *Greek Revival Architecture in America*. New York: Oxford University Press, 1944.

Hammond, Harold E. "A Commoner's Judge: The Life and Times of Charles Patrick Daly." Ph.D. diss., Columbia University, 1951.

Hardenbrook, William T. E. *Financial New York: A History of the Banking and Financial Institutions of the Metropolis*. New York and Chicago, 1897.

BIBLIOGRAPHY

Harlow, Alvin F. *Old Bowery Days.* New York: D. Appleton, 1931.

Harper, J. Henry. *The House of Harper.* New York: Harper and Bros., 1912.

Harris, Neil. *The Artist in American Society: The Formative Years, 1790–1860.* New York: G. Braziller, 1966.

Harris, Thomas L. *Juvenile Depravity and Crime in Our City.* New York, 1850.

Hartley, Isaac S. *Memorial of Robert Milham Hartley.* Utica, N.Y., 1882.

Hassard, John R. G. *Life of the Most Reverend John Hughes.* New York, 1866.

Haswell, Charles H. *Reminiscences of an Octogenarian.* New York, 1897.

Hazelton, Henry I. *The Boroughs of Brooklyn and Queens, Counties of Nassau and Suffolk.* 7 vols. New York and Chicago: Lewis Historical Publishing Co., 1925.

Headley, Joel T. *The Great Riots of New York, 1712–1873.* Indianapolis and New York: Bobbs-Merrill, 1970.

Hedrick, Ulysses P. *A History of Agriculture in the State of New York.* Albany: New York State Agricultural Society, 1933.

—— *A History of Horticulture in America to 1860.* New York: Oxford University Press, 1950.

Henlein, Paul G. *Cattle Kingdom in the Ohio Valley, 1783–1860.* Lexington: University of Kentucky Press, 1959.

Hidy, Ralph W. *The House of Baring in American Trade and Finance.* Cambridge: Harvard University Press, 1949, repr. 1970.

Hoffman, Murray. *A Digest of the Charters, Statutes and Ordinances of, and Relating to, the Corporation of the City of New York.* 3 vols. New York, 1865 and 1869.

—— *A Treatise upon the Estate and Rights of the Corporation of the City of New York, As Proprietors.* New York, 1853.

Hone, Philip. *Diary, 1828–1851.* Allan Nevins, ed. New York: Dodd, Mead, 1936.

Hopkins, John H. *Poor Trinity. The Report of a Committee on the Condition of Trinity Church Examined.* New York, 1859.

Horan, James D. *Mathew Brady: Historian with a Camera.* New York: Crown, 1955.

Horlick, Allan S. *Boys and Merchant Princes: The Social Control of Young Men in New York.* Lewisburg, Pa.: Bucknell University Press, 1975.

Hufeland, Otto. *Early Mount Vernon.* Mount Vernon, N.Y.: Mount Vernon Public Library, 1940.

Hughes, Glenn. *A History of the American Theatre, 1700–1950.* New York: S. French, 1951.

Hughes, John. *Complete Works of the Most Rev. John Hughes.* Lawrence Kehoe, ed. 2 vols. New York, 1866.

Hungerford, Edward. *Men and Iron: The History of the New York Central.* New York: Thomas Y. Crowell, 1938.

—— *Men of Erie.* New York: Random House, 1946.

—— *Wells Fargo.* New York: Random House, 1949.

BOOKS, PAMPHLETS AND DISSERTATIONS

Hunt, Freeman, *Worth and Wealth: A Collection of Maxims, Morals and Miscellanies for Merchants and Men of Business.* New York, 1856.
—— *Lives of American Merchants.* 2 vols. New York, 1856–58.
Hutchinson, E. P. *Immigrants and Their Children, 1850–1950.* New York: Wiley, 1956.
Hyndman, H. M. *Commercial Crises of the Nineteenth Century.* London, 1892, repr. 1967.
[Ingraham, Abijah]. *A Biography of Fernando Wood. A History of the Forgeries, Perjuries and Other Crimes of Our "Model Mayor."* No. 1. N.p., n.d.
Inness, George, Jr. *Life, Art, and Letters of George Inness.* New York: The Century Co., 1917.
Irving, Pierre M. *The Life and Letters of Washington Irving.* 4 vols. New York, 1863–64.
Jacoby, George P. *Catholic Child Care in Nineteenth Century New York.* Washington, D.C.: Catholic University of America Press, 1941.
James, Henry. *Washington Square.* New York, 1881; repr. New York: Harper, 1956.
Jay, William. *A Letter to Rev. William Berrian, D.D., on the Resources, Present Position, and Duties of Trinity Church.* New York, 1856.
Johnson, Emory R., *et al. History of Domestic and Foreign Commerce of the United States.* 2 vols. Washington, D.C.: Carnegie Institution, 1915.
Jones, Chester L. *The Economic History of the Anthracite-Tidewater Canals.* Philadelphia: University of Pennsylvania Press, 1908.
Jones, Fred M. *Middlemen in the Domestic Trade of the United States, 1800–1860.* Urbana: University of Illinois Press, 1937.
Judson, Edward Z. C. ["Ned Buntline"]. *Mysteries of New York.* London, n.d.
Kaestle, Carl F. *The Evolution of an Urban School System, New York City, 1750–1850.* Cambridge: Harvard University Press, 1973.
Kapp, Friedrich. *Immigration and the Commissioners of Emigration.* New York, 1870.
Katz, Irving. *August Belmont: A Political Biography.* New York: Columbia University Press, 1968.
Katz, Michael. *The Irony of Early School Reform: Educational Innovation in Mid-Nineteenth Century Massachusetts.* Cambridge: Harvard University Press, 1968.
Kavaler, Lucy. *The Astors: A Family Chronicle of Pomp and Power.* New York: Dodd, Mead, 1966.
[Kendall, Isaac C.] *The Growth of New York.* New York, 1865.
King, Charles. *History of the New York Chamber of Commerce.* New York, 1856.
—— *Progress of the City of New York During the Last Fifty Years.* New York, 1852.
Kirkland, Edward C. *Men, Cities and Transportation: A Study in New England History, 1820–1900.* 2 vols. Cambridge: Harvard University Press, 1948.
Kouwenhoven, John A. *Partners in Banking . . . Brown Brothers Harriman & Co., 1818–1968.* New York: Doubleday, 1968.

BIBLIOGRAPHY

Krehbiel, Henry E. *Chapters of Opera*. 3rd. ed. New York: Holt, 1911.
Ladies of the Mission. *The Old Brewery and the New Mission House at the Five Points*. New York, 1854, repr. 1970.
Lancaster, Clay. *New York's First Suburb: Old Brooklyn Heights*. Rutland, Vt.: Tuttle, 1961.
Landy, Jacob. *The Architecture of Minard Lafever*. New York: Columbia University Press, 1970.
Lane, Francis E. *American Charities and the Child of the Immigrant*. Washington, D.C.: Catholic University of America Press, 1932.
Lane, Roger. *Policing the City: Boston, 1822–1885*. New York: Atheneum, 1971.
Langsam, Miriam Z. *Children West: A History of the Placing-Out System of the New York Children's Aid Society, 1853–1890*. Madison: University of Wisconsin Press, 1964.
Lanier, Henry W. *A Century of Banking in New York, 1822–1922*. New York: George H. Doran, 1922.
Lee, James M. *History of American Journalism*. Garden City, N.Y.: Garden City Publishing Co., 1923.
Lehmann-Haupt, Hellmut. *The Book in America*. 2nd ed. New York: Bowker, 1952.
Leonard, Ira M. "New York City Politics, 1841–1844: Nativism and Reform." Ph.D. diss., New York University, 1965.
Leonard, Ira M. and Robert D. Parmet. *American Nativism, 1830–1860*. New York: Van Nostrand, 1971.
Lester, Charles E. *Glances at the Metropolis*. New York, 1854.
Levine, Edward M. *The Irish and Irish Politicians: A Study of Cultural and Social Alienation*. Notre Dame, Ind.: University of Notre Dame Press, 1966.
Lewis, Harold M. *Physical Conditions and Public Services* (vol. 8 of the *Regional Survey of New York*). New York: Regional Plan of New York, 1929.
Leyda, Jay. *The Melville Log*. 2 vols. New York: Harcourt, Brace, 1951.
Lightner, Otto C. *The History of Business Depressions*. New York: The Northeastern Press, 1922.
Lindstrom, Diane. *Economic Development in the Philadelphia Region, 1810–1850*. New York: Columbia University Press, 1978.
Lockwood, Charles. *Manhattan Moves Uptown: An Illustrated History*. Boston, Houghton Mifflin, 1976.
Loop, Anne S. *History and Development of Sewage Treatment in New York City*. New York, 1964.
Lossing, Benson J. *History of New York City*. 2 vols. New York, 1884.
Low, Seth. *New York in 1850 and in 1890*. New York, 1892.
Lowitt, Richard. *A Merchant Prince of the Nineteenth Century: William E. Dodge*. New York: Columbia University Press, 1954.
Lynch, Dennis T. *"Boss" Tweed*. New York: Boni and Liveright, 1927.
McAdam, David, et al. *History of the Bench and Bar of New York*. 2 vols. New York, 1897.

BOOKS, PAMPHLETS AND DISSERTATIONS

McAllister, Ward. *Society as I Have Found It.* New York, 1890.

McElrath, Thomas. *A Dictionary of Words and Phrases Used in Commerce.* New York, 1871.

Mack, Edward C. *Peter Cooper.* New York: Duell, Sloan and Pearce, 1949.

McLean, Alexander. *History of Jersey City.* 2 vols. Jersey City, N.J., 1895.

MacLeod, Donald. *Biography of Hon. Fernando Wood.* New York, 1856.

McLoughlin, William G. *The Meaning of Henry Ward Beecher.* New York: Knopf, 1970.

[McVickar, William A.] *City Missions.* New York, 1857.

Mandelbaum, Seymour. *Boss Tweed's New York.* New York: Wiley, 1965.

Manning, James H. *Century of American Savings Banks.* New York: B. F. Buck, 1917.

Marcuse, Maxwell F. *This Was New York!* New York: Carlton Press, 1965.

Martin, Edgar. *The Standard of Living in 1860.* Chicago: University of Chicago Press, 1942.

Marvin, Winthrop. *The American Merchant Marine.* New York: Scribner, 1910.

Masquerier, Lewis. *Sociology: or, The Reconstruction of Society, Government and Property.* New York, 1877.

Mathews, Cornelius. *Big Abel and the Little Manhattan.* New York, 1845.

—— *A Pen-And-Ink Panorama of New York City.* New York, 1853.

Matthiessen, F. O. *The James Family.* New York: Knopf, 1947.

Maverick, August. *Henry J. Raymond and the New York Press.* Hartford, Conn., 1870, repr. 1970.

Mayo, A. D. *Symbols of the Capital; or, Civilization in New York.* New York, 1859.

Medbery, James K. *Men and Mysteries of Wall Street.* New York, 1870; repr. Wells, Vt.: Fraser, 1968.

Mennel, Robert M. *Thorns and Thistles: Juvenile Delinquents in the United States, 1825–1940.* Hanover, N.H.: University Press of New England, 1973.

Merritt, Raymond H. *Engineering in American Society, 1850–1875.* Lexington: University Press of Kentucky, 1969.

Meyer, Balthasar H., et al. *History of Transportation in the United States before 1860.* Washington, D.C.: Carnegie Institute, 1917; repr. 1948.

Miller, Douglas T. *Jacksonian Aristocracy: Class and Democracy in New York, 1830–1860.* New York: Oxford University Press, 1967.

Miller, Harry E. *Banking Theories in the United States before 1860.* Cambridge: Harvard University Press, 1927.

Miller, Lillian B. *Patrons and Patriotism: The Encouragement of the Fine Arts in the United States, 1790–1860.* Chicago: University of Chicago Press, 1966.

Miller, Nathan. *The Enterprise of a Free People.* Ithaca, N.Y.: Cornell University Press, 1962.

Miller, Perry. *The Life of the Mind in America: From the Revolution to the Civil War.* New York: Harcourt, Brace, 1965.

Miller, Wilbur R. *Cops and Bobbies: Police Authority in New York and London, 1830–1870.* Chicago: University of Chicago Press, 1977.

BIBLIOGRAPHY

Miller, Zane. *Boss Cox's Cincinnati*. New York: Oxford University Press, 1968.
Moody, Richard. *Edwin Forrest: First Star of the American Stage*. New York: Knopf, 1960.
Monaghan, Jay. *The Great Rascal: The Life and Adventures of Ned Buntline*. Boston: Little, Brown, 1952.
Morrison, John H. *History of American Steam Navigation*. New York: W. F. Sametz, 1903; repr. 1958.
—— *History of New York Ship Yards*. New York: W. F. Sametz, 1909.
Mott, Frank L. *A History of American Magazines, 1741–1850*. New York: Appleton, 1930.
—— *A History of American Magazines, 1850–1865*. Cambridge: Harvard University Press, 1938.
Mumford, Lewis. *Roots of Contemporary Architecture*. New York: Reinhold, 1952.
—— *Sticks and Stones: A Study of American Architecture and Civilization*. New York: Boni and Liveright, 1924.
Mushkat, Jerome. *Tammany: The Evolution of a Political Machine, 1789–1865*. Syracuse, N.Y.: Syracuse University Press, 1971.
Myers, Gustavus. *The History of Tammany Hall*. New York: B. Franklin, 1917; repr. 1968.
Myers, Margaret. *The New York Money Market. Volume 1: Origins and Development*. New York: Columbia University Press, 1931.
Nelson, William and Charles A. Shriner. *History of Paterson and Its Environs*. 3 vols. New York and Chicago: Lewis Historical Publishing Co., 1920.
Nevins, Allan. *Abram S. Hewitt, With Some Account of Peter Cooper*. New York: Harper, 1935.
—— *The Evening Post*. New York: Boni and Liveright, 1922.
—— *Hamilton Fish*. New York: Dodd, Mead, 1936.
—— *History of the Bank of New York and Trust Company, 1784 to 1934*. New York: Private printing, 1934.
Newton, William W. *Dr. Muhlenberg*. Boston and New York, 1891.
Nichols, L. Nelson. *History of the Broadway Tabernacle*. New Haven, Conn.: Tuttle, Morehouse and Taylor, 1940.
Nichols, Thomas L. *Forty Years of American Life*. New York: Stackpole Sons, 1937.
North, C. C. *The Extension of Albany Street*. New York, 1855.
Nye, Russel B. *Society and Culture in America, 1830–1860*. New York: Harper and Row, 1974.
Obituary Addresses on the . . . Death of the Hon. Robert H. Morris. New York, 1855.
O'Brien, Frank M. *The Story of the Sun*. New York: D. Appleton, 1928.
Odell, George C. D. *Annals of the New York Stage*. 15 vols. New York: Columbia University Press, 1927–39.
Olmsted, Frederick Law. *Walks and Talks of an American Farmer in England*. Ann Arbor, Mich.: University of Michigan Press, 1967.
Olmsted, Frederick Law, Jr. and Theodora Kimball. *Frederick Law Olmsted,*

BOOKS, PAMPHLETS AND DISSERTATIONS

Landscape Architect, 1822–1903. 2 vols. New York: Putnam, 1928.

Overton, Grant. *Portrait of a Publisher, And First Hundred Years of the House of Appleton, 1825–1925.* New York: D. Appleton, 1925.

Parton, James. *Famous Americans of Recent Times.* Boston and New York, 1895.

Penny, Virginia. *The Employments of Women: A Cyclopaedia of Woman's Work.* Boston, 1863.

Persons, Stow. *The Decline of American Gentility.* New York: Columbia University Press, 1973.

Pessen, Edward. *Riches, Class, and Power before the Civil War.* Lexington, Mass.: D. C. Heath, 1973.

Pickett, Robert S. *House of Refuge: Origins of Juvenile Reform in New York State, 1815–1857.* Syracuse, N.Y.: Syracuse University Press, 1969.

Pierce, Bradford K. *A Half Century with Juvenile Delinquents; or, The New York House of Refuge.* New York, 1869.

[Pierrepont, H. E.] *Historical Sketch of Fulton Ferry.* Brooklyn, 1879.

Pine, John B. *The Story of Gramercy Park.* New York: Gramercy Park Associates, 1921.

Pleasants, Samuel A. *Fernando Wood of New York.* New York: Columbia University Press, 1948.

Poe, Edgar Allan. *Doings of Gotham.* Jacob E. Spannuth and Thomas O. Mabbott, eds. Pottsville, Pa.: J. E. Spannuth, 1929.

Poor, Henry Varnum. *History of Railroads and Canals of the United States.* New York, 1860.

Pope, Jesse E. *The Clothing Industry in New York.* Columbia: University of Missouri Press, 1905.

Porter, Glenn, ed. *Regional Economic History: The Mid-Atlantic Area since 1700.* Wilmington, Del.: Eleutherian Mills-Hagley Foundation, 1976.

Porter, Kenneth W. *John Jacob Astor, Business Man.* 2 vols. Cambridge: Harvard University Press, 1931.

Pound, Arthur. *The Golden Earth: The Story of Manhattan's Landed Wealth.* New York: Macmillan, 1935.

Pratt, Edward E. *Industrial Causes of Congestion of Population in New York City.* New York: Longmans, 1911.

Pratt, John W. *Religion, Politics and Diversity: The Church–State Theme in New York History.* Ithaca, N.Y.: Cornell University Press, 1967.

Pray, Isaac. *Memoirs of James Gordon Bennett and His Times.* New York, 1855.

Pred, Allan R. *The Spatial Dynamics of U.S. Urban-Industrial Growth, 1800–1914.* Cambridge: MIT Press, 1966.

—— *Urban Growth and the Circulation of Information: The United States System of Cities, 1790–1840.* Cambridge: Harvard University Press, 1973.

Presbrey, Frank. *The History of American Advertising.* Garden City, N.Y.: Doubleday, 1929.

Prime, Samuel I. *Life in New York.* New York, 1847.

Pumphrey, Ralph E. and Muriel W. Pumphrey, eds. *The Heritage of American Social Work.* New York: Columbia University Press, 1961.

BIBLIOGRAPHY

Putnam, George H. *George Palmer Putnam*. New York: Putnam, 1912.
—— *Memories of My Youth*. New York: Putnam, 1914.
Ravitch, Diana. *The Great School Wars: New York City, 1805–1973*. New York: Basic Books, 1974.
Reed, Thomas H. and Paul Webbink. *Documents Illustrative of American Municipal Government*. New York: The Century Co., 1926.
Rezneck, Samuel. *Business Depressions and Financial Panics*. New York: Greenwood, 1968.
Richardson, James F. *New York Police, Colonial Times to 1901*. New York: Oxford University Press, 1970.
Richardson, William H. *Jersey City*. Jersey City, N.J.: The Jersey Journal, 1927.
Richmond, J. P. *New York and Its Institutions, 1609–1872*. New York, 1872.
Riegel, Robert E. *American Women*. Rutherford, N.J.: Farleigh Dickinson University Press, 1970.
Robinson, Solon. *Hot Corn Stories*. New York, 1854.
—— *How to Live: Saving and Wasting*. New York, 1874.
—— *Solon Robinson: Pioneer and Agriculturist: Selected Writings, 1825–1851*. 2 vols. Indianapolis: Indiana Historical Bureau, 1936.
Rodgers, Cleveland. *New York Plans for the Future*. New York: Harper, 1943.
Roper, Laura W. *FLO: A Biography of Frederick Law Olmsted*. Baltimore: Johns Hopkins University Press, 1973.
Rosenberg, Carroll S. *Religion and the Rise of the American City: The New York City Mission Movement, 1812–1870*. Ithaca, N.Y.: Cornell University Press, 1971.
Rosenwaike, Ira. *Population History of New York City*. Syracuse, N.Y.: Syracuse University Press, 1972.
Rosewater, Victor. *Special Assessments: A Study in Municipal Finance*. 2nd ed. New York, 1898.
Ross, Joel E. *What I Saw in New York*. Auburn, N.Y., 1851.
Rothman, David J. *The Discovery of the Asylum*. Boston: Little, Brown, 1971.
Rubin, Joseph J. and Charles H. Brown. *Walt Whitman of the New York Aurora*. State College, Pa.: Pennsylvania State University Press, 1950.
Rudy, S. Willis. *The College of the City of New York*. New York: City College Press, 1949.
Ruggles, Samuel B. *Letters on Rapid Transit*. New York, 1875.
—— *Memorial . . . on the Social and Fiscal Importance of Open Squares in the City of New York*. New York, 1878.
—— *Writings and Speeches*. New York, 1860.
Russel, Robert R. *Improvement of Communication with the Pacific Coast as an Issue in American Politics, 1783–1864*. Cedar Rapids, Ia.: Torch Press, 1948.
Sanger, William W. *The History of Prostitution*. New York: Eugenics Publishing Co., 1937.
Savage, Theodore F. *The Presbyterian Church in New York City*. New York: Presbytery of New York, 1949.

BOOKS, PAMPHLETS AND DISSERTATIONS

Scharf, J. Thomas. *History of Westchester County.* 2 vols. Philadelphia, 1886.

Schmidt, Hubert G. *Agriculture in New Jersey.* New Brunswick, N.J.: Rutgers University Press, 1973.

Schneider, David M. *The History of Public Welfare in New York State, 1609–1866.* Chicago: University of Chicago Press, 1938.

Schwab, John C. *History of the New York Property Tax.* American Economic Association. *Publications.* Vol. 5, no. 5.

Scisco, Louis D. *Political Nativism in New York State.* New York: Columbia University Press, 1901.

[Scoville, Joseph] *The Old Merchants of New York City. By Walter Barrett, Clerk.* 4 vols. New York, 1863–66.

Serrell, James E. *Plan and Description Proposing to Re-Model the City of New York,* 1869.

Seyfried, Vincent F. *The Long Island Railroad: A Comprehensive History.* 3 vols. Garden City, N.Y.: Long Island Press, 1961–66.

Shaughnessy, Jim. *Delaware & Hudson.* Berkeley, Ca.: Howell-North Books, 1967.

Shaw, Ronald E. *Erie Water West: A History of the Erie Canal, 1792–1854.* Lexington: University of Kentucky Press, 1966.

Shultz, William J. and M. R. Caine. *Financial Development of the United States.* New York: Prentice-Hall, 1937.

Smith, John T. *The Catholic Church in New York.* 2 vols. New York: Hall and Locke, 1905.

Smith, Matthew Hale. *Sunshine and Shadow in New York.* Hartford, Conn., 1868.

Smith, Timothy L. *Revivalism and Social Reform in Mid-Nineteenth Century America.* New York: Abingdon Press, 1957.

Smith, Walter B. and Arthur H. Cole. *Fluctuations in American Business, 1790–1860.* Cambridge: Harvard University Press, 1935.

Sobel, Robert. *The Big Board: A History of the New York Stock Market.* New York: Free Press, 1965.

Somers, Dale A. *The Rise of Sports in New Orleans, 1850–1900.* Baton Rouge: Louisiana State University Press, 1972.

Soulé, Frank et al. *The Annals of San Francisco.* New York, 1854.

Spann, Edward K. *Ideals and Politics: New York Intellectuals and Liberal Democracy, 1820–1880.* Albany, N.Y.: State University of New York Press, 1972.

Spring, Gardiner. *Personal Reminiscences.* 2 vols. New York, 1866.

Stiles, Henry R. *A History of the City of Brooklyn.* 3 vols. Brooklyn, N.Y.

Still, Bayrd. *Mirror for Gotham: New York as Seen by Contemporaries from Dutch Days to the Present.* New York: New York University Press, 1956.

Stimson, A. L. *History of the Express Companies.* New York, 1859.

Stokes, I. N. Phelps. *The Iconography of Manhattan Island, 1498–1909.* 6 vols. New York: R. H. Dodd, 1915–1928.

Stone, William L. *History of New York City.* New York, 1868.

Stow, F. H. *The Capitalist's Guide and Railway Annual.* New York, 1859.

BIBLIOGRAPHY

Strong, George Templeton. *Diary.* Allan Nevins and Milton H. Thomas, eds. 4 vols. New York: Macmillan, 1952.

Taft, Henry W. *A Century and A Half at the New York Bar.* New York: Private printing, 1938.

Tappan, Henry P. *The Growth of Cities.* New York, 1855.

Tappan, Lewis. *The Life of Arthur Tappan.* New York, 1871, repr. 1970.

Taylor, Bayard. *Hannah Thurston.* New York, 1891.

—— *John Godrey's Fortunes.* New York, 1888.

—— *Unpublished Letters.* John R. Schultz, ed. San Marino, Cal.: Huntington Library, 1937.

Taylor, George R. *The Transportation Revolution.* New York: Harper and Row, 1951.

Temin, Peter. *The Jacksonian Economy.* New York: Norton, 1969.

Thernstrom, Stephen. *The Other Bostonians: Poverty and Progress in the American Metropolis, 1880–1970.* Cambridge: Harvard University Press, 1973.

Thomlinson, Ralph. *Population Dynamics.* New York: Random House, 1965.

Thompson, D. G. Brinton, *Ruggles of New York: A Life of Samuel B. Ruggles.* New York: Columbia University Press, 1946.

Thompson, Robert L. *Wiring a Continent: The History of the Telegraph Industry in the United States, 1832–1866.* Princeton, N.J.: Princeton University Press, 1947.

Train, George Francis. *Young America in Wall Street.* New York, 1857; repr. 1968.

Troen, Selwyn K. *The Public and the Schools: Shaping the St. Louis System, 1838–1920.* Columbia: University of Missouri Press, 1975.

Tryon, Rolla M. *Household Manufactures in the United States, 1640–1860.* New York: A. M. Kelly, repr. 1966.

Tunnard, Christopher. *The City of Man.* 2nd ed. New York: Scribner, 1970.

Tyack, David B. *The One Best System: A History of American Urban Education.* Cambridge: Harvard University Press, 1974.

Upjohn, Everard M. *Richard Upjohn: Architect and Churchman.* New York: Columbia University Press, 1939.

Upton, William T. *William Henry Fry: American Journalist and Music Critic.* New York: Crowell, 1954.

Van Deusen, Glyndon G. *Horace Greeley.* Philadelphia: University of Pennsylvania Press, 1953.

Van Every, Edward. *Sins of New York.* New York, 1930; repr., New York: Benjamin Blom, 1972.

Van Vleck, George W. *The Panic of 1857: An Analytical Study.* New York: Columbia University Press, 1943; repr. 1967.

Van Winkle, Daniel. *History of the Municipalities of Hudson County, New Jersey.* 3 vols. New York and Chicago: Lewis Historical Publishing Co., 1924.

Van Zandt, Roland, *Chronicle of the Hudson.* New Brunswick, N.J.: Rutgers University Press, 1971.

Veiller, Lawrence. *Tenement House Reform in New York, 1834–1900.* New York: Evening Post Job Printing House, 1900.

BOOKS, PAMPHLETS AND DISSERTATIONS

Vose, John D. *Fresh Leaves from the Diary of a Broadway Dandy.* New York, 1852.

Vose, Reuben. *Despotism; or The Last Days of the American Republic.* New York, 1856.

—— *The Rich Men of New York.* 2nd series. New York, 1861.

Walsh, James J. *History of Medicine in New York.* 3 vols. New York: National Americana Society, 1919.

Walsh, Michael. *Sketches of the Speeches and Writings.* Compiled by the Spartan Association. New York, 1843.

Ward, David. *Cities and Immigrants.* New York: Oxford University Press, 1971.

Warner, Sam Bass, Jr. *The Private City: Philadelphia in Three Periods of Its Growth.* Philadelphia: University of Pennsylvania Press, 1968.

Watson, Frank D. *The Charity Organization Movement in the United States.* New York: Macmillan, 1922.

Weber, Adna F. *The Growth of Cities in the Nineteenth Century.* New York, 1899.

Wecter, Dixon. *The Sage of American Society.* New York: Scribner, 1937.

Weeks, Lyman H., ed. *Prominent Families of New York.* Revised ed. New York, 1898.

Wegmann, Edward. *The Water-Supply of the City of New York, 1658–1895.* New York, 1896.

Wheatley, Richard. *The Life and Letters of Mrs. Phoebe Palmer.* New York, 1876.

White, Philip L. *The Beekmans of New York . . . 1647–1877.* New York: New York Historical Society, 1956.

Whitman, Walt. *New York Dissected.* Emory Holloway and Ralph Adimori, eds. New York: R. R. Wilson, 1936.

—— *Specimen Days.* repr. New York: New American Library, 1961.

Whitney, Thomas R. *A Defence of the American Policy, as Opposed to the Encroachment of Foreign Influence.* New York, 1856.

Williams, David A. *David C. Broderick: A Political Portrait.* San Marino, Ca.: Huntington Library, 1969.

Williamson, Jefferson. *The American Hotel.* New York: Knopf, 1930.

Willis, N. Parker. *People I Have Met.* Detroit, 1853.

Wilson, James G., ed. *The Memorial History of the City of New-York.* 4 vols. New York, 1893.

Wittke, Carl. *The Irish in America.* Baton Rouge: Louisiana State University Press, 1956.

Whortley, Lady Emmeline Stuart. *Travels in the United States.* 3 vols. London, 1851.

Woodman, Harold D. *King Cotton and His Retainers.* Lexington: University of Kentucky Press, 1968.

Wyllie, Irvin G. *The Self-Made Man in America.* New Brunswick, N.J.: Rutgers University Press, 1954.

Wyman, Mary A. *Two American Pioneers: Seba Smith and Elizabeth Oakes Smith.* New York: Columbia University Press, 1927.

INDEX

INDEX

INDEX

INDEX

INDEX

INDEX

INDEX

INDEX

INDEX

INDEX

INDEX

INDEX